MACROECONOMICS

MACROECONOMICS

FOURTH EDITION

PAUL WONNACOTT / RONALD WONNACOTT
UNIVERSITY OF MARYLAND / UNIVERSITY OF WESTERN ONTARIO

JOHN WILEY & SONS

NEW YORK / CHICHESTER / BRISBANE / TORONTO / SINGAPORE

Acquisitions Editor: John Woods
Cover Illustrator: Jana Brenning
Cover Calligrapher: Stuart David
Text Designer: Madelyn Lesure
Developmental Editors: Barbara Heaney and Georgene Gallagher
Managing Editor: Joan Kalkut
Copy editing Supervisor: Gilda Stahl; Copy editor: Betty Pessagno
Production Manager: Joe Ford; Production: Hudson River Studio
Photo Research: John Wiley Photo Research Department

Library of Congress Cataloging in Publication Data:

Wonnacott, Paul.
     Macroeconomics / Paul Wonnacott, Ronald Wonnacott. — 4th ed.
        p.   cm.
     Includes bibliographical references.
     ISBN 0-471-50829-2
     1. Macroeconomics.   I. Wonnacott, Ronald J.   II. Title.
HB172.5.W67   1990   89-39544
339—dc20   CIP

Printed in the United States of America

10 9 8 7 6 5 4 3 2 1

Ronald J. Wonnacott received his Ph.D. in economics from Harvard in 1959, and has taught at that university, the University of Western Ontario, and the University of Minnesota. He has written widely on the subject of U.S.-Canadian trade and on the economics of customs unions and free trade areas—much of this with his brother Paul. Their joint book, *Free Trade between the United States and Canada: The Potential Economic Effects* (Harvard University Press, 1967) was one of the studies that led to a twenty-year debate in Canada and to the recent Free Trade Agreement between the United States and Canada. Ron Wonnacott has also co-authored books on statistics and econometrics with a third brother, Tom (also published by John Wiley). He is a past president of the Canadian Economics Association and a Fellow of the Royal Society of Canada. He shares an enthusiasm for tennis and skiing with Paul. He loves the music of Mozart, and is a member of the Honourable Company of Edinburgh Golfers.

Paul Wonnacott studied history as an undergraduate at the University of Western Ontario. He then switched to his second and greatest academic love—economics—receiving his Ph.D. from Princeton. He was on the faculty of Columbia University before taking his present post at the University of Maryland. He has written extensively on international economics. In joint work with brother Ron on the theory of customs unions, the two authors emphasize the gains achieved when a trading partner reduces its barriers to imports. Paul Wonnacott has a keen interest in economic policy. While with the Council of Economic Advisers, he participated in work which led to the decision to adopt flexible exchange rates in the early 1970s. He has also served on the staffs of the Canadian Royal Commission on Banking and Finance, the Federal Reserve Board, and the U.S. Treasury. He is currently on leave from the University of Maryland, serving as the economic adviser to the Undersecretary of State.

To
David
Ann
Alan
Bruce

PREFACE

TO THE INSTRUCTOR

The fourth edition of *Macroeconomics* represents the most comprehensive revision to date. The extensive revisions build on and refine the framework of earlier editions. Details on "What's New" in this edition are provided in the next section.

This book was inspired by two major questions that arose in our teaching—and by our uneasiness regarding the answers.

For macroeconomics, the principal question that led us to write this book was the following: After studying introductory economics, are students able to understand public controversies over such topics as the level of government spending and taxation, the rising national debt, and monetary policy? Are we training our students to understand the front pages of the newspaper? For many years the introductory course was aimed at teaching students how policy should be run, that is, at providing a cookbook of "right" answers. While many books express more doubts and qualifications than was the case a decade ago, we have altered the focus of the course even more by building up to the seven controversial questions in Parts IV and V:

■ How can inflation exist at the same time as a high rate of unemployment?

■ In the face of an unemployment-inflation dilemma, what options do policymakers have?

■ How does the economy adjust to inflation, and what complications does inflation present to the policymaker?

■ Why have productivity and growth been disappointing since 1973?

■ Is fiscal or monetary policy the key to aggregate demand?

■ Should the authorities attempt to "fine tune" aggregate demand?

■ Should exchange rates be fixed or flexible? What complications do international transactions introduce into monetary and fiscal policies?

While there are no simple, indisputably "correct" answers to these questions, we believe that the major issues can be presented clearly to beginning students of economics, providing them with an understanding of important, recurring public debates over macroeconomic policy.

For microeconomics (covered in the companion volume, *Microeconomics*), the principal question was the following. Does the introductory study of microeonomics lack coherence? To the student, does microeconomics tend to become just one thing after another—a guided tour through the economist's workshop, introducing as many polished pieces of analytic machinery as possible for use later in more advanced courses in our view there is little point in concentrating on analytic techniques for their own sake, when the time could instead be spent applying basic economic theory to interesting policy issues. Even for those students who continue in economics, we doubt that it is useful to focus heavily on analytic techniques. True, such a focus gives students some headstart in their later courses, but it also increases the risk that they will be bored by repetition and will miss some of the forest while concentrating on the trees. Therefore, we follow a simple rule of thumb: In introducing analytic concepts, we focus on those most useful in studying policy issues.

We have attempted to make microeconomics more interesting and understandable by organizing our discussion around two continuing themes: **efficiency** and **equity,** which provide the focus of the companion volume, *Microeconomics.*

These, then, are the first two objectives of our work:

1. To provide an understanding of the major, controversial policy questions.

2. To provide coherence and interest to microeconomics by focusing on the two major themes of efficiency and equity.

THE FOURTH EDITION: WHAT'S NEW?

The biggest single innovation in the fourth edition is a new recurring theme: LIVING IN A GLOBAL ECONOMY. This new theme was inspired by the increasingly close ties between the United States and the international economy. In 1950 exports plus imports of goods and services were equal to only 9.3% of U.S. gross national product; less than 10% of our economy was tied directly to international trade. By 1970 the figure had grown to 12.7%, and by 1988, to 23.3%. With the relaxation of capital controls and improvements in communications, financial ties have grown even stronger. Furthermore, major new economic policy issues have arisen in international relations—such as the protection of the environment.

Topics under the general heading of LIVING IN A GLOBAL ECONOMY include:

■ Why **office rents** vary among the major financial and economic centers, such as London, Tokyo, Hong Kong, and New York. (This illustrates the concepts of demand and supply in Ch. 4, pp. 58–59.)

■ Why **unemployment rates** are **so high** in Western Europe, even though they were generally much lower than U.S. rates during the 1960s and 1970s (Ch. 14, pp. 256–258).

■ The recent **free trade agreement between the United States and Canada** (Ch. 3, pp. 43–44)—a topic in which we have had a personal interest since the 1960s, when Harvard published our book, *Free Trade Between the United States and Canada: The Potential Economic Effects.*

■ The move toward **privatization** of government-owned enterprises in a number of countries, such as the United Kingdom. (This section, in Ch. 5, pp. 77–78, includes our favorite quotation: Sir John Egan's observation that Prime Minister Margaret Thatcher "has never liked owning car companies. She barely puts up with owning the police.")

■ The **four tigers** of East Asia—South Korea, Taiwan, Hong Kong, and Singapore—and their impressive growth (Ch. 16, pp. 285–288).

Other important changes include:

■ **Full color,** used for a functional purpose. Costs and supply are shown in red, while demand is shown in blue. Green—the color of money—is often used to represent dollar values.

■ A number of **summary tables,** for example, tables that compare
  —**Rational expectations** theory with early **monetarism** (p. 256).
  —The views of **Keynesians** with the views of those in the **classical/monetarist** tradition (p. 327).

■ A number of **new boxes** and **appendixes** (and the elimination of some old ones). New items include:
  —**What Should Banks Do?** (Box 12-2, pp. 218–219). This box describes the Savings and Loan crisis and explains some of the problems that can arise when institutions are allowed to gamble with the government's money. It also outlines suggested steps to prevent a repeat of the crisis.
  —**Outlawing Deficits** (Box 10-1, pp. 180–181). This box explains the Gramm-Rudman Act and why outlawing deficits does not provide a simple solution.
  —How the response of consumers may weaken fiscal policy (Appendix on pp. 311–312). This appendix includes the **Barro-Ricardo** theorem.

■ A new discussion of **economic growth in the developing world** (Ch. 16).

■ A discussion of how social security taxes help the government to balance its budget, and the problems that may arise in the twenty-first century as a result. See the section entitled **Social Security to the Rescue? The Twelve Trillion Dollar Temptation,** pp. 180–182.

■ A completely revised discussion of **rational expectations** to make it more precise, yet substantially simpler (pp. 253–255).

■ A discussion of some of the **problems facing the Bush administration** during its first year (p. 71), and why the administration's policy did not seem designed to maximize the president's chances of reelection (p. 323).

■ The use of the term **aggregate expenditures** rather than aggregate demand in Keynesian diagrams, in response to suggestions by users. (For our distinction between the concepts of aggregate expenditures and aggregate demand, see the bottom of p. 139.)

SLOW, ORDERLY EXPOSITION

One of our major objectives has been to explain important ideas as simply as possible, in slow, orderly steps. In some cases, this has meant the addition of more detail. For example, our introduction to the concepts of aggregate demand and aggregate supply is more detailed (and, in our opinion, much more precise) than that of most competing books. In particular, we explain why aggregate demand and aggregate supply curves can have the shapes and slopes that we draw. (See especially the introduction to Ch. 8, pp. 119–120.) This, we believe, is important. Aggregate demand is not simply an addition of demand curves for individual products (nor is aggregate supply simply a sum of individual supply curves). The principal reason why an *individual* demand curve slopes downward to the right is that, as the price of a product falls, buyers have an incentive to *switch* away from other products and buy this one instead. For aggregate demand—dealing with the economy as a whole—no such switching takes place, for the very simple reason that there are no other products. We, like other authors, emphasize the importance of switching in explaining the demand and supply for an individual product in the early chapters. But such switching becomes irrelevant when looking at aggregate demand or aggregate supply. Compared to other authors, we provide more detail and a tighter explanation of what the aggregate demand and aggregate supply curves look like, and why. This additional material makes the introduction to macroeconomics *easier*. It fills gaps in the theory; students are less likely to be puzzled about where the aggregate demand and supply curves come from.

In other cases, the desire to proceed in slow, orderly steps has meant cutting difficult topics that are not essential to the argument. For example, once the focus is on aggregate demand and aggregate supply, the discussion of savings and investment in Say's Law becomes a distraction; it adds a puzzling and complicated step to the introduction of macroeconomics. In contrast to some other authors, we take Say's Law out of the introduction to macroeconomic theory and put it in an appendix. Not only is this desirable as a way of avoiding a tangled and difficult topic in the introduction to macroeconomics; it provides better balance to the book. Say's Law was one of the less sensible parts of classical theory (as explained in Appendix 9-B, pp. 158–159). For a balanced presentation, it is important to look first at the most—not the least—sensible elements of a theory. (Keynes used Say's Law as a convenient target, but his objective was to replace classical theory, not explain it.)

In summary, we have made the slow, methodical development of theory one of our principal goals. Students have responded favorably to our organization and writing style.

SUPPLEMENTS

There are five supplements available to users of *Economics*, Fourth Edition. They are also available to users of this text:

1. **Study Guide,** which includes:
   - A statement of the purpose of each chapter.
   - A list of learning objectives.
   - A detailed summary highlighting all the important ideas covered.
   - Exercises in matching important terms and their definitions.
   - True-False practice exam-type questions.
   - Multiple-Choice practice exam-type questions.
   - Numerical and graphical exercises.

2. **Instructor's Resource Guide,** which includes for each chapter:
   - Learning objectives.
   - Teaching Hints.
   - Lecture outline, also available on disk with **Lecture Maker** lecture customizing software for IBM PCs.
   - Answers to end-of-chapter problems.
   - Transparency masters for text art not included in transparency package.

3. **Test Bank.** Expanded for this macroeconomic edition, this includes about 1500 multiple-choice and true-false questions. It is available in computerized format for the IBM and Macintosh computers.

4. **Transparencies.** Approximately 100 two-color transparencies will be available to adopters.

5. **Software.** Developed by Steven Albert of Northwestern University, this software includes a number of innovative graphical, numerical, and other types of exercises to reinforce fundamental macro and micro concepts.

TO THE STUDENT

Economics is like the music of Mozart. On one level, it holds great simplicity: Its basic ideas can be quickly grasped by those who first encounter it. On another level, below the surface there are fascinating subtleties that remain a challenge—even to those who spend a lifetime in its study. We therefore hold out this promise: In this introductory study, you will learn a great deal about how the economy works—the basic principles governing economic life that must be recognized by those in government and business who make policy decisions. At the same time, we can also promise that you won't be able to master it all. You should be left with an appreciation of the difficult and challenging problems of economics that remain unsolved.

Perhaps someday you will contribute to their solution.

HOW TO USE THIS BOOK

Our objective has been to make the basic propositions of economics as easy as possible to grasp. As you encounter each new topic, essential terms are printed in **boldface** and are followed by definitions set apart from the main text. These key terms should be studied carefully during the first reading and during later review. (A glossary is provided at the end of the book, defining terms used in this text as well as other common economics terms that you may encounter in class or in readings.) The basic ideas of each chapter are summarized in the Key Points at the end of the chapter; new concepts introduced in the chapter are also listed.

When you read a chapter for the first time, concentrate on the main text. Don't worry about the boxes. They are set aside from the text to keep the main text as simple and straightforward as possible. The boxes fall into two broad categories: First are the boxes that provide interesting and occasionally amusing asides, for example, Box 18-1 (pp. 322–323) which addresses the question of whether business cycles are generated by politicians in their eagerness to be reelected. Second are the boxes that present detailed theoretical explanations that are not needed to grasp the main ideas in the text. If you want to glance at the boxes that are fun and easy to read, fine. But when you first read a chapter, don't worry about those that contain more difficult material. On the first reading, you may also skip appendixes and starred (*) footnotes; these also tend to be more difficult and are not essential to the thread of the main story. Come back to them after you have mastered the basic ideas.

Economics is not a spectator sport. You cannot learn just from observation; you must work at it. When you have finished reading a chapter, work on the problems listed at the end; they are designed to reinforce your understanding of important concepts. [The starred (*) problems either are based on material in a box or they are more difficult questions designed to provide a challenge to students who want to do more advanced work.] Because each chapter builds on preceding ones, and because the solution to some of the problems depends on those that come before, remember this important rule: Don't fall behind. In this regard, economics is similar to mathematics. If you don't keep up, you won't understand what's going on in class. To help you keep up, we recommend the *Study Guide* (fourth edition) which is designed specially to assist you in working through each chapter. It should be available in your bookstore.

Bon voyage!

ACKNOWLEDGMENTS

During the work on this fourth edition, we have accumulated many debts. First and foremost, our thanks go to John Woods, who had overall responsibility for the development of the book and supplements. He has tirelessly contributed to the final product in ways too numerous to list. For editorial assistance, we thank Georgene Gallagher, Barbara Heaney, Gilda Stahl, and Betty Pessagno. The unstinting work of Joe Ford, Ed and Lorraine Burke, and Joan Kalkut kept production of the book on schedule. We thank Maddy Lesure for an outstandingly attractive design of the text, and Ron Blue for his imaginative layout of the *Study Guide*.

We are particularly indebted to teachers and scholars who have advised us or reviewed the book in its many drafts, and have provided a wealth of suggestions. To all, we extend our thanks.

David Able
Mankato State University

Jack Adams
University of Arkansas

Morris Adelman
M.I.T.

Lyndell Avery
Penn Valley Community College

Charles A. Berry
University of Cincinnati

Benjamin Blankenship
U.S. Department of Agriculture

Ake Blomqvist
University of Western Ontario

Frank Brechling
University of Maryland

Gerold Bregor
University of South Carolina

Charles R. Britton
University of Arkansas

Mario Cantu
Northern Virginia Community College

John Cochran
Arizona State University

John M. Cooper
Moorhead State University

Harvey Cutler
Colorado State University

Padma Desai
Columbia University

Donald Ellickson
University of Wisconsin, Eau Claire

Paul Farnham
Georgia State University

Rudy Fichtenbaum
Wright State University

Richard Freeman
Harvard University

Bernard Gaucy
Hollins College

Howard Gilbert
South Dakota State University

Allen Goodman
Wayne State University

Gordon Green
Bureau of the Census

Loren Guffey
University of Central Arkansas

Ralph Gunderson
University of Wisconsin, Oshkosh

George Hoffer
Virginia Commonwealth University

Ig Horstmann
University of Western Ontario

Sheng Hu
Purdue University

Richard H. Keehn
University of Wisconsin,
    Parkside

David Laidler
University of Western Ontario

William Lastrapes
Louisiana State University

Edward Montgomery
Michigan State University

Peter Morgan
University of Western Ontario

Mark Morlock
California State University, Chico

Dwight Perkins
Harvard University

Wayne Plumly, Jr.
Valdosta State College

Robert Puth
University of New Hampshire

Charles Register
University of Baltimore

Judy Roberts
California State University

Kenneth G. Scalet
York College of Pennsylvania

Robert Schwab
University of Maryland

William Schworm
University of British Columbia

Alden Shiers
California Polytechnic State
    University

Calvin Siebert
University of Iowa

Andre Simmons
University of Nevada

Timothy Smeeding
University of Utah

Rebecca M. Summary
Southeast Missouri State
    University

Robert W. Thomas
Iowa State University

Ralph Townsend
University of Maine

John Vahaly
University of Louisville

Paul Weinstein
University of Maryland

John Whalley
University of Western Ontario

C. G. Williams
University of South Carolina

Mark E. Wohar
University of Nebraska

BRIEF CONTENTS

Part I   BASIC ECONOMIC CONCEPTS

1. Economic Problems and Economic Goals   2
2. Scarcity and Choice: *The* Economic Problem   25
3. Specialization, Exchange, and Money   36
4. Demand and Supply: The Market Mechanism   46
5. The Economic Role of Government   65

Part II   AN INTRODUCTION TO MACROECONOMICS:
High Employment, Price Stability, and Growth

6. Measuring National Product and National Income   82
7. Fluctuations in Economic Activity   100
8. Aggregate Demand and Aggregate Supply: Classical and Keynesian Equilibria   119
9. Equilibrium with Unemployment: The Keynesian Approach   134

Part III   AGGREGATE DEMAND POLICIES

10. Fiscal Policy   164
11. Money and the Banking System   187
12. The Federal Reserve and Monetary Policy   206

Part IV   GREAT MACROECONOMIC ISSUES:
Aggregate Supply

13. How Can Inflation and Unemployment Coexist?   226
14. How Do We Deal with the Unemployment-Inflation Dilemma?   242
15. How Does Inflation Affect the Economy?   261
16. Growth and Productivity: Why Have They Varied So?   277

Part V   GREAT MACROECONOMIC ISSUES:
Aggregate Demand

17. Monetary Policy and Fiscal Policy: Which Is the Key to Aggregate Demand?   296
18. Fine Tuning or Stable Policy Settings?   313
19. Fixed or Flexible Exchange Rates?   339

CONTENTS

Part I   BASIC ECONOMIC CONCEPTS

1. ECONOMIC PROBLEMS AND ECONOMIC GOALS   2

Economic Progress   2
Economic Problems   3
Economic Policy   5
   The Controversial Role of Government   5
Box 1-1   Karl Marx   6
Economic Goals   7
   1. A Low Rate of Unemployment   7
   2. Stability of the Average Price Level   9
   3. Efficiency   10
   4. An Equitable Distribution of Income   11
   5. Growth   12
Interrelations Among Economic Goals   13
A Preview   14
Key Points   14
Key Concepts   15
Problems   15

Appendix. DIAGRAMS USED IN ECONOMICS   16

1. A Simple Comparison of Two Facts   16
   Things to Watch   16
2. Time Series: How Something Changes Through Time   18
   Should We Measure from Zero?   18
   How Should Growth Be Illustrated?   19
   Real or Monetary Measures?   21
   Relative Measures   21
3. Relationships Between Variables   21

2. SCARCITY AND CHOICE: *The* Economic Problem   25

Unlimited Wants. . .   25
. . . And Scarce Resources   26
Scarcity and Choice: The Production Possibilities Curve   27
   The Shape of the Production Possibilities Curve: Increasing Opportunity Costs   28
The Production Possibilities Curve Is a Frontier   29
Growth: The Outward Shift of the Production Possibilities Curve   30
Growth: The Choice Between Consumer Goods and Capital Goods   31

An Introduction to Economic Theory: The Need to Simplify   **31**
    Theory Necessarily Means Simplification   **32**
    The Distinction Between Positive and Normative Economics   **33**
Key Points   **34**
Key Concepts   **35**
Problems   **35**

3. SPECIALIZATION, EXCHANGE, AND MONEY   36
Exchange: The Barter Economy   **36**
Exchange with Money   **37**
    The Circular Flow of Expenditures and Income   **37**
The Monetary System   **38**
    Monetary Problems in the POW Camp   **40**
Comparative Advantage: A Reason to Specialize   **41**
Box 3–1   Illustration of Comparative Advantage   **42**
Economies of Scale: Another Reason to Specialize   **42**
Living In a Global Economy   Economies of Scale and the U.S.-Canadian Free Trade
    Agreement   **43**
Key Points   **44**
Key Concepts   **45**
Problems   **45**

4. DEMAND AND SUPPLY: The Market Mechanism   46
Decisions by Private Markets and by the Government   **46**
How Private Markets Operate   **47**
Perfect and Imperfect Competition   **48**
Demand and Supply   **49**
    Demand   **49**
    Supply   **50**
    The Equilibrium of Demand and Supply   **51**
Shifts in the Demand Curve   **52**
    Demand Shifters   **53**
What Is Produced: The Response to a Change in Taste   **54**
Shifts in Supply   **54**
    Supply Shifters   **55**
    The Response to a Shift in the Supply Curve   **55**
    Shifts in a Curve and Movements Along the Curve   **56**
The Interconnected Questions of What, How, and For Whom   **56**
    How? and For Whom?   **58**
Living in a Global Economy   Renting an Office in Tokyo, London, or Hong Kong   **58**
The Market Mechanism: A Preliminary Evaluation   **59**
    Strengths of the Market   **59**
    The Alternative of Price Controls: Some Problems   **59**
    The Market Mechanism: Limitations and Problems   **60**

Box 4-1   What's the Price of Justice?   **61**
Key Points   **62**
Key Concepts   **63**
Problems   **63**

5. THE ECONOMIC ROLE OF GOVERNMENT   65

Government Expenditures   **66**
    Government Purchases Versus Transfers   **66**
    Expenditures of the Federal Government   **68**
Tax Revenues   **69**
Expenditures, Revenues, and Deficits   **70**
    Reaganomics   **70**
    The Early Bush Administration   **71**
Principles of Taxation   **72**
    1. Neutrality   **72**
    2. Nonneutrality: Meeting Social Objectives by Tax Incentives   **72**
    3. Equity   **72**
    4. Simplicity   **73**
The Tax Reform Act of 1986   **73**
Government Regulation   **74**
The Role of the Government   **75**
    1. Providing What the Private Market Cannot   **76**
    2. Dealing with Externalities   **76**
    3. Encouraging the Use of Merit Goods   **76**
    4. Helping the Poor   **77**
    5. Promoting Economic Stability   **77**
Living in a Global Economy   The Privatization of Public Enterprise   **77**
Key Points   **78**
Key Concepts   **79**
Problems   **79**

Part II   AN INTRODUCTION TO MACROECONOMICS:
High Employment, Stability, and Growth

6. MEASURING NATIONAL PRODUCT AND NATIONAL INCOME   82

The Market as a Way of Production   **82**
Two Approaches: National Product and National Income   **83**
National Product   **83**
    1. Personal Consumption Expenditures (C)   **85**
    2. Government Purchases of Goods and Services (G)   **85**
    3. Private Domestic Investment (I)   **86**
    4. Exports of Goods and Services (X)   **87**
    5. A Subtraction: Imports of Goods and Services (M)   **87**

National Product: A Summary Statement   87
The Complication of Depreciation: GNP and NNP   87
Net National Product and National Income: The Complication of the Sales Tax   90
Other Income Measures   90
    Personal Income (PI)   91
    Disposable Income (DI)   91
    Relative Magnitudes   91
Nominal and Real GNP   91
    Price Indexes   92
    Other Real Measures   93
A Measure of Economic Welfare   93
    1. Emphasis on Additional Social Indicators   94
    2. A Comprehensive Measure of Economic Welfare (MEW)   94
The Underground Economy: The Case of the Missing GNP   96
Key Points   97
Key Concepts   98
Problems   98

7. FLUCTUATIONS IN ECONOMIC ACTIVITY   100
The Four Phases of the Business Cycle   101
Box 7-1   Seasonal Adjustment of Economic Data   103
Living in a Global Economy   The International Depression of the 1930s   103
The U.S. Economy During Recent Business Cycles   105
    Consumption and Investment During Recession   105
Unemployment   108
    Calculating the Unemployment Rate   108
    Underemployment   108
    Who Are the Unemployed?   110
    Types of Unemployment   110
How Much Employment Is "Full Employment"?   114
Economic Costs of Recession   115
Box 7-2   Recession Can Be Harmful to Your Health   115
Key Points   117
Key Concepts   117
Problems   117

8. AGGREGATE DEMAND AND AGGREGATE SUPPLY:
Classical and Keynesian Equilibria   119
The Classical Approach   120
    Aggregate Supply: The Classical Approach   121
    Equilibrium at Full Employment   121
    The Classical Explanation of the Depression   122

Classical Macroeconomics: A Preliminary Summary   **123**
The Keynesian Approach   **124**
The Simple Keynesian Aggregate Supply Function   **125**
Aggregate Demand: The Keynesian Approach   **127**
Classical Economics and Keynesian Economics: A Summary   **127**
Areas of Agreement   **128**
Areas of Disagreement   **129**
Key Points   **130**
Key Concepts   **131**
Problems   **131**

Appendix. THE AGGREGATE DEMAND CURVE OF KEYNESIAN ECONOMICS   132

9. EQUILIBRIUM WITH UNEMPLOYMENT: The Keynesian Approach   134
Personal Consumption Expenditures   **135**
Saving   **136**
The Marginal Propensity to Consume   **138**
The Simplest Equilibrium: An Economy with No Government   **139**
Equilibrium with Large-Scale Unemployment   **142**
An Alternative Approach: Saving and Investment   **142**
The Circular Flow of Expenditures: Leakages and Injections   **143**
The Equilibrium of Saving and Desired Investment   **143**
Changes in Desired Investment: The Multiplier   **145**
The Multiplier Process: A More Detailed Look   **145**
The Multiplier: The Saving-Investment Approach   **148**
The Multiplier When Prices Change   **149**
When Prices Are Constant   **149**
Changing Prices: Equilibrium with an Upward-Sloping Aggregate Supply Curve   **150**
Key Points   **151**
Key Concepts   **152**
Problems   **152**

Appendix 9-A. CONSUMPTION IN THE SHORT RUN AND THE LONG RUN   154
Time   **154**
Expectations   **155**
Wealth   **155**

Appendix 9-B. CLASSICAL ECONOMICS: Equilibrium with Full Employment   156
Saving and Investment   **156**
The Keynesian Rebuttal   **157**
Say's Law   **158**

Appendix 9-C. CHANGES IN THE DESIRE TO SAVE: The Paradox of Thrift   160

Part III   AGGREGATE DEMAND POLICIES

10. FISCAL POLICY   164

Government Purchases   164
Taxes   166
    A Lump-Sum Tax   166
    Adding Realism: A Proportional Tax   168
Taxes Reduce the Size of the Multiplier   168
    Injections and Leakages   169
Exports and Imports   169
Automatic Stabilizers   170
Two Complications   171
    1. A Policy Trap: Attempting to Balance the Budget Every Year   171
    2. Measuring Fiscal Policy: The Full-Employment Budget   172
    The Full-Employment Budget Since 1960   173
The Supply-Side Tax Cuts of the 1980s   173
    The Supply-Side Case   174
    Criticisms   174
The National Debt   176
    The Burden of Deficits and Debt   176
    Could the Government "Go Broke"?   177
The Issue of Restraint   179
    1. Balance the Full-Employment Budget Every Year   179
    2. Balance the Budget Over the Business Cycle   179
    3. Limit Government Spending   179
    Formal Constraints   179
Box 10-1   Outlawing Deficits   180
Social Security to the Rescue? The Twelve Trillion Dollar Temptation   180
Key Points   182
Key Concepts   183
Problems   184

Appendix. CAN TAXES BE CUT WITHOUT LOSING REVENUES?   185

11. MONEY AND THE BANKING SYSTEM   187

The Functions of Money   188
Money in the U.S. Economy   188
    A Broader Concept of Money: M2   189
Banking as a Business   190
    The Goldsmith: The Embryonic Bank as a Warehouse   190
    Keeping the Books: The Balance Sheet   191
    Fractional-Reserve Banking   191
    Bank Runs and Panics   192
The Modern U.S. Banking System   193

The Federal Reserve 193

The Commercial Banks 193

Other Depository Institutions 194

Remaining Regulations 195

Banks and the Creation of Money 195

How a Check Is Cleared 197

Why a Bank Can Safely Lend No More Than Its Excess Reserves 198

The Multiple Expansion of Bank Deposits 198

Two Complications 202

Key Points 203

Key Concepts 204

Problems 204

12. THE FEDERAL RESERVE AND MONETARY POLICY 206

The Organization of the Federal Reserve 206

Controlling the Money Supply: Open Market Operations 208

Restrictive Open Market Operations 211

Controlling the Money Supply: Discount Policy 211

Controlling the Money Supply: Changes in Reserve Requirements 211

Monetary Policy and Interest Rates 212

Box 12-1 Bond Prices and Interest Rates 213

Other Monetary Tools 214

Selective Control in the Stock Market: Margin Requirements 214

Moral Suasion 215

The Balance Sheet of the Federal Reserve 215

What Backs Our Money? 216

What Backs Checking Deposits? 216

Why Not Gold? 217

Box 12-2 Federal Insurance and Bank Risks: What Should Banks Do? 218

Money Misbehaving: Procyclical Movements in the Money Stock 220

How an Interest Rate Target Can Destabilize the Money Stock 220

Key Points 222

Key Concepts 223

Problems 223

Part IV   GREAT MACROECONOMIC ISSUES: Aggregate Supply

13. HOW CAN INFLATION AND UNEMPLOYMENT COEXIST? 226

The Facts 228

The Phillips Curve of the 1960s 228

The Policy Dilemma of the 1960s: The Tradeoff Between Inflation and Unemployment 230

The Record Since 1970: Higher Inflation and Higher Unemployment 231

Cost-Push Versus Demand-Pull Inflation 231

Price Expectations and the Wage-Price Spiral: The Accelerationist Theory   233
    Limiting Inflation   235
    The Vertical Long-Run Phillips Curve   235
The Problem of Unwinding Inflationary Expectations   238
    Gradualism   239
Box 13-1   The Natural Rate Theory and the Great Depression   239
Key Points   240
Key Concepts   240
Problems   241

14. HOW DO WE DEAL WITH THE UNEMPLOYMENT-INFLATION DILEMMA?   242
What Can Be Done to Reduce the Natural Rate of Unemployment?   242
    Increases in the Rate of Unemployment   243
    Steps to Reduce the Natural Rate of Unemployment   244
Direct Restraints on Wages and Prices: Income Policies   245
    The Kennedy-Johnson Guideposts   246
    The Wage-Price Freeze of 1971   246
    Income Policies Under Carter: Pay and Price Standards   246
    Income Policies: Controversial Issues   247
    Income Policies: A Final Word   248
Other Proposals to Ease the Transition to Lower Inflation   248
    Indexation of Wages   248
    The Share Economy   250
Expectations When People Anticipate Policies   250
    Large Shifts in the Short-Run Phillips Curve   251
    Unwinding Inflation   252
    Credibility   253
Rational Expectations   253
    Ineffective Policies?   253
    Criticisms   255
Living in a Global Economy   Why Is the Unemployment Rate So High In Europe?   256
Key Points   258
Key Concepts   259
Problems   259

15. HOW DOES INFLATION AFFECT THE ECONOMY?   261
Unexpected Inflation: Who Loses and Who Gains?   262
    Losers   263
    Winners   263
Adjusting to Expected Inflation: The Real Rate of Interest   263
The Real Interest Rate in the United States   265
Inflation and the Taxation of Interest   267

Inflation Causes Uncertainty   **268**
    Erratic Inflation Makes the Bond Market Shrink   **269**
    Adjustable-Rate Mortgages   **269**
Inflation Causes a Front-Loading of Debt   **269**
    Graduated-Payment Mortgages   **270**
    Graduated-Payment Mortgages and Adjustable-Rate Mortgages: A Comparison   **271**
Box 15-1.   The Rule of 70: How Long Does It Take for Prices to Double?   **271**
Macroeconomic Policy in an Inflationary Environment   **272**
    Calculating the Real Deficit   **272**
    An Alternative View   **272**
    Monetary Policy in an Inflationary Environment   **274**
Key Points   **275**
Key Concepts   **275**
Problems   **276**

16. GROWTH AND PRODUCTIVITY: Why Have They Varied So Much?   277
Productivity and Economic Growth in the United States   **277**
    Increases in Labor Hours and Productivity   **278**
    The Increase in U.S. Productivity, 1948–1973   **279**
    The Puzzle of the 1970s: What Went Wrong?   **280**
    International Comparisons   **281**
The Least Developed Countries: The Vicious Circle of Poverty   **282**
Breaking the Vicious Circle   **285**
    Development and the International Economy   **285**
Living in a Global Economy   The "Four Tigers" of East Asia   **285**
    Their International Economic Relations   **286**
    The Role of the Government   **287**
The International Debt Crisis   **288**
Key Points   **290**
Key Concepts   **291**
Problems   **291**

Appendix. WILL POPULATION EXPLODE? The Malthusian Problem   292

Part V   GREAT MACROECONOMIC ISSUES: Aggregate Demand

17. MONETARY POLICY AND FISCAL POLICY:
Which Is the Key to Aggregate Demand   296
The Effects of Monetary Policy: The Keynesian View   **297**
    Step 1. Monetary Policy and the Interest Rate: The Stock of Money and the Demand for It   **297**
    Step 2. The Interest Rate and Investment Demand   **299**
    Problems with Monetary Policy   **301**

Monetary Policy: The Monetarist View   301
    The Quantity Theory of Money   302
    Why Should Velocity Be Stable? The Demand for Money   303
Monetarist Doubts About Fiscal Policy: Crowding Out   304
Living in a Global Economy   Budget Deficits and Trade Deficits   305
The Uncertain Lesson of Recent History   306
    The Rise and Fall of Monetarism   306
    The Recent Reliance on Monetary Policy   308
The Case for Using Monetary and Fiscal Policies Together   308
Key Points   309
Key Concepts   310
Problems   310

Appendix. DOUBTS ABOUT FISCAL POLICY: How Do Consumers Respond?   311
Barro-Ricardo   311

18. FINE TUNING OR STABLE POLICY SETTINGS?   313
Aiming for a Stable High-Employment Economy: The Active Keynesian Approach   314
    An Example   315
The Case Against Activism: Lags   315
    The Helmsman's Dilemma   317
The Case Against Activism: The Overestimation of Potential   317
The Case for a Monetary Rule   320
The Case Against a Monetary Rule   321
    1. Can There Be a Rigid Rule?   321
    2. Would Aggregate Demand be Insufficient?   322
    3. Would a Monetary Rule Make the Growth of Aggregate Demand More Stable?   323
Box 18-1.   The Problem of Goals: Is There A Political Business Cycle?   322
The Outcome of the Debate   325
    Which Target?   325
Forecasting   326
    Forecasting with a Model   326
    Turning Points   328
    The Proof the Pudding   329
Key Points   331
Key Concepts   332
Problems   332

Appendix. THE ACCELERATOR: A Nonmonetary Explanation Of Business Fluctuations   333
Investment Demand: The Simple Accelerator   333
Modification of the Simple Accelerator: Lags in Investment   335
Interactions Between the Accelerator and the Multiplier   336
    The Downswing and Lower Turning Point   336
Key Points   337
Problems   338

19. FIXED OR FLEXIBLE EXCHANGE RATES?   339

Exchange Rates   339

The Foreign Exchange Market   341

Disequilibrium in the Exchange Market   341

The Gold Standard   343

    The Adjustment Mechanism of the Gold Standard   343

    Problems with the Gold Standard   343

The Adjustable Peg: The IMF System, 1945-1971   344

The IMF System: The Problems of Adjustment and Confidence   345

The Breakdown of the Adjustable Peg System, 1971-1973   346

Flexible Exchange Rates   347

    Real and Nominal Exchange Rates   348

    The Fluctuating Dollar   348

Toward a Compromise System?   352

The European Monetary System   352

Key Points   353

Key Concepts   354

Problems   354

Appendix. BALANCE-OF-PAYMENT ACCOUNTS   355

The Current Account   356

The Capital Accounts   357

    A. Changes in Nonreserve Assets   357

    B. Changes in Reserve Assets   357

    C. The Statistical Discrepancy   357

The Balance of Payments   357

Glossary   359

Index   391

MACROECONOMICS

PART I

BASIC ECONOMIC CONCEPTS

Alfred Marshall, the great teacher and scholar of a century ago, described economics as the "study of mankind in the ordinary business of life." Within this broad description, economics deals with many specific questions. To list but a few:

- Why is it so difficult to get a job at some times and so easy at others?

- Why did our nation produce so much more in 1989 than in 1939?

- What determines the relative prices of goods? Why is water cheap, even though it is necessary to life itself? Why are diamonds expensive, even though they are an unessential luxury?

- How do business executives decide which goods to produce?

Those are some of the questions that you will encounter in this book.

CHAPTER 1
ECONOMIC PROBLEMS AND ECONOMIC GOALS

Economy is the art of making the most out of life.
GEORGE BERNARD SHAW

Some years ago, a Japanese mass-circulation newspaper, the *Mainichi,* conducted a survey of 4,000 people, asking them what they thought of first when they heard the word *takai* (high). "Mount Fuji," said 12%. The overwhelming majority—88%—said, "Prices." In the United States, only two presidents have failed in their bids for reelection in the past 75 years. In 1932, Herbert Hoover was defeated by Franklin D. Roosevelt. At that time, the economy was approaching the low point of the Great Depression; more than one worker in five was out of a job. Roosevelt promised hope. In 1980, Jimmy Carter lost to Ronald Reagan. In that year, the increase in the average level of prices—that is, the inflation rate—was 12.4%. Those two elections showed how much the American public cares about the problems of unemployment and inflation. With the rare exception of the individual who inherits great wealth, most of us are concerned with the jobs available to us and with the purchasing power of the incomes we earn.

Economics is a study of problems, such as inflation and unemployment. It is also a study of success.

ECONOMIC PROGRESS

From the vantage point of our comfortable homes of the late twentieth century, it is easy for us to forget how many people, through history, have been losers in the struggle to make a living. Unvarnished economic history is the story of deprivation, of 80-hour weeks, of child labor—and of starvation. However, it is also the story of the slow climb of civilization toward the goal of relative affluence, where the general public as well as the fortunate few can have a degree of material well-being and leisure.

One of the most notable features of the U.S. economy has been its growth. Although there have been interruptions and setbacks, economic progress has been remarkable. Figure 1-1 shows one of the standard measures of success—the increase in total production per person.[1] The average American now produces more than twice as much as the average American in 1945 and about six times as much as the average American at the turn of the century. Furthermore, the higher output is produced with less effort: The average number of hours worked by those in manufacturing has declined about 25% during this century (Fig. 1-1). Thus economic progress in the United States has been reflected both in an increase in the goods and

---

[1]The measure of output in this diagram is *gross national product,* or GNP for short. This concept will be explained in Chapter 6.

2

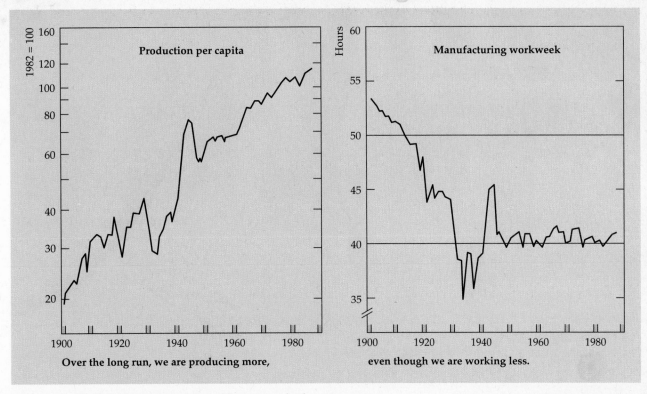

FIGURE 1-1   Production per person and hours worked.

(Source: Board of Governors of the Federal Reserve, *1988 Historical Chart Book*.)

services that we produce and enjoy, and in a greater amount of leisure time. (However, not everyone enjoys more leisure. A 1988 poll by Louis Harris indicated that professional people average 52.2 hours per week and that people in small businesses work 57.3 hours.)

A similar tale of success has occurred in many other countries. In the period from 1960 to 1987, national output grew at an average annual rate of 3.8% in France, 3.0% in Germany, 3.6% in Italy, 3.2% in the United States, and 4.2% in Canada. Nor has growth been confined to the countries of Europe and North America. Particularly notable has been the growth of the Japanese economy. From the ashes of the Second World War, Japan has emerged as one of the leading nations in the world. As a result of a rapid growth averaging 6.7% per year between 1960 and 1987, Japan now ranks with Switzerland, the United States, Norway, and Canada as one of the highest income countries in the world. Other stories of success have come from

the middle-income areas of East Asia, such as South Korea, Hong Kong, and Singapore. Figure 1-2 shows the growth rates in a number of countries and continents.

ECONOMIC PROBLEMS

Although rapid growth has occurred in many countries, it has been neither universal nor automatic. In a number of the poorest countries, the standard of living remains abysmally low, with an average income per person of less than $200 *per year*. The World Bank—an international institution whose major purpose is to lend to the low-income countries—estimates that, between 1965 and 1986, output per person rose at an average annual rate of only 1.25% in the 30 poorest countries (excluding China). The record is even bleaker in 10 of these countries, where population has outrun the

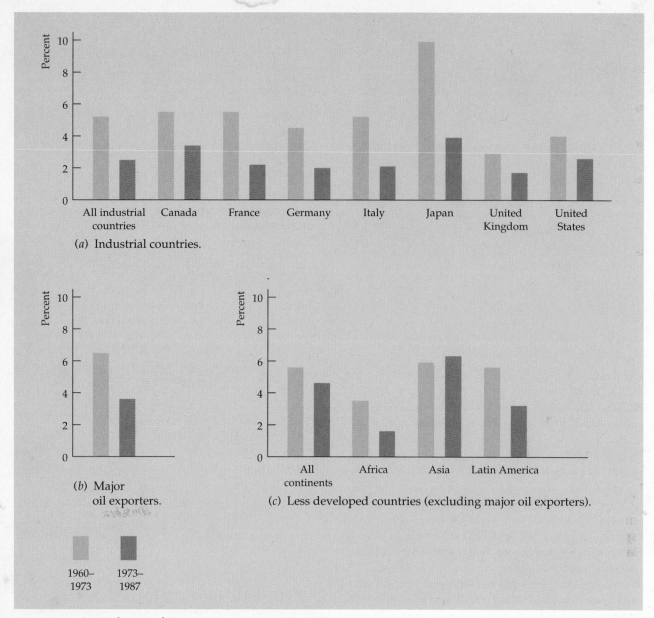

FIGURE 1-2   Annual rates of increase in output, 1960–1987.

Output has grown rapidly in many countries, particularly Japan. Note that for most countries, growth slowed down after 1973—with the rapidly developing economies of Asia being an exception. The slower growth may be traced in part to the disruptions caused by the rapid increase in the price of oil. (Source: World Bank, *World Development Report*, various issues.)

increase in production and output per person has actually declined.[2]

In both rich countries and poor, substantial economic problems remain. Even in the relatively prosperous United States, we may wonder:

■ Why are some people unable to find work when so much needs to be done?

■ Why do pockets of poverty remain in an affluent society?

■ Why have prices marched upward?

■ Are we really producing the right things? Should we produce more housing and fewer cars? Or more subways and fewer office buildings?

■ Why is pollution such a problem? What should be done about it?

ECONOMIC POLICY

Why? and *What should be done?* are the two key questions in economics. The ultimate objective of economics is to *develop policies to deal with our problems.* However, before we can formulate policies, we must first make every effort to understand how the economy has worked in the past and how it works today. Otherwise, well-intentioned policies may go astray and lead to unforeseen and unfortunate consequences.

When economic policies are studied, the center of attention is often the policies of the government—policies such as taxation, government spending programs, and the regulation of particular industries such as electric power. However, the policies of private businesses are also important. How can they best organize production in order to make goods at the lowest possible cost? What prices does a business charge if it wants to maximize profits? When should a supermarket increase the stocks of goods in its warehouse?

THE CONTROVERSIAL ROLE OF GOVERNMENT

For more than 200 years, economics has been dominated by a controversy over the proper role of gov-

ernment. In what circumstances should government take an active role? When is it best for government to leave decisions to the private participants in the economy? On this topic, the giants of economics have repeatedly met to do battle.

In 1776, Scottish scholar **Adam Smith** published his pathbreaking book, *An Inquiry into the Nature and Causes of the Wealth of Nations.*[3] Modern economics may be dated from that historic year, which was also notable for the Declaration of Independence. Smith's message was clear: Private markets should be liberated from the tyranny of government control. In pursuit of their private interests, individual producers will make the goods that consumers want. It is not, said Smith, "from the benevolence of the butcher, the brewer, or the baker that we expect our dinner, but from their regard to their own interest." There is an "invisible hand," he wrote, that causes the producer to promote the interests of society. Indeed, "by pursuing his own interest he frequently promotes that of the society more effectually than when he really intends to promote it." In general, said Smith, the government should be cautious about interfering with the operations of the private market. According to Smith, the best policy is generally one of **laissez faire**—leave it alone. Government intervention usually makes things worse. For example, government imposition of a tariff is generally harmful. (A *tariff*, or *duty*, is a tax on a foreign-produced good as it enters the country.) Even though a tariff generally helps domestic producers who are thereby given an advantage over foreign producers, the country as a whole loses. Specifically, a tariff increases the cost of goods available to consumers, and this cost to consumers generally outweighs the benefits to producers. Smith's work has been refined and modified during the past 200 years, but many of his laissez-faire conclusions have stood the test of time. For example, there is still a very strong economic argument against high tariffs on imported goods. In recent decades, one of the principal areas of international cooperation has been the negotiation of lower tariffs.

---

[2]World Bank, *World Development Report 1988* (Washington, D.C., 1988), pp. 222–223.

[3]Available in the Modern Library edition (New York: Random House, 1937). Smith's book is commonly referred to as *The Wealth of Nations.*

During the Great Depression of the 1930s—a century and a half after the appearance of the *Wealth of Nations*—the laissez-faire tradition in economics came under attack. In 1936, **John Maynard Keynes** published his *General Theory of Employment, Interest and Money* (also known, more simply, as the *General Theory*). In this book, Keynes (which rhymes with Danes) argued that the government has the duty to intervene in the economy to put the unemployed back to work. Of the several ways in which this could be done, one stood out in its simplicity. By building public works, such as roads, post offices, and dams, the government could provide jobs directly and thus provide a cure for the depression.

With his proposals for a more active role for government, Keynes drew the ire of many business executives. They feared that, as a result of his recommendations, the government would become larger and private enterprise would gradually be pushed out of the picture. But Keynes did not foresee this result. He believed that, by providing jobs, the government could remove the explosive frustrations caused by the mass unemployment of the 1930s, and could make it possible for Western political and economic institutions to survive. His objective was to modify our economic system and make it better. Unlike Karl Marx, he was not trying to destroy it. (For a brief introduction to the revolutionary ideas of Marx, see Box 1–1.)[4]

Thus Smith and Keynes took apparently contradictory positions—Smith arguing for less govenment and Keynes for more.[5] It is possible, of

---

[4]Throughout this book, the boxes present illustrative and supplementary materials. They can be omitted without losing the main thread of the discussion.

[5]Conflicting views over the proper role of government may be found in the works of two retired professors: the University of Chicago's Milton Friedman (who argues for less government) and Harvard's John Kenneth Galbraith (who argues for more). See John Kenneth Galbraith, *The Affluent Society* (Boston: Houghton Mifflin, 1958) and Milton Friedman and Rose Friedman, *Free to Choose* (New York: Harcourt Brace Jovanovich, 1980). We recommend that if you read one of these books, you also read the other. Each puts forth a convincing case. Nevertheless, they are flatly contradictory .

BOX 1–1 *Karl Marx*

The main text refers to two towering economists—Adam Smith and John Maynard Keynes. In the formation of the intellectual heritage of most American economists, Smith and Keynes have played leading roles. If, however, we consider the intellectual heritage of the world as a whole, Karl Marx is probably the most influential economist of all. The current economic systems in a number of countries—most notably the Soviet Union and China—were founded on Marx's theories.

Many business executives viewed Keynes as a revolutionary because he openly attacked accepted opinion and proposed fundamental changes in economic policy. But by revolutionary standards, Keynes pales beside Marx. The Marxist call to revolution was shrill and direct: "Workers of the world, unite! You have nothing to lose but your chains."

Why did they have nothing to lose? Because, said Marx, workers are responsible for the production of all goods. Labor is the sole source of value. But workers get only part of the fruits of their labor. A large—and in Marx's view, unjustified—share goes to the exploiting class of capitalists. (Capitalists are the owners of factories, machinery, and other equipment.) Marx believed that, by taking up arms and overthrowing capitalism, workers could end exploitation and obtain their rightful rewards.

On our main topic—the role of government—Marx was strangely ambivalent. Who would own the factories and machines once the communist revolution had eliminated the capitalist class? Ownership by the state was the obvious solution; in fact, this has been the path taken by countries such as the Soviet Union. The revolution has led to state ownership of the means of production. Yet, Marx also believed that the revolution would eventually lead to the "withering away" of the state. However, there has been no perceptible sign of this withering away in Marxist societies.

course, that each was right. Perhaps the government should do more in some respects and less in others. Economic analysis does not lead inevitably to either an activist or a passive position on the part of the government. The economist's rallying cry should not be, "Do something." Rather, it should be, "Think first."

ECONOMIC GOALS

The ultimate goal of economics is to develop better policies to minimize our problems and to maximize the benefits from our daily toil. More specifically, economists focus on a number of major goals:

1.   *A low rate of unemployment.* People willing to work should be able to find jobs reasonably quickly. Widespread unemployment is demoralizing, and it represents an economic waste. Society foregoes the goods and services that the unemployed could have produced.

2.   *Price stability.* It is desirable to avoid rapid increases—or decreases—in the average level of prices.

3.   *Efficiency.* When we work, we want to get as much as we reasonably can out of our productive efforts.

4.   *An equitable distribution of income.* When many live in affluence, no group of citizens should suffer stark poverty.

5.   *Growth.* Continuing growth, which would make possible an even higher standard of living in the future, is generally considered an important objective.

The list is far from complete. Not only do we want to produce more, but we also want to do so without the degradation of our environment; the **reduction of pollution** is important. **Economic freedom**—the right of people to choose their own occupations, to enter contracts, and to spend their incomes as they please—is a desirable goal. So, too, is **economic security**—freedom from the fear that chronic illness or other catastrophe will place an individual or a family in a desperate financial situation.

The achievement of our economic goals provides the principal focus of this book. As a background for later chapters, let us look at the major goals in more detail.

1.   A LOW RATE OF UNEMPLOYMENT

The importance of full employment was illustrated most clearly during the **Great Depression** of the 1930s, when the United States and many other countries conspicuously failed to achieve it. During the sharp contraction from 1929 to 1933, total output in the United States fell almost one-third, and spending for new buildings, machinery, and equipment declined by almost 80%. As the economy slid downward, more and more workers were thrown out of jobs. By 1933, one-quarter of the labor force was unemployed (Fig. 1-3). Long lines of the jobless gathered at factory gates in the hope of work; disappointment was their common fate. Nor was the problem quickly solved. The downward slide into the depths of the depression went on for more than three years, and the road back to a high level of employment was even longer. It was not until the beginning of the 1940s, when American industry began working around the clock to produce weapons, that many of the unemployed were able to find jobs. There was not a single year during the whole decade 1931–1940 that unemployment averaged less than 14% of the labor force.

A *depression* exists when there is a very high rate of unemployment over a long period of time.

Something had clearly gone wrong—disastrously wrong. Large-scale unemployment represents tremendous waste; time lost in involuntary idleness is gone forever. The costs of unemployment go beyond the loss of output: Unemployment also involves the dashing of hopes. Those unable to find work suffer frustration and a sense of worthlessness, and they lose skills as they remain idle.

The term **unemployed** is reserved for those who are willing and able to work but are unable to find jobs. Thus, those of you who are full-time college students are not included among the unemployed. Your immediate task is to get an education, not a job. Similarly, the 70-year-old retiree is not included in the statistics of the unemployed, nor are those in prisons or mental institutions, since they are not available for jobs.

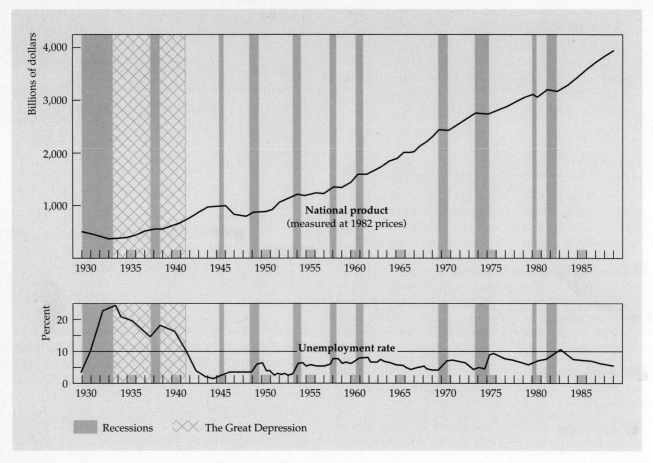

FIGURE 1-3   Output and unemployment in the United States, 1929–1988.
During the Great Depression, output fell and the unemployment rate rose sharply to 25%.
In recent decades, the unemployment rate has been much lower.

A person is *unemployed* if he or she is available and looking for work but has not found it.

At the end of the Second World War, the Great Depression was still a fresh memory. The public, the politician, and the economist shared a common determination that a repeat of the 1930s could not be permitted. This determination was reflected in the **Employment Act of 1946,** which declared:

It is the continuing responsibility of the Federal Government to use all practical means. . . to promote maximum employment, production, and purchasing power.

Since the end of the Second World War, we have been successful in avoiding a depression; there has been no repetition of the high unemployment rates of the 1930s. However, the past four decades have not been an unbroken story of success. From time to time, there have been downturns in the economy—much more moderate, it is true, than the slide of 1929 to 1933, but downward movements nonetheless. These more moderate declines, or **recessions,** have been accompanied by an increase in the unemployment rate. In December 1982, during the worst recession of the past four decades, the unemployment rate rose to a peak of 10.6%. Although we have been successful in avoiding big depressions, the problem of periodic recessions has not been solved.

A *recession* is a decline in total output, income, employment, and trade, usually lasting 6 months to a year, and marked by widespread contractions in many sectors of the economy. (The decline is not confined to just one or two industries, such as steel or aircraft.)

2. STABILITY OF THE AVERAGE PRICE LEVEL

Unemployment caused the downfall of Herbert Hoover in 1932. **Inflation** was a significant reason for the defeat of Jimmy Carter in 1980.

Inflation is an increase in the average level of prices. *Deflation* is a fall in the average level of prices.

Observe in Figure 1-4 how the average of prices paid by consumers has risen through most of our recent history, with the period 1920–1933 being a notable exception. Prices rose most rapidly during and after World War I and for a brief period

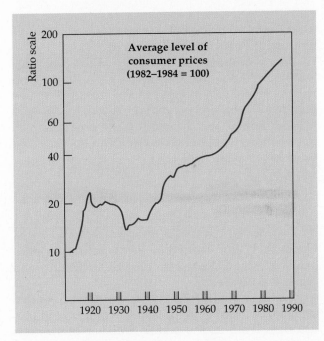

FIGURE 1-4   Consumer prices.

Occasionally prices have fallen—for example, during the early 1930s. In recent decades, however, the trend of prices has been clearly upward. In 1974, and again in 1979 and 1980, the United States suffered from "double-digit" inflation—a rise in the average level of prices by more than 10% per year.

after World War II. Between 1973 and 1981, inflation was unusually severe for peacetime periods. (Details on how to draw and interpret diagrams may be found in the appendix to this chapter and in the *Study Guide* that accompanies this text.)

Whereas unemployment represents sheer waste—society loses the goods that might have been produced by those out of work—the problem with inflation is less obvious. When a price rises, there is both a winner and a loser. The loser is the buyer who has to pay more. However, there is a benefit to the seller, who gets more. On balance, it is not clear whether the society is better or worse off.

It is true, of course, that there is much resentment of inflation, but perhaps at least some of this resentment reflects a peculiarity of human nature. When people find the goods they *sell* rising in price, they see the increase as perfectly right, normal, and justified. On the other hand, when they find the goods they *buy* rising in price, they often view the increase as evidence of the seller's greed. When the price of wheat rises, farmers see themselves at last getting a reasonable return from their toil. When the price of oil increases, the oil companies argue that they are getting no more than the return necessary to finance the search for more oil. When the price of books rises, authors feel they are getting no more than a "just" return for their creative efforts, and book publishers insist they are being no more than adequately compensated for their risks. However, when the farmer, the oil company, the author, and the book publisher find that the prices of the goods they *buy* have increased, they believe they have been cheated by inflation. We may all be the victims of an illusion—the illusion that each of us can and should have a rise in the price of what we sell, but that the price of what we buy should remain stable. For the economy as a whole, this is not possible.

This two-sided nature of price increases—a gain to the seller but a loss to the buyer—means that it is difficult to evaluate the dangers of inflation. Indeed, there has been considerable controversy as to whether a low rate of inflation (say, 1% or 2% per annum) is dangerous, or whether, on the contrary, it may actually be beneficial to society. Some say that a small rate of inflation makes it easier for the economy to adjust to changes and to maintain a high level of employment.

When inflation gets beyond a moderate rate,

however, there is widespread agreement that it becomes a menace. It becomes more than a mere transfer of money from the buyer to the seller; it interferes with the production and exchange of goods. This has most clearly been the situation during very rapid inflations, when economic activity was severely disrupted. **Hyperinflation**—that is, a skyrocketing of prices at annual rates of 1,000% or more—occurs most commonly during or soon after a military conflict, when government spending shoots upward—for example, in the South during the civil war, in Germany during the early 1920s, and in China during its civil war in the late 1940s. A hyperinflation means that money rapidly loses its ability to buy goods. People are anxious to spend money as quickly as possible while they can still get something for it.

Clearly, hyperinflation of 1,000% or more per year is an extreme example. However, lower rates of inflation, amounting to 10% or less per year, can also have serious consequences:

1. Inflation hurts people living on fixed incomes and people who have saved fixed amounts of money for their retirement or for "a rainy day" (future illness or accident). The couple who put aside $1,000 in 1960 for their retirement suffered a rude shock: In 1989, $1,000 bought no more than $250 bought in 1960.

2. Inflation can cause business mistakes. For good decisions, businesses need an accurate picture of what is going on. When prices are rising rapidly, the picture becomes obscured and out of focus. Decision makers cannot see clearly. (For example, business accounting is done in dollar terms. When there is rapid inflation, some businesses may report profits when, on a more accurate calculation, they might actually be suffering losses. Consequently, inflation can temporarily hide problems.) Our economy is complex, and it depends on a continuous flow of accurate information. *Prices are an important link in the information chain.* For example, a high price should provide a signal to producers that consumers are especially anxious to get more of a particular product. But in a severe inflation, producers find it difficult to know whether this is the message, or whether the price of their product is rising simply because all prices are rising. In brief, *a severe inflation obscures the message carried by prices.*

Here, it is important to distinguish between a rise in the **average level of prices** (inflation) and a change in **relative** prices. Even if the average level of prices were perfectly stable (that is, no inflation existed), some *individual* prices would still change as conditions changed in specific markets. For example, new inventions have cut the cost of producing computers, and as a result computer companies have been able to cut prices sharply. At the same time, energy prices (for oil, gasoline, electricity, etc.) have risen during the past 20 years, particularly in 1973 and 1979. The resulting fall in the price of computers relative to the price of oil has performed a useful function. It has encouraged businesses to use more of the relatively cheap computers in their operations and to conserve on the relatively expensive oil. (This is not, of course, to deny that the rise in the price of oil was painful, particularly to those living in the colder areas of the country.)

3. EFFICIENCY

This illustration—of how businesses use more computers when they become cheaper—is one example of economic **efficiency.**

In an economy, both the unemployment rate and the inflation rate may be very low, but performance may still be poor. For example, fully employed workers may be engaged in a lot of wasted motion, and the goods being produced may not be those that are needed most. In this case, the economy is inefficient.

Efficiency is the goal of getting the most out of our productive efforts.

Under this broad definition, two types of efficiency can be distinguished: **technological efficiency** and **allocative efficiency.**

To illustrate *technological efficiency* (also known as *technical* efficiency), consider two bicycle manufacturers. One uses a certain number of workers and machines to produce 1,000 bicycles. The other uses the same number of workers and machines to produce 1,200 bicycles. The second manufacturer is not a magician but simply a better manager. The second manufacturer is technologically efficient, whereas the first is inefficient. Technological inefficiency exists when more output can be produced with the existing machines and workers, working at a reasonable pace. (Technological efficiency does not require a sweatshop.) Because technological inefficiency involves wasted motion and sloppy management, better management is the solution.

Allocative efficiency, on the other hand, occurs when the *best combination of goods* is produced with the *lowest cost combination of inputs*. How much food should we produce? How many houses? Suppose we produce only food and do so in a technologically efficient way, with no wasted motion. We will still not have achieved the goal of allocative efficiency because consumers want both food and housing.

Thus allocative efficiency involves the choice of the best combination of outputs. It also involves using the best (lowest cost) combination of inputs. Consider the earlier illustration. The cost of computers is coming down, while the cost of imported oil has risen. If businesses fail to adjust—and fail to conserve oil and to use computers more—there is allocative inefficiency.

Relative prices perform a key role in encouraging allocative efficiency. As we have noted, the decrease in the price of computers encourages businesses to use more computers and less of other, relatively more expensive inputs. While it is undesirable to have large changes in the *average* level of prices (inflation or deflation), changes in *relative* prices may perform a very useful function, encouraging businesses and consumers to conserve on scarce goods and to use cheaper alternatives instead.

4. AN EQUITABLE DISTRIBUTION OF INCOME

Ours is an affluent society, yet many people remain so poor they have difficulty buying the basic necessities of life, such as food, clothing, and shelter. In the midst of plenty, some live in dire need. Should some people have so much while others have so little?

When the question is put this way, the compelling answer must surely be no. Compassion requires that assistance be given to those crushed by illness and to those born and raised in cruel deprivation.

Our sense of equity, or justice, is offended by extreme differences. Thus most people think of *equity* as a move toward *equality*. But not all the way. The two words are far from synonymous. While there is widespread agreement that the least fortunate should be helped, there is no consensus that the objective of society should be an equal income for all. Some individuals are willing to work overtime; it is generally recognized as both just and desirable for them to have a higher income as a consequence. Otherwise, why should they work longer hours? Similarly, it is generally considered right for the hardworking to have a larger share of the nation's income pie, since they have contributed more to the production of the pie in the first place.

There is no agreement on how far we should go toward complete equality of incomes. The best division (or distribution) of income is ill defined. Therefore much of the discussion of income distribution has been focused on narrower questions, such as: What is happening to those at the bottom of the ladder? What is happening to the families who live in poverty?

Poverty is difficult to define in precise dollar terms. For one thing, not everyone's needs are the same. The sickly have the greatest need for medical care. Large families have the most compelling need for food and clothing. There is no simple, single measure of the "poverty line," below which families may be judged to be poor. Reasonable standards may, however, be established by taking into consideration such obvious complications as the number of individuals in a family. The poverty standards defined by the U.S. government in 1988 are shown in Table 1-1.

There are two ways of raising people above the

TABLE 1-1 Poverty Standards, 1988

Size of Family	Poverty Line
One person	$6,000
Two persons	7,690
Three persons	9,420
Four persons	12,075
Five persons	14,290

According to U.S. government standards, families are poor if their incomes fall below these figures. For example, a four-person family is poor if it has an income of less than $12,075.

poverty line. The first is to increase the size of overall national income. As income rises throughout the economy, the incomes of those at the lower end will also generally rise. In the words of President John Kennedy, "A rising tide lifts all boats."

A second way to reduce poverty is to increase the share of the nation's income going to the poorest people. Thus poverty may be combated by a **redistribution of income.** For example, the well-to-do may be taxed in order to finance government programs aimed at helping the poor. A number of government programs have attempted to raise the share of the nation's income going to the poorest families.

During the 1950s and 1960s, progress was made toward that goal. Between 1950 and 1969, the share of the poorest 20% of families rose from 4.5% to 5.6% of total income. Furthermore, a rising tide was lifting all boats. Because of the vigorous expansion of the economy, average family income rose about 40%—even after adjusting for inflation. The rising tide of income, together with the larger percentage going to the poor, combined to raise the incomes of the poorest fifth by more than 70% (again, after adjusting for inflation). Thus the poorest of 1969 were much better off than the poorest of 1950. Nevertheless, they were still very poor by the overall standards of society.

Figure 1-5 shows the steady decline in the percentage of the population living in poverty during the 1960s, from 22.1% to 12.1%. After a brief reversal during the recession of 1970, the downward trend continued, reaching a low of 11.1% in 1973. Until 1978 there was little change, but between 1978 and 1983, the rate increased to 15.2%. Since 1983, the rate has again declined, although it remains above the lows of the 1970s. We are still far short of the objective of eliminating poverty. Why is this task so difficult? One reason is unemployment; many of the poor are unemployed. The poverty rate increased between 1978 and 1983 when the economy was in recession and the unemployment rate was increasing. Both poverty and unemployment decreased during the long expansion after 1983.

Unemployment has not been the only reason for poverty. Although the unemployment rate was no higher in 1981 than in 1976, the percentage of the population living in poverty was substantially

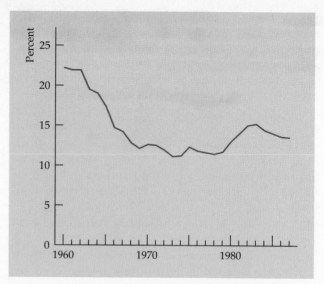

FIGURE 1-5   The percentage of the population living in poverty.

During the long expansion of the 1960s there was a substantial decline in the percentage of the population living in poverty. After 1979, the percentage living in poverty increased. (Source: *Annual Report of the President, 1989,* p. 342.)

higher (14.0% compared with 11.8%). Poverty is a perplexing problem.

5. GROWTH

In an economy with large-scale unemployment, output can be increased by putting the unemployed back to work. Slack in the economy can be reduced, and productive capacity can be used more fully. Once the economy approaches its capacity, however, additional increases in output require an increase in the productive capacity itself. Capacity can be raised either by an addition to the available resources (for example, an increase in the number of factories and machines) or an improvement in technology (that is, the invention of new, more productive machines or new ways of organizing production). When economists speak of growth, they typically mean an *increase in the productive capacity* of the economy that results from technological improvement and additional factories, machines, or other resources.

The advantages of growth are obvious. If the

economy grows, our incomes will be higher in the future. We and our children will have higher standards of material comfort. Moreover, some of the rising production can be used to benefit the poor without reducing the incomes of the rich.

Emphasis on growth as an economic objective has changed substantially over the years. During the Kennedy administration in the early 1960s, growth became a prominent national goal, both because of its economic advantages and the importance of "keeping ahead of the Russians." During the late 1960s and early 1970s, doubts began to develop. While the advantages of growth are obvious, it comes at a cost. If we are to grow more rapidly, more of our current efforts will have to be directed toward the production of machines and away from the production of consumption goods. In the future, of course, as the new machines begin operating, they will turn out more consumption goods—more clothing, furniture, or cars. Thus current policies to stimulate growth will make possible higher consumption in the future. For the moment, however, consumption will be lower. Thus, in order to evaluate a high-growth policy, we have to compare the advantage of higher *future* consumption with the sacrifice of lower *current* consumption.

Seen in this light, it is not clear that the faster the rate of growth, the better. Future generations should be considered, but so should the present one.

Even if we were concerned solely with the welfare of coming generations, it would not be so clear that the more growth, the better. Very rapid rates of growth may harm the environment. If our primary objective is to produce more steel and more automobiles, we may pay too little heed to the belching smoke of the steel mills or to the effect of the automobile on the quality of the air we breathe. Thus during the 1970s there was less emphasis on growth than there had been during the early 1960s and more emphasis on other goals, such as the preservation of the environment.

During the Reagan administration, the pendulum swung back toward growth as an objective. Vigorous growth was again seen as a way of dealing with many economic problems, including poverty. Kennedy's remark—"A rising tide lifts all boats"—again became popular in Washington. (In rebuttal, Herbert Stein observed: "Unfortunately,

that is not true. A rising tide does not lift the boats that are under water.... Many kinds of poverty will not be significantly relieved by faster growth.")[6]

INTERRELATIONS AMONG ECONOMIC GOALS

The achievement of one goal may help in the achievement of others. As already noted, growth may make it easier to reduce the problem of poverty. Additional income may be provided to the poor out of the growth in total income, without reducing the income of those at the top. Thus social conflicts over the share of income may be reduced if the size of the nation's total income is increasing.

Similarly, the poverty problem is easier to solve if the unemployment rate is kept low, so that large numbers of unemployed do not swell the ranks of the poor. When goals are **complementary** like this (that is, when achieving one helps to achieve the other), economic policymaking is relatively easy. By attacking on a broad front and striving for several goals, we can increase our chances of achieving each.

Unfortunately, however, economic goals are not always complementary. In some cases, they are in conflict. For example, when unemployment is reduced, inflation generally gets worse. There is a reason for this phenomenon. Heavy purchasing by the public tends to reduce unemployment, but it also tends to increase inflation. It reduces unemployment because, as the public buys more cars, unemployed workers get jobs again in the auto factories; when families buy more homes, construction workers find it easier to find jobs. At the same time, heavy purchasing tends to increase inflation because producers are more likely to raise their prices if buyers are clamoring for their products. Such **conflicts among goals** test the wisdom of policymakers. They feel torn in deciding which objective to pursue.

---

[6]Herbert Stein, "Economic Policy, Conservatively Speaking," *Public Opinion,* February 1981, p. 4. (Stein was chairman of the Council of Economic Advisers from 1972 to 1974.)

A PREVIEW

These, then, are the five major objectives of economic policy: *high employment, price stability, efficiency, an equitable distribution of income,* and *growth.* The first two goals are related to the stability of the economy. If the economy is unstable, moving along like a roller coaster, its performance will be very unsatisfactory. As it heads downhill into recession, large numbers of people will be thrown out of work. Then, as it heads upward into a runaway boom, prices will soar as the public scrambles to buy the available goods. The first two goals may, therefore, be viewed as two aspects of a single objective: that of achieving an **equilibrium** with stable prices and a low unemployment rate. This will be the major topic in Parts II–V (Chapters 6 through 19) of this book.

Equilibrium is the first of the three main "E's" of economics. The second E—**efficiency**—will be studied in Parts VI–VIII (Chapters 20 through 34).

Are we getting the most out of our productive efforts? When does the free market—where buyers and sellers come together without government interference—encourage efficiency? When the free market does not encourage efficiency, what (if anything) should be done?

Part IX (Chapters 35 through 40) deals primarily with the third E—**equity.** If the government takes a laissez-faire attitude, how much income will go to the workers? To the owners of land? To others? How do labor unions affect the incomes of their members? How can the government improve the lot of the poor?

The final major objective—growth—cuts across a number of other major topics and thus appears periodically throughout the book. However, before we get into the meat of the three issues of equilibrium, efficiency, and equity, we must first set the stage with some of the basic concepts and tools of economics. To that task we now turn in Chapters 2 through 5.

KEY POINTS

1. During the twentieth century, substantial economic progress has been made in the United States and many other countries. We are producing much more, even though we spend less time at work than did our grandparents.

2. Nevertheless, substantial economic problems remain: problems such as poverty in the less developed countries and at home, high rates of unemployment, and inflation.

3. One of the things that economists study is how to deal with problems, either through private action or through government policies.

4. In the history of economic thought, the role of government has been controversial. Adam Smith in 1776 called for the liberation of markets from the tyranny of government control. By 1936, John Maynard Keynes was appealing to the government to accept its responsibilities and to undertake public works in order to get the economy out of the depression.

5. Important economic goals include:

  (a) An equilibrium with high employment and price stability.

  (b) Efficiency. *Allocative efficiency* involves the production of the right combination of goods, using the lowest cost combination of inputs. *Technological efficiency* occurs when people produce the maximum quantity of output with a given quantity of inputs, while working at a reasonable pace.

  (c) Equity in the distribution of income.

  (d) A satisfactory rate of growth.

6. Large changes in the *average* level of prices are undesirable. However, changes in *relative* prices may be desirable as a way of encouraging people to conserve scarce goods and to use more plentiful, cheaper alternatives instead.

7. Goals are complementary if the achievement of one helps in the achievement of the other. For example, a reduction in unemployment also generally reduces poverty. However, goals may be in conflict. An increase in spending works to reduce unemployment, but it can also increase the rate of inflation.

KEY CONCEPTS

laissez faire
depression
recession
unemployment
inflation
deflation

hyperinflation
average level of prices
relative prices
allocative efficiency
technological efficiency
poverty

equal distribution of income
equitable distribution of income
redistribution of income
growth
complementary goals
conflicting goals

PROBLEMS

1-1. According to Smith's "invisible hand," we are able to obtain meat, not because of the butcher's benevolence, but because of his self-interest. Why is it in the butcher's self-interest to provide us with meat? What does the butcher get in return?

1-2. Suppose another depression were to occur like the depression of the 1930s. How would it affect you? (Thinking about this question provided a major motivation for a generation of economists. They were appalled at the prospect and determined to play a role in preventing a repetition of the Great Depression.)

1-3. The section on an equitable distribution of income reflects two views regarding the proper approach to poverty:

(a) The important thing is to meet the basic needs of the poor—that is, to provide at least a minimum income for the purchase of food, shelter, and other necessities.

(b) The important thing is to reduce inequality—that is, to reduce the gap between the rich and the poor.

These two views are not the same. For example, if there is rapid growth in the economy, objective (a) may be accomplished without any progress being made toward (b). Which is the more important objective? Why? Do you feel strongly about your choice? Why?

1-4. In Figure 1-1, observe that the strong downward trend in the length of the workweek ended about 1950. Before that date, part of the gains of the average worker came in the form of shorter hours. Since 1950, practically all the gains have consisted of higher wages and fringe benefits. Can you provide any reason why the workweek leveled out in 1950?

1-5. Explain how an upswing in purchases by the public will affect (a) unemployment and (b) inflation. Does this result illustrate economic goals that are complementary or conflicting?

DIAGRAMS USED IN ECONOMICS

Chapter 1 contains diagrams that illustrate important points, such as the increase in production per person since 1900 (Fig. 1-1) and the fact that economic growth slowed down after 1973 (Fig. 1-2). In the study of economics, diagrams are used frequently—as you may see by flipping through this book. A picture is often worth a thousand words. Diagrams can fix important ideas in our minds. They present information in a vivid and eye-catching way. Unfortunately, they can also mislead. The first and lasting impression may be the wrong impression. This appendix explains some of the major types of diagrams used in economics and some of the ways in which diagrams may be used to impress or mislead rather than inform.

Three major types of diagrams will be considered:

1. Diagrams that present and compare two facts.

2. Diagrams that show how something changes through time. For example, Figure 1-4 illustrates how the average level of prices has usually risen but has sometimes fallen.

3. Diagrams that show how two variables are related—for example, how an increase in family income (variable 1) results in an increase in spending (variable 2).

1. A SIMPLE COMPARISON OF TWO FACTS

The simplest type of diagram brings together two facts for comparison. Often, the best method of presenting two facts—and the least likely to mislead—is to use a *bar chart* like the one shown back in Figure 1-2. In the top left corner, the first bar shows that the average rate of increase in output in industrial countries was 5.2% per year between 1960 and 1973, while the next bar shows that the rate was only 2.5% between 1973 and 1987. By comparing the heights of the bars, we immediately see how the rate has changed.

THINGS TO WATCH

Even such a simple diagram may carry a misleading message. There are several "tricks" which an unscrupulous writer can use to fool the reader.

Suppose, for example, that someone wants to present the performance of a country or a corporation in the most favorable light. Consider an example—a country whose steel production rose from 10 million tons in 1980 to 20 million tons in 1990.

Figure 1-6 is a bar chart illustrating this comparison in the simplest, most straightforward way. Glancing at the height of the two bars in this diagram, the reader gets the correct impression—steel production has doubled.

This is a very good performance but not a spectacular one. Suppose someone wants to make things look even better. Two easy ways of doing so—without actually lying—are illustrated in Figure 1-7.

The left panel is designed to mislead because part of the diagram is omitted. The heights of the bars are measured from 5 million tons rather than

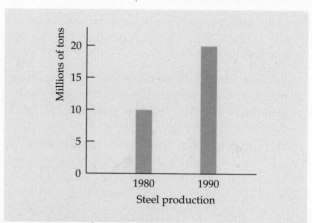

FIGURE 1-6   A simple bar chart.

The simplest bar chart provides a comparison of two numbers, in this case the production of steel in two years. We see correctly that steel production has doubled.

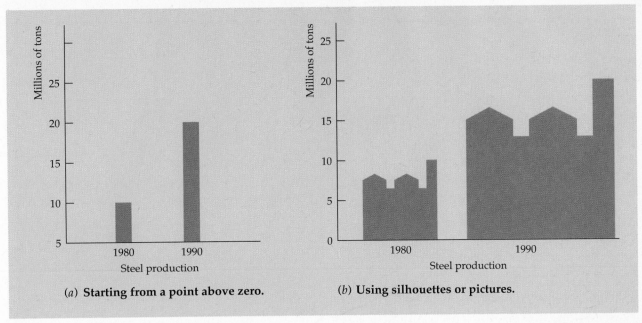

FIGURE 1-7   Variations on the simple bar chart.

Readers may be misled by variations on the simple bar chart. Both of the above panels
present the same information as in Figure 1-6. In the left panel, the vertical axis begins
with 5 million tons, rather than zero. In the right panel, pictures are used, rather than bars.
In each case, the reader may be left with the erroneous impression that steel production
has more than doubled.

zero. Thus the 1990 bar is three times as high as the
1980 bar, and the unwary reader may be left with
the wrong impression—that steel production is
three times as high, whereas in fact it is only twice
as high. This, then, is the first thing to watch out
for: Do the numbers on the vertical axis start from
zero? If not, the diagram may give the wrong
impression.

The right panel shows another way in which
the reader may be fooled. The bars of Figure 1-6 are
replaced with something more interesting— pictures of steel mills. Because production has doubled, the steel mill on the right is twice as high as
that on the left. But notice how this picture gives
the wrong impression. The mill on the right is not
only twice as high. It is also twice as wide, and we
can visualize it as being twice as deep, too.
Therefore, it isn't just twice as large as the mill on
the left; it is many times as large. Thus the casual
reader may again be left with the wrong impression—that steel output has increased manyfold,
when in fact it has only doubled. This, then, is the

second reason to be wary: Look carefully and skep-
tically at diagrams that use silhouettes or pictures.
Do they leave you with an exaggerated impression
of the changes that have actually occurred?

Figure 1-8 illustrates a third way to mislead
readers.[7] In both panels, the facts are correct
regarding the average price of common stock in the
United States. (Each share of common stock represents part ownership of a company.) The left panel
shows that, between 1929 and 1953, the average
price of stocks did not change at all. The right panel shows facts that are equally true. Between 1932
and 1953—almost the same period of comparison—stock prices increased *six fold*. How can *both*
of these panels be correct? The answer: Between
1929 and 1932, the most spectacular stock market

---

[7]For more detail on how readers may be misled, see the
sprightly book by Darrell Huff, *How to Lie with Statistics*
(New York: W.W. Norton, 1954).

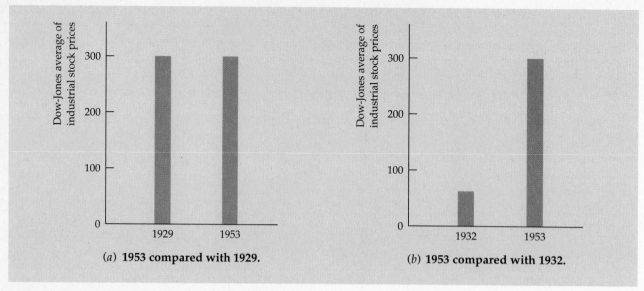

FIGURE 1-8   Comparisons depend on the times chosen.

Comparisons may change even when seemingly minor changes are made in the dates. In 1953, stock prices were no higher on average than in 1929 (left panel). However, they were six times as high in 1953 as they had been in 1932.

collapse in American history occurred, with stocks losing five-sixths of their value.

Notice the contrast between the two panels. The left one implies that not much can be gained by entering the stock market. The right panel gives exactly the opposite impression: The stock market is the place to get rich. Thus, an author can give two completely different messages, depending on the choice of the initial "base" year (1929 or 1932). So beware. In any diagram showing how something has changed over time, ask yourself: Has the author slanted the results by selecting years designed to mislead?

2. TIME SERIES: HOW SOMETHING CHANGES THROUGH TIME

That last problem can be avoided by providing more information to the reader with a **time series** diagram, showing stock prices *every* year, not just a beginning and final year. Even better is to show stock prices every month. With a more detailed figure, the reader can see a much more complete story, including both the collapse of 1929–1932 and

the way in which stock prices have risen since 1932.

> A *time series* diagram shows how something (such as the price of stocks, the output of steel, or the unemployment rate) has changed through time.

However, even when we provide a detailed time series, a number of issues remain. Here are some of the most important.

SHOULD WE MEASURE FROM ZERO?

In discussing a simple comparison between two facts, we seem to have settled the question of how we should measure up the vertical axis of a diagram. To start at any figure other than zero can be misleading—as in Figure 1-7a, when steel production was measured up from a starting point of 5 million tons.

Once we provide the detailed information of a time series, we should reopen the question of how to measure along the vertical axis. The problem is that we now have two conflicting considerations.

We would like to start from zero to avoid misleading the reader. On the other hand, starting from some other point may make the details of a diagram much easier to see.

This is illustrated in Figure 1-9, which shows the rate of unemployment in each year from 1978 to 1988. In the left panel, the unemployment rate is measured vertically, starting from zero. This gives us the best picture of how the overall unemployment rate compares in any two years we might like to choose (for example, 1979 and 1982). Contrast this with the right panel, where the measurement of unemployment starts above zero. Like Figure 1-7a, this panel can be misleading. For example, it might leave the impression that the unemployment rate tripled between 1979 and 1982, whereas in fact it increased by far less (approximately from 6% to 10%).

However, the right panel has a major compensating advantage. It provides a much clearer picture of how the unemployment rate *changes* from year to year; the year-to-year differences are much more conspicuous. These year-to-year changes are very important, as they are one measure of fluctua-tions in the economy. Consequently, the right-hand diagram can be more informative.

If panel *b* is chosen, readers must be warned that we have not started from zero. One way is to leave a gap in the vertical bars to show that something has been left out. Another way, also shown in panel b, is to leave a gap in the vertical axis itself.

HOW SHOULD GROWTH BE ILLUSTRATED?

Some time series—such as a nation's popula-tion—have a strong tendency to grow through time. If we measure in the normal way along the vertical axis, the curve becomes steeper through time, as shown in the left panel of Figure 1-10. There is nothing necessarily wrong with this pre-sentation; the increase in the population between 1970 and 1980 (23 million) was in fact much greater than the increase between 1870 and 1880 (10 mil-lion).

However, there are two related problems with this figure. First, the numbers in the early years—

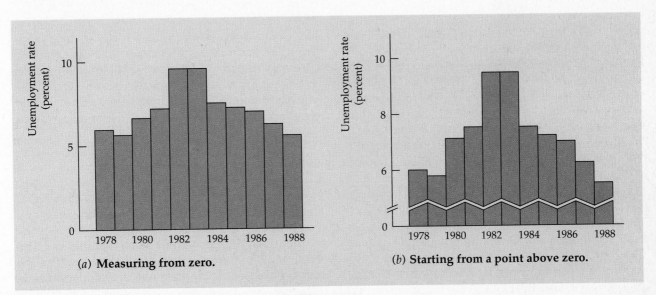

(a) **Measuring from zero.**   (b) **Starting from a point above zero.**

FIGURE 1-9   A time series: The unemployment rate, 1978–1988.

The reader is provided much more information with a time series showing every year or every month rather than just two years. In this diagram, there is an advantage in starting the vertical measurement above zero. Observe that the detailed year-to-year changes stand out more clearly in the right panel than in the left. To warn the reader that something has been left out, a gap is left in the vertical bars.

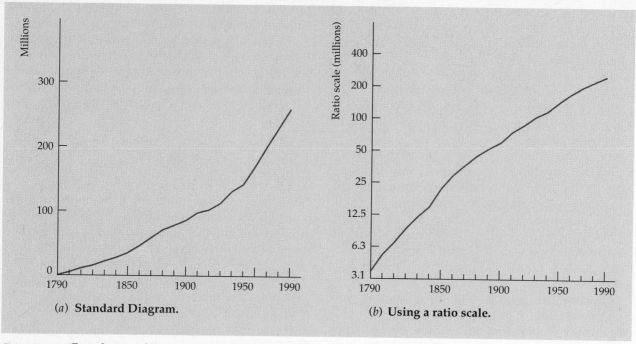

FIGURE 1-10   Population of the United States, 1790–1990.

A ratio scale allows us to identify the period when the rate of population growth was most rapid. It occurred when the slope of the curve in the right panel was steepest.

before, say, 1820—are so small that details can scarcely be seen. Second, we may be interested not just in the absolute numbers but in the *rate* at which population is growing. Thus the 10 million increase in population in the 1870s represents a much greater rate of increase (2.3% per year) than the 23 million increase of the 1970s (1.1% per year).

To highlight the rate of growth, a **ratio** or **logarithmic** scale is used on the vertical axis in panel *b* of Figure 1-10. On such a scale, equal *percentage* changes show up as equal distances. For example, the vertical distance from 50 million to 100 million (an increase of 100%) is the same as the distance from 100 million to 200 million (also an increase of 100%). In such a diagram, if something grows at a *constant rate* (for example, by 2% per year), it traces out a *straight line*. By looking for the steepest sections of the time series, we can identify the periods when population has grown at the most rapid rate. (Similarly, back in Fig. 1-4, which is also drawn on a ratio scale, the steepest parts of the curve show when the most rapid rates of inflation occurred.)

A ratio scale is appropriate for a time series—like population—that grows. However, it is inappropriate for a series that does not have a strong tendency to grow. For example, there is no reason to expect a greater and greater percentage of the population to be living in poverty, and it would therefore be inappropriate to use a logarithmic scale in a figure showing the poverty rate.

Finally, note that, when a logarithmic scale is used, the question of whether the vertical axis is measured from zero becomes irrelevant, since zero *cannot* appear on such a diagram. By looking at Figure 1-10*b*, we can see why. Each time we go up 1 centimeter (one notch on the vertical axis), the population doubles—from 50 to 100 million, and then to 200 million. We can make exactly the same statement the other way around: Each time we go down a centimeter, the population falls by half—from 50 million to 25 million, then 12.5 million, and so on. No matter how far we extend the diagram downward, each additional centimeter will reduce the population by one-half. Therefore the vertical axis can *never* reach zero on such a diagram.

REAL OR MONETARY MEASURES?

People often complain that the federal government is getting too big. Suppose we wanted to look at the size of the government. How would we do so?

The most obvious way is to look at the amount the government spends. Measured in dollars, the growth of government spending has been truly stupendous over the past half century (Fig. 1-11). There are, however, several shortcomings to this simple measure.

The first has to do with prices, which have risen substantially during the past half century. Inflation means that, even if the government had remained exactly the same size—building the same number of roads, keeping the same number of soldiers in the army—it would have spent many more dollars; its expenditures in dollar or **nominal** terms would have gone up rapidly. In order to eliminate the effects of inflation, government statisticians calculate what government expenditures *would have been if prices had not gone up*—that is, if prices had remained at the level existing in a single year. Such a measure of government expenditures—in **constant-dollar** or **real** terms—is shown in panel *a* of Figure 1-12. Observe how much more slowly government expenditures have grown when the effects of inflation are eliminated. Chapter 6 will provide details on how real expenditures are calculated.

RELATIVE MEASURES

Even when measured in real terms, government expenditures have risen substantially. Does this, in itself, mean that the government is too big? The answer is, not necessarily. One reason is that, as the government has grown, so has the overall economy. Thus we may ask the question: Has the government grown *relative to the economy*? (As in Fig. 1-1, the size of the economy is measured by gross national product, or GNP.) In Figure 1-12, panel *b*, observe that government expenditures have not grown much relative to the economy (that is, as a percentage of GNP) in recent decades.

In passing, we note that, even if government spending is rising relative to the size of the overall economy, this does not, in itself, mean that the government is "too big;" nor would a downward trend necessarily mean that the government was "too small." During the 1930s, government spending was rising relative to the size of the economy, yet defense spending was still too low to meet the growing threat from Hitler. On the other hand, as we come to an accommodation with the Soviet Union, it may be clear that we can reduce military spending in relative safety.

3. RELATIONSHIPS BETWEEN VARIABLES

Frequently, economists want to keep track of the relationship between two variables. Table 1-2 provides an illustration—the relationship between the incomes of households and their expenditures for the basic necessities (housing, food, and clothing).

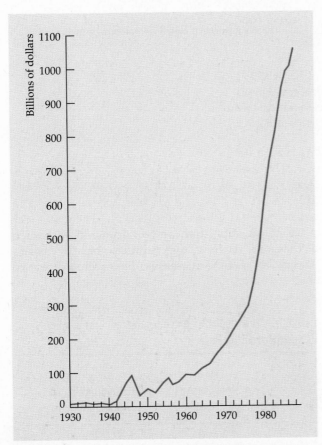

FIGURE 1-11   Federal government expenditures, measured in dollars.

As measured by the number of dollars spent, the size of the federal government has expanded very rapidly.

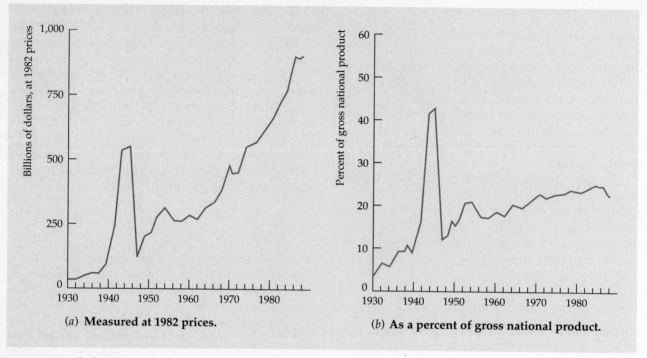

(a) **Measured at 1982 prices.**

(b) **As a percent of gross national product.**

FIGURE 1-12   Federal government expenditures: Alternative presentations.

When the effects of inflation are removed in the left panel, the growth of government
spending is much less spectacular than in Figure 1-11. The right panel shows that the size
of the federal government has grown relatively slowly as a fraction of gross national
product.

The top row (row *A*) indicates that the American
family with an income of $10,000 spends $7,000 on
the basic necessities. Similarly, row *B* shows that a
family with an income of $20,000 spends $11,000 on
these basics.

The data in Table 1-2 may be graphed as Figure
1-13, where income is measured along the horizontal axis and expenditures for basics up the vertical
axis. (The lower left corner, labeled "0," is the **origin**—that is, the starting point from which both
income and basic expenditures are measured.) To
plot the data in row *A* of the table, we measure
$10,000 in income along the horizontal axis and
$7,000 in spending for basics up the vertical axis.
This gives us point *A* in the diagram. Similarly,
points *B, C,* and *D* represent corresponding rows *B,
C,* and *D* in Table 1-2.

One question that can be addressed with such
a diagram is how expenditures on the basics
change as income increases. For example, as in-

TABLE 1-2   Household Income and
Expenditures for Basics

Family	(1) Household Income (after taxes)	(2) Expenditures for Basics
A	$10,000	$7,000
B	20,000	11,000
C	30,000	14,500
D	40,000	17,500

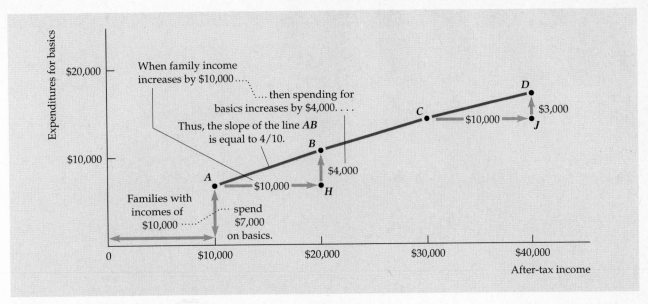

FIGURE 1-13   How expenditures for basics are related to income.

As family income increases (along the horizontal axis), the family's expenditures for the basics increase (as measured up the vertical axis). The *slope* of the line between any two points—such as *A* and *B*—shows how strongly expenditures for basics respond (*HB*) to an increase in income (*AH*).

come increases from $10,000 at point *A* to $20,000 at point *B*, basic expenditures rise from $7,000 to $11,000; that is, expenditures on the basics rise by $4,000 in response to the $10,000 increase in income.

This relation can be illustrated by drawing a line between points *A* and *B*, and looking at its **slope**—slope being defined as the *vertical change* or *rise* (*HB*) *divided by the horizontal change* or *run* (*AH*). In this example, the slope is $4,000/$10,000 = 4/10. As incomes increase from point *A* to point *B*, families spend 40% of the increase on the basics.

Observe in this diagram that the slope becomes smaller as incomes increase and we go further to the right. Whereas the slope is 4/10 between *A* and *B*, it is only $3,000/$10,000, or 3/10, between *C* and *D*. This smaller slope makes sense. Families with high incomes already have good houses, food, and clothing. When their income goes up another $10,000, they don't spend much more on the

basics; they have other things to do with their income.

Nevertheless, no matter how far to the right this diagram is extended, the line joining any two points will always slope *upward*—that is, the slope is always *positive*. The reason is that, as people's incomes rise, they are always willing to pay somewhat more in order to get better houses, food, and clothing.

In some relationships, however, there may be a downward-sloping curve. Figure 1-14 illustrates the situation facing a company producing a small business aircraft. The costs facing such a company are high: It has the expense of designing the aircraft, and it requires an expensive plant for production. If the firm produces only a few units each year (say, 10 aircraft, measured along the horizontal axis), it will operate at point *A*. It will be unable to charge a price high enough to cover its costs, and it will therefore suffer a loss—that is, its profit

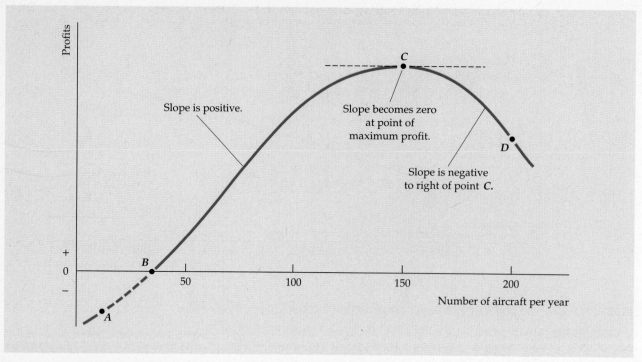

FIGURE 1-14   Output and profits.

If the firm produces only a few planes, it cannot cover its costs. It suffers losses. (Profits are negative.) As production increases, its losses shrink as it approaches point B. Then, to the right of B, the firm begins to make profits. As long as output is less than 150 units, the profits curve has a *positive* slope; that is, it slopes upward. Profits reach a peak at point C and thereafter begin to decline. Thus to the right of C the curve has a *negative* slope. At the point where the curve reaches its peak, it is horizontal. The slope is zero.

(measured along the vertical axis) will be negative. As it sells more, its revenues will rise, and it will begin to make profits to the right of point B.

Profits do not rise indefinitely. If the company were to produce a large number of planes—say, 200—it would have to slash prices in order to sell them. This would reduce its profits. Thus the profit curve at first slopes upward, reaches a peak at C, and then slopes downward.

Point C is very significant for the firm. At this point, the firm *maximizes its profits*. The curve ceases to slope upward and is just about to slope downward; the slope is just about to switch from being positive to becoming negative. Thus, at the point of maximum profit, the slope of the curve is *zero*.

CHAPTER 2
SCARCITY AND CHOICE
The Economic Problem

Economics studies human behaviour as a relationship between ends and scarce means.
LIONEL ROBBINS

When Neil Armstrong stepped on the moon in 1969, the space program achieved its most spectacular success. Now, 20 years later, Carl Sagan, the noted Cornell astronomer and author of the best-selling *Cosmos*, has proposed a new space adventure. He has urged that a space ship be sent to Mars with a U. S. and Soviet crew. The time has come, he believes, for human eyes to look directly at that mysterious planet.

Sagan's proposal has met with skepticism. The reason is cost. The U.S. share of such a project would be huge—perhaps as much as $100 billion. How could we pay for it? Through additional taxes that would require the public to give up income in order to finance the space program? Through cutbacks in other spending by the federal government—for roads, social security, or defense? Sagan's proposal has run directly into the central **economic problem.** We must make **choices.** We cannot have everything we want, because:

1. Our material **wants** are virtually **unlimited.**
2. Economic **resources** are **scarce.**

If we use our productive capacity to send a spaceship with human passengers to Mars, we will have less for other things.

The economic problem is the need to make choices among the options permitted by our scarce resources.

Economics is the study of how scarce resources are allocated to satisfy alternative, competing human wants.

To *economize* is to achieve a specific benefit at the lowest cost in terms of the resources used.

UNLIMITED WANTS. . .

Consider, first, our wants. If we can survive in a simple one-bedroom bungalow, why do we aspire to much larger homes filled with gadgets? Why do our material wants never seem to be satisfied? Material wants arise for two reasons. First, each of us has basic biological needs: the need for food, shelter, and clothing. But there is also a second reason. Clearly, we are prepared to work more than is required to meet our minimum needs. We want more than the basic diet of vegetables and water needed to sustain life. We want more than the minimum clothing needed to protect us from the cold. In other words, we want not only the essential goods and services that make life possible, but also some of the nonessentials that make life pleasant. Of course, the two basic reasons for material wants cannot be sharply separated. When we sit down to a gourmet meal at a restaurant, we are getting the food essential for satisfying our biological requirements. But we are getting something more. When we savor exotic foods in a comfortable and stylish atmosphere, we are also getting luxuries. Such nonessentials are sufficiently pleasant that we are willing to work to obtain them.

The range of consumer wants is exceedingly broad. We want **goods,** such as houses, cars, shoes, and tennis rackets. Similarly, we want **services,** such as medical care and transportation. When we get what we want, it may whet our appetites for something more. We may become dissatisfied with the old lawnmower and want a self-propelled one instead. After we buy a house, we may wish to replace the carpets and drapes. Furthermore, as new products are introduced, we may want them too. We want video recorders, home computers, and a host of other products never dreamed of by earlier generations. Even though it is conceivable that, some day, we will say, "Enough," that day seems far away. Our material wants show no sign of being completely satisfied.

. . . AND SCARCE RESOURCES

Not all wants can be satisfied because of the second fundamental fact. Although our productive capacity is large, it is not without limit. There are only so many workers in the labor force, only a given amount of land, and only a certain number of machines and factories. In other words, our resources are limited.

Resources are the basic inputs used in the production of goods and services. Therefore, they are also frequently known as **factors of production.** They can be categorized under three main headings: land, capital, and labor.

1. Land. Economists use this term in a broad sense, to include not only the land cultivated by farmers and the land in cities used as building lots, but also the other gifts of nature that come with the land. Thus the minerals that are found under the soil, and the water and sunlight that fall on the soil, are all part of the land resource.

2. Capital. This term refers to buildings, equipment, and inventories of materials (such as steel) to be used in the productive process. An automobile factory is "capital," and so are the machines in the plant and the steel with which automobiles will be built. In contrast to land, which has been *given* to us by nature, capital has been *produced* at some time in the past. It may have been the distant past; the factory may have been built 25 years ago. Or it may have been the recent past; the steel may have been manufactured last month. The process of producing and accumulating capital is known as **investment.**

Unlike *consumer goods* (such as shoes, cars, or food), *capital goods* or investment goods (such as tractors, factories, or machinery in the factories) are not produced to satisfy human wants directly. Rather, they are intended for use in the production of other goods. Capital produced now will satisfy wants only indirectly and at a later time, when it is used in the production of consumer goods. The production of capital therefore means that someone is *willing to wait.* When a machine is produced rather than a car, the choice is made to forego the car now in order to produce the machine, thus making it possible to produce more cars or other goods in the future. Capital formation therefore involves a choice between consumption *now* and more consumption *in the future.*

One point of terminology should be emphasized here. Unless otherwise specified, economists use the term "capital" to mean **real capital,** not financial capital. In previous paragraphs, we've been referring to real capital—the factories and machinery used to produce other goods. On the other hand, **financial capital** consists of financial assets such as common stocks, bonds, or bank deposits. Such assets are important. The holder of a stock or bond, for example, has a form of wealth that is likely to produce income in the future, in the form of dividends on the stock or interest on the bond. But, while an individual might consider 100 shares of General Motors stock as part of his or her "capital," they are not capital in the economic sense. They are not a resource with which goods and services can be produced.

Similarly, when economists talk of investment, they generally mean **real investment**—the accumulation of machines and other real capital—and not financial investment, such as the purchase of a government bond.

3. Labor. This term refers to the human resource— the physical and mental talents that people apply to the production of goods and services. The construction worker provides labor, and so does the college professor or the physician. The professor produces educational services, and the doctor produces medical services.[1]

One particular human resource deserves special emphasis: **entrepreneurial ability**. Entrepreneur is a French word that means "someone who undertakes." More specifically, it means someone who

a. *Organizes production*, bringing together the factors of production—land, labor, and capital—to make goods and services.

b. *Makes business decisions*, figuring out what goods to produce and how to produce them.

c. *Takes risk*, knowing that there is no guarantee that business decisions will turn out to be correct.

d. *Innovates*, introducing new products, new technology, and new ways of organizing business.

In order to be successful, an entrepreneur needs to be aware of changes in the economy. Is the market for adding machines declining, while that of computers is expanding? If so, the successful entrepreneur will not build a new assembly line for adding machines but will instead consider the production of computers. Some entrepreneurs are spectacularly successful. For example, Steve Jobs and Steve Wozniak set up Apple Computer while they were still in their twenties. Their mushrooming sales helped to make the microcomputer a common household appliance—and made them multi-millionaires in the process. Other entrepreneurs are engaged in much more prosaic, everyday enterprises. The teenager who offers to cut a neighbor's lawn for $10 is an entrepreneur. So is the college student who has a business typing other students' papers. The key questions facing an entrepreneur are these: Are people willing to pay for what I can produce? Can I sell the good or service for a price high enough to cover costs and have some profit left over?

Because entrepreneurs are the ones who undertake the production of new goods, they play a strategic role in determining the dynamism and growth of the economy.

SCARCITY AND CHOICE: THE PRODUCTION POSSIBILITIES CURVE

With unlimited wants and limited resources, we face the fundamental economic problem of **scarcity**. We cannot have everything we want; we must make *choices*.

The problem of scarcity—and the need to make choices—can be illustrated with a **production possibilities curve** (PPC). This curve shows what can be produced with our existing resources (land, labor, and capital) and with our existing technology. Although our resources are limited and our capacity to produce is likewise limited, we have an option as to what goods and services we produce. We may produce fewer cars and more aircraft or less wheat and more corn.

In an economy with thousands of products, the choices before us are complex. In order to reduce this complexity, consider a very basic economy with only two goods (cotton clothing and wheat) where a decision to produce more food (wheat) will leave us able to produce less clothing.

The options open to us are illustrated in the hypothetical production possibilities curve in Figure 2-1. Consider first an extreme example, in which all our resources are directed toward the production of food. In this case, illustrated by option *A*, we would produce 20 million tons of food but no clothing. This clearly does not repre-

---

[1]The preceding paragraphs have presented the traditional division of the factors of production into the categories of land, labor, and capital. While this traditional division is still popular, present-day economists do not universally subscribe to it. In particular, some economists now talk of "human capital." This term may be defined as the education and training that add to the productivity of labor. Human capital has two of the important characteristics of physical capital: (1) it requires a willingness to wait during the training period, when the trainee does not produce goods or services; and (2) it results in an increase in the productive capacity of the economy, since a trained worker can produce more than an untrained one.

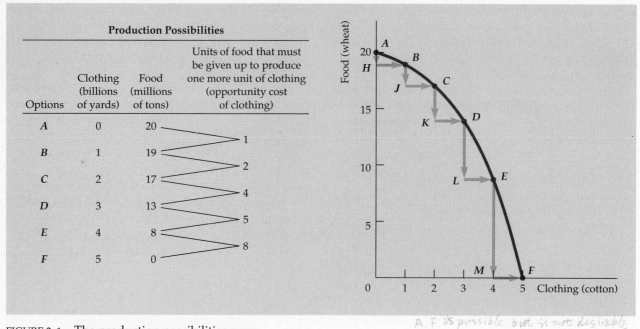

FIGURE 2–1   The production possibilities curve.

The curve shows the combinations of two goods that can be produced with limited
resources of land, labor and capital.

A.F is possible but is not desirable

sent a desirable composition of output. Although we would be well fed, we would be running around naked. However, no claim has been made that the points on the production possibilities curve are necessarily *desirable;* the only claim is that they are *possible.* And point A is possible.

At the other extreme, if we produced nothing but clothing, we would make 5 billion yards, as illustrated by point F. Again, this is a possible outcome but not a desirable one. We would be well dressed as we faced starvation.

THE SHAPE OF THE PRODUCTION POSSIBILITIES CURVE: INCREASING OPPORTUNITY COSTS

More reasonable cases are those in which we produce some quantities of each good. Consider how the economy might move from point A toward point F. At point A, nothing is produced but food. It is grown on all types of arable land throughout the nation. In order to begin the production of clothing, cotton would be planted in the areas that were comparatively best suited for cotton produc-

tion—those in Alabama and Mississippi. From these lands, we would get a lot of cotton, while giving up just a small amount of food that might have been grown there. This is illustrated in the move from point A to point B on the production possibilities curve. Only one unit of food is given up in order to produce the first unit of clothing.

As more cotton is produced, however, land must be used that is somewhat less suited to its production. As a result, the second unit of clothing does not come quite so easily. To produce it, more than one unit of food must be given up. This is illustrated in the move from point B to point C. As clothing production is increased by one more unit (from one unit to two), food production falls by two units (from 19 to 17). The **opportunity cost** of the second unit of clothing—the food we have to give up to acquire it—is thus greater than the opportunity cost of the first unit.

Further increases in the production of clothing come at higher and higher opportunity costs in terms of food foregone. As we move to the third unit of clothing (from point C to D), we must start planting cotton in the corn belt of Iowa. A lot of food must be given up to produce that third unit of clothing. Finally, in the last move from point *E* to point *F,* all our resources are switched into the production of clothing. The last unit of clothing comes at an extremely high opportunity cost in terms of food. Wheat production is stopped on the farms of North Dakota and Minnesota, which are no good at all for producing cotton. The wheat lands remain idle, and the farmers of North Dakota and Minnesota migrate further south, where they can make only minor contributions to cotton production. Thus the last unit of clothing (the move from point *E* to *F*) comes at a very high cost of eight units of food.

The *opportunity cost* of a product is the alternative that is given up to produce that product. In the illustration, the opportunity cost of a unit of clothing is the food that is given up when that unit of clothing is produced.

Therefore the *increasing opportunity cost of cotton is a reflection of the specialized characteristics of resources.* Resources are not completely adaptable to alternative uses. The lands of Minnesota and Mississippi are not equally well suited to the production of cotton and wheat. Thus the opportunity cost of cotton rises as its production is increased.

As a result of increasing opportunity cost, the production possibilities curve in Figure 2-1 *bows outward.* Technically, this curve is described as *concave to the origin.* The arrows in this figure illustrate why. The horizontal increases in clothing production—from point *H* to *B,* from *J* to *C,* from *K* to *D,* and so on—are each one unit. The resulting reductions in food production—measured vertically from *A* to *H, B* to *J, C* to *K,* and so on—become larger and larger, making the curve increasingly steep as we move to the right.

While opportunity costs generally increase, as shown in Figure 2-1, it is not logically necessary that they must do so. In some cases, it is possible for opportunity costs to be constant. For example, beef cattle and dairy cattle can graze on similar land; it is possible that the resources used to raise beef are equally suited for dairy cattle. Thus the opportunity cost of beef in terms of milk may be constant. If so, a production possibilities curve drawn with milk on one axis and beef on the other would be a straight line.

THE PRODUCTION POSSIBILITIES CURVE IS A FRONTIER

The production possibilities curve in Figure 2-1 illustrates what an economy is capable of producing. It shows the *maximum* possible combined output of the two goods. In practice, actual production can fall short of our capabilities. Obviously, if there is large-scale unemployment, labor resources are being wasted. The same is true if workers are employed but are wasting their time on the job. In either case, the result is a point like *U,* inside the production possibilities curve in Figure 2-2. Beginning at such a point, it is possible to produce more food *and* more clothing (and move to point *D*) by getting those who are wasting their time or are

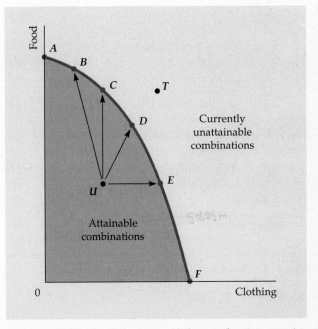

FIGURE 2-2   Unemployment and the production possibilities curve.

Point *U* represents a position of large-scale unemployment. If people are put back to work, the economy can be moved to point *D,* with more food *and* more clothing.

With its limited resources, the society can choose any point along the production possibilities curve, or any point within it. Points in the shaded area within the curve are undesirable; the society could do better by moving out to the curve. Points beyond the curve are unattainable with the resources currently at our disposal.

unemployed back to work. (With full employ-ment, we alternatively could choose any other point on the production possibilities curve, such as *B*, *C*, or *E*.)

Thus, although the production possibilities curve represents options open to the society, it does not include all conceivable options. The attainable options include not only the points on the curve, but also all points in the shaded area inside the curve.

The production possibilities curve therefore traces out a *frontier* or *boundary* of the options open to us. We can pick a point on the frontier if we don't waste resources and maintain a high level of employment. Or we can end up inside the curve if we use resources in a wasteful way or mismanage the economy into a depression. But points such as *T* outside the curve are currently unattainable. We cannot reach them with our present quantities of land, labor, and capital, and with our present tech-nology.

In summary, the production possibilities curve illustrates three important concepts: scarcity, choice, and opportunity cost.

1. *Scarcity* is illustrated by the fact that combina-tions outside the curve cannot be attained. Even though we might want such combinations, we can-not have them with the resources available to us.

2. Because we cannot have combinations outside the curve, we must settle for a *choice* of one of the attainable combinations outlined by the PPC.

3. *Opportunity cost* is illustrated by the downward slope of the production possibilities curve. When we reallocate our resources to produce more of one good, we produce less of another.

GROWTH: THE OUTWARD SHIFT OF THE PRODUCTION POSSIBILITIES CURVE

As time passes, a point such as *T* (Fig. 2-2) may come within our grasp as our productive capacity increases and the economy grows. There are three main sources of growth:

1. Technological improvement, representing new and better methods of producing goods.

2. An increase in the quantity of capital.

3. An increase in the number of workers, and in their skills and educational levels.

Consider a technological improvement. Suppose a new type of fertilizer is developed that substantial-ly increases the output of our land, whether cotton or wheat is being grown. Then we will be able to produce more wheat and more cotton. The produc-tion possibilities curve will shift out to the new curve (PPC$_2$) shown in Figure 2-3.

Growth is defined as an increase in the productive capacity of the nation. It is illustrated by an outward movement of the production possibilities curve.

Although the new fertilizer illustrated in Figure 2-3 increases our ability to produce *both* wheat and cotton, other types of technological improvement may increase our ability to produce only *one* of them. For example, the development of

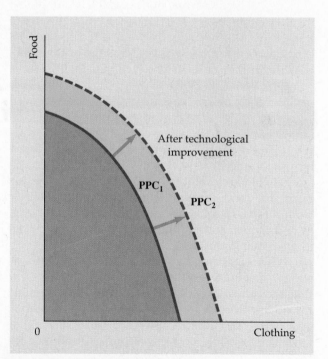

FIGURE 2-3   Technological improvement.

As a result of the development of a new fertilizer, productive. capabilities increase. The production possibilities curve moves outward.

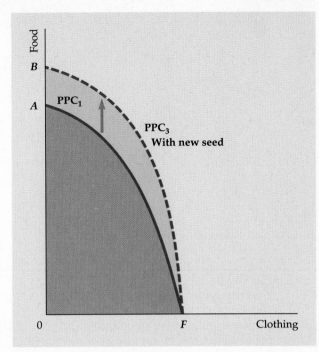

FIGURE 2-4   Technological improvement in a single good.

When a new, improved strain of wheat is developed, the production possibilities curve moves out to PPC$_3$.

a new disease-resistant strain of wheat will increase our ability to produce wheat but not cotton. In this case, illustrated in Figure 2-4, nothing will happen to the place where the production possibilities curve meets the axis for clothing. If we direct all our resources to the production of clothing, we can still produce no more than is shown by point F. However, if we direct all our resources to wheat, we can produce more; the other end of the PPC moves upward along the food axis, from A to B. The development of the new strain of wheat therefore causes the PPC to move upward, from PPC$_1$ to PPC$_3$.

GROWTH: THE CHOICE BETWEEN CONSUMER GOODS AND CAPITAL GOODS

As an alternative to technological change, consider the second source of growth listed above: an increase in the quantity of capital. The capital we have today is limited. However, capital itself can be produced. The quantity of capital we will have in the year 2020 will be determined in large part by how much of our resources we choose to devote this year and in coming years to producing capital, rather than consumer goods.

In order to study this choice, we must look at a different production possibilities curve—not one showing food and clothing, but rather, one showing the choice between the production of *capital goods* (such as machines and factories) and the production of *consumer goods* (such as food, clothing, and television sets).

In Figure 2-5, two hypothetical countries are compared. Starting in 1990, these two countries face the same initial production possibilities curve (PPC$_{1990}$). The citizens of country A (on the left) believe in living for the moment. They produce mostly consumption goods and very few capital goods, at point C. As a result, their capital stock will not be much greater in 2020 than it is today, so their PPC will shift out very little. In contrast, the citizens of country B (on the right) keep down the production of consumer goods in order to build more capital goods, at point F. By the year 2020, their productive capacity will be greatly increased, as shown by the large outward movement of the PPC. Because they have given up so much consumption today, their income and ability to consume will be much greater in the future. Thus any society faces a choice: How much consumption should it sacrifice now in order to be able to consume more in the future?

AN INTRODUCTION TO ECONOMIC THEORY: THE NEED TO SIMPLIFY

The production possibilities curve is the first piece of theoretical equipment the beginning economics student typically encounters. There will be many more. At this early stage, it is appropriate to address directly a problem that often bothers both beginning and advanced students. The production possibilities curve, like many other theoretical tools that will be introduced in later chapters, represents a gross simplification of the real world. When the PPC is drawn, it is assumed that only two types of

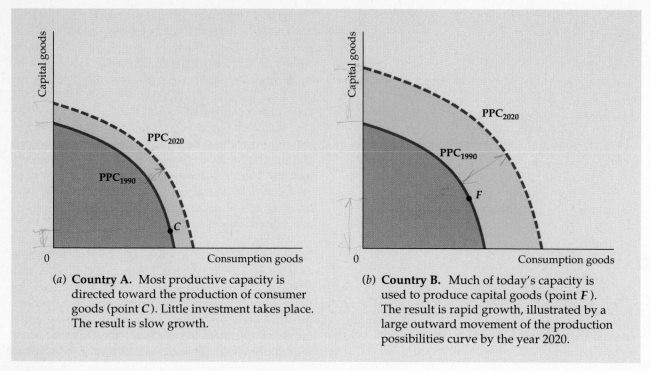

(a) **Country A.** Most productive capacity is directed toward the production of consumer goods (point **C**). Little investment takes place. The result is slow growth.

(b) **Country B.** Much of today's capacity is used to produce capital goods (point **F**). The result is rapid growth, illustrated by a large outward movement of the production possibilities curve by the year 2020.

FIGURE 2-5   Capital formation now helps to determine future productive capacity.

This figure illustrates the choice between consumer goods and capital goods. The country on the left consumes most of its current output and does not invest very much in new capital equipment. It therefore grows slowly. In contrast, the country on the right is willing to direct a large fraction of its current production into investment. It grows rapidly as a result.

goods can be produced—food and clothing, or consumer goods and capital goods. Diagrams are limited to two alternatives because the printed page has only two dimensions. Yet obviously, there are thousands of goods produced in the modern economy. This raises a question: With our simple approach, can we say anything of relevance to the real world?

THEORY NECESSARILY MEANS SIMPLIFICATION

If we wished to describe the real world in detail, we could go on without end. A complete description would be useless as a guide to private behavior or public policy; it would be too complex. In a sense, theory is like a map. A road map is necessarily incomplete. In many ways, it is not very accurate, and, indeed, it is downright wrong. Towns and villages are not round circles. Roads of various qualities do not really come in different colors. If a road map were more realistic, it would be less useful for its intended purpose. If it tried to show every house and every tree, it would be an incomprehensible jumble of detail. A road map is useful precisely because it is a simplification that shows in stark outline the various roads that may be traveled. Similarly, the objective of economic theory is to draw in stark outline the important relationships among producers and consumers.

When details are left out of a road map, it becomes more useful as a guide for the auto traveler. However, it becomes less useful for other purposes. A road map is a poor guide for airplane pilots, who instead need a map with the height of mountains marked clearly. A road map is also a poor guide for sales managers, who need a map showing regional sales targets and staff assignments. The way in which a map is constructed depends on its intended use. Various maps are "true," but they do not represent the "whole truth." An important question for a map user thus becomes: Do I have the best map for my purpose?

The same generalization holds for economic theory. If we wish to study long-run growth, we may use quite different theoretical tools from those we would use to study short-term fluctuations. If we want to study the consequences of price controls on the housing market, we may use different tools from those we would choose to investigate the economic consequences of a cut in the defense budget. Just as in the case of the map, the "best" theory cannot be identified unless we know the purposes for which it is to be used.

The production possibilities curve is a theoretical tool whose purpose is to illustrate the concept of scarcity. *If* we begin on the PPC, with our resources fully employed, then we can come to a significant conclusion: To produce more of one good, we will have to cut back on the production of some other good or service. The "if" clause is important. It tells us that when we consider points along the PPC, we are making an assumption—that resources are fully utilized. When the "if" clause is violated—that is, when the economy begins with large-scale unemployment—then we reach quite a different conclusion: The economy *can* produce more consumer goods and more capital goods at the same time. Thus the "if" clause acts as a label on our theoretical road map. It makes clear the assumptions we are making and tells us when the map can be used.

For the novice and old hand alike, it is essential to recognize and remember such "if" clauses. We must pay attention to the set of assumptions underlying any theory that we use. If we don't, we may use the wrong theory and make serious policy mistakes—just as the pilot who uses the wrong map may fly a plane into the nearest mountain top.

THE DISTINCTION BETWEEN POSITIVE AND NORMATIVE ECONOMICS

The uses of theory are many, but they may be divided into two main families. **Positive or descriptive** economics aims at understanding how the economy works. It is directed toward explaining the world as *it is,* and how various forces can cause it to change. In contrast, **normative** economics deals with the way the world (or some small segment of it) **ought to be.**

A debate over a *positive* statement can often be settled by looking at the facts. For example, the following is a positive statement: "U.S. steel production last year was 100 million tons." By looking up the statistics, we can find out whether this was true. A more complicated positive statement is: "There are millions of barrels of oil in the rocks of Colorado." With a geological study, we can discover whether this claim is likely to be so. A third positive statement is this: "If a ton of dynamite is exploded 100 feet below the surface, 1,000 barrels of oil will be released from the rocks." By experimentation, we can discover whether this is generally true.

A *normative* statement is more complex: for example, "We ought to extract large quantities of oil from the Colorado rocks." Facts are relevant here. If there is no oil in the rocks of Colorado (a positive conclusion), then the normative statement that we ought to extract oil must be rejected for the very simple reason that it cannot be done. However, facts alone will seldom settle a dispute over a normative statement, since it is based on something more—on a view regarding appropriate goals or ethical values. A normative statement involves a value judgment, a judgment about what ought to be. It is possible for well-informed individuals to disagree over normative statements, even when they agree completely regarding the facts. For example, they may agree that, in fact, a large quantity of oil is locked in the rocks of Colorado. Nevertheless, they may disagree whether it should be extracted. Perhaps these differences may develop over the relative importance of a plentiful supply of heating oil as compared with the environmental damage that might accompany the extraction of oil.

Although some positive statements may be

easily settled by looking at the facts, others may be much more difficult to judge. This is particularly true of statements making claims about causation. They may be quite controversial because the facts are not easily untangled. For example: "If there is no growth in the money stock next year, then inflation will fall to zero"; or, "If income tax rates are increased by 1%, government revenues will increase by $20 billion next year"; or, "Rent controls have little effect on the number of apartments offered for rent."

In evaluating such statements, economists and other social scientists have two major disadvantages as compared with natural scientists. First, experiments are difficult or impossible in many instances. Society is not the plaything of economists. They do not have the power to conduct an experiment in which one large city is subjected to rent control while a similar city is not, simply to estimate the effects of rent control. Nevertheless, economists do have factual evidence to study. By looking at situations in which rent controls have actually been imposed by the government, they may be able to estimate the effects of those controls. Moreover, in special situations, economic experiments *are* possible, particularly when the

government is eager to know the results. For example, experiments have been undertaken to determine whether people work less when they are provided with a minimum income by the government. (The results will be reported in Chapter 39.)

The second disadvantage is that the social sciences deal with the behavior of people, and behavior can change. Suppose we estimate corporate profits next year to be $200 billion. We might carelessly conclude that, if the profits tax is raised by 10%, the government will receive an additional $20 billion in revenues. But this is not necessarily so. With a higher tax rate, businesses may behave differently, in order to reduce the taxes they have to pay. Furthermore, even if we have evidence on how businesses have responded to a 10% tax increase in the past, we cannot be certain that they will respond the same way in the future. As time passes, they may become more imaginative in finding ways to avoid taxes. The possibility that people will learn and change has been one of the most interesting areas of research in economics in recent years.

In contrast, physical scientists study a relatively stable and unchanging universe. Gravity works the same today as it did in Newton's time.

KEY POINTS

1. *Scarcity* is a fundamental economic problem. Because wants are virtually unlimited and resources are scarce, we must make *choices*.

2. The choices open to society are illustrated by the *production possibilities curve*. This illustrates the concept of the *opportunity cost* of a good *A*, which is the amount of another good *B* that must be sacrificed to produce *A*.

3. Not all resources are identical. For example, the land of Mississippi is different from the land of Minnesota. As a consequence, opportunity cost generally increases as more of a good is produced. For example, as more cotton is produced, more and more wheat must be given up for each additional unit of cotton. As a result, the production possibilities curve normally bows outward.

4. The production possibilities curve is a frontier, representing the choices open to society—*if there is* full utilization of land, labor, and capital. If there is large-scale unemployment, then production occurs at a point within this frontier.

5. The economy can grow and the production possibilities curve can move outward if

    (a) Technology improves.

    (b) The capital stock grows.

    (c) And/or the labor force grows.

6. By giving up consumer goods at present, we can produce more capital goods and thus have a growing economy. The production of capital goods (investment) therefore represents a choice of more future production instead of present consumption.

7. Like other theoretical concepts, the production possibilities curve represents a simplification. Because the world is so complex, theory cannot reflect the "whole truth." Nevertheless, a theory—like a road map—can be valuable if it is used correctly. In order to determine the appropriate uses of a theory, it is important to identify the assumptions on which the theory was developed. As theories are developed in this book, it will be essential to pay attention to the assumptions underlying each.

KEY CONCEPTS

scarcity	factors of production	production possibilities curve
goods	land	opportunity cost
services	labor	growth
resources	capital	positive economics
the economic problem	investment	normative economics
economics	entrepreneur	

PROBLEMS

2-1. "Wants aren't insatiable. The economic wants of David Rockefeller have been satisfied. There is no prospect that he will spend all his money before he dies. His consumption is not limited by his income." Do you agree? Does your answer raise problems for the main theme of this chapter, that wants cannot all be satisfied with the goods and services produced from our limited resources? Why or why not?

2-2. "The more capital goods we produce, the more the U.S. economy will grow, and the more we and our children will be able to consume in the future. Therefore, the government should encourage capital formation." Do you agree or disagree? Why? Can any case be made on the other side?

2-3. Is your answer to Problem 2-2 an example of "positive" or "normative" economics? Why?

CHAPTER 3
SPECIALIZATION, EXCHANGE, AND MONEY

Money... is not of the wheels of trade: it is the oil which renders the motion of the wheels smooth and easy.

DAVID HUME

The early French colony at Quebec was a forbidding place in winter, with temperatures often falling to 20° below zero. Keeping warm was the first problem. Getting supplies from France was a close second. During the winter, the St. Lawrence River was clogged with ice.

Of the many things the colony lacked, money was one. Not only did ships have difficulty sailing up the river, but even when they did come, they had little currency; the colony's sponsors in France were reluctant to send money. The colonists found that barter—for example, the trade of a bushel of wheat for a bag of salt—was very cumbersome; even in a simple economy, money was essential. What could they do? They hit upon an ingenious solution. They used playing cards as money. The man with an ace in his pocket often had a smile on his face.

In the modern economy, as in the early colonies, money plays a central role. Over the decades, production has become increasingly specialized with the development of new machinery and equipment. **Specialization** contributes to efficiency; often, workers can produce more by specializing. But **specialization necessitates exchange.** A farmer who produces only beef wants to exchange some of that beef for clothing, cars, medical services, and a whole list of other products.

This chapter will

■ Describe the two types of exchange:

1. barter.

2. exchange with money.

■ Explain why exchange using money is so much simpler than barter.

■ Provide more detail on how people can gain from specialization and exchange.

EXCHANGE: THE BARTER ECONOMY

In a **barter** system, no money is used: One good or service is exchanged directly for another. The farmer specializing in beef must find a hungry barber and thus get a haircut, or find a hungry tailor and thus exchange meat for a suit of clothes, or find a hungry doctor and thus obtain medical treatment. A simple barter transaction is illustrated in Figure 3-1. In a barter economy, there are dozens of such bilateral (two-way) transactions: between the farmer and the tailor; between the farmer and the doctor; between the doctor and the tailor; and so on.

Barter can be very inefficient. Farmers may spend half their time producing beef and the other

36

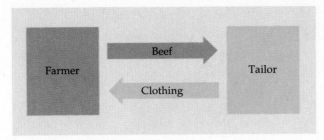

FIGURE 3-1   Barter.

With barter, no money is used. The farmer exchanges beef directly for clothing. Transactions involve only two parties—in this case, the farmer and the tailor.

half searching for someone willing to make the right trade. Barter requires a **coincidence of wants:** Each of those engaged in barter must have a product that the other wants. The farmer not only must find someone who wants beef, but that someone must also be able to provide something in exchange that the farmer wants. Furthermore, with barter, there is a problem of **indivisibility.** A suit of clothes—or an automobile, or a house—should be bought all at once, and not in pieces. To illustrate, suppose that a beef farmer who wants a suit of clothes has been lucky enough to find a tailor who wants meat and is willing to make a trade. The suit of clothes may be worth 100 pounds of beef, and the farmer may be quite willing to give up this amount. The problem is that the tailor may not be *that* hungry and perhaps only wants 50 pounds of beef. In a barter economy, what is the farmer to do? Get only the jacket from this tailor and set out to find another hungry tailor in order to obtain a pair of pants? If the farmer does so, what are the chances that the pants will match?

EXCHANGE WITH MONEY

With money, exchange is much easier. It is no longer necessary for wants to coincide. In order to get a suit of clothing, the farmer need not find a hungry tailor, but only someone willing to buy the beef. The farmer can then take the money from the sale of the beef and buy a suit of clothes. Money represents **general purchasing power**—that is, it can be used to buy *any* of the goods and services offered for sale. Therefore, complex transactions

among many parties are possible with money. Figure 3-2 presents a simple illustration with three parties. Actual transactions in a monetary economy may be very complex, with dozens or even hundreds of participants.

Note how money solves the problem of indivisibility. The farmer can sell the whole carcass of beef for money and use the proceeds to buy a complete set of clothes. It doesn't matter how much beef the tailor wants.

In the simple barter economy, there is no clear distinction between seller and buyer, or between producer and consumer. When bartering beef for clothing, the farmer is at the same time both the seller (of beef) and the buyer (of clothing). In contrast, in a monetary economy, there is a *clear distinction between seller and buyer.* In the beef market, the farmer is the seller; the tailor is the buyer. The farmer is the producer; the tailor is the consumer.

THE CIRCULAR FLOW OF EXPENDITURES AND INCOME

The distinction between the producer and the consumer in a money economy is illustrated in Figure 3-3. Producers—or businesses—are in the right-hand box; consumers—or households—in the left. Transactions between the two groups are illustrated in the loops. The top loops show consumer expenditures for goods and services. Beef, clothing, and a host of other products are bought with money.

The lower loops show transactions in economic resources. In a complex exchange economy, not only are consumer goods bought and sold for money; so, too, are resources. In order to be able to buy food and other goods, households must have money income. They acquire money by providing the labor and other resources which are the inputs of the business sector. For example, workers provide their labor in exchange for wages and salaries, and owners of land provide their property in exchange for rents.

Figure 3-3 is simplified. For example, it does not include government or foreign purchases of goods and services, which are very important. Remember the purpose of simplification discussed in Chapter 2: to show in sharp outline the relationships on which we want to concentrate. Figure 3-3 shows the circular flow of payments—that is, how businesses use the receipts from sales to pay their

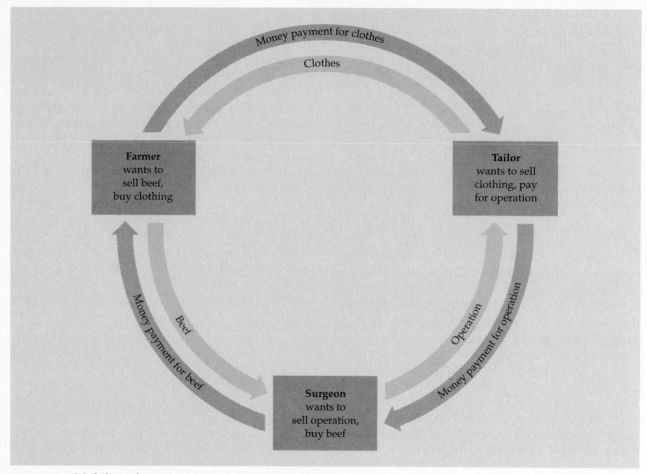

FIGURE 3-2   Multilateral transactions in a money economy.

In a money economy, multilateral transactions among many participants are possible. The farmer gets clothing from the tailor, even though the tailor does not want to buy the farmer's beef. Flows of money are shown in green.

wages, salaries, and other costs of production, while households use their income receipts from wages, salaries, and so on, to buy consumer goods.

THE MONETARY SYSTEM

Because barter is so inefficient, there is a natural tendency for something to become accepted as money. One example was the early colony at Quebec, where playing cards were used as money.

The powerful tendency for money to appear may also be illustrated by the prisoner-of-war camp of World War II.[1] Economic relations in such a camp were primitive and the range of goods was very limited. However, some things were available: rations supplied by the German captors and the Red Cross parcels that arrived periodically. Each person received a parcel containing a variety of items such as cheese, jam, margarine, and cigarettes. Nonsmokers who received cigarettes were eager to trade them for other items. Thus the basis was established for exchange.

_____

[1]This illustration is based on R. A. Radford, "The Economic Organization of a POW Camp," *Economica* (November 1945), pp. 189–201.

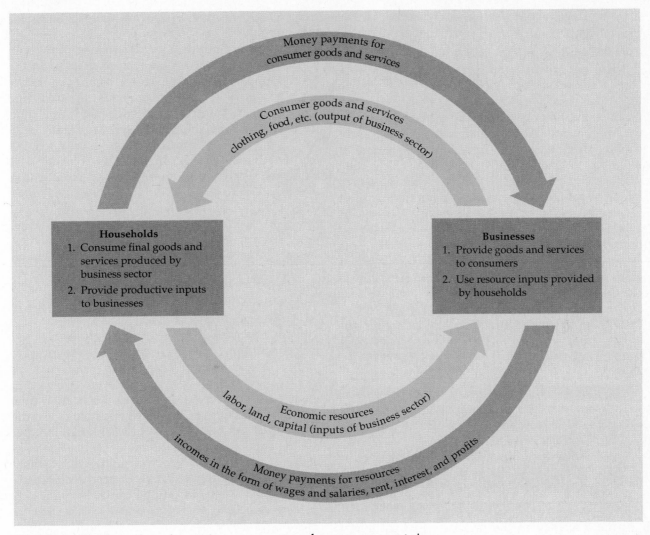

FIGURE 3-3   The flow of goods, services, resources, and money payments in a simple economy.

Monetary payments are shown in the outer loop. These pay for the flow of goods and services and resources shown in the inner loop.

At first, trading was rough and ready, with no clear picture of the relative values of the various items. In one instance, a prisoner started walking around the camp with only a can of cheese and five cigarettes, and returned with a complete Red Cross parcel. He did so by buying goods where they were cheap and selling them where they were expensive. As time went by, the relative prices of various goods became more stable, and all prices came to be quoted in terms of cigarettes. For example, a can of cheese was worth twenty cigarettes.

Not only did cigarettes become the measuring rod for quoting prices, but they were also used as the common **medium of exchange**—that is, cigarettes were the item used to buy goods. Cigarettes became the money of the POW camp. This was a natural evolution; there was no government to decree that cigarettes were money, and no authority to enforce that choice. At other times and in other societies, other items have been used as money—items as diverse as beads, porpoise teeth, rice, salt, wampum, stones, and even woodpecker scalps.

MONETARY PROBLEMS
IN THE POW CAMP

Cigarette money made the primitive economy of the prisoner-of-war camp more efficient. But problems occurred, including problems quite similar to those of more advanced monetary systems. Distinctions among various brands of cigarettes became blurred. Although all cigarettes were not equally desirable to smokers, all were equal as money. In paying for beef or other items, a cigarette was a cigarette. What was the consequence? Smokers held back the desirable brands for their personal use and spent the others. The less desirable cigarettes therefore were the ones used as money; the "good" cigarettes were smoked. This example illustrates **Gresham's law**. This law, first enunciated by Elizabethan financier Sir Thomas Gresham (1519–1579), is popularly and loosely abbreviated: "Bad money drives out good." In this case, "bad" cigarettes drove "good" cigarettes out of circulation as money. (The good cigarettes were smoked instead.)

Gresham's law: If there are two types of money whose values in exchange are equal while their values in another use (like consumption) are different, the more valuable item will be retained for its other use while the less valuable item will continue to circulate as money. Thus the "bad" (less valuable) money drives the "good" (more valuable) money out of circulation.

The tendency of the prisoners to treat every cigarette as equal to every other cigarette caused another monetary problem. As a cigarette was a cigarette, prisoners often pulled out a few strands of tobacco before passing a cigarette along. This development corresponds precisely to a problem that has occurred whenever gold coins have circulated: People have "clipped" coins by chipping off bits of gold. Furthermore, the cigarette currency became debased: Some enterprising prisoners rolled cigarettes from pipe tobacco or broke down cigarettes and rerolled them, reducing the amount of tobacco in each. Similarly, governments have from time to time given in to the temptation to debase gold coins by melting them down and reissuing them with a smaller gold content. (Private entrepreneurs have had a strong incentive to do the same, but they have been discouraged throughout history by severe punishments for counterfeiters.)

It was not clipping or debasement, however, that led to the greatest monetary problems in the POW camp. As long as there was a balanced inflow of both cigarettes and other goods, the exchange system of the camp worked reasonably well. But, from time to time, the weekly Red Cross issue of 25 or 50 cigarettes per prisoner was interrupted. As the existing stock of cigarettes was consumed by smokers, cigarettes became more and more scarce. Desperate smokers had to offer more and more to get cigarettes; their value skyrocketed. To put the same point another way: Other goods were now exchanged for fewer and fewer cigarettes. A can of cheese that previously sold for 20 cigarettes dropped in value to 15, 10, or even fewer cigarettes. Thus there was deflation—a decline in the prices of other goods, measured in terms of money (cigarettes).

As cigarettes became increasingly scarce and prices continued to fall, prisoners began to revert to barter in exchanging other goods. Smokers who had the few remaining cigarettes were reluctant to give them up to make purchases. Then, from time to time, thousands of cigarettes would arrive at the camp during a brief period. Prices soared; in other words, the value of cigarettes fell. Prisoners became reluctant to accept cigarettes in payment for other goods. Once again, barter became common. Thus *the monetary system worked smoothly only as long as a reasonable balance was kept between the quantity of money (cigarettes) and the quantity of other goods.*

Two characteristics of a good monetary system may be drawn out of this story of the "cigarette standard:"

1. A smoothly operating monetary system should be made up of money whose value is **uniform.** Nonuniform money will set Gresham's law into operation, with "bad" money driving "good" money out of circulation. In the United States, the Federal Reserve System issues our paper currency and is responsible for assuring that money is uniform. One dollar bill is as good as another. It doesn't matter whether the $1 bill I have in my pocket is crisp and new, or whether it is tattered and soiled. The Federal Reserve will replace it with a new bill of equal value when it becomes excessively worn. This uniformity in the value of each dollar bill obviously adds to the ease of exchange—and it means that Gresham's law does not operate in our modern economy.

2. A second important characteristic of a good monetary system is that there be the **proper quantity of money,** neither too much nor too little. In the United States, the responsibility for controlling the quantity of money also lies with the Federal Reserve. This important topic will be studied in Part III of this book.

COMPARATIVE ADVANTAGE: A REASON TO SPECIALIZE

The beginning of this chapter described three key elements in the development of an economy. People **specialize.** For example, the farmer concentrates on producing beef. Specialization then requires **exchange.** The farmer exchanges beef to get other goods and services. Finally, **money** makes specialization and exchange run smoothly. However, money doesn't explain why specialization and exchange are advantageous in the first place. Why are specialization and exchange efficient? Why do they increase the goods and services we enjoy, and thus provide the propellant that drives the wheels of commerce?

One answer is provided by the **principle of comparative advantage.** To understand this principle, it is useful to look first at the simpler concept of **absolute advantage.**

A good is often made in the place that is best suited for its production: steel near the coal mines of Pennsylvania, corn in the fertile fields of Iowa, bananas in the tropical lands of Central America, coffee in the cool highlands of Colombia, and so on. In technical terms, there is some tendency for a good to be produced in the area that has an *absolute advantage* in its production.

A country (or region or individual) has an *absolute advantage* in the production of a good if it can produce that good with fewer resources (less land, labor, and capital) than can other countries (or regions or individuals).

To illustrate how this principle applies to specialization between individuals, consider the case of the lawyer and the professional gardener. The lawyer is better at drawing up legal documents and the gardener generally is better at gardening, so it is in the interest of each to specialize in the occupation in which he or she has an absolute advantage.

The truth is often more complicated than this, however. By looking at the complications, we will be led to the idea of comparative advantage. Suppose a certain lawyer is better at gardening than the gardener; she's faster and more effective—in short, she has a "greener thumb." She has an absolute advantage in both the law and gardening. If absolute advantage were the key, she would practice law and do her own gardening as well. Does this necessarily happen? The answer is no. Unless this lawyer positively enjoys gardening as a recreation, she will leave the gardening to the professional. Why? Even though the lawyer, being an excellent gardener, can do as much gardening in 1 hour (let us say) as the gardener could in 2, she will be better off to stick to law and hire the gardener to work on the flowers and shrubbery. Why? In 1 hour's work, the lawyer can draw up a will, for which she charges $100. The gardener's time, in contrast, is worth only $10 per hour. By spending the hour on the law rather than on gardening, the lawyer comes out ahead. She earns $100 and can hire the gardener for $20 to put in 2 hours to get the gardening done. By sticking to law for that 1 hour, the lawyer gains $80, which she can then use to buy more goods and services. To sum up: Because of specialization and exchange, she ends up with more goods and services. (This principle is explained in more detail in Box 3-1.)

The gardener also gains through specialization and exchange. Although he has to work 10 hours in order to earn the $100 needed to hire the lawyer to draw up his will, at least he gets a will. If he spent that 10 hours instead trying to draw up a will himself, he might end up with no will at all, or "half a will"—a piece of paper that might or might not be valid, because the only law he would know would be whatever he might be able to pick up in that brief 10 hours. Thus by specialization and exchange, the gardener gets a better will than he could acquire by producing it himself.

BOX 3–1   *Illustration of Comparative Advantage*

A.   Assume the following:

   1.   In 1 hour, the lawyer can plant 20 flowers.

   2.   In 1 hour, the gardener can plant 10 flowers. (Therefore the lawyer has the **absolute advantage** in gardening.)

   3.   The lawyer's time, in the practice of law, is worth $100 per hour.

   4.   The gardener's time, in gardening, is worth $10 per hour.

B.   *Question:*

   How should the lawyer have 20 flowers planted?

   Option 1: Do it herself, spending 1 hour.

       Cost: She gives up the $100 she could have earned by practicing law for that hour.

   Option 2: Stick to the law, and hire the gardener to plant the 20 flowers.

       Cost: Two hours of gardener's time at $10 per hour, making a total of $20.

C.   *Decision:* Choose option 2.

   Spend the available hour practicing law, earning $100.

   Hire the gardener to do the planting for $20.

   Net advantage over option 1: The difference of $80 that can be spent on other goods.

D.   *Conclusion:* The lawyer has the *comparative advantage* in law. By specializing in this and exchanging, she ends up with $80 more goods and services. This is her incentive to specialize.

This example leads to two important conclusions:

1.   There are *mutual benefits* from specialization and exchange. The lawyer gains by specializing and hiring someone else to do the gardening. The gardener likewise gains by specializing and hiring someone else to provide legal services.

2.   Absolute advantage is *not* necessary for mutually beneficial specialization. The lawyer has an absolute advantage in both gardening and law; the gardener has an absolute disadvantage in both. The lawyer specializes in the law where she has a *comparative advantage*. In gardening, she is only twice as productive as the gardener, but in law she is many, many times as productive.

British economist **David Ricardo** enunciated the principle of comparative advantage in the early nineteenth century to illustrate how countries gain from international trade. But comparative advantage provides a general explanation of the advantages of specialization; it is just as relevant to domestic as to international trade. Nevertheless, it is customary to follow Ricardo and consider this principle as part of the study of international economics. We will follow the custom, and put off our detailed analysis of comparative advantage to Chapter 33 on international trade.

Comparative advantage, then, provides one reason for specialization and exchange. But there is a second fundamental reason.

ECONOMIES OF SCALE: ANOTHER REASON TO SPECIALIZE

Consider two small cities that are identical in all respects. Suppose that the citizens of these cities want both bicycles and lawnmowers but that neither city has any advantage in the production of either good. Will each city then produce its own, without any trade existing between the two? Probably not. It is likely that one city will specialize in bicycles, and the other in lawnmowers. Why?

The answer is **economies of scale.** To understand what this term means, first assume that there is no specialization. Each city directs half its productive resources into the manufacture of bicycles and half into the manufacture of lawnmowers, thus producing 1,000 bicycles and 1,000 lawnmowers. But if either city specializes by directing all its productive resources toward the manufacture of bicycles, it can acquire specialized machinery and produce 2,500 bicycles. Similarly, if the other city directs all its productive resources toward the manufacture of lawnmowers, it can produce 2,500. Note that each city, by doubling all inputs into the production of a single item, can more than double its output of that item from 1,000 to 2,500 units. Thus economies of scale exist.

Economies of scale exist if an increase of x% in the quantity of every input causes the quantity of output to increase by more than x%. (For example, if all inputs are doubled, then output more than doubles.)

Even though neither city has any initial advantage in the production of either product, both can gain by specialization. Before specialization, their combined output was 2,000 bicycles and 2,000 lawnmowers. After specialization, they together make 2,500 bicycles and 2,500 lawnmowers.

While Ricardo's theory of comparative advantage dates back to the early nineteenth century, the explanation of economies of scale goes back even further, to Adam Smith's *Wealth of Nations* (1776). In Smith's first chapter, "Of the Division of Labour," there is a famous description of pin-making:

> A workman not educated to this business . . . could scarce, perhaps, . . . make one pin in a day, and certainly not twenty. But in the way in which this business is now carried on, not only the whole work is a peculiar trade, but it is divided into a number of branches. . . . One man draws out the wire, another straightens it, a third cuts it, a fourth points it, a fifth grinds it at the top for receiving the head. . . . Ten persons, therefore, could make among them upwards of forty-eight thousand pins in a day. Each person, therefore, . . . might be considered as making four thousand and eight hundred pins in a day.[2]

What is the reason for the gain that comes from the division of pin-making into a number of separate steps? Certainly, it is not that some individuals are particularly suited to drawing the wire, whereas others have a particular gift for straightening it. On the contrary, if two individuals are employed, it

---

[2]Adam Smith, *An Inquiry into the Nature and Causes of the Wealth of Nations* (Modern Library edition, New York: Random House, 1937), pp. 4–5.

matters little which activity each is assigned. Adam Smith's "production line" is efficient because of economies of scale which depend on

1. The introduction of specialized machinery.

2. Specialization of the labor force on that machinery.

Modern corporations also derive economies of scale from a third major source:

3. Specialized research and development, which make possible the development of new equipment and technology.

In the modern world, economies of scale provide the second important reason for specialization and exchange—along with comparative advantage. Economies of scale help to explain why the manufacturers of automobiles and mainframe computers are few in number and large in size. It is partly because of economies of scale that the automobile industry is concentrated in the Detroit area, with Michigan shipping cars to other areas in exchange for a host of other products.

However, economies of scale explain much more than the trade among the regions, states, and cities *within* a country. They also are an important explanation of trade *between* countries. For example, economies of scale in the production of large passenger aircraft go on long after the U.S. market is met. Thus Boeing achieves a major advantage by producing aircraft for the world market. There are gains to the aircraft buyers, too. For example, Australians can buy a Boeing 747 for a small fraction of what it would cost to manufacture a comparable airplane in Australia.

LIVING IN A GLOBAL ECONOMY

ECONOMIES OF SCALE AND THE U.S.-CANADIAN FREE TRADE AGREEMENT

Even the huge U.S. market is not large enough for some producers to capture all the economies of scale—for example, the manufacturers of aircraft and mainframe computers. But it is large enough for the producers of many other goods, such as automobiles. In fact, U.S. auto firms can offer a wide variety of models and still produce most of them at the high volume needed to gain substantially all the economies of scale. Thus these producers can achieve low cost and at the same time provide a wide choice of models to consumers.

The United States is unique, however, because it is such a large economy. Smaller economies—like Canada's—cannot produce a wide range of cars and at the same time achieve the high-volume output necessary to achieve low cost. Thus in producing cars, Canada has a choice among three options.

1. It can produce a variety of models, each at a small scale and therefore at high cost, for the domestic Canadian market. This option would provide car buyers with a choice among models, but at high cost.

2. It can produce a small number of models, each at high volume, for the domestic market. This alternative would provide the advantage of low cost, but consumers would not have much choice.

3. It can gain both advantages (high-volume, low-cost production and a wide variety of models) by engaging in international trade. Produce only a few models in Canada, at high volume and low cost. Export many of these cars, in exchange for a variety of imported models.

Historically, up to the early 1960s, Canadian automotive policy was based on the first choice. But the twin advantages of the third option are clear and can come about only through international trade. In order to gain these advantages, Canada entered a special agreement with the United States in 1965, allowing tariff-free passage of cars both ways across the border.

The favorable experience with the auto agreement encouraged the two nations to negotiate a broad free trade agreement, which came into effect at the beginning of 1989. Under this comprehensive agreement, tariffs between the two countries on all goods will be phased out by 1998. In addition, the agreement provides for freer trade in services (such as banking services) and in energy, and for greater freedom of investment across the border.

For Canada, economies of scale provide the main advantage of the free trade agreement. Canadian businesses are now in the process of reorganization, cutting down the number of products and models they produce, but increasing the output of each. Much of the output from the longer production runs is destined for the U.S. market.

The agreement also promises gains for the United States. Northeastern states will find it easier to purchase inexpensive hydroelectric power from Quebec. U.S. firms will have freer access to the Canadian market; Canada will be phasing out tariffs that are generally two or three times as high as U.S. tariffs. The Canadian market will become even more important for U.S. exporters. Before the free trade agreement, Canada already was the largest market for U.S. exports. Indeed, a single Canadian province (Ontario) bought more U.S. exports than did Japan.

In this chapter, the advantages of specialization and exchange have been studied. Exchange takes place in markets; how markets operate will be the subject of the next chapter.

KEY POINTS

1. By specializing, people become more productive. But specialization requires exchange. Specialization and exchange make the economy more efficient; that is, we end up with more goods and services as a consequence.

2. The most primitive form of exchange is barter. Its disadvantage is that it requires a coincidence of wants. Producers waste a lot of time searching for the right trade.

3. Exchange is much easier and more efficient with money. Thus money has developed even in the absence of government action—as happened in the prisoner-of-war camp.

4. In the prisoner-of-war camp, some cigarettes were more desirable than others. The desirable cigarettes were smoked, leaving the less desirable cigarettes to circulate as money. This illustrated Gresham's law: "Bad money drives out good." In the modern U.S. economy, the Federal Reserve provides the currency, with every dollar bill worth the same as every other one; there is no "bad" money to drive "good" money out of circulation.

5. There are two major reasons why specialization and exchange increase efficiency, and thus increase the quantity of goods and services we can acquire. (a) Comparative advantage and (b) economies of scale.

6. Our example of *comparative advantage* is the lawyer who is better than the gardener at both the law and gardening. Even so, she does not do her gardening herself, because she has an even greater advantage in the law. She can gain by specializing in law (her comparative advantage) and hiring the gardener to do the gardening.

7. Economies of scale exist if an increase of x% in the quantity of every input causes the quantity of output to increase by more than x%.

KEY CONCEPTS

specialization	indivisibility	debasement of the currency
exchange	general purchasing power	absolute advantage
barter	medium of exchange	comparative advantage
coincidence of wants	Gresham's law	economies of scale

PROBLEMS

3-1. (a) Among the goods the United States exports are commercial aircraft, computers, and agricultural products such as soybeans and wheat. Why are these goods exported?

(b) Imports include automobiles, television sets, oil, and agricultural products such as coffee and bananas. Why are these goods imported?

(c) The United States exports some agricultural products and imports others. Why? The United States exports many aircraft, but it also imports some. Why are we both exporters and importers of aircraft? The United States and Canada export large numbers of cars to one another. Why?

3-2. Suppose that one individual at your college is outstanding, being the best teacher and a superb administrator. If you were the college president, would you ask this individual to teach or to become the administrative vice-president? Why?

3-3. Most jobs are more specialized than they were 100 years ago. Why? What are the advantages of greater specialization? Are there any disadvantages?

3-4. Draw a production possibilities curve (PPC) for the lawyer mentioned on p. 41 and in Box 3-1, putting the number of wills drawn up in a week on one axis and flowers planted on the other. (Assume that the lawyer works 40 hours per week.) How does the shape of this PPC differ from that in Chapter 2?

* 3-5.   Draw the production possibilities curve of one of the two identical cities described in the section on economies of scale. Which way does the curve bend? Does the opportunity cost of bicycles increase or decrease as more bicycles are produced?

----

*Problems marked with asterisks are more difficult than the others. They are designed to provide a challenge to students who want to do more advanced work.

CHAPTER 4

DEMAND AND SUPPLY:
The Market Mechanism

Do you know,
Considering the market, there are more
Poems produced than any other thing?
No wonder poets sometimes have to seem
So much more business-like than business men.
Their wares are so much harder to get rid of.
                    ROBERT FROST, *NEW HAMPSHIRE*

Although some countries are much richer than others, the resources of every country are limited. Choices must be made. Moreover, every economy is specialized to some degree. In every economy, therefore, some mechanism is needed to answer the fundamental questions raised by specialization and by the need to make choices:

■ **What** goods and services will be produced? Which of the options on the production possibilities curve will be chosen?

■ **How** will these goods and services be produced? For example, will cars be produced by relatively few workers using a great deal of machinery, or by many workers using relatively little capital equipment?

■ **For whom** will the goods and services be produced? Once goods are produced, who will consume them?

DECISIONS BY PRIVATE MARKETS AND BY THE GOVERNMENT

There are two principal mechanisms by which the three questions above can be answered. First, answers can be provided by Adam Smith's "invisible hand." If people are left alone to make their own transactions, then the butcher and baker will provide the beef and bread for our dinner. In other words, answers may be provided by transactions among individuals and corporations in the **market.**

In a *market,* an item is bought and sold. When transactions between buyers and sellers take place with little or no government interference, then a *private* or *free* market exists.

The government provides the second method for determining what goods and services will be produced, how they will be produced, and for whom.

Conceivably, a nation might depend almost exclusively on private markets to make the three fundamental decisions. The government might be confined to a very limited role, providing defense, police, the courts, roads, and little else. At the other extreme, the government might try to decide almost everything, specifying what is to be produced and using a system of rationing and allocations to decide who gets the products. But the real world is one of compromise. In every actual economy, there is some *mixture* of markets and government decision-making.

However, reliance on the market varies substantially among countries. By international standards, the U.S. government plays a restricted role; most choices are made in private markets. In the United States, most factories, machinery, and other forms of capital are owned by private individuals and corporations. The U.S. government owns only a limited amount of capital—for example, the power plants of the Tennessee Valley Authority—and undertakes less than 5% of the nation's overall investment. In most other countries, government enterprises undertake between 10% and 25% of investment. In many foreign countries, the government owns the telephone system, railroads, and all the major electric power plants—and in some cases, even factories that produce steel, automobiles, and other goods.

At the other end of the spectrum from the United States are centrally planned economies such as those in the Soviet Union and Eastern Europe, where the government owns most of the capital. In these countries governments decide what is to be produced with this capital. For example, the Soviet Union has a central planning agency that issues detailed directives to the various sectors of the economy to produce specific quantities of goods. It would be a mistake, however, to conclude that government planning is all-pervasive. Markets for goods exist in the Soviet Union, as in other centrally planned economies. Moreover, the Soviet Union is currently engaged in experiments to reduce the influence of the government and place more reliance on markets.

A *capitalist* or *free enterprise economy* is one in which most capital is privately owned, and decisions are made primarily through the price system (that is, in markets).

A *centrally planned economy* is one in which the government owns most of the capital and makes many of the economic decisions.

Because of their importance in the United States, private markets will be our initial concern. Later chapters will deal with the economic role of the government.

HOW PRIVATE MARKETS OPERATE

In most markets, the buyer and the seller come face to face. When you buy clothes, you go to the store selling them; when you buy groceries, you physically enter the supermarket. However, physical proximity is not required to make a market. For example, in a typical stock market transaction, someone in Georgia puts in a call to his broker to buy 100 shares of IBM common stock. About the same time, someone in Pennsylvania calls her broker to sell 100 shares. The transaction takes place on the floor of the New York Stock Exchange, where representatives of the two brokerage houses meet. The buyer and the seller of the stock do not leave their respective homes in Georgia and Pennsylvania.

Some markets are quite simple. For example, a barbershop is a market, since haircuts are bought and sold there. The transaction is obvious and straightforward; the service of haircutting is produced on the spot. In other cases, markets are much more complex. Even the simplest everyday activity may be the culmination of a complicated series of market transactions.

As you sat at breakfast this morning drinking a cup of coffee, you were using products from distant areas. The coffee itself was probably produced in Brazil. The brew was made with water that perhaps had been delivered in pipes manufactured in Pennsylvania and purified with chemicals produced in Delaware. The sugar for the coffee may have been produced in Louisiana or the Caribbean.

Perhaps you used artificial cream made from soybeans grown in Missouri. Possibly, your coffee was poured into a cup made in New York State and stirred with a spoon manufactured in Taiwan from Japanese stainless steel which used Canadian nickel in its production. All this was for one cup of coffee. Imagine the far more complex story of where a computer or car originates!

In such a complicated economy, something is needed to keep things straight, to bring order out of potential chaos. **Prices** bring order by performing two important, interrelated functions:

1. Prices provide **information.**
2. Prices provide **incentives.**

To illustrate, suppose we start with an example of chaos, with too much coffee in New York and none in New Jersey. Coffee lovers in New Jersey would clamor for coffee, even at very high prices. The high price is a signal, providing *information* to coffee owners that there are eager buyers in New Jersey. It also provides them with an *incentive* to send coffee from New York to New Jersey. In any market, the price provides the focus for interactions between buyers and sellers.

PERFECT AND IMPERFECT COMPETITION

Some markets are dominated by a few large firms; other markets have thousands of sellers. The "big three" automobile manufacturers (General Motors, Ford, and Chrysler) make most of the cars sold in the United States, with the rest provided by foreign firms. Such an industry, which is dominated by a few sellers, is an **oligopoly.** Some markets are even more concentrated. For example, there is just one supplier of local telephone services to homes in your area; the telephone company therefore has a **monopoly** on local service. On the other hand, there are thousands of wheat producers.

A *monopoly* exists when there is only *one seller.* An *oligopoly* exists when a *few sellers* dominate a market.

The number of participants in a market has a significant effect on how the price is determined. In the wheat market, where there are thousands of

buyers and thousands of sellers, no individual farmer produces more than a tiny fraction of the total supply. No single farmer can affect the price of wheat. For each farmer, the price is given; the individual farmer's decision is limited to the amount of wheat to sell. Similarly, millers realize that they are each buying only a small fraction of the wheat supplied. They realize that they cannot, as individuals, affect the price of wheat. Each miller's decision is limited to the amount of wheat to be bought at the existing market price. In such a **perfectly competitive** market, *there is no pricing decision* for the individual seller and the individual buyer to make. Each buyer and seller is a **price taker.**

When there are so many buyers and sellers that no single buyer or seller has any influence over the price, the result is *perfect competition* (sometimes shortened simply to *competition*).

In contrast, individual producers in an oligopolistic or a monopolistic market know that they have some control over price. For example, IBM sets the prices of its computers. That does not mean, of course, that it can set *any* price it wants and still be assured of making a profit. It can offer to sell at a high price, in which case it will sell only a few computers. Or it can charge a lower price, in which case it will sell more.

A *buyer* may also be large enough to influence price. General Motors is a large enough purchaser of steel to be able to bargain with the steel companies over the price of steel. When individual buyers or sellers can influence price, **imperfect competition** exists.

Imperfect competition exists when any buyer or any seller is able to influence the price. Such a buyer or seller is said to have *market power.*

Note that the term *competition* is used differently in economics and in business. Don't try to tell someone from Chrysler that the automobile market isn't competitive; Chrysler is very much aware of the competition from General Motors, Ford, and the Japanese. Yet, according to the economist's definition, the automobile industry is far *less* competitive than the wheat industry.

An *industry* refers to all the producers of a good or service. For example, we may speak of the automobile industry, the wheat industry, or the accounting industry. Note that the term *industry* can refer to *any* good or service; it need not be manufactured.

A *firm* is a business organization that produces goods and/or services. A *plant* is an establishment at a single location used in the production of a good or service—for example, a factory, mine, farm, or store. Some firms, such as General Motors, have many plants. Others have only one—for example, the local independent drug store.

Because price is determined by impersonal forces in a perfectly competitive market, the competitive market is simplest and will therefore be considered first. The perfectly competitive market is also given priority because competitive markets generally operate more efficiently than imperfect markets, as we will eventually show in Chapters 25 and 26.

DEMAND AND SUPPLY

In a perfectly competitive market, price is determined by demand and supply.

DEMAND

Consider, as an example, the market for apples, in which there are many buyers and many sellers, with none having any control over the price. For the buyer, a high price acts as a deterrent. The higher the price, the fewer apples buyers purchase. Why is this so? As the price of apples rises, consumers switch to oranges or grapefruit, or they simply cut down on their total consumption of fruit. Conversely, the lower the price, the more apples are bought. A lower price brings new purchasers into the market, and each purchaser tends to buy more. The response of buyers to various possible prices is illustrated in the **demand curve** in Figure 4-1. Points *A*, *B*, *C*, and *D* correspond to

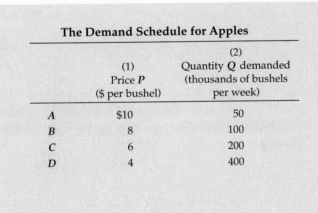

The Demand Schedule for Apples

	(1) Price *P* ($ per bushel)	(2) Quantity *Q* demanded (thousands of bushels per week)
A	$10	50
B	8	100
C	6	200
D	4	400

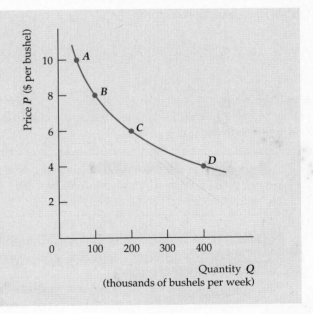

FIGURE 4-1 The demand curve.

At each of the possible prices specified, there is a certain quantity of apples that people would be willing and able to buy. This information is shown in two ways: in tabular form and as a diagram. On the vertical axis, the possible prices are shown. In each case, the quantity of apples that would be bought is measured along the horizontal axis. Since people are more willing to buy at a low price than at a high price, the demand curve slopes downward to the right. Demand curves are shown throughout this book in blue.

The Supply Schedule for Apples

	(1) Price P ($ per bushel)	(2) Quantity Q supplied (thousands of bushels per week)
F	$10	260
G	8	240
H	6	200
K	4	150

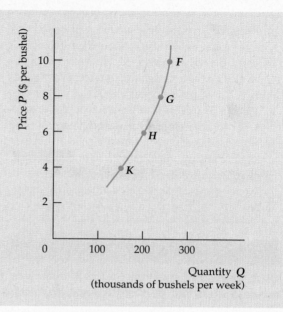

FIGURE 4-2   The supply curve for apples.

For each of the possible prices specified, the supply schedule indicates how many units the sellers would be willing to sell. This information is illustrated graphically in this figure, which shows how the supply curve slopes upward to the right. At a high price, suppliers will be encouraged to step up production and offer more apples for sale. Supply curves are shown throughout this book in red.

rows *A, B, C,* and *D* in the **demand schedule** shown beside the figure.

A *demand curve* or a *demand schedule* shows the quantities of a good or service which buyers would be willing and able to purchase at various market prices.

It should be emphasized that a demand curve reflects not just what people want, but also *what they are willing and able to pay for.*

The demand curve or demand schedule applies to a *specific population* and to a *specific time period.* Clearly, the number of apples demanded during a month will exceed the number demanded during a week, and the number demanded by the people of Virginia will be less than the number demanded in the whole United States. In a general discussion of theoretical issues, the population and time framework are not always stated explicitly,

but it nevertheless should be understood that a demand curve applies to a specific time and population.

SUPPLY

Whereas the demand curve illustrates how buyers behave, the supply curve illustrates how sellers behave; it shows how much they would be willing to sell at various prices. Needless to say, buyers and sellers look at high prices in a different light. A high price discourages buyers and causes them to switch to alternative products, but a high price encourages suppliers to produce and sell more of the good. Thus, the higher the price, the higher the quantity supplied. This is shown in the **supply curve** in Figure 4-2. As in the case of the demand curve, the points on the supply curve (*F, G, H,* and *K*) are drawn from the numbers in the corresponding rows of the **supply schedule** beside the figure.

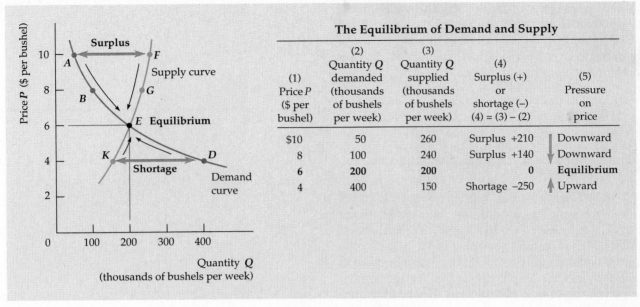

FIGURE 4-3   How demand and supply determine equilibrium price and quantity.

Equilibrium exists at point *E,* where the quantity demanded equals the quantity supplied. At any higher price, the quantity supplied exceeds the quantity demanded. Because of the pressure of unsold stocks, competition among sellers causes the price to be bid down to the equilibrium of $6. Similarly, at a price less than the $6 equilibrium, forces are set in motion which raise the price. Because the quantity demanded exceeds the quantity supplied, eager buyers clamor for more apples and bid the price up to the equilibrium at $6.

A *supply curve* or a *supply schedule* shows the quantities of a good or service that sellers would be willing and able to sell at various market prices.

THE EQUILIBRIUM OF DEMAND AND SUPPLY

The demand and supply curves may now be brought together in Figure 4-3. The **market equilibrium** occurs at point *E,* where the demand and supply curves intersect. At this equilibrium, the price is $6 per bushel, and sales are 200,000 bushels per week.

An *equilibrium* is a situation in which there is no tendency to change.

To see why *E* is the equilibrium, consider what happens if the market price is initially at some other level. Suppose, for example, that the initial price is $10, which is above the equilibrium price. What happens? Purchasers buy only 50,000 bushels (shown by point *A* in Figure 4-3), while sellers want to sell 260,000 bushels (point *F*). Therefore, there is a large **surplus** of 210,000 bushels. Some sellers are disappointed: They sell much less than they wish at the price of $10. Unsold apples begin to pile up. In order to get them moving, sellers now begin to accept a lower price. The price starts to come down—to $9, then $8. Still there is a surplus, or an excess of the quantity supplied over the quantity demanded. The price continues to fall. It does not stop falling until it reaches $6, the equilibrium. At this price, buyers purchase 200,000 bushels, which is just the amount the sellers want to sell; in other words, the "market is cleared." Both buyers and sellers are now satisfied with the quantity of their purchases or sales at the existing market price of $6. Therefore, there is no further pressure on the price to change.

A *surplus* exists when the quantity supplied exceeds the quantity demanded. (The price is above the equilibrium.)

Now consider what happens when the initial price is below the equilibrium, at, say, $4. Eager buyers are willing to purchase 400,000 bushels (at point *D*), yet producers are willing to sell only 150,000 bushels (at point *K*). There is a **shortage** of 250,000 bushels. As buyers clamor for the limited supplies, the price is bid upward. The price continues to rise until it reaches $6, the equilibrium where there is no longer any shortage because the quantity demanded is equal to the quantity supplied. At point *E*, and only at point *E*, will the price be stable.

A *shortage* exists when the quantity demanded exceeds the quantity supplied. (The price is below the equilibrium.)

SHIFTS IN THE DEMAND CURVE

The quantity of a product that buyers want to purchase depends on the price. As we have seen, the demand curve illustrates this relationship between price and the quantity demanded. But the quantity that people want to purchase also depends on other influences. For example, if incomes rise, people will want to buy more apples—and more of a whole host of other products, too.

The purpose of a demand curve is to show how the quantity demanded is affected by price, **and by price alone.** When we ask how much people want to buy at various prices, it is important that our answer not be disturbed by other influences. In other words, when we draw a demand

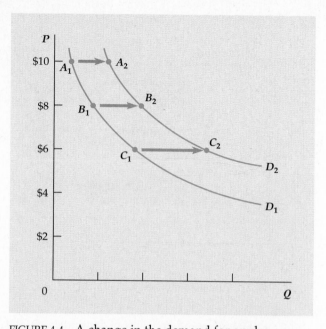

FIGURE 4-4   A change in the demand for apples.

When incomes rise, there is an increase in the number of apples that people want to buy at any particular price. At a price of $10, for example, the quantity of apples demanded increases from point A_1 to A_2. At other prices, the increase in incomes also causes an increase in the number of apples demanded. Thus, the whole demand curve shifts to the right, from D_1 to D_2.

curve for a good, we must *hold constant incomes and everything else that can affect the quantity demanded,* with the sole exception of the price of the good. We make the **ceteris paribus** assumption—that all other things remain unchanged. (*Ceteris* is the same Latin word that appears in *et cetera,* which literally means "and other things." *Paribus* means "equal" or "unchanged.")

Of course, as time passes, other things do *not* remain constant. Through time, for example, incomes generally rise. When that happens, there is an increase in the quantity of apples demanded. The whole demand curve shifts to the right, as illustrated in Figure 4-4. Since *economists use the term "demand" to mean the whole demand curve or demand schedule,* we may speak of this rightward shift in the curve more simply as an *increase in demand.*

DEMAND SHIFTERS

A shift in the demand curve—that is, a change in demand—may be caused by a change in any one of a whole host of other things. Some of the most important are income, prices of related goods, and tastes.

1. *Income.* When incomes rise, people are able to buy more. And people do in fact buy more of the typical or **normal good.** For such a good, the number of units demanded at each price increases as incomes rise. Thus the demand curve shifts to the right with rising incomes, as illustrated in Figure 4-4.

Not all goods are normal, however. As incomes rise, people may buy *less* of a good. For example, they may demand less margarine, since they are now able to afford butter. Or they may stop buying day-old bread since they can afford fresh bread instead. When the increase in income causes a leftward shift of the demand curve, the item is an **inferior good.**

If an increase in income	Shifts the demand curve for a good to the right	It is a *normal* good (or a superior good)
If an increase in income	Shifts the demand curve for a good to the *left*	It is an *inferior* good

2. *Prices of Related Goods.* A rise in the price of one good can cause a shift in the demand curve for another good.

For example, if the price of oranges were to double while the price of apples remained the same, buyers would be encouraged to buy apples instead of oranges. Thus a rise in the price of oranges causes a rightward shift in the demand curve for apples. Goods such as apples and oranges—which satisfy similar needs or desires—are **substitutes.** Other examples are tea and coffee,

butter and margarine, bus and train tickets, or heating oil and insulating materials.

For **complements** or **complementary goods,** exactly the opposite relationship holds. In contrast to substitutes—which are used *instead of* each other—complements are used *together*, as a package. For example, gasoline and automobiles are complementary goods. If the price of gasoline spirals upward, people become less eager to own automobiles. The demand curve for cars therefore shifts to the left. So it is with other complements, such as tennis rackets and tennis balls, or formal clothing rentals and tickets to a formal dance.

Finally, many goods are basically *unrelated*, in the sense that a rise in the price of one has no significant effect on the demand curve of the others. Thus bus tickets and butter are unrelated, as are coffee and cameras.

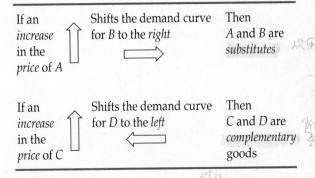

If an increase in the price of A	Shifts the demand curve for B to the *right*	Then A and B are *substitutes*
If an increase in the price of C	Shifts the demand curve for D to the *left*	Then C and D are *complementary* goods

3. *Tastes.* Tastes change over time. Because of increased interest in physical fitness, more people are jogging. This activity increases the demand for running shoes. Tastes, and therefore demand, are quite volatile for some products, particularly for fads like video games.

This list covers some of the most important demand shifters, but it is far from complete. To see how it might be extended, consider the following questions:

1. If the weather changes, how will the change affect the demand for skiing equipment? For snow tires?

2. If people expect cars to be priced $2,000 higher next year, what effect will this expected increase have on the demand for cars this year?

3. As more and more families get video cassette recorders, and thereby become able to skip through the commercials with the fast scan button, how will this affect the demand by companies buying television ads? (A. C. Neilsen, a firm that rates TV shows as a service for advertisers, has found that, when people watch taped shows, half of them do in fact "zap" the commercials.)

WHAT IS PRODUCED: THE RESPONSE TO A CHANGE IN TASTES

At the beginning of this chapter, three basic questions were listed. To see how the market mechanism can help to answer the first of these—"*What will be produced?*"—consider what happens when there is a change in tastes. Suppose, for example, that people develop a desire to drink more tea and less coffee. This change in tastes is illustrated by a rightward shift in the demand curve for tea and a leftward shift in the demand curve for coffee.

As the demand for tea increases, the price is bid up by eager buyers. With a higher price, growers in Sri Lanka and elsewhere are encouraged to plant more tea. At the new equilibrium, shown as point E_2 in Figure 4-5, the price of tea is higher than it was originally (at E_1), and the consumers buy a larger quantity of tea. In the coffee market, the results are the opposite. At the new equilibrium (F_2), the price is lower and a smaller quantity is bought.

Thus, competitive market forces cause producers to "dance to the consumers' tune." In response to a change in consumer tastes, prices change. Tea producers are given an incentive to step up production, and coffee production is discouraged.

SHIFTS IN SUPPLY

While the market encourages producers to "dance to the consumers' tune," the opposite is also true. As we will now see, consumers also "dance to the producers' tune." The market involves a complex

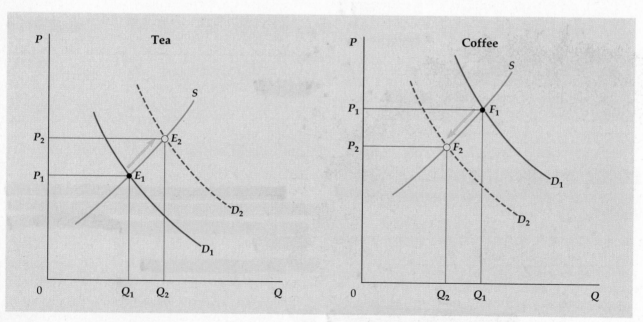

FIGURE 4-5   A change in tastes.

A change in tastes causes the demand for tea to increase and the demand for coffee to decrease. As a result, more tea is bought, at a higher price. Less coffee is bought, and the price of coffee falls.

interaction: Sellers respond to the desires of buyers, and buyers respond to the willingness of producers to sell.

Just as the demand curve reflects the desires of buyers, so the supply curve illustrates the willingness of producers to sell. In an important respect, the two curves are similar. The objective of each is to show **how the quantity is affected by the price of the good, and by this price alone.** Thus, when we draw the supply curve, once again we make the *ceteris paribus* assumption. Everything except the price of the good itself is held constant.

SUPPLY SHIFTERS

As in the case of demand, the other things that affect supply can change through time, causing the supply curve to shift. Some of these other things are the following:

1. *The Cost of Inputs.* For example, if the price of fertilizer goes up, farmers will be less willing to produce wheat at the previously prevailing price. The supply curve will shift to the left.

2. *Technology.* Suppose there is an improvement in technology that causes costs of production to fall. With lower costs, producers will be willing to supply more at any particular price. The supply curve will shift to the right.

3. *Weather.* This is particularly important for agricultural products. For example, a drought will cause a decrease in the supply of wheat (that is, a leftward shift in the supply curve), and a freeze in Florida will cause a decrease in the supply of oranges.

4. *The Prices of Related Goods.* Just as items can be substitutes or complements in consumption, so they can be substitutes or complements in production.

We saw earlier that substitutes in consumption are goods that can be consumed as *alternatives* to one another, satisfying the same wants—for example, apples and oranges. Similarly, **substitutes in production** are goods that can be produced as *alternatives* to one another, using the same factors of production. Thus, corn and soybeans are substitutes in production; they can be grown on similar land. If the price of corn increases, farmers are encouraged to switch their lands out of the production of soybeans and into the production of corn.

The amount of soybeans they are willing to supply at any given price decreases; the supply curve for soybeans shifts to the left.

Earlier, we also observed that complements in consumption are used *together*—for example, gasoline and automobiles. Similarly, **complements in production** or **joint products** are produced together, as a package. Beef and hides provide an example. When more cattle are slaughtered for beef, more hides are produced in the process. An increase in the price of beef causes an increase in beef production, which in turn causes an increase in the production of hides—that is, a rightward shift of the supply curve of hides.

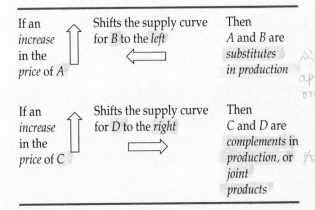

| If an *increase* in the price of A | Shifts the supply curve for B to the *left* | Then A and B are *substitutes in production* |
| If an *increase* in the price of C | Shifts the supply curve for D to the *right* | Then C and D are *complements* in *production*, or *joint products* |

THE RESPONSE TO A SHIFT IN THE SUPPLY CURVE

To illustrate how "consumers dance to the producers' tune," suppose there is a frost in Brazil, which wipes out part of the coffee crop. As a result, the supply curve shifts to the left, as illustrated in Figure 4-6. With less coffee available, the price is bid upward. At the new equilibrium (G_2), the price is higher and the quantity sold is smaller.

How do consumers respond to the change in supply? Because of the higher price of coffee, consumers are discouraged from buying. For example, some may decide to drink coffee only once a day, rather than twice. Anyone who is willing and able to pay the high price will get coffee; those who are unwilling or unable to pay the price will not get it. Thus *the high price acts as a way of allocating the limited supply among buyers.* The coffee goes only to buyers who are sufficiently eager to be willing to pay the high price, and sufficiently affluent to be able to afford it.

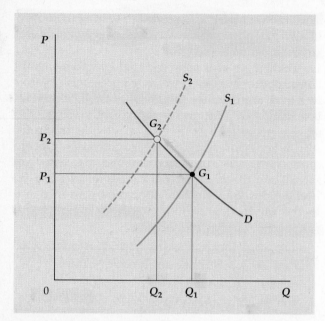

FIGURE 4-6   A shift in supply.

A freeze in Brazil causes a leftward shift in the supply curve of coffee. The result is a movement of the equilibrium along the demand curve from G_1 to G_2. At the new equilibrium, there is a higher price, and a smaller quantity is sold.

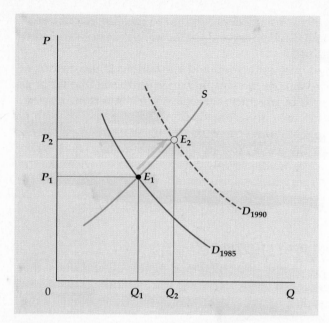

FIGURE 4-7   A shift in the demand for tea.

This diagram, based on the left panel of Figure 4-5, shows that there is an increase in the quantity of tea supplied as the equilibrium moves from E_1 to E_2. However, supply does not change, since the supply curve does not move.

SHIFTS IN A CURVE AND MOVEMENTS ALONG A CURVE

Because the term *supply* applies to a supply schedule or a supply curve, a change in supply means a *shift* in the entire curve. Such a shift took place in Figure 4-6 as a result of a freeze in Brazil.

In this figure, observe that the demand curve has not moved. However, as the supply curve shifts and the price consequently changes, there is a movement *along* the demand curve from G_1 to G_2. At the second point, less is bought than at the original point. The quantity of coffee demanded is less at G_2 than at G_1.

The distinction between *a shift in a curve* and a *movement along a curve* should be emphasized. What can we say about the move from G_1 to G_2?

1. It is correct to say that "supply has decreased." Why? Because the entire supply curve has shifted to the left.

2. It is *not* correct to say that "demand has decreased." Why? Because the demand curve has not moved.

3. It is, however, correct to say that "the quantity demanded has decreased." Why? Because a smaller quantity is demanded at G_2 than at G_1.

A similar distinction should be made when the demand curve shifts. This is shown in Figure 4-7, based on the left panel of Figure 4-5, where the demand for tea increases because of a change in tastes. The rightward movement of the demand curve causes the equilibrium to move *along* the *supply* curve, from E_1 to E_2. It is *not* correct to say that supply increases, since the supply curve does not move. However, the *quantity supplied* does increase as the price rises. Quantity Q_2 is greater than Q_1.

THE INTERCONNECTED QUESTIONS OF WHAT, HOW, AND FOR WHOM

We have explored how two tunes are played. Demand is the tune played by consumers, and supply is the tune played by producers. Each group dances to the tune played by the other.

If we now want to go beyond the question of *what* will be produced to the other questions— *how?* and *for whom?*—we must recognize that the world is even more complex. More than two tunes are being played. In fact, there is a whole orchestra, with the tune played on any one instrument related to the tunes played on all the others.

The major segments of the economy are illus- trated in Figure 4-8, which adds detail to Figure 3-3 (in Chapter 3). The **product markets** for apples, coffee, bread, housing, and so forth, are represent- ed by the upper box; these are the markets studied thus far. The box at the bottom indicates that there are similar **markets for factors of production,** with their own demands and supplies. For example, to produce wheat, farmers need land; they create a

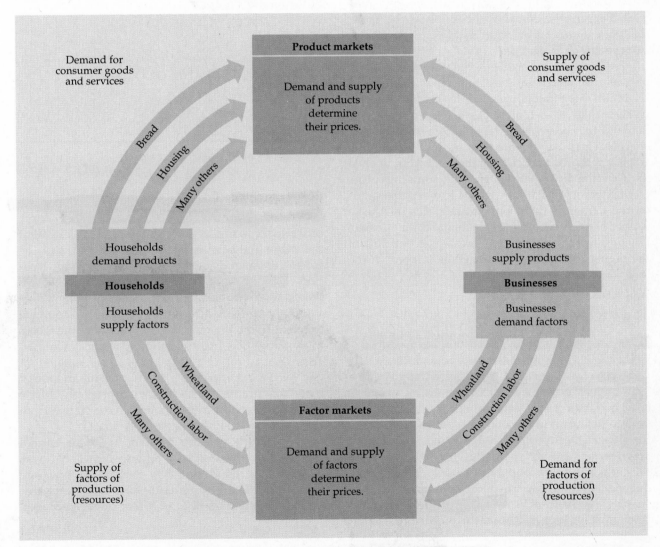

FIGURE 4-8 **Markets answer the basic questions of what, how, and for whom.**

The product markets (top box) are most important in determining *what* is produced, and the factor markets (lower box) in determining *how* goods are produced and *for whom.* However, there are many interrelationships among the two boxes. For example, incomes change in response to changing demand and supply conditions in the lower box, and these changing incomes in turn influence the demand for products in the upper box.

demand for land. At the same time, those with land are willing to sell or rent it if the price is attractive; they create a supply of land.

To answer the question *"What* will be produced?" we begin by looking at the top box, where the demand and supply for products come together. If there is a large demand for bread, producers will respond by producing a lot. But eventually it is necessary to look at the lower box, too, where the demand and supply for the factors of production come together. Why are the factor markets relevant? Because the demand and supply in the upper box are influenced by what happens in the factor markets in the lower box.

For example, consider what happened when oil was discovered in Alaska several decades ago. To build the pipeline needed to get the oil out, workers had to be hired. As a consequence, the demand for construction labor in Alaska increased sharply. The price of labor (that is, the wage rate) in Alaska shot up, and construction workers flocked in from the lower 48 states. The spiraling wage payments in Alaska (lower box) had repercussions on the demands for goods and services in Alaska (upper box). For example, the demand for Alaskan housing in the upper box increased as a result of the higher earnings of construction workers in the lower box.

HOW? AND FOR WHOM?

To answer the question *"What* will be produced?" we began by looking at the product markets in the upper box of Figure 4-8. To answer the questions *how?* and *for whom?* we look first at the lower box.

The factor prices established in the lower box help to determine *how* goods are produced. During the Black Death of 1348–1350 and subsequent plagues, an estimated quarter to a third of the Western European population died. As a consequence, labor supply was reduced and wages rose sharply, by 30 to 40%. Because of the scarcity of labor and its high price, wheat producers had an incentive to farm their lands with less labor. Wheat was produced in a different way, with a different combination of labor and land. In those days, as today, the market mechanism helped to determine how the society conserved its scarce supply of a factor—in this case, labor.

The answer to the question *"For whom* is the nation's output produced?" depends on incomes, which are determined by the interplay of supply and demand in factor markets (lower box in Figure 4-8). For example, the supply of doctors is small compared with the demand for doctors. The price of medical "labor" is therefore high; doctors generally have high incomes. On the other hand, unskilled labor is in large supply and is therefore cheap. Consequently, the unskilled worker receives a low income and is able to buy only a small share of the nation's output.

LIVING IN A GLOBAL ECONOMY

RENTING AN OFFICE IN TOKYO, LONDON, OR HONG KONG

While Japan is rich, the Japanese are not.

CLYDE PRESTOWITZ[1]

In real estate, so the saying goes, three things are important: location, location, and location. Prime office space is similar in design and quality in all of the major financial capitals of the world. But the price it commands depends very much on the location. Demand and supply can differ greatly between cities, resulting in quite different rents.

Buoyant demand and limited supply combine to make Tokyo the most expensive city in the world to rent an office. In 1988, office space in downtown Tokyo rented for an average of $175 per square foot per year. For a space 12' × 9', that meant an annual rental of almost $19,000. Not surprisingly, many junior executives found themselves cramped in offices that were little bigger than closets.

New York was far behind, with an annual rental of "only" $45 per square foot. That was cheaper than London ($155), Paris ($70), or Hong Kong ($65). Hong Kong is in surprising company, for it is often classified as a less developed area.

---

[1]*Trading Places: How We Allowed Japan to Take the Lead* (New York: Basic Books, 1988), p. 311. Prestowitz was counselor for Japanese Affairs, U.S. Department of Commerce.

How can offices be so expensive then? One reason is the short supply of land: Hong Kong has 5.5 million people crowded in an area about 20 miles square. Another reason is the booming economy. Hong Kong is one of the best places to do business in all of East Asia, and firms are willing to pay the high rents.

THE MARKET MECHANISM: A PRELIMINARY EVALUATION

Some see private enterprise as a predatory target to be shot, others as a cow to be milked; but few are those who see it as a sturdy horse pulling the wagon.

WINSTON CHURCHILL

There are thousands of markets in the United States and millions of interconnections among the markets. Changes in market conditions are reflected in changes in prices. As we have seen, prices provide information to market participants; they provide them with incentives to respond to changing conditions; and they bring order out of a potentially chaotic situation.

STRENGTHS OF THE MARKET

In some ways, the market mechanism works very well. Specifically:

1. The market *gives producers an incentive to produce the goods that consumers want.* If people want more tea, the price of tea is bid up, and producers are encouraged to produce more.

2. The market *provides an incentive to acquire useful skills.* For example, the high fees that doctors charge give students an incentive to undertake the long, difficult, and expensive training necessary to become a physician.

3. The market *encourages consumers to use scarce goods carefully.* For example, when the coffee crop is partially destroyed by bad weather, the price is driven up and people use coffee sparingly. Those who are relatively indifferent are encouraged to switch to tea. Even those who feel they must have coffee are motivated to conserve. With the high price of coffee, they are careful not to brew three cups when they intend to use only two.

4. Similarly, the price system *encourages producers to conserve scarce resources.* In the pasturelands of Texas, land is plentiful and cheap; it is used to raise cattle. In contrast, in Japan land is relatively scarce and expensive; cattle don't "run the range" over huge acreages of land the way they do in the United States.

5. The market involves a *high degree of economic freedom.* Nobody forces people to do business with specific individuals or firms. People are not directed into specific lines of work by government officials; they are free to choose their own occupations. Moreover, if people save, they are free to use their savings to set themselves up in their own independent businesses.

6. Markets provide *information on local conditions.* For example, if an unusual amount of hay-producing land in a specific county is plowed up to grow corn, then the price of hay in that county will tend to rise. The higher price of hay will signal farmers that they should put some of the land in this county back into hay. No government agency can hope to keep up-to-date and detailed information on the millions of localized markets like this one, each with its own conditions. Note the amount of information that is relevant, even for this simple decision on whether hay or corn should be planted: the quality of the land, particularly its relative productivity in hay and corn; the number of cattle and horses that eat hay; the cost of fertilizer for hay and for corn; the cost of seed for each; and so on and on.

In evaluating how well a market works, we should keep in mind the most important question of all: *compared to what?* Even a poor market may work better than the alternatives. Thus, one of the strongest arguments for the market parallels Winston Churchill's case for democracy: It may not work very well, but it does work better than the alternatives that have been tried from time to time.

THE ALTERNATIVE OF PRICE CONTROLS: SOME PROBLEMS

Consider what happens if the government tries to keep a price down by setting a *price ceiling.* Specifically, suppose it sets the price at P_1, below the equilibrium at E in Figure 4-9. The result is a shortage AB. Eager buyers have trouble finding the

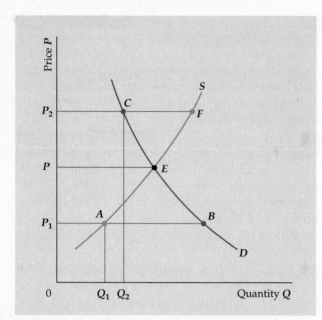

FIGURE 4-9 Price-setting by government.

If the government sets a price ceiling at P_1 to keep the price below the equilibrium at E, the result is a shortage AB. Observe that consumers end up with less; the quantity supplied at A is less than at equilibrium E.

On the other hand, if the government sets a price floor at P_2, the result is a surplus. The government can keep the price at P_2 if it is willing to buy the surplus CF. Again the public ends up with less—at C—than it would get at equilibrium E. Thus, when the government sets the price, consumers get a smaller quantity, *whether the price is set above or below its equilibrium.*

good. Thus, when the United States had a ceiling on gasoline prices in 1979, drivers had to wait in long lines at gas stations. Obviously, they wasted time—not to mention the gasoline they wasted while waiting in line.

Moreover, as a result of price controls, goods may disappear from regular distribution channels and flow instead into illegal **black markets.** In this case, the scarce goods go to those willing to break the law. Furthermore, the public may end up paying more for black market goods than it would pay in a free market. Black marketeers charge higher prices because they want compensation for the risks and because they have to use informal, inefficient marketing arrangements.

A **black market** is one in which sales take place at a price above the legal maximum.

Price controls can create other problems. For example, in its desire to prevent labor unrest, the Polish government kept bread fixed at a low price—so low that it was less than the price of the grain that went into making the bread. Therefore it was cheaper for farmers to feed their livestock bread rather than grain. When they did so, the labor and other resources that had been used to make grain into bread were wasted.

THE MARKET MECHANISM: LIMITATIONS AND PROBLEMS

Although the market has impressive strengths, it is also the target of substantial criticisms:

1. While the market provides a high degree of freedom for participants in the economy, *it may give the weak and the helpless little more than the freedom to starve.* In a market, producers do not respond solely to the needs of consumers. Rather, they respond to the desires of consumers that are backed up with cash. Thus under a system of *laissez faire,* the pets of the rich may have better meals and better health care than the children of the poor.

2. Markets *simply won't work* in some parts of the economy. When there is a military threat, individuals cannot provide their own defense. An individual who buys a rifle has no hope of standing against a foreign power. Defense is provided by the government, with organized military forces. The police and the judicial system are other services that can best be provided by the government. No matter how well the market works in general, people can't be permitted to "buy" a judge. (Even though the government provides the judicial system, a problem may still arise. See Box 4–1.)

3. In a system of laissez faire, *prices are not always the result of impersonal market forces.* In many markets, one or more participants have the power to influence price. *The monopolist or oligopolist may restrict production* in order to keep the price high, as we will see in detail in later chapters.

4. Activities by private consumers or producers may have undesirable *side effects.* Nobody owns the

BOX 4–1   What's the Price of Justice?

The bizarre case of Pennzoil vs Texaco raised a troubling question: What's the price of justice? According to press reports, one month after Pennzoil lodged a $15 billion suit against Texaco in 1984, Pennzoil's lead lawyer gave $10,000 to Judge Anthony Farris of the district court of Harris County, Texas, to help the judge finance his reelection campaign. When Texaco's lawyers found out, they expressed their shock and moved that Farris be disqualified. The motion was denied by a judge who offered a quaint explanation: if judges had to step aside for the mere appearance of impropriety, it would play havoc with the system. Texaco's lawyers decided they had to do something. They raised the bid, distributing $72,700 in campaign contributions to seven justices of the Texas Supreme Court who were expected to make a final ruling in the case—including three who weren't even running for reelection. Was this enough? Hardly. Texaco's lawyers were cheapskates. Pennzoil's lawyers responded with $315,000, including contributions to four justices who weren't running. One of the supreme court justices was so appalled that he resigned to campaign for reform.

Texans are not alone in wondering whether money is undermining the integrity of their judicial system. Although Texas is one of just a handful of states that still elect all their judges, most states—39, to be exact—have elections for at least some judges. At one time, judicial elections were inexpensive. But with television and highly paid campaign consultants, some contests have become very costly.

And what of the Pennzoil-Texaco case? Pennzoil's suit was based on the complaint that Texaco had taken over Getty Oil in spite of Getty's prior commitment to sell out to Pennzoil. The jury awarded Pennzoil $10.5 billion, plus interest—much more than the total value of Getty. The award drove Texaco temporarily into bankruptcy while a settlement was being worked out.

Sources: "Pennzoil and the Judge," *The Washington Post,* July 30, 1987: William P. Barrett, "The Best Justice Money Can Buy," *Forbes,* June 1, 1987; and Sheila Kaplan, "What Price Justice? Oh, About $10,000," *The Washington Post,* May 17, 1987.

---

air or the rivers. Consequently, in the absence of government restraints, manufacturers may use them as garbage dumps, harming those downwind or downstream. The market provides no incentive to limit such negative side effects.

5. An unregulated system of private enterprise *may be quite unstable,* with periods of inflationary boom giving way to sharp recessions. Economic instability was a particularly severe problem in the early 1930s, when the economies of many countries collapsed into a deep depression. (On this and some other occasions, instability in the economy was compounded by ill-advised policies by the government.)

6. In a system of laissez faire, businesses may do an excellent job of satisfying consumer wants as expressed in the marketplace. But should the businesses be given high marks if they have *created the wants in the first place by advertising?* In the words of retired Harvard Professor John Kenneth Galbraith, "It involves an exercise of imagination to suppose that the taste so expressed originates with the con-

sumer."[2] In this case, the producer is sovereign, not the consumer. According to Galbraith, the consumer is a puppet, manipulated by producers with the aid of Madison Avenue's bag of advertising tricks. Many of the wants that producers create and then satisfy are trivial: for example, the demands for automobile chrome and junk food.

Without arguing the merits of each and every product, defenders of the market system question Galbraith's point. In part, their defense of the market is based on the question "Compared with what?" If market demands are dismissed, who then is to decide which products are "meritorious" and which are not? Government officials? Should not people be permitted the freedom to make their

---

[2]John Kenneth Galbraith, "Economics as a System of Belief," *American Economic Review* (May 1970): 474. See also Galbraith, *The New Industrial State* (Boston: Houghton Mifflin, 1967).

own mistakes? And why should we assume that created wants are without merit? After all, we are not born with a taste for art or good music. Our taste for good music is created when we listen to it. Galbraith certainly would not suggest that symphony orchestras are without merit, simply because they statisfy the desire for good music which they have created. But who then is to decide which created wants are socially desirable?

If these criticisms of the market are taken far enough, they can be made into a case for replacing the market with an alternative system. Those favoring centrally controlled economies lay particular emphasis on points 1, 5, and 6 in their argument that the market should be replaced with government direction of the economy.

However, these criticisms are also often made by those who seek to reform, rather than replace, the market system. The recent economic history of Western Europe, North America, and many other parts of the globe has to a significant extent been written by such reformers. If the market does not provide a living for the weak and the helpless, then its outcome should be modified by private and public assistance programs. If monopolies have excessive market power, they can be broken up or their market power restrained by the government. If the production of a good creates pollution or other undesirable side effects, such side effects can be limited by taxation or controls. So say the reformers.

Although the market is a vital mechanism, it has sufficient weaknesses and limitations to provide the government with a major economic role. This role will be the subject of the next chapter.

KEY POINTS

1. Every economy has limited resources and involves specialization and exchange. In every economy, a mechanism is needed to answer three fundamental questions:

  (a) What will be produced?
  (b) How will it be produced?
  (c) For whom will it be produced?

2. The two principal mechanisms for answering these questions are the government and private markets.

In the real world, all countries rely on a *mixture* of markets and government actions. However, the mixture differs among countries. The United States places a relatively heavy reliance on the market. In centrally planned countries such as the USSR and other nations in Eastern Europe, the government has much more pervasive influence.

3. *Prices* play a key role in markets, providing information and incentives to buyers and sellers.

4. Markets vary substantially, with some being dominated by one or a few producers, whereas others have many producers and consumers. A market is *perfectly competitive* if there are many buyers and many sellers, with no single buyer or seller having any influence over the price.

5. In a perfectly competitive market, equilibrium price and quantity are established by the intersection of the demand and supply curves.

6. In drawing both the demand and supply curves, the *ceteris paribus* assumption is made—that "other things" do not change. Everything that can affect the quantity demanded or supplied—with the sole exception of price—is held constant when a demand or supply curve is constructed.

7. If any of these "other things"—such as consumer incomes or the prices of other goods—do change, the demand or supply curve will shift.

8. *What* the economy produces is determined primarily in the market for goods and services in the upper box of Figure 4-8. On the other hand, *how* and *for whom* are determined primarily in the factor markets (the lower box). However, there are numerous interactions among markets. The answer to each of the three questions depends on what happens in both the upper and lower boxes.

9. A substantial case can be made for the market system because it encourages firms to produce what people demand, and because it encourages the careful use of scarce goods and resources. Nevertheless, the market also has significant weaknesses, which provide the government with an important economic role.

KEY CONCEPTS

market	market power	*ceteris paribus*
capitalist economy	industry	demand shifter
free enterprise	firm	normal good
central planning	plant	inferior good
mixed economy	demand	substitutes
monopoly	supply	complements
oligopoly	equilibrium	supply shifter
perfect competition	surplus	joint products
imperfect competition	shortage	black market

PROBLEMS

4-1. Figure 4-6 illustrates the effect of a Brazilian freeze on the coffee market. How might the resulting change in the price of coffee affect the tea market? Explain with the help of a diagram showing the demand and supply for tea.

4-2. The relatively high incomes of doctors give students an incentive to study medicine. Other than the expected income and costs of training, what important factors affect career decisions?

4-3. It is often said that "the market has no ethics. It is impersonal." But individual participants in the market do have ethical values, and these values may be backed up with social pressures. Suppose that, in a certain society, it is considered not quite proper to be associated with a distillery. With the help of demand and supply diagrams, explain how this view will affect:

(a) The demand and/or supply of labor in the alcohol industry.

(b) The willingness of people to invest their funds in the alcohol industry, and the profitability of that industry.

4-4. Suppose that social sanctions are backed up by law and that people caught selling marijuana are given stiff jail sentences. How will this affect the demand and supply of marijuana? The price of marijuana? The quantity sold? The incomes of those selling marijuana?

* 4-5. In distinguishing between substitutes and complements, the text lists a number of simple examples. Tea and coffee are substitutes, whereas cars and gasoline are complements.

It is worth looking more closely at one example, however, that may not seem quite so simple: heating oil and insulation. How would you correct or rebut the following erroneous argument:

> "Heating oil and insulation are complements, not substitutes, because they are used together. In Alaska, they use a lot of heating oil and a lot of insulation. In California, they don't use much of either."

---

*Problems marked with asterisks are more difficult than the others. They are designed to provide a challenge for students who want to do more advanced work.

Try to answer this question without looking at the following hints. But if you have difficulty, consider these hints:

(a) Think about the market for heating oil and insulation in a single city, say, St. Louis. When the price of heating oil goes up in St. Louis, do you think that this causes the demand curve for insulation to shift to the right or to the left? Does this make insulation a complement or substitute for heating oil, according to the definitions in the text?

(b) Are natural gas and oil substitutes or complements? Suppose the incorrect statement in quotation marks above had mentioned heating oil and natural gas rather than heating oil and insulation.

(c) If we accept the erroneous statement shown above in quotation marks, can't we argue in a similar manner that there are no such things as substitutes? For example, wouldn't we also accept the following incorrect conclusion: "In California, more apples and more oranges are sold than in Alaska. Therefore, apples and oranges are used together. They are complements, not substitutes." Do you see that this statement is incorrect, because it departs from the standard assumption that "other things remain unchanged?" In identifying complements and substitutes, we must not switch from one location and population (Alaska) to another (California); we must look at a single set of people (the St. Louis example in part a). Do you see why economists emphasize the assumption that "other things remain unchanged" (*ceteris paribus*)?

CHAPTER 5
THE ECONOMIC ROLE OF GOVERNMENT

Government does not go beyond its sphere in attempting to make life livable. . . .
OLIVER WENDELL HOLMES

When Franklin Delano Roosevelt became president in 1933, the nation was mired in the Great Depression. Roosevelt believed that the government had the responsibility to do something to alleviate the widespread economic misery. He summarized his view: "As new . . . problems arise beyond the power of men and women to meet as individuals, it becomes the responsibility of the Government itself to find new remedies." Quite a different opinion was expressed by President Ronald Reagan in 1980. Government, said Reagan, "is not the solution to our problem. Government *is* the problem."

Government affects the economy in four ways, by

■ Spending.

■ Taxation.

■ Regulation.

■ Operating public enterprises, such as power plants.

Chapter 4 pointed out that public enterprise is quite limited in the United States; it is much less important here than in other countries. Accordingly, this chapter will concentrate on the other three ways in which the government affects the U.S. economy—spending, taxation, and regulation.

A final section of the chapter describes the changing attitudes toward public enterprises in Britain and a number of other countries.

The government's decisions to spend, tax, regulate, or establish public enterprises all help to answer the questions highlighted in Chapter 4: *What* goods and services will be produced? *How?* and *For whom?*

1. *Spending.* When the government pays social security pensions to retirees, it influences *who* gets society's output; the recipient of a pension is able to buy more goods and services. When the government builds roads or buys aircraft, it affects *what* is produced. When the government spends money for agricultural research, it influences *how* food will be produced.

2. *Taxes.* When the government collects taxes, it influences *who* gets society's output. When you pay taxes, you have less left to buy goods and services. Taxes also affect *what* is produced. For example, the tax on gasoline is much higher in Europe than in the United States. That is one reason why European cars are smaller, on average, than U.S. cars. Finally, the tax system may also influence *how* goods are produced. For example, by changing tax laws, the government can encourage businesses to use more machinery.

3. *Regulation.* Governmental regulations also influence what, how, and for whom goods and services are produced. For example, the government prohibits some pesticides and requires seat belts in cars. It thereby affects *what* is produced. By requiring producers of steel to limit their emissions of smoke, the government influences *how* goods are produced. It also regulates some prices—for example, some city governments impose rent ceilings so that people with low and moderate incomes can afford to keep their apartments. Such ceilings affect *who* gets the output of society. More of the present tenants stay, and fewer apartments are available for newcomers and young people.

In the private market, people have an option of buying or not buying products such as television sets and cars. In contrast, government activities generally involve compulsion. Taxes *must* be paid; people are not allowed to opt out of the system when the time comes to pay income taxes. Similarly, government regulations are enforced by compulsion; car manufacturers *must* install safety equipment. Compulsion sometimes exists even in a government spending program. Young people *must* go to school—although their parents do have the option of choosing a private school rather than one run by the government.

Having presented a broad overview, we now look at government spending, taxation, and regulation in more detail.

GOVERNMENT EXPENDITURES

During the nineteenth and early twentieth centuries, government expenditures covered little more than the expenses of the army and navy, a few public works, and the salaries of a small number of government officials. Except for wartime periods when spending skyrocketed to pay for munitions, weapons, and personnel, government spending was small. As late as 1929, all levels of government—federal, state, and local—together spent less than $11 billion a year. Of this total, about three-quarters was spent at the state and local levels. Highway maintenance and education were typical government programs. This does not mean, however, that a rigid policy of laissez faire was followed. Even during the nineteenth century, governments at both the state and local levels participated in some important sectors of the economy.

For example, governments helped railroads and canal systems to expand.

With the depression of the 1930s, a major increase in government activity began. Distress and unemployment were widespread, and the government became more active. During the decade 1929–1939, federal government spending increased from $3 billion to $9 billion. Part of the increase was specifically aimed at providing jobs through new agencies, such as the Civilian Conservation Corps (CCC). Then, when the United States entered the Second World War in 1941, the government undertook huge spending to pay for military equipment and personnel. By 1944, defense amounted to more than 40% of gross national product (GNP).

When the war ended in 1945, the nation demobilized and government spending fell by more than 50%. Expenditures never fell to the low levels of 1929, however, because the government had taken on new peacetime responsibilities. For example, during the 1930s it began the *social security* system, whose principal function is the payment of pensions to retired people. More recently, the government has introduced *medicare* to provide medical assistance to the elderly, and *medicaid* to provide such assistance to the needy. Expenditures for weapons and other military purposes have also remained high for the past four decades.

GOVERNMENT PURCHASES VERSUS TRANSFERS

Government expenditures may be classified into two major categories:

- **Purchases of goods and services.**
- **Transfer payments.**

Government *purchases* of goods include items such as paper, computers, and aircraft. The government purchases services when it hires schoolteachers, police officers, and employees for government departments. When the government purchases goods and services, *it makes a direct claim on the productive capacity of the nation.* For example, when the government orders a computer, the manufacturer uses glass, plastic, copper, silicon chips, machines, and labor to make the computer. Similarly, the purchase of services involves a claim on productive resources. The police officer hired by the government must spend time on the beat and thus becomes unavailable for work in the private sector.

Government ***transfer payments,*** on the other hand, are payments *for which the recipient does not provide any good or service in return.* Transfer payments include social security and medicare benefits for the elderly and welfare payments such as medicaid. Of the transfer payments, social security and medicare are by far the largest, accounting for 28% of total federal government expenditures in 1988.

A ***transfer payment*** is a payment by the government to an individual, for which the individual does not provide a good or service in return. Social security benefits, unemployment compensation, and welfare payments are examples of transfers.

When the government purchases goods or services, it makes a claim on the productive capacity of the economy. For example, when it buys computers, labor and materials have to be used to produce those computers. In contrast, transfer payments represent no direct claim by the government on the productive capacity of the nation. It is true, of course, that when the government collects social security taxes from workers and pays benefits to retirees, the pattern of consumer spending is affected. The old have more to spend and workers have less.

The left panel of Figure 5-1 shows total government expenditures, including transfers. The right panel shows government purchases of goods and services; that is, it excludes transfers. These are the expenditures that make a direct claim on the productive resources of the economy. In each panel,

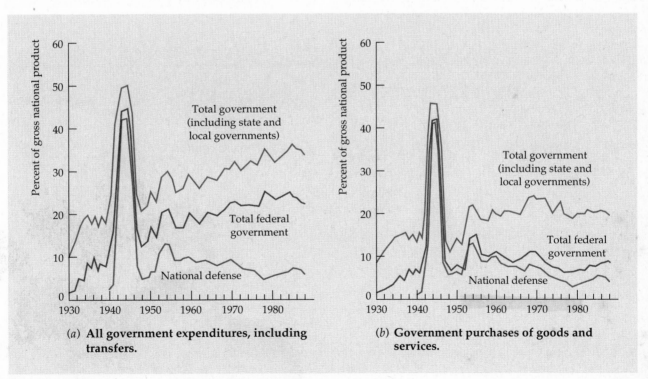

(a) **All government expenditures, including transfers.**

(b) **Government purchases of goods and services.**

FIGURE 5-1   Government expenditures, 1930–1988 (as percentage of gross national product).

The left panel shows how total government expenditures, including expenditures on goods and services and the amounts redistributed in the form of transfers, have grown as a percentage of gross national product. The right panel shows only the expenditures for goods and services. As a percentage of GNP, these expenditures have not changed much over the past three decades.

expenditures are shown as a percentage of the overall size of the economy, as measured by gross national product or GNP. (Chapter 6 will explain in detail how GNP is measured.) Observe that as a percentage of GNP, government purchases of goods and services are approximately what they were three decades ago (right panel). Purchases by state and local governments have gone up, but these increases have been approximately matched by the declining percentage for the federal government. In 1988, federal government purchases of goods and services were only two-thirds as large as the combined purchases of state and local governments.

The two panels give two quite different impressions of the size of government. If we look only at purchases of goods and services in the right panel, then the percentage of national product going to the government has been quite stable over the past three and a half decades. If, on the other hand, we include transfers and look at total government expenditures in the left panel, the government's percentage is increasing. In brief, the government is not directly claiming a larger and larger share of the nation's product for itself (right panel). It *is*, however, claiming a larger share when account is taken of what it *redistributes* in the form of social security and other transfer payments.

EXPENDITURES OF THE FEDERAL GOVERNMENT

Figure 5-2 shows expenditures of the federal government in more detail. Notice how much defense expenditures have changed through the years. In the 1960s, they ran between 7% and 10% of GNP. By 1979, they fell below 5%. During the 1980s, they rose above 6%.

This figure also shows the increase in social security and medicare expenditures through the years. The combined social security and medicare program surpassed defense expenditures in 1976 to

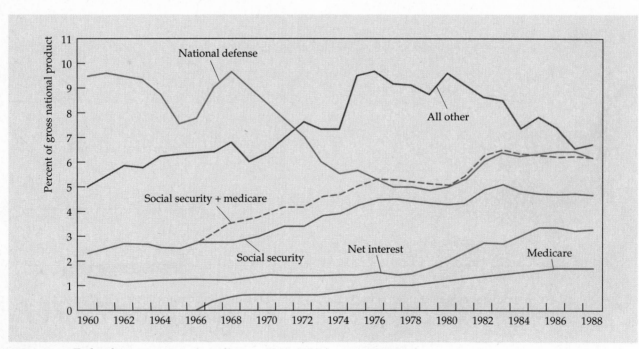

FIGURE 5-2   Federal government expenditures, 1960–1988 (as percentage of gross national product).

Federal government expenditures for interest, social security, and medicare have increased rapidly.

become the largest single spending category. Interest payments have also been rising rapidly, from a little over 1% of GNP in the early 1960s to more than 3% by the late 1980s. There are two reasons for this rapid increase in interest payments: (1) interest rates rose; and (2) the government's debt, on which interest must be paid, grew rapidly during the 1980s.

TAX REVENUES

Figure 5-3 presents a breakdown of the revenues of the federal government. The **personal income tax** provides the greatest share of revenues. This tax is levied on taxable personal income—that is, on the incomes of individuals and families after the subtraction of various exemptions and deductions.

For a married couple with two children, the income tax was levied at the rates shown in Table 5-1 in 1989. Because of exemptions and deductions,

TABLE 5-1   Federal Income Tax, 1989[†]

(1) Income	(2) Tax	(3) Average Tax Rate (3) = (2) ÷ (1)	(4) Marginal Tax Rate (tax on additional income)
$10,000	0	0	0
$20,000	$1,020	5.1%	15%
$50,000	$6,280	12.6%	28%
$100,000	$20,878	20.9%	33%
$200,000	$53,878	26.9%	33%
$250,000	$68,544	27.4%	28%
$500,000	$138,544	27.7%	28%
$1,000,000	$278,544	27.9%	28%

[†]For a married couple with two children, filing jointly and claiming the standard deduction.

such a couple did not have to pay tax on the first $13,200 of income. The *average tax rate* (col. 3) is simply the total tax divided by income. Observe that, as income rises, the percentage of income paid in tax also rises. Therefore, the income tax is **progressive**. Note, however, that at very high incomes, the progressivity practically disappears and the tax is approximately **proportional**, between 27% and 28%.

If a tax takes a larger percentage of income as income rises, the tax is *progressive.*

If a tax takes a smaller percentage of income as income rises, the tax is *regressive.*

If a tax takes a constant percentage of income, the tax is *proportional.*

The **marginal tax rate** is shown in the last column; it is the tax rate on *additional* income. For example, at an income of $20,000, a couple is in the 15% marginal tax bracket and accordingly pays 15¢ tax on each additional dollar of income. The marginal tax rate increases to 28% and then to 33%.

The last column shows something peculiar. As income rises to $250,000, the marginal tax rate comes *down* again to 28%. This peculiarity is explained by the political compromises that led to the Tax Reform Act of 1986. The Congress and the administration wanted to advertise that they were

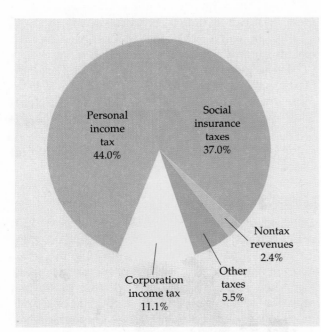

FIGURE 5-3   Federal government receipts, 1990 (projected).

The personal income tax is the largest single source of revenue for the federal government. Social insurance taxes—mainly for social security—are in second place.

cutting the *maximum* tax rate to 28%. This is in a sense true: The *average* tax rate (col. 3) does not rise above 28%. However, the marginal rate does rise above 28%—to 33% over a range.

Although the personal income tax remains the largest single component of federal government revenues, social insurance taxes (to pay for social security and unemployment insurance) have risen rapidly, from 16% of total federal revenues in 1960 to 37% in 1988. Social security contributions, or taxes, are paid to finance old-age pensions and payments to the families of contributors who die or are disabled. In 1989, the tax stood at 15.02% of wages and salaries up to a maximum income of $48,000; half the tax is collected from the employer and half from the employee. In order to finance the rapid increase in social security payouts, the social security tax has been increased repeatedly. It was 6% in 1960, 9.6% in 1970, and 12.25% in 1980. The maximum income subject to tax has also been rising.

The social security tax is *regressive.* While it is collected at a flat percentage on incomes up to a limit of $48,000 in 1989, any additional income is exempt from the tax. Thus the tax constitutes a higher percentage of the income of an individual making $48,000 per year than of someone making three times that much, who gets most income free of this tax. Nevertheless, if we look at the social security system *as a whole*—both taxes and benefits—we find that it favors lower income people. They receive bigger benefits, compared to the taxes they have paid, than do high-income people. While lower income people pay a disproportionate share of the social security tax, they receive an even larger share of the benefits.

The tax on corporate income (profits) constitutes the third most important source of federal revenue. In recent decades, the corporate income tax has become less important as a source of revenue—falling from about 25% of total federal revenues in the 1950s to about 11% in 1988.

Minor amounts of revenues are brought in by other taxes, such as excise taxes—on items such as cigarettes, alcoholic beverages, and gasoline—and customs duties imposed on goods imported into the United States. The government also has small receipts from nontax sources, such as fees paid by users of some government services.

EXPENDITURES, REVENUES, AND DEFICITS

When the government's revenues fall short of its expenditures, its budget is in *deficit.* In order to pay for the shortfall, the government has to borrow the difference. When it does so, its outstanding *debt* increases.

If a government's revenues exceed its expenditures, it has a budget *surplus.*

If a government's revenues fall short of its expenditures, it has a budget *deficit.*

If a government's revenues equal its expenditures, its budget is *balanced.* (The term *balanced budget* is often used loosely to mean that the budget is either in balance or in surplus; that is, revenues are at least as great as expenditures.)

The government's *debt* is the amount it owes. The debt increases when the government runs a deficit and borrows.

In the past quarter century, the U.S. government has run a deficit every year except 1969. During the early 1980s, the deficits grew rapidly, reaching a peak of 6.3% of GNP in 1983 (Fig. 5-4).

Large government deficits pushed up the size of the national debt from $909 billion in 1980 to more than $3 trillion in 1990. The large deficits were especially surprising because they occurred during the presidency of Ronald Reagan, who had vigorously attacked deficits prior to his election in 1980.

REAGANOMICS

The large deficits are one indication of how difficult it is to develop and execute an overall economic strategy—particularly when the objective is to make major changes in the role of the government.

When he came into office, President Reagan intended to change policy sharply. His economic program—which quickly was given the label of "Reaganomics"—included the following objectives:

1. Increase defense expenditures.

2. Restrain and, where possible, reduce other expenditures by the federal government.

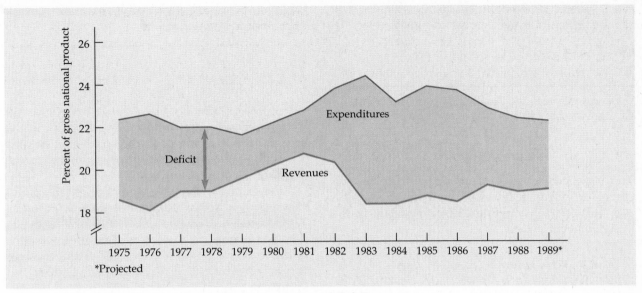

FIGURE 5-4   The federal budget: Expenditures, receipts, and deficits
(as percentages of gross national product).

Over the past decade, expenditures of the federal government have been substantially
higher than projected revenues, resulting in budget deficits.

3. Reduce government regulation.

4. Cut tax rates.

These policies were based on a philosophy of
what the government should and should not do. In
President Reagan's view, the major responsibilities
of the government were to provide protection from
external enemies and to provide the basis for an
orderly society. He believed that government had
gone far beyond its appropriate role. One of his
objectives, said Reagan, was to "get the government off the backs of the people."

President Reagan achieved some of his objectives. The tax law enacted in 1981 provided for cuts
in tax rates over the period from 1981 to 1984.
Defense expenditures were increased, both in dollar terms and as a percentage of national product.
But other expenditures were much more difficult to
cut than expected, even though some programs
were slashed. The early hopes of the Reagan
administration—that the budget could be balanced
by 1984—were dashed. In fact, deficits ballooned.

The high deficits meant that the national debt
grew rapidly. As a result, interest on the debt also

grew rapidly. The high interest expenditures will
make it even more difficult to balance the budget in
the future.

THE EARLY BUSH ADMINISTRATION

The large deficits severely limited President George
Bush's options when he entered the White House
in 1989. He had a number of goals that were not
easily reconciled:

■ Additional government spending on children,
the homeless, and education, as a way of building a
"kinder, gentler nation."

■ No new taxes, in line with his unequivocal
campaign promise.

■ A reduction and elimination of the budget
deficit by the early 1990s.

To help reduce the deficit, the president suggested
broad categories on which spending was to be cut
back, but he did not identify specific programs.
Congress was invited to join in the politically difficult process of picking the actual programs to be

cut. It seems likely that the budgetary situation will remain difficult throughout his administration.

PRINCIPLES OF TAXATION

The art of taxation consists of plucking the goose so as to obtain the largest amount of feathers with the least possible amount of hissing.

JEAN BAPTISTE COLBERT
SEVENTEENTH-CENTURY FRENCH STATESMAN

The major objective of taxation is to raise revenues—to obtain feathers without too much hissing. But other objectives are also important in the design of a tax system.

1. NEUTRALITY

In many ways, the market system works admirably. Adam Smith's invisible hand provides the consuming public with a vast flow of goods and services. As a starting point, therefore, a tax system should be designed to be *neutral*. That is, it should disturb market forces as little as possible, unless there is a good reason to the contrary.

For the sake of illustration, consider a far-fetched example. Suppose that blue cars were taxed at 10% and green cars not at all. This tax would clearly not be neutral between blue and green cars. People would have an incentive to buy green cars; blue cars would practically disappear from the market. A tax that introduces such a distortion would make no sense.

While this illustration is trivial, actual taxes do introduce distortions. For example, several centuries ago, houses in parts of Europe were taxed according to the number of windows. As a result, houses were built with fewer windows. To a lesser degree, the current property tax introduces a perverse incentive. If you have your house repaired, the government's evaluation of your house (the assessed value) may be raised and your taxes increased as a consequence. Therefore property taxes encourage you to let your property deteriorate.

The problem is that every tax provides an incentive to do something to avoid it. As long as taxes must be collected, complete neutrality is impossible. The objective of the tax system must therefore be more modest: to aim toward neutrality. As a starting point in the design of a tax system,

the disturbance to the market that comes from taxation should be minimized.

2. NONNEUTRALITY: MEETING SOCIAL OBJECTIVES BY TAX INCENTIVES

There is, however, an important modification that must be made to the neutrality principle. In some cases, it may be desirable to disturb the private market.

For example, the government might tax polluting activities, so that firms will do less polluting. The market is disturbed but in a desirable way. Another example is the tax on cigarettes, which, in addition to its prime objective of raising revenue for the government, also discourages cigarette consumption.

3. EQUITY

Taxation represents coercion; taxes are collected by force if necessary. Therefore it is important that taxes both be fair and give the appearance of being fair. There are, however, two different principles for judging fairness.

The Benefit Principle. This principle recognizes that the purpose of taxation is to pay for government services. Therefore, let those who gain the most from government services pay the most.

If this principle is adopted, then a question arises: Why not simply set prices for government services which people can voluntarily pay if they want the services? In other words, why not charge a price for a government service, just as General Motors charges for cars? This approach may work—for example, for a toll road from which drivers can be excluded if they do not pay. But it will not work for public goods that benefit people even if they do not pay—for example, police, disease control programs, and air traffic control. Everyone will enjoy them, but no one will offer to pay for them. It is the function of the government to determine whether such programs are worthwhile. Once the decision is made to go ahead, people must be required to support the program through taxes. If the **benefit principle** of taxation is followed, the government estimates how much various individuals and groups benefit, and sets taxes accordingly.

Ability to Pay. If the government sets taxes according to the benefit principle, it does not redistribute income. The people who are taxed also get benefits from government programs. If the government wishes to redistribute income, it can set taxes according to the *ability to pay.* The basic measures of the ability to pay are income and wealth.

If taxes are imposed according to the *benefit* principle, people pay taxes in proportion to the benefits they receive from government spending.

If taxes are imposed according to the *ability to pay* principle, higher taxes are paid by those with greater ability to pay, as measured by income and/or wealth.

If the government were to levy a progressive income tax and an inheritance tax, and at the same time provide assistance to those at the bottom of the economic ladder, it would substantially redistribute income from the rich to the poor. But the world is not so simple. The government levies many other taxes as well, and some of these are proportional or even regressive. Overall, high-income groups pay only a slightly higher percentage of their incomes in taxes than do low-income groups.[1] It is on the expenditure side that the government has its greatest effect in redistributing income. We have already noted that the social security system as a whole favors lower income people. Even though they pay more than a proportionate share of social security taxes, they get an even larger share of benefits.

4. SIMPLICITY

To anyone who has spent the first two lovely weekends of April sweating over an income tax form,

---

[1]It is surprisingly difficult to tell who pays some of the taxes. For example, do corporate taxes come out of the pockets of the owners of corporations, who on average have higher incomes than the general public? Or are they passed on to the general public, in the form of higher prices? This issue is studied in detail by Joseph Pechman, *Who Paid the Taxes, 1965-85?* (Washington, D.C.: Brookings Institution, 1985).

simplicity of the tax system is devoutly to be desired. Of course, we live in a complex world, and the tax code must to some degree reflect this complexity. But, as a result of decades of tinkering, the U.S. income tax has become ridiculously complicated. Indeed, it has become so complicated that the Internal Revenue Service (IRS) itself gives incorrect answers to taxpayer inquiries about one-third of the time. Mortimer Caplin, a former commissioner of the IRS, found that the tax code had grown so "horrendously complex" that he turned to an accounting firm to prepare his own return. So did Wilbur Mills, the ex-chairman of the House Ways and Means Committee—a committee that is largely responsible for writing the tax laws. (However, Donald Alexander, another former IRS chief, prepares his own tax return, since he thinks that those who write and enforce the law "should have to undergo the ordeal to see what it's like.")

A number of proposals have been made to simplify the tax system. Some people have flippantly suggested an ultra-simple, two-line tax form:

line 1: What did you make last year? $___ .

line 2: Send it in.

THE TAX REFORM ACT OF 1986

Widespread dissatisfaction with the existing tax system led to the Tax Reform Act of 1986. This act had broad bipartisan support, including the president and congressional leaders such as Senator William Bradley and Congressman Dan Rostenkowski.

The Tax Reform Act had two major features:

1. It plugged or restricted a number of *loopholes* that had allowed people to avoid taxes on some of their income. For example, the investment tax credit—which had given businesses a tax break as a reward for investing—was eliminated. Tax advantages for owners of real estate were reduced. Capital gains (that is, gains on the sales of stocks, bonds, or other assets) are now taxed at the same rate as earned income, rather than at the lower, preferential rates that existed before 1986.

2. It cut tax rates. For example, the average tax for individuals with incomes less than $10,000 was cut by more than half. Toward the upper end of the income scale, the highest marginal tax rate on personal income was reduced from 50% to 33%. The tax rate on corporate profits was cut from 46% to 34%.

The closing of loopholes (point #1) means that more income is now taxed. As a result, it is possible to reduce tax rates (point #2) while still maintaining total revenues. The objective of the 1986 act was to reform taxes and make them fairer; it was not designed to raise or lower the total amount the government was taking from the public.

The tax system not only became fairer; it also moved in the direction of neutrality. Because loopholes were restricted and tax rates reduced, people now have less incentive to look for special ways to avoid taxes. They have less incentive to look for tax gimmicks when they make investments, and more incentive to focus on profitability instead. In this way, tax reform has contributed to the efficiency of the economy.

In addition to increasing fairness and neutrality, the proponents of the 1986 legislation at first hoped to achieve a third goal, also—to make the tax system simpler. However, very early in the debate, Congress recognized that, whatever the virtues of the proposed reform, it would not simplify taxes. The word "simplification" was quietly dropped from the title of the bill. But two objectives out of three is not bad. In the tax reform debate, Congress turned in a distinguished performance.

GOVERNMENT REGULATION

The government's budget, amounting to hundreds of billions of dollars, has a substantial effect on the types of goods produced and on who gets these goods. In addition, the government affects the economy through its regulatory agencies, such as the Environmental Protection Agency (EPA) which controls pollution. The cost of *administering* such agencies—which amounts to only 2% to 3% of the federal government's budget—is an inadequate measure of their importance. The cost to businesses of *complying* with these regulations is far higher. For example, it costs a steel mill much more to install pollution-control devices than it costs the EPA to administer the regulations. The gains to the public—in the form of cleaner air—are likewise much greater than the small amounts that appear in the federal budget.

During the past century, a number of steps have been taken to limit the most flagrant abuses of private business. In 1890, the Sherman Act declared business mergers that create monopolies to be illegal. Then the Federal Trade Commission (FTC) was established in 1914 in the belief that monopolies should be prevented before the fact, rather than punished after they are created.

Regulation goes far beyond the control of monopoly. For example, the Food and Drug Administration (FDA) determines the effectiveness and safety of drugs before they are permitted on the market. The financial shenanigans of the 1920s—which contributed to the collapse into the depression—led in 1933 to the establishment of the Securities and Exchange Commission (SEC) to regulate financial markets. The SEC requires corporations to disclose information about their finances. Banks are extensively regulated by the Federal Reserve System, the Federal Deposit Insurance Corporation, the Comptroller of the Currency, and state regulatory agencies. The Federal Aviation Administration (FAA) sets and enforces safety standards for aircraft.

In the 1960s and 1970s, there was an upswing in regulatory activity, with the addition of such agencies as the Equal Employment Opportunity Commission (EEOC), the Environmental Protection Agency (EPA), the Commodity Futures Trading Commission (CFTC), and the Occupational Safety and Health Administration (OSHA).

In many areas, regulation is relatively uncontroversial. For example, few people complain when the Federal Aviation Administration enforces safety standards for the airlines. Similarly, there is widespread support for government regulation aimed at keeping unsafe drugs off the market. The FDA drew particular praise because it had blocked the distribution of thalidomide, a drug to relieve nausea that caused birth defects when it was used in Europe.

However, doubts set in after the flurry of regulatory activity of the 1960s and 1970s. In particular, there were growing concerns that some government regulations were working at cross purposes. For example, the Justice Department and the FTC were charged with the responsibility of reducing monopoly abuse and increasing competition in the U.S. economy. But, at the same time, the Civil Aeronautics Board (CAB) was *limiting* competition among airlines. In order to fly a new route in competition with existing carriers, an airline needed approval of the CAB, and the CAB regularly turned down such requests. In addition, banking regulation set the interest rate that banks could offer to depositors, and limited competition between banks and other financial institutions. During the Carter and Reagan administrations, major steps were taken to reduce regulation of banks and airlines. At the end of 1984, the CAB went out of business.

Under the Reagan administration, with its desire to reduce the regulatory hassles faced by business, enforcement of safety and environmental regulations became less vigorous. Particularly with respect to the environment, the policies of the administration stirred controversy. The EPA became a demoralized agency, touched by scandal. Critics of the administration pointed out that the EPA performed an essential function. Without it, there would be nothing in the competitive market system to give businesses any strong incentive to restrain pollution.

What is needed is a sense of balance. The private market mechanism has substantial defects. For example, corporations cannot on their own be counted on to pay sufficient attention to limiting pollution. But government agencies also have defects; they are not run by superhumans capable of solving all our problems. Furthermore, government regulation can be costly. While we use government agencies to deal with major defects in the market, we should be prepared to live with minor failures, where the cure may be worse than the defects themselves.[2]

Regulation in the public interest is made particularly difficult because of the political clout of producers. When regulations are being developed, the affected industry makes its views known forcefully. But the views of consumers are diffuse and often underrepresented. In an extensive study of regulatory agencies, the Senate Government Operations Committee concluded that the public is outnumbered and outspent by industry in regulatory proceedings. The committee chairman observed that regulatory hearings "can be likened to the biblical battle of David and Goliath—except that David rarely wins." This conclusion should come as no surprise. For decades, an irreverent definition has circulated in Washington: A sick industry is one that cannot capture control of its regulatory agency.

The heavy influence of producers is not simply the result of a conspiracy of wealth. Rather, it is an intrinsic feature of a highly specialized economy. Each of us has a major, narrow, special interest as a producer, and each of us has a minor interest in a wide range of industries whose goods we consume. We are much more likely to react when our particular industry is affected by government policy; we are much less likely to express our diffuse interest as consumers. The political clout of producers is primarily the result of modern technology and a high degree of specialization; it is not primarily a result of our particular system. It exists in a wide variety of political-economic systems, including those of Britain, France, Germany, Japan, and the Soviet Union.

THE ROLE OF THE GOVERNMENT

With government budgets reaching hundreds of billions of dollars, and with an extensive list of government regulations, the U.S. economy is clearly a substantial distance away from a pure market system of laissez faire. What principles and objectives guide the government when it intervenes?

In part, government intervention is based on deep social attitudes that are often difficult to explain. Thirty years ago, Americans could look askance at government-financed, "socialized" medicine in Britain. Yet at the same time they could consider British education "undemocratic" because many well-to-do Britons sent their children to privately financed elementary and secondary schools. The British, on the other hand, were proud of their educational system and were puzzled by what they considered a quaint, emotional American objection

---

[2]The government does not, however, always exercise common sense. Many bizarre laws are on the books. For example, it is illegal in Seattle to carry a concealed weapon more than 6 feet long. An ordinance in Danville, Pennsylvania, requires that "fire hydrants must be checked one hour before fires." Sault Ste. Marie had a law against spitting into the wind. In Washington, D.C., it was illegal to punch a bull in the nose. These examples are taken from Laurence J. Peter, *Why Things Go Wrong* (New York: Morrow, 1984) and Barbara Seuling, *You Can't Eat Peanuts in Church and Other Little-Known Laws* (New York: Doubleday, 1975).

to public financing of medical care. During the past three decades, the gap between the two societies has narrowed, with increasing governmental involvement in medicine in the United States and a decline in the importance of privately financed education in Britain.

The government intervenes in the economy for many reasons; it is hard to summarize them all. We will look at five of the main ones.

1. PROVIDING WHAT THE PRIVATE MARKET CANNOT

Consider defense expenditures. For obvious political reasons, defense cannot be left to the private market. The prospect of private armies marching around the country is too painful to contemplate. But there also is an impelling economic reason why defense is a responsibility of the government.

The difference between defense and an average good is the following. If I buy food at the store, I get to eat it; if I buy a movie ticket, I get to see the film; if I buy a car, I get to drive it. But defense is different. If I want a larger, better equipped army, my offer to purchase a rifle for the army will not add in any measurable way to my own security. My neighbor, and the average person in Alaska, Michigan, or Texas, will benefit as much from the extra rifle as I do. In other words, the benefit from defense expenditures *goes broadly to all citizens; it does not go specifically to the individual who pays.* If defense is to be provided, it must be financed by the government.

Such goods—where the benefit goes to the public regardless of who pays—are sometimes known as **public goods.**

2. DEALING WITH EXTERNALITIES

An *externality* is a side effect—good or bad—of production or consumption. For example, when individuals are immunized against an infectious disease, they receive a substantial benefit; they are assured that they won't get the disease. But there is an *external benefit* as well, because others gain too; they are assured that the inoculated individuals will not catch the disease and pass it along to them. Similarly, there is an external benefit when people have their houses painted. The neighborhood becomes more attractive.

An *external cost* occurs when a factory pollutes the air. The cost is borne by those who breathe the polluted air. Similarly, someone who drives an unsafe car imposes an external cost. He may kill not only himself, but others too.

An *externality* is a side effect of production or consumption. Persons or businesses other than the producer or consumer are affected. An externality may be either positive (for example, vaccinations) or negative (for example, pollution).

Because of the effects on others, the government may wish to encourage activities that create external benefits and to discourage those with external costs. It can do so with any of its three major tools: expenditures, regulations, or taxes. The government spends money for public health programs, for the immunization of the young. In many states, regulations require the inspection of automobiles, to keep cars with poor brakes off the highways. And some states impose higher taxes on leaded than on unleaded gasoline in order to reduce pollution.

3. ENCOURAGING THE USE OF MERIT GOODS

Government intervention may also be based on the view that people are not in all cases the best judges of what is good for them. According to this view, the government should encourage **merit goods**—those that are deemed particularly desirable—and discourage the consumption of harmful products. People's inability to pick the "right" goods may be the result of short-sightedness, ignorance, or addiction.

In some cases, the government attempts merely to correct ignorance in areas where the public may have difficulty determining (or facing?) the facts. The requirement of a health warning on cigarette packages is an example. In other instances, the government goes further, to outright prohibition, as in the case of heroin and other hard drugs.

The government intervenes relatively sparingly to tell adults what they should or should not consume. (Children are another matter, however; they are not allowed to reject the "merit" good, education.) However, substantial government direction does occur in welfare programs, presumably on the ground that those who get themselves into financial difficulties are least likely to make wise consumption decisions. Thus part of the assistance to the poor consists of food stamps and housing programs rather than outright grants of money. In this way, the government attempts to direct consumption toward housing and milk for the children, rather than (perhaps) toward liquor for an alcoholic parent.

4. HELPING THE POOR

The market provides the goods and services desired by those with the money to buy, but it provides little for the poor. In order to help the impoverished and move toward a more humane society, government programs have been established to provide assistance for old people, the handicapped, and the needy.

5. PROMOTING ECONOMIC STABILITY

Finally, if we go back to the beginning of the upswing in government activity—to the depression of the thirties—we find that the primary motivation was not to affect the kinds of products made in the economy, nor specifically to aid the poor. Rather, the problem was the quantity of production. With unemployment rates running over 15% of the labor force year after year, the problem was to produce more, because more of almost anything would help put people back to work. Since the dark days of the 1930s, the government has been held responsible for maintaining a reasonably stable economy, with a low rate of unemployment.

LIVING IN A GLOBAL ECONOMY

THE PRIVATIZATION OF PUBLIC ENTERPRISE

In the half century from 1929 to 1979, governments in many countries undertook new responsibilities. The general trend was toward more government—more government spending, more taxation, more regulation, and more government enterprises. This trend has been broken in the past decade. In the

United States, the Reagan administration pushed through a cut in income tax rates. A number of countries have begun a process of *privatization*, selling their government enterprises to private owners.

Britain has been a leader in privatization since the election of the Conservative government under Margaret Thatcher in 1979. During her first term (1979–1983), the most important part of the privatization program was the sale of 600,000 units of government-owned housing to the tenants for a total of £4.5 billion (approximately $6 billion, or an average of $10,000 per unit). Since 1983, housing sales have continued, but the sales of government corporations have become even more important. The British government has sold its interests in British Aerospace, British Airways, British Gas, British Telecom, Rolls Royce, and the Jaguar/ Rover automotive group, to name some of the more significant. Sir John Egan, chairman of Jaguar, observed that "The Prime Minister [Margaret Thatcher] has never liked owning car companies. She barely puts up with owning the police."

In its privatization program, the British government had a number of objectives.

1. The government *raised funds* by selling enterprises—over £400 million in 1980–1981 and £5.1 billion in 1987–1988. However, receipts from the sale of enterprises did not represent a net gain to the government. Until 1987, almost all the firms offered for sale were profitable. Thus the government was giving up a flow of future profits.

2. The government hoped and expected that there would be a *gain in efficiency.* Freed from the heavy hand of government supervision and spurred on by the profit motive, private firms would have an incentive to adopt more productive methods. The government therefore hoped that the nation would reap a long-term gain, in terms of a greater output of goods and services.

3. The government hoped to increase the *mobility of the labor force* by selling government-owned housing to the tenants. Workers living in such housing had traditionally been discouraged from moving to take new employment opportunities. Once they left government-subsidized housing, they might have great difficulty finding comparable housing elsewhere because of long waiting lists. When the government sold the houses to the tenants, the new owners were free to sell them and move to new job opportunities.

4.   The government was eager to promote an *ethic of ownership and enterprise.* In the words of one member of the Thatcher government:

> Our aim is to build upon our property-owning democracy and to establish a people's capital market, to bring capitalism to the place of work, to the high street and even to the home. . . .
> These policies also increase personal independence and freedom, and by establishing a new breed of owner, have an important effect on attitudes. They tend to break down the division between owners and earners.[3]

It is not surprising that privatization has been a subject of intense ideological debate. Proponents of "people's capitalism" urge the government on. Opponents are concentrated in the Labour Party and labor unions. They argue that privatization is disruptive; it costs the government future revenues

---

[3]John Moore, financial secretary of the Treasury, as quoted in Raymond Vernon, ed., *The Promise of Privatization* (New York: Council on Foreign Relations, 1988), p. 41.

when profitable enterprises are sold; and it leads privatized firms in the telecommunications and airline industries to "skim cream." That is, they introduce new services only in profitable locations and shirk their responsibility to provide services to the more remote and less affluent regions. So say the critics.

Substantial steps toward privatization have also been taken in a few other countries: Bangladesh, Chile, and France. Other countries are planning major privatization programs, including New Zealand, the Philippines, and Turkey. More limited divestitures have occurred in Ecuador, Italy, Mexico, and Senegal. Critics insist that privatization is more talk than action. Nevertheless, Raymond Vernon of Harvard University concludes that "the sheer number and diversity of the countries involved suggest that the movement is more than a rash of children's crusades."[4] Vernon points out that attitudes shifted abruptly in favor of privatization in many countries during the early 1980s. Even the Chinese and Soviet governments seem to be moving away from tight and comprehensive control of their enterprises.

---

[4]Vernon, *The Promise of Privatization*, p. 1.

KEY POINTS

1. The government affects the economy through expenditures, taxation, regulation, and publicly owned enterprises.

2. Except for the period of demobilization after World War II, total government spending (including transfers) has been on an upward trend as a percentage of gross national product (GNP). If, however, only purchases of goods and services are counted, the government's share of GNP has been quite stable over the past three decades. State and local governments have grown, while federal government purchases of goods and services have declined as a percentage of GNP.

3. Federal transfer payments have risen rapidly as a percentage of GNP. Social security is the largest transfer program.

4. Personal income taxes and social security taxes are the two main sources of revenue for the federal government, with corporate income taxes coming in a distant third.

5. Federal government revenues have fallen far short of expenditures. As a result, the federal government has run large deficits, running as high as 6.3% of GNP in 1983.

6. Government regulatory agencies are active in many areas, regulating monopoly and protecting the public from misleading advertising, unsafe drugs, and pollution.

7. The primary reasons for government intervention in the economy are to:

(a) Provide public goods that cannot be supplied by the market because individuals have no incentive to buy them. Individuals get the benefits regardless of who pays.

(b) Deal with externalities, such as pollution.

(c) Encourage the use of merit goods and discourage or prohibit harmful products.

(d) Help the poor.

(e) Help stabilize the economy.

8. A number of objectives are important in the design of a tax system:

(a) In general, neutrality is a desirable objective.

(b) In some cases, however, the government should alter market signals by taxation. For example, a tax can be used to discourage pollution.

(c) Taxes should be reasonably simple and easily understood.

(d) Taxes should be fair. There are two ways of judging fairness: the benefit principle and ability to pay.

KEY CONCEPTS

purchase of goods and services	regressive tax	benefit principle
transfer payment	proportional tax	ability-to-pay principle
income tax	deficit	public good
average tax rate	surplus	merit good
marginal tax rate	balanced budget	externality
progressive tax	tax neutrality	privatization

PROBLEMS

5-1. "That government governs best which governs least." Do you agree? Why or why not? Does the government perform more functions than it should? If so, what activities would you like it to reduce or stop altogether? Are there any additional functions that the government should undertake? If so, which ones? How should they be paid for?

5-2. "State and local governments are closer to the people than the federal government. Therefore, they should be given some of the functions of the federal government." Are there federal functions that might be turned over to the states and localities? Do you think they should be turned over? Why or why not? Are there federal functions that the states are incapable of handling?

5-3. The government engages in research. For example, the government has agricultural experimental stations, and during the Second World War, the government developed the atomic bomb through the Manhattan Project. Why do you think the government engages in these two types of research, while leaving most research to private business? Does the government have any major advantages in undertaking research? Any major disadvantages?

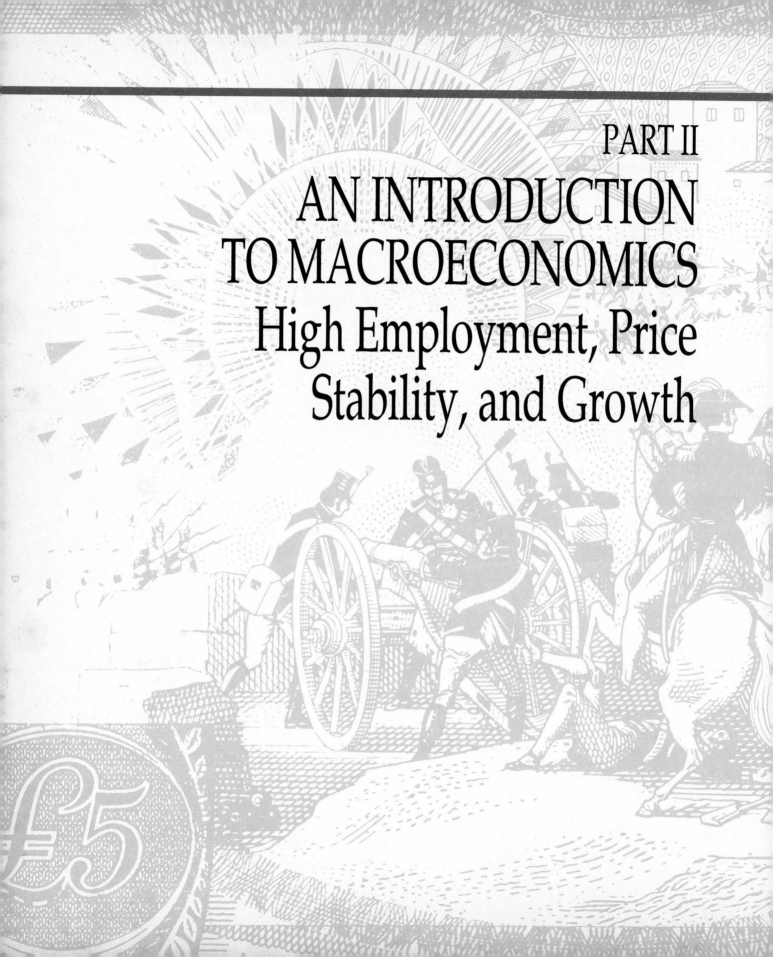

PART II
AN INTRODUCTION TO MACROECONOMICS
High Employment, Price Stability, and Growth

Parts 2, 3, and 4 will focus on the *macroeconomic* goals of:

- High employment.

- Price stability.

- Growth.

Macroeconomic objectives focus on the overall magnitudes in the economy: How many workers are employed in the economy *as a whole*? What is happening to the *average* level of prices? What is happening to the *total output* of the economy?

Specifically, Part 2 covers

- The measurement of gross national product (Chapter 6).

- Changes in output, employment, and prices over the past 60 years (Chapter 7).

- The concepts of *aggregate demand* and *aggregate supply*, and how they can be used to explain fluctuations in output, employment, and prices (Chapter 8).

- The causes of large-scale unemployment (Chapter 9).

CHAPTER 6
MEASURING NATIONAL PRODUCT AND NATIONAL INCOME

Never ask of money spent
Where the spender thinks it went
Nobody was ever meant
To remember or invent
What he did with every cent.

ROBERT FROST
"THE HARDSHIP OF ACCOUNTING"

In our modern economy, we produce a vast array of goods and services, including food, housing, clothing, medical care, and cars. One way of judging the performance of the economy is to measure the production of all these goods and services. A measure of total production does not, of course, give a complete picture of the welfare of the nation. When we acquire more goods, we do not necessarily become happier. Other things are obviously important too, notably, the sense of accomplishment that comes from our work, and the quality of our environment. Nevertheless, the total amount we produce is one important measure of economic success.

THE MARKET AS A WAY OF MEASURING PRODUCTION

The wide range of products poses a problem: How are we to add them all up into a single measure of

national product? How do we add apples and oranges?

Market prices provide an answer. If apples sell for $1 per pound and oranges for 50¢ per pound, the market indicates that 1 pound of apples is worth 2 pounds of oranges. Thus, when market prices are used, oranges and apples can be compared and added, as shown in the example in Table 6-1. In our complex economy, the total value of output can be found in a similar way. By taking the quantity times the market price, we find expenditures on a particular product. By adding up the expenditures for the many goods and services produced—clothing, food, automobiles, and so on—we can get a dollar measure of national product during the year.

National product is the money value of the goods and services produced by a nation during a specific time period, such as a year.

82

TABLE 6-1   Using Market Prices to Add Apples and Oranges

	(1) Quantity (pounds)	times	(2) Price (per pound)	equals		(3) Market Value (1) × (2) = (3)
Apples	1,000	×	$1.00	=		$1,000
Oranges	4,000	×	$0.50	=		$2,000
					Total	$3,000

TWO APPROACHES: NATIONAL PRODUCT AND NATIONAL INCOME

When we produce more goods and services, we also acquire more income. For example, when General Motors produces and sells more cars, it hires more people to work on the assembly line. The wage incomes of workers rise, as do the profits of General Motors. When we produce, we generate income. This idea was first illustrated in Figure 3-3 for a simple economy that produces only consumer goods and services. This idea is repeated here as Figure 6-1.

The performance of this simple economy can be measured by looking at the money payments in either the upper loop or the lower loop. The upper loop shows expenditures by households buying the goods produced by business. Once business has received these payments, where do they go? The lower loop shows that they go to those who have provided the productive inputs: wages and salaries go to the labor force; rents to suppliers of land and buildings; and interest and profits to the suppliers of capital. Profits are what is left over after other payments—such as wages, salaries, and interest—have been made. Thus, in the very simple economy shown in Figure 6-1, both green loops give exactly the same total. We may look at the upper loop, which shows the expenditures for *national product.* Alternatively, we may look at the lower loop, which measures *national income.*

National income is the sum of all income derived from providing the factors of production. It includes wages and salaries, rents, interest, and profits.

This chapter provides a detailed discussion of how national product and national income are measured.

NATIONAL PRODUCT

To calculate national product, we look at the upper loop, examining expenditures on the goods and services that have been produced. When we calculate what has been produced, it is important to

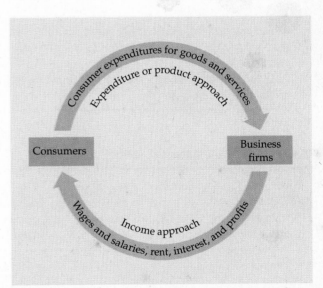

FIGURE 6-1   The circular flow of payments: A simple economy.

In the top loop, we see the payments for the goods and services produced. This loop measures national product. In the bottom loop, we see where the receipts of businesses go: to pay wages, salaries, rents, interest, and profits. This loop measures national income.

count everything *once*, but *only once.* Unless we are careful, we may make a mistake and count some things more than once. The reason is that most products go through a number of stages in the process of production; they are sold a number of times before reaching the hands of the final user. For example, copper wiring and silicon chips are sold to electronics companies, which use them to manufacture television sets. In calculating national product, government statisticians include the television sets sold to consumers, but they do not also count separately the wiring and chips that went into the sets. Similarly, they count the bread purchased by the consumer, but they do not also count separately the flour that was used in producing the bread. To do so would mean that the flour would be counted twice.

The television sets and bread bought by consumers are **final products,** whereas the wheat that went into the bread and the chips that went into the television sets are **intermediate products.** As a first approximation, national product is found by adding up just the expenditures on final products. In this way, double counting is avoided.

A *final product* is a good or service that is purchased by the ultimate user, and not intended for resale or further processing.

An *intermediate product* is one that is intended for resale or further processing.

Note that it is the *intended use,* rather than the physical characteristics of a product, which determines whether or not it is a final good. When gasoline is bought by a service station, it is an intermediate good; it is intended for resale to the public. When it is bought by a farmer or trucker, it is also an intermediate product, since it will be used to harvest grain or produce trucking services. However, when it is purchased by a tourist on vacation, it is a final good.

The distinction between final products and intermediate products is illustrated in Table 6-2, which shows a simplified productive process with only four stages. The first step in the production of a loaf of bread occurs when the farmer grows 20 cents' worth of wheat. The second stage is the milling of this wheat into flour, which is then worth 45 cents. In other words, 25 cents of *value is added* to the 20 cents' worth of wheat when it is made into flour. Similarly, the table shows how value is added during the last two stages, when the flour is baked into bread and when the bread is delivered to the consumer. How much has been produced? The answer: the $1.25 loaf of bread. In calculating national product, we use only the $1.25 value of the bread. We must not add up the value of all the transactions in the first column. Such **double counting** would give an erroneous total of $2.85.

In the calculation of national product, final products are divided into four categories: (1) personal consumption expenditures, (2) government

TABLE 6-2   Final and Intermediate Products

Stage of Production	(1) Value of Sales	less	(2) Cost of Intermediate Products	equals	(3) Value Added (1) − (2) = (3)
Intermediate goods					
Wheat	$0.20	−	0	=	$0.20
Flour	0.45	−	$0.20	=	0.25
Bread, at wholesale	0.95	−	0.45	=	0.50
Final good					
Bread, at retail	$1.25	−	0.95	=	0.30
				Total	$1.25

Value is added at the various stages of production. Note that the sum of all the value-added items in the last column ($1.25) is equal to the value of the final product.

expenditures for goods and services, (3) private domestic investment, and (4) net exports—that is, exports minus imports. By including government, investment, and net exports, we are now recognizing that the world is more complicated than the simple one shown in Figure 6-1, where consumers buy all the final goods produced in the economy.

Value added is the difference between the value of a firm's product and the cost of intermediate products bought from outside suppliers.

---

1. PERSONAL CONSUMPTION EXPENDITURES (C)

Consumption is the ultimate objective of economic activity; people work and produce in order to obtain goods and services to consume. Personal consumption expenditures (C) constitute the largest component of national product. They may be divided into three main components: *durable goods*, such as cars or washing machines; *nondurable goods*, such as food or clothing; and *services*, such as medical services or haircuts (Table 6-3).

2. GOVERNMENT PURCHASES OF GOODS AND SERVICES (G)

Consumer goods and services are not the only things produced in the economy. The government hires teachers; educational services are produced. The government spends money for road repairs; better roads are produced. Governments at all levels—federal, state, and local—undertake expenditures for the public good.[1]

Although government expenditures on goods and services (G) are included in the national product, transfer payments are not. When the government buys an airplane, the airplane is produced. However, when the government makes transfer payments—such as social security payments to retirees—the recipients are not required to produce

---

*[1]The inclusion of all government expenditures for goods and services in national product is a problem. Some government purchases are for "final" use, but other government spending is for intermediate products. A road, for example, can carry both vacation traffic (a "final" or consumption type of use) and trucks loaded with goods (an "intermediate" stage in the productive process). Thus it might be argued that, insofar as roads are used for "intermediate" purposes, this portion of the expenditure for roads should not be included in national product. National product accountants have avoided this problem. They simply assume that all goods and services purchased by the government are for "final" use, and they therefore include all such purchases in national product.

The problems in defining national product are surveyed in Robert Eisner, "Extended Accounts for National Income and Product," *Journal of Economic Literature*, December 1988, pp. 1611–1685.

TABLE 6-3   Composition of Personal Consumption Expenditures, 1988

Type	Billions of Dollars	Percent of Total	
Durable goods	451	14.0%	
Automobiles and parts	209		6.5%
Furniture and household equipment	159		4.9%
Other	83		2.6%
Nondurable goods	1047	32.4%	
Food	552		17.1%
Clothing	187		5.8%
Other	308		9.5%
Services	1729	53.6%	
Housing	501		15.5%
Medical cure	404		12.5%
Household operation	197		6.1%
Transportation	117		3.6%
Other	510		15.8%

anything in return. Therefore, government expenditures on aircraft are included in national product, but transfer payments are not.

3. PRIVATE DOMESTIC INVESTMENT (*I*)

Each year, we produce not only goods and services purchased by consumers and government, but also capital goods that help in production in future years. Private domestic investment includes three categories: (a) business investment in *plant* and *equipment;* (b) *residential construction;* and (c) *changes in inventories.*

Plant and Equipment. This category includes the construction of factories, warehouses, stores, and other nonresidential structures used by businesses, and the acquisition of machinery and other equipment.

Residential Construction. The construction of residences is included in the investment segment of national product. Apartment buildings are included in investment because, like a factory or machine, they are intended to be income-producing assets. In future years, the apartment building will produce shelter, for which the owner will charge rent.

There is a substantial advantage in treating all residential construction similarly in the national product accounts. When housing of any kind is built, families have shelter, whether they rent the new housing or own it. For consistency, construction of new owner-occupied housing is included in the investment category. More specifically, national product accountants treat owner-occupied housing *as if* the family had originally invested in the home and then, in future years, rented the house to itself. Note that houses are treated differently from consumer durables such as refrigerators: houses are included in investment, whereas refrigerators are part of consumption expenditures.

Changes in Inventories. We have seen that wheat that goes into bread is not counted separately in the national product, because its cost is included as part of the total cost of bread and is accounted for in the price of the bread. But what about any wheat above and beyond the amount we currently con-

sume? What happens to it? The answer is that it is either exported (a possibility we will consider in just a moment), or it is used to build up our inventories of wheat. Any such increases in our stocks of wheat represent something we have produced this year. Therefore, they are included in this year's national product.

Similarly, increases in inventories of steel are included in national product—for example, the additional inventories of steel held by refrigerator manufacturers, or the increase in the inventory of unsold steel held by a steel company. However, we do not include the steel that went into the production of refrigerators or machines, since it has already been included when we count consumer purchases of refrigerators and investment in equipment.

Earlier, it was noted that, as a first approximation, national product is found by adding up only expenditures on final products. That is an acceptable and commonly used generalization. It is 99% right, and that is not bad. But it is not precisely accurate. National product includes not only final products in the form of consumer goods and services, government purchases, and equipment and buildings, but also the intermediate products that have been added to inventories. The precisely correct statement is perhaps worth reiterating: we should measure all goods and services *once,* and *only once.*

Changes in inventories can be either positive or negative. In a bad crop year, there may be less wheat on hand at the end of the year than at the beginning. When we take more out of our stocks than we have put back in, changes in inventories are negative, and they are subtracted in measuring national product.

Finally, note that the private domestic investment category (*I*) includes only *private* investment, since government investment—in roads, dams, and the like—is included elsewhere as part of government expenditures for goods and services. Moreover, it includes only *domestic* investment in the United States, since it is U.S. national product that is being estimated. If General Motors builds a factory in Germany, its value is included in German national product, not in U.S. national product. On the other hand, if Volkswagen builds a plant in the United States, that plant is included in U.S. national product.

4. EXPORTS OF GOODS AND SERVICES (X)

The wheat that is exported is part of our total production of wheat and therefore should be included in national product. Because such wheat does not appear in the first three categories (C, G, I), it is included here—in exports of goods and services (X).

The way we export a good, such as wheat, is obvious: we simply put it on a ship and send it abroad. But how do we export services, such as haircuts and surgical operations? The answer is as follows. A tourist from Tokyo visiting Hawaii has expenditures for hotel accommodations, for taxi rides, for haircuts, and for medical services. Since these services have been produced by Americans, they must be counted as part of the U.S. national product. Since they are paid for by the foreigner, they are considered exports of services, even though the hotel, the taxi, the barber shop, and the hospital remain in the United States.

Interest paid by foreigners to Americans, and the profits of U.S. subsidiaries abroad, are also considered exports of services. They represent income to the United States for the services provided by our capital; that is, they represent returns from our past investments abroad.

5. A SUBTRACTION: IMPORTS OF GOODS AND SERVICES (M)

When the Japanese buy our wheat, this export is included in our national product. What happens, on the other side, when we buy Japanese automobiles? Such purchases of imports are included in the U.S. consumption expenditures category, but they have not been produced in the United States. Therefore they should not be counted as part of our national product. Thus we must take them out. We must subtract imports of cars, and of other goods and services, in order to complete our calculation of national product.

NATIONAL PRODUCT: A SUMMARY STATEMENT

In summary:

$$NP = C + I + G + X - M \qquad (6\text{-}1)$$

where

NP = national product

C = personal consumption expenditures

I = private domestic investment

G = government purchases of goods and services

$X - M$ = exports minus imports = net exports

Finally, recall that national product includes only goods and services produced *during the year*. Therefore it does not include expenditures for used goods, such as cars or houses. They were produced in a previous year and were included in that year's national product. However, renovations of old buildings are included, as are repairs to automobiles. They represent current production. Also included in current national product are the brokerage fees for selling houses and other buildings. They represent payments for a valuable service—namely, assistance in the transfer of the building to someone who wants it.

THE COMPLICATION OF DEPRECIATION: GNP AND NNP

Each year, businesses add new buildings, plant, and equipment to their stock of capital. However, the quantity of capital does not increase by the full value of buildings and equipment produced during this year. The reason is that existing buildings and equipment have deteriorated—or *depreciated*—during the year from wear and obsolescence.

Depreciation is the decline in the value of a capital good because of wear and obsolescence.

If we want to know how much our capital stock has increased during the year, we must make an adjustment for depreciation (Fig. 6-2). Accordingly, two concepts of investment should be distinguished:

Gross private domestic investment (I_g) is equal to total expenditures for new plant, equipment, and residential buildings, plus the change in inventories.

Net private domestic investment (I_n) is the increase in the capital stock. I_n is equal to gross private domestic investment (I_g), less depreciation.[2]

Corresponding to these two concepts of investment are two concepts of national product: *gross national product* (GNP) and *net national product* (NNP).

$$GNP = C + I_g + G + X - M \qquad (6\text{-}2)$$
$$NNP = C + I_n + G + X - M \qquad (6\text{-}3)$$

_____

*[2]More precisely, to go from I_g to I_n, national product accountants subtract *Capital Consumption Allowances* (CCA). These allowances include not only depreciation, but also adjustments for the effects of inflation on the measurement of capital. This is a fine point, which we henceforth ignore; we use the simpler concept of depreciation in place of CCA.

The only difference between GNP and NNP is that GNP includes gross investment, whereas NNP includes net investment. But:

$$I_n = I_g - \text{depreciation} \qquad (6\text{-}4)$$

Therefore,

$$NNP = GNP - \text{depreciation} \qquad (6\text{-}5)$$

This relationship between GNP and NNP is illustrated in the first two columns of Figure 6-3.

In theory, NNP is a better measure than GNP, because NNP takes into account the obsolescence and physical deterioration of machinery and buildings during the year. It therefore measures the goods and services that may be used by society without running down the capital stock. But, why, then, is so much more attention paid to GNP than to NNP in newspapers and economics books? The reason is that, although NNP is the best measure conceptually, it is difficult to estimate in practice.

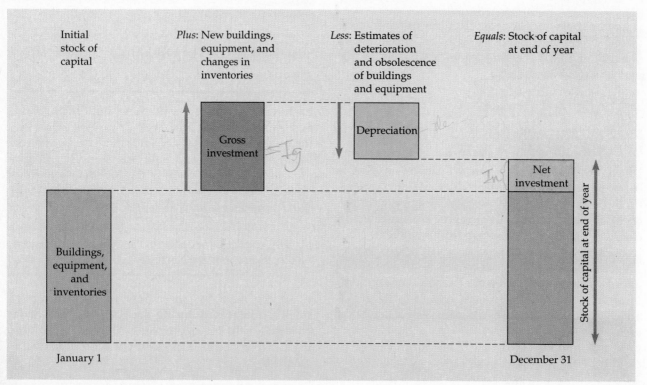

FIGURE 6-2   Net investment: A change in the stock of capital.

During the year the stock of capital increases by gross investment, less depreciation.

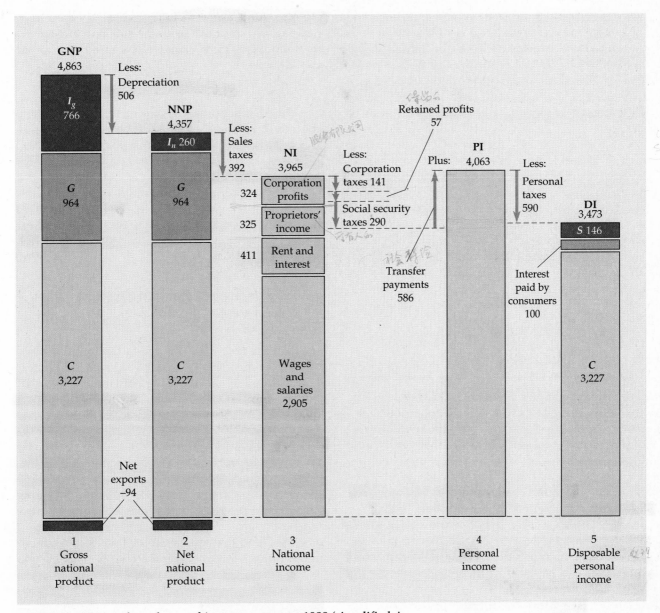

FIGURE 6-3   National product and income accounts, 1988 (simplified; in billions of dollars).

GNP = Gross national product   C = Personal consumption expenditures
NNP = Net national product   G = Government expenditures for goods and services
NI = National income I_g = Gross private domestic investment
PI = Personal income I_n = Net private domestic investment
DI = Disposable personal income   S = Personal saving

Gross investment—the value of new buildings and equipment, as well as additions to inventories—is relatively easy to measure. To estimate net investment, however, we need to measure depreciation, which raises difficult questions. How rapidly will a machine really wear out? Will it become obsolete before it is physically worn out? If it is to be scrapped in 10 years, does its value decline in a "straight line," by 10% each year? Or does it lose most of its productive value in the first few years? Because of such questions, we cannot be confident about estimates of depreciation. In practice, therefore, GNP is used *much* more commonly than NNP.

In the first two columns of Figure 6-3, observe that net exports were negative in 1988. The United States imported substantially more than it exported.

NET NATIONAL PRODUCT AND NATIONAL INCOME: THE COMPLICATION OF THE SALES TAX

Earlier in this chapter, Figure 6-1 illustrated the circular flow of payments in which upper-loop payments represented national product and lower-loop payments national income. In that very simple diagram, the two loops were equal, and net national product and national income were exactly the same size. In our complex, real-world economy, they are closely related but not precisely equal.

Net National Product (NNP) is the total quantity of goods and services produced during the year, measured at market prices. *National income* is the sum of all income paid to those who provide the factors of production. How can they possibly be different? They may be different because the factors of production do not get all the proceeds from the sale of a good. Part of it goes to the government in the form of sales taxes.

To illustrate, consider a package of razors priced at $1.99 plus a sales tax of 10¢. The $1.99 goes into the wages and salaries, rents, interest, and profits of those who contribute at various stages to the production of the razors. *This $1.99 is included in national income.* Of course, when you get to the cash register, you will pay the full $2.09. Because net national product is measured at mar-

ket prices, *it includes the whole $2.09.* Accordingly, net national product exceeds national income by the amount of sales taxes (and a number of other similar taxes).[3]

$$NI = NNP - \text{sales taxes}$$

This distinction shows up in Figure 6-3, where column 2 measures NNP. Sales taxes (and other similar taxes) are subtracted to get column 3, which shows the national income earned by the suppliers of productive resources.

The tax complication should not obscure a conclusion that is worth repeating. With the exception of sales taxes, the proceeds from the sale of the final product become incomes of the factors of production. Thus:

> **The process of production is also the process of generating income.**

Column 3 of Figure 6-3 lists the familiar components of income—wages and salaries, rent, interest, and profits—as well as an item not encountered before: "proprietors' income." To understand this item, note that for a corporation such as General Motors, wages are sharply distinguishable from profits. Wages go to the workers, while profits are the return to the owners of the corporation. However, for some businesses—such as a family farm or a mom and pop store—it is not feasible to separate wages, profits, and other income shares. How much of a farmer's income is the result of the family's labor, and how much a return on its investment in buildings, equipment, and so on? It is not easy to say. Accordingly, no attempt is made to subdivide such income, and so it is included as a single sum: proprietors' income.

OTHER INCOME MEASURES

Figure 6-3 illustrates two other important measures, namely, personal income and disposable personal income.

---

*3Other similar taxes include customs duties on imports, property taxes, and excise taxes on cigarettes and other items.

PERSONAL INCOME (PI)

Although most of *national income* is received by households as their personal income (PI), national income and personal income are not exactly the same. One reason is that some parts of national income do not flow through the business sector to become the *personal income* of households:

■ Part of corporate profit is taken by the government in the form of corporate income taxes.

■ Part of profit is retained by corporations to finance expansion. Thus dividends are the only portion of corporate profits that *do* flow from corporations to households as personal income.

■ Taxes are paid into the social security fund; these taxes have to be deducted from national income before we get personal income.

The other reason why personal income is not the same as national income lies in transfer payments, such as social security pensions and payments by the government to the unemployed. Such transfers are a source of personal income to households, but they are not payments to households for providing factors of production. Therefore, they are not included in national income.

Thus, to find personal income (col. 4, Fig. 6-3), we begin with national income (col. 3) and then make several adjustments. We *subtract* corporate taxes, profits retained by corporations, and social security taxes, and *add* transfer payments. Personal income is the measure that corresponds most closely to the everyday meaning of "income."

DISPOSABLE INCOME (DI)

Not all personal income is available to the individual or family for personal use, however; the government takes a sizable chunk in the form of personal taxes. These are mainly personal income taxes, but also include other items such as inheritance taxes. After these taxes are paid, disposable personal income (DI) remains. Households can do three things with this income: spend it on consumption, use it to pay interest on consumer debt, or save it. Disposable income is an important concept, because consumers look at this income when they decide how much to spend.

RELATIVE MAGNITUDES

Before leaving Figure 6-3, observe the relative magnitudes of the major boxes. Consumption is by far the largest component of GNP, amounting to 66% of GNP in 1988. In that year government expenditures for goods and services constituted the next largest component, 20%. Although gross investment was also substantial, most of it went to cover depreciation, leaving a relatively small proportion as net investment.

In the third column, wages and salaries were by far the largest component of national income, 73%. Corporate profits were 8.2% of national income (and 6.7% of GNP). In the last column, saving was only 4.2% of disposable income.

Although most of these items are relatively stable, a few change quite sharply from year to year. Net exports can be either positive or negative; they were usually positive in the years prior to 1983 but in recent years they have been a large negative number—sometimes in excess of $100 billion. Net investment has been quite volatile, rising sharply during periods of business prosperity and falling during recessions. In the three decades from 1959 to 1988, gross investment ranged from a low of 13.3% of GNP in 1975 to a high of 17.9% in 1978. Corporate profits are even more responsive to business conditions—reaching a high of 13.9% of national income in 1965, and a low of 6.8% in 1982.

NOMINAL AND REAL GNP

Dollar prices provide a satisfactory basis for calculating national product in any one year; they allow us to add apples and oranges, medical services, and cars. However, if we wish to evaluate the performance of the economy over a number of years, we face a major problem. The dollar is a shrinking yardstick; because of inflation, its value goes down. On average, the dollar in 1989 bought only 62% of what it bought in 1979.

As the years pass, the dollar measure of GNP increases for two quite different reasons. First, there is an increase in the *quantity* of goods and services produced. This increase is desirable, because we have more goods and services at our disposal. Second, the *prices* of goods and services increase.

TABLE 6-4   Current-dollar and Constant-dollar GNP

1982 current-dollar GNP		1990 current-dollar GNP		1990 constant-dollar GNP	
10 cars	@ $8,000 = $ 80,000	12 cars	@ $11,000 = $132,000	12 cars	@ $8,000 = $ 96,000
10 computers	@ $2,000 = $ 20,000	12 computers	@ $ 1,500 = $ 18,000	12 computers	@ $2,000 = $ 24,000
	Total $100,000		Total $150,000		Total $120,000

This increase is undesirable, because it reflects a failure to combat inflation. To judge the performance of the economy, *it is essential to separate the desirable increase in the quantity of output from the undesirable increase in prices.*

In order to do this, economists use the concept of *constant-dollar GNP,* also known as *real GNP.* This is calculated by valuing GNP at the prices that existed in a beginning or *base year,* not at the prices that actually exist while the GNP is being produced. (The U.S. government uses 1982 as the base year in GNP calculations.) Table 6-4 gives a hypothetical example of a simple economy producing only two goods, cars and computers.

If we examined only *nominal* or *current-dollar GNP* in the first two columns, we might come to the erroneous conclusion that output had risen by 50%—up from $100,000 in 1982 to $150,000 in 1990. But this clearly misstates the increase in the quantity of goods and services produced. Observe that the quantities of cars and computers have both increased by only 20%. By measuring 1990 output at 1982 prices in the final column, we find constant-dollar GNP to be $120,000. Comparing this number with 1982 GNP of $100,000, we come to the correct conclusion: Real output has increased by 20%.

Obviously, this example is very simplified. Figure 6-4 shows the actual figures for current-dollar and constant-dollar GNP. Observe how much more rapidly the current-dollar series has risen. Much of the increase in nominal GNP has been caused by a rise in prices.

PRICE INDEXES

More specifically, we can use current-dollar and constant-dollar GNP to calculate *how much* the average level of prices has risen since the base year. Returning to the example in Table 6-4, observe that nominal GNP in 1990 is 1.25 times as high as real GNP in that year ($150,000 ÷ $120,000 = 1.25).

By convention, the average price in the **base year** is given a value of 100 when calculating a **price index.** Thus, in the example in Table 6-4, the

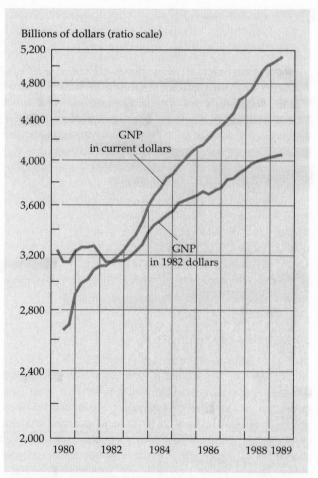

FIGURE 6-4   Gross national product (GNP), measured in current dollars and 1982 dollars.

Much of the increase in current-dollar national product has been the result of inflation. Observe that national product has grown much more slowly in constant (1982) dollars than in current dollars.

index of prices in 1990 is 125 (that is, 1.25 times the base of 100); the average level of prices has risen by 25%.

An *index* is a number that shows how an average (of prices, or wages, or some other economic measure) has changed over time.

The index calculated from nominal and real GNP figures is known as the *implicit GNP price deflator,* or, more simply, as the *GNP deflator.* In general, it is calculated as:

$$\text{GNP price deflator} = \frac{\text{Nominal GNP}}{\text{Real GNP}} \times 100 \quad (6\text{-}6)$$

Although the GNP deflator measures the change in the average price of the goods and services we have *produced,* another index—the *consumer price index* (CPI)—measures the change in the average price of the goods and services *bought* by the typical household. Specifically, the CPI measures changes in the cost of a basket of goods and services purchased by the typical urban family—food, automobiles, housing, furniture, doctor's services, and so on.

When the prices of the goods and services that we produce rise, so generally do the prices of what we purchase—for the simple reason that we consume most of what we produce. Therefore, it is not surprising that the GNP price deflator and the CPI tend to move together, particularly over extended periods of time. Thus the GNP deflator rose by 27% between 1982 and 1989 while the CPI rose by 28%. However, there may be signficant short-run differences in the two indexes—most notably in 1979, when the CPI rose 11.3% while the GNP deflator increased by a more moderate 8.7%. Both indexes reflected the steep rise in oil prices during that year. But the effect was stronger on the CPI, because it covers all the oil consumed in the United States, including both the oil produced at home *and* the large quantity of imported oil. (On the other hand, the GNP deflator covers only the oil produced in the United States.)

OTHER REAL MEASURES

Equation 6-6 may be rearranged:

$$\text{Real GNP} = \frac{\text{Nominal GNP}}{\text{GNP price deflator}} \times 100 \quad (6\text{-}7)$$

This process—of dividing by a price index—is known as **deflating.** Similar equations may be used to calculate other real measures. For example:

$$\text{Real consumption} = \frac{\text{Nominal consumption}}{\text{CPI}} \times 100 \quad (6\text{-}8)$$

$$\text{Real wage} = \frac{\text{Nominal wage}}{\text{CPI}} \times 100 \quad (6\text{-}9)$$

Suppose the nominal or money wage rises from $10.00 to $10.70 per hour, while the CPI rises by 5%. Then, using Equation 6-9, we find:

$$\text{Real wage} = \frac{\$10.70}{105} \times 100 = \$10.19 \quad (6\text{-}10)$$

The real wage has increased from $10.00 to $10.19, or by 1.9%. That is, a worker's wage will buy almost 2% more goods and services. Observe that, in deflating the nominal wage to find the real wage, we use the CPI. This is the most appropriate price index, since it measures changes in the prices of the goods and services that the typical family buys.

Equation 6-9 gives the precise answer, but it is cumbersome. A much simpler procedure is often used to find the approximate change:

$$\text{Change in real wage} \approx$$
$$\text{change in money wage} - \text{change in CPI} =$$
$$7\% - 5\% = 2\% \quad (6\text{-}11)$$

A MEASURE OF ECONOMIC WELFARE

Real GNP is one of the most frequently used measures of economic performance. Large changes in GNP may in fact reflect severe problems or impressive gains. When the nation's real GNP fell by 30% between 1929 and 1933, the performance of the economy was very unsatisfactory. In contrast, the large increase in real GNP in Japan in recent decades has reflected a rapid rise in the material standard of living.

Yet real GNP cannot be taken as a precise measure of the standard of living. The most obvious difficulty arises because an increase of, say, 10% in real GNP doesn't mean that the average person has 10% more goods and services. The reason is that population is growing. Rather than using total GNP figures, it is appropriate to estimate changes in the standard of living by looking at real GNP *per capita;* that is, real GNP divided by the population.

Other, more subtle problems arise because market sales are taken as the starting point in calculating GNP. When you hire a professional carpenter to build bookcases, the amount you pay appears in GNP. But if you build bookcases for your home, only the wood and materials are included in GNP; the value of your time as a carpenter is not. Similarly, a restaurant meal appears in GNP. But when you prepare an even better meal at home, only the ingredients bought from the store are included. Thus GNP does not include some important items, simply because they do not go through the market.

In calculating GNP, however, government statisticians do not adhere mindlessly to the idea that GNP should include all market transactions and nothing else. GNP includes some *imputed* items that do not go through the market. We have already seen that owner-occupied housing is treated *as if* its owners rent to themselves. Imputed rents on such housing are included in GNP, even though people do not actually pay themselves rent. Other imputations include consumption of home-grown food by farmers.

On the other hand, some items that actually do go through the market are excluded from GNP, and quite properly so. Because GNP is taken as a measure of the economy's performance, illegal products—such as heroin—are excluded from GNP on the ground that lawmakers have decided they are "bads" rather than "goods."

Nevertheless, a number of dubious items remain in GNP. When international relations become more tense, higher expenditures for weapons are included in GNP, but our situation has scarcely improved. If there is an increase in crime, additional expenditures for police, courts, and prisons are included in GNP. Yet society is certainly no better off than it was before the increase in crime.

Furthermore, some goods are included, whereas the "bads" they create are ignored. For example, GNP includes the production of automobiles, but there is no downward adjustment for the resulting pollution. Indeed, if people need medical attention as a result, GNP will go up, since doctor's services are included in GNP.[4]

Naturally enough, economists are bothered by the shortcomings of GNP as a measure of well-being. During the past two decades, a number of attempts have been made to deal with some of the inadequacies. These attempts fall under two main headings.

1. EMPHASIS ON ADDITIONAL SOCIAL INDICATORS

The first approach is to downplay GNP as the measure of how the economy and society are performing and to realize that it is only one of a number of important indicators of performance. Rather than focusing on GNP, policymakers can look at a set of indicators that, taken together, provide both a way of judging performance and a set of objectives for policymakers. In addition to real GNP, important indicators of well-being include life expectancy, infant mortality rates, the availability of health care, education and literacy, the amount of leisure, the quality of the environment, and the degree of urban crowding.

2. A COMPREHENSIVE MEASURE OF ECONOMIC WELFARE (MEW)

The second approach is more ambitious: to provide a comprehensive single measure of economic performance, including not only national product, but also additions for the value of leisure and subtractions for pollution and other disadvantages of crowded urban living. Such a measure of economic welfare (MEW) has been presented by two economists at Yale University, William Nordhaus and James Tobin.[5]

---

[4]See Kenneth E. Boulding, "Fun and Games with the Gross National Product," in Harold W. Helfrich, Jr., *The Environmental Crisis* (New Haven, Conn.: Yale University Press, 1962).

[5]William Nordhaus and James Tobin, "Is Growth Obsolete?" in *Economic Growth, Fiftieth Anniversary Colloquium* (New York: National Bureau of Economic Research, 1972).

The difficulties they encountered were formidable. The most interesting implication of their study is that an entirely satisfactory index *cannot* be constructed. To see why, consider the problem posed by leisure. As our ability to produce has increased, the working population has taken only part of the gain in the form of higher wages and other measured incomes; a significant part of the gain has come in the form of a shorter workweek. Specifically, Nordhaus and Tobin calculated that the average number of leisure hours increased by 22% between 1929 and 1965, while real per capita net national product rose by 90%.

The question is, What should be made of these facts? Specifically, which of the following conclusions is correct?

1. Production per person went up by 90%, and we had more leisure, too. Therefore, economic welfare improved by more than 90%; it rose *more* than NNP.

2. Production per person went up by 90%, but leisure increased by less than 90%—specifically, by only 22%. Therefore, economic welfare rose by some average of the 90% and the 22%, that is, by *less* than NNP.

It is far from clear which of these conclusions is "correct." Therefore, Nordhaus and Tobin presented two alternative estimates of MEW, reflecting the two alternative assumptions regarding leisure. These alternatives are shown in Figure 6-5, together with the growth of NNP per capita.

The choice between conclusions 1 and 2 is difficult, but it is only the beginning of the problems associated with evaluating economic welfare in a more comprehensive way. For example, observe that the Nordhaus-Tobin estimates of MEW do not drop during the Great Depression, and, indeed, they actually rise between 1929 and 1935. How can this be? Were we really becoming better off as the economy slid into depression? The explanation for this quirk: Nordhaus and Tobin have included leisure as an element of welfare, and leisure certainly increased as people were thrown out of work. But surely something is wrong here. Leisure after a good day's work may be bliss, but it's not pleasant to be idle when you've lost your job.

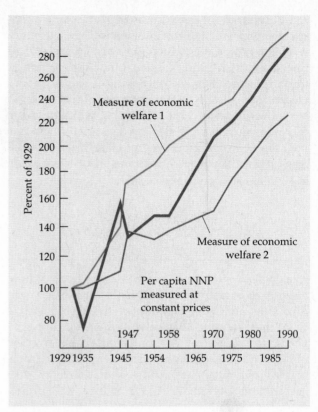

FIGURE 6-5 **Measures of economic welfare.**

Nordhaus and Tobin found the measure of economic welfare to be *extremely* sensitive to the treatment of leisure. Measure 1 is based on the view that welfare has gone up by more than NNP, since we have gotten the increase in output and more leisure, too. Measure 2 reflects the view that welfare has gone up by an average of the increase in NNP and the (smaller) increase in leisure. (Data for 1929–1965 are from the Nordhaus-Tobin study. We have added our estimates for the period since 1965.)

The ultimate test of economic success is the contribution which economic activity makes to the goal of human happiness. But developing a single, summary measure of this contribution is impossible. In the words of the late Arthur Okun, a former chairman of the Council of Economic Advisers, the calculation of "a summary measure of social welfare is a job for a philosopher king."[6]

---

[6]Arthur M. Okun, "Should GNP Measure Social Welfare?" *Brookings Bulletin* (Washington, D.C., Summer 1971).

Because it is impossible to develop a single comprehensive measure of welfare, we are stuck with the national product accounts. In spite of all their defects and shortcomings, they do provide an important measure of the health of our economy. Downturns in real GNP act as a signal that we have been unable to prevent recessions, while long-run increases in real GNP per capita are an important indicator of economic progress. GNP is a significant and useful social indicator—but we should not view it as the last word.

THE UNDERGROUND ECONOMY: THE CASE OF THE MISSING GNP

The logical question of what statisticians should attempt to measure is not the only controversy surrounding the GNP accounts. Another involves what they are able to measure *in practice*. In recent years, a number of economists and government officials have expressed concern that many transactions escape the attention of national product accountants, resulting in a substantial underestimate of GNP.

The reason is that plumbers, carpenters, and doctors—to name but a few—have an incentive to perform services without reporting their income, in order to evade taxes. When such income is unreported, it disappears not only from the Treasury's tax records, but also from the GNP accounts. Moonlighting, and the income of illegal aliens, are particularly unlikely to be reported. Such "subterranean" or "irregular" activities are by no means confined to the United States: the French have their *travail au noir* (work in the dark); the British their *fiddle;* and the Germans their *Schattenwirtschaft* (shadow economy). The **underground economy** includes not only unreported illegal activities—which, as we have noted, national income accountants intentionally exclude from the GNP—but also such socially desirable services as the work of the moonlighting plumber, whose only illegal aspect is tax evasion. If we want an accurate measure of the goods and services produced in our economy, we should certainly include such socially desirable services.

The problem, of course, is to get information, since those in the underground economy are trying to keep their activities secret. Thus it is difficult to measure the size of the underground economy directly. Rather, economists have looked for the traces left by irregular activities. What might these traces be?

The most obvious way to keep transactions secret is to use currency rather than checks. Thus economic sleuths looking for traces of the underground economy have usually begun by studying the amount of currency in the hands of the public. For example, in 1979, Peter Gutman of the City University of New York wryly noted that "There is now about $460 of currency in circulation in the United States for every man, woman, and child. . . . [We] may want to ponder . . . what all this currency is used for."[7] Gutman's conclusion was that much of the money was used in a large underground economy, which he estimated at 10% of measured GNP by the late 1970s. Other writers have found evidence that the underground economy is even larger and is growing rapidly.[8]

If, in fact, the legal segment of the underground economy is not only large but also growing relative to reported GNP, we can reach a number of important conclusions: (1) Official statistics understate the growth of the economy; (2) official statistics overstate the true rate of inflation, because people in the rapidly growing underground sector generally charge lower prices to gain customers; and (3) unemployment statistics overstate the true amount of unemployment. People collecting unemployment insurance—but also working "off the record" in the underground economy—are not likely to tell interviewers from the Labor Department that they are employed. In other words, things may be better than the official statistics would suggest.

---

[7]Peter M. Gutman, "Statistical Illusions, Mistaken Policies," *Challenge*, November 1979, p. 16.

[8]Recent work includes Edgar L. Feige, ed., *The Underground Economies: Tax Evasion and Information Distortion* (Cambridge: Cambridge University Press, 1989). This book includes estimates of the underground economies in a number of countries, including France, Germany, Italy, Sweden, the Soviet Union, the United Kingdom, and the United States.

The same is true in a number of other countries. Recent estimates suggest that the legal segment of the *economia somersa* (submerged economy) in Italy is 25% or 30% as large as measured GNP; its inclusion would have increased the growth of real Italian GNP by 0.7% per year during the 1980s. In Argentina, the underground economy is estimated to be as high as 60% of reported GNP.

KEY POINTS

1. National product is the value of the goods and services produced by a nation during a specific time period, such as a year. National income is the sum of all income derived from providing the factors of production. It includes wages and salaries, rent, interest, profits, and proprietors' income.

2. The market provides a way of adding apples, oranges, automobiles, and the many other goods and services produced during the year. Items are included in national product at their market prices.

3. In measuring national product, everything should be measured once, and only once. Intermediate products (such as wheat or steel) used in the production of other goods (such as bread or automobiles) should not be counted separately, since they are already included when we count the final product (bread or automobiles).

4. Depreciation is a measure of the decline in the value of capital because of wear and obsolescence. Net investment equals gross investment minus depreciation. Net investment is a measure of the increase in the capital stock (Fig. 6-2).

5. $GNP = C + I_g + G + X - M$
$NNP = GNP - depreciation$

Because depreciation is difficult to measure accurately, statisticans have more confidence in the measure of GNP than NNP. Therefore, GNP is used more commonly.

6. Receipts from the sale of products are distributed to those who contribute to the productive process by providing labor, capital, or land. In a simple economy, all the proceeds from the sale of goods would be distributed in the form of income payments to the factors of production. Net national product and national income would be the same. However, in a real-world economy, national income is less, because some of the proceeds from the sale of goods goes to the government in the form of sales taxes. Thus:

National income = NNP – sales taxes.

7. Review Figure 6-3 for the relationships among NNP, national income, personal income, and disposable personal income.

8. Market prices provide a good way to add up the many different goods and services produced in a *single* year, but they would be a misleading way of comparing the national product in *different* years. The reason is that the value of the dollar shrinks as a result of inflation. A rise in current-dollar national product reflects both an increase in prices and an increase in real production.

9. To estimate the increase in real output, constant-dollar figures are used. These are found by measuring GNP at the prices existing in a base year.

10. By "deflating" current data with the appropriate price index, it is possible to get a real measure of other important economic variables, such as the real wage.

11. Real GNP (or real NNP) per capita is not a good measure of economic welfare. However, when Nordhaus and Tobin tried to calculate a more comprehensive measure of economic welfare, they ran into the insoluble problem of how to deal with leisure.

12. The "underground" economy is made up of two components:

  (a) Unreported income whose only illegal aspect is the failure of the income earner to report this income—for example, unreported income of plumbers, carpenters, doctors, or farmers. The services themselves are legal and socially useful, and they would be included in GNP if government statisticians knew how large they were.

(b) Income from illegal activities such as the drug trade. Since congress has decided that these activities represent social "bads," they would not be included in GNP even if statisticians knew how large they were.

Circumstantial evidence suggests that (a) is growing in proportion to reported GNP. Thus the official GNP statistics understate the growth of real GNP.

KEY CONCEPTS

final product	exports of goods and services	personal income (PI)
intermediate product	imports of goods and services	disposable personal income (DI)
value added	gross private domestic investment	consumer price index (CPI)
consumption	gross national product (GNP)	GNP deflator
investment	net national product (NNP)	real GNP
inventories	depreciation	base year
government purchases of goods and services	national income (NI)	real wage
		underground economy

PROBLEMS

6-1. Consider an economy in which the following quantities are measured in billions of dollars:

Consumption expenditures	$1,000
Purchases of secondhand cars	100
Gross private domestic investment	300
Government transfer payments	100
Sales taxes	50
Government purchases of goods and services	200
Corporate income taxes	200
Personal income taxes	100
Exports minus imports	10
Depreciation	75

    (a) Calculate GNP. (Be careful. Not all the items are included.)

    (b) Calculate NNP.

6-2. The change in inventories can be negative. Can net investment also be negative? Explain.

6-3. Give an example of an import of a service.

6-4. Which of the following government expenditures are included in GNP?

(a) The purchase of an aircraft for the Air Force.

(b) The purchase of a computer for the Treasury Department.

(c) The payment of unemployment insurance benefits to those who have lost their jobs.

(d) The salary paid to maintenance workers who mow the grass beside the highways.

6-5. Last year a family engaged in the following activities. What items are included in GNP? In each case explain why the item is included or excluded.

(a) They purchased a used car.

(b) They deposited $1,000 in a savings deposit at the bank.

(c) They purchased $2,000 worth of groceries.

(d) They flew to London for a vacation.

6-6. For 1988 (shown in Fig. 6-3):

(a) Which was larger: government purchases of goods and services or gross investment?

(b) Approximately what percentage of NNP was net investment?

(c) Approximately how large a percentage of national income were wages and salaries? Corporate profits? Rent and interest?

(d) Approximately what fraction of disposable income was saved?

6-7. Of Nordhaus and Tobin's two measures of economic welfare, do you think one is better than the other? If so, which one, and why?

6-8. For each of the following, state whether you agree or disagree. If you agree, explain why; if you disagree, correct the statement.

(a) When a trucker buys gasoline, the intended use is for the production of trucking services for others, not for pleasure trips. Therefore, this gasoline is an intermediate product, whereas the trucking service is a final product.

(b) Bread purchased by a household is a final product, but bread purchased by a supermarket or a restaurant is an intermediate product.

(c) Defense expenditures provide no direct satisfaction to the public. They only protect our freedom to enjoy other goods and services. Therefore, defense expenditures are considered an intermediate product and are not included separately in the calculation of GNP.

6-9. Equation 6-11 shows a simplified way of estimating the approximate change in the real wage. To see how close this approximation is, find the true change in the real wage (from Eq. 6-9), and compare it to the estimate found with Equation 6-11 in each of the following cases:

(a) When the money wage increases by 10%, while the CPI increases by 2%.

(b) When the money wage increases by 30%, while the CPI increases by 22%.

(c) When the money wage increases by 200%, while the CPI increases by 100%.

Do your results from these examples suggest any circumstances under which it would be wise to avoid the use of Equation 6-11?

CHAPTER 7
FLUCTUATIONS IN ECONOMIC ACTIVITY

A recession is when your neighbor is out of work. A depression is when you're out of work.
HARRY S. TRUMAN

The Great Depression left an indelible impression on the American mind. Between 1929 and the depth of the depression in 1933, real GNP declined by 30% and the unemployment rate shot up to almost 25% of the labor force. Many of those thrown out of work could find no other job. In his book, *Hard Times*, Studs Terkel quotes an unemployed San Francisco worker:

I'd get up at five in the morning and head for the waterfront. Outside the Spreckles Sugar Refinery, outside the gates, there would be a thousand men. You know dang well there's only three or four jobs. . . .

There'd be this kind of futile struggle, because somehow you never expected to win. We had a built-in losing complex. . . . By now, it's one o'clock, and everybody's hungry. These were fathers, eighty percent of them. They had held jobs and didn't want to kick society to pieces. They just wanted to go to work and they couldn't understand.[1]

Fortunately, the depression of the 1930s was unique. But even in more normal times, economic

_____

[1]Terkel, *Hard Times* (New York: Avon Books, 1971).

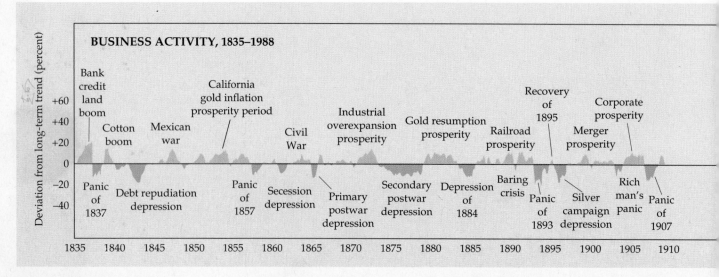

BUSINESS ACTIVITY, 1835–1988

conditions rarely stand still. Figure 7-1 shows the ups and downs of American business over the past century and a half.

The collapse of 1929–1933 was followed by a long and painful recovery. It was not until the government bought huge quantities of munitions during World War II that the economy recovered fully. After the war, there was a temporary drop in output as factories were converted from weapons to peacetime products. In the four decades since that time, there have been eight recessions—an average of one every five years.

Fluctuations in economic activity are irregular. No two recessions are exactly alike, nor are any two expansions. Some last for years, the most notable examples being the expansions of 1961–1969 and 1982–? Other expansions are short-lived, such as the expansion of 1958–1960 (24 months) and the expansion of 1980–1981, which gave way to a new recession after only 12 months. The economy is not a pendulum swinging regularly at specific intervals. If it were, the analysis of business fluctuations would be simple: the movement of a pendulum is easily predicted.

THE FOUR PHASES OF THE BUSINESS CYCLE

Because business fluctuations are so irregular, it is perhaps surprising that they are called "cycles." However, they all have the same four phases: recession, trough, expansion, and peak (Fig. 7-2).

The key to identifying a business cycle is to identify a *recession*—the period when economic activity is declining. The question that immediately arises is, how far down does the economy have to go before we call it a recession? A private research organization—the National Bureau of Economic Research (NBER)—determines what is called a recession. Not every slight downward jiggle of the economy can be called a recession; rather, the decline should be significant. The NBER's major test is historical: Is the downswing as long and as severe as declines of the past that were labeled "recessions"? But some simpler definition is needed, since we cannot always pause to review the historical record when using such a common term as recession. Geoffrey H. Moore of Rutgers University—who studied business cycles for many years

FIGURE 7-1   Business activity, 1835–1988.

Business activity fluctuates irregularly. The biggest swing occurred between 1929 and 1945, with the economy first collapsing into the Great Depression and then rising to a peak of war production. Earlier booms were associated with such events as the California gold rush and railroad construction. Early recessions generally came in the aftermath of wars or as a result of financial disturbances, such as the Panic of 1907. (*Source:* Ameritrust Corp., Cleveland.)

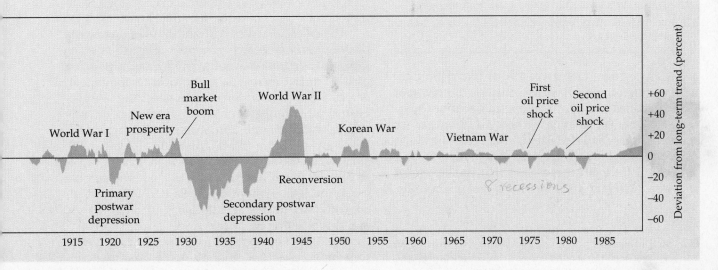

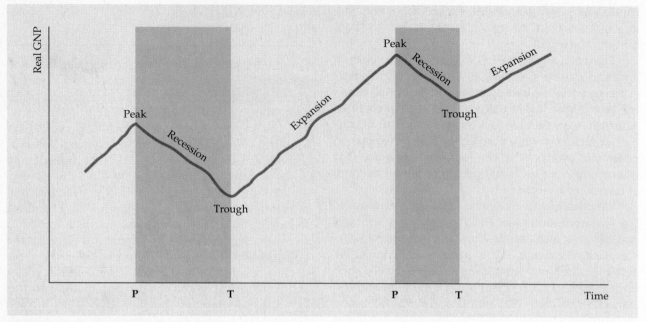

FIGURE 7-2   The four phases of the business cycle.

Periods of expansion and recession alternate, with peaks and troughs in between. The National Bureau of Economic Research identifies each recession, the peak month that precedes it, and the trough month that ends it. Not every expansion reaches a high degree of prosperity with a low unemployment rate; an expansion sometimes ends prematurely and a new recession begins.

with the NBER—offered the summary definition that has already appeared in Chapter 1:

> A *recession* is a decline in total output, income, employment, and trade, usually lasting six months to a year and marked by widespread contractions in many sectors of the economy.[2]

Many writers prefer a much simpler definition: a recession occurs when seasonally adjusted real GNP declines for two or more consecutive quarters. (For an explanation of how GNP and other data are "seasonally adjusted," see Box 7-1.) However, the NBER never accepted this definition, and in 1980, it declared a recession that did not meet this test. Although the recession lasted six months,

from February to July, real GNP fell in only one quarter—the second quarter, from April to June. (Problem 7-5 at the end of this chapter helps to show how this apparent paradox is possible. Output may fall for six months, even though GNP figures show only one quarter of decline.)

The recession ends with the *trough,* that is, the *turning point* at which economic activity is at its lowest. The trough is followed by the *expansion* phase. Output increases, and profits, employment, wages, prices, and interest rates generally rise too. Historically, the *peak* or upper turning point was often associated with a financial panic, such as the Panic of 1907 or "Black Tuesday"—October 29, 1929, when the stock market crashed. Recent peaks have been much less spectacular, with one notable exception. The economic peak in late 1973 coincided with war in the Middle East, an oil embargo, and skyrocketing oil prices.

Not only is it difficult to decide when a downturn becomes strong enough to be classified as a recession. It is also difficult to decide when a seri-

---

[2]On the problem of defining a recession, see Geoffrey H. Moore, *Business Cycles, Inflation, and Forecasting* (Cambridge, Mass.: Balinger, 2d ed., 1983), Chapter 1.

BOX 7–1 *Seasonal Adjustment of Economic Data*

Not all ups and downs in business represent a misbehavior of the economy. Crops are harvested in the summer and autumn months. The month-to-month changes in food production reflect a law of nature with which we learn to live. Retail sales boom in December, only to fall in January.

Such regular month-to-month swings are no cause for concern. The decline in retail sales in January is the aftermath of the December buying boom; it is not a symptom of an oncoming recession. In order to identify a recession, we must remove the seasonal effects from business activity. That is, we must *seasonally adjust* our data on production, sales, and the like. The following technique is used.

From past information, suppose the statistician discovers that December sales of toys typically run at three times the average monthly rate, only to drop to one-half the average monthly rate in January. The raw data for toy sales can then be seasonally adjusted by dividing December's sales by 3 and multiplying January's sales by 2. (In fact, more complicated techniques are used, but this is the general idea.) Similarly, quarterly data for GNP or monthly indexes of industrial production can be adjusted to remove seasonal fluctuations and this can help to identify fundamental movements in the economy.

---

ous recession should be labeled a **depression.** There is no commonly accepted definition of a depression, except, perhaps, Harry Truman's quip which introduced this chapter. Because the depression of the 1930s was so deep and long-lasting, unemployment would have to be severe and persistent before we could talk of a depression. Perhaps the definition should require that unemployment remain at double-digit levels—that is, 10% or more—for a full two years. By this criterion, the severe recession of 1981–1982 did not qualify as a depression. Although the seasonally adjusted unemployment rate reached a peak of 10.6% in December 1982, it exceeded 10% for only eight months. Regardless of how a depression is defined, there is no doubt that this term should be used to describe the collapse of the 1930s when unemployment rates soared in the United States and many other countries.

LIVING IN A GLOBAL ECONOMY

THE INTERNATIONAL DEPRESSION OF THE 1930s

The Great Depression was characterized by

1. High Unemployment Rates. By 1933, the unemployment rate exceeded 15% of the labor force in many countries, including Canada, France, Germany, and Italy.

2. Collapsing Commodity Prices. Between 1929 and 1932, the prices of internationally traded commodities collapsed. For example, the prices of wheat, sugar, tin, and tea all fell more than 50%; cotton and silk by more than 60%; and rubber by more than 75%. For the less developed nations that were heavily dependent on commodity exports, the collapse in prices was a disaster.

3. Falling Industrial Production. In a single year—1930—industrial production fell about 8% in Britain, Italy, and Japan; almost 15% in Austria, Canada, and Germany; and almost 20% in the United States.

Demand fell sharply for both manufactured products and commodities. However, the prices of manufactures did not collapse the way commodity prices did; falling demand showed up primarily in the form of lower output, not lower prices.[3] For example, within the United States, the prices of automobiles and farm implements fell by less than

---

*[3]Technical note: There were two reasons for this difference between the prices of manufactures and basic commodities. (1) Many manufacturers do not operate in perfectly competitive markets; they have some control over their selling price. (2) During periods of slack demand, manufacturers often do better by reducing production rather than price. If they cut their price, it may no longer cover wages, parts, and materials. If they cut production, they can lay off workers, reduce their expenditures on parts and materials, and cut their losses. In contrast, on many farms, the labor is that of the farm family itself. If farmers cut production, they save relatively little on costs. They may feel they have no alternative but to keep producing, and accept whatever low price they may get from the sale of their commodities.

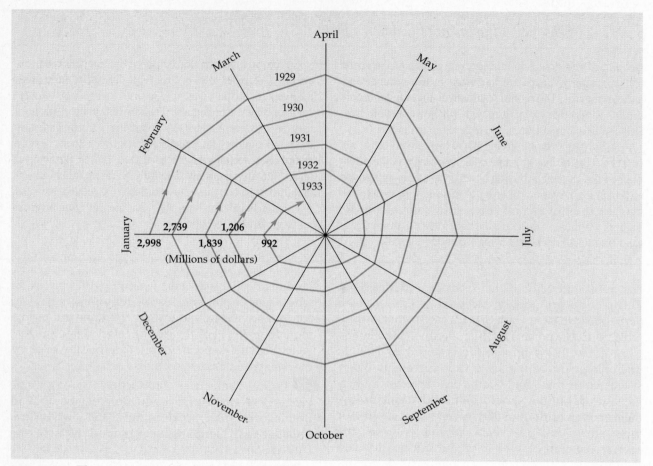

FIGURE 7-3   The contracting spiral of trade, 1929–1933.

This figure shows how the total imports of 75 nations fell as the world economy slid into depression. In fact, imports declined more than GNP in the 75 nations. (*Source:* Charles P. Kindleberger, *The World in Depression, 1929–1939* (Berkeley: University of California Press, rev. ed., © 1986), p. 170, based on League of Nations Statistics.)

10% between 1929 and 1933, even though output was plummeting.

4. Collapsing International Trade. Figure 7-3 illustrates how the dollar value of international trade spiralled downward between 1929 and 1933. Both prices and quantities of trade declined sharply.

In fact, international trade declined more than domestic production; imports fell as a percentage of GNP, particularly in Japan, Germany, and Italy. The depression thus marked a sharp contrast to the

long historical trend: over the past 250 years, imports have increased as a percentage of GNP. (Imports of the major industrial countries have on average risen about twice as rapidly as GNP over that long period.)

Why was the Great Depression international in scope? Surprisingly, the detailed causes of the depression are still being debated, but there is one clear way in which the economies of the nations are tied together. When GNP and national income fall in a single country, so do its imports. When people have lower incomes, they buy fewer goods, including fewer imports. The decline in imports means that other countries export less; the hard times spread to them.

The international depression had profound political consequences. The German depression was one of the factors that brought Hitler to power, with his promises of full employment and military conquest.

The Great Depression also laid the foundation for modern macroeconomics. Politicians, economists, and the general public were determined to prevent a repeat of the 1930s. So far, we have been successful.

THE U.S. ECONOMY DURING RECENT BUSINESS CYCLES

In spite of successes since the Great Depression, some problems remain. The economy has continued to fluctuate, and, perhaps most disconcerting of all, its performance has not improved with time. Recessions have *not* been getting more and more mild. On the contrary, two of the most recent recessions—1973–1975 and 1981–1982—have been the most severe since the Great Depression.

Figure 7-4 shows how output, unemployment, profits, money wages, and inflation have changed since 1959. As is customary, recessions are marked with shaded bars, and the peaks and troughs are identified with the letters *P* and *T,* respectively. Observe that:

■ During recessions, when production is falling, the unemployment rate rises. Since less is being produced, firms need fewer workers. During an expansion, production increases and the unemployment rate falls.

■ During recessions, when output is declining, inflation generally declines too. When the economy is expanding, the rate of inflation generally accelerates.

■ During recessions, profits fall by a much larger percentage than output. They rise rapidly during expansions.

Wages and profits behave quite differently during recessions. Although profits fall sharply, money wages remain *much* more stable. Indeed, recessions

had no readily apparent effect on the wage series shown in Figure 7-4, except for the slowing of the rate of increase in money wages after the severe recession of 1981–1982. Recessions hit workers primarily in the form of unemployment, not lower wages.

Observe, too, that *inflation responds slowly* to changing business conditions. During the first few years of the long expansion of the 1960s, for example, prices were quite stable. It was only after 1964 that inflation began to accelerate. During the expansion of 1970–1973, inflation was likewise concentrated in the later years. The same was true during the expansion of 1975–1979. In 1986, the rate of inflation was actually lower than it had been when the long expansion began in 1982.

Recessions generally bring the inflation rate down, but once again, inflation is slow to respond. The upward momentum of inflation may continue into the early part of a recession, as it did in 1974. Generally, it is toward the end of recessions that economic slack has its strongest effect in bringing inflation down. Inflation often continues to slow down during the early recovery—for example, in 1971 and 1975.

The slowness of prices to respond introduces an important complication into the government's task of stabilizing the economy, as we will see when we get to the more advanced macroeconomic topics of Part 4 (Chapters 13 and 14).

CONSUMPTION AND INVESTMENT DURING RECESSION

During recessions, some parts of GNP decline much more than others. This is illustrated in Figure 7-5, which shows the changes in various segments of output between the last quarter of 1979 (which marked the end of the expansion of the 1970s) and the last quarter of 1982 (when the economy reached a trough).

Consumption. Over this period, real GNP declined by 0.6%, but real consumption expenditures actually rose, by 4.4%. Expenditures for both services and nondurables increased, while consumers cut back their real spending for durables by 2.1%.

This difference in the behavior of durables, on the one hand, and services and nondurables, on the other, can be explained as follows. Because dur-

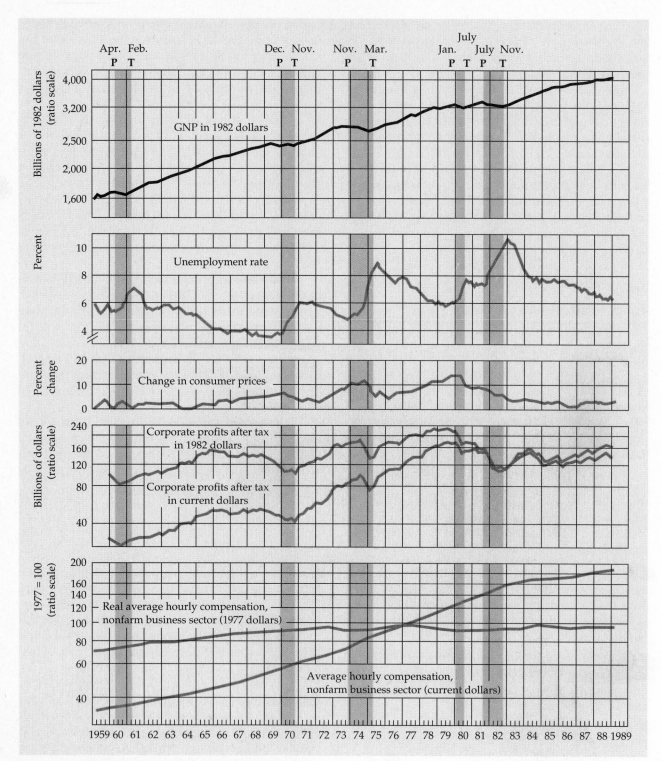

FIGURE 7-4   Business fluctuations in the United States.

(*Source:* Department of Commerce, *Business Conditions Digest.*)

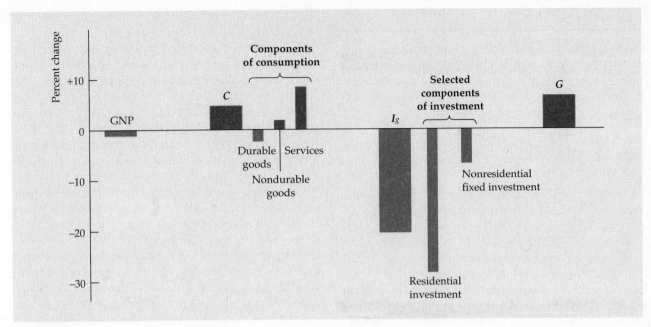

FIGURE 7-5   The downturn of 1980–1982.

The economy reached a cyclical peak in the last quarter of 1979. There were then two quick recessions, with the trough of the second occurring in the last quarter of 1982. This figure shows how some components of GNP declined much more than others between the last quarter of 1979 and the last quarter of 1982. In fact, both consumption and government purchases of goods and services increased in real terms. The recession was concentrated in the investment sector.

ables last, people have the option of postponing purchases during hard times, when they are having trouble paying their bills. For example, as incomes decline, people may decide to fix up their old cars or old refrigerators rather than splurging on new ones. They can continue to enjoy the use of durables, even if they are not currently buying them. In contrast, services such as medical services must be produced at the time when people are ready to consume them; they cannot be stored. Similarly, purchases of nondurable goods are closely tied to consumption. Purchases of food represent one of the last things people will cut back during recessions.

Investment. Much larger fluctuations occur in the investment sector. By the last quarter of 1982, overall investment had fallen by 20.8% from its level of three years earlier. Residential investment declined by no less than 28.4%. Nonresidential fixed invest-

ment (which includes both plant and equipment) fell by a less spectacular 6.9%. Inventory accumulation, which had been consistently positive in every quarter from the beginning of 1976 until the third quarter of 1979, had become a large negative figure (-$22.7 billion) by the last quarter of 1982.

Instability of investment has been a continuing feature of business cycles; fluctuations in investment have accounted for a large fraction of overall fluctuations in the economy. Furthermore, the decline in inventories in 1982 was typical for a period of recession. Inventory investment has become negative in every U.S. recession since the Second World War, with only one exception (1970). Moreover, swings in inventory investment have been large, on average accounting for more than half of the total decline in real GNP during the recessions of the past four decades. Not surprisingly, then, the declines of the past four decades have frequently been referred to as *inventory recessions*.

UNEMPLOYMENT

The two principal features of a recession are a fall in output and a rise in the unemployment rate. Changes in output are measured by the national product accounts. Changes in unemployment are measured by the unemployment rate.

CALCULATING THE UNEMPLOYMENT RATE

The unemployment rate is estimated each month by the Bureau of Labor Statistics (BLS) using an obvious, direct approach: It asks people. Because it would be prohibitively expensive and time consuming to ask everybody, a sample of about 65,000 households is surveyed. Questions are asked regarding each member of the household who is over 16, except those unavailable for work because they are in institutions such as prisons or mental hospitals. Each individual is classified in one of three categories: (1) employed, (2) unemployed, or (2) not in the labor force.

All those who have worked in the week of the survey are counted as employed, even part-time employees who have worked as little as one hour. People are counted as unemployed if they are without work and (a) are on temporary layoff but expect to be recalled, (b) are waiting to report to a new job within four weeks, or (c) say they have actively looked for work during the previous four weeks and are currently available for work. Those not in the labor force include retirees, full-time students without paying jobs, and those who stay out of the labor force in order to look after young children. The unemployment rate is calculated as the number of unemployed, as a percentage of the labor force (Table 7-1, line 4a).

The BLS also calculates the unemployment rate in a second way, as a percentage of the *civilian* labor force (Table 7-1, line 4b). In order to make this calculation, it subtracts the number in the armed forces from the labor force. Until recent years, the unemployment rate was generally quoted in this way, as a percentage of the civilian labor force. However, the standard practice now is to quote unemployment as a percentage of the whole labor force, including the military. When the armed forces are included, the labor force is somewhat larger, and the unemployment rate is therefore

slightly lower—generally 0.1% less than when just the civilian labor force is used.

The method used in calculating the unemployment rate has caused controversy. (1) Some critics think the official unemployment rate overstates the true figure, pointing out that there is no check on those who say they are looking for work; they are simply asked. (2) Others observe that, during hard times, workers may become *discouraged* and quit looking for work after they have been repeatedly rebuffed. They thereby drop out of the labor force. Thus, during recessions, the rise in the unemployment rate may not measure the full deterioration in the employment situation. This interpretation is supported by the behavior of the labor force. During recessions, it generally grows very slowly and sometimes even declines because of the departure of discouraged workers. In contrast, it grows rapidly during recoveries. When jobs are easier to get, people are more likely to enter the labor force and less likely to drop out.

Discouraged workers are those who want work but are no longer actively looking for it because they think no jobs are available. When they stop looking for work, they are no longer counted either as part of the labor force or as unemployed.

Finally, during recessions, there is an increase in the number of people who can't get full-time jobs, and who are therefore involuntarily limited to part-time work. Such *underemployment* does not show up in the unemployment statistics, but information on this point is available. The BLS calculates hours lost for this reason and includes them in the *labor force time lost* (Table 7-1, line 5). Because this figure includes both the unemployed and the underemployed on a shortened workweek, it is higher than the unemployment rate. As we would expect, the gap between the two figures becomes larger during recessions, when more workers are limited to part-time work.

UNDEREMPLOYMENT

We have just considered one group of the underemployed: those who can find only part-time work when they want full-time jobs. Underemployment

TABLE 7-1   The Labor Force and Unemployment, Dec. 1988 (in millions)

1. Total population		247.2
Less: those not in labor force		122.9
2. Equals: labor force		124.3
Less: armed forces		1.7
3. Equals: civilian labor force		122.6
(a) employed	116.0	
(b) unemployed	6.6	
4. Unemployment rate		

(a) as percentage of the labor force

$$\frac{\text{line 3 (b)}}{\text{line 2}} = \frac{6.6}{124.3} = 5.3\%$$

(b) as percentage of the civilian labor force

$$\frac{\text{line 3 (b)}}{\text{line 3}} = \frac{6.6}{122.6} = 5.4\%$$

Addenda

5. Labor force time lost
   6.3%

6. Labor force participation rates for those over 19

	Male	Female
1950	88.4%	33.3%
1960	86.0%	37.6%
1970	82.6%	43.3%
1980	79.4%	51.3%
1988	77.9%	56.8%

Source: Bureau of Labor Statistics.

also takes a second form, which results from the way in which businesses respond to falling sales.

During recessions, businesses do not change the number of employees quickly. As the economy begins to weaken, businesses are more likely to cancel overtime than to lay off workers. Thus employment falls less rapidly than output. Even after overtime has been substantially eliminated, employers are reluctant to lay off workers. One reason is that a person who has been laid off may take a job somewhere else. When sales revive, the business will then have to go through the time-consuming and expensive task of hiring and training a replacement. Thus managers often conclude that it is better to keep workers on the job, even if they are not kept busy. Such workers are underemployed in the sense that they produce significantly less than they could. As the economy declines into recession, the *productivity of labor* consequently declines.

Workers are *underemployed* if (1) they can find only part-time work when they want full-time work; or (2) they are being paid full time but are not kept busy because of low demand for the firm's products.

The *productivity of labor* is the average amount produced in an hour of work. It is measured as total output divided by the number of hours of labor input.

When the economy finally does recover, labor productivity increases very rapidly. Because many businesses have developed slack during the recession, they have underemployed labor and machinery. During the early stages of a recovery, businesses can therefore increase their output substantially before they need to add many more workers.

As a result, output fluctuates more than unemployment during the business cycle. Specifically, for every cyclical change of 2% to 3% in output, the unemployment rate moves 1% in the opposite direction. This tendency for output to fluctuate much more strongly than unemployment is known as *Okun's Law,* after the late Arthur Okun, whose distinguished career included a professorship at Yale University and service as chairman of President Lyndon Johnson's Council of Economic Advisers.

WHO ARE THE UNEMPLOYED?

Unemployment does not fall equally on all members of society. The unemployment rate for teenagers, for example, is much higher than that for adults (Fig. 7-6). The rate for blacks is about twice as high as that for whites. The unemployment rate among black teenagers is staggering—almost 51% during the summer of 1982 when the economy was approaching the trough, and still 32% in 1988, after five years of economic expansion. Historically, the unemployment rate for women has generally been somewhat above that for men. However, the difference has generally declined during recessions, which hit male-dominated construction and heavy manufacturing jobs particularly hard. During the recession of 1981–1982, the rate for men rose above that for women and remained above the female rate throughout the recovery year of 1983. By the latter part of the 1980s, there was little difference between male and female unemployment rates.

Figure 7-7 illustrates two other important features about the unemployed—how they came to be unemployed, and how long they are unemployed. The duration of unemployment increases sharply during recessions, as unemployed workers experience more and more difficulty in finding jobs. At the end of the prosperous year 1979, less than 10% of the unemployed had been out of work more than six months. By the end of the recession in late 1982, this figure had risen to more than 20%. The

increase has important implications. Short-term unemployment can be painful but is scarcely catastrophic. It is long-term unemployment that is so demoralizing. During recessions, this type of unemployment accounts for a larger share of the rising overall unemployment rate. Thus the unemployment situation becomes even worse than it appears in the overall unemployment numbers. For example, while the overall number of the unemployed almost doubled from 6.1 million in December 1979 to 12.0 million in December 1982, the number of long-term unemployed (over 15 weeks) almost *quadrupled,* from 1.2 million to 4.7 million people.

During recessions, people are much more likely to lose their jobs, either through layoff or discharge (Fig. 7-7, lower panel). However, even during recessions, it is unusual if more than 60% of the unemployed have actually lost their previous jobs. The other 40% are new entrants (young people who are looking but have not yet found work after leaving school); reentrants (many of whom are reentering the labor force after caring for young families); and people who have quit their last jobs to look for something better. Of course, people are more reluctant to quit during hard times, when other jobs are scarce. However, even as the unemployment rate hit its peak of 10.6% in December 1982, 0.8% of those who had jobs quit during that month.

Thus the U.S. labor force is quite mobile. Many people are ready to quit their jobs to look for something better. The mobility of the U.S. labor force is illustrated in Figure 7-8. The arrows show the many ways people move into and out of employment and into and out of the labor force. Because of this mobility, it is difficult to define precisely what is meant by "full employment." Clearly, the government is not striving for an economy in which the unemployment rate is zero. To accomplish such a goal, the government would have to forbid people from leaving one job until they already had another lined up.

TYPES OF UNEMPLOYMENT

Before attempting to define the elusive concept of "full employment," let us consider the various

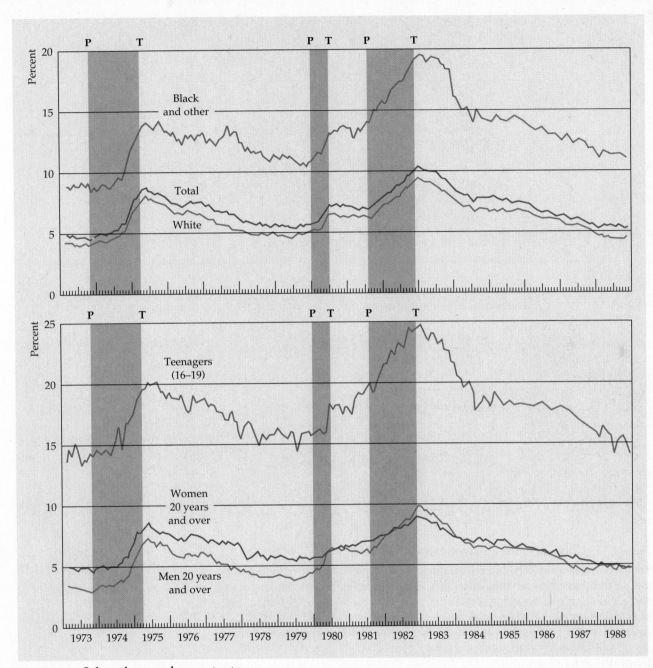

FIGURE 7-6   Selected unemployment rates.

Unemployment rates vary greatly among different groups of the population. Blacks have an
unemployment rate that is about twice as high as that of whites. Historically, women have
had higher unemployment rates than men, but the rate for men rose above the women's
rate during the recession of 1982. Teenagers have the highest unemployment rate of all.
Even during the relatively prosperous years of the late 1980s, the teenage unemployment
rate still averaged more than 15%. During the recession year of 1982, it was more than 23%.

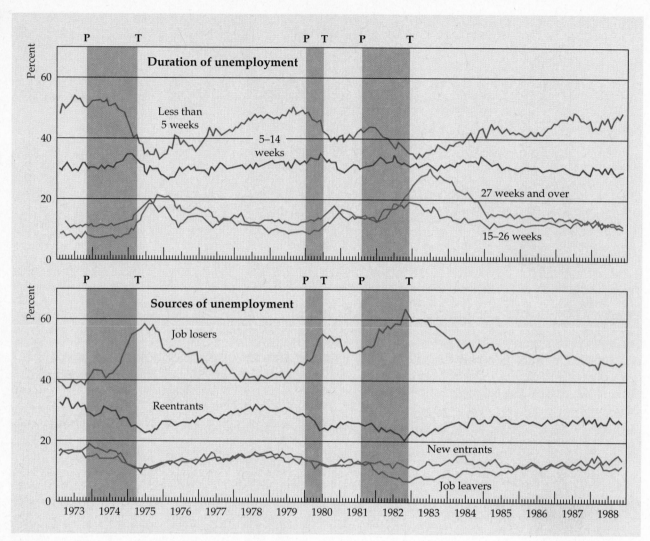

FIGURE 7-7   Duration of unemployment and its sources.

The top panel shows how the duration of unemployment increases during recessions and into the early recovery, when people are still having difficulty finding jobs. The lower panel shows the sources of unemployment. During prosperous periods such as 1979 and 1988, most of the unemployed are not people who have lost their jobs through layoff or firing. Rather, the majority are people who have quit their jobs and labor-force entrants who have not yet found work. However, during the recessions of 1973–1975, 1980, and 1981–1982, more than half the unemployed had lost their jobs—as many as 60% in late 1982.

types of unemployment. One type has already been discussed: *cyclical unemployment.* During recessions, workers are laid off. Cyclical unemployment is the most important type of unemployment and the one on which macroeconomic analysis is focused. There are other types as well.

Cyclical unemployment is the unemployment caused by general downturns in the economy.

Frictional Unemployment.   There will always be some people between jobs or looking for their first job.

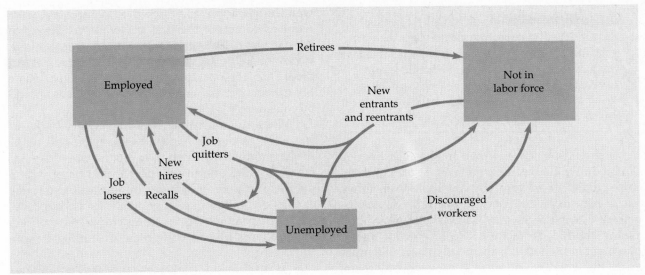

FIGURE 7-8 The changing labor force.

The labor force is quite mobile. Not only do many people move from job to job, but many move into and out of the labor force and into and out of the pool of unemployed.

Others may be temporarily out of work because of the weather—for example, those employed in construction work.

Frictional unemployment is temporary unemployment associated with adjustments in a changing, dynamic economy. It arises for a number of reasons. For example, some new entrants into the labor force take time to find jobs, some workers with jobs quit to look for something better, and some are unemployed by temporary disturbances (for example, bad weather or a temporary shutdown of an automobile factory to retool for a new model).

Such frictional unemployment is practically inevitable. It is difficult to see how it could be eliminated without an oppressive government directing people to the first available jobs. Moreover, at least some frictional unemployment is desirable. For example, people often want to spend some time looking for a job. Such time can be well spent, since the first available job may be quite inappropriate. Having people search for high-paying, high-productivity jobs is not only good for them, but it also contributes to the overall efficiency of the economy. Similarly, it is desirable to have people engaged in building houses, even though the inevitable result will be some unemployment because some construction jobs cannot be done in bad weather.

In our dynamic, changing economy, some industries decline and others rise. In many cases, when one firm goes bankrupt, others rise to take its place, and the labor force can move to the new jobs quite quickly and easily. Such transitional unemployment is also classified as frictional; people are temporarily between jobs as they hunt for new ones.

Structural Unemployment. In other cases, the changing pattern of jobs may permanently eliminate some jobs. For example, in the 1950s and 1960s, many coal mines shut down in Appalachia because oil was displacing coal. Many of the unemployed miners were unable to find local jobs; to find work, they would have had to move hundreds of miles and learn new skills. Similarly, a loss of part of the market to Japanese cars, combined with automation on the assembly line, has permanently reduced the number of jobs in the automobile industry, leaving some workers stranded. These are illustrations of *structural unemployment*.

Structural unemployment results when the location and/or skills of the labor force do not match the available jobs. It can occur because of declining demand for a product, because of automation or other changes in technology, because industry is moving to a different location, or because new entrants into the labor force do not have the training for available jobs.

It should be obvious that no sharp distinction can be drawn between frictional and structural unemployment. If an auto parts factory closes down and a bicycle factory opens up a mile away, displaced auto workers may quickly and easily find jobs in the bicycle factory. The temporary unemployment is frictional. If the new jobs are 150 miles away, the workers will have to move to take them. During the extended period before they actually do move, they may be classified among the structurally unemployed. But what if the new job is 30 miles away, near the limit of the commuting range? This case is not so clear. The difference between frictional and structural unemployment is one of degree. Structural unemployment lasts longer, because to get a new job, a greater change in location or a more extensive acquisition of new skills is required.

Because it is longer lasting and more painful than frictional unemployment, structural unemployment is a greater social problem. Once again, however, it may represent a painful side effect of the desirable flexibility of the economy. After the invention of the transistor, it would have made no sense to protect glass workers' jobs by requiring that radios and computers use traditional vacuum tubes. However, the pain associated with such structural unemployment does make a case for government assistance to ease the adjustment process, for example, by subsidized retraining for displaced workers. The society that benefits from the new transistor technology can help to reduce the burden that falls on a group of glassworkers who have lost their jobs.

HOW MUCH EMPLOYMENT IS "FULL EMPLOYMENT"?

It is impossible—and undesirable—to eliminate unemployment completely. Few people would

want an economy in which the unemployed were required to accept the first job available. Hence, if the concept of *full employment* is to be meaningful, it cannot be defined as an unemployment rate of zero. Over the past quarter century, a lively debate has arisen over the unemployment rate that should be considered "full employment."

When the unemployment rate is very high—at 9%, 10%, or higher—a rapid expansion will make the economy work better in many ways. An increase in total output will go hand in hand with a decrease in unemployment. In addition, economic expansion will typically generate rapid improvements in productivity as underemployed workers and underemployed equipment are utilized more fully.

As expansion continues and the unemployment rate is reduced, problems can occur, however. Producers hire more workers when the demand for their products is increasing. Rising demand can also lead to inflation. One way to define full employment is the situation that exists when the unemployment rate has been brought down as much as possible, without causing an inflationary overheating of the economy. Formally:

Full employment exists when the unemployment rate is brought down as low as possible, without causing an increase in the rate of inflation.

According to this widely used definition, full employment is not defined in terms of any specific number; the full-employment rate of unemployment can change as a result of changes in labor market institutions or changes elsewhere in the economy. For example, frictional and structural unemployment may be high when technology is changing rapidly and many old products are becoming obsolete.

During the 1960s, an unemployment rate of 4% was taken as the target of government policy; this was the rate on which economists focused when they discussed the concept of full employment. By 1966, the 4% goal was reached, and in 1969, the rate fell even further, to 3.5%. Inflation was accelerating, however. The economy was overheating, in part because of the large government expenditures on the war in Vietnam.

During the 1970s, the government found itself struggling to control inflation, even though the annual unemployment rate never fell below 4.9%.

A 4% rate of unemployment came to be viewed as an unrealistic objective, in the sense that it could be achieved only during temporary periods when the economy was overheating and inflation accelerating. Frictional and structural unemployment seemed to be higher than in the 1950s and 1960s; one reason was the adjustments caused by the volatile price of oil. As a result, the unemployment rate considered to be full employment was revised upward; discussions of full employment focused on the range between 5.5% and 6.5%.

In 1988, the unemployment rate fell below 5.5% without generating strong inflationary pressures. The concept of full employment is now often identified with the unemployment range between 5% and 5.5%.

ECONOMIC COSTS OF RECESSION

Whenever the economy slips into recession, potential output is lost, never to be recovered. The weeks and months which the unemployed spend in idleness are gone forever. Furthermore, the unemployed are subject to great stress and hardship. Unemployment is costly not only in terms of the output foregone, but also in terms of demoralization of the population (Box 7-2).

The lost output is illustrated in Figure 7-9. The smooth curve is an estimate of the path the economy would have followed in the absence of recessions and business cycles—that is, if full employment had been consistently maintained. This path can accordingly be labeled *full-employment GNP*

BOX 7–2   *Recessions Can Be Harmful to Your Health*

Harvey Brenner of Johns Hopkins University has found that unemployment and other economic problems have adverse effects on physical and mental health, and shorten life spans. The following excerpts are from his report to the U.S. Congress:[†]

> In addition to a high unemployment rate, three other factors—decline in labor force participation, decline in average weekly hours worked, and an increase in the rate of business failures—are strongly associated with increased mortality. . . .
>
> Economic inequality is associated with deterioration in mental health and well-being, manifest in increased rates of homicide, crime, and mental hospital admissions.
>
> . . . The report presents new evidence on the relationship between pathological [economic] conditions and . . . per capita alcohol consumption; cigarette consumption; illicit drug traffic and use; divorce rates; and the proportion of the population living alone.

Between 1973 and 1974, the unemployment rate rose from 4.9% to 5.6% of the civilian labor force. The chart shows Brenner's estimate of the additional stress-related deaths and crimes associated with this increase in unemployment.

[†]M. Harvey Brenner, *Estimating the Effects of Economic Change on National Health and Social Well-Being* (Washington, D.C.: U.S. Congress, Joint Economic Committee, June 1984), pp. 2–3.

The statistical relationships found by Brenner do not *prove* that the recession *caused* these results, but the evidence is strong enough to provide a warning: recessions can be harmful to your health.

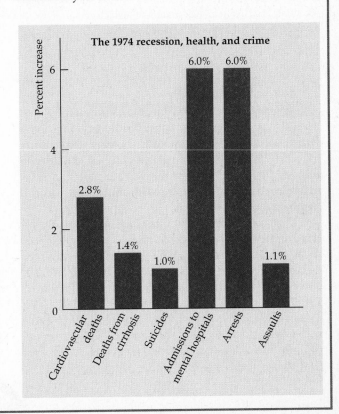

The 1974 recession, health, and crime

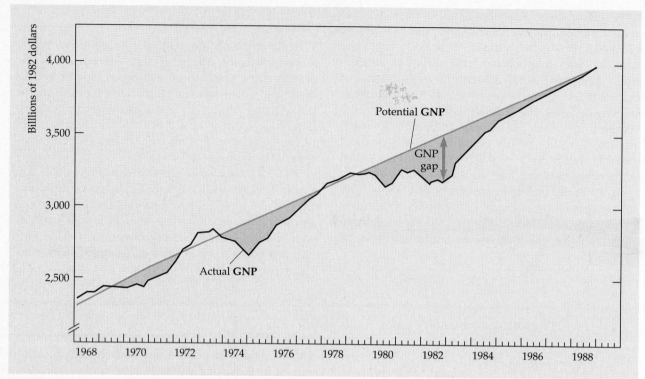

FIGURE 7-9   The cost of recession: The GNP gap.

During periods of slack in the economy, production is less than the full-employment potential. The GNP gap—the amount by which actual GNP falls below potential—is a measure of output lost because of recessions.

or *high-employment GNP* or *potential GNP.* Needless to say, economists cannot identify this path with precision. As just noted, there is uncertainty over how much employment should be considered full employment. Nevertheless, this path is useful in estimating the approximate amount of output lost because of recessions.

Lost output is known as the *GNP gap.* By far the greatest gap occurred during the Great Depression. In recent decades, the largest gap occurred during the severe recession of 1981–1982 and the early recovery that followed. Between 1981 and 1985, the gap averaged about 6% of GNP. This meant a total loss in output of about $1,000 billion, measured at 1982 prices, or about $4,000 for every person in the United States. (The reader is warned that these numbers can change substantially if different estimates of potential output are made.

Problems in estimating the potential path will be studied in detail in Chapter 18.)

The *GNP gap* is the amount by which actual GNP falls below potential GNP.

Finally, observe in Figure 7-9 that actual GNP has on occasion exceeded the estimate of potential—for example, in 1968–1969, 1972–1973, and 1978. This may seem puzzling: How can the economy possibly produce more than its potential? The answer is that the economy is capable of short-term bursts of activity which are unsustainable in the long run because of their cumulative adverse effects on the economy. Most notably, the short bursts of activity can cause the economy to overheat and inflation to accelerate.

KEY POINTS

1. The U.S. economy does not expand steadily. From time to time, expansion is interrupted by a recession.

2. During recessions, output declines and the unemployment rate rises. Profits fall sharply. Inflation generally declines in the later part of a recession and in the early recovery.

3. During recessions, the increase in the unemployment rate does not reflect all the pressures on the labor force. Some workers are limited to part-time work, even though they want full-time employment. Some of the unemployed become discouraged. When they stop looking for work and drop out of the labor force, they are no longer counted among the unemployed.

4. During recessions, output declines to a greater extent than employment. Although the unemployment rate rises, it rises by a smaller percentage than the change in output.

5. The unemployment rate for teenagers and minorities exceeds that for the labor force as a whole. Until 1980, women had a higher unemployment rate than men.

6. Unemployment may be classified as

(a) Cyclical unemployment.
(b) Frictional unemployment.
(c) Structural unemployment.

Cyclical unemployment, as the name suggests, is attributable to instability in the economy. Of the three types of unemployment, frictional unemployment represents the smallest problem: people are temporarily out of work as they hunt for jobs. Structural unemployment is more serious since workers have to move or obtain additional skills in order to find jobs.

7. "Full employment" does not mean an unemployment rate of zero. During the 1960s, an unemployment rate of 4% was interpreted as full employment. However, full employment is now generally considered to exist when unemployment is in the range between 5% and 5.5%.

8. The *GNP gap* measures how much actual output falls short of the full-employment potential. The gap is an important measure of the cost of recessions; it measures how much potential output has been lost. However, it does not include all the social costs, such as the demoralization of those who are out of work.

KEY CONCEPTS

recession	unemployment rate	frictional unemployment
trough	underemployment	structural unemployment
expansion	discouraged workers	full employment
peak	productivity of labor	potential or full-employment
turning point	Okun's Law	output
depression	cyclical unemployment	GNP gap

PROBLEMS

7-1. In Figure 7-1, a number of important events have been associated with periods of prosperity. Choose three of these events. Can you explain why each of them contributed to prosperity? (Take one from the period 1835–1865, one from 1865–1900, and one from the twentieth century.)

7-2. Why is it difficult to identify a recession? Why doesn't the National Bureau of Economic Research (NBER) just declare a recession whenever real output declines?

7-3. The text notes that inflation may respond slowly to changing economic conditions. For example, the downward pressure on prices may be concentrated in the later stages of recession and continue into the early recovery. Why might inflation be slow to respond?

7-4. During business cycles:

(a) Why do consumer durable purchases fluctuate more than consumer purchases of nondurables and services?

(b) Why does output fluctuate more than the unemployment rate?

* **7-5.** In 1980, the NBER estimated that the downward movement of the economy lasted six months—February to July, inclusive. Yet real GNP data show only one quarter of decline—the second quarter, from April to June. It seems that there may be something wrong here. We might expect that, if output fell for six months, GNP would decline for two quarters.

To show that there is, in fact, nothing wrong, construct a hypothetical set of monthly output figures from October 1979 to September 1980 that satisfy the following conditions: (1) Real GNP reaches a peak value of, say, $1,000 billion in January 1980. (2) Output declines every month from February until the trough month of July. (3) Quarterly output falls only once: second-quarter output is less than that of the first quarter of 1980, but the third quarter is above the second, and the first quarter of 1980 is above the last quarter of 1979.

When you have met these conditions, note that you have a series in which GNP does decline for a full six months, but the decline shows up in only one quarterly figure.

CHAPTER 8
AGGREGATE DEMAND AND AGGREGATE SUPPLY
Classical and Keynesian Equilibria

I believe myself to be writing a book on economic theory which will largely revolutionize—not, I suppose, at once but in the course of the next ten years—the way the world thinks about economic problems.

JOHN MAYNARD KEYNES
THE GENERAL THEORY OF EMPLOYMENT, INTEREST, AND MONEY (1936)

In studying the market for an individual product—such as apples—we illustrated the concepts of demand and supply in a diagram, with the horizontal axis showing the quantity of apples and the vertical axis showing the price of apples. This diagram was very useful. For example, by shifting the demand and supply curves, we could see how price and quantity respond to changing conditions of demand and supply (Figs. 4-5 and 4-6).

In macroeconomics, the concepts of **aggregate demand** and **aggregate supply** are useful in a similar way. For example, they can be used to explain why economic activity fluctuates. Since we are now dealing with the overall magnitudes in the economy, we use the horizontal axis to show the *overall* or *aggregate* quantity of output—that is, real national product. On the vertical axis, we put the *average* level of prices.

In drawing the aggregate demand and aggre-

gate supply curves, we must be careful. *We cannot assume that the aggregate demand curve slopes downward to the right simply because the demand curve for an individual product slopes this way. Nor can we assume that the aggregate supply curve slopes upward to the right simply because the supply curve for an individual product does.*

To see why, reconsider the earlier explanation in Chapter 4 of why the demand curve for apples slopes downward to the right. This curve is drawn on the assumption that the price of apples is the *only* price that changes; when we draw the demand curve for apples, we assume that the prices of all other goods remain stable. Thus, when the price of apples falls, it declines *relative to the prices* of all other goods. With apples becoming a "better buy," people are encouraged to *switch* their purchases away from other goods and to buy more apples instead. Such switching is the principal reason why the demand curve for an individual product slopes downward to the right.

Now consider what happens when we turn to the macroeconomic demand curve, with total output on the horizontal axis and the average level of prices on the vertical. For the economy as a whole, a fall in the level of all prices cannot cause buyers to switch from "other goods." There are no such other goods. It is not obvious how the aggregate demand curve should be drawn.

A similar problem arises on the supply side. In drawing the supply curve for a single product, such as apples, we assume that the prices of all other goods remain stable. Thus, when the price of apples rises, it increases *relative to the prices* of other goods. Farmers therefore have an incentive to *switch* away from the production of other goods and to produce more apples instead. When we look at macroeconomics—studying the economy as a whole—producers can't switch away from other goods because there aren't any. We cannot assume that the aggregate supply curve slopes upward to the right just because the supply curve for an individual product does.

How, then, are we to draw aggregate demand and aggregate supply? Historically, there have been two approaches to this question. The first is the classical approach—the accepted, mainstream approach of most economists up to the 1930s, an approach which has had a strong revival during the past three decades. The second approach was introduced by John Maynard Keynes during the 1930s as a way of understanding and combatting the Great Depression.

Because they had quite different ideas about aggregate demand and aggregate supply, Keynes and the classical economists came to quite different conclusions. This chapter will explain their sharp disagreement. In the view of classical economists, the market economy has an *automatic tendency toward full employment*; the economy will move to an *equilibrium with full employment*. Keynes disputed this theory, maintaining that the economy could reach an *equilibrium with large-scale unemployment*. Because the market mechanism could not be counted on to ensure full employment, Keynes believed that the government had the responsibility to restore full employment.

THE CLASSICAL APPROACH

Classical economists believed that the aggregate quantity of goods and services demanded would increase as the average price level fell, as illustrated in Figure 8-1. The reason is this. Suppose that all prices fall by, say, 50%, as illustrated by the move from P_1 to P_2. Then, each dollar buys more; the *purchasing power* of money has increased. Finding that they can buy more with their money, people step up their purchases. Thus the aggregate demand curve slopes downward to the right. (But remember: the additional purchases do not come about as a result of *switching* among goods. People buy more goods *in total*.)

Classical economists went beyond this general statement and became more specific. With prices only half as high at P_2 as at P_1, each dollar would buy twice as much. Therefore, classical economists said, the quantity of goods and services purchased at B would be about twice as great as at A. Alternatively, if prices had doubled, from P_1 to P_3, each dollar would buy only half as much as it did originally, and people would therefore buy only about half as much at C as at A.

In this theory, classical economists *put money at*

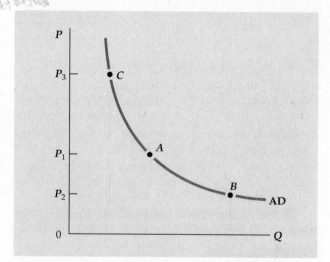

FIGURE 8-1   The classical aggregate demand function.

According to classical economists, the aggregate demand function slopes downward to the right. As prices fall, the money in the hands of the public will buy more. As a result, the public does buy more goods and services at B than at A.

the center of aggregate demand. In their view, the willingness and ability of people to buy goods depends on the quantity of money in their possession and on the purchasing power of that money.

The *purchasing power of money* is the real quantity of goods and services that one dollar will buy. When the price level rises, the purchasing power of money *falls.* For example, when the price level doubles, the purchasing power of money falls to half its previous level.

AGGREGATE SUPPLY: THE CLASSICAL APPROACH

Classical economists argued that the aggregate supply function was vertical at the *potential* or *full-employment* quantity of output, as illustrated in Figure 8-2. Why?

To answer this question, consider what happens if the economy is initially at point *F,* with full employment. Now, suppose that all prices double, including the price of labor (that is, the wage rate).

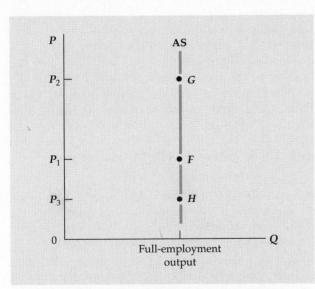

FIGURE 8-2   The classical aggregate supply function.
According to classical economists, the aggregate supply function is vertical, at the full-employment or potential quantity of national product. A general rise or fall in prices and wages does not make producers any more—or any less—willing to supply goods and services.

In other words, there is a *general inflation,* with *relative* prices and wages unaffected. Workers are basically in the same position as before. Although their money wages have doubled, so have prices. The real wage—the quantity of goods and services which the wage will buy—is unchanged. Therefore workers' willingness to work remains the same. Businesses also are in basically the same situation as before. Their productive capacity remains unchanged, and the relationship between costs and prices also remains unchanged. As a result, businesses offer the same amount of goods and services for sale. Thus point *G* on the aggregate supply curve is directly above point *F.* Similarly, classical economists argued that the quantity of goods and services offered for sale would remain unchanged if all wages and prices fell by 50%, as illustrated by the move from P_1 to P_3. Thus point *H* is directly below point *F.*

There is a *general inflation* when all prices increase by the same percentage, leaving relative prices unchanged.

EQUILIBRIUM AT FULL EMPLOYMENT

When we bring together the aggregate demand and aggregate supply curves of classical economics, we find the equilibrium at *E* in Figure 8-3. Classical economists believed that the economy would be in equilibrium only at full employment, at a point like *E,* and that market forces would automatically lead the economy to full employment.

To explain this classical view, suppose that the economy is initially at a position of large-scale unemployment, such as point *B* in Figure 8-3. The high unemployment rate occurs because, at the initial price level P_1, the quantity of goods and services demanded (at *B*) is substantially less than the full-employment output (at *A*). What will happen, according to classical economists? At P_1, the quantity of goods and services demanded is less than producers are willing to supply. In order to sell more goods, businesses will cut their prices. They will reduce the wage they pay, since the large number of unemployed will be so eager to get jobs that they will be willing to work for less than the pre-

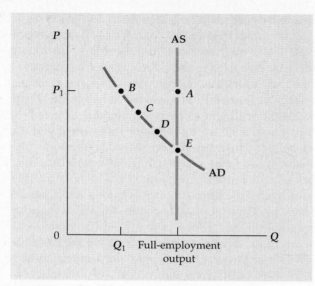

FIGURE 8-3   Equilibrium in classical economics.

According to classical economists, large-scale unemployment would result in an automatic movement back to full employment. Under the pressure of market forces, prices and wages would fall. The economy would gradually move down the aggregate demand curve toward full-employment equilibrium E.

vailing wage. Thus both prices and money wages will fall. With prices falling below P_1, the purchasing power of the money in the hands of the public will increase and they will buy more. There will be a move along the aggregate demand curve from B to C to D. This process will continue until the economy gets to equilibrium E, with full employment. Once this equilibrium has been reached, there will no longer be downward pressures on prices and wages.

THE CLASSICAL EXPLANATION OF THE DEPRESSION

Since classical economists believed that there would always be full employment when the economy was in equilibrium, how did they explain recessions? In particular, how did they explain the biggest recession of all—the decline into the Great Depression between 1929 and 1933? Their answer was that large-scale unemployment existed only when the economy was in *disequilibrium;* it was the result of *disturbances* to the economy.

Most notably, the economy could be disturbed by a *shift* in the aggregate demand curve. As we have already seen, classical economists focused on money and its purchasing power in their analysis of aggregate demand. In drawing any single aggregate demand function (as in Fig. 8-1), classical economists assumed that the quantity of money was constant. That is, the number of dollars was fixed. Any changes in the quantity of money would cause a shift in the aggregate demand function. It would shift to the right if the quantity of money increased or to the left if the quantity of money decreased.

Thus a classical explanation of the depression goes something like this.[1] In 1929, the economy was close to a full-employment equilibrium at A in Figure 8-4, with aggregate demand AD_{1929}. Then, because of disturbances in the banking and financial system, the stock of money in the hands of the public fell by about 30% between 1929 and 1933. As a result of the decline in the money stock, aggregate demand shifted to the left, to AD_{1933}.

Even with this fall in demand, full employment would still have been possible if prices and wages had fallen all the way to P_E. In this event, full employment would have occurred at new equilibrium E. But prices and wages were **sticky** in a downward direction; that is, they did not fall quickly in the face of slack demand and high unemployment. One reason for stickiness is that it takes some time for job searchers to realize that they will not find the job they want, at the wage they expect. It is only after a frustrating search that they will be willing to settle for a lower wage.[2]

---

[1]Details may be found in the very readable chapter on the depression in Milton Friedman and Anna Schwartz, *A Monetary History of the United States, 1867-1960* (Princeton, N.J.: Princeton University Press, 1963).

*[2]Two other reasons for stickiness were provided in Chapter 7, footnote 3, which explained why the prices of manufactures fell much less than those of agricultural commodities between 1929 and 1933.

Some classical economists argued that distortions among *relative* prices made the depression even more severe. We skip this argument because it was quite complex. In this section, we consider only the effects of a *general*, across-the-board inflation or deflation, in which all prices and wages move by the same percentage, leaving relative prices unchanged. This allows us to grasp the central points of classical theory.

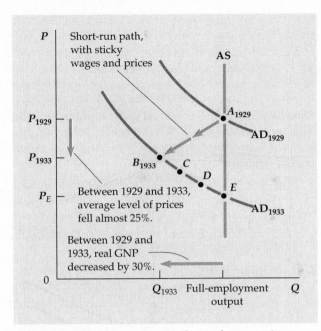

FIGURE 8-4 The depression in classical economics.

Classical economists believed that the principal cause of the Great Depression was a collapse in demand, caused by a sharp decline in the money stock. Because wages and prices are sticky, the economy did not move directly to its new full-employment equilibrium, *E*, but rather to *B*.

Because of stickiness, prices fell only to P_{1933} by 1933. With prices remaining higher than required for the new equilibrium, the amount of goods and services purchased was far less than the economy's full-employment potential. Specifically, at the price level P_{1933}, aggregate demand was only great enough to buy the quantity of output at point B_{1933}. The economy was in a deep depression.

Thus wage and price stickiness kept the economy from moving directly downward along the aggregate supply function in the face of a collapse in demand. As demand fell, the economy instead moved along the short-run path from *A* to *B*. In the absence of any further disturbance in demand, price and wage adjustments could be expected to gradually restore full employment. Although it would take time, the economy would move along the new aggregate demand curve from *B* to *C* to *D*, and finally to the new full-employment equilibrium *E*. So argued classical economists.

In other words, the classical aggregate supply curve illustrated where the economy would *eventu-*

ally go. Over the **long run,** classical economists were confident that wages and prices would in fact adjust, restoring full employment.

In classical macroeconomics, the *long run* is the period over which prices and wages adjust completely.

This approach led classical economists to suggest two possible solutions for a depression:

1. The initial source of the disturbance might be eliminated. Steps might be taken to prevent a decline in the quantity of money in the first place, or to restore the quantity of money once it had fallen. If the money supply had been held stable, aggregate demand would never have collapsed, and the economy would not have fallen into the depression.

2. Workers and businesses might be encouraged to accept lower wages and prices quickly, so the economy could move more rapidly to its new full-employment equilibrium *E*. The more willing workers and businesses were to accept lower wages and prices, the shorter would be the temporary period of unemployment. Note that the classical "long run" is not any fixed number of months or years. It is whatever period is needed for wages and prices to adjust. The faster they adjust, the sooner the economy reaches its long-run equilibrium with full employment.

Many classical economists were quite skeptical that the government could provide much help in promoting downward wage and price flexibility. Indeed, many believed that when the government became involved in markets, it was likely in practice to keep prices up and to *increase* their stickiness. Thus many classical economists argued for a policy of laissez faire. In macroeconomic as in microeconomic questions, they saw little role for the government; the operation of market forces would work to restore full employment. There was one very important exception, however: the government controlled the quantity of money. Its key responsibility was to keep the money stock stable and prevent a depression in the first place.

CLASSICAL MACROECONOMICS: A PRELIMINARY SUMMARY

Before proceeding, let us summarize the main

points of classical macroeconomics developed thus far.

1. The aggregate demand curve slopes downward to the right. As prices fall, each dollar will buy more, and people accordingly do buy more. A single aggregate demand curve is drawn on the assumption that the nominal quantity of money is constant.

2. If the quantity of money increases, the aggregate demand curve shifts to the right. If the quantity of money decreases, aggregate demand shifts left.

3. The aggregate supply curve is vertical at the full-employment output.

4. In the long run, a shift in the aggregate demand curve causes a change in prices, not in output. The reason is that, in the long run, the economy moves back to equilibrium on the vertical aggregate supply curve. At equilibrium, there is full employment.

5. In the short run, however—when wages and prices have not yet adjusted fully—a collapse in aggregate demand can cause a depression, as illustrated by the move from *A* to *B* in Figure 8-4. An increase in demand can cause a recovery—that is, a movement from *B* back toward *A*.

6. The major economic responsibility of the government is to stabilize the quantity of money and thereby stabilize aggregate demand. In most other respects, laissez faire is the best policy.

THE KEYNESIAN APPROACH

Prior to the Great Depression, most economists considered unemployment to be a relatively minor and temporary problem, associated with fluctuations in the economy. The decade-long depression of the 1930s shattered this confidence and provided the backdrop for a new theory of unemployment, proposed by British economist John Maynard Keynes. His major work—*The General Theory of Employment, Interest and Money*—attacked the prevailing classical view. Specifically, Keynes offered three major propositions:

1. *Unemployment in the market economy.* In contrast to classical economists, Keynes argued that a market economy might not have a strong tendency to move to full employment. On the contrary, a market economy might come to rest in *an equilibrium with large-scale unemployment*—often referred to, more briefly, as an **unemployment equilibrium.** Furthermore, even if the economy did temporarily reach full employment, it might be quite unstable and fall back into depression. In other words, Keynes said that the market economy was defective in two important ways:

> **(a)** It might fall into a *persistent depression,* such as the depression of the 1930s.
>
> **(b)** It might be quite *unstable,* so that even if it did reach full employment, this happy state of affairs might be short-lived.

2. *The cause of unemployment.* Keynes argued that large-scale unemployment was due to an *insufficiency of aggregate demand*—that is, too little spending for goods and services.

3. *The cure for unemployment.* To cure unemployment, aggregate demand should be increased. The best way to do that, said Keynes, was by an *increase in government spending.*

This, then, is the main policy message of Keynes' *General Theory:* the government has the ability—and the *responsibility*—to *manage aggregate demand,* and thus to ensure continuing prosperity. Cast aside was the classical view, that market forces would solve the unemployment problem and that the government should strictly limit its interference in the economy. Keynes was particularly impatient with economists who were willing to wait for the "long run," when they expected market forces to reestablish full employment. *"In the long run* we are all dead," he retorted.[3]

Keynes held out the promise that the government could increase aggregate demand and thus solve the appalling unemployment problem of the 1930s. His book was a spectacular success; it ranks with Adam Smith's *Wealth of Nations* and Karl Marx's *Das Kapital* as one of the most influential economics books ever written. The *General Theory* led to a sharp change in economic thinking. With its appearance in 1936, the *Keynesian Revolution* was underway.

---

[3]J. M. Keynes, *Monetary Reform* (New York: Harcourt Brace, 1924), p. 88 (italics in original).

To support his three propositions, Keynes suggested a new theoretical framework, including an approach to aggregate demand and aggregate supply which was quite different from that of classical economists.

THE SIMPLE KEYNESIAN AGGREGATE SUPPLY FUNCTION

Classical economists, recognizing that prices and wages might temporarily be sticky, had used this stickiness to explain *transitional* periods of large-scale unemployment when aggregate demand decreased. Keynes placed even more emphasis on stickiness. In his view, workers and businesses would strongly resist any cut in wages and prices. As a result, wages and prices would remain *rigid*

for an indefinitely long period in the face of large-scale unemployment.

This meant that there was a horizontal section in the Keynesian aggregate supply function, as illustrated by section *BA* in the left-hand panel of Figure 8-5. Here's why. If, from an initial position of full employment at point *A*, there was a decline in aggregate demand, prices would remain stable. The fall in demand would show up in terms of a decrease in output, not in prices. This is shown by the movement from *A* to *B*. Furthermore, there would be little tendency, even in the long run, for prices and wages to fall. If aggregate demand remained low, the economy would remain in a depression at *B*.

According to Keynes, the cure was to increase aggregate demand. In response, producers would

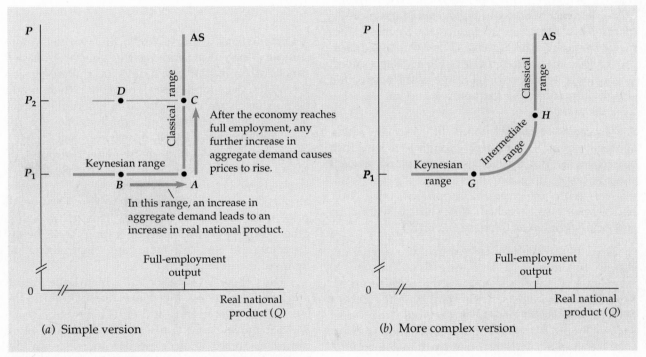

FIGURE 8-5   The Keynesian aggregate supply function.

There are two main segments of the simple Keynesian aggregate supply function (panel *a*). In the horizontal section, prices are stable, and a change in aggregate demand causes a change in output and employment. In the vertical section, an increase in demand causes an increase in prices.

Panel *b* shows the more complicated version of the Keynesian aggregate supply function. Because of bottlenecks, the prices of some goods rise before the economy reaches full employment. This causes an intermediate, curved section in aggregate supply.

step up production. Because of the large numbers of unemployed workers and the large quantity of unused machinery, more could be produced at existing prices. Output would increase, and the economy would move to the right, along the horizontal range of the aggregate supply function back toward A.

Once the economy got to A—to a point of full employment—Keynes had no major objection to the classical approach to aggregate supply. Because the economy was already operating at capacity, any further increase in aggregate demand would be reflected in higher prices. The economy would move vertically upward toward C. In short, the Keynesian aggregate supply function had two quite different ranges, a horizontal range and a vertical range.

1.   The *horizontal range* was relevant for analyzing periods of depression and recession, when inadequate demand resulted in high rates of unemployment. This range most interested Keynes. The major purpose of his *General Theory* was to explain the causes and cures of the Great Depression. Accordingly, this horizontal range of the aggregate supply function is frequently known as the *Keynesian range*.

2.   The *vertical range* would be reached when aggregate demand was high enough to ensure full employment. Further increases in demand would simply cause inflation. Because Keynes had no quarrel with the classical approach once full employment was reached, this vertical section is sometimes known as the *classical range*.[4]

Together, these two ranges give the aggregate supply function BAC in Figure 8-5a, forming a reversed L. (This figure follows the convention of Keynesian economists, with "real national product" on the horizontal axis. Previous diagrams, such as Figure 8-4, followed the convention of classical economists, with the quantity of real output Q

on the axis. Q is the same as real national product, and the two terms may be used interchangeably.)

Through time, the horizontal section of the Keynesian aggregate supply curve can *ratchet* upward. From initial point B, suppose that aggregate demand increases enough to move the economy not just to A, but beyond that all the way to C, with prices rising to P_2. Once C is reached, any reduction in demand does not lead the economy to retrace its path back toward A because prices and wages do not move down from the new level established at C; businesses and labor resist such a move. Instead, the response to a fall in aggregate demand is a decrease in output. The economy moves toward D, along the horizontal line.

In brief, the simple Keynesian aggregate supply function is a reversed L, with the horizontal part of the L ratcheting upward every time a new, higher price level is established.

A Complication.   Unfortunately, the world is more complex than indicated by the simple L-shaped function. From the early days of the Keynesian Revolution, economists recognized that there might be no sharply defined point at A where the economy suddenly reaches full employment. As the economy expands, not all industries reach capacity at exactly the same time. Bottlenecks can occur, as some industries reach their capacity in spite of slack elsewhere in the economy. In the industries already at capacity, prices begin to rise. The overall price index begins to creep up. This occurs while other industries are still operating well below capacity, and are still increasing their output as demand increases.

Thus there is a period in which both output and prices are increasing. The economy follows the curved path between G and H in Figure 8-5, panel *b*. As it moves from G toward H, more and more industries reach their capacity; increases in demand show up more and more in terms of higher prices, and less and less in terms of increases in real output. The curve becomes increasingly steep, finally reaching point H.

The horizontal range of aggregate supply was used by Keynesians in their explanation of the Great Depression. The curved *intermediate range* between G and H is important in more normal

---

[4]Both Keynesian and classical economists recognized a complication that is avoided here. As time passes, the economy grows, with the full-employment or potential output increasing. Therefore the vertical section of the aggregate supply function shifts gradually to the right with the passage of time.

times, when the economy is neither in an inflationary boom (the vertical section) nor in a depression (the horizontal part).

AGGREGATE DEMAND: THE KEYNESIAN APPROACH

To study aggregate demand, Keynes broke it down into four components, which correspond to the components of national product:

1. *Personal consumption expenditures.*

2. *Investment demand*—that is, the demand for plant, equipment, housing, and additional inventories.

3. *Government purchases of goods and services.*

4. *Net exports.*

Although consumption is the largest component of aggregate demand, investment demand and government spending play central roles in Keynesian economics.

Investment demand is important because it is the major *cause* of economic instability. Keynes emphasized that businesses are willing to invest only when they expect the new plant and equipment to add to profits. Expectations are fragile. Once the economy starts to decline, business executives become pessimistic; they therefore cut back on investment, increasing the downward momentum. In other words, Keynes highlighted investment demand in order to emphasize how unstable a market economy might be. This view contrasts to the classical view of an economy that moves toward an equilibrium at full employment and is basically stable—provided that the quantity of money is stable.

Government spending plays a key role in Keynesian economics as a *cure* for economic instability. Although the depression was caused by a collapse of investment demand, it was unrealistic to expect investment demand to move the economy out of the depression. Business executives had become too pessimistic. Therefore it was up to the government to provide a cure by increasing the component of aggregate demand directly under its control. That is, it was desirable to increase government spending to compensate for the decline in investment demand and thus restore full employment. During more moderate recessions, the government likewise had a responsibility to increase

its spending in order to maintain the overall level of spending in the economy.

In brief, Keynesian economists see unstable investment demand as the source of economic instability. Government spending can be used as a cure. When investment demand falls, government spending can be increased. When investment demand soars, government spending can be cut back, once again stabilizing aggregate demand. Government spending can thus be used to *compensate* for fluctuations in investment demand.

We reemphasize that the four components of aggregate demand highlighted by Keynesian theory correspond to the four components of national product studied in Chapter 6. Two major innovations in macroeconomics—the development of national product accounts and the new Keynesian theory of employment—interacted and reinforced one another during the 1930s and 1940s.

Finally, observe that in Figure 8-5, we have drawn no aggregate demand curve. Thus something is missing from our introduction to Keynesian theory. We have not shown how the demand for goods and services responds to a change in the average level of prices. Because Keynes' views on this topic were complicated, they are left to the appendix at the end of this chapter. All we need to note here is the principal conclusions. Keynesian theory suggests that the aggregate demand curve slopes downward to the right during normal times. In a depression, things could be different; the aggregate demand function might slope downward to the left. In the Keynesian view, the classical interpretation of the depression (Fig. 8-4) was simply wrong.

CLASSICAL ECONOMICS AND KEYNESIAN ECONOMICS: A SUMMARY

In his *General Theory*, Keynes launched an attack on classical economists, on two grounds: (1) their theory was wrong; and, even more importantly, (2) they had no adequate proposals for dealing with the severe unemployment problem of the 1930s. A heated debate ensued, both over policies and over the proper theoretical framework for studying macroeconomic problems.

Differences between Keynesians and the inheritors of the classical school continue to the present day. These differences attract considerable attention. While debates can be interesting, the fact that differences still exist should not obscure an even more important fact: on many issues, there is general agreement among macroeconomists, regardless of their intellectual heritage.

AREAS OF AGREEMENT

Those in the classical and Keynesian traditions agree that

1. A *sharp decline in aggregate demand* was the principal cause of the collapse into the Great Depression of the 1930s.

2. *Fluctuations in aggregate demand* have been the major cause of fluctuations in output in recent decades.

3. Therefore, the *stabilization of aggregate demand* should be an important macroeconomic objective.

4. When the economy is already operating at its full-employment potential, *any large increase in aggregate demand will spill over into inflation.* Both the classical and Keynesian aggregate supply functions are vertical at full-employment output. When the economy is at full employment, higher demand causes higher prices.

The second point is worth explaining in more detail. Consider Figure 8-6, with a normal, downward-sloping aggregate demand function, AD_1. The aggregate supply function slopes upward to the right; it corresponds to the intermediate range

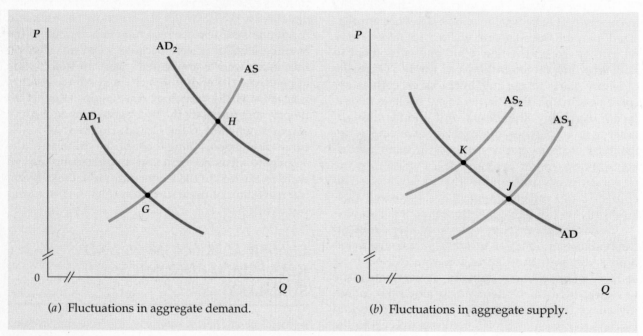

(a) Fluctuations in aggregate demand.

(b) Fluctuations in aggregate supply.

FIGURE 8-6   Short-run fluctuations in aggregate demand and supply.

In panel *a*, aggregate demand fluctuates. During the expansion, output increases and there is upward pressure on prices, as illustrated by the movement from *G* to *H*. This is the pattern actually observed in most business expansions.

The right-hand panel illustrates what happens if aggregate supply fluctuates. Upward pressures on prices occur during recessions, with 1973–1974 providing an example. However, the inflationary recession of 1973–1974 was unusual. Typically, inflationary pressures grow during periods of expansion, as illustrated in panel *a*.

of the Keynesian supply function in Figure 8-5*b*. Panel *a* of Figure 8-6, in which aggregate demand shifts, is broadly consistent with the pattern already observed in Chapter 7: during expansion, output increases and inflation generally accelerates.

If shifts in aggregate supply had been the main cause of business cycles (panel *b*), we would expect inflation to rise during recessions (as the economy moves from *J* to *K*). But this is not in fact what usually happens. Therefore, we may conclude that shifts in aggregate demand are the major cause of business fluctuations, not shifts in aggregate supply. Not surprisingly, then, we will focus on the aggregate demand side in our early study of macroeconomics in Chapters 9-12. (Although the outcome in panel *b* is unusual, it occasionally occurs. For example, the rate of inflation increased as the economy fell into a recession in 1973–1974. This unusual case will be studied when we look at shifts in aggregate supply in Chapter 13.)

AREAS OF DISAGREEMENT

There are four topics of continuing disagreement:

1. *Which is more important: monetary policy or fiscal policy?* We have seen how economists in the classical tradition attributed the depression to a decline in the money stock. Depressions could be avoided by keeping the money stock more stable (a better monetary policy). In contrast, Keynes emphasized government spending (fiscal policy) as a way of increasing aggregate demand and combatting the depression.

There is a continuing difference as to whether monetary policy or fiscal policy has the stronger and more predictable effect on aggregate demand. Those in the classical tradition focus on **monetary policy,** whereas those in the Keynesian tradition are most likely to think first of **fiscal policy.** However, it should be emphasized that *most modern macroeconomists believe that both monetary and fiscal policies are important.*

Monetary policy involves a change in the rate of growth of the money stock.

Fiscal policy involves a change in government expenditures or in tax rates.

---

2. *A policy rule, or active management?* While macroeconomists agree that it would be desirable for aggregate demand to be more stable, they differ sharply over how stability is best achieved. Those in the Keynesian tradition emphasize the defects and instabilities of a market economy and believe that the government has the responsibility to *actively manage aggregate demand* in order to reduce the amplitude of business fluctuations.

Those in the classical tradition generally believe that the market economy will be reasonably stable, *if* monetary conditions are kept stable. As a result, they recommend a **monetary policy rule:** the authorities should aim for a *steady, moderate increase in the money stock*, at something like 3% or 4% per year. A steady growth is appropriate, because we live in a growing economy. More money is needed to buy the increasing volume of goods and services that can be produced.

Because of their emphasis on money, modern inheritors of the classical tradition are frequently known as **monetarists.** They do not argue that adherence to a monetary rule will create a perfectly stable economy, because aggregate demand will not expand in a perfectly stable way even if money does. But they are very skeptical that the government can make things better by active policy management. Like the earlier classical economists, they fear that the government is, on average, likely to make things worse. (The reasons for this fear will be explained in Chapter 18.)

This disagreement—between those who argue for *active management* by government and those who advocate a *policy rule*—is probably the most important single policy dispute among macroeconomists.

3. *The role of government.* Because of their belief in the effectiveness of market forces, and because of their skepticism about the ability of governments to substantially improve the operation of the economy, monetarists generally believe that the government's role should be narrowly circumscribed.[5]

---

[5]For example, Milton Friedman and Rose Friedman, *Free to Choose* (New York: Harcourt Brace Jovanovich, 1979). The Friedmans would reduce the role of the government in many areas, including education. They recommend that the government support education by giving vouchers to parents, to be used in the school of the parents' choice.

Those in the Keynesian tradition are much more likely to favor a large role for the government. They not only believe in the active management of aggregate demand, but also are generally sympathetic toward other government activities aimed at domestic economic problems—for example, public housing and job training programs. Those who argue for active management of aggregate demand are not required, by the logic of their case, to argue that the government should also undertake other tasks. But it is not surprising that those who are confident of the government in one area—demand management—tend to be confident of its abilities in other respects as well.

4. *The nature of equilibrium.* Economists in the clas-

sical tradition associate equilibrium with full employment. High rates of unemployment represent a *temporary* problem caused by economic fluctuations and short-run *disequilibrium.* In contrast, Keynesian theory offers the possibility that the economy might fall into an unemployment equilibrium, with a *continuing* problem of inadequate aggregate demand and high rates of unemployment.

While the possibility of an unemployment equilibrium remains a point of difference between those in the Keynesian and classical traditions, this issue has become less important with the passage of time. Half a century has passed since the Great Depression, and Keynesians are much less worried about a lengthy depression than they used to be.

KEY POINTS

1. Just as demand and supply are useful in microeconomics, so they are also useful in macroeconomics. However, we cannot assume that the aggregate demand and supply curves will necessarily have slopes similar to those of the demand and supply curves for individual products. (Microeconomics deals with individual products, such as wheat or apples. Macroeonomics deals with the overall economic aggregates, such as GNP.)

2. There are two main approaches to aggregate demand and aggregate supply: the classical and the Keynesian approaches.

3. According to the classical view, there will be full employment whenever the economy is in equilibrium; a market economy has a natural tendency to move toward full employment. According to Keynes, the economy can reach an equilibrium with large-scale unemployment.

4. Classical theory stresses the importance of money as a determinant of aggregate demand. In drawing a single aggregate demand curve, classical economists assume that the nominal quantity of money is held constant. When prices fall, the purchasing power of this fixed nominal quantity increases. Therefore, people purchase more goods

and services. Accordingly, the classical aggregate demand curve slopes downward to the right.

5. According to classical theory, the aggregate supply curve is vertical, at potential or full-employment output.

6. Therefore, in the classical equilibrium—where aggregate demand and aggregate supply intersect—there is full employment.

7. According to classical economists, the depression was the result of a leftward shift in the aggregate demand curve, which in turn resulted from a fall in the money stock. In time—in the "long run"—classical economists believed that wages and prices would fall enough to restore full employment.

8. Keynes emphasized the downward rigidity of wages and prices. In its simplest form, the Keynesian aggregate supply function forms a reversed L, as illustrated in Figure 8-5. In the horizontal part of the aggregate supply function, there could be an equilibrium with large-scale unemployment.

9. According to Keynes, the principal cause of the depression was the collapse of the investment component of aggregate demand. The solution lay in additional government expenditures, whose purpose would be to increase aggregate demand to the full-employment level. Thus Keynes rejected the laissez-faire conclusions of many classical economists.

10. Keynesian economists often stress fiscal policy as a tool for managing demand, whereas those in the classical tradition emphasize the importance of money. However, most modern economists believe that *both* fiscal and monetary policies can have an important effect on demand.

11. A significant debate continues over how actively the authorities should manage aggregate demand. Keynesians generally favor active management, whereas those in the classical tradition generally favor a monetary rule: the authorities should aim for a steady, moderate increase in the quantity of money.

KEY CONCEPTS

aggregate demand and supply
purchasing power of money
general inflation
equilibrium at full employment
stickiness of wages and prices
long run

equilibrium with large-scale
    unemployment
reversed-L aggregate supply
    function
Keynesian and classical ranges of
    aggregate supply

monetary policy
fiscal policy
active management of demand
monetary policy rule
monetarist

PROBLEMS

8-1. The demand curve for a specific good, such as wheat, slopes downward to the right. Why can't we simply conclude that, as a result, the aggregate demand curve will have the same general shape?

8-2. Draw a diagram showing the classical aggregate demand function. Why does it have the slope you have shown?

8-3. Why is the classical aggregate supply function vertical?

8-4. If the economy starts with high unemploy-ment, explain two ways in which full employment might be restored in the classical system.

8-5. What is the reason for the horizontal section of the Keynesian aggregate supply function?

8-6. According to Keynes, what was the best way to get out of a depression?

8-7. What evidence suggests that fluctuations in aggregate demand, rather than fluctuations in aggregate supply, have been the principal reason for fluctuations in real GNP?

THE AGGREGATE DEMAND CURVE OF KEYNESIAN ECONOMICS

In order to complete our story about aggregate demand and aggregate supply, we need to look at what Keynes said about the slope of the aggregate demand function in his *General Theory*. Suppose that in the face of a depressed economy at B (Fig. 8-7), a general deflation did occur, with prices and wages all falling by 40%, from P_1 to P_2. The horizontal segment of the aggregate supply curve would then be at the new prevailing price level P_2; aggregate supply would have shifted down from AS_1 to AS_2. What would the result be? What would happen to the aggregate quantity of goods and services demanded? To answer this question, said Keynes, we have to look at what will happen to the major components of demand, particularly consumption and investment.

1. *Consumption demand.* The amount which people consume depends primarily on their incomes. As wages and incomes fall by the same proportion, people find that they are no better off: their *real wages* remain unchanged. Accordingly, said Keynes, we would not expect any change in the quantity of goods and services they consume. In other words, if we look only at consumption—the largest single component of aggregate demand—we will expect the aggregate demand function to be *vertical*. If it has any tendency to slope downward to the right or left, it will have to be because of the behavior of other components of demand, most notably investment.

2. *Investment demand.* Investment demand depends in part on what is happening to consumer purchases. For example, a rise in the sales of automobiles will encourage auto manufacturers to invest by buying more plant and machinery. How-

ever, if consumption is stable in the face of deflation—for reasons explained in point 1—then there is no reason to expect investment to change on this account.

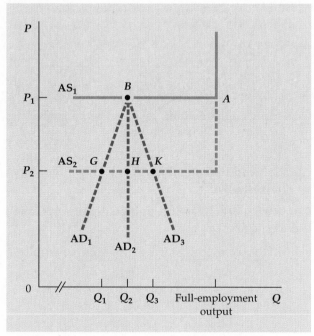

FIGURE 8-7   Aggregate demand in Keynesian economics.

If prices and wages fall during a depression, the result may be an increase in the quantity of goods and services demanded, as illustrated by the movement from B to K. But this outcome is unlikely, according to Keynes. The likely outcome is a decreasing quantity, at point G. Thus the aggregate demand function is likely to look like AD_1 during a depression. Deflation will cause a decrease, not an increase in economic activity.

To identify the effects of price changes on investment, we have to look instead at two other forces:

1. *The interest-rate effect.* As prices and wages fall, the amount of money in the system increases in *real* terms; that is, in terms of what it will buy. There are the same number of dollars, but each dollar is worth more. Because individuals and businesses have more real money, they are more willing to lend it; interest rates fall as a result. With lower interest rates, businesses find it cheaper to borrow the money with which to buy equipment. Investment should increase on this account.

2. *The expectations effect.* Investment also depends on people's expectations regarding the future. If prices are expected to rise, for example, businesses have an incentive to buy buildings or equipment quickly, in order to avoid the higher prices later. In extreme cases, there can be strong speculation in real estate; there is a rush to get in while the getting is good. On the other hand, expectations of a fall in prices can cause businesses to put off investment, in the hopes of buying the plant or equipment even more cheaply in the future. It is this characteristic, said Keynes, that makes deflation so dangerous. As prices fall, people may come to expect a continuing deflation, which can cause a weakening of investment demand.

Accordingly, there are two opposite forces at work as prices decline—the interest-rate effect, working to increase investment, and the expectations effect, working to depress it. Keynes was particularly dubious about the interest-rate effect when the economy was suffering substantial slack. During such periods, interest rates may already be very low. For example, the interest rates on long-term government bonds fell below 3% during the Great Depression. No matter how far prices fall, interest rates cannot fall much further. Clearly, interest rates cannot become negative; people would simply refuse to buy bonds yielding negative rates and would hold money instead.

Thus Keynes argued that, during a depression, a weak interest-rate effect is likely to be overpowered by a negative expectations effect. In this case, a fall in the price level would lead to a decrease in investment and to a decrease in the total quantity of goods and services demanded. The aggregate demand curve would go through point *G* in Figure 8-7. It is conceivable that the opposite might happen: the interest rate effect *might* under some circumstances be strong. In this case, a fall in prices would lead to an increase in investment, and the aggregate demand curve would go through *K*. However, Keynes believed that this outcome was very unlikely. A fall in prices was likely to cause a decline, not a rise, in investment demand.

In brief, Keynes presented two reasons for rejecting the classical argument that full employment could be restored by a general fall in prices and wages:

1. In the first place, prices and wages *won't* fall much; they are rigid in a downward direction. The downward shift of the aggregate supply curve illustrated in Figure 8-7 will not in fact occur.

2. *Even if* prices and wages *did* fall, the market could not be counted on to restore full employment. A more likely outcome would be a movement toward *G* (Fig. 8-7); deflation would *worsen* the depression.

In arguing that market forces would not lead automatically to full employment, even in the long run, Keynes came to his central policy conclusion. If the economy is at a point like *B*, the government should not stand idly by while millions remain out of work. It should accept its responsibilities and increase its spending in order to shift aggregate demand to the right and restore full employment at *A*.

PROBLEMS

* **8-8.** As part of Franklin Roosevelt's program to combat the Great Depression of the 1930s, the National Recovery Act contained provisions to keep prices up. Explain why someone in the classical tradition might consider such legislation a blunder. Explain why a Keynesian would be much more likely to favor such legislation.

CHAPTER 9
EQUILIBRIUM WITH UNEMPLOYMENT
The Keynesian Approach

The economic system in which we live . . . seems capable of remaining in a chronic condition of sub-normal activity for a considerable period without any marked tendency either towards recovery or towards complete collapse. Moreover, . . . full, or even approximately full employment is of rare and short-lived occurrence.

JOHN MAYNARD KEYNES,
THE GENERAL THEORY OF EMPLOYMENT, INTEREST AND MONEY (1936)

Of all our economic problems, unemployment is perhaps the most vexing. Unemployment represents an obvious waste: Society foregoes the goods and services which the unemployed might have produced. Unemployed people suffer the demoralization, frustration, and loss of self-respect that come with idleness.

As we saw in Chapter 8, the deep depression of the 1930s led to a new theory of unemployment, advanced by John Maynard Keynes. This chapter will explain Keynes' major theoretical proposition, that the economy may reach an equilibrium with large-scale unemployment. (The next chapter will outline Keynes' major policy proposals—namely, what the government can do to combat unemployment.)

Equilibrium in an economy is determined by aggregate supply and aggregate demand. To explain Keynesian theory, we begin where Keynes did, focusing on the horizontal section of the aggregate supply function (Fig. 8-5), where prices are

stable and where changes in spending lead to changes in real output. To determine how large national output will be, we need to know the aggregate quantity of goods and services demanded. Recall from Chapter 8 that aggregate demand is made up of four components:

1. Personal consumption expenditures.

2. Investment demand.

3. Government purchases of goods and services.

4. Net exports (that is, exports minus imports).

The basic point of Keynesian theory—that the economy may reach an equilibrium with large-scale unemployment—can be illustrated most easily in a simple economy with only the first two components: consumption and investment. This chapter describes such a simple economy. Government expenditures and net exports will be added in Chapter 10.

PERSONAL CONSUMPTION EXPENDITURES

Of all the components of total spending, personal consumption is by far the largest. In 1988, for example, personal consumption expenditures were $3.2 trillion (in current dollars), or about two thirds of total spending for goods and services in the United States.

People spend more when their disposable (after-tax) income increases; they can afford to spend more, and they do so. Figure 9-1 illustrates the relationship between consumption and disposable in-

come. The vertical axis measures consumption expenditures and the horizontal axis measures disposable income. (Both are measured in real terms, adjusted for inflation.) Each point on this diagram represents a single year. In 1982, for example, disposable income totaled $2,262 billion (measured horizontally), while consumption measured $2,051 billion (measured vertically). In 1933, disposable income was only $371 billion (in 1982 prices), and consumption was $379 billion (again, measured in 1982 prices).

Now let us consider a simple, imaginary economy with no government and no taxes, and with the relationship between consumption and dispos-

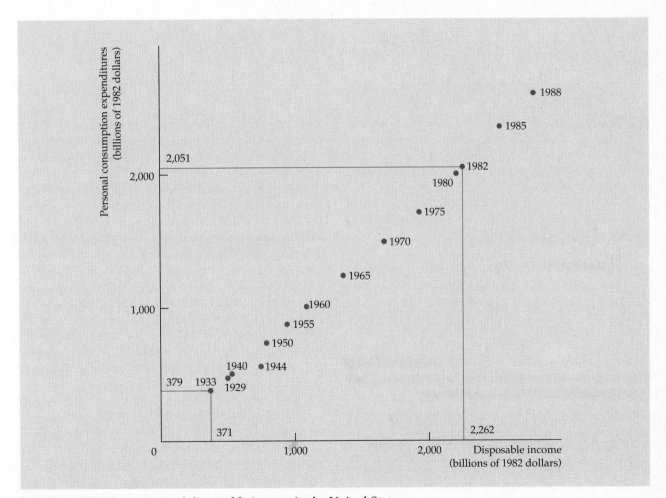

FIGURE 9-1   Consumption and disposable income in the United States, 1929–1988 (selected years).

Consumption depends on disposable income. As disposable income increases, so does consumption. (*Source:* U.S. Department of Commerce.)

TABLE 9-1 Consumption and Saving (billions of dollars at constant prices)

	(1) DI Disposable Income	(2) C Consumption	(3) Marginal Propensity to Consume $MPC = \dfrac{\Delta C}{\Delta DI}$	(4) S Saving (4) = (1) − (2)	(5) Marginal Propensity to Save $MPS = \dfrac{\Delta S}{\Delta DI}$
A	$ 500	$ 600		−100	
			$\dfrac{400}{500} = 0.8$		$\dfrac{100}{500} = 0.2$
B	1,000	1,000		0	
			$\dfrac{400}{500} = 0.8$		$\dfrac{100}{500} = 0.2$
C	1,500	1,400		+100	
			$\dfrac{400}{500} = 0.8$		$\dfrac{100}{500} = 0.2$
D	2,000	1,800		+200	

able income shown in Table 9-1. The numbers in this table are illustrated in Figure 9-2. For example, point A in Figure 9-2 corresponds to line A of the table. Disposable income is $500 billion, and consumption is $600 billion.

The relationship between consumption and disposable income is known as the **consumption function.**

The *consumption function* shows how consumption expenditures change when disposable income changes.

SAVING

From the numbers for consumption and disposable income, saving can be calculated. Saving is what people have left of disposable income after they make their consumption expenditures:

Saving = disposable income − consumption[1]   (9-1)

Using this equation, we can calculate saving in Table 9-1. For example, in line D, disposable in-

---

[1]More precisely, saving equals disposable income less consumption expenditures less interest paid by consumers, as noted in Chapter 6. However, when explaining the basic Keynesian theory, it is standard practice to ignore the interest complication and use the simplified equation shown here.

come is $2,000 billion and consumption is $1,800 billion. Saving is therefore $200 billion—the amount people have left over after their consumption expenditures.

Saving can also be derived from the consumption function in Figure 9-2. To show how, it is helpful to draw a 45° line from the origin. The 45° line has an important property: *Any point on it is the same distance from the two axes.* Consider, for example, an economy in which disposable income is $2,000 billion, as shown by the horizontal distance between the origin and point G in Figure 9-2. Then the vertical distance from G up to point H on the 45° line is also $2,000 billion. Thus this disposable income (*DI*) of $2,000 billion may be measured either along the horizontal axis from the origin to point G, or as the vertical distance from G up to the 45° line at H.

Saving is the vertical distance between the consumption function and the 45° line. When income is $2,000 billion (the height of the 45° line, *GH*), consumption is $1,800 billion (the height of the consumption function, *GD*). Saving is the difference, $200 billion (*DH*). This $200 billion is carried down to the **saving function** in Figure 9-3. At an income of $2,000 billion, saving is shown as the $200 billion height of point D.

If disposable income decreases to $1,000 billion

FIGURE 9-2 The consumption function (billions of dollars at constant prices).

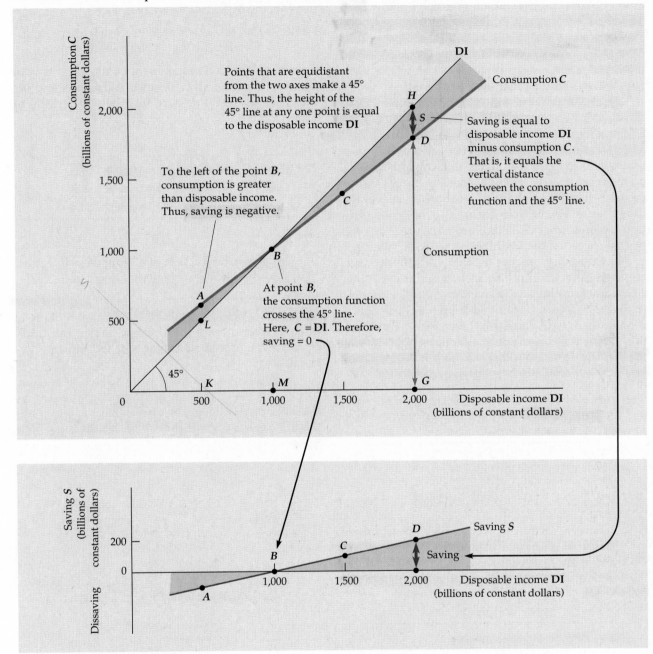

FIGURE 9-3 The saving function (billions of dollars at constant prices).

and we move to the left to point *M*, we can once again measure income as the height of the 45° line—in this case the height of point *B*. But *B* is also on the consumption function; thus the vertical distance to *B* also measures consumption. Therefore, at point *B*, *where the consumption function and the 45° line intersect*, consumption and disposable income are equal, and *saving is zero*. At corresponding point *B* in Figure 9-3, saving is shown as zero; point *B* is on the axis.

Suppose, now, that disposable income decreases even more, to $500 billion at point *K*. Now consumption *KA* is *more* than disposable income *KL*. Saving is negative; people on average *dissave*. This dissaving—distance *AL*—is carried down to the lower diagram, where point *A* is below the horizontal axis, showing that saving is negative.

How can that be? How can individuals possibly spend more than their incomes? The answer is by running into debt or by drawing on assets they have accumulated in the past. For the economy as a whole, it is extremely unlikely that consumers will, on average, dissave. But it is possible. In 1933, after incomes had fallen sharply, consumers on average did dissave. Recall from Figure 9-1 that consumption expenditures ($379 billion, measured in 1982 prices) exceeded disposable income ($371 billion).

In summary, saving is the vertical distance between the consumption function and the 45° line. The points on the saving function—*A*, *B*, *C*, and *D* in Figure 9-3—can be derived from the corresponding points *A*, *B*, *C*, and *D* on the consumption function. Thus, the consumption function (Fig. 9-2) and the saving function (Fig. 9-3) are *two alternative ways of illustrating precisely the same information.*

The *saving function* shows how saving changes when disposable income changes.

THE MARGINAL PROPENSITY TO CONSUME

As consumers' incomes increase, they spend more. The **marginal propensity to consume,** or MPC, measures how much more. Formally, the MPC is the fraction of *additional* disposable income that is consumed:

Marginal propensity to consume =
$$\frac{\text{change in consumption}}{\text{change in disposable income}} \qquad (9\text{-}2)$$

In abbreviated notation, this is written:

$$\text{MPC} = \frac{\Delta C}{\Delta DI} \qquad (9\text{-}3)$$

where Δ means "change in."

If we think of a small $1 increase in disposable income, the MPC can be written:

MPC = the fraction of a $1 increase in disposable income that is consumed

This is an obvious restatement of the idea: If your income increases by $1 and your consumption increases by $0.80 as a result, then your MPC is $0.80/$1.00 = 0.80.

Similarly,

Marginal propensity to save (MPS) =
$$\frac{\text{change in saving}}{\text{change in disposable income}} = \frac{\Delta S}{\Delta DI} \qquad (9\text{-}4)$$

Or:

MPS = the fraction of a $1 increase in disposable income that is saved

In passing, note that economists use the term *marginal* to mean "extra" or "additional." Thus, in later chapters, marginal revenue will mean additional revenue and marginal cost will mean additional cost.

In Figure 9-4, the MPC is illustrated. It is equal to the vertical change in consumption, divided by the horizontal change in disposable income. Thus *the MPC is equal to the slope of the consumption function.* Consequently, if the MPC is constant (as it is in

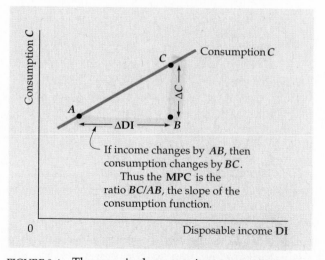

FIGURE 9-4 The marginal propensity to consume.

The slope of the consumption function equals the MPC. If the MPC is constant, the consumption function is a straight line.

our simple numerical example), then the consumption function has a constant slope; it is a straight line. Similarly, the MPS is the slope of the saving function.

In our example, the MPC is 0.8 and the MPS is 0.2 (Table 9-1, cols. 3 and 5). Observe that

$$MPC + MPS = 1 \qquad (9-5)$$

This must be the case. If a person gets $1 more in income, whatever is not consumed is saved. For example, if the MPC were only 0.75, an increase of $1 in income would lead to an increase of 75¢ in consumption. The remaining 25¢ would be saved; the MPS would be 0.25.

In our hypothetical example, the MPC of 0.8 is somewhat lower than the long-run MPC in the United States. Over long periods of time, U.S. consumers have increased their consumption expenditures by more than 90¢ for every $1.00 increase in disposable income. For example, in the four decades between 1948 and 1988, the increase in consumption was 92% of the increase in disposable income. However, in the short run, the response of consumption is less strong; it takes time for people to adjust to a change in income. An MPC of 0.8 may be taken as an approximation of the MPC during short-run business fluctuations. Appendix 9-A provides further details on the consumption function in the long run and the short.

THE SIMPLEST EQUILIBRIUM: AN ECONOMY WITH NO GOVERNMENT

Keynes' objective was to demonstrate that laissez-faire, market economies contain a fundamental defect: they may come to rest at a very high rate of unemployment. In order to explain this central proposition as clearly and as quickly as possible, we look at a bare-bones economy, with no international trade, no government spending, no taxes, no depreciation, and no retained corporate profits. In this very simple economy, GNP = NNP = national income = disposable income. In other words, all the receipts from the sale of national product flow through the business sector to become the disposable income of the household sector; there are none of the subtractions explained in detail back in Chapter 6.

The absence of government and international transactions means that there are only two groups to buy the final goods and services of the economy—households that buy consumption goods and businesses that invest in plant, machinery, and other types of capital. (We reiterate that, when macroeconomists write of investment, they mean acquisitions of new equipment, plant, housing, and additional inventories. They do not include financial investment, such as the purchase of stocks or bonds, or the acquisition of secondhand plant, equipment, or housing.)

To make the task even simpler, we initially assume that businesses spend a constant $200 billion for investment goods. We do not claim that this assumption is realistic. Indeed, as noted in previous chapters, investment is one of the most volatile components of GNP. Therefore, as soon as we complete the simple example, we will want to consider what happens when investment spending *does* change.

In Table 9-2 (col. 5) and in Figure 9-5, the $200 billion of investment spending are added to personal consumption expenditures to find **aggregate expenditures.** The term *aggregate expenditures* is used to show how spending depends on national product. The term *aggregate demand* is reserved for a different curve, which shows how the quantity demanded depends on the average level of prices—as illustrated in the last chapter (for example, Fig. 8-1).

The *aggregate expenditures* function shows how the aggregate quantity of goods and services demanded depends on national income or national product.

The *aggregate demand* function shows how the aggregate quantity of goods and services demanded depends on the average price level.

This idea—that quantity demanded can depend on both price and income—is not new. Chapter 4 pointed out that the quantity of an individual good demanded can depend on both price and income.

In Figure 9-5, observe that the horizontal axis and the 45° line show national product NP instead of the disposable income DI shown earlier in the consumption function (Fig. 9-2). In the simple economy studied here, disposable income equals national product (and NNP = GNP).

TABLE 9-2   Equilibrium National Product   (billions of dollars)

	(1) NP National Product (equals disposable income in this simple economy)	(2) C Consumption Expenditures	(3) S Saving (3) = (1) − (2)	(4) I* Desired Investment (assumed constant)	(5) AE Aggregate Expenditures = C + I* (5) = (2) + (4)	(6) Relation of Aggregate Expenditures (5) to National Product (1)		(7) Economy Will
H	$1,000	$1,000	0	$200	$1,200	Higher	⇓	Expand
J	1,500	1,400	100	200	1,600	Higher		Expand
K	2,000	1,800	200	200	2,000	Same		Stay at equilibrium
L	2,500	2,200	300	200	2,400	Lower	⇑	Contract
M	3,000	2,600	400	200	2,800	Lower		Contract

Equilibrium occurs when aggregate expenditures equal national product. Comparing columns 1 and 5 in Table 9-2, we see that equilibrium occurs at an output of $2,000 billion. The same equilibrium of $2,000 billion is shown in Figure 9-5 at point *E*, where the aggregate expenditures function cuts the 45° national product line.

To see why this is the equilibrium, observe that aggregate expenditures would not be sufficient to buy any larger output—say the $2,500 billion measured from the origin to point *L* on the horizontal axis and also vertically from *L* to point *N* on the 45° line. National product *LN* is made up of the dark blue line, plus the light blue line, plus the red line. Aggregate expenditures are less than that, however. They are just the dark blue line (consumer expenditures) plus the light blue line (investment demand). Thus, at an output of $2,500 billion, the amount we produce (national product) exceeds the quantity of goods and services that consumers and businesses want to purchase.

What happens to the excess production, shown by the red line? It remains unsold; it piles up on retailers' shelves and in warehouses. It represents **undesired inventory accumulation.** As unwanted goods accumulate, retailers, wholesalers, and other businesses cut back on their orders. Output falls and continues to contract as long as the aggregate expenditures line remains below the 45° national product line. In other words, output continues to fall until the economy reaches equilibrium E, where national product NP = aggregate expenditures AE and there is no further pressure of unsold goods. Therefore $2,000 billion is the equilibrium quantity of output.

At a disequilibrium quantity of national product, such as $2,500 billion, it is important to distinguish between **actual investment** and **desired investment.** Actual investment—the quantity that shows up in the official national product accounts in Chapter 6—includes all investment in plant, equipment, housing, and inventories, whether or not that investment is desired. Thus, for an economy producing at $2,500 billion, the investment figure that appears in the national product accounts will be the light blue line *plus* the red line. ("Red line goods" for which there is no demand, and which therefore pile up as **undesired inventory accumulation,** have clearly been produced during the year and must therefore be included in the national product statistics.) In contrast with actual investment, desired investment—also known as **planned investment** or **investment demand**—is only the investment which businesses want, that is, the light blue line. In order to preserve the important distinction between desired investment and

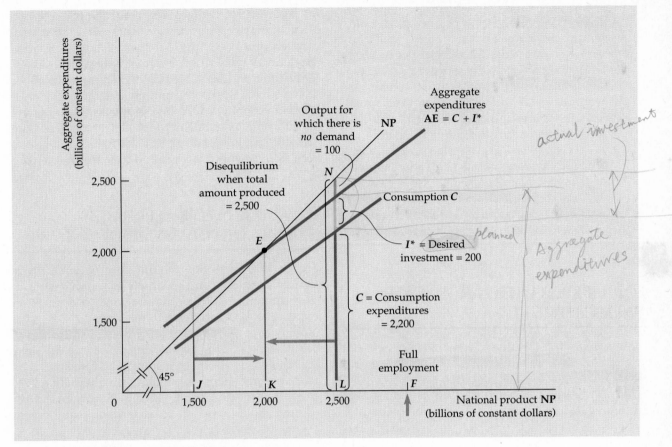

FIGURE 9-5   Equilibrium national product.

Point E represents equilibrium, with output of $2,000 billion. Here aggregate expenditures equal national product. A higher rate of production, such as $2,500 billion, is not stable, as we can see by looking at the line LN and its colored components. National product equals the vertical distance to the 45° line, that is, distance LN. For most of this product, there is a market. The quantity of consumer goods demanded is equal to the dark blue line. The quantity of investment goods demanded is equal to the light blue line. But for the red line, there is no demand. Unsold goods pile up in the warehouses. Businesses cut back on production. Output falls to its equilibrium of $2,000 billion.

actual investment, we use the symbol I^* with an asterisk to represent desired investment. As in Chapter 6, a plain I will stand for actual investment—that is, investment as shown in the GNP accounts.

Just as an output initially greater than equilibrium results in contraction, so an output initially less than equilibrium generates expansion. Consider an output of $1,500 billion, at point J. Here, the aggregate expenditures line is higher than the

45° national product line. Buyers want to purchase more goods than are currently being produced. Retailers and wholesalers find it difficult to keep goods in stock. Inventories are run down below their desired levels; there is an *undesired decrease in inventories*. Because retailers and wholesalers want to rebuild their inventories, they step up their orders. To fill their larger orders, manufacturers and other producers expand production toward the equilibrium, E.

Actual investment I is the amount of new plant, equipment, and housing acquired during a time period, plus the increase in inventories. All inventory accumulation is included, *whether or not the inventories were desired.*

Desired investment I*—also known as *planned investment* or *investment demand*—is the amount of new plant, equipment, and housing acquired during the period, plus *additions to inventories that businesses wanted to acquire.* It excludes undesired inventory accumulation.

Undesired inventory accumulation is actual investment (*I*) less desired investment (*I**)

Undesired decrease in inventories is equal to desired investment (*I**) minus actual investment (*I*). It exists when undesired inventory accumulation is negative.

EQUILIBRIUM WITH LARGE-SCALE UNEMPLOYMENT

Now we are in a position to illustrate Keynes' key contention, that the *equilibrium national product need not be at the quantity necessary to ensure full employment.* Equilibrium national product is determined by aggregate expenditures, as illustrated by point *E*

in Figure 9-5. On the other hand, the full-employment national product represents what the economy can produce with its current resources of labor, land, and capital; it is shown at national product *F*. The situation which Keynes feared, and which he believed would be a common outcome of a free-market economy, is the one shown in this diagram. Equilibrium national product at *E* is far less than the full-employment quantity at *F*. (See the quotation from Keynes which introduces this chapter.)

AN ALTERNATIVE APPROACH: SAVING AND INVESTMENT

Figure 9-5 shows how equilibrium national product is determined in the simple economy (with no government, etc.) by putting together consumption expenditures *C* and desired investment *I**. We have already seen, however, that the saving function is an alternative way of presenting *exactly the same information* as in the consumption function. It is therefore not surprising that, as an alternative to *C* plus *I**, we can bring saving *S* together with desired investment *I** to determine equilibrium

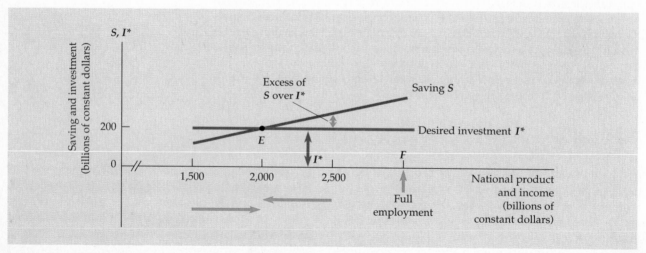

FIGURE 9-6   The equilibrium of saving and desired investment.

Equilibrium occurs at output of $2,000 billion, where saving = desired investment. At a greater national product, such as $2,500 billion, disequilibrium exists. Because the leakages from the spending stream (in the form of saving) are greater than the injections (in the form of investment), national product falls toward its equilibrium at $2,000 billion.

national product. This is done in Figure 9-6. In the simple economy, *equilibrium occurs when saving equals desired investment*—that is, at point *E* where national product is $2,000 billion. We may confirm in Table 9-2 that saving (col. 3) equals desired investment (col. 4) at the same $2,000 billion equilibrium output at which aggregate expenditures (col. 5) equal national product (col. 1).

THE CIRCULAR FLOW OF EXPENDITURES: LEAKAGES AND INJECTIONS

To explain *why* equilibrium occurs when saving equals investment demand, it is helpful to call again on the circular flow of payments previously used in Chapter 6. Figure 9-7 shows an extremely simple economy in which there is no desired investment and in which consumers buy all the goods produced. Suppose that producers sell $1,000 billion of goods during an initial period. In turn, they pay this $1,000 billion to households in the form of wages, salaries, rents, and other incomes, as shown in the lower loop of the diagram. Suppose, more-

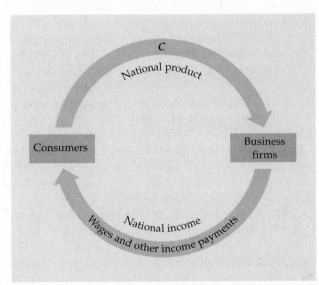

FIGURE 9-7   The simplest circular flow of payments. (All income is spent for consumer goods and services.)

The simplest economy is one in which people consume all their income. Income is used to buy consumer goods and services. In turn, the receipts from the sale of consumer goods and services are again paid out as income, in the form of wages, salaries, and so on. Once more, people use all their income to buy consumer goods and services. Round and round the payments go.

over, that the households turn around and spend all their $1,000 billion of income on consumer goods in the upper loop. Once more, the producers sell $1,000 billion in goods and services, and once more they pay out this amount in incomes to the households. Round and round this $1,000 billion of payments go; national product is stable at this level.

Now let us introduce complications, starting with saving. Suppose that instead of consuming all their incomes of $1,000 billion, people decide they would like to save $100 billion. They spend only $900 billion on consumer goods. Producers have made $1,000 billion in goods, but they sell only $900 billion. Unsold goods pile up, and producers cut back on production. When they do so, they pay out less in wages and other incomes. The circular flow of national product and income shrinks. Thus saving represents a leakage from the circular spending stream; it acts as a drag on national product and income.

Now, consider investment demand. Suppose that businesses decide to increase their capital stock and that they order $100 billion worth of machinery. In response to the demand, $100 billion of machinery is produced. The machinery companies pay out the $100 billion in wages, salaries, and other incomes. Incomes rise, people consume more, and the circular flow of national product and income increases. Investment therefore acts as a stimulus to national product and income.

THE EQUILIBRIUM OF SAVING AND DESIRED INVESTMENT

In terms of their effect on aggregate expenditures and output, saving and investment have offsetting effects. Saving is a **leakage** from the circular spending stream; an increase in the desire to save leads to a decrease in national product. Investment represents an **injection** into the circular spending stream; an increase in desired investment leads to an increase in national product. Equilibrium exists when the forces of contraction and expansion are in balance—that is, when saving equals desired investment. In Figure 9-6, this happens at point *E*, where national product is $2,000 billion.

At any greater national income, such as $2,500 billion, the leakage from the circular flow of spending—in the form of saving—exceeds the injection of investment spending, and output decreases. If, on the other hand, national product is initially at a

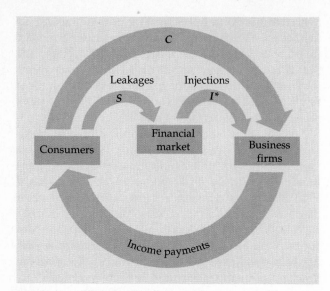

FIGURE 9-8 The circular flow, with saving and investment.

Investment expenditures work to broaden the spending stream. Leakages into saving narrow it. Equilibrium is reached when leakages from the stream (saving) are equal to injections (investment).

point to the left of the $2,000 billion equilibrium, the injection of investment spending exceeds the leakage into saving and national product increases. This can be visualized in Figure 9-8: when more investment is pumped in, the income flow becomes greater. The larger flow causes more leakages into saving at the other side. (When income increases, so does saving.) The flow stabilizes when the injections and leakages are equal.

Some saving and investment decisions are made by the same people. For example, business executives may decide not to pay dividends. Instead, they may save their profits in order to have the funds to invest in more equipment. In this case, the decision to save can be closely tied to the decision to invest. Sometimes, however, saving and investment decisions are made by different groups. Households may save to send their children to college or for retirement; they save without investing. (Remember that here we are talking about real investment—the purchase of new buildings or equipment—and not about the acquisition of bonds or bank accounts.) Investment decisions are made

principally by business executives. They buy additional plant and equipment when their profit prospects are good, even though they may have to borrow to do so. In this case, they invest more than they save. The question that therefore arises is, what forces bring saving and investment into equilibrium?

Here, there is a sharp difference between Keynesian economics and classical economics. In Keynes' view, the separation of saving and investment decisions means that *there is no assurance that, if an economy begins at full employment, desired investment will be as great as saving.* If it is not—as illustrated at full-employment output *F* in Figure 9-6—then national product will decrease and unemployment will result. In other words, national income will fall by a sufficient amount to make saving equal to desired investment.

In classical economics, there is an alternative mechanism that can equate saving and desired investment—namely, the *interest rate.* (Appendix 9-B provides details on how the interest rate is determined in the financial market.) In a nutshell, the main point is this. Classical economists believed that, if saving were plentiful, savers would be eager to lend; they would bid down the interest rate. As a result, businesses would be able to finance their investment projects more cheaply, and they would therefore decide to invest in more plant and equipment. The interest rate would continue to fall and desired investment would increase, until saving and investment were brought into equality—at full employment. Keynes was skeptical that financial markets would work this well. Consumers might want to save more than business executives wanted to invest. The result would be a contraction in output and large-scale unemployment, as illustrated in Figure 9-6.

The two approaches in Figures 9-5 and 9-6 are exact equivalents; either diagram can be derived from the other. To summarize, the condition for equilibrium can be stated in several different ways:

1. Equilibrium exists when national output is equal to aggregate expenditures. This is the **output-expenditures approach** to determining equilibrium and is illustrated by point *E* in Figure 9-5.

2. Equilibrium exists when actual investment *I* equals desired investment *I**—that is, when inventories are at their desired level. There is no undesired change in inventories, such as that shown by the red line in Figure 9-5.

3. Equilibrium exists when saving and desired investment are equal, as illustrated by point *E* in Figure 9-6. This is the **leakages-injections approach.**

These three statements are different ways of expressing the same basic point.

The reason for unemployment may be stated in two alternative ways. There will be an *unemployment equilibrium* if

1. Aggregate expenditures shown in the line AE are too low to buy the full-employment quantity of national product NP. For example, at full-employment point *F* in Figure 9-5, the aggregate expenditures line is below the 45° NP line.

2. The injections of desired investment are less than the leakages into saving when national product is at the full-employment quantity. For example, at full-employment point *F* in Figure 9-6, *I** is below *S.*

CHANGES IN DESIRED INVESTMENT: THE MULTIPLIER

Investment is a flighty bird.

J. R. HICKS

The basic Keynesian diagrams (Figs. 9-5 and 9-6) illustrate how the economy can reach an equilibrium at less than full employment. They can also be used to illustrate how economic activity can change, with the economy periodically moving from boom to recession and back.

During the business cycle, investment is quite unstable. Consider what happens if desired investment increases. Suppose that business executives become more optimistic about the future. They will plan to expand their operations, undertaking more investment in plant and equipment. Suppose, specifically, that desired investment increases by $100 billion.

The results are shown in Figure 9-9. When the increase in desired investment is added, the aggregate expenditures function shifts upward by $100 billion, from AE$_1$ to AE$_2$. Equilibrium once more occurs where aggregate expenditures and national

product are equal—that is, where the new aggregate expenditures function AE$_2$ cuts the 45° line at *H*. Thus the increase in desired investment moves the equilibrium from *E* to *H*. Observe that something very important has happened. The equilibrium national product has increased *by $500 billion, which is far more than the $100 billion increase in investment demand.*

How can that be? The answer is this. As businesses build more factories and order more equipment, people are put to work producing factories and equipment. They earn more wages. As their incomes rise, they increase their consumption expenditures. Thus the nation produces not only more capital goods, such as factories and equipment, but *also* more consumer goods. National product rises by more than investment. Specifically, as the equilibrium moves from *E* to *H*, national product increases by $500 billion. This sum includes not only the $100 billion increase in investment spending on capital goods (shown as ΔI^* in Fig. 9-9), but also an increase of $400 billion in spending on consumer goods (shown as ΔC). These are the additional goods consumers buy as their incomes rise, and they accordingly move along the consumption function from *G* to *R*.

The $100 billion increase in desired investment therefore has a *multiplied* effect on national product. The relationship between the increase in national product and the increase in desired investment is known as the *investment multiplier*, or, more simply, as the **multiplier.** Formally, it is defined:

$$\text{Multiplier} = \frac{\text{change in equilibrium national product}}{\text{change in desired investment}} = \frac{\Delta NP}{\Delta I^*} \qquad (9\text{-}6)$$

In our illustration, equilibrium national product rises by $500 billion when desired investment increases by $100 billion. Therefore the multiplier is 5.

THE MULTIPLIER PROCESS: A MORE DETAILED LOOK

The multiplier process may be better understood by looking in more detail at what happens when there is an additional $100 billion of investment

FIGURE 9-9   The multiplier.

With an MPC = 0.8, a $100 billion increase in investment demand causes a $500 billion increase in national product.

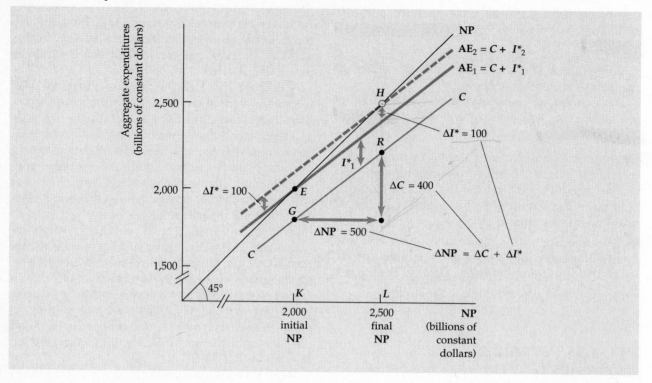

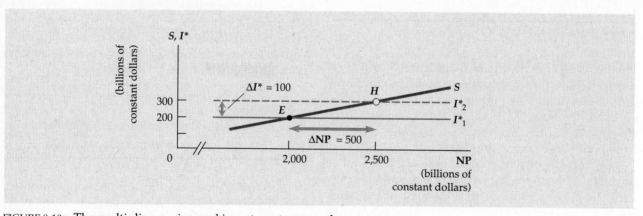

FIGURE 9-10   The multiplier: saving and investment approach.

With an MPS = 0.2, an increase of $100 billion in desired investment (from I^*_1 to I^*_2) causes an increase of $500 billion in national product.

expenditures on capital goods. The *direct impact* is a $100 billion increase in national product; more machines and other capital goods are produced. This is not the end of the story, however. The $100 billion spent for plant and equipment goes in the form of wages, rents, profits, and other incomes to those who provide the resources used to produce the capital goods. In other words, disposable incomes are $100 billion higher. (Remember, we are dealing with a highly simplified economy in which there is no government to take a tax bite.) Consumers now spend most of this increase in their disposable income, with the precise amount depending on their marginal propensity to consume (MPC). For example, if the MPC is 0.8, consumers are induced to spend $80 billion more, as shown in

the "second round" increase in the national product in Figure 9-11.

Again, this is not the end of the story. When consumers spend $80 billion more for clothing, food, and other consumer goods, that $80 billion in spending becomes income for producers. Thus the incomes of textile workers, farmers, and others who produce these consumer goods rise by $80 billion. With an MPC of 0.8, these people spend $80 billion × 0.8 = $64 billion. Once more, national product has risen, this time by $64 billion. The story goes on and on, with each round of consumer spending giving rise to another, smaller round.

Observe that, with an MPC = 0.8, the total spending resulting from each dollar of initial investment expenditure forms the series $1x(1 + 0.8

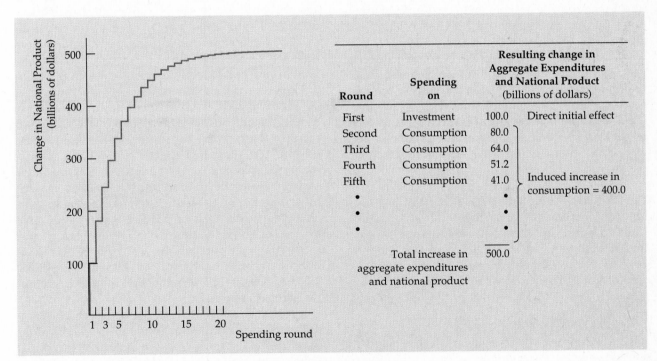

Round	Spending on	Resulting change in Aggregate Expenditures and National Product (billions of dollars)	
First	Investment	100.0	Direct initial effect
Second	Consumption	80.0	
Third	Consumption	64.0	
Fourth	Consumption	51.2	
Fifth	Consumption	41.0	Induced increase in consumption = 400.0
•		•	
•		•	
•		•	
Total increase in aggregate expenditures and national product		500.0	

FIGURE 9-11   The multiplier process: The buildup of national product.

This figure portrays the various rounds of spending that result from an initial increase of $100 billion in investment in round 1. Notice how national product builds up toward its equilibrium increase of $500 billion.

$+ 0.8^2 + 0.8^3 \ldots$). It can be shown[2] that the sum of such a series is:

$$\$1 \left(\frac{1}{1 - 0.8} \right) = \$5 \qquad (9\text{-}7)$$

That is:

$$\begin{pmatrix} \text{initial } \$1 \\ \text{increase in} \\ \text{investment} \end{pmatrix} \begin{pmatrix} \text{multiplier} \\ \text{of } 5 \end{pmatrix} \begin{pmatrix} \text{eventual} \\ \text{increase in} \\ \text{national product} \end{pmatrix}$$

In this case, because the MPC is 0.8, the multiplier is 5. More generally:

$$\text{Multiplier} = \frac{1}{1 - \text{MPC}} = \frac{1}{\text{MPS}} \qquad (9\text{-}8)$$

Thus the size of the multiplier depends on the size of the MPC—that is, on the slope of the consumption function. The steeper the consumption function—that is, the higher the MPC—the larger the multiplier.

Observe also how Figure 9-11 confirms Figure 9-9. Both show that a $100 billion increase in investment causes a $500 billion increase in national product. This $500 billion is made up of the original $100 billion increase in investment, plus $400 billion in *induced* consumption that occurs as people spend more when their disposable incomes rise.

The Multiplier Works Both Ways. We have just seen how an increase in investment (of $100 billion) leads to a multiplied increase in national product (of $500 billion). The multiplier works in a similar way when investment decreases. For example, a "first round" reduction of $100 billion in invest-

ment causes a direct reduction of $100 billion in national product and income. Because of the $100 billion fall in their incomes, consumers will cut their spending by $80 billion in the "second round." They will buy fewer books, shirts, or movie tickets. This in turn will reduce the incomes of authors, textile workers, and movie producers. As a result, their consumption will fall, and, as in the earlier example, there will be a series of "rounds." The sum of all these rounds will be a $500 billion decrease in national product.

THE MULTIPLIER: THE SAVING-INVESTMENT APPROACH

Just as the saving-investment diagram may be used to show an unemployment equilibrium, so it may also be used to illustrate the multiplier. This is done in Figure 9-10, which once again provides exactly the same information as the diagram above it. When desired investment increases by $100 billion, from I^*_1 to I^*_2, equilibrium moves from E to H. Once again, observe that national product increases by more than the initial increase in investment. Indeed, income increases until people are willing to increase their saving by the full $100 billion injected into the spending stream by the new investment. People are not willing to increase their saving by this $100 billion until their incomes have increased by $500 billion. Remember: their marginal propensity to save (MPS) is $\frac{1}{5}$; they only save $1 out of every additional $5 they earn. Thus, from this other perspective, we confirm that equilibrium income rises by $500 billion. (Appendix 9-C provides a further elaboration of the saving-investment approach.)

With the saving-investment approach, the multiplier may be defined in terms of the MPS rather than the MPC. To do so, first note that income is either consumed or saved. Therefore:

$$\text{MPS} = 1 - \text{MPC} \qquad (9\text{-}9, \text{ from } 9\text{-}5)$$

Thus Equation 9-8 can be rewritten:

$$\text{Multiplier} = \frac{1}{\text{MPS}} \qquad (9\text{-}10)$$

It should be emphasized that output increases by the amount shown in Equation 9-10—or in similar Equation 9-8—*only in the very simple economy considered so far.*

---

[2]Let c stand for the MPC. As long as c is less than 1 (in our case, 0.8), then the sum of the series

$$1 + c + c^2 + c^3 \ldots = \frac{1}{1 - c}$$

This can be shown by actually doing the division on the right side. In other words, divide 1 by $(1 - c)$, as follows:

$$\begin{array}{r} 1 + c + c^2 \ldots \\ 1 - c \overline{)1} \\ \underline{1 - c} \\ c \\ \underline{c - c^2} \\ c^2 \ldots \end{array}$$

In practice, the increase in real national product will be smaller than indicated by Equations 9-8 and 9-10 because of two complications:

1. Part of the increase in spending may show up in terms of *higher prices*, rather than in terms of a larger real national product. prices↑ ΔC↓ MPC↓

2. *Taxes* and *imports* act as additional leakages from the spending stream. These additional leakages depress the size of the multiplier, even in a world in which prices are stable.

The second point will be explored in Chapter 10. In this chapter, we look at the first.

THE MULTIPLIER WHEN PRICES CHANGE

The Keynesian multiplier model was developed as a way of explaining how output and employment can change as spending changes. In the simple form presented thus far, an increase in spending shows up entirely as an increase in real national product. This means that the economy is moving along the horizontal section of the aggregate supply curve, where prices do not change.

WHEN PRICES ARE CONSTANT

Figure 9-12 illustrates this fixed-price case and shows how the aggregate expenditures approach of this chapter is related to the aggregate demand–aggregate supply approach of the previous chapter.

Panel *a* repeats the idea of the multiplier. A $100 billion increase in investment leads to a $100 billion upward shift of the aggregate expenditure line and to a $500 billion increase in output as equilibrium moves from *E* to *H*.

Panel *b* shows the corresponding points of equilibrium in an aggregate demand–aggregate supply diagram. The initial increase of $100 billion in investment spending, plus the induced increase of $400 billion in consumer spending, mean that the aggregate demand curve shifts to the right by $500 billion. National product also increases by $500 billion, as equilibrium moves from *E* to *H*.

Observe that an increase in desired investment leads to an *upward* shift in the aggregate expendi-

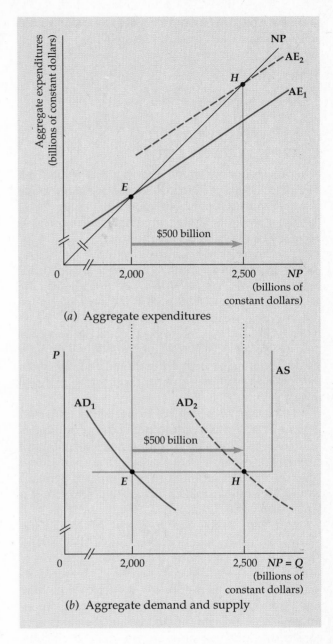

(a) Aggregate expenditures

(b) Aggregate demand and supply

FIGURE 9-12   The economy with rigid prices.

The upper panel repeats the multiplier idea in Figure 9-9. A $100 billion increase in investment spending causes a $500 billion increase in output.

The lower panel shows what's happening with the aggregate demand/aggregate supply approach. As expenditures increase, the aggregate demand function shifts to the right by $500 billion and equilibrium output increases from *E* to *H*. The full $500 billion in additional spending shows up as a $500 billion increase in real output.

ture line AE (panel *a*) and to a *rightward* shift of the aggregate demand curve AD (panel *b*).

CHANGING PRICES: EQUILIBRIUM WITH AN UPWARD-SLOPING AGGREGATE SUPPLY CURVE

Once the economy enters the range at which the aggregate supply function slopes upward, price changes can no longer be ignored. In Figure 9-13, the lower panel—showing what happens to prices—becomes an essential part of the story.

The lower panel again shows how the aggregate demand curve shifts to the right by $500 billion. However, point *H* can no longer be the equilibrium because it is not on the aggregate supply curve. Instead, the new equilibrium is at *K*, where AD$_2$ and AS intersect. Part of the $500 billion increase in aggregate demand shows up as a $300 billion increase in real national product, with the remainder showing up in terms of an increase in prices (from P_1 to P_2).

The extent to which spending will be reflected in prices rather than output depends on the slopes of the aggregate supply and aggregate demand curves. For example, if the aggregate supply curve AS were steeper, an increase in aggregate demand would generate a smaller increase in output and a larger increase in prices.

Now let's double back to see what's happening in the upper aggregate expenditures diagram in Figure 9-13. *H* can no longer be the equilibrium, since part of the additional spending is being dissipated in terms of higher prices. As prices rise, there will be a smaller increase in aggregate real expenditures—the amount of goods and services that consumers and investors are buying. Specifically, the rise in prices will mean that real spending, as measured by the aggregate expenditures line, will rise to only AE$_3$ rather than AE$_2$. The result will be an equilibrium at *K*.

Finally, it is possible that all the additional spending will show up entirely in terms of higher prices, not additional output. This will happen if the aggregate supply curve is vertical. In this case, an increase in investment spending will not cause any increase in real output at all. The AE curve won't rise at all but will remain at AE$_1$.

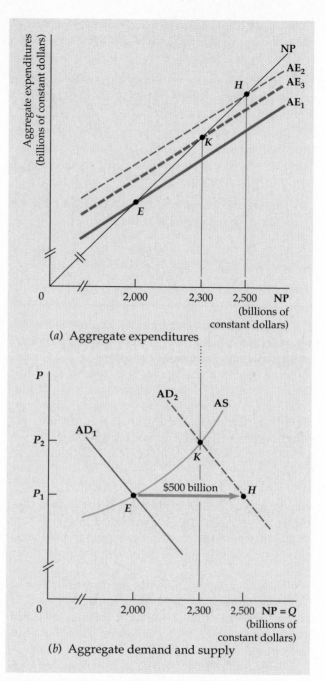

(*a*) Aggregate expenditures

(*b*) Aggregate demand and supply

FIGURE 9-13   An upward-sloping aggregate supply curve.

If, in the lower panel, the aggregate supply curve slopes upward, then a rightward shift of $500 billion in the aggregate demand curve will not cause a full $500 billion increase in output. Equilibrium moves to *K*, not *H*.

Because spending is dissipated in paying higher prices, real expenditures in the upper panel rise only from AE$_1$ to AE$_3$. The new equilibrium is at *K* in both panels.

KEY POINTS

1. During the Great Depression of the 1930s, British economist John Maynard Keynes introduced a new theory of unemployment, arguing that

(a) A market economy can come to rest at an equilibrium with large-scale unemployment.

(b) The cause of unemployment is insufficient aggregate demand.

(c) The most straightforward cure for unemployment is an increase in government spending. (This point will be studied in Chapter 10.)

2. The components of aggregate demand are:

(a) Personal consumption expenditures.

(b) Investment demand—that is, the demand for buildings, equipment, and additional inventories.

(c) Government purchases of goods and services.

(d) Net exports (that is, exports minus imports).

3. This chapter explains the Keynesian theory of an unemployment equilibrium in a simple economy with only two types of spending for final goods, namely, consumption and investment.

4. Consumption expenditures depend primarily on disposable personal income. As incomes rise, people consume more. The change in consumption, as a fraction of a change in disposable income, is known as the *marginal propensity to consume* (MPC).

5. The *aggregate expenditures* function shows how the aggregate quantity of goods and services demanded depends on national income or national product. In contrast, the *aggregate demand* function shows how the aggregate quantity of goods and services demanded depends on the average price level.

6. Equilibrium national product occurs when the aggregate expenditures function cuts the 45° line. A larger national product would be unsustainable, because expenditures would fall short of production and unsold goods would pile up in inventories.

7. In Keynesian theory, equilibrium national product may be less than the full-employment quantity.

8. There are several alternative ways of stating the condition for equilibrium. It exists when

(a) Aggregate expenditures and national product are equal—that is, when the aggregate expenditure function cuts the 45° national product line (Fig. 9-5).

(b) Inventories are at their desired level—that is, when actual investment equals desired investment and there is no undesired buildup or reduction in inventories (Fig. 9-5).

(c) Desired investment and saving are equal (Fig. 9-6).

9. An increase in desired investment raises national product and income, and induces people to consume more. In the simple economy, real national product increases by the rise in investment times the multiplier, where the multiplier is:

$$\text{Multiplier} = \frac{1}{1 - \text{MPC}}$$

Because saving equals income minus consumption,

$$\text{Marginal propensity to save} = 1 - \text{MPC}$$

Thus the multiplier in the simple economy may alternatively be expressed as:

$$\text{Multiplier} = \frac{1}{\text{MPS}}$$

10. In practice, the increase in real national product will be smaller than indicated by these two multiplier equations because of several complications:

(a) Part of the increase in spending may show up in terms of *higher prices*, not in terms of larger real national product.

(b) *Taxes* and *imports* act as additional leakages from the spending stream. (This point will be explained in Chapter 10.)

11. If the aggregate supply function slopes upward to the right, only part of any increase in aggregate demand shows up in terms of larger output. Part goes to pay higher prices.

KEY CONCEPTS

consumption function

saving function

45° line

marginal propensity to consume (MPC)

marginal propensity to save (MPS)

aggregate expenditures

desired or planned investment (I^*)

actual investment (I)

undesired inventory accumulation

saving-investment approach

circular flow of spending

leakage

injection

output-expenditures approach

leakages-injections approach

multiplier

PROBLEMS

9-1. Draw a diagram showing the consumption function, the aggregate expenditures function, and the 45° line. What quantity of NP represents the equilibrium? Explain why a smaller NP would lead to an increase in output.

9-2. The consumption function and the saving function are two alternative ways of presenting the same information. The text explains how the saving function can be derived from the consumption function. Draw a saving function first and then show how the consumption function can be derived from it.

9-3. Draw a diagram showing desired investment and the saving function. What is the equilibrium national product? Explain why a higher national product would be unsustainable. Also explain why national product will expand, if it initially is smaller than the equilibrium quantity.

9-4. The mathematical formula for the multiplier shows that a high MPC causes a high multiplier. By tracing the effects of $100 billion in additional investment through a number of "rounds" of spending, show that the multiplier is higher with an MPC of 0.9 than with an MPC of 0.8. (As a starting point, refer to the table beside Figure 9-11.)

9-5. On a sheet of graph paper, draw a large diagram similar to Figure 9-10, showing the multiplier effects of a $100 billion increase in investment

demand when the MPS = 0.2. Now suppose that the MPS increases to 0.5. Draw in a new savings function, going through the same initial equilibrium E. When investment demand increases by $100 billion, what is the new equilibrium national product? What is the size of the multiplier now?

9-6. What is the difference between actual investment (I) and desired investment (I^*)? What happens if desired investment is greater than actual investment? Why?

9-7. Consider an economy with the relationship between consumption and income shown in the table below.

Disposable Income = NP ($ billions)	Consumption ($ billions)	Saving ($ billions)	Initial Aggregate Expenditures ($ billions)	Later Aggregate Expenditures ($ billions)
1,000	900			
1,100	975			
1,200	1,050			
1,300	1,125			
1,400	1,200			
1,500	1,275			
1,600	1,350			
1,700	1,425			
1,800	1,500			

(a) Fill in the blanks in the Saving column.

(b) What is the MPC? The MPS?

(c) Investment demand is originally $200 billion. Fill in the blanks in the Initial Aggregate Expenditures column.

(d) What is the equilibrium national product?

(e) Now assume that desired investment rises to $300 billion. What does this do to aggregate expenditures? (Fill in the Later Aggregate Ex-penditures column.) What is equilibrium national product now?

(f) Comparing your answers to *d* and *e*, find the multiplier.

9-8. Redraw Figure 9-13 with a vertical, "classical" aggregate supply curve. Now suppose businesses spend $100 billion more on plant and equipment. In both panels of this diagram, show what happens to equilibrium real national product.

CONSUMPTION IN THE SHORT RUN AND THE LONG RUN

Over long periods, consumption responds strongly to increases in disposable income. The consumption function is steep, and the marginal propensity to consume (MPC) is more than 0.9. However, during short-run periods when disposable income is fluctuating, consumption responds more weakly; the MPC is smaller.

The distinction between the short-run and long-run consumption function is illustrated in Figure 9-14. During periods when incomes increase slowly and steadily, consumption moves up along the steep long-run consumption function C_L, along path F, G, H. However, as incomes fall during recessions, consumption does not retreat from H back toward G. Rather, it declines less sharply, following the short-run consumption function C_{s1} from H toward D. Then, as the economy recovers, consumption again follows the relatively flat consumption function from D back toward H.

Consumers will then respond to a continued expansion by moving from H to K. Another downswing into recession will once again result in a movement along a relatively flat short-run consumption function—in this case, along C_{s2} toward R. In brief:

1. The long-run consumption function is steep, with an MPC of more than 0.9. Over long periods of time, saving is quite small and stable as a fraction of disposable income. The long-run consumption function is a straight line going through the origin.

2. During the business cycle, the consumption function is flatter. (An MPC of 0.75 or 0.8 is a reasonable number to use when talking about an average recession.) As time passes, the short-run consumption function shifts upward from C_{s1} to C_{s2}, and so on.

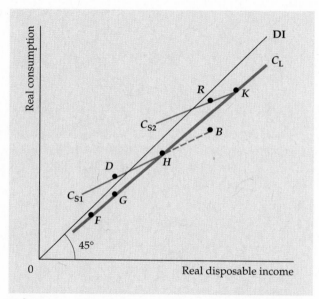

FIGURE 9-14 The long-run and short-run consumption functions.

The short-run consumption function is flatter than the long-run function. During a recession, consumption moves to the left along a short-run consumption function. Over time, the short-run consumption function shifts upward.

Economists have identified some of the important variables that can affect consumption, and explain the upward shift of the short-run consumption function.

TIME

One explanation emphasizes that consumers are creatures of habit; it takes *time* for them to adjust to a new standard of living. This is particularly true in a recession. Consumers have gotten used to the good life. Even though their incomes are decreasing, they try to maintain their standards of consumption; they do not cut back consumption sharply.[3] This explains the relatively flat short-run consumption function. It also explains why the function can shift upward. Over time, people gradually get used to their higher incomes and consume more.

EXPECTATIONS

Another explanation is based on the view that consumers do not simply look at their current disposable incomes when deciding how much to spend. Rather, they take their expected future incomes into account, too. Thus, for example, students often dissave—for a very good reason. They will have higher incomes in the future, and it will be easier to save then. A second example occurs during a recession, when people recognize that their current incomes are unusually low. They expect higher incomes in the future, and therefore they save little or nothing.

According to this view, consumption depends not simply on current income, but on expected normal income—or *permanent income*, to use Milton Friedman's label.[4] As time passes, people come to expect higher incomes; the short-run consumption function shifts upward.

---

[3]This explanation was suggested by Harvard's James Duesenberry in his early study, *Income, Saving, and the Theory of Consumer Behavior* (Cambridge, Mass.: Harvard University Press, 1949).

[4]Milton Friedman, *A Theory of the Consumption Function* (Princeton, N.J.: Princeton University Press, 1957). When he wrote this book, Friedman was a professor at the University of Chicago.

WEALTH

Wealth also causes an upward shift of the short-run consumption function. Wealth and income are not synonymous. For example, a retired person may have a small income and yet still own considerable wealth. This person is likely to consume more than current income, running down wealth in the process.

For the economy as a whole, wealth has gradually increased as more capital has been accumulated. This increase in wealth has caused a gradual upward shift of the short-run consumption function.

The classical theory explained in Chapter 8 is a variation on this theme. According to the classical view, consumers are strongly influenced by a particular type of wealth—namely, the wealth they hold in the form of money balances.

It is now standard practice for economists to use a consumption function that includes both wealth and "permanent income."

Finally, two details might be noted. A recession may be very deep, ending in a depression. In this case, consumers may move a considerable distance to the left along the short-run consumption function. They may reach a point to the left of the 45° line, such as D in Figure 9-14, where consumption exceeds disposable income. This in fact happened at the depth of the depression in 1933.

On the other hand, an upswing may be very strong, ending in a boom. Then the upward momentum may take consumers along short-run consumption function C_{s1} from D to H and all the way to B, to the right of the long-run consumption function. Here, consumers are saving a large percentage of their incomes. It makes sense for them to do so because the boom conditions may not last. Consumption was furthest to the right of the long-run consumption function in 1944, at the height of the wartime boom in the U.S. economy. In that year, consumption was also kept down because few consumer durables were available; auto companies were producing tanks, not cars.

APPENDIX 9-B
CLASSICAL ECONOMICS
Equilibrium With Full Employment

Chapter 8 described the main difference between Keynesian and classical theories. Although classical economists believed that equilibrium occurs at full employment, some of them conceded that large-scale unemployment could occur temporarily, as a result of disturbances. However, market forces would move the economy back toward its equilibrium with full employment.

This chapter has explained the revolutionary idea in Keynes' *General Theory*, that there could be an equilibrium with large-scale unemployment. The purpose of this appendix is to look in more detail at the contrasting classical argument.

The main point in the classical case was explained in Chapter 8, especially Figure 8-3. In the face of large-scale unemployment, prices fall, increasing the real quantity of money. Because households have more purchasing power at their disposal, they buy more goods and services. This process continues until full employment is restored.

SAVING AND INVESTMENT

There was, however, also a second strand to the classical theory of full employment, related to the Keynesian theory of saving and investment studied in this chapter. Like Keynes, classical economists recognized that desired investment and saving would have to be equal for the economy to be in equilibrium. But unlike Keynes (Fig. 9-6), they did not believe that real national product would have to decrease if desired investment was less than saving.

Rather, classical economists argued that the price mechanism will bring desired investment and saving into equilibrium at full employment. The key price that does this is the interest rate. The interest rate is the reward received by savers, and it is also the price corporations and others pay for borrowed funds with which they construct buildings or engage in other investment projects.

Suppose that, when the economy is at full employment, desired investment falls short of sav-

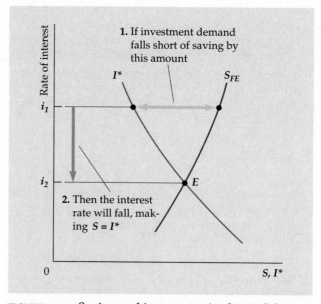

FIGURE 9-15 Saving and investment in classical theory.

The S_{FE} curve shows how much will be saved at various interest rates in a fully employed economy. The I^* curve shows how much businesses will borrow to finance investment projects at various interest rates. Classical economists argued that if saving exceeded investment demand, the interest rate would fall until saving and investment were equalized—without large-scale unemployment.

ing. Savers have large quantities of funds. In their eagerness to acquire bonds and other earning assets, they are willing to settle for a lower interest rate. As the interest rate falls, businesses find it cheaper to borrow, and they are encouraged to undertake more investment projects. In other words, desired investment increases. The rate of interest continues to drop until desired investment and saving are brought into equality, as illustrated in Figure 9-15. Full employment is maintained.

In other words, classical economists argued that there was something wrong with Keynes' plumbing. Savings do not simply leak from the economy; rather, an increase in saving causes a fall in interest rates, which in turn causes an increase in investment. Thus the financial markets, where savers supply funds to investors, provide a connection between saving and investment in Figure 9-8 (page 144); they provide a mechanism that brings saving leakages back into the spending stream in the form of investment demand.

THE KEYNESIAN REBUTTAL

In response, Keynes said that classical economists were in error when they counted on the interest rate to fall enough to equate saving and investment at full employment. In his *General Theory* (p. 182), he argued that there is "no guarantee" that the full-employment saving curve intersects investment demand "anywhere at all" when the interest rate is positive. This possibility is illustrated in Figure 9-16. Here, no full-employment equilibrium exists, since I^* and S_{FE} intersect at a negative interest rate. However, it is not possible for interest rates to fall below zero, since people would be unwilling to lend money; they would simply lock it up in a bank vault instead. Keynes went one step further and argued that the minimum interest rate is not zero but at some positive rate, shown as i_{min} in Figure 9-16.

Now, if the economy were temporarily at full employment, saving would exceed desired invest-

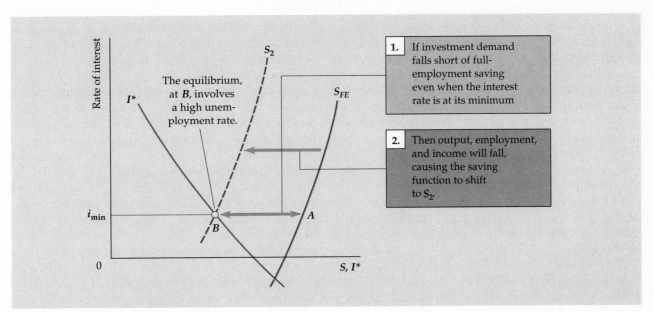

FIGURE 9-16   The Keynesian rebuttal.

Keynes argued that there was something wrong with the classical approach to saving and investment illustrated in Figure 9-15. Specifically, he said that the full-employment saving curve (S_{FE}) might intersect the investment demand curve I^* at an interest rate below the minimum (i_{min}) which can occur in financial markets. In this case, the gap AB between saving and investment demand cannot be closed by a fall in the interest rate. It is closed by a fall in output, causing the saving function to shift to S_2.

ment by quantity *BA*. Being at a minimum, the interest rate cannot fall to bring saving and investment demand into equilibrium. Something has to give. According to Keynes, the things that will give will be output and employment. As leakages into saving exceed injections of investment spending, national product and employment will decrease. With smaller incomes, people will save less; the saving function in Figure 9-16 will shift to the left, all the way to S_2. Now there is an equilibrium because saving and investment demand are equal. However, there is large-scale unemployment at this equilibrium.

Incidentally, Figure 9-16 is based on the only diagram in Keynes' *General Theory* (on p. 180). Clearly, Keynes felt strongly about the classical idea that a change in the interest rate would bring saving and investment into equality at full employment.

The differences between Keynes and the classical economists may be summarized as follows. Classical economists argued that *an increase in saving,* by depressing interest rates, *causes an increase in investment* and thus stimulates growth. As such, saving is a benefit to society; it makes us better off in the future. In contrast, Keynes argued that this isn't necessarily so. Saving may be antisocial. It may decrease national product and employment (a possibility explored in Appendix 9-C). Furthermore, Keynes believed that it is more correct to argue that *a change in investment demand causes a change in saving* (Fig. 9-10 page 146) than to argue, as the classical economists did, that a change in the desire to save causes a change in investment. Thus, said Keynes, classical economists had gotten the relationship between saving and investment backwards. Because of their confusion, they had overlooked the possibility that the economy might reach an equilibrium with a high rate of unemployment.

In rebuttal, classical economists fell back on their general price mechanism to explain why the economy would reach equilibrium at full employment—an argument already explained in Chapter 8. To recapitulate, they said that, in the face of large-scale unemployment, prices would fall. This decline would increase the purchasing power of money; the real quantity of money would rise. As a result, people would buy a greater quantity of goods and services. This process would continue

until full employment was restored. Because this process was described by Cambridge professor A. C. Pigou, the idea that an increase in the real quantity of money will cause an increase in purchases is sometimes known as the *Pigou Effect.* Alternatively, it is known as the *real balance effect,* because it is the proposition that people will buy more when their real money balances increase.

In summary, classical economists counted on price flexibility to help to restore full employment in *two* ways.

1. *General* price flexibility, illustrated in Chapter 8, Figure 8-3. In the presence of large-scale unemployment, prices would fall, restoring full employment.

2. Flexibility of a *specific* price, namely, the interest rate. If saving exceeded desired investment when the economy was at full employment, the interest rate would fall, bringing saving and investment into equality (Fig. 9-15).

SAY'S LAW

There was also a third, less precise proposition in classical theory, known as *Say's law,* after nineteenth-century economist J. B. Say.

Say proposed the disarmingly simple idea that *supply creates its own demand.* When people sell a good or service, they do so in order to be able to buy some other good or service. The very act of supplying one good or service thus creates a demand for some other good or service. There can be too much supply for some specific product, such as shoes, but, if so, there is too much demand and not enough supply of some other product. Surpluses and shortages can exist in an *individual* market. Nevertheless, for the economy as a whole, there cannot be an excess of supply over demand.

Keynes put his finger on the problem with Say's simple idea. When people create goods and services, it is true that they earn income. The income from the production of all the goods and services is sufficient to buy those goods and services. The problem is that people do not spend all their incomes; they save part of it. Therefore, demand can fall short of production. This shortfall may be offset by investment demand. However, if investment demand is less than full-employment saving, there will be an overall inadequacy of demand and unemployment will result.

Therefore Say's law is a weak foundation on which to build the idea that the economy will provide full employment. Say simply assumed that people would spend all their income; his theory provided no mechanism for restoring full employment. In contrast, the main body of classical theory *did* provide two mechanisms: the general flexibility of prices (point 1, above), and the flexibility of the interest rate (point 2).

Say's law should not be considered the main classical defense against the Keynesian idea of an unemployment equilibrium. Indeed, Say's law is inconsistent with the main body of classical economics. According to Say's law, there can be no excess of supply over demand, *regardless of the general price level.* However, according to the more sensible version of classical theory presented in Chapter 8, the supply of output will exceed demand whenever the average level of prices is above equilibrium. The demand for national output will be equal to its supply only when the price level is at equilibrium (as explained earlier in Fig. 8-3).

APPENDIX 9-C

CHANGES IN THE DESIRE TO SAVE
The Paradox of Thrift

Keynesian theory explains how equilibrium national product NP changes if there is a change in desired investment—as we saw in Figure 9-10. Now let's consider what happens if the saving function shifts upward—or, what amounts to the same thing, the consumption function shifts downward.

Suppose that people become more thrifty, and they save more out of any given income. This causes the saving function to shift upward from S_1 to S_2 in Figure 9-17. Consider what happens at the initial national product, A, as a result. The leakage into saving (AG) now exceeds the injections in the form of desired investment (AE_1). National product therefore decreases to its new equilibrium, B, where saving and desired investment are again equal. In this simple case in which desired investment is horizontal, an increase in the desire to save has no effect on the equilibrium quantity of saving or investment. The amount saved and invested is the same at BE_2 as it was originally at AE_1. The only effect is a decrease in output.

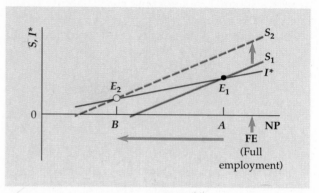

FIGURE 9-18 The paradox of thrift.

With the investment function sloping upward to the right, an increase in the desire to save results in a movement from E_1 to E_2. In equilibrium, the quantity of saving decreases, since E_2 is not as high as E_1.

That is not the worst of it, however. In order to simplify the analysis, desired investment has been assumed to be constant thus far. Clearly, that need not be the case; desired investment can change. Specifically, it may increase as NP increases. As more goods are produced, there is a need for more machines and factories. In this case, desired investment slopes upward, as shown in Figure 9-18.

Now a shift in the saving function becomes particularly potent. An increase in the desire to save, moving the saving function from S_1 to S_2, causes a very large decrease in equilibrium national product from A to B. Furthermore, the effects on the equilibrium amount of saving and investment are paradoxical. *As a result of the upward shift in the saving function,* observe that *the amount of saving and investment in equilibrium falls,* from distance AE_1 to BE_2. This is the **paradox of thrift.**

What happens is this: Beginning at the initial equilibrium E_1, an increase in the desire to save causes an increase in leakages from the spending

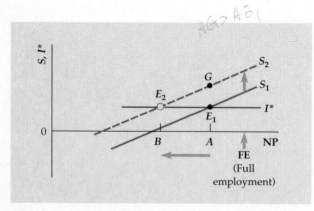

FIGURE 9-17 An increase in the desire to save.

An increase in the desire to save does not increase equilibrium saving. Instead, it results in a decrease in output.

160

stream and output falls. Accordingly, businesses decide they need fewer machines and factories. There is a decline in the quantity of investment as the economy moves to the left along the investment function. Equilibrium is restored only when national product has fallen enough so that people are content to save an amount that is no more than the diminished quantity of investment, at point E_2. Because the quantity of investment decreases as national product falls, and because national product must fall by enough to bring saving into equality with investment, saving declines in the move from E_1 to E_2.

The *paradox of thrift* occurs when an increase in the desire to save (a shift from S_1 to S_2) causes a fall in actual saving (from AE_1 to BE_2).

The paradox of thrift illustrates how macroeconomic conclusions—covering the economy as a whole—may be quite different from conclusions for a single individual. If a single individual becomes more thrifty, saving more out of any level of income, then he or she will end up with more saving. But we cannot conclude that, just because this is true for a single individual, it will also be true for the economy as a whole. Such a conclusion would be an illustration of the **fallacy of composition.** Figure 9-18 depicts a case in which the results for the society as a whole are exactly the opposite from the results for an individual: for the society, a stronger effort to save means less actual saving.

The *fallacy of composition* involves the unwarranted conclusion that a proposition true for a single individual or single market is necessarily true for the economy as a whole.

The paradox of thrift is part of Keynesian theory, whose underlying assumptions should be reemphasized at this point. The Keynesian analysis *deals with the situation in which there is large-scale unemployment.* The economy is on the horizontal section of the aggregate supply function; *changes in spending lead to changes in output and no change in prices.*

If, on the other hand, the economy is experiencing booming demand conditions and is in the inflationary vertical range of the aggregate supply function, the Keynesian analysis of thrift must be completely reversed. The macroeconomic problem is eased by an increase in the desire to save—that is, by a downward shift in the consumption function. As consumption and aggregate demand fall, inflationary forces are weakened. Furthermore, since the economy is at full employment and is therefore fully utilizing its resources, a decrease in consumption releases resources from the production of consumer goods. These resources become available for the production of capital goods. Thus an increase in the willingness to save indeed adds to the amount of factories and machinery produced; the real saving of society is augmented. *In a world of inflationary excess demand, the paradox of thrift does not hold.*

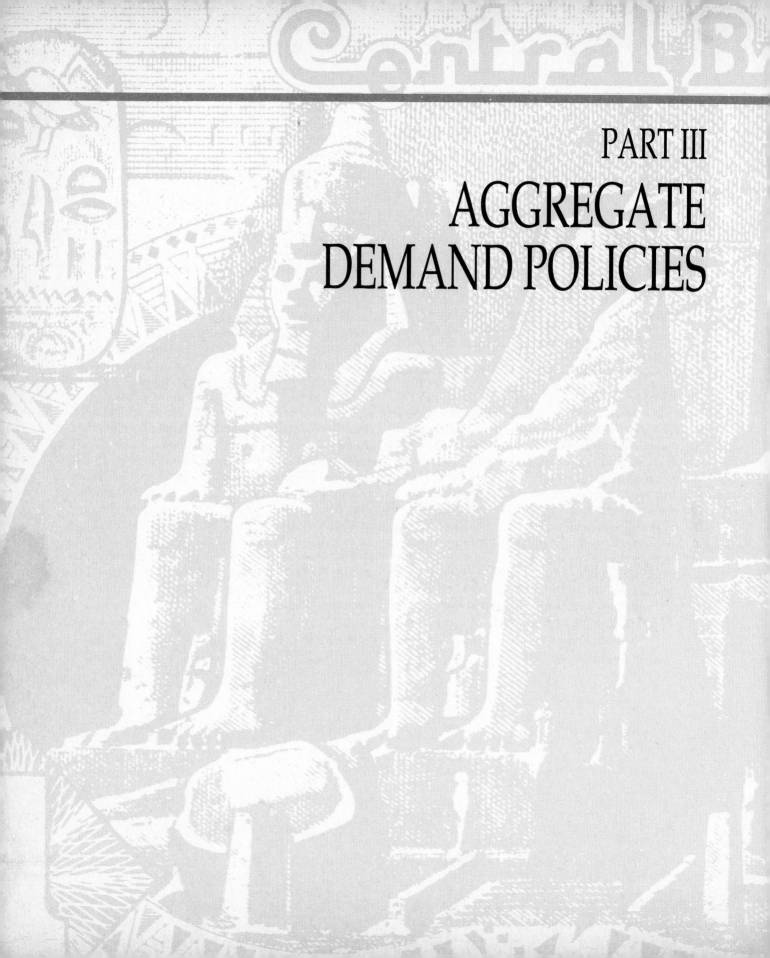

PART III
AGGREGATE DEMAND POLICIES

Recessions and depressions are caused by a fall in spending. Inflation is caused by too much spending.

To combat depressions or recessions, governments can stimulate aggregate demand. Two aggregate demand policies are available:

■ *Fiscal policy*—that is, changes in government spending or tax rates (Chapter 10).

■ *Monetary policy*—that is, a change in the rate of growth of the money stock (Chapters 11 and 12).

If the government increases its spending for projects such as roads or dams, it directly increases the demand for cement, steel, and other materials. Aggregate demand increases.

If taxes are cut or the money supply is increased, the public is encouraged to spend. Again, aggregate demand increases.

CHAPTER 10
FISCAL POLICY

Fiscal policy has to be put on constant . . . alert. . . . The management of prosperity is a full-time job.

WALTER W. HELLER
CHAIRMAN, COUNCIL OF ECONOMIC ADVISERS, 1961–1964

Recessions and depressions are caused by too little spending. By taking steps to increase aggregate spending during a recession or depression, the government can increase the amount of national product and put the unemployed back to work. At other times, aggregate demand is increasing too rapidly; the economy is at full employment and prices are rising. By restraining aggregate demand, the government can slow the inflation.

The government can use two major policy tools to influence aggregate demand: *fiscal policy* and *monetary policy*. The purpose of this chapter is to study the first of these, fiscal policy.

A change in fiscal policy occurs when the government changes its spending programs or when it alters tax rates. In the bare-bones economy discussed in Chapter 9, the government was completely ignored; there was no government spending or taxation. In order to study fiscal policy in simple steps, we first introduce the effects of government spending; we will ignore taxes until a later point.

GOVERNMENT PURCHASES

Like investment and consumption expenditures, government purchases of goods and services are a component of aggregate expenditures. Once government spending is added to the bare-bones economy of Chapter 9, aggregate expenditures become:

Aggregate expenditures (AE) =
consumption expenditures (C)
+ desired investment (I*)
+ government purchases of goods and services (G)

Government expenditures for goods and services (G) can be added vertically to consumption and desired investment to get the aggregate expenditures line shown in Figure 10-1. Note that when government purchases of $100 billion are added vertically to consumption expenditures plus desired investment, the equilibrium moves from point D to point E. The increase in national product, measured by the $500 billion distance AB on the horizontal axis, is a multiple of the $100 billion of government spending. *The multiplier process works on government spending* just as it worked on investment spending. For example, when workers receive income from building roads, a whole series of spending and respending decisions is set in motion. The workers spend most of their wages for consumer goods such as clothing and cars. Additional employees are hired by the clothing and automobile industries, and these employees also spend more as a consequence of their rising incomes. The process is similar to that illustrated in the last chapter, when investment increased.

In spite of government spending, aggregate expenditures may nevertheless still fall short of

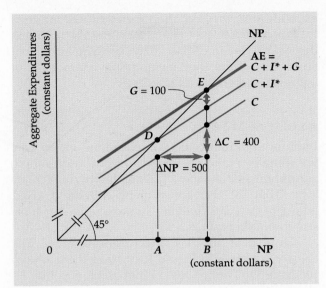

FIGURE 10-1   Equilibrium with government spending.

Government spending is added vertically to consumption and investment demand in order to get aggregate expenditures: AE = $C + I^* + G$. Observe that the multiplier process works on government expenditures. Without government spending, the equilibrium would be at point D (as we saw in Chapter 9). With government spending, the equilibrium is at E. The increase in national product (AB = $500 billion) is a multiple of the $100 billion of government spending. As people's incomes rise, they move along the consumption function, consuming $400 billion more.

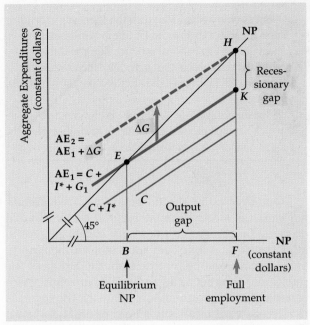

FIGURE 10-2   Fiscal policy for full employment.

At initial equilibrium E, there is large-scale unemployment; national product B falls far short of the full-employment national product at F. To reach full employment, government spending (G_1) should be increased by HK, the amount of the recessionary gap. This will shift aggregate expenditures up to AE_2 and move the economy to a full-employment equilibrium at H. Note that HK, the recessionary gap, is the vertical distance between the aggregate expenditures line (AE_1) and the 45° line, measured at the full-employment national product.

what is needed for full employment. This was the case during the depression of the 1930s. This situation is illustrated in Figure 10-2, where equilibrium E is far to the left of the full-employment national product.

If the economy is to reach full employment, aggregate expenditures must shift upward. One way for this shift to take place is by an increase in government spending. The question is, how much more government spending is needed to restore full employment? Observe that at the full-employment quantity of national product (F), the aggregate expenditures function (AE_1) falls below the 45° line by distance HK. This is known as the **recessionary gap.**

In order to get to full employment, the aggregate expenditures function must be shifted up by the amount of the recessionary gap, HK. Thus HK is the amount of additional government purchases that are needed. Hence we come to the first and

most important rule of thumb for fiscal policy:

> **By increasing its purchases of goods and services by the amount of the recessionary gap, the government can eliminate the gap and move the economy to full employment.**

When the government increases its spending, once again the multiplier process is at work. In Figure 10-2, note that an increase of government spending equal to the recessionary gap (HK) causes output to increase by an even larger amount, BF—that is, by enough to eliminate the output gap and restore full employment. We can put the same point another way: Because of the multiplier, the output gap (BF) is larger than the recessionary gap (HK, the amount of government spending needed to restore full employment).

A *recessionary gap* exists when the aggregate expenditures function is below the 45° line at the full-employment quantity of national product. The gap is the vertical distance from the aggregate expenditures line up to the 45° line, measured at full-employment national product.

The *output gap*—or *GNP gap*—is the amount by which national product falls short of the full-employment quantity. It is measured along the horizontal axis.

One final point should be emphasized. *For the full impact of the multiplier to occur, it is essential that taxes not be increased to pay for the additional government spending.* As we will soon see, an increase in taxes would remove income from the hands of the public and thus act as a drag on consumption. With consumption discouraged in this way, the increase in aggregate expenditures would be smaller than it would be if tax rates were kept stable.

This, then, is a key policy conclusion of Keynesian economics: During a depression, when a large increase in aggregate expenditures is needed to restore full employment, *government spending should not be limited to the government's tax receipts.* Spending should be increased without increasing taxes. But if taxes are not raised, how is the government to finance its spending? The answer is, by borrowing—that is, by adding to the public debt. *Deficit spending is not unsound during a depression.* On the contrary, it will stimulate aggregate expenditures and reduce unemployment.

At other times, aggregate demand is too large; the economy is at full employment and prices are rising. In such circumstances, the appropriate government policy is one of restraint. By keeping its spending down, the government can reduce inflationary pressures.

TAXES

There is one difference between a tax collector and a taxidermist—the taxidermist leaves the hide.

MORTIMER CAPLIN,
FORMER COMMISSIONER OF THE INTERNAL REVENUE SERVICE

Government spending is only one side of fiscal policy; the other is taxation. Although taxes do not show up directly as a component of aggregate expenditures, they do affect expenditures indirectly. When people pay taxes, they are left with less disposable income, and they consequently consume less. Thus the consumption component of aggregate expenditures is reduced.

A LUMP-SUM TAX

In order to introduce tax complications one by one, we initially make an unrealistic but very simple assumption—that taxes (*T*) are levied in a *lump sum*. That is, the government collects a fixed amount—say, $100 billion—in taxes *regardless of the size of national product.*

How does this tax affect consumption? The answer is shown in Figure 10-3. After the tax, people have $100 billion less in disposable income. As a consequence, their consumption declines. By how much? With a marginal propensity to consume (MPC) of 0.8, they consume $80 billion less. They also save $20 billion less. Thus the $100 billion fall in disposable income is reflected in a $20 billion decline in saving and a $80 billion decline in consumption.

This $80 billion decrease in consumption is carried over to Figure 10-4. Point *B* on the after-tax consumption function C_2 is $80 billion below *A*. Similarly, every other point on the original con-

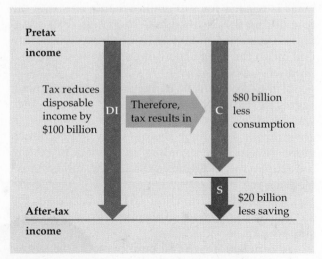

FIGURE 10-3   A tax depresses consumption.

If the MPC is 0.8, a $100 billion tax reduces consumption by $80 billion and saving by $20 billion.

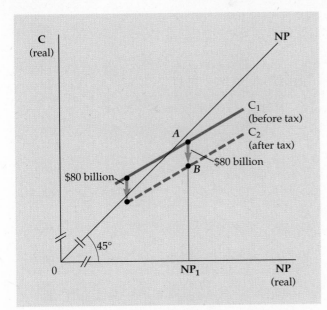

FIGURE 10-4   Effect of a $100 billion lump-sum tax.

If the MPC is 0.8, a lump-sum tax of $100 billion causes the consumption function to shift down by $80 billion—that is, the tax times the MPC.

sumption function also shifts down by $80 billion. The new after-tax function is parallel to the original consumption function but $80 billion lower. In general:

> **A lump-sum tax causes the consumption function to shift down by the amount of the tax times the MPC.**

When taxes are increased and the consumption function shifts downward, the aggregate expenditures line likewise shifts downward. Thus, when aggregate expenditures are too high and prices are rising, an *increase* in taxes is the appropriate policy step. On the other side, a *cut* in taxes represents a *stimulative* policy; the reduction in taxes will increase disposable income and shift the consumption function and aggregate expenditures *upward*.

Note that a change in taxes is almost as powerful a tool for controlling aggregate expenditures as a change in government purchases of goods and services—almost, but not quite. An increase of $100 billion in government purchases causes aggregate expenditures to shift upward by the full $100 billion. However, a decrease in taxes of $100 billion

shifts aggregate expenditures up by only $80 billion—that is, $100 billion times the MPC.

Because government purchases of goods and services are more powerful, dollar for dollar, than a change in taxes, there is reason to turn to government purchases when major changes are desired in aggregate demand. During the early Keynesian period, economists did concentrate on government purchases in their fiscal policy recommendations. However, since 1962, tax changes have become a more prominent way to manage aggregate demand. Thus President John F. Kennedy's program to "get the economy moving again" included a $10 billion cut in taxes. In 1968, a temporary tax surcharge was imposed to reduce the inflationary pressures associated with the Vietnam War and the Great Society's spending programs. In early 1975, taxes were cut in order to stimulate the economy, which was suffering from the worst recession since the 1930s. (Not all tax changes, however, are aimed primarily at managing demand. The tax cuts enacted in 1981 were aimed at the "supply side." Specifically, they were intended to increase the incentives to produce. In practice, however, they had an important effect on aggregate demand. Their timing was fortunate: They helped to stimulate the recovery from the deep recession of 1982. The "supply side" will be considered later.)

Tax changes have become an important component of fiscal policy because

1. A tax cut is generally *less controversial* than an increase in government spending as a way of stimulating the economy. This is true in part because of skepticism over the government's ability to spend money wisely and because of fears that the government will grow bigger and bigger.

2. Tax changes may be put into effect *more quickly* than changes in government spending. For example, an increase in spending for highways, government buildings, dams, or other public works requires considerable planning, which takes time.

To summarize the policy conclusions thus far:

1. *To stimulate aggregate demand* and thus combat unemployment, the appropriate fiscal policy is an increase in government spending and/or a cut in taxes—that is, *steps that increase the government's deficit* or reduce its surplus.

2. *To restrain aggregate demand* and thus combat

inflation, the appropriate fiscal policy is a cut in government spending and/or an increase in taxes—that is, *steps that move the government's budget toward surplus.*

> A rising government deficit acts as a stimulus to aggregate demand. A reduction in the government's deficit, or an increase in its surplus, acts as a drag.

ADDING REALISM: A PROPORTIONAL TAX

These two important policy conclusions have been illustrated by studying a simple lump-sum tax that was $100 billion no matter what national product might be. However, this tax isn't realistic. Actually, tax collections rise and fall with national income and national product. This is obviously true of income taxes; the more people earn, the more taxes they pay. It is also true of sales taxes: If national product and total sales rise, government revenues from sales taxes likewise rise.

We may take a giant step toward realism by discarding the lump-sum tax and instead studying a tax that does rise and fall with national product. The tax we will consider is a **proportional tax**—that is, a tax yielding revenues that are a constant percentage of national product.

As we saw in Figure 10-4, a lump-sum tax shifts the consumption function down by a constant amount. However, the effects are different with a proportional tax. If national product doubles, tax collections likewise double, and the depressing effects on the consumption function also double. For example, suppose there is a 20% proportional tax. At national product NP_1 in Figure 10-5, this tax depresses consumption from point B to D. If national product is twice as great at NP_2, this same tax depresses consumption by twice as much—from K to L.

Of course, a 30% tax depresses consumption even more than a 20% tax. Thus consumption function C_3 lies below C_2. In general, the heavier the tax, the more the consumption function rotates clockwise, as shown in Figure 10-5.

Note two important effects of a proportional tax:

1. It *lowers* the consumption function. On this first

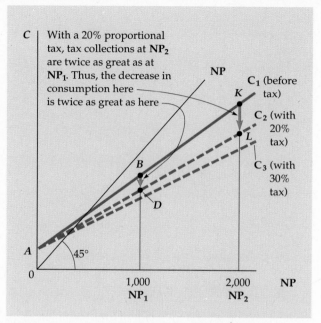

FIGURE 10-5   A proportional tax: Effect on consumption.

When a proportional tax is imposed, the consumption function rotates clockwise around point A. The higher the tax rate, the more the consumption function rotates. As the tax rate rises from 20% to 30%, the consumption function becomes *lower* and *flatter.*

point, then, a proportional tax is similar to a lump-sum tax.

2. It makes the consumption function *flatter* than in a tax-free economy. On this second point, a proportional tax is different from a lump-sum tax. (A lump-sum tax doesn't affect the slope of the consumption function.)

TAXES REDUCE THE SIZE OF THE MULTIPLIER

When taxes make the consumption function flatter, they reduce the size of the multiplier. (Chapter 9 explained that the size of the multiplier depends on the slope of the consumption function.) Moreover, taxes can make the multiplier *much* smaller. Recall that, with no taxes and an MPC of 0.8, the multiplier was 5. When a proportional tax of 25% is imposed, the multiplier drops sharply, to only 2.5.

To see why, suppose investment increases by $100 million. This is the initial injection; it represents the "first round" of the multiplier process. National product goes up by the full $100 million in investment. What happens in the second round?

Because of the 25% tax, each dollar of investment results in an increase of only 75¢ in disposable income. With an MPC of 0.8, consumers spend 60¢. This 60¢ is the "second round" of spending. Each successive round is likewise 60% of the previous round. For each $1 initial increase in investment, this gives total spending of $1(1 + 0.6 + 0.6² + 0.6³ + . . .). Applying Equation 9-7 from the previous chapter,[1] we find the sum of this series:

$$\frac{1}{1 - 0.6} = \$2.50$$

Thus the multiplier is only 2.5.

INJECTIONS AND LEAKAGES

The previous chapter explained a very simplified economy, with only consumption and investment and no government sector or international transactions. Such an economy reaches equilibrium when the injections into the spending stream, in the form of investment spending, are just equal to the leakages from the spending stream, in the form of saving.

---

*[1] In an economy with taxes (but still with no international trade), the formula for the multiplier is:

$$\text{Multiplier} = \frac{1}{s + t - st}$$

where

> s is the marginal propensity to save
>
> t is the marginal tax rate—that is, the change in tax collections as a fraction of the change in national product

We do not derive this equation in this book. However, you can use it to confirm that, when $s = 0.2$ and $t = 0.25$, the multiplier is 2.5.

A similar proposition still holds in a more complex economy; equilibrium still exists when injections and leakages are equal. However, as the economy becomes more complex, additional leakages and additional injections occur.

Specifically, government spending is an injection into the spending stream, similar to investment spending. When the government spends more for roads or buildings, the producers of these roads and buildings earn higher incomes, and their consumption consequently rises.

On the other side, taxes represent a leakage, similar to saving. Income taken in taxes cannot be used by the public for consumption expenditures. Because taxes are a leakage, they reduce the size of the multiplier.

EXPORTS AND IMPORTS

International transactions make things more complicated. There is one more injection and one more leakage.

Exports are the injection. Larger exports of wheat or computers add to U.S. national product. Farmers and workers on the computer assembly-line have larger incomes, and they consequently step up their consumption expenditures. Thus the multiplier process is set in motion by additional exports, as well as by an increase in investment or government spending.

Imports are the leakage, and they make the multiplier even smaller. Consider what happens if IBM builds a new factory. This investment is the initial injection. In the "first round," national product goes up by the full amount of the factory. What is the "second round" effect?

Because the government takes a slice in taxes—say, 25%—only 75¢ of each dollar spent to build the factory gets into the hands of consumers as disposable income. Of this 75¢, consumers save, say, one fifth (15¢), leaving only 60¢ in consumption. Not all of this amount is spent on U.S. goods and services, however. A portion—say, 10¢—goes to purchase imported goods. As a result, the "second round" increase in national product is only 50¢ for each initial injection of $1.

At this second round, one half of each $1 in income leaks out into taxes, saving, and imports;

only 50¢ is spent by consumers for domestically produced goods. Similarly, in later rounds of spending, one half is consumed and one half leaks out of the domestic spending stream. For each $1 in initial injection, this gives a sum of all rounds equal to:

$$\$1(1 + 0.5 + 0.5^2 + 0.5^3 + \dots)$$

Using Equation 9-7 once more, we find:

$$\text{Sum} = \$1\left(\frac{1}{1 - 0.5}\right) = \$2.00$$

Therefore, the multiplier in this example is 2.

In an economy with international transactions:

1. The multiplier is smaller because of the additional leakage into imports.[2]

2. Equilibrium once again occurs when total injections equal total leakages. Specifically, when:

$$I^* + G + X = S + T + M$$

where:

I^* is desired investment

G is government expenditures for goods and services

X is exports

S is saving

T is tax collections

M is imports

---

[2]Advanced texts derive the formula for the multiplier in an economy with taxes and international trade:

$$\text{Multiplier} = \frac{1}{s + t + m - st}$$

where

s is the marginal propensity to save

t is the marginal tax rate

m is the marginal propensity to import—that is, the change in imports as a fraction of the change in national product

Obviously, the multiplier is becoming complicated. There is one simplification that may help. In all cases:

$$\text{Multiplier} = \frac{1}{\text{marginal rate of leakages}}$$

The larger are leakages, the lower is the multiplier.

Because one country's imports represent another's exports, international trade has contrasting effects on the two trading partners. An expansion originating in the United States causes an increase in our imports, weakening our upswing. Because our imports represent the exports of another country, such as Mexico, the economy of that country expands: Mexican employment and output rise because Americans buy more Mexican goods. Although imports weaken our upswing, they create an expansion elsewhere. *Prosperity spreads across international boundaries.* Similarly, a recession in one country has a depressing effect on incomes elsewhere. If U.S. income falls, Americans buy less from Mexico, reducing output and employment in that country.

AUTOMATIC STABILIZERS

Because taxes and imports lower the size of the multiplier, they make the economy more stable. In an economy with a high tax rate and a high propensity to import, the multiplier is small. Therefore a fall in desired investment causes only a moderate decline in national product. On the other side, a runaway boom is less likely in such an economy, because so much of the increase in income leaks away into taxes and imports.

Tax revenues that vary with national product are a **built-in stabilizer** or **automatic stabilizer.** The way that taxes act to stabilize the economy is illustrated in Figure 10-6. In this example, taxes (T) are just adequate to cover government expenditure (G) when the economy is at the initial national product NP_1; the budget is balanced ($G = T$). Now suppose the economy slips into a recession, with national product decreasing to NP_2. Tax collections fall, and the budget automatically moves into deficit. This fall in tax collections helps to keep aggregate expenditures up: Disposable income is left in the hands of the public, and consumption therefore falls less sharply. As the government's budget moves into deficit, it provides stimulus to the economy and thus reduces the downward momentum. Similarly, the tax system acts as a restraint on an upswing. As national product increases, tax collections rise. The government's budget moves toward surplus, and the upward movement of the economy is slowed.

An *automatic stabilizer* is any feature of the economic system that reduces the strength of recessions and/or the strength of upswings in demand, *without policy changes being made.*

An automatic stabilizer should be distinguished from a *discretionary policy action,* such as a cut in tax *rates* or the introduction of new government spending programs.

The degree of automatic stabilization from the tax system depends on how strongly tax payments respond to changes in national product. That is, it depends on the *marginal tax rate* for the economy as a whole—the fraction of an increase in national product that is paid in taxes. The greater the marginal tax rate, the steeper is the taxation function (T) in Figure 10-6 and the stronger the automatic stabilization.

Some government expenditures may also provide automatic stabilization (not shown in Fig. 10-6). As the economy slides into a recession, there is an automatic increase in government spending for unemployment insurance benefits and for welfare. The additional government spending sustains

disposable income and therefore slows the downswing.

Automatic stabilizers reduce the severity of economic fluctuations. However, they do not eliminate them. The objective of discretionary fiscal policy is to reduce the fluctuations even more.

TWO COMPLICATIONS

The tendency of the government's budget to swing automatically into deficit during recessions, and into surplus during inflationary booms, helps to stabilize the economy. The automatic swings may therefore be regarded as a plus. However, they also introduce two important complications into fiscal policy.

1. A POLICY TRAP: ATTEMPTING TO BALANCE THE BUDGET EVERY YEAR

When the budget automatically swings into deficit during hard times, it sets a trap for the unwary policymaker. Suppose that the government tries to balance the budget every year. As the economy enters a recession, tax collections decline, causing deficits. If policymakers are determined to balance the budget, they will have two choices: they can cut government spending or they can increase tax rates. *Either step will depress aggregate expenditures and make the recession worse. By raising taxes or cutting expenditures, the government will offset the automatic stabilizers built into the tax system. Trying to balance the budget each year is a policy trap.*

President Hoover fell into this trap during the early years of the Great Depression. He shared the prevailing view that the government should balance its budget.[3] As tax revenues fell and deficits

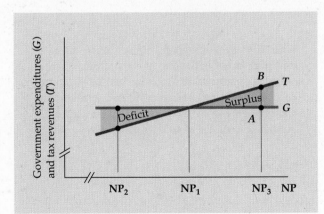

FIGURE 10-6   Automatic fiscal stabilization.

As national product increases from NP_1 toward NP_3, the government's budget automatically moves into surplus. This slows down the increases in disposable income and consumption and thus slows down the expansion. Conversely, the budget automatically moves into deficit during recessions as national product decreases from NP_1 toward NP_2. The government deficit helps to keep up disposable income and consumption and thus alleviates the recession.

[3]For example, in his 1932 presidential campaign against Hoover, Franklin Roosevelt urged his Pittsburgh audience: "Let us have the courage to stop borrowing to meet continuing deficits. Stop the deficits."

As deficits mounted during his first administration, this statement became an embarrassment. It inspired a story that circulated in Washington. When Roosevelt was returning to Pittsburgh several years later, he reportedly turned to one of his speechwriters and asked how he would explain away his earlier Pittsburgh speech. The reply was, "Deny you were ever in Pittsburgh."

mounted, he was convinced that the elimination of the deficit was essential to restore business confidence and hasten economic recovery. In 1932, he recommended that taxes be increased to get the budget back into balance. Congress agreed. The result was one of the largest peacetime increases in taxes in U.S. history. Fiscal policy was precisely the opposite of what was needed to promote recovery. Rather than the needed stimulus, the country got a large dose of restraint. The stage was set for the collapse into the deepest point of the depression in 1933. Ironically, the policy did not succeed in its goal of balancing the budget. Partly because of the added fiscal restraint, the economy collapsed. As it collapsed, tax revenues fell and the deficit persisted.

Hoover was not alone in falling into the trap; a number of other countries also increased tax rates during the depression. These blunders of the 1930s set the stage for the Keynesian Revolution with its important message: Spending and tax policies should be aimed at the goals of full employment and price stability, and not at the goal of balancing the budget. Keynes argued that *fiscal policy should be designed to balance the economy, not the budget.* The government has the ability—*and the responsibility*—to manage aggregate demand and thus ensure continuing prosperity.

2. MEASURING FISCAL POLICY: THE FULL-EMPLOYMENT BUDGET

Because the government's budget swings *automatically* toward deficit during recessions and toward surplus during booms, the state of the budget cannot be taken as a measure of how fiscal *policy* has changed. For example, the ballooning deficits in 1931-1932 did not mean that Hoover was following an expansive fiscal policy; in fact, he was doing the opposite.

In order to determine whether fiscal policy is moving in an expansive or restrictive direction, some measure other than the actual budgetary deficit or surplus is therefore needed. What might that measure be?

To answer this question, economists divide the government's deficit into two components, as illustrated in Figure 10-7. In this figure, the economy is in a recession; national product NP_1 falls short of full employment. The actual budget deficit is *BD*,

the excess of government spending (G) over tax revenues (T). The two components are:

1. The part *BC* of the deficit that is attributable to cyclical downturns in the economy. As the economy moves into recession, tax receipts are automatically depressed, and the deficit is thereby pushed up. This part of the deficit is called the *cyclical* component.

2. The deficit, *KH = CD*, which would occur *even if* there were no business cycles and the economy were always at full employment. This deficit is due to the structure of the tax and the government's spending programs. It is accordingly known as the **structural** deficit, the **full-employment** deficit, or the **cyclically adjusted** deficit.

The *full-employment budget* or *structural budget* measures what the government's deficit or surplus would be with existing tax rates and spending programs, *if* the economy were at full employment.

The full-employment budget provides an answer to the question posed earlier. *It provides a measure of what is happening to fiscal policy* because it changes only in response to changes in tax rates and spending programs, and not in response to business cycles. Specifically:

When the full-employment budget is moving towards a larger deficit (or smaller surplus), fiscal policy is expansive. Tax rates are being cut, or government spending increased. When the full-employment budget is moving towards a larger surplus (or smaller deficit), fiscal policy is restrictive.

Figure 10-7 shows what happens during a recession. As the economy contracts from full-employment F toward A, the cyclical component of the deficit grows; the gap between the actual deficit and the full-employment deficit increases. It remains large during the early recovery (while the economy is still quite close to A). During prosperity, the actual and full-employment deficits are the same. (Both are equal to *KH* when the economy is at full employment F.)

Finally, if tax rates are cut, T moves down, increasing both the actual and full-employment deficits (or decreasing the surplus). An increase

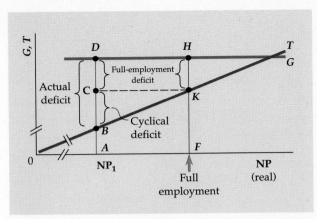

FIGURE 10-7   The full-employment deficit and the cyclical deficit.

This figure illustrates how the actual budget deficit BD can be broken down into its structural component CD and its cyclical component BC. The economy is in a recession; national product NP_1 is less than the full-employment quantity. The actual budget deficit is BD—that is, government spending AD less tax revenues AB. The full-employment or structural deficit, however, is only $HK = CD$. The cyclical component of the deficit BC is the difference between the actual deficit BD and the full-employment deficit CD.

in government spending G likewise causes an increase in both the actual and full-employment deficits.

THE FULL-EMPLOYMENT BUDGET SINCE 1960

Figure 10-8 confirms that the gap between the two budgets has in fact increased in every recession; the actual deficit became larger than the full-employment deficit. The gap between the two persisted during the early years of every recovery, while the economy was still short of full employment.

Movements in the full-employment budget can be used to identify some important changes in fiscal policy. Observe how the surplus in the full-employment budget declined in 1964, reflecting the expansionary tax cut of that year. On the other hand, the full-employment budget swung from deficit to surplus in 1968–1969 as a result of the policies designed to reduce inflationary pressures—the 1968 tax increase and restraints on gov-

ernment spending. In 1975, the full-employment budget moved sharply into deficit as a result of the tax cut and increases in government spending designed to lift the economy out of the recession of 1973–1975.

Figure 10-8 also shows some disquieting aspects of our fiscal history. Consider what happened from 1965 to 1967. The stagnation of the early 1960s was a thing of the past; the unemployment rate was low and inflation was gaining momentum. The proper fiscal stance was restraint. Yet fiscal policy was moving in the opposite direction. The full-employment budget was moving further into deficit, applying more stimulus to an economy that was already overheated. During these years, fiscal policy destabilized the economy, making the inflationary problem worse. How did that happen? The answer is, the government has many other concerns besides the stabilization of the economy. In the late 1960s, President Johnson was caught in the quagmire of an unpopular and frustrating war, and he shied away from an increase in taxes to finance higher government spending. For several years, he overruled the recommendations of his economic advisers that taxes be increased to restrain inflation. The tax increase was not passed until 1968, when it was long overdue.

THE SUPPLY-SIDE TAX CUTS OF THE 1980s

Also disturbing were the budgetary developments of the 1980s. During the first three years of the Reagan administration (1981–1983), full-employment deficits grew rapidly. There were two principal reasons: (1) a large increase in military spending, and (2) cuts in tax rates enacted in 1981.

At first, the deficits provided a desirable stimulus as the economy fell into recession in 1982. Within a few years, however, the economy was approaching full employment. A reduction in the deficit was in order. Yet large structural deficits persisted into the late 1980s, averaging over 3% of GNP. These deficits were not motivated by a desire to manage aggregate demand. In fact, the Reagan administration was skeptical of the whole idea of using fiscal policy to manage demand. It was following a new approach, which focused on the "supply side."

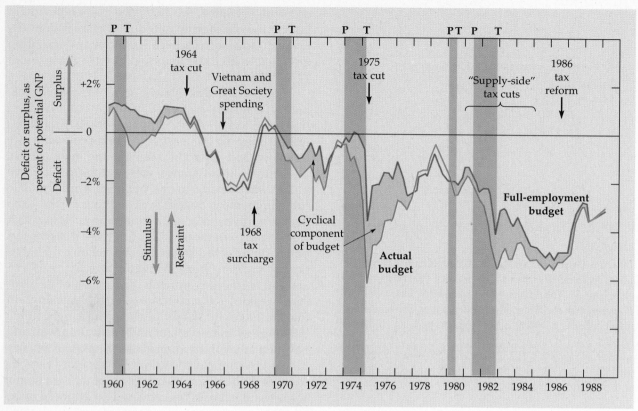

FIGURE 10-8   The full-employment budget and the actual budget, 1960–1988.

When the economy is operating below the full-employment level, tax revenues are
depressed and the actual budget shows a larger deficit (or smaller surplus) than the full-
employment budget. The full-employment budget shows changes in fiscal policy—for
example, the tax cuts of 1964 and 1975 designed to stimulate the economy.

THE SUPPLY-SIDE CASE

The idea behind the supply-side tax cuts was part
of the overall philosophy of the president. The
administration sought to get government regula-
tors off the backs of business and to stop tax collectors from taking so much out of the public's
pockets. Then the private sector of the economy
would be free to do what it did best: produce more
and provide vigorous growth. The issue here was
not one of short-run, countercyclical management;
rather, it had to do with the basic incentives in the
economic system.

Figure 10-9 illustrates the supply-side case. The
left panel shows the traditional view of a tax cut or
other expansive fiscal policy, which shifts the
aggregate demand curve to the right. Output increases, but there is a disadvantage: prices rise. The

right panel shows the double advantage of a tax
cut that increases incentives to produce. When the
aggregate supply curve shifts to the right, there is
more output *and* less inflation.

How, specifically, can tax cuts stimulate supply? Advocates of the supply-side approach suggested three ways:

1.   By encouraging people to work more.
2.   By encouraging saving and investment.
3.   By promoting the efficient use of resources.

CRITICISMS 批评

Critics pointed out that the supply-side tax cuts
would have undesirable side effects: higher government deficits and a less equal distribution of

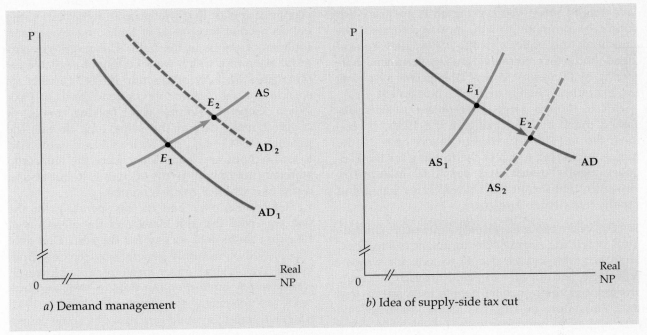

FIGURE 10-9   Tax cuts: demand management versus supply side.

Panel *a* shows the traditional case for a tax cut; it shifts the aggregate demand curve to the right. The idea behind a supply-side cut is that it will increase the productive capacity of the economy, shifting the aggregate supply curve to the right, as shown in panel *b*. If this is successful, output will be increased and inflation reduced.

income as tax rates on high-income taxpayers were cut. Critics also doubted that the program would work as advertised, and questioned the three main pillars of the supply-side case:

1. *Do tax cuts encourage work?* Lower tax rates leave workers with more after-tax income. It seems plausible that they should be willing to work more because the rewards are higher. However, this conclusion is not necessarily correct. With higher after-tax incomes, people can afford more leisure; they may actually work less. In Chapter 1, we saw that people in fact worked fewer hours as incomes rose during the first half of the twentieth century.

Studies of the labor market indicate that, at present, higher after-tax rewards generally do lead to more work, but this effect is not very strong. Charles Schultze, the chief economic adviser to President Jimmy Carter, quipped: "There's nothing wrong with supply-side economics that division by ten wouldn't cure."

2. *Do tax cuts encourage saving and investment?* By leaving people with more disposable income, tax cuts do encourage personal saving. However, it is not clear that more saving will mean more investment.

The difficulty is that tax cuts push the government's deficit up, forcing the government to borrow more.[4] When it does so, it gets the public's savings; they do not go into investment after all. In other words, the public's saving may be offset—or more than offset—by government deficits. This in fact happened during the 1980s; government deficits rose much more rapidly than saving. This is not surprising. When taxes are cut by $10 and the deficit thereby rises, people with an MPS of 0.1

----

[4]Some of the more enthusiastic supply siders suggested that cuts in tax rates would actually *reduce* the government's deficits, not increase them. This idea is explained in the appendix to this chapter.

save only $1 more. When economists are asked for policies to promote growth, most recommend the *opposite* of the policies of the 1980s; they recommend budgetary *restraint*. Less government borrowing will absorb less of the public's saving, leaving more available to finance investment.

Even though large government deficits absorbed much of U.S. saving in the 1980s, investment did not dry up. Foreign savers came to the rescue, providing much of the funding for the U.S. government's deficit and for U.S. investment. However, that meant the United States was going rapidly into debt to foreigners.

3. *Do lower tax rates promote efficiency?* On this third point, the supply-side argument is strongest. High tax rates induce people to look for ways—both legal and illegal—to avoid taxes. If tax rates are reduced, high-income people may spend less time and effort looking for loopholes. With this time and effort no longer wasted, they are likely to produce more. Furthermore, tax cuts will encourage more efficient investment, as investors look more closely at the productivity of their investment and less at the tax implications.

THE NATIONAL DEBT

Whenever the government runs a deficit, it borrows to pay for expenditures in excess of its revenues. When it borrows, its debt increases. Thus a deficit this year adds to the total national debt. The national debt represents the sum of all annual deficits going back to the beginning of the nation.

The government has run particularly large deficits—and the national debt has consequently grown very rapidly—during two periods: the Second World War and the period beginning in 1982. The large deficits of recent years have revived an old debate. Aren't we passing a crushing burden of debt to future generations? Surprisingly, there is no simple "yes" or "no" answer to this question.

Consider, first, the very large deficits that the government ran during the Second World War. Who bore the burden of that war—the people of the time, or their children who inherited the very large debt?

The answer is, *it was borne mostly by the people at the time*. To see why, consider what the primary

economic cost of that war was. To fight battles, the nation needed thousands of tanks and planes and millions of troops in the field. This required enormous resources which were no longer available for other uses. Military production in 1943 came *at the opportunity cost of giving up consumer goods in 1943*. When General Motors was making tanks, it couldn't make cars at the same time. It was the people of 1943—and not their children—who had to do without new cars. They were the ones who suffered, not only in terms of lives lost, but also in terms of consumer goods foregone.

Of course, only part of the spending for the war was paid through taxes, and the government ran up a large debt to pay for the rest. This debt was passed on to future generations; the debt from World War II has never been repaid. However, when we pay interest on this debt in 1990, we obviously are not paying the people who lived in 1943. Rather, interest payments are made by some people in 1990 to other people in 1990. Specifically, the government collects taxes from the general public and uses some of the taxes to pay interest to bondholders. Thus government debt—indeed, any debt—transfers funds from one group *now* to another group *now*. It does *not* transfer funds from people in one time period to people in an earlier period.

THE BURDEN OF DEFICITS AND DEBT

Nevertheless, deficit spending and the accumulation of public debt can impose burdens on future generations in a number of ways:

1. Government deficits can act as a *drag on investment*. When the government runs a deficit by increasing its spending, it is using resources that could have gone into investment instead. Unless the government itself is spending on investment projects—such as roads, sewers, or power plants—deficit spending can impose a burden on future generations. They may *inherit a smaller capital stock than they otherwise would have*.

Deficit spending does not always reduce investment, however. It depends on how close the economy is to full employment. If the economy is in a depression or major recession, it is operating inside the production possibilities curve. In this case, producing more goods for the government does not require a reduction in consumption or investment. On the contrary, because of the multiplier, we produce more consumption goods too. As more consumer goods are produced, investment is stimulated: To produce more cars and refrigerators, businesses need more machines and factories. Thus deficit spending *during a depression* generates benefits rather than burdens for future generations. It stimulates the production of consumer goods for the present generation and more capital stock for future generations.

2. To help finance its deficits, the U.S. government has *borrowed abroad.* By 1988, foreigners had accumulated $330 billion of the federal government's debt—about 13% of the total (and equal to about 7% of GNP). If the government sells bonds to Americans, they will get the future interest payments. As a nation, we will "owe the debt to ourselves." However, this is not the case for foreign-owned debt. As a nation, we will have to pay interest to foreigners.

3. When the government collects taxes to pay interest on the debt—whether held at home or abroad—there is another cost: the **excess burden** of taxation. When taxes are imposed, the public has an incentive to alter its behavior to avoid paying taxes. For example, people have an incentive to hire lawyers to hunt for tax loopholes and to divert their savings into tax-sheltered investments—that is, investments on which little or no tax is paid. As a result, the efficiency of the economy is reduced.

The *excess burden of taxes* is the decrease in the efficiency of the economy that results when people change their behavior to avoid paying taxes. It should be distinguished from the *primary burden,* which is measured by the amount of taxes people actually pay.

Note that the excess burden of taxes strengthens the supply-side argument for tax reductions in one way, but weakens it in another. The clearest supply-side advantage in cutting taxes is the improvement in the efficiency of the economy—that is, a reduction in the excess burden of taxes today. However, if lower taxes today mean a higher debt and therefore higher taxes in the future to pay interest, then more efficiency today comes at a cost: less efficiency in the future.

4. The need for the government to pay interest may lead to an *undesirable redistribution of income.* Whether it does so depends on who has to pay the taxes and who receives the interest. (It also depends on what we consider a "desirable" distribution of income.)

5. The need to pay interest on a rising debt may also cause *inflation.* Inflation may result if the government finances its rising interest payments, not by collecting more taxes, but instead by borrowing and thus running up its deficit even more. The rising deficits stimulate aggregate demand and add to inflationary pressures. The inflationary effects are particularly strong if the Federal Reserve (our central bank) creates new money and lends it to the government in order to help the government make its interest payments.

6. The national debt can *feed on itself.* As the debt rises, the government's interest payments also rise. These interest payments are part of the government's expenditures, and they make it more difficult to get deficits under control. By 1988, the federal government's interest payments were $152 billion—almost as much as the deficit in that year—and about 14% of total federal government spending (Table 10-1). If the government can't keep deficits down now, how will it be able to do so in the future, when it must make even larger interest payments?

7. The danger of the debt "feeding on itself" has become severe enough that *we may have lost our ability to use fiscal policy to combat future recessions.* If we run large deficits even in the prosperous years of the late 1980s, what will happen if we use fiscal policy vigorously to combat the next recession? With even larger deficits, won't we generate an unstoppable tide of debt and even greater interest payments and deficits in the future?

COULD THE GOVERNMENT "GO BROKE"?

If it gets more and more deeply into debt, could the federal government, like a business corporation, go bankrupt? The answer is no, but the reason why it won't "go broke" should be carefully stated.

First, consider one common, but inaccurate, argument. It is frequently asserted that the govern-

TABLE 10-1   The Public Debt and Interest Payments, 1929–1990

Year	(1) Public Debt	(2) Gross National Product	(3) Interest Payments	(4) Public Debt, as Percentage of GNP (1) ÷ (2)	(5) Interest Payments, as Percentage of GNP (3) ÷ (2)	(6) Interest Payments, as Percentage of Federal Government Expenditures	(7) Per Capita Public Debt (current dollars)	(8) Per Capita Public Debt (1982 dollars)
	(billions of current dollars)							
1929	$ 16	$ 103	$ 0.7	16%	0.7%	23.4%	$ 135	886
1940	45	100	1.1	45	1.1	11.6	340	2,520
1945	278	212	4.1	131	1.9	4.3	1,986	11,266
1950	257	287	4.5	90	1.6	10.8	1,689	6,779
1960	290	507	6.8	57	1.3	8.9	1,602	5,070
1970	370	993	13.5	37	1.4	7.1	1,805	4,244
1975	533	1,549	21.7	34	1.4	7.2	2,468	4,218
1980	908	2,627	51.2	35	1.9	8.9	4,009	4,678
1985	1,817	3,952	129.4	46	3.3	13.7	7,603	6,850
1988	2,601	4,780	151.7	54	3.2	14.3	10,564	8,681
1990[a]	3,107	5,476	170.1	57	3.1	14.8	12,378	9,380

[a]As estimated in *Economic Report of the President, 1989*, pp. 397–399.

ment cannot go bankrupt because it has the authority to tax. Thus it has the power to extract from the public whatever amounts are necessary to service the debt. Surely there is something wrong with this argument. State and local governments also have the power to tax, yet they can go broke, as the holders of Cleveland and New York City bonds discovered in the 1970s. At times, these cities were unable to make payments on their debt. In a democracy, the government must face elections. Even dictatorships depend on public support. As a result, there are political and practical limits to taxes. The holder of a government bond does not have a guarantee of repayment merely because the government has the right to tax.

The federal government cannot go bankrupt for quite a different reason. It has a power even more potent than the power to tax: It has the constitutional power to print money to pay interest or principal, and thus prevent a default on the national debt. (Congress has delegated the power to print money to the Federal Reserve. However, Congress could reclaim this power if the Federal Reserve were unwilling to print money to prevent a de-

fault.) In other words, a national government does not go bankrupt because bonds are repayable in something—money—which national governments can create.

However, if large quantities of money are created to help make payments on the public debt, the consequence will be a rise in prices. (Recall what happened in the prisoner-of-war camp when large quantities of cigarette "money" suddenly came on the scene.) Thus an excessive national debt has quite different consequences from an excessive corporate debt: It causes excess demand and inflation, not bankruptcy.

Nevertheless, there is one situation in which even a national government may default on its debts—namely, if it has borrowed another country's currency. For example, many countries borrow U.S. dollars on the international financial markets. They cannot escape this debt by printing dollars; they can print only their own currencies. During the past decade, a number of governments that had borrowed heavily in U.S. dollars have been in default or in danger of default—for example, Argentina, Brazil, Mexico, and Poland.

THE ISSUE OF RESTRAINT

Keynesian economics throws into question the old rule that the government should try to balance its budget every year. But if there is no rule, what will prevent the government from careless increases in spending or tax cuts? We may warn of the dangers of excess, but can we really expect restraint? With the large deficits of the 1980s, these old questions are posed again.

A number of alternative guidelines have been suggested to provide restraint, while avoiding the destabilizing fiscal policies that can occur if the government tries to balance its actual budget every year.

1. BALANCE THE FULL-EMPLOYMENT BUDGET EVERY YEAR

Remember why the old balanced-budget rule was destabilizing. As the economy moves into recession and a budget deficit automatically appears, the balanced-budget rule requires an increase in tax rates or a cut in government spending. Both actions can make the recession worse. Such destabilizing actions can be avoided if the government aims at balancing the *full-employment* budget rather than the actual budget. Because the full-employment budget does not automatically swing into deficit during recessions, it does not give a false signal that a tax increase or spending cut is needed. Thus the full-employment budget has two major uses: as a **way of measuring** fiscal policy and as a **guide** to fiscal policy.

This first rule represents an unambitious strategy. All it does is allow the automatic stabilizers to combat the recession; it does not allow the government to go one step further and actively fight the recession by introducing fiscal stimulus. (Such stimulus—for example, a cut in tax rates—would violate the rule, because it would put the full-employment budget into deficit.) Thus its aim is to avoid destabilizing actions, not to actively stabilize the economy. It therefore is reminiscent of the doctor's motto: *Primo non nocere*, "First, do no harm."

2. BALANCE THE BUDGET OVER THE BUSINESS CYCLE

An alternative rule would permit an active fiscal policy. Under this rule, the government would be committed to balance the actual budget over the whole business cycle, not every year. During recessions, tax rates could be cut and spending increased to stimulate aggregate expenditures. During good times, the government would run sufficient surpluses to cover the deficits run during the recessions.

3. LIMIT GOVERNMENT SPENDING

Another approach is to *limit federal government spending as a fraction of GNP.* Presidents Carter and Reagan both subscribed to this objective. President Carter committed himself to reduce spending to 21% of GNP compared to 22% in 1976. This objective was reached by 1979. However, the percentage bounced back to 22.1% in 1980. A large increase in interest payments pushed up expenditures (the numerator), while recession kept down GNP (the denominator).

In his first months in office, President Reagan proposed to reduce federal government spending to 20% of GNP by 1984. However, substantial increases in expenditures and lower-than-expected growth pushed the percentage up to 23.1% by 1984. In the last year of his administration in 1988, it was 22.3%.

FORMAL CONSTRAINTS

Some critics of government spending argue that it is unrealistic to expect the government to be restrained by any of the guidelines listed above. No matter what policy the administration and Congress proclaim, they are likely to choose the path of least resistance, giving in to those clamoring for bigger spending programs and cutting taxes to increase their popularity at the polls. Consequently, these critics argue that the government should be constrained by an enforceable rule, written into the Constitution or into law. Enough escape clauses are generally suggested to avoid the need to cut spending or raise taxes during a depression. In broad terms, the proposals require only that the full-

BOX 10–1   Outlawing Deficits

President Reagan suggested a constitutional amendment requiring a balanced budget. Congress was unenthusiastic, since an amendment would limit its powers. It therefore refused to pass an amendment for the states to ratify. Proponents then sought to bypass Congress by having two-thirds (34) of the states petition for a constitutional convention. By 1984, 32 states had submitted such petitions, and proponents of the amendment were hoping for two more. However, they were disappointed. In 1988, after Kentucky came close to becoming the thirty-third petitioner, some of the earlier states had second thoughts. A number—including Alabama and Florida—rescinded their petitions. The balanced budget amendment was dead.

Opponents of an amendment killed it with a number of objections. They pointed out that it would limit the power of Congress to deal with emergencies. Furthermore, they argued that the Reagan administration was inconsistent. It proposed an amendment but nevertheless submitted budgets with huge deficits. If the administration really believed in a balanced budget, said the critics, it should submit one to the Congress.

GRAMM-RUDMAN

Although Congress rejected a balanced-budget amendment to the Constitution, it enacted the same general idea into law in the Balanced Budget and Emergency Deficit Control Act of 1985, commonly known as Gramm-Rudman after its two principal sponsors. This act established a numerical timetable for a gradual elimination of the budget deficit. Congress was, however, mindful of President Hoover's sad history, and therefore permitted higher deficits in the event of recession.

The Gramm-Rudman Act avoided the rigidity of a constitutional amendment. Because it was a law passed by Congress, it could also be changed by Congress. In fact, it was changed. The original act, passed in 1985, called for a balanced budget by 1991. By 1987, this goal seemed impossibly difficult, and Congress amended the act, putting off the date for a balanced budget until 1993. As the budget targets become more difficult in the next several years, Congress may face a dilemma: Will it raise taxes, cut spending, or change the act?

Like the administration, Congress can be schizophrenic over deficits. The same Congress that passed the Balanced Budget Act also passed the appropriations that resulted in a deficit of $212 billion in 1986.

It was a classic case of wanting to have your cake and eat it, too. Congress wanted lower deficits. However, it was loath to increase taxes over the objections of the administration, particularly after 1984. In the presidential election of that year, Democratic contender Walter Mondale said he would raise taxes; not much has been heard of him since. Congress was also reluctant to cut spending.

Consider an example. It does not represent large sums—"only" $1 billion or so a year—but it does illustrate

employment budget be balanced (as in point 1 above).

In fact, Congress did pass the Gramm-Rudman Act in 1985, requiring a gradual reduction in deficits (Box 10-1).

SOCIAL SECURITY TO THE RESCUE? THE TWELVE TRILLION DOLLAR TEMPTATION

Is the government putting a burden on future generations? Nowhere is that question more relevant than in the financing of social security.

Until recently, social security was on a pay-as-you-go basis. The common perception—that each individual worker's social security taxes were put aside in a fund for his or her own retirement—was a misperception. Very little was saved; most of the current year's taxes were used to pay current retirees. At the end of 1980, the Social Security Trust Fund was a pitiful $26 billion—less than $300 for every working man and woman in the United States. Social security was a giant machine for transfers. The working population was paying taxes to support their retired parents and grandparents.

As long as there were many workers for every retiree, this system could go along quite smoothly. The current generation was supporting their parents, but they could count on getting similar support from their children when it came time to retire in 2020.

the problem. For many years, the Defense Department wanted to close dozens of obsolete bases, but Congress insisted on keeping them open. Examples included Fort Douglas in Utah, which protected stagecoach routes; Fort Monroe in Virginia, which had a moat to protect it from the British in the War of 1812; and Loring Air Base in Maine, which was built 40 years ago to place bombers closer to Soviet targets. In the missile age, it became useless. To prevent the Defense Department from closing unwanted bases, Congress passed a law requiring an "environmental impact statement" first. The procedure—obscure, complex, and open to challenge in court—prevented the Defense Department from closing any domestic base between 1977 and 1988. The Pentagon actually did complete an environmental study on Loring. A senator from Maine struck back. He sponsored a law that forbade the Air Force from spending any money to close it.

The problem was that individual members of Congress felt compelled to keep money flowing to their constituencies. For the nation as a whole, this practice was clearly wasteful. In order to finesse the political problem, Congress established a bipartisan commission in 1988 to recommend a list of bases to be closed. Congress undertook to vote yes or no on the whole list, with no exceptions. Thus, when closings began in 1989, individual members of Congress avoided blame for the closing of bases in their particular districts.

On the budget, Congress and the administration would like to make three decisions—on tax rates, spending, and the deficit. In fact, however, there are only two decisions to be made. If Congress and the administration set tax rates and spending programs, the deficit is determined. If they set taxes and the deficit, then they cannot be free to do as they like on the spending side. Gramm-Rudman was designed to put spending at the end of the line in the decision process, and thus exert restraint at that point. If the Gramm-Rudman deficit ceilings are exceeded, expenditures are to be cut automatically, more or less across-the-board, with social security and interest payments exempted.

Needless to say, tension over three sets of inconsistent decisions has made the budgetary process even more complex and Byzantine. It has invited petty cheating, such as the creative bookkeeping that helped to keep the 1987 deficit (almost) within the Gramm-Rudman limit at $149 billion. A number of identifiable groups have emerged in Congress: those who want higher taxes to pay for more spending; those who want a rigid budget rule to curb spending; those who want to forget about deficits. The details are strictly for connoisseurs. One small tip may be helpful, however. To figure out what's going on in the political game, you need to know that the teams changed ends at halftime—about 1983. Prior to that time, "conservatives" (mainly Republicans) expressed shock at high deficits. Since that time, "liberals" (mainly Democrats) have been the most vocal critics.

Or could they? By 1983, Congress awoke to a disturbing fact. Because of the baby boom between 1946 and 1964, there will be many retirements after 2020, and fewer workers to support every retired person. In 1984, there were 4 workers for every American over the age of 65; by 2030 there will be only 2.6. A pay-as-you-go system would impose a crushing burden on the workers of 2030. Would they revolt? Was the stage being set for economic warfare between the young and the old?[5]

Faced with this disturbing question, Congress put aside the pressures of the moment to address the problems of the distant future. Since the workers of 2030 could not be expected to bear the full burden of supporting their retired parents, current workers would have to start saving for their own retirement now. The sham of the Social Security Trust Fund would have to end; it would have to become a trust fund in reality. Social security tax rates were raised substantially to provide for an estimated buildup of the trust fund to $12 trillion by 2030. This is a huge figure—$12 million million, or four times the national debt in 1990. However, it will not be too much. By the middle of the twenty-first century, it will be exhausted as baby boomers draw their pensions.

What happens as the $12 trillion builds up?

[5]Henry J. Aaron, Barry P. Bosworth, and Gary Burtless, *Can America Afford to Grow Old? Paying for Social Security* (Washington, D.C.: Brookings Institution, 1989), and Frank Levy, *Dollars and Dreams* (New York: Russell Sage Foundation, 1987).

The social security system is included in the budget of the U.S. government. Large surpluses of the social security system are already helping to keep down the overall deficit of the government; they are helping to hide the rising deficits elsewhere in the budget (Fig. 10-10).

This situation worries some observers. Will the social security surpluses simply be frittered away in other spending programs? Will the Social Security Trust Fund become a "twelve trillion dollar temptation" as critics fear? Some argue that we should change our objectives. Instead of trying to balance the overall budget (as specified by the Gramm-Rudman Act), they argue that we should attempt to balance the budget *excluding* social security. This would mean large overall surpluses as the Social Security Trust funds are built up.

It is true, of course, that when the baby boomers retire in the 2020s, their retirement income will be spent on goods and services produced at that time. The medical services and food that they buy will have to be produced by those in the labor force at the time; they cannot be stored from current production. (There are some exceptions. For example, housing built now will still provide homes in 2030.) In a very real sense, people who are young in 2030 will face the burden of producing for a large number of retirees.

That burden may be lightened, however. If the government runs overall budget surpluses, it will help in two ways already noted. First, more resources will be available for investment. In 2030, the nation's capital will be higher than otherwise. As a result, productive capacity will also be higher. The nation will be in a better position to produce goods and services for the elderly.

Second, lower deficits or higher surpluses can

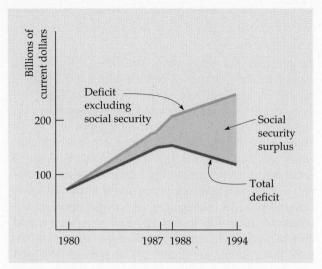

FIGURE 10-10   Social security surpluses and overall budget deficits.

The surplus in the social security system has been building up, keeping down the overall deficit of the federal government. With current tax rates and spending programs, the overall deficit will continue to fall in the early 1990s. However, the deficit excluding social security will continue to rise. (*Note:* In this diagram, social security includes Medicare. Estimates for 1994 are taken from Aaron, Bosworth, and Burtless, *Can America Afford to Grow Old?*, p. 7.)

help reduce the amount that the United States borrows abroad. Smaller interest payments will be made to foreign nations by the taxpayers of 2030, who will thus find it easier to bear the burden of supporting old people.

Whatever the government does, social security will be one of the most important—and controversial—budgetary issues of the next several decades.

KEY POINTS

1. A change in fiscal policy occurs when the government changes its spending programs or when it alters tax rates.

2. An increase in government spending causes an increase in equilibrium national product. An increase in taxes causes a decrease in equilibrium national product.

3. When aggregate expenditures are low and the rate of unemployment is high, fiscal policy should be expansionary. That is, the government should increase spending and/or cut tax rates. These steps increase the government's deficit.

4. When excess aggregate expenditures are causing inflation, fiscal policy should be restrictive; the government should cut spending and/or increase tax rates. These steps will move the government's budget toward surplus.

5. Tax collections automatically rise as national product increases and fall as national product falls. Thus the government budget *automatically* tends to move into deficit during a recession and into surplus during expansion. This tendency helps to reduce the amplitude of cyclical swings and thus provides *built-in stability* to the economy.

6. Because the government's budget automatically responds to changes in national product, the actual budget cannot be taken as a *measure* of fiscal policy actions. The appropriate measure is the *full-employment budget,* which indicates what the surplus or deficit would be with current tax and spending legislation, if the economy were at full employment.

7. If the government attempts to balance the actual budget every year, it will fall into a *policy trap* and take destabilizing actions. During a downturn in economic activity, when the budget automatically moves toward deficit, the government will cut expenditures or raise taxes in an effort to balance the budget, thereby making the downturn worse. The Hoover administration fell into this policy trap in 1932, when it recommended a large tax increase.

8. This trap can be avoided if the full-employment budget—rather than the actual budget—is used as a policy guide. The full-employment budget has no tendency to swing automatically into deficit during recessions; therefore it does not erroneously suggest that taxes should be raised. Accordingly, the full-employment budget has two major functions: (1) as a *measure* of fiscal policy; and (2) as a *guide* for fiscal policy.

9. The tax cuts of 1981 were not aimed at managing aggregate demand. Rather, their objective was to stimulate the productive capacity of the economy by

   (a) Encouraging people to work more.

   (b) Encouraging saving and investment.

   (c) Promoting the efficient use of resources.

The most valid of these points is (c).

10. A deficit causes a change in the total debt outstanding. The national debt now is the cumulative total of all deficits run by the U.S. government, back to the beginning of the republic.

11. Government deficits and a large national debt can create a number of problems:

   (a) When the government engages in deficit spending, it may use resources that would otherwise have been used to produce capital. Thus large deficits may mean less capital for future generations.

   (b) Insofar as the debt is held abroad, people at home will be taxed to pay interest to foreigners.

   (c) When taxes are imposed to pay interest on the debt, there will be a loss of economic efficiency as people look for ways to avoid taxes. This loss of efficiency is called the "excess burden of taxes."

   (d) If the government pays interest by borrowing rather than taxing, it can add to inflationary pressures.

   (e) The debt can "feed on itself." A large debt requires large interest payments. This makes it difficult to avoid future deficits, which add to the size of the debt.

   (f) Since a large debt requires large interest payments, it can cause such large deficits that the government feels that it has lost the ability to fight recessions with additional deficit spending.

KEY CONCEPTS

fiscal policy	deficit spending	actual budget
recessionary gap	automatic stabilizers	supply-side tax cut
output gap or GNP gap	discretionary policy action	primary burden of tax
lump-sum tax	full-employment or structural budget	excess burden of tax
proportional tax		

PROBLEMS

10-1. Using a diagram, explain the difference between the recessionary gap and the output gap. Which is larger? How are these two measures related to the multiplier?

10-2. During the Great Depression, Keynes argued that it would be better for the government to build pyramids than to do nothing. Do you agree or disagree? Why? Are there any policies better than building pyramids? That is, can you think of any policies that would give all the advantages of building pyramids, plus additional advantages? Explain.

10-3. During the Great Depression, the following argument was frequently made:

> A market economy tends to generate large-scale unemployment. Military spending can reduce unemployment. Therefore, capitalism requires wars and the threat of wars if it is to survive.

What part or parts of this argument are correct? Which are wrong? Explain what is wrong with the incorrect part(s). Rewrite the statement, correcting whatever is incorrect.

10-4. In 1964 and 1975, when the government wanted to stimulate aggregate demand, it cut tax rates. What are the advantages of cutting tax rates rather than increasing government spending? What are the disadvantages? When restraint is needed, would you favor increases in taxes, cuts in government spending, or a combination of the two? Why?

10-5. Assume that full employment initially exists and that the actual budget is in balance.

(a) If the economy then slips down into a recession and there are no policy changes, will the actual budget and the full-employment budget behave the same way? Explain your answer. (For help with this question, refer to Figs. 10-6 and 10-7.)

(b) Suppose, as an alternative, that the government takes strong fiscal policy steps to combat the recession. Will there be a difference in the behavior of the actual budget and the full-employment budget? Explain.

10-6. Attempting to balance the budget every year can set a trap for policymakers. It leads to incorrect policies during a depression. Does such a balanced-budget rule also lead to incorrect policies during an inflationary boom? Why?

10-7. In what way is the federal budgetary deficit of recent years different from that of 1943? Is the deficit a problem now? Explain.

APPENDIX

CAN TAXES BE CUT WITHOUT LOSING REVENUES?

Some of the more enthusiastic supply-side economists believed that tax rates could be cut without the government losing revenue.

This idea was put forward most explicitly by Arthur Laffer of the University of Southern California, who drew the *Laffer curve* shown in green in Figure 10-11. This curve illustrates the relationship between tax rates and total government revenues.

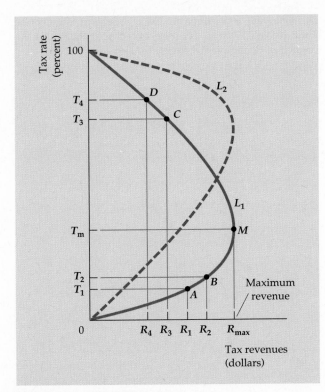

FIGURE 10-11   The Laffer curve.

The Laffer curve illustrates the relationship between tax rates and government revenues. If the tax rate is either zero or 100%, no revenues are collected. At some intermediate point, *M*, tax revenues are maximized.

If the tax rate is zero, no revenues are collected. On the other hand, if the tax rate is 100%, once again revenues are zero; nobody will work to earn income if the government taxes it all away. People will either loaf or, more likely, spend their time finding ways—legal or otherwise—to avoid the tax.

At some intermediate tax rate, T_m, revenues are at a maximum. If the tax rate is below this level, say, at T_1, a tax increase will cause little change in work effort and tax avoidance. Therefore a tax increase will cause a rise in government revenues. For example, as taxes rise from T_1 to T_2, revenues increase from R_1 to R_2. On the other hand, if taxes are initially *above* T_m—at T_3, for example—then a further increase in the rate to T_4 will cause enough idleness and tax evasion that the total taxes collected by the government will decrease, from R_3 to R_4.

The question is whether the initial tax rate is above or below the maximum revenue rate, T_m. Although we know that revenues are zero if the tax rate is either zero or 100%, we do not know how high T_m is. For example, the curve could be L_2 rather than L_1, in which case the revenue-maximizing tax rate would be much higher. Laffer believed that we were already above T_m in 1980, in the range where a tax increase leads to a fall in government revenue. In other words, a *cut* in the tax rate would lead to an *increase* in revenues. Thus a tax cut would be a painless policy, benefiting the public while reducing the government's deficits.

For the tax system as a whole, Laffer's claim was implausible. Suppose, for example, that personal income is initially $4,000 billion and the average tax rate is 25%. The government collects $1,000 billion. If the tax rate is now cut by one fifth, to 20%, taxable personal income will have to increase to $5,000 billion if government revenues are to remain stable ($5,000 x 20% = $1,000). It is not clear how a cut in the tax rate could cause such a huge

185

increase in taxable income, unless tax cheating was rampant and people suddenly decided to pay their taxes when the tax rate dropped to 20%.

This is not to suggest that Laffer's idea should be completely dismissed. For some taxes—those that are most easily avoided—the revenue-maximizing rate may be lower than for other taxes. For example, capital gains taxes can be avoided simply by holding on to assets; they are levied only when an asset is sold. Because people have so much discretion as to when to sell assets, there is a lively debate as to whether a cut in the capital gains tax from its current maximum of 28% would lead to an increase in revenues. Statistical studies are inconclusive, some suggesting an increase and others a decrease. Note, however, that the capital gains tax is special. Most incomes, in the form of wages and salaries, allow no such discretion by the taxpayers. Thus the revenue-maximizing tax rate for such income is higher than that for a capital gains tax.

The Laffer curve was frequently mentioned in the press. However, it is unclear how important it was as an inspiration for the tax cut of 1981. It is true that the idea was appealing to Mr. Reagan. For example, he implied that he agreed with it during the campaign of 1980 (Flint, Mich., May 17):

> We would use the increase in revenues the federal government would get from the tax decrease to build our defense capabilities.

Nevertheless, once it got down to the gritty details of actual budget planning, Laffer's rosy idea of a revenue-enhancing tax cut was discarded. The budget was to be balanced by major reductions in domestic spending. Indeed, the administration hoped that tax cuts would *cause* cuts in spending, because of the deficits that would otherwise occur.

In the event, the tax revenues did fall, but the expected cut in expenditures did not occur. Deficits rose rapidly. These deficits, observed Herbert Stein, cast doubt on Laffer's idea and, more broadly, act as a warning "about the search for novel ideas whose chief claim to validity is that they would be nice if true."[6]

----

[6]*Memorandum* (Washington, D.C.: American Enterprise Institute, Fall 1988), p. 5. Stein served as chairman of the Council of Economic Advisers, 1972–1974.

CHAPTER 11
MONEY AND THE BANKING SYSTEM

Lack of money is the root of all evil.
GEORGE BERNARD SHAW

Fiscal policy is one tool for managing aggregate demand. Monetary policy is another. Monetary policy involves control over the quantity of money in our economy. If the quantity of money is increased, spending is encouraged; aggregate demand rises. Similarly, if the quantity of money decreases, aggregate demand is restrained. By adjusting the quantity of money, the authorities can affect aggregate demand.

There is another reason why money is an important topic in macroeconomics. Money not only provides a *tool to stabilize the economy*; it can also represent a *source of problems*. Indeed, monetary disturbances have been associated with some of the most spectacularly unstable episodes in economic history. Two examples stand out. One occurred in the years following the First World War, when Germany went through a period of hyperinflation. In December 1919, there were about 50 billion marks in circulation. Four years later, this figure had risen to almost 500,000,000,000 billion marks—an increase of 10,000,000,000 times! Because money was so plentiful, it became practically worthless; prices skyrocketed. Indeed, money lost its value so quickly that people were anxious to spend it as soon as possible, while they could still buy something with it. If the value of your money is going to fall by half by tomorrow—as it did during the German hyperinflation—then you want to spend it today.

The second illustration occurred in the United States between 1929 and 1933. Monetary disturbances accompanied the collapse into the Great Depression. As the economy slid downward, the quantity of money fell from $26.2 billion in mid-1929 to $19.2 billion in mid-1933—or by 27%. By the time Roosevelt became president in 1933, many banks had gone bankrupt and many bank deposits had become worthless.

In the coming chapters, we will investigate:

1. Monetary *problems.* What are the forces that cause monetary disturbances? What has been done in the past, and what can be done in the future, to reduce such disturbances and make the economy more stable?

2. Monetary *opportunities.* What monetary policies are most likely to stabilize aggregate demand and minimize fluctuations in economic activity?

As background, this chapter explains:

■ The functions of money.

■ The various types of money.

■ How the money stock increases when banks make loans.

THE FUNCTIONS OF MONEY

Without money, specialized producers would have to resort to barter. Because barter is so cumbersome, a monetary system will naturally evolve, even in the absence of a government—as the development of a cigarette money in the prisoner-of-war camp illustrated (Chapter 3).

Money has three interrelated functions. Money acts as

1. The **medium of exchange.** That is, it is used to buy goods and services.

2. The **unit of account** or *standard of value*. Prices are quoted in money. For example, a car is priced at $10,000 and a pair of shoes at $50.

3. A **store of value.** Because it can be used to buy goods or services whenever the need arises, money is a convenient way to hold wealth.

Of course, money is not a perfect store of value because its *purchasing power* can change. Inflation means that the purchasing power of money is declining; each dollar buys less. Furthermore, even if the average level of prices were perfectly stable, money would not be the best way to hold large amounts of wealth. Once you hold a moderate amount of money, it is generally better to put most additional wealth into government bonds or other assets that earn interest. People want to hold some money because it is the most *convenient* asset; it can be used directly to buy goods and services.

MONEY IN THE U.S. ECONOMY

If it waddles like a duck,
And quacks like a duck,
Then it is a duck.

ANONYMOUS

Money is what money does. To define money, we should begin by looking at *what is actually used* to buy goods and services. What is used by the householder paying the electric bill? By the customer at the supermarket? By the child buying candy? By the employer paying wages?

Coins (nickels, dimes, etc.) and paper currency ($1 bills, $10 bills, etc.), which together are known as **currency,** are used in many transactions—but certainly not in all. Indeed, most payments are made by check. When you write a check, it is an order to your bank or savings and loan association to make payment out of your checking account. Other payments are made with travelers' checks. These three items—currency, checking deposits, and travelers' checks—are what people actually use when making purchases. They constitute the most basic and important concept of money, and they are represented by the symbol M1. Unless otherwise specified, this is what economists mean when they speak of "money."

M1 = currency + checking deposits + travelers' checks

Checking deposits are by far the largest component of M1, amounting to $553 billion in February 1989, compared with only $212 billion in currency and $7 billion in travelers' checks.

Several complications should be noted about the basic definition of money, M1. M1 has been identified as the items that are *actually used* in making transactions. However, something seems to have been left out. When shopping, people often use credit cards rather than either currency or checks. Yet there is no mention of credit cards in the definition of money. There are two related reasons. First, in a fundamental sense, people don't "pay" with credit cards. They simply defer the payment for a few weeks or months. When the credit card bill comes, it must be paid with a check (or, conceivably, with currency). Thus it is the final payment with a check, rather than the initial charging with a credit card, that represents the fundamental payment. It is the balance in the checking account that is money, not the credit card. Second, people *own* currency and checking accounts. Credit cards, on the other hand, represent an easy way to run up debt. If, as the result of a sudden windfall, I acquire an extra $1,000 that I deposit in my bank account, I will be very much aware of the fact and will clearly be better off as a result. On the other hand, if the credit card issuer informs me that I can charge an extra $1,000, I will not necessarily be better off. Indeed, I may scarcely notice.

The second complication is a small, but important, technical point regarding the data in Figure 11-1. When the quantity of money is calculated, currency and deposits are counted only when they are held *by the public*—that is, by individuals and

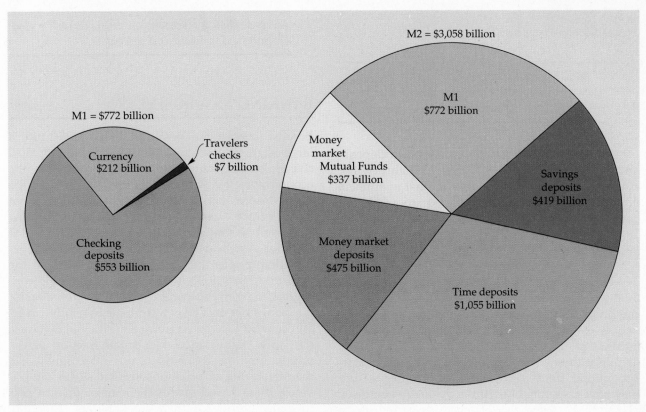

FIGURE 11-1   Composition of the money stock (February 1989)

Checking deposits are by far the most important component of M1. M1 is about 25% of M2, a much broader definition of money.

nonbank institutions such as manufacturing corporations. Holdings by the federal government, the Federal Reserve, and deposit-accepting institutions (such as commercial banks) are excluded from the money stock, since these are the institutions that create money. This exclusion makes sense. For example, if the Federal Reserve has a million $1 bills printed up and stored in its vaults, it makes little sense to say that the money stock has gone up by $1 million. That currency gains significance and becomes "money" only when it passes out of the hands of the Federal Reserve and into the hands of the public.

A BROADER CONCEPT OF MONEY: M2

Money is important because it is used in transactions; it makes the exchange of goods and services work much more smoothly and efficiently than a barter system. Money is also important because it can affect aggregate demand. When people have more money, they are likely to spend more.

Once we concentrate on the effect of money on spending, it is not clear that M1 is unique. Consider *savings deposits* against which checks cannot be written. It is true that such deposits cannot be used directly to make payments. However, they can easily be transferred into checking deposits, which in turn can be spent. The spending patterns of someone with $1,000 in a noncheckable savings account may not be very different from the spending of a person with $1,000 in a checking account.

Thus, when economists are studying the determinants of aggregate demand, they frequently broaden their horizons beyond the narrowly defined M1. Specifically, they often use a broader definition, M2, which includes noncheckable savings deposits and other close substitutes for M1:

M2 = M1 + noncheckable savings deposits +
time deposits[1] + money market deposits +
money market mutual funds

A *time deposit* is similar to a savings deposit, except that it has a specific time to maturity. For example, if you have a time deposit that matures in three months, your money is tied up until that date. If you want it sooner, you must pay a penalty. Time deposits are the largest single component of M2, as illustrated in Figure 11-1.

Banks also accept *money market deposits.* These deposits pay market-determined interest rates, as do the *money market mutual funds* offered by brokerage houses and mutual fund organizations. These two assets are examples of the many innovations introduced by financial institutions in recent decades. Money market deposits and money market mutual funds offer checking privileges, and they have therefore blurred the distinction between M1 and M2. Even though checks can be drawn against them, they are not included in M1 because they cannot be used in the unrestricted way that currency or regular checking deposits can. Holders may be restricted to two or three checks per month, or they may be prohibited from writing checks for less than $500.

It is possible to go further, to M3 and even broader concepts. The problem is that there is no obvious place to stop. There is a whole spectrum of assets with varying degrees of **liquidity.** Money market funds are highly liquid; time deposits are slightly less so. As we move along the spectrum, we would soon encounter short-term marketable government securities, which, while highly liquid, would not generally be considered money. There is no sharp, obvious distinction between money and **near monies.**

---

[1]Only time deposits of less than $100,000 are included in M2. Time deposits of $100,000 or more are generally held by businesses and are included in an even broader definition of money, M3.

An asset is *liquid* if it can be converted into cash at a stable price, and with little cost and bother.

BANKING AS A BUSINESS

Because checking deposits in banks constitute a large share of the money used in everyday purchases, banks occupy a strategic position in the economy. Never was this more clear than in the Great Depression, when many banks throughout the country went bankrupt. When Franklin Roosevelt became president in March 1933, the U.S. banking system was in a state of collapse. Monetary disruptions added to the other woes of the economy. Early 1933, with its chaotic banking conditions, marked the lowest point of the depression.

Banks not only play a strategic role in the overall operation of the economy, but they also have a particular significance to a small fraction of the population: the stockholders of banks. Banks, like manufacturing corporations or retail stores, are privately owned, and one of their major objectives is to make profits for their stockholders. Therefore two questions are relevant in an analysis of banking operations: (1) How do banks earn profits? and (2) how can banks be used by the authorities to stabilize the economy?

THE GOLDSMITH: THE EMBRYONIC BANK AS A WAREHOUSE

The quest for profits led to the development of the modern bank. How this happened can be illustrated by dipping briefly into the history of the ancestors of banks—the medieval goldsmiths.

As their name implies, goldsmiths worked and shaped the precious metal. But they also undertook another function. Because gold wares were extremely valuable, customers looked to the goldsmith for safe storage of their treasures. In return for the deposit of a valuable, the goldsmith would provide the customer with a warehouse receipt—the promise to return the valuable to the customer on demand. Thus the goldsmiths performed a service for a rich elite that was basically similar to the service that a baggage checkroom performs for you or me. They stored packages for a fee and returned them to the owner on demand.

When unique gold ornaments were deposited, the customer naturally wanted to get back precisely the item that had been left with the goldsmith. But goldsmiths held not only unique items for their customers; gold coins were also deposited. It was not essential to the depositor to get back *exactly* the same coins that had been deposited. Thus the basis for the development of banks was laid.

KEEPING THE BOOKS: THE BALANCE SHEET

To see how the banking business developed, the **balance sheet** is a useful device. It lists (1) the firm's **assets** (what the firm owns), (2) **liabilities** (what the firm *owes*), and (3) the **net worth** of the firm. Net worth is equal to assets minus liabilities. For example, if a firm owns $10,000 in assets and has $6,000 in liabilities, its net worth is the difference of $4,000. Thus:

$$\text{Net worth} = \text{Assets - liabilities}$$

This may be rearranged:

$$\text{Assets} = \text{liabilities} + \text{net worth}$$

The balance sheet lists assets on one side, with liabilities and net worth on the other. The two sides must be equal because of the way in which net worth is defined (assets less liabilities). **The balance sheet must balance.**

FRACTIONAL-RESERVE BANKING

Now let's go back to the early goldsmith. Suppose he owned a building worth 10,000 "dollars." The building was an asset; it appeared on the left-hand asset side of the goldsmith's balance sheet. Suppose also that the goldsmith accepted $100,000 in gold coins for safekeeping. As the coins were in his possession, they appeared on the asset side. But the owners of the gold had the right to withdraw them at any time upon demand. The goldsmith had *demand deposit liabilities* of $100,000; he had to be prepared to provide the depositors with this much gold whenever they requested it. Thus the early goldsmith had the balance sheet shown in Table 11-1.

At this stage, a fundamental question arose regarding the goldsmith's business. If it operated simply as a warehouse, holding the $100,000 in gold coins that the customers had deposited, it would not be very profitable. Its sole source of profits would be the amount charged for safeguarding gold.

After some years of experience holding gold for many different depositors, the goldsmith might have noticed something interesting. Although he was committed to repay the gold of the depositors on demand, he did not actually repay all at once in the normal course of events. Each week some people withdrew gold, but others made deposits. There was a flow of gold out of the warehouse, but there was also an inflow. There was some fluctuation in the goldsmith's total holdings of gold; nonetheless, a sizable quantity remained on deposit at all times.

Sooner or later a question therefore occurred to the goldsmith. Why not lend out some of this gold

TABLE 11-1   Balance Sheet of the Early Goldsmith

Assets		Liabilities and Net Worth	
Gold coins	$100,000	Demand deposit liabilities	$100,000
Building	$ 10,000	Net worth	$ 10,000
Total	$110,000	Total	$110,000

The early goldsmith operated a warehouse, holding $1 in gold for every $1 in deposits.

that was just sitting in the vaults, "collecting dust"? Since the depositors did not all try to withdraw their gold simultaneously, the goldsmith did not need to have all the gold on hand. Some could be put to work earning interest. We can therefore imagine the goldsmith beginning to experiment by making loans. Undoubtedly, he started cautiously, keeping a relatively large quantity of gold in his vaults. Specifically, suppose that he kept a large reserve of $40,000 in gold to pay off depositors in the event that a group of them suddenly demanded their gold back. He lent the remaining $60,000 in gold, with the borrowers giving him promissory notes stating their commitment to pay interest and repay the principal after a period of time. Then the goldsmith's balance sheet changed to the one shown in Table 11-2. The only difference was on the asset side: The goldsmith had exchanged $60,000 of gold for $60,000 in promissory notes (shown simply as "Loans").

In making loans, the goldsmith went beyond warehousing and entered the **fractional-reserve banking** business. That is, *he held gold reserves that were only a fraction of his demand deposit liabilities.* In normal times, things worked out well. The goldsmith kept enough gold to pay off all depositors who wanted to make withdrawals, and he earned interest on the loans he had made.

As time passed and goldsmiths gained confidence in the banking business, they experimented by keeping gold reserves that were lower and lower fractions of their deposit liabilities. Sometimes they had only 20% in reserve or even less. They had an incentive to reduce reserves because each additional dollar taken out of reserves and lent out meant that additional interest could be earned. But, while the entry into fractional-reserve banking allowed goldsmiths to prosper, they faced two major risks in their new banking business:

1.   Their loans might go sour. That is, goldsmiths might lend to businesses or individuals who became unable to repay. Clearly, then, the *evaluation of credit risks* (the estimation of the chances that borrowers would be unable to repay) became an important part of goldsmithing—and of modern banking.

2.   Because they kept reserves equal to only a fraction of their deposit liabilities, the goldsmith-bankers were counting on a reasonably stable flow of deposits and withdrawals. In normal times, these flows were indeed likely to be stable. But the goldsmith-banker could not count on times being normal. If for some reason depositors became frightened, they would appear in droves to make withdrawals. In other words, there would be a *run* on the bank.

BANK RUNS AND PANICS

During business downturns, people were particularly likely to become frightened and to look for safety. What could be safer than holding gold? In crises, then, the public tended to switch into gold—that is, they withdrew gold from their banks. But the banks, operating with gold reserves equal to only a fraction of their deposits, could not meet the demand if all their depositors wanted gold at the same time. *Unlike the original goldsmith who held 100% reserves—and acted simply as a warehouse—the*

TABLE 11-2   The Goldsmith Becomes a Banker

Assets		Liabilities and Net Worth		
Reserve of gold coins	$ 40,000	Demand deposits	$100,000	When the goldsmith loans gold coins . . .
Loans	$ 60,000	Net worth	$ 10,000	. . . reserves decline . . .
Building	$ 10,000			. . . and are now only a fraction of deposit liabilities.
Total	$110,000	Total	$110,000	

Once the goldsmith had begun to lend the deposited gold and kept gold reserves equal to only a fraction of demand deposit liabilities, the business ceased to be a simple warehouse and became a bank.

fractional-reserve bank simply did not have enough gold to pay off all its depositors. A panic, with a run on the banks, was the result. Since banks could not possibly pay off all their deposit liabilities, every individual depositor had an incentive to withdraw his or her deposit before the bank ran out of gold and was forced to close. For all depositors as a group, this was self-destructive behavior. The run could push banks into bankruptcy, with some depositors losing their money forever. But individual depositors could not be expected to commit financial suicide for the common good; they could not be expected to stay out of a lineup of those making withdrawals. At the earliest sign of a run, each depositor had a personal interest to be *first* in line to get back his or her gold.

THE MODERN U.S. BANKING SYSTEM

This account is obviously an extremely simplified version of the history of banks. Nonetheless, it does help to explain why the U.S. banking system was periodically shaken with crises at the turn of the century. These banking crises added to the instability of the economy. Following the Panic of 1907, a National Monetary Commission was established to study monetary and banking problems. The result was the Federal Reserve Act of 1913.

THE FEDERAL RESERVE

The Federal Reserve—also known informally as the "Fed"—is the central bank of the United States. It is the American equivalent of foreign central banks, such as the Bank of England, the Deutsche Bundesbank of Germany, the Bank of Canada, and the Bank of Japan. As the central bank, the Federal Reserve

1. Has the responsibility to *control the quantity of money* in the United States.

2. *Issues paper currency* (dollar bills).

3. *Acts as the "bankers' bank."* While you and I keep our deposits in the commercial banks, commercial banks in turn keep deposits in the Federal Reserve. While you and I—and business corporations—can go to the commercial banks for loans, commercial banks in turn can borrow from the Federal Reserve. The Federal Reserve also helps the commercial banks to make the system of payment by check work smoothly and inexpensively.

4. *Supervises and inspects* commercial banks. (The U.S. Treasury, the Federal Deposit Insurance Corporation, and state banking authorities share this responsibility with the Fed.)

5. Acts as the *federal government's bank.* The government keeps some of its deposits in the Fed, and the Fed administers the sale of government bonds and their repayment when they come due. The Fed also acts on behalf of the government in buying and selling foreign currencies, such as German marks or Swiss francs.

How the Federal Reserve carries out these responsibilities will be major topics in future chapters.

THE COMMERCIAL BANKS

The commercial banks are the most direct descendants of the goldsmiths of old. They perform the two functions of the goldsmith-banker illustrated in Table 11-2. That is, they accept deposits, and they make loans to businesses and individuals. These two key functions show up clearly in the combined balance sheet of commercial banks shown in Table 11-3. Deposits are shown in items 7 and 8, and loans to businesses and individuals in item 4.

A number of other items on the balance sheet are also worthy of note, beginning with the first entry—reserves. Unlike the goldsmiths and the early banks, modern banks do not hold gold as reserves; gold is no longer the basic money of the United States or of other countries. Instead, banks hold two kinds of reserve: deposits in the Federal Reserve and currency. Banks are *required by law* to keep reserves equal to certain percentages of their deposits, the percentages being specified by the Federal Reserve within the legal limits set by Congress. Note that reserves, which appear on the *asset* side of the balance sheet, must meet the required percentages of the deposits (items 7 and 8) on the *liabilities* side of the bank's balance sheet. For example, with a required reserve ratio of 10%, a bank with $50 million in deposit liabilities would have to hold $5 million of its assets in the form of reserves.

TABLE 11-3 Combined Balance Sheet, Commercial
Banks, February 1989   (billions of dollars)

Assets		Liabilities and Net Worth	
(1) Reserves		(7) Checking deposits	601
Currency	27	(8) Other savings and	
Reserve deposits		time deposits	1,521
in Federal Reserve	28	(9) Other liabilities	713
(2) Deposits held in other		(10) Total liabilities	2,835
banks, and other cash items	171	(11) Net worth	196
(3) Securities			
U.S. government	353		
Other	183		
(4) Loans			
Commercial and			
industrial loans	667		
Other	1,218		
(5) Other assets	384	(12) Total liabilities	
(6) Total assets	3,031	and net worth	3,031

Source: *Federal Reserve Bulletin*, May 1989, p. A18.

Required reserves are reserves that deposit-accepting institutions are required to hold in order to meet their legal obligations. These reserves are specified as percentages of deposit liabilities. Required reserves are held in the form of currency or deposits in the Federal Reserve.

Continuing down the asset side of the balance sheet, note that loans are the largest category of assets (item 4). The banks also hold substantial amounts of bonds and short-term securities issued by the federal and state governments (item 3).

OTHER DEPOSITORY INSTITUTIONS

Until the early 1970s, commercial banks played a unique role in the U.S. economy. They alone could accept checking deposits from the public. These deposits—known technically as *demand* deposits—paid no interest.

There were, however, a number of other financial institutions that could accept other types of deposits. Most important were thrift institutions such as the savings and loan associations (S&Ls) and mutual savings banks, which accepted *savings* deposits from the public. Checking was not permitted against such deposits. The thrift institutions used the deposited funds mainly to lend to home buyers. When they made such loans, they obtained mortgages on the homes of the borrowers. Thus the most important item on the asset side of their balance sheet was a portfolio of mortgages.

During the 1970s, the distinction between commercial banks and the thrift institutions began to break down. In 1972, a number of New England thrift institutions were eager to attract new deposits and began to offer a new type of interest-bearing savings account against which a *negotiable order of withdrawal* (NOW) could be written. In effect, such an order was a check, and the thrift institutions had gotten around the prohibition against checkable savings deposits. At first, the authorities resisted this change. NOW accounts were limited to New England.

In 1980, however, Congress took steps to deregulate financial institutions and encourage competition among them. Thrift institutions throughout the country were permitted to accept checking accounts. Commercial banks, which had previously been prohibited from paying interest on their checking accounts, were now permitted to do so. Thus the principal distinctions between commercial banks and thrift institutions were eliminated. (When we write about "commercial banks" in the following pages, the reader should understand that we mean "commercial banks and other depository institutions, such as savings and loan associations.")

REMAINING REGULATIONS

In spite of the substantial deregulation of recent years, commercial banks and other depository institutions remain subject to regulations:

First, and most important, they are required to hold reserves as a fraction of their deposit liabilities. This regulation plays a key role in helping the Federal Reserve to control the quantity of money, as we will see.

Second, they are inspected by a number of agencies, such as the Federal Reserve and the U.S. Treasury. A major purpose of inspection is to prevent unsound practices that might threaten the survival of the institutions.

Third, many banks are still prevented from doing business outside their home state.

The historical prohibition against interstate banking is breaking down, however. One reason is the increasing number of failures of banks and S&Ls. State authorities have at times permitted out-of-state banks to take over troubled banks and S&Ls; the out-of-state banks were often willing to pay for the privilege of setting up business and thus relieve the state authorities of some of the costs of compensating the depositors of failing institutions. Furthermore, a number of states have passed laws permitting regional banking. Banks from neighboring states are allowed in if the neighboring states grant reciprocal privileges and let their banks in.

Banking has become a highly competitive and rapidly changing business, and it promises to remain so in the future.

BANKS AND THE CREATION OF MONEY

The public's use of checking deposits as money would be reason enough to look carefully at the operation of banks. But banks require attention for an additional reason—and one of great importance. In the normal course of their operations, they create money. Most people have heard of this power in a vague and imprecise way. Banks are consequently looked on with a mixture of awe and resentment. How did they acquire this almost magical power, and why should they be allowed to exercise it? These attitudes reflect a lack of understanding of banking. There is in fact nothing magical in the process whereby money is created. Your local bank does not have a fountain pen with which it can create unlimited amounts of money out of thin air.

The operations of banks, and how they create money, can be understood most easily by looking at the balance sheets of individual banks. An individual commercial bank, like the aggregate of commercial banks shown in Table 11-3, has a list of assets and liabilities. To avoid being burdened with detail, we simplify the following tables by showing only the *changes* in the balance sheet of a bank. (Like the whole balance sheet, changes in the balance sheet *must* balance.) To avoid untidy fractions, we assume that the required reserves of banks are a nice round figure—20% of their checking deposit liabilities—even though requirements are not, in fact, this high. To simplify further, we assume that banks initially have just enough reserves to meet the legal reserve requirement.

Now, suppose your eccentric old uncle dies. In his will, he leaves you $100,000 that he has been keeping in a shoe box in his attic. You rush to your local bank to put the $100,000 into your checking account. As a result, your bank—call it bank A—has $100,000 more in currency on the asset side of its balance sheet (Table 11-4). It also has $100,000 more in liabilities, since you have a $100,000 claim on the bank in the form of a checking deposit. (This $100,000 deposit represents an *asset* to you; it is something you own. However, this same $100,000 deposit is a *liability* to the bank; the bank must be prepared to pay you $100,000 in currency if you ask.)

As a result of this deposit, what has happened to the quantity of money? The answer is: nothing. You initially held the $100,000 in currency; you exchanged the currency for $100,000 in checking deposit money. Once the deposit is made, the $100,000 in dollar bills ceases to be counted as part of the money stock, since it is held by the bank. (Remember the technical point regarding the data in Fig. 11-1: Currency and checking deposits are included in the money stock only when they are held by the public, but not when they are held by the Federal Reserve, the U.S. Treasury, commercial banks, or other deposit-accepting institutions.) The *composition* of the money stock has changed; the

TABLE 11-4 Changes in Assets and Liabilities
When Commercial Bank Receives Deposit

Commercial bank A

Assets		Liabilities	
Reserves of currency	+$100,000	Checking deposits	+$100,000
Required $20,000			
Excess $80,000			
Total	$100,000	Total	$100,000

When you deposit $100,000 in currency. . .

. . . bank reserves also rise by $100,000.

Your balance sheet

Assets		Liabilities	
Currency	–$100,000	No change	
Checking deposit	+$100,000		
Total	0	Total	0

When commercial bank A receives your $100,000 deposit, both its assets and liabilities rise by $100,000. But your holdings of money do not change. You have merely switched from one type of money (currency) to another (a checking deposit).

public now holds $100,000 more in checking deposits and $100,000 less in currency. At this point, however, the total amount of money has not yet changed.

This is not the end of the story because the bank now has excess reserves. Its checking deposit liabilities have gone up by your $100,000. Therefore its required reserves have risen by $20,000 (that is, $100,000 times the required reserve ratio of 20%). However, its total reserves have risen by the $100,000 in currency that you deposited. Thus it now has $80,000 in **excess reserves.** Like the goldsmith of old, it is in a position to make loans to businesses and other customers.

Suppose that a local shoe store wants to expand its operations. It goes to the bank to borrow $80,000, an amount that just happens to equal the excess reserves of the bank. The bank agrees to make the loan (Table 11-5). Mechanically, what happens? The bank could presumably hand over

TABLE 11-5 Bank A Makes a Loan

Assets		Liabilities	
Reserves of currency	$100,000	Checking deposits	
		of you	$100,000
Loan[†]	+$ 80,000	of shoe store[†]	+$ 80,000
Total	$180,000	Total	$180,000

When a bank makes a loan . . .

. . . checking deposits increase.

When the bank lends $80,000, checking deposits increase by $80,000. This represents a net increase in the money stock.

[†]Items resulting from the loan.

$80,000 in dollar bills to the store owner in exchange for a promissory note that commits the store to repay the loan. However, the bank does not normally operate this way. Instead, when it makes the loan, it simply adds $80,000 to the checking deposit of the borrower. This arrangement is entirely satisfactory to the borrower, who can write a check against the deposit. As a result of this loan, the balance sheet of the commercial bank is modified, as shown in Table 11-5.

Now, what has happened to the money supply? Observe that *when the bank makes a loan, the stock of money in the hands of the public increases.* Specifically, there now is $80,000 more in checking deposit money.

Excess reserves are reserves, in the form of currency or deposits in the Federal Reserve, that are in excess of those that a commercial bank or other depository institution is required to hold.

Excess reserves = total reserves − required reserves

HOW A CHECK IS CLEARED

So far, so good. However, the story has just begun. It is continued in Figure 11-2. The shoe store borrowed from the bank in order to buy inventory, not

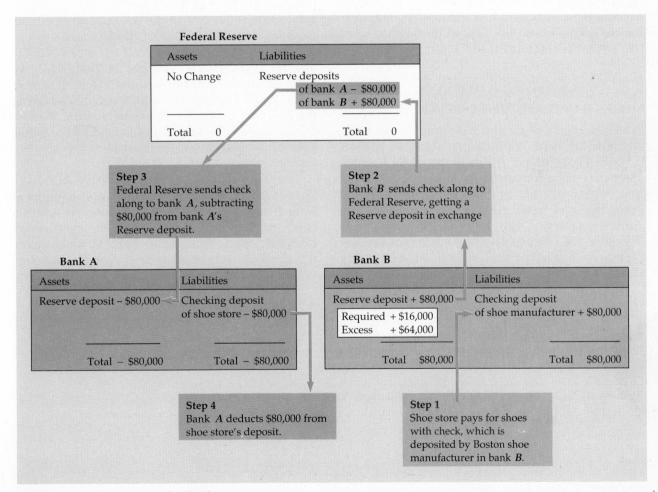

FIGURE 11-2   The clearing of a check

In the check-clearing process, the bank in which the check was deposited (bank B) acquires reserves, whereas the bank on which the check was drawn (bank A) loses reserves.

to leave its money sitting idly in a checking account. Suppose that the shoe store orders shoes from a Boston manufacturer, sending a check for $80,000 in payment. The shoe company in Boston deposits the check in its bank (bank B). This sets in motion the process of **check clearing**—which straightens out accounts between bank A in your home town and bank B in Boston (Fig. 11-2). Bank B sends the check along to the Federal Reserve, receiving in exchange a reserve deposit of $80,000. Bank B's accounts balance, since its assets in the form of reserves have gone up by the same amount ($80,000) as its checking deposit liabilities to the shoe manufacturer. (The $80,000 reserve deposit represents an *asset* to bank B and a *liability* to the Federal Reserve.)

The Fed, in turn, sends the check along to bank A, subtracting the $80,000 from bank A's reserve deposit. Bank A balances its accounts by subtracting the $80,000 from the deposit of the shoe store that wrote the check in the first place.

WHY A BANK CAN SAFELY LEND NO MORE THAN ITS EXCESS RESERVES

When the effects of the check clearing (in Fig. 11-2) are added to bank A's earlier transactions (shown in Table 11-5), the net effects on bank A's balance sheet may be summarized in Table 11-6. Observe that, as a result of the check clearing, bank A's excess reserves have completely disappeared. (Its currency reserves rose by $100,000 when you deposited the original $100,000, but its reserve deposit in the Fed fell by $80,000 when the shoe store's check cleared. Thus its net change in reserves is

$20,000, just enough to provide the required reserve for its $100,000 checking deposit liability to you.) The $80,000 in excess reserves disappeared as a result of bank A's $80,000 loan to the shoe store. Thus we come to a fundamental proposition:

> **A bank may prudently lend an amount up to, but no greater than, its excess reserves.**

THE MULTIPLE EXPANSION OF BANK DEPOSITS

We have seen how bank A's excess reserves are eliminated when the shoe store's $80,000 check clears. But observe (in Fig. 11-2) that bank B now has excess reserves of $64,000—that is, the difference between the $80,000 increase in its actual reserves and the $16,000 increase in its required reserves ($16,000 = 20% of the $80,000 increase in its checking deposit liabilities).

Bank B may prudently lend up to $64,000, the amount of its excess reserves. In Table 11-7, we suppose that it lends this amount to a local camera store. When the loan is made, $64,000 is added to the checking deposit of the camera store. Because the amount of checking deposits held by the public goes up by $64,000, *the money stock increases by this amount.*

Suppose that the camera store has borrowed the $64,000 to buy film, cameras, and equipment from Kodak. To pay for its purchases, it writes a check to Kodak. Kodak deposits the check in its Rochester, New York, bank—bank C. Once again, the check-clearing mechanism is set in operation. When bank C sends the check to the Federal

TABLE 11-6   Net Effects on Bank A
(check clearing combined with earlier transactions)

Assets		Liabilities	
Reserves	$ 20,000	Checking deposits of you	$100,000
Required $20,000 Excess 0			
Loan	$ 80,000		
Total	$100,000	Total	$100,000

This table gives the combined effect on bank A of check clearing (Fig. 11-2) and earlier transactions (Table 11-5). After the check is cleared, bank A has no excess reserves.

TABLE 11-7 Bank B Lends to Camera Store

Assets		Liabilities	
Reserve deposit	$ 80,000	Checking deposits of shoe manufacturer	$ 80,000
Loan[†]	+$ 64,000	of camera store[†]	+$ 64,000
Total	$144,000	Total	$144,000

When bank B lends $64,000 . . .

. . . checking deposits increase by $64,000.

As a result of the second round of lending, the money stock increases by $64,000.

[†]Items resulting from the loan.

Reserve, it receives a reserve deposit of $64,000 (Table 11-8). But when the check is sent along to bank B (the camera store's bank), that bank loses $64,000 in reserves and no longer has any excess reserves.

Observe, however, that bank C now has excess reserves of $51,200; it can safely lend that amount. When it does so, it creates a new checking deposit of $51,200, thus increasing the money stock once again. The process continues. As a result of your initial deposit of $100,000, there can be a chain reaction of loans, as shown in Figure 11-3 and Table 11-9. At each stage, the amount of loans that can be made (and the amount of deposits that can thereby be created) is 80% of the amount made in the previous stage. The total increase in deposits is the sum of the series: $100,000 + $100,000 \times 0.8 + $100,000 \times 0.8^2$. . . . If this series is taken to its limit—with an

TABLE 11-8 The Creation of Money: After the Second Round

Bank B

Assets		Liabilities	
Reserves	$16,000	Checking deposits of shoe manufacturer	$80,000
Required $16,000			
Excess 0			
Loans	$64,000		
Total	$80,000	Total	$80,000

Bank C

Assets		Liabilities	
Reserves	$64,000	Checking deposits of Kodak	$64,000
Required $12,800			
Excess $51,200			
Total	$64,000	Total	$64,000

When bank C receives deposits and reserves of $64,000, it can prudently lend $51,200. And so the process continues.

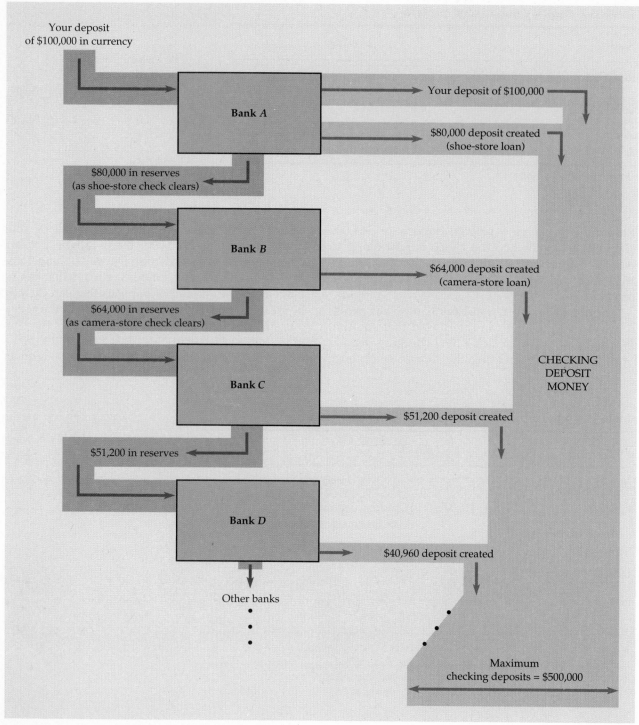

FIGURE 11-3   The multiple expansion of bank deposits

The banking system as a whole can do what no single bank can do. It can transform the original deposit of $100,000 in currency into as much as $500,000 in checking deposit money.

TABLE 11-9 The Multiple Expansion of Bank Deposits

A. The chain reaction

Bank	(1) Acquired Reserves and Checking Deposits	(2) Required Reserves (2) = (1) × 0.20	(3) Excess Reserves = Loans Which Banks Can Make (3) = (1) – (2)	(4) Changes in Money Stock (4) = (3)
A	$100,000 (yours)	$20,000	$80,000	$80,000
B	$80,000 (shoe manufacturer's)	$16,000	$64,000	$64,000
C	$64,000 (Kodak's)	$12,800	$51,200	$51,200
D	$51,200	$10,240	$40,960	$40,960
.	.	.	.	.
.	.	.	.	.
.	.	.	.	.
Maximum sum	$500,000	$100,000	$400,000	$400,000

B. Effects on consolidated balance sheet of all commercial banks (with maximum permissible expansion)

Assets		Liabilities	
Reserves	$100,000	Checking deposits	$500,000
Required $100,000 Excess 0			
Loans	$400,000		
Total	$500,000	Total	$500,000

As much as $500,000 in checking deposits can result when the banking system receives an additional $100,000 in reserves.

infinite number of rounds—then, by a basic algebraic proposition,[2] the sum is equal to $100,000 ÷ (1 – 0.8) = $500,000.

When the banking system acquires additional reserves, it can therefore increase checking deposits by a multiple of the initial increase in reserves.

_____

[2]Mathematically, this is the same theorem used in the derivation of the multiplier in Chapter 9 (footnote 2). However, the economic issues are *very* different in the two cases. In the multiplier, the total effects of various rounds of spending are derived. Here, changes in the stock of money are calculated.

The checking deposit multiplier D is equal to the reciprocal of the required reserve ratio R:

$$D = \frac{1}{R}$$

In our example:

$$D = \frac{1}{20\%} = 5$$

The initial acquisition of $100,000 in reserves made possible an increase in checking deposits of $500,000 (that is, $100,000 × 1/0.2). Alternatively, if the required reserve ratio were lower—say, 10%— the banking system would have been capable of creating as much as $1,000,000 (that is, $100,000 × 1/0.1) in checking deposits on the basis of $100,000 in reserves. A lower reserve requirement would mean a greater increase in the money supply because required reserves at each stage would be less. Consequently, there would be greater excess reserves that could be loaned at each stage, resulting in a larger increase in the money supply.

Thus, *when the Federal Reserve changes the required reserve ratio,* as it is permitted to do, *it can have a powerful effect on the amount of loans which the banks can make and on the amount of checking deposits which they can create.*

During the **multiple expansion of deposits,** the banking system as a whole does something no single bank can do. *The banking system as a whole can create deposits equal to a multiple of the reserves that it acquires. But any single bank can create deposits by an amount equal to only a fraction (80% in our illustration) of the reserves that it acquires.*

TWO COMPLICATIONS

With a required reserve ratio of 20%, $500,000 is the *maximum* increase in checking deposits following a $100,000 acquisition of reserves by the banking system. In practice, the actual increase in checking deposits is likely to be considerably less, because of two complications:

1. Banks may decide not to lend out the maximum permitted but to hold some excess reserves instead. During prosperous times, this is not an important complication because banks hold only small amounts of excess reserves. Banks receive no interest on their excess reserves, and they have a strong incentive to make loans in order to increase their interest earnings. They typically continue to lend until their excess reserves fall well below 1% of their total reserves.

During a depression, however, bankers may be panic-stricken. They may be afraid to make loans because they doubt the ability of borrowers to repay. They may decide to keep their funds secure by holding them as excess reserves rather than making additional loans. During the Great Depression, excess reserves skyrocketed, reaching almost 50% of total reserves by 1935. This unwillingness of the banks to lend kept down the amount of money in the hands of the public and slowed the recovery. Thus bank holdings of excess reserves may fluctuate in a *perverse manner.* Banks may hold large excess reserves during a depression, thereby keeping down the quantity of money. But this is precisely the time when it is *most* desirable for the quantity of money to expand.

2. As loans are made and people get more checking deposit money, they may want to hold more currency, too. In other words, they may withdraw cash from their deposits. Insofar as this happens, the reserves of the banks are reduced; the initial deposit of currency that started off the expansion is partially reversed. As a consequence, the total amount of monetary expansion is reduced.

When currency is held by the public, it is, in a sense, just ordinary money. The dollar I hold in my pocket is only a dollar. On the other hand, when currency is deposited in a bank, it becomes "high-powered." Although the dollar ceases to count directly in the money stock (since bank holdings of currency are excluded from the definition of money), that dollar bill is a bank reserve. On this reserve base, the banking system can build a superstructure of as much as $5 of checking deposit money if the required reserve ratio is 20%. The large amount of checking deposit money, built on a much smaller base of reserves, can be represented graphically by an inverted *pyramid* (Fig. 11-4).

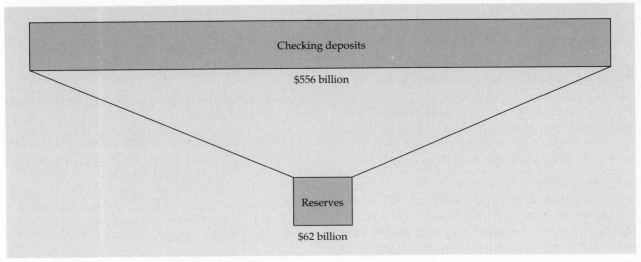

FIGURE 11-4   The inverted monetary pyramid

On its reserve base of currency and reserve deposits, the commercial banking system can build a superstructure of checking deposits—of as much as $1/R$ times the base. (Data are for September 1988.)

KEY POINTS

1. Money is important in the study of macroeconomics because

   (a) The authorities can take steps to alter the quantity of money and thus affect aggregate demand. *Monetary policy* is a powerful tool for managing aggregate demand. The details of monetary policy will be explained in Chapter 12.

   (b) At times, strong disturbances have occurred in the monetary system—for example, during the Panic of 1907 and the Great Depression of the 1930s. Such disturbances can make the economy unstable.

2. Money has three interrelated functions. It acts as

   (a) The medium of exchange.

   (b) The unit of account, that is, the standard of value.

   (c) A store of value.

3. Because currency, checking deposits, and travelers' checks are used in transactions, they are included in the basic definition of the money stock, M1. Checking deposits constitute by far the largest component of M1.

4. Noncheckable savings and time deposits are close substitutes for M1. When studying how money and the banking system affect aggregate demand, economists thus sometimes focus on an alternative definition of money, M2.

   M2 = M1 + noncheckable savings deposits +
         time deposits + money market deposits +
         money market mutual funds

5. The Federal Reserve is the central bank of the United States. As such:

   (a) It has the responsibility to control the quantity of money.

   (b) It issues paper currency.

   (c) It acts as the bankers' bank.

   (d) It supervises and inspects commercial banks.

   (e) It acts as the federal government's bank.

6. Banks have two principal functions: to accept deposits and to make loans. When a bank makes a loan, it increases the stock of money.

7. Commercial banks and other depository institutions are required to hold reserves in the form of currency or reserve deposits in the Federal Reserve. These reserves must meet required percentages of the commercial bank's deposit liabilities. The purpose of required reserves is to limit the quantity of money that banks can create.

8. When a *single* bank acquires additional deposits and reserves, it can safely lend out only a *fraction* of these reserves—specifically, an amount equal to its excess reserves. However, the banking *system* (all banks and other depository institutions as a whole) can make loans and therby create deposits that are a *multiple* of any new reserves that it acquires.

9. The maximum increase in checking deposits

that can be created by the banking system is:

$$\frac{1}{R} \times \text{the acquisition of reserves}$$

where R is the required reserve ratio.

10. In practice, the increase is likely to be less than the maximum, since

(a) Banks sometimes hold substantial excess reserves. This happened during the depression of the 1930s. However, banks normally do not hold large amounts of excess reserves. It would be expensive for them to do so; they would forego the interest they would receive by making additional loans.

(b) As people get more checking deposit money, they are likely to want to hold more currency, too. When they withdraw currency from their deposits, the reserves held by the banks are reduced.

KEY CONCEPTS

medium of exchange	money market deposits	required reserves
unit of account	money market mutual funds	excess reserves
store of value	M1 and M2	clearing of a check
currency	liquid asset	multiple expansion of bank deposits
checking deposit	fractional-reserve banking	
savings deposit	balance sheet	checking deposit multiplier
time deposit	bank run	monetary pyramid

PROBLEMS

11-1. (a) A corporation that previously paid its workers in cash decides to pay them by check instead. As a result, it decides to deposit $10,000 which it has held in currency in its safe. Show how this deposit will affect the balance sheets of (1) the corporation and (2) its bank (the First National Bank of Buffalo).

(b) Does this deposit of $10,000 affect the money stock? Explain your answer.

(c) How much can the First National Bank of Buffalo now lend, if there is a required reserve ratio of 10%? If it lends this amount to a farmer to buy machinery, show the direct

effect of the loan on the bank's balance sheet. Then show the First National Bank of Buffalo's balance sheet after the farmer spends the loan to buy machinery and the farmer's check is cleared.

(d) As a result of the original deposit (in part (a) of this problem), what is the maximum increase in checking deposits that can occur if the required reserve ratio is 10%? The maximum amount of bank lending? The maximum increase in the money stock?

11-2. Suppose that a bank receives a deposit of $100,000 and decides to lend the full $100,000.

Explain how this decision can get the bank into difficulty.

11-3. If all banks are required to keep reserves equal to 100% of their checking deposits, what will be the consequences of a deposit of $100,000 of currency in bank A?

11-4. During the 1930s, banks held large excess reserves. Now they hold practically none. Why? If you were a banker, would you hold excess reserves? How much? Does your answer depend on the size of individual deposits in your bank? On interest rates? On other things?

11-5. Suppose that there is a single huge commercial bank that holds a monopoly on all banking in the United States. If this bank receives $100,000 in deposits, and if the required reserve ratio is 20%, how much can the bank safely lend? Explain. [*Hints:* (a) Study Table 11-9, Part B. (b) In Figure 11-2, bank A lost reserves to bank B. If there is only one bank, will it lose reserves in this way?]

11-6. During the 1930s, the U.S. banking system did not work well. Banking disturbances contributed to the depth and duration of the depression.

(a) Explain how, during a financial crisis, individual bank depositors have an incentive to behave in a manner that makes the crisis worse. Do you think that an educational campaign to teach depositors the dangers of such actions would help to solve this problem? If so, explain how. If not, explain why not.

(b) Explain how, during the Great Depression, individual banks had an incentive to behave in a manner that made the depression deeper and longer lasting. If you were a banker, would you behave in this way? Do you think that an educational campaign to teach bankers the dangers of such actions would have helped to solve this problem? If so, explain how. If not, explain why not.

CHAPTER 12
THE FEDERAL RESERVE AND MONETARY POLICY

You can't appreciate home till you've left it, [nor] money till it's spent.

O. HENRY

"There have," said humorist Will Rogers, "been three great inventions since the beginning of time: fire, the wheel, and central banking." Why did Rogers, even in jest, put central banking on the list? The answer: A central bank—such as the Federal Reserve, the Bank of England, or the Bank of Mexico—has a unique power. It controls the quantity of money in an economy. With this power comes a grave responsibility. If the central bank creates too much money, it will cause inflation. If it creates too little—or allows the money stock to decline—the economy is likely to fall into a recession or a depression.

This chapter describes the three principal policy tools the Federal Reserve can use to control the quantity of money:

1. Open market operations—that is, purchases or sales of government bonds or shorter term securities by the Federal Reserve.

2. Changes in the **discount rate.** This is the interest rate at which the Federal Reserve lends to banks.

3. Changes in **required reserve ratios** that banks must hold as percentages of their checking and time deposits.

The latter parts of the chapter will explain

■ A number of minor policy tools.

■ Some of the problems that can arise in monetary policy.

Before describing the Fed's tools in detail, let us look briefly at the way the Federal Reserve is organized.

THE ORGANIZATION OF THE FEDERAL RESERVE

When the Federal Reserve Act was passed in 1913, the very concept of a central bank was controversial. Those who opposed the creation of a central bank feared that it would result in a concentration of monetary power, with serious political consequences. This fear was not new. The Second Bank of the United States, which had acted as a rudimentary central bank in the early nineteenth century, had come to an abrupt end at the hands of President Andrew Jackson, who attacked its political power. "The bank," said Jackson, "is trying to kill me, *but I will kill it.*"[1] And he did so.

The political controversies and compromises that surrounded the establishment of the Federal

---

[1]Arthur M. Schlesinger, Jr., *The Age of Jackson,* abr. ed. (New York: Mentor, 1949), p. 42.

Reserve are reflected in its untidy organization. In order to diffuse power, the Federal Reserve was organized with 12 regional Federal Reserve Banks, in Boston, New York, Philadelphia, and other major cities (Fig. 12-1). These 12 district banks handle most of the everyday operations of the Fed, including the clearing of checks and the issuing of new currency. (If you look to the left of George Washington's picture on a dollar bill, you will find a seal that identifies the Federal Reserve Bank that issued it.) In Washington D.C., overall coordination is provided by the seven-member Board of Governors of the Federal Reserve System—also known, more simply, as the Federal Reserve Board.

The members of the Federal Reserve Board are appointed by the president of the United States, subject to congressional approval. In order to provide the Board with a degree of independence from political pressures and thus to strengthen its ability to fight inflation, members of the Board are appointed for extended 14-year terms, with one position becoming vacant every 2 years. The chair serves for a 4-year term, which may be renewed.

During the history of the Fed, there have been numerous power struggles between the Board and the district banks. In the 1920s, the Board was overshadowed by the forceful president of the Federal Reserve Bank of New York, Benjamin Strong. More recently, the Fed has been dominated by the chairmen of the Federal Reserve Board—William McChesney Martin, who headed the Board from 1951 to 1970; his successor, Arthur F. Burns (1970–1978); Paul Volcker (1979–1987); and, most recently, Alan Greenspan (1987–   ).

There have been many revisions in the Federal Reserve Act. The major current powers of the

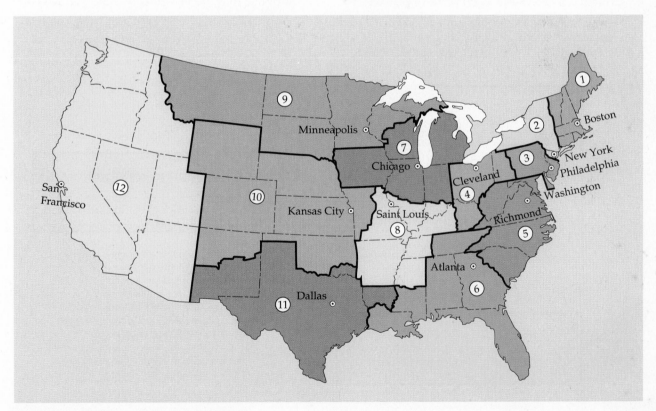

FIGURE 12-1   The Federal Reserve System

The United States is divided into 12 Federal Reserve districts, each with a Federal Reserve bank. (Alaska and Hawaii are part of the district served by the Federal Reserve Bank of San Francisco.)

Board and the 12 regional Federal Reserve Banks are listed in Figure 12-2. Each of the principal tools of the Federal Reserve is handled differently.

1.   Open market operations. This tool, the most important of all, is controlled by the Federal Open Market Committee (FOMC), which consists of the seven members of the Board of Governors and five of the presidents of the 12 district Federal Reserve Banks. The president of the New York Fed is a permanent member of the FOMC, with the other regional presidents serving on a rotating basis. The FOMC issues directives to the trading desk in the New York Fed, which handles the actual purchase or sale of securities.

2.   Changes in the discount rate. Proposals for change are made by the regional Federal Reserve Banks, subject to the approval of the Federal Reserve Board.

3.   Changes in required reserve ratios. Power to change these ratios is held by the Federal Reserve Board in Washington, subject to limits prescribed by Congress.

CONTROLLING THE MONEY SUPPLY: OPEN MARKET OPERATIONS

The Federal Reserve can increase the quantity of commercial bank reserves—and thereby increase the quantity of checking deposit money which the banks can create—by purchasing U.S. government securities on the open market. To make such a purchase, the Fed puts in a bid on the securities market; the seller may be a bank or a member of the general public who is willing to sell. But whether the government security is sold by a bank or by the public, the results are similar.

Suppose that the Fed puts in a bid for $100,000

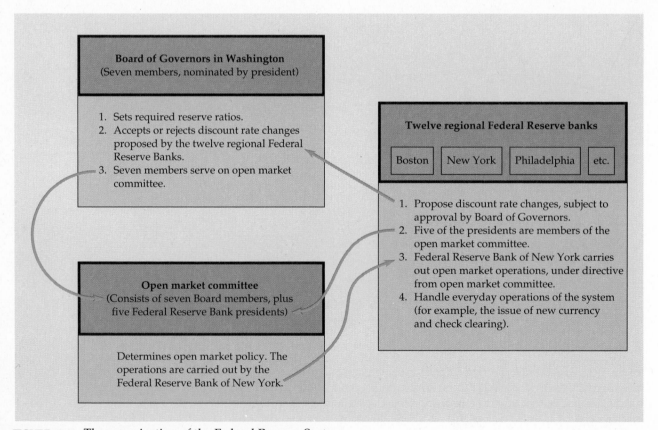

FIGURE 12-2   The organization of the Federal Reserve System

worth of government securities and that General Motors is the seller. General Motors delivers the securities and gets a check for $100,000 in return. GM deposits this check in its commercial bank (bank A). In turn, bank A sends the check along to the Federal Reserve and has its deposit with the Fed increased by $100,000. The changes in the balance sheets of the Fed and commercial bank A are shown in Table 12-1. Observe that, *when the Federal Reserve buys government securities, it increases the reserves of the commercial banking system.*

At the initial step shown in Table 12-1, the money supply has gone up by $100,000. Why? The answer is: GM's $100,000 checking deposit is counted as part of the money stock. (The government security which GM gave up was not part of the money stock.) Furthermore, *the stage is set for an additional expansion* because of the new reserves held by bank A. Specifically, bank A now has $80,000 in excess reserves and can safely lend that amount. A whole series of loans, similar to those

already described in Chapter 11, can take place. Thus, with a 20% required reserve ratio, the $100,000 open market purchase makes possible a maximum increase of $500,000 in checking deposits—that is, an increase of $500,000 in the money stock. (Again, as explained in Chapter 11, this is a maximum. In practice, the actual increase will be less, insofar as the public decides to hold more currency along with its higher checking deposits, and insofar as commercial banks hold excess reserves.)

This, then, is the power of open market operations. The Fed carries out the simple transaction of buying a government security, and the reserves of the banking system increase as a result. Thus the Fed makes possible an increase in the nation's money supply.

Suppose now that the Fed buys the $100,000 worth of government securities from a commercial bank rather than from General Motors. The end result is the same. The maximum increase in the money stock is once again $500,000, although the

TABLE 12-1   An Open Market Purchase: Initial Effects   (thousands of dollars)

Federal Reserve

Assets		Liabilities	
Government securities	+100	Reserve deposits of bank A	+100
Total	100	Total	100

Fed gets government securities.
Commercial bank gets reserve deposit.
GM gets checking deposit.

Commercial bank A

Assets		Liabilities	
Reserve deposit	+100	Checking deposits of GM	+100
Required 20 Excess 80			
Total	100	Total	100

At this stage, the money supply has increased by $100,000, because GM has a checking deposit of that amount.

Commercial bank A has excess reserves, and therefore a further expansion of the money supply can take place.

TABLE 12-2   Open Market Purchase, When a Commercial Bank Is the Seller
(initial effects, in thousands of dollars)

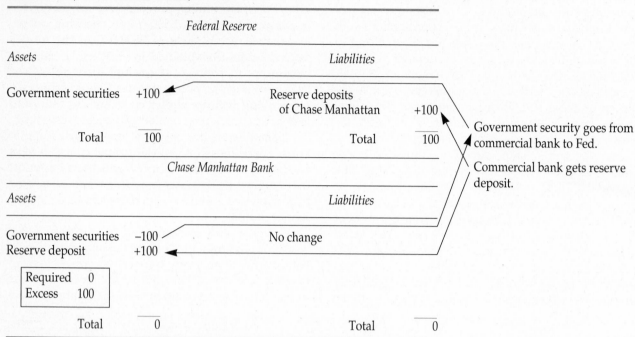

Federal Reserve

Assets		Liabilities	
Government securities	+100	Reserve deposits of Chase Manhattan	+100
Total	100	Total	100

Government security goes from commercial bank to Fed.

Commercial bank gets reserve deposit.

Chase Manhattan Bank

Assets		Liabilities	
Government securities	–100	No change	
Reserve deposit	+100		

Required	0
Excess	100

Total	0	Total	0

If the Fed buys the government security from a comercial bank (say, Chase Manhattan), no change takes place in the money stock at this initial stage. However, Chase Manhattan now has a full $100,000 in excess reserves, and it can therefore lend that amount.

mechanics are slightly different. Table 12-2 shows the initial effects of an open market operation if the Fed buys the government securities from the Chase Manhattan Bank. Chase sends the government securities to the Fed. The Fed pays for the securities by adding $100,000 to the reserves of the Chase Manhattan Bank. Once again, commercial bank reserves have increased when the Fed pays for its open market purchase. However, observe that, at the initial stage shown in Table 12-2, no change has yet taken place in the money stock. Why? The reason is: Nothing has yet happened to the public's holdings of currency or checking deposits. But note that Chase now has the full $100,000 in excess reserves, since its total reserves have gone up by $100,000 while its deposit liabilities—and therefore its required reserves—have not changed. Chase can safely lend the full $100,000, creating a $100,000 checking deposit when it does so. Once again, the

maximum checking deposit expansion is the series $100,000 + $80,000 + $64,000 + . . . , giving a total of $500,000.

In both examples of an open market purchase (Tables 12-1 and 12-2), note that when the Federal Reserve acquires assets (the government securities), its liabilities also go up. This is scarcely surprising, since the balance sheet must balance. The increase in Federal Reserve liabilities takes the form of reserve deposits, which act as the reserves of the commercial banks. To summarize briefly:

> When the Fed wants to increase the quantity of money, it purchases government securities on the open market. When it pays for these securities, it creates new bank reserves. The additional bank reserves make possible a multiple expansion of the money stock.

RESTRICTIVE OPEN MARKET OPERATIONS

Just as the Fed purchases securities when it wants to increase the money supply, so it sells securities when it wants to decrease the money supply. The numbers on the balance sheets are the same as in Tables 12-1 and 12-2, but the signs are the opposite. For example, when the Fed sells $100,000 in securities to the Chase Manhattan bank, the Fed's holdings of government securities go down by $100,000, and the reserve deposits of Chase also go down by $100,000.

An actual open market sale might lead to very tight monetary conditions, however. We live in a growing economy in which productive capacity increases. It is appropriate for the money stock to grow through time, in order to encourage aggregate demand to grow and keep the economy at full employment. Thus restrictive policies by the Federal Reserve normally do not involve actual sales of securities. Rather, *a reduction in the rate of security purchases*, aimed at reducing the *rate of growth* of the money stock, generally provides monetary conditions that are as tight as the Fed wishes in its fight against inflation.

CONTROLLING THE MONEY SUPPLY: DISCOUNT POLICY

The Federal Reserve acts as the banker's bank. Just as commercial banks lend to the general public, so the Fed may lend to commercial banks. For historical reasons, the interest rate on such loans is usually known as the **discount rate**, although it is sometimes called the *Federal Reserve Bank interest rate*. (In most other countries, it is known more simply as the *bank rate*.)

In Chapter 11, we saw how a commercial bank provides its customer with a checking deposit when it makes a loan. The transaction between the Fed and a commercial bank is similar. When the Fed grants a loan to a bank, it increases that bank's reserve deposit in the Fed, as shown in Table 12-3. Thus *such loans—or "discounts"—add to the total reserves of the banking system* and therefore they permit the banking system to increase the money supply.

Unlike open market operations, Fed lending is at the initiative of the commercial banks rather than the Fed; the commercial banks must take the first step by asking for the loans. However, the Fed has two ways of controlling the amount it lends to the commercial banks.

1. It can *change the discount rate.* A higher discount rate makes it more expensive for commercial banks to borrow from the Fed and thus discourages such borrowing.

2. It can *refuse to lend* when the banks ask. Borrowing is intended as a temporary way for banks to bring their reserves up to required levels when they have been run down by unexpected deposit withdrawals or other unforeseen circumstances. Banks are expected to confine their borrowing to periods when it is needed, and not simply use it as a way of expanding their operations.

CONTROLLING THE MONEY SUPPLY: CHANGES IN RESERVE REQUIREMENTS

The quantity of deposits that the commercial banks can create depends on the size of their reserves and on the required reserve ratio. The last chapter explained, specifically, that the maximum amount

---

TABLE 12-3 The Federal Reserve Grants a Loan to a Bank   (thousands of dollars)

Federal Reserve				
Assets		*Liabilities*		The Fed makes a loan to a commercial bank.
Loan to bank	+100	Reserve deposit of bank	+100	As a result, bank reserves increase.
Total	100	Total	100	

of deposits that can be created is equal to the amount of the reserves times $1/R$. Thus an *increase* in R (the required reserve ratio) will *decrease* the amount of deposits that can be created.

Since 1935, the Federal Reserve has had the power to change required reserve ratios within limits set by law. The details of the law are rather complicated, but, basically, the Fed is now authorized to set the required reserve ratio on checking deposits anywhere in the range from 8% to 14%.

The Fed's power to change required reserve ratios is a potent tool. With total reserves of, say, $100 million, an increase in the required reserve ratio from 10% to 11% would reduce the maximum quantity of checking deposits from $1,000 million to approximately $900 million.

The Federal Reserve learned the power of this tool the hard way, as a result of one of its policy blunders during the Great Depression. Between August 1936 and May 1937, the Fed *doubled* required reserve ratios. The restrictive effects were less strong than they otherwise might have been because banks initially had large excess reserves; the banks already had most of the reserves needed to meet the new requirements. The economy nevertheless suffered a blow. Banks felt compelled to cut back their loans. This derailed the recovery then in progress; unemployment shot up from 14.3% in 1937 to 19.0% in 1938. Since that unfortunate event, the Federal Reserve has recognized that a change in reserve ratios can act like a sledgehammer. It has therefore been very careful. When changes have been made in recent decades, they have been quite small, usually no more than one-half of 1%.

MONETARY POLICY AND INTEREST RATES

When the Federal Reserve takes steps to increase the quantity of money, it thereby creates downward pressures on interest rates.

To see why, let's look first at the Fed's most important tool—open market operations. When the Federal Reserve goes on the open market to buy government securities, it increases the demand for these securities. As a result, it bids up

their prices. But higher security prices mean lower interest rates.

As an example, consider *U.S. Treasury bills.* These are the short-term government securities which the Fed usually purchases in its open market operations. Unlike a government bond, which provides semiannual interest payments, a Treasury bill involves no explicit interest payment. It simply represents a promise by the government to pay, say, $100,000 on a specific date, usually three months after the date of issue. The purchaser obtains a yield by purchasing the bill at a discount, paying less than the full $100,000 face value. For example, a buyer who pays $97,000 for a three-month bill gets $3,000 more than the purchase price when the bill reaches maturity. Thus the interest or yield on that bill is approximately 3% for the three-month period—that is, 12% per annum. (By convention, interest is quoted at an annual rate, even for securities with less than one year to maturity.)

Suppose that the Fed enters the market, bidding for Treasury bills and pushing their price up from $97,000 to $98,000. What can now be gained by purchasing a bill at this price? Only $2,000. This is approximately 2% for the 3 months, or 8% per annum. Thus we see that:

> Security prices and interest rates *move in opposite directions.* A "rise in the price of Treasury bills" (from $97,000 to $98,000 in our example) is just another way of saying "a fall in the interest rate on Treasury bills" (from 12% to 8% in our example). Similarly, a fall in the price of securities represents a rise in the interest rate.

Thus when the Federal Reserve purchases government securities on the open market and bids up their prices, it is thereby bidding down interest rates. The proposition that a rise in security prices means a fall in interest yields also holds for long-term bonds, as explained in Box 12-1.

The secondary effects of the open market purchase also work to reduce interest rates. As the reserves of commercial banks rise, they step up their lending activities. In their eagerness to make additional loans, banks have an incentive to reduce the interest rate they charge. Specifically, they may

BOX 12–1   Bond Prices and Interest Rates

The relationship between bond prices and interest rates can be seen most easily by considering a *perpetuity*—a bond that has no maturity date and is never paid off. It represents a commitment to pay, say, $80 in interest per year forever, regardless of what happens to current interest rates. Although the U.S. government does not issue such bonds, a number of foreign examples might be cited—the British *consols* or the *rentes perpetuelles* of France.

Like other bonds, perpetuities may be sold by their initial owners. A buyer willing to pay $1,000 for such a perpetuity would obtain an interest rate or yield of 8%—that is, $80 per year on the purchase price of $1,000. However, if the price fell, and the buyer could get the perpetuity for $800, the annual $80 payment would provide a yield of 10%. (The $80 represents a 10% yield on the $800 paid.) Again, we see that *a fall in the price of a security means a rise in the interest rate or yield on the security.*

A bond with a specific maturity of, say, 10 years requires a much more complex calculation. The holder of such a bond receives two types of payments: (1) *Coupon* payments—that is, interest payments made periodically (normally semiannually), and (2) the repayment of the *face value* or *principal* of the bond when it reaches maturity at the end of the 10 years.

As a background to seeing what happens to the price of a bond, note that if $100 is deposited in an account paying 10% per annum, the deposit rises to a total of $110 at the end of the first year. During the second year, 10% interest is paid on this $110. That is, interest is paid not only on the original deposit of $100, but also on the first year's interest of $10. When interest is paid on interest in this way, interest is being *compounded*. In this example, interest during the second year is $11 (that is, $110 × 10%), raising the deposit to a total of $121 by the end of the second year.

This can be expressed:

$$\$100\,(1 + 0.10)^2 = \$121$$

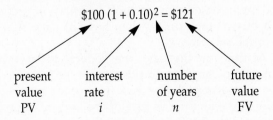

present	interest	number	future
value	rate	of years	value
PV	*i*	*n*	FV

In general, this can be rewritten:

$$PV\,(1 + i)^n = FV$$

This relationship is often written in an alternative way:

$$PV = \frac{FV}{(1 + i)^n}$$

In our example:

$$\$100 = \frac{\$121}{(1 + 0.10)^2}$$

This tells us that, if the interest rate is 10%, an asset that has a future value or payoff of $121 in two years time is worth $100 today.

For many assets, the payoff is strung out over many years. In other words, there are many terms on the right-hand side of the present value equation. For example, a bond with a 10-year maturity and annual coupon payments of $8 will have a payoff of $8 each year until the tenth year, when the owner receives a final payoff of $8 plus the face value of $100. For the standard bond, the annual coupon payments and the principal are determined when the bond is first sold; they do not change when interest rates change.

If the market interest rate is, say, 9%, the present value of this bond (the price at which it can be bought or sold today) is calculated as follows:

$$PV = \frac{\$8}{1.09} + \frac{\$8}{(1.09)^2} + \frac{\$8}{(1.09)^3} + \ldots + \frac{\$8 + \$100}{(1.09)^{10}}$$
$$= \$93.58$$

Or, in general,

$$\text{Price (PV) of bond} = \frac{C}{1 + i} + \frac{C}{(1 + i)^2} + \ldots + \frac{C + \$100}{(1 + i)^n}$$

where C is the coupon payment.

From this equation, we can calculate the price if we know the rate of interest (i), or we can calculate the interest rate if we know the price of the bond. The higher the one is, the lower the other will be. Thus once again we see that the higher the price of bonds, the lower the interest rate.

shave their prime rate—that is, their publicly announced interest rate for short-term loans.[2]

A cut in the discount rate or a reduction in the required reserve ratio likewise acts to reduce interest rates. In each case, banks are able to lend more, and they are encouraged to cut their prime rate in order to attract new customers.

In summary, the Fed has three tools to expand the money stock and stimulate aggregate demand:

- Open market purchases.
- A cut in the discount rate.
- A reduction in the required reserve ratio.

These policy actions have three interrelated effects. They

- Make it possible for banks to lend more.
- Increase the money stock.
- Lower interest rates.

Chapter 17 will explain in detail how expansive policies can stimulate aggregate demand and thus make recessions less severe.

During times when aggregate demand is too high and inflation is accelerating, tighter policies are appropriate: a reduction in open market purchases, an increase in the discount rate, and/or a cautious increase in the required reserve ratio.

OTHER MONETARY TOOLS

Open market operations, changes in the discount rate, and changes in reserve requirements are *quantitative controls;* they help the Fed control the quantity of money in the U.S. economy. They are supplemented by (1) *selective* or *qualitative controls,* which can affect the supply of funds to specific markets, and (2) *moral suasion.*

---

[2]Traditionally, the prime rate was defined as the bank's lowest rate, available only to its most creditworthy customers. However, this is no longer the case. Since 1980, banks have made some loans at rates below the prime. Thus the prime should now be considered simply the announced rate of a bank, not necessarily its lowest rate.

SELECTIVE CONTROL IN THE STOCK MARKET: MARGIN REQUIREMENTS

The Great Depression of the 1930s was preceded by the Crash of 1929. In order to prevent a repeat of the speculative excesses of the 1920s, Congress granted the Fed the power to set **margin requirements,** which limit the amount that people can borrow when they buy stocks or bonds.

Margin requirements limit the amount that can be borrowed to purchase stocks or bonds. For example, if the margin requirement on stock is 60%, buyers of stock must put up 60% of the purchase price in their own money and can borrow no more than 40%.

A healthy stock market can add to the overall health of the economy; collapsing stock prices will reduce the wealth of stockholders and may depress consumption and investment. (However, the importance of the stock market should not be exaggerated. The economy maintained a healthy growth in 1988 in spite of the sharp decline in the stock market in October 1987.) In turn, a healthy stock market requires that stockholders be able to face temporary setbacks without being forced to sell their shares. If they have borrowed most of the money to buy stocks, they may have to dump their stocks when prices decline, pushing prices down even further. Stockholders gain staying power when they have their own money invested.

The Fed can cut margin requirements to revive a low or declining market, and it can raise margin requirements to restrain a speculative burst in stock prices. In recent years, the Fed has not used this power. It has kept the requirement steady at 50% since the last change in 1974. However, even a fixed requirement can reduce speculation; people can't buy a stock unless they have at least 50% of the purchase price.

At times in the past, the Federal Reserve has been empowered to impose other selective controls. For example, the Fed imposed controls on credit card spending as part of the anti-inflationary program of 1980. There were delays in working out detailed regulations, and the credit card controls took effect too late, after the economy was already headed down into a recession. The Fed's power to control credit card spending was allowed to lapse by Congress.

MORAL SUASION

In addition to its formal tools—such as open market operations or changes in the discount rate—the Federal Reserve may attempt to influence the behavior of member banks in less formal ways. Specifically, it may resort to *jawboning*—that is, exhorting bankers to refrain from certain actions or encouraging them to take others. From time to time, for example, the Federal Reserve has recommended that banks reduce the amount of their new loans or increase their net worth in order to ensure their ability to weather storms. (A bank can increase its net worth by retaining its profits rather than paying them out in dividends. An addition to net worth increases the amount by which a bank's assets exceed its liabilities. Thus the bank is protected if some of its assets disappear—for example, if some of its loans turn out to be uncollectable.)

The Federal Reserve can use a number of levers to fortify its moral suasion and to ensure that the banks do not completely ignore its exhortations. For example, borrowing through the Fed's discount window is a privilege, not a right; if a bank ignores the recommendations of the Fed, it may find the Fed less willing to lend. In addition, the Fed must approve certain bank activities, such as the opening of a branch in a foreign country. The Fed can refuse such permission if it feels that the net worth of the bank is inadequate.

THE BALANCE SHEET OF THE FEDERAL RESERVE

Some actions of the Federal Reserve do not show up directly on its balance sheet—for example, moral suasion, or changes in reserve requirements. But other acts do—for example, its open market operations. Thus the balance sheet of the Federal Reserve can provide insights into some of the Fed's activities.

The consolidated balance sheet of the 12 Federal Reserve banks is shown in Table 12-4. Two entries on the right side are particularly worth noting. First is the large amount of Federal Reserve notes—the ordinary dollar bills that people hold. This item is very large because of the public's desire to hold more currency as its overall holdings of money have increased. Although open market

TABLE 12-4 Consolidated Balance Sheet of the 12 Federal Reserve Banks, February 28, 1989   (billions of dollars)

Assets		Liabilities and Net Worth	
U.S. government securities	229	Deposits	
Loans to depository		Reserve deposits of	
institutions	2	depository institutions	37
		U.S. Treasury	6
Other assets	54	Foreign and other	1
		Federal Reserve notes	223
		Other liabilities	13
		Total liabilities	280
		Net Worth	5
Total	285	Total	285

In the Federal Reserve's balance sheet, U.S. government securities are the main asset, and Federal Reserve notes the largest liability.

operations and other Fed policies affect the *amount* of money in the economy, the public is free to choose the *form* in which it holds its money—whether in currency or bank deposits.

The second noteworthy item on the right side is the small net worth of the Federal Reserve. If the Fed were a private corporation, this would be cause for alarm. The slightest reversal in its fortunes might cause the value of its assets to dip below the amount of its liabilities, wiping out its net worth and threatening bankruptcy. But the Fed is no ordinary corporation. It is a part of the government, and a very special part, since it has the power to create money. Because of this special power, the Fed need not worry about building up its net worth; it has an assured flow of profits. It earns interest on the large holdings of government securities on the asset side, while it pays no interest on most of its liabilities—in particular, reserve deposits and Federal Reserve notes. The Fed turns most of its profits over to the U.S. Treasury, and, as a result, its net worth remains low.

On the asset side of the Fed's balance sheet, U.S. government securities are by far the largest entry; these securities have been accumulated through past open market operations. Loans (discounts) to commercial banks and other depository institutions are generally not very large—only $2 billion at the end of February 1989.

WHAT BACKS OUR MONEY?

Money is debt. The largest component of the money stock—namely, checking deposits—is debt of the commercial banks and other deposit-accepting institutions. Federal Reserve notes—the currency of everyday use—are liabilities (debt) of the 12 Federal Reserve banks.

In a sense, the money supply is backed by the assets of the banking system. Checking deposits are backed by the loans, bonds, and reserves held by the commercial banks and other depository institutions. Federal Reserve notes and reserve deposits are backed by the assets of the Federal Reserve, mainly federal government securities. What, in turn, backs the government securities? The answer is: the government's promise to pay, based in the first instance on its ability to tax, but in the final analysis on its ability to borrow newly created money from the Federal Reserve or to print money directly. (Recall the section in Chapter 10 entitled: "Could the Government Go Broke?")

Clearly, we have gone in a circle. Currency is backed with government debt, and government debt is ultimately backed by the ability of the federal authorities to print more currency. In a sense, the whole game is played with mirrors; money is money because the government says it is. Until a few years ago, Federal Reserve notes boldly proclaimed that "the United States of America will pay to the bearer on demand" the face value of the Federal Reserve note. What would happen if an individual submitted a $1 bill and demanded payment? He or she would receive another $1 bill in exchange. This does not make much sense, and the bold proclamation has been eliminated from Federal Reserve notes. Now, we can say simply: a dollar is a dollar is a dollar.

What, then, determines the value of a Federal Reserve note? Dollar bills have value because of

1. Their scarcity compared to the demand for them.
2. Their general acceptability.

As long as the Federal Reserve keeps the supply of money in reasonable balance with the demand for it, money retains its value, even though it has no backing with precious metal or any other tangible commodity.

Dollar bills are generally acceptable by such diverse people as the taxi driver, the house painter, and the doctor. They all know they can turn around and buy other goods and services with the dollar bills. In part, general acceptability is a matter of convention—as in the case of cigarettes in the POW camp. But convention and habit are reinforced by the status of Federal Reserve notes as **legal tender.** Creditors *must* accept them in payment of a debt.

Legal tender is the item that creditors must accept in payment of debts.

WHAT BACKS CHECKING DEPOSITS?

How about checking deposits? What protects their role as part of the money stock? Unlike currency, checking deposits are not legal tender. A gas station is not obliged to accept a personal check and usually won't do so.

People are willing to hold money in the form of checking deposits because of the convenience of paying by check and because they are confident they can get currency for the deposits when they want it. But what assurance do depositors have of actually being able to get $100 in currency for every $100 they hold in deposits?

The first assurance lies in the assets of the banks—their reserves and earning assets of loans and securities. If a bank finds that people are withdrawing more than they are depositing, it may cover the difference by liquidating some of its assets—for example, by selling some of its bonds, or by using the proceeds of its loans as they are repaid. However, bank assets may not always be enough. Indeed, they proved to be woefully inadequate during the depression of the 1930s. As the economy collapsed, many businesses could not repay their bank loans, and the value of bank assets shrank. As their assets fell to less than their deposit liabilities, the banks were driven into bankruptcy, and many depositors suffered heavy losses.

This situation clearly was dangerous because bank runs are contagious. When some banks fail, depositors become frightened and are more likely to run on other banks, too. In early 1933, the contagion spread like wildfire, and the banking system collapsed. In order to prevent a repetition of the 1930s, an important additional backing was provided for depositors. The government set up the **Federal Deposit Insurance Corporation** (FDIC) to insure bank deposits up to a sizable limit, currently $100,000 per deposit. For this insurance, the banks pay premiums to the FDIC. A similar institution—the *Federal Savings and Loan Insurance Corporation* (FSLIC)—guarantees deposits in savings and loan associations up to the same limit. Because deposits are now guaranteed by the government, people no longer have the same incentive to run on their banks, and the U.S. banking system is much more secure than it was in the early 1930s. Thus deposit insurance has two interrelated objectives:

■ To protect depositors from losses.

■ To reduce the threat of a run on the banking system.

Deposit insurance has contributed to the stabil-ity of the U.S. economy. Nevertheless, the large increase in failures among banks and S&Ls since 1980 has raised fundamental questions regarding the insurance system, as explained in Box 12-2.

WHY NOT GOLD?

There is an obvious problem with **fiat money**—paper currency that is money because the government says it is. The government or central bank can create such money at will. What, then, is to restrain the authorities from creating and spending money recklessly, generating a runaway inflation?

This question provided a rationale for the old *gold standard*, under which the currency issued by the government and/or the central bank was convertible into gold. The authorities could not create money recklessly. Like the goldsmith of old, they had to keep a gold backing equal to a reasonable fraction of their currency liabilities. This was the original design of the Federal Reserve when it was established in 1914. The Fed was required to keep gold reserves to back its currency and deposit obligations. Under the old gold standard, the Fed itself was a fractional-reserve bank. It could create liabilities—in the form of currency and reserve deposits—that were a multiple of its gold reserves. However, it did not have the power to create an unlimited amount of such liabilities.

The gold standard fulfilled its objective of restraining the reckless creation of money, but it had a serious flaw. The quantity of money could fluctuate as a result of changes in the quantity of gold. When the Fed bought gold flowing into the country from abroad or from U.S. gold mines, the effects were similar to those of an open market operation: Commercial bank reserves increased. (The effects on the Fed's balance sheet were similar to those from the open market operation shown in Table 12-1, except that the asset acquired by the Fed was gold rather than government securities.) A gold inflow could lead to a large increase in the money stock. Similarly, a gold outflow could have a very powerful contractionary effect. There was no assurance that the gold standard would provide the quantity of money needed for a full-employment, noninflationary economy.

Problems with the gold standard became acute during the early depression of the 1930s. As unemployment and business bankruptcies shot upward,

BOX 12–2 Federal Insurance and Bank Risks: What Should Banks Do?

Federal deposit insurance has been successful in its main objective: There have been no large-scale runs on banks since the FDIC was established during the depression. A few runs have occurred, but they have been due mainly to gaps in the insurance system. In 1985, there were runs on a number of S&Ls in Ohio and Maryland. However, these S&Ls were chartered by the state and were not required to have federal deposit insurance. Depositors ran for a very good reason: Their S&Ls were on the verge of bankruptcy, and their deposits had no backing by the federal government. To deal with the crisis, the legislatures of the two states decided that state-chartered S&Ls would henceforth be required to get federal insurance. This experience confirmed the value of federal insurance.

As failures of banks and S&Ls increased during the 1980s, concerns grew regarding the potential cost to the taxpayer of making good on the deposit insurance. The failures were attributable to a number of causes:

1. *The rise in interest rates* in the late 1970s and early 1980s. This point may seem paradoxical. With higher interest rates, banks can charge more for their loans. But, in the short run, banks lose when interest rates rise; there is a decline in the value of the bonds they own. (Box 12-1 explained how high interest rates mean low bond prices.) S&Ls are hit particularly hard. They hold many long-term mortgages with interest rates set at low levels. If they must pay higher interest rates on their deposits than they receive on the mortgages they own, they will suffer losses. In brief, a rise in interest rates can hurt banks and can hurt S&Ls even more.

2. *Long-run weakness in the oil states.* The skyrocketing price of oil in the 1970s created short-term prosperity in Texas and Oklahoma, and pushed up real estate prices. However, when oil prices fell during the 1980s, there was an extended period of business bankruptcies and falling real estate values. Banks that had loaned heavily to the oil

business suffered when their loans became uncollectable. Again, S&Ls were particularly hard hit: Some home owners simply walked away from their property when the market value fell below the amount of the mortgage.

3. *Rapid changes in the financial markets.* Traditionally, commercial loans—that is, short-term loans to businesses—were the core of the banking business, providing good returns at moderate risk. But the borrowing pattern of many high-quality, low-risk businesses has been changing. As an alternative to borrowing from the banks, they have increasingly borrowed from the financial markets by selling their *commercial paper* (a type of promissory note), just as the U.S. government borrows by selling Treasury bills. As the traditional lending business has shrunk, banks have looked elsewhere, making large loans to developing countries and to high-risk businesses such as oil.

4. *Financial deregulation,* which has contributed to the pressures on banks in some ways. For example, regulations at one time prevented banks from paying interest on checking deposits. This provided them with a source of low-cost funds. With deregulation, banks now pay interest and compete more actively for deposits.

5. *Fraud.* In a large number of failures, dishonesty was a factor. In some cases, officers or employees of banks and S&Ls syphoned off funds for their personal use.

GAMBLING WITH THE GOVERNMENT'S MONEY

By the mid-1980s, a number of S&Ls were technically bankrupt: Their assets had shrunk to less than their liabilities. Nonetheless, most remained in business. Their depositors were protected by the Federal Savings and Loan Insurance Corporation (FSLIC) and felt no pressure to withdraw their deposits.

Unfortunately, an institution with a negative net worth

people became frightened. They tried to switch their assets into safer forms. They switched out of bank deposits into paper currency and gold. Foreign holders of dollars were particularly anxious to convert them into gold after the British decided to stop converting pounds into gold. They were afraid that the United States would also stop converting its currency into gold, and wanted to get

gold from the United States while they still could. Between August and October of 1931, the Federal Reserve's holdings of gold dropped by 16%. The money supply came under strong contractionary pressures when the economy was already headed downward into the depth of the depression.

The Federal Reserve might have offset the contractionary effects of the gold outflow by engaging (that is, with assets less than liabilities) faces different incentives than a healthy institution. One of the things that a healthy financial institution does is to weigh risks carefully. It does not undertake loans unless it believes that the potential returns compensate for the risks. In a sense, it is willing to gamble but only if the odds are in its favor.

For a bankrupt S&L, the game changes. If risky loans are made at high interest rates and if these loans are repaid, the S&L may work its way out of bankruptcy. However, if the loans turn sour, the losses can eventually be unloaded on the FSLIC; it will have the unpleasant task of paying off depositors at the end. In a sense, the bankrupt S&L is gambling with the government's money. If it wins, it keeps the gains; if it loses, the government—which backs the FSLIC—accepts the losses. Heads, the S&L wins; tails, FSLIC loses. In these circumstances, why be cautious?

Thus FSLIC faces a problem of *moral hazard:* Some S&Ls behave recklessly because they are insured. One way the FSLIC could protect itself would be to close down the bankrupt S&Ls and accept the existing losses before they mushroom. But in the short run, this would be costly.

FSLIC had limited funds and it temporized. Losses mounted. FSLIC was granted additional funds by Congress, but these were not adequate to deal with the problem. By the late 1980s, bankruptcies were mounting, and the FSLIC faced potential losses of perhaps as much as $100 billion. One of the first acts of President Bush was to propose a plan to close down some bankrupt S&Ls and reduce the losses of the Savings & Loan system.

WHAT SHOULD BANKS DO?

Some financial observers suggest that the authorities should do more than simply close bankrupt institutions. They should also address the fundamental question of how deposit insurance should work in a changing world of financial deregulation and rapid technological change.

A few argue that there is no way to solve the problem of moral hazard: as long as federal insurance exists, institutions will have an incentive to gamble with the government's money. They therefore suggest that deposit insurance be reduced or eliminated. But this suggestion ignores one of the main lessons of the 1930s. Uninsured banks are subject to runs, and widespread runs can disrupt the whole economy.

A more promising proposal is to limit what insured institutions can do. Robert E. Litan of the Brookings Institution, a Washington-based public policy organization, suggests that deposits continue to be insured but that, in return, banks (and other deposit-accepting institutions) be required to avoid risks. Specifically, they would be forbidden to make loans, and required to hold short-term government securities as backing for their deposits.* These banks could be subsidiaries of larger financial institutions, which could make loans to businesses, consumers, and others. But insurance would cover only the banks themselves, and not the larger financial institutions. There would be a wall preventing the larger parent institutions from using the bank deposits. Litan argues that, although many of the results of financial deregulation are desirable, deposit insurance implies that there should be government restrictions on what deposit-accepting institutions can do. Otherwise, banks and S&Ls will continue to gamble with the government's money, and the taxpayer may be stuck with huge losses.

---

*Robert E. Litan, *What Should Banks Do?* (Washington, D.C.: Brookings Institution, 1987).

in vigorous open market purchases. But the Fed was paralyzed by the unfolding depression; its open market purchases were half-hearted and sporadic.

To limit the damage, President Roosevelt changed the rules of the game. The United States raised its official price of gold; as a result, gold began to flow in from abroad. To prevent the public from withdrawing gold from the banking system, U.S. citizens were forbidden to hold gold (with a few exceptions, such as jewelry or dental work). It wasn't until the beginning of 1975 that the public was allowed to hold gold again, and by then gold no longer played an important role in the monetary system.

The biggest problem with the gold standard,

then, is that it does not provide a *steady* and measured restraint. Rather, it exerts restraint in the form of a *threat of disaster*. If a crisis of confidence occurs, the public will switch away from paper money and into gold. As the banking system loses its gold reserves, it will be under powerful pressures to contract the money stock. As long as the authorities are lucky, with gold flowing in steadily from mines or from foreign countries, and as long as they follow farsighted policies that prevent any crisis of confidence, it is possible that the system may work reasonably well. But in the period between the two world wars, the authorities were neither farsighted nor lucky.

The history of the gold standard, and, in particular, the role of gold in the early depression, gained in importance in 1979–1980 as inflation accelerated into double digits (above 10%). Because governments and central banks appeared unwilling or unable to exercise enough restraint to control inflation, some observers concluded that the only way to restore a sound monetary system was to reestablish some link to gold and thus impose an external constraint on monetary policy. But this would be a mistake. The gold standard contributed to the depression of the 1930s; it can make the economy unstable.

MONEY MISBEHAVING: PROCYCLICAL MOVEMENTS IN THE MONEY STOCK

At the beginning of Chapter 11, two reasons were given for studying money:

■ Monetary policy can be used to stabilize aggregate demand and reduce fluctuations in the economy.

■ Money can be a source of problems. Instability in the money stock can cause instability in the economy.

Much of this chapter has been devoted to the first point, explaining how the Federal Reserve can change the quantity of money in an effort to stabilize the economy. The second point is also important: money can be a source of economic instability. The money stock has often moved in a *procyclical*

way, increasing rapidly during good times and contracting during bad times, thereby making business cycles worse.

Many examples might be cited. We have seen how the money stock declined during the early depression, adding to the downward momentum of the economy. In the 1940s and 1970s, large increases in the quantity of money were a cause of rapid inflation. Declines in the rate of growth of the money stock often foreshadow a coming recession. For example, the recessions of 1969–1970, 1973–1975, and 1980 were all preceded or accompanied by declines in the rate of growth of the money stock (Fig. 12-3).

Why might money move in a procyclical way, adding to economic instability? Some of the reasons are quite subtle, and will be deferred to Chapter 18. However, here are some of the most important:

1. *War.* War is perhaps the most obvious reason for monetary instability. To finance military operations, the money stock is often increased rapidly. Sometimes a government prints money directly; sometimes it borrows from the central bank. As a result, wars are often accompanied by rapid inflation.

2. *The gold standard.* As noted in the previous section, the old gold standard was a source of instability during the early years of the Great Depression. Because the gold standard has been discarded, it is mainly of historical interest.

3. *An interest rate target.* Critics charge that the Federal Reserve destabilizes the money stock because it often aims at the wrong target, attempting to stabilize interest rates. To understand this criticism, it is necessary to look at the policy decisions facing the Fed.

HOW AN INTEREST RATE TARGET CAN DESTABILIZE THE MONEY STOCK

The ultimate objectives of the Federal Reserve are full employment and price stability. However, the Fed does not control employment or the level of prices directly. Rather, it adjusts the levers of monetary policy and, in particular, open market operations. It is only by affecting the quantity of money

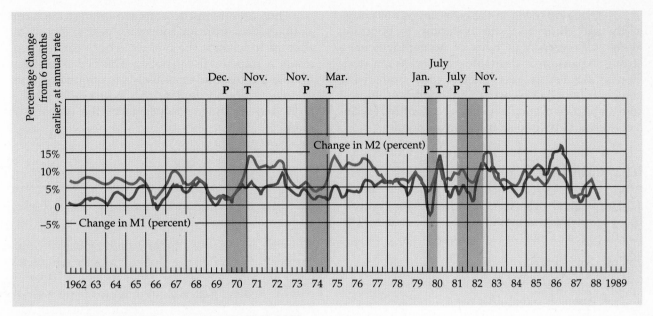

FIGURE 12-3   Changes in the money stock, 1960–1988

The rate of growth of the money stock generally slows down before recessions begin.
(*Source:* U. S. Department of Commerce, *Business Conditions Digest,* based on data of the
Federal Reserve).

and interest rates that the Fed affects employment and prices.

In formulating policy, the Federal Open Market Committee (FOMC) has a decision to make. Should it give the trading desk at the New York Fed instructions to aim for a certain level of interest rates? Or should the trading desk be ordered to aim for a specific increase in the quantity of money? Or some combination of the two? A controversy has raged over this question for decades. Critics of the Fed argue that it has generally concentrated on interest rates and that, as a result, its actions have sometimes destabilized the economy.

To see how this might happen, suppose that the Federal Reserve has decided to keep the interest rate near the existing rate of, say, 8% per annum. Then suppose that an upturn in the economy occurs. Business executives become more optimistic and undertake additional investment; aggregate demand rises. To finance their new plant and equipment, they borrow. The additional demand for funds creates pressures for interest rates to rise

and bond prices to fall. If the Fed wants to keep interest rates from rising—that is, to keep bond prices from falling—it now has to buy bonds on the open market. However, such open market purchases increase bank reserves and lead to an increase in the money stock. As a consequence, there is an additional increase in aggregate demand. As demand rises, businesses are encouraged to revise their investment plans upward once more; the expansion gathers momentum. There is a *cumulative upward movement,* with increases in aggregate demand and increases in the money stock reinforcing one another.

The Fed cannot control both the money stock and the interest rate. If it wants to control the money stock, it must let interest rates rise in the face of a large increase in the demand for loans.

If it decides to control interest rates, it loses control of the money stock. The result can be a vicious circle, with higher demand initially causing an increase in the money stock, and the increase in the money stock in turn causing a further increase in demand; and so on.

A strong upswing in the economy is not necessarily bad. Indeed, if the economy is bumping along with very high rates of unemployment, a strong expansion is desirable. In this case, a decision by the Fed to keep interest rates from rising can contribute to a recovery. But a policy of interest rate stabilization may also cause a healthy expansion to run away into an inflationary boom.

Thus an attempt to stabilize interest rates can at times be a trap for monetary policy, just as an attempt to balance the budget every year can represent a trap for fiscal policy. The Fed is inviting trouble if it responds passively, creating more money whenever the demand for borrowed funds is high, and creating less whenever the demand is slack.

KEY POINTS

1. The Federal Reserve is responsible for controlling the quantity of money in the U.S. economy. It has three major tools at its command:

   (a) Open market operations.

   (b) Changes in the discount rate.

   (c) Changes in required reserve ratios.

2. The Federal Reserve's untidy organizational chart is the result of an early controversy over the desirable degree of centralization. There are 12 regional Federal Reserve Banks and a Board of Governors in Washington. For monetary policy, the most important body is the Federal Open Market Committee (FOMC).

3. When the Fed purchases securities on the open market, it increases bank reserves; when it sells securities, it reduces reserves. Changes in reserves affect the amount of checking deposit money that commercial banks and other depository institutions can create.

4. A decrease in the discount rate encourages bank borrowing from the Fed. Such borrowing creates bank reserves.

5. When it reduces required reserve ratios, the Fed increases the quantity of checking deposits the banks can create on any given reserve base.

6. An open market purchase by the Fed increases the demand for government securities, bidding up their prices. When this happens, the yields (interest rates) on securities are bid down.

7. Less important tools of the Federal Reserve include margin requirements for purchases of stocks, and moral suasion.

8. In the last analysis, there is nothing backing our currency: "A dollar is a dollar." Money retains its value *because it is scarce.* Even though it doesn't cost the Federal Reserve anything to create reserve deposits, and the costs of printing currency are small, the Fed does not create money recklessly. If it did so, there would be a wild inflation.

9. Under the old gold standard, the Fed was required to hold gold reserves equal to a fraction of its deposit and note liabilities. Since this system was based on gold, and gold "can't be printed," there was a restraint on irresponsible money creation. However, the gold standard had an enormous defect: The amount of money that could be created on the available gold base was not necessarily the quantity needed for full employment with stable prices. In fact, changes in gold reserves and in the money stock could make economic instability worse. In 1931, the decline in the quantity of gold held in the U.S. banking system caused a contraction of the money stock and added to the downward momentum of the economy.

10. Chapter 10 explained how the makers of fiscal policy could fall into a trap if they followed a policy of balancing the budget every year. The central bank also faces a policy trap. If it stabilizes interest rates, it may lose control of the money stock. The result can be a vicious circle, with higher demand causing an increase in the money stock, and the increase in the money stock in turn causing a further increase in demand.

KEY CONCEPTS

open market operation	quantitative controls	Federal Deposit Insurance Corporation (FDIC)
discount rate	qualitative controls	fiat money
required reserve ratio	margin requirement	gold standard
Treasury bill	moral suasion (jawboning)	monetary policy trap
prime rate	legal tender	

PROBLEMS

12-1. What are the three major tools of the Federal Reserve for controlling the quantity of money? Which of these tools affect the quantity of reserves of the commercial banks?

12-2. Suppose that the Federal Reserve purchases $100,000 in Treasury bills from commercial bank A. Explain how the balance sheets of the Fed and commercial bank A are affected. How much can commercial bank A now safely lend? (Assume that bank A's reserves were just adequate prior to the purchase by the Fed.)

12-3. Table 12-1 shows the changes in the balance sheets of the Fed and a commercial bank when the Fed purchased a government security from General Motors. Show how the balance sheet of GM changed as a result of this open market transaction.

12-4. Suppose that the price of a three-month, $100,000 Treasury bill is $96,000. What is the approximate yield on this bill? (Following the conventional practice, quote the yield at an annual rate.) Now suppose that the price of three-month bills falls to $95,000. What happens to the yield?

12-5. "Counterfeiting is generally an antisocial act. But if there is a depression, all counterfeiters should be let out of jail." Do you agree or disagree? Explain why.

12-6. What backing do Federal Reserve notes have? Why are these notes valuable?

12-7. Why can the Fed fall into a policy trap if it tries to stabilize interest rates? For review, also explain the trap facing the makers of fiscal policy.

*12-8. Suppose, for some reason, that the public decides that it wants to switch out of checking deposits and hold most of its deposit money in the form of currency instead.

   (a) What effect would this switch have on the reserves of the commercial banks?

   (b) What effect would it have on the money stock? Explain why.

   (c) What, if anything, should the open market committee do in response to this switch?

   (d) If, in part (c), you recommend large open market purchases or sales, how would you respond to a critic who argues that the Fed should keep its open market operations small and gradual, in order to stabilize the economy? If you recommend that the Fed do nothing, do you consider the change in the money stock in (b) to be healthy for the economy?

PART IV

GREAT MACROECONOMIC ISSUES

Aggregate Supply

Previous chapters presented the bare bones of macroeconomics. The theory was simple. However, the real world is complex. Part 4 will deal with four complications:

1. How can inflation and high unemployment exist at the same time? (Chapter 13) Previous chapters explained how inflation can be caused by too much spending, and unemployment by too little. This theory is too simple. If inflation and unemployment were always caused in this way, they would not occur at the same time. But sometimes they do. Why?

2. How do policymakers deal with a combination of inflation and high unemployment? (Chapter 14)

3. How does inflation affect the economy? In the presence of inflation, what can the public do to protect itself? (Chapter 15)

4. Why do growth rates vary so much from decade to decade and from country to country? (Chapter 16)

To answer these questions, we must look closely at aggregate supply.

CHAPTER 13
HOW CAN INFLATION AND UNEMPLOYMENT COEXIST?

The first panacea for a mismanaged nation is inflation of the currency; the second is war. Both bring a temporary prosperity; both bring a permanent ruin. But both are the refuge of political and economic opportunists.

ERNEST HEMINGWAY

In the three decades following the Great Depression, macroeconomists were preoccupied with aggregate demand. How could we prevent a repeat of the depression, with its decade-long inadequacy of demand? How, and to what extent, could we hope to manage aggregate demand in order to reduce short-run fluctuations in the economy? Then, beginning in the 1960s, macroeconomists also began to pay close attention to aggregate supply. Any study of macroeconomics is now incomplete without an investigation of *both* demand and supply.

The last three chapters have dealt with the demand side, and, in particular, with the use of monetary and fiscal policies to affect aggregate demand. In the next four chapters, we study aggregate supply.

Chapter 8 introduced the aggregate supply function of Keynesian theory, repeated here as Figure 13-1. According to this view, if there initially is a deep depression at *A*, with output falling far short of the economy's full-employment potential, then an increase in aggregate demand will cause the economy to move toward *B*. In the horizontal range *AB*, the increase in demand will be reflected entirely in an increase in output, and prices will

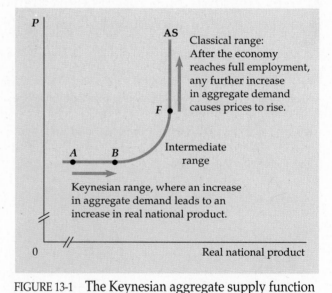

FIGURE 13-1   The Keynesian aggregate supply function

This figure repeats the aggregate supply function of earlier chapters. If the economy begins at a point of depression, such as *A*, an increase in demand will increase real output. The economy will move from *A* toward *B*, with prices remaining stable. Once full employment has been reached at point *F*, a further increase in aggregate demand will cause inflation, but no change in output or employment. The economy will move upward from *F*.

remain stable. At the other end, if an economy begins on the vertical section at *F,* an increase in demand will be reflected entirely in terms of higher prices, as the economy moves upward from *F.* Finally, there is an intermediate range, between *B* and *F.* As the economy approaches full employment, an increase in demand will be reflected partly in higher output and partly in higher prices.

In passing, we reemphasize a point already encountered several times. A change in *demand* causes a movement *along* a *supply* curve. For example, an increase in aggregate demand causes a movement along the aggregate supply curve from *B* to *F* in Figure 13-1.

In all probability, the reader has become increasingly uncomfortable with the view of the world represented by Figure 13-1. It doesn't seem to fit the facts very well. In particular, it suggests that, whenever inflation is a serious problem (at *F* or above), the economy should be at full employment. On the other hand, prices should be stable whenever unemployment is high (to the left of *B*). Yet there have been times when *both* unemployment and inflation have been high, particularly in the early 1980s. In 1981, for example, inflation was almost 9%, while unemployment averaged 7.5%. Although Figure 13-1 has been useful as an introduction to the idea of aggregate supply, it is too simple. It is not consistent with what has happened in recent decades. The time has come to look closely at the facts.

To do so, economists use a slightly different approach from Figure 13-1. Instead of looking at how prices and output change, they use a diagram with the two central macroeconomic problems—inflation and unemployment—on the axes, as shown in Figure 13-2. In this diagram, the three general ideas behind Figure 13-1 can be illustrated:

1. First is the idea that prices will be stable in a deep depression. This is illustrated by points *A* and *B* in Figure 13-2. When prices are stable, the rate of inflation is zero. Thus points *A* and *B* are on the horizontal axis. If, starting from a point of severe depression with high unemployment at *A,* aggregate demand rises, output will increase and unemployment will fall. The fall in unemployment shows up as a *leftward* move from *A* to *B* in Figure 13-2. This corresponds to a *rightward* move when output increases in Figure 13-1.

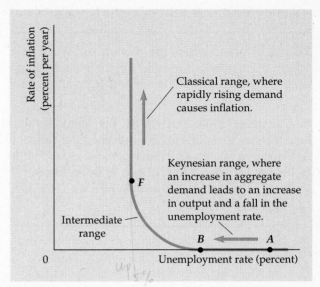

FIGURE 13-2   An alternative presentation: Inflation and unemployment

The major ideas in Figure 13-1 are repeated in this diagram. Starting from a point of depression, such as *A,* an increase in demand will leave prices stable. The rate of inflation will be zero. Output will increase. Unemployment will fall, as illustrated by the leftward movement to *B.* In the intermediate range from *B* to *F,* an increase in aggregate demand is reflected partly in inflation, and partly in output and employment. Once full employment has been established at *F,* a more rapid growth in aggregate demand is reflected entirely in terms of inflation, with no change in the unemployment rate.

2. The second idea from Figure 13-1 is this: Whenever there is rapid inflation, the economy is at full employment. This idea is illustrated by the vertical range above *F* in Figure 13-2. Because of frictional unemployment, there is some unemployment—perhaps 5%—even at points of "full employment." In the range above *F,* a faster growth in aggregate demand will mean more inflation, with no change in output or employment.

3. Third is the intermediate range, as demand is increased and the economy moves from *B* to *F.* The increase in demand is reflected partly in higher prices and partly in terms of rising output and falling unemployment.

Just as Figure 13-1 was too simple, so too is the curve in Figure 13-2. Many of the facts do not fit this figure.

THE FACTS

Historical observations are plotted in Figure 13-3, where each point shows the inflation rate and the unemployment rate in one of the years since 1960. Two major points stand out:

1. Between 1961 and 1969, the data form a smooth curve, similar to the intermediate range of the curve in Figure 13-2. Such a curve is known as a **Phillips curve,** after British economist A. W. Phillips, who found that British data for 1861–1957 fit a similar curve.[1]

When the rate of inflation (or the rate of change of money wages)[2] is put on the vertical axis and the rate of unemployment on the horizontal axis, historical data sometimes trace out a smooth curve bending upward to the left—for example, the curve traced out by the United States data for the 1960s. Such a curve is known as a *Phillips curve.*

2. With the sole exception of 1986, all the observations since 1969 are above and to the right of the Phillips curve traced out by the 1960s. Since 1969, we have frequently suffered from high rates of both inflation and unemployment. To use an inelegant but common term, we have suffered from **stagflation.**

Stagflation exists when a high rate of unemployment (stagnation) and a high rate of inflation occur at the same time.

[1]A. W. Phillips, "The Relation Between Unemployment and the Rate of Change of Money Wages in the United Kingdom," *Economica,* November 1958, pp. 282-299. For a readable account of the controversies over the Phillips curve, on which this chapter focuses, see Robert M. Solow, "Down the Phillips Curve with Gun and Camera," in David A. Belsley and others, eds., *Inflation, Trade and Taxes* (Columbus: Ohio State University Press, 1976), pp. 3–32.

[2]The original Phillips curve showed the rate of change of money wages—rather than inflation—on the vertical axis. Since money wages rise rapidly during periods of high inflation, a similar curve is traced out in either case.

In the rest of this chapter, we will look closely at these two points. First, we will examine why the economy might move along a Phillips curve, as it did during the 1960s. Second, we will consider the puzzle presented by the 1970s and 1980s. Why did things get worse after 1969, with higher inflation *and* higher unemployment?

The importance of answering the second question can scarcely be exaggerated. Suppose we cannot figure out what is happening. Suppose the economy does not behave in a predictable manner—it does not move along a predictable aggregate supply curve or Phillips curve in response to a change in aggregate demand. Then the basis for the demand management policies discussed in earlier chapters is undercut. If expansive fiscal and monetary policies are introduced during a recession, can we count on an increase in output? Or will we get more inflation instead? On the other hand, if we apply restraint during an inflationary boom, can we count on a reduction in the rate of inflation? Or will we merely get less output? In other words, demand management policies require *both* a knowledge of how monetary and fiscal policies affect aggregate demand, and a knowledge of how the economy responds to changes in aggregate demand. Making sense of what has happened since 1969 is therefore one of the major tasks of macroeconomic theorists. Before turning to this central question, we will lay the background by looking at the Phillips curve traced out in the 1960s.

THE PHILLIPS CURVE OF THE 1960s

During the 1960s, available empirical evidence—including the purple curve traced out by U.S. data in Figure 13-3 and Phillips' similar British curve—pointed strongly to the conclusion that increases in aggregate demand move the economy along a smooth, stable Phillips curve. Increases in aggregate demand had an effect partly on output and employment, and partly on prices. As the economy moved further and further to the left up the Phillips curve, this curve became steeper. In other words, each additional increase in demand caused more inflation and a smaller decline in the unemployment rate. Why might the economy move

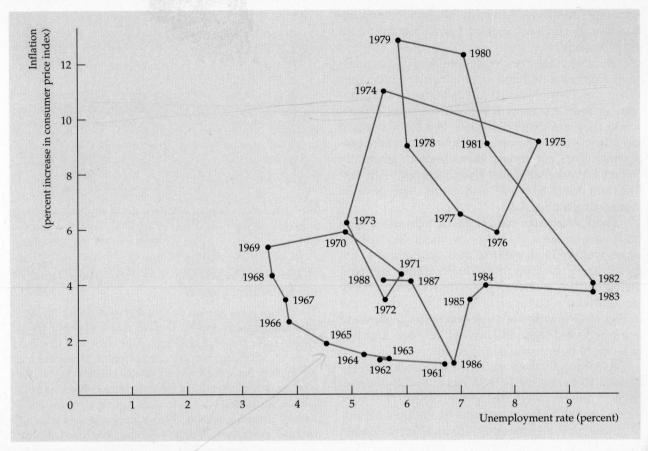

FIGURE 13-3   Inflation and unemployment

The 1960s trace out a *Phillips curve*. Points for the 1970s and 1980s are generally higher and further to the right, reflecting higher inflation *and* more unemployment.

along such a curve in response to changes in demand?

Consider, first, the position of businesses. When there is large-scale unemployment of the labor force, plant and equipment are also likely to be used at much less than capacity. If demand increases in these circumstances, the primary response of businesses is to increase output rather than prices. An increase in output will allow the fuller utilization of plant and equipment and result in rising profits. Furthermore, businesses may be skeptical about their ability to make price increases stick. If they raise prices rapidly, their competitors—who also have excess capacity—will be only too eager to capture a larger share of the market.

As the expansion continues and plant and equipment are used more fully, businesses respond differently to an increase in demand. They have less excess capacity. Therefore, as demand increases, they have less opportunity to raise profits by increasing output. At the same time, they are in a better position to raise prices. Higher prices involve less risk of a loss of markets to competitors, since the competitors are also approaching capacity and are in no position to expand output rapidly to capture additional sales. Furthermore, as the unemployment rate falls, businesses find it harder to hire and keep workers. As the labor market tightens, businesses become increasingly aggressive in their bidding for workers, offering higher wages.

As wage rates move upward, the costs of production rise. Businesses respond by raising the prices of their products.

Similarly, labor responds differently to increases in aggregate demand as employment increases. When the unemployment rate is high, the first concern of workers is with jobs. If they are offered work, they are generally quick to take it without too much quibbling over pay. However, as economic expansion continues, the situation gradually changes. Workers become less concerned with getting and keeping a job, and more aggressive in demanding higher pay.

These changing conditions, which affect both business and labor, do not come about suddenly at some well-defined point of full employment. On the contrary, they occur gradually. When demand increases, the economy may consequently move smoothly up a Phillips curve like the purple curve in Figure 13-3, with successive increases in demand being reflected more in terms of inflation and less in terms of output and employment.

Accordingly, there were two reasons for policymakers to believe that they faced a well-defined, stable Phillips curve during the 1960s. (1) It conformed to the facts—most notably, Phillips' historical study and the unfolding situation in the United States. (2) It seemed plausible from a theoretical viewpoint.

THE POLICY DILEMMA OF THE 1960s: THE TRADEOFF BETWEEN INFLATION AND UNEMPLOYMENT

This belief by policymakers—that they faced a well-defined Phillips curve—presented them with a **policy dilemma.** By adjusting aggregate demand policies, they could move the economy along the Phillips curve. But what point should they pick? A point like G in Figure 13-4, with low inflation and a high rate of unemployment? Or a point like H, with low unemployment but a high rate of inflation? Or some point in between? Facing a **tradeoff** between the goals of high unemployment and price stability, what relative importance should they attach to the two objectives?

Faced with this dilemma, the government responded in two ways. One was to emphasize the objective of high employment. After all, unemployment represents a clear and unambiguous loss to

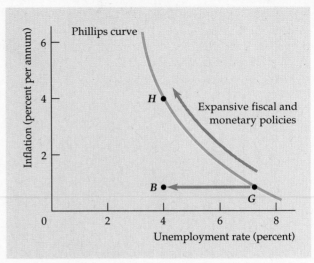

FIGURE 13-4   The problem of the 1960s: The inflation-unemployment tradeoff

The Phillips curve presents policymakers with a dilemma. By adjusting aggregate demand, they can choose a point on the Phillips curve. But what point should they choose? G provides a low rate of inflation but high unemployment. H provides high employment but at the cost of substantial inflation. In 1961, the economy was at point G. The objective of the Kennedy and Johnson administrations was to reduce unemployment—but without increasing inflation. By restraining wage and price increases as aggregate demand expanded, they hoped to move the economy toward point B.

the economy, whereas the costs of inflation are much more difficult to identify. Thus the Kennedy and Johnson administrations undertook a policy of expanding aggregate demand, aimed at reducing the unemployment rate toward a target of 4%. By itself, such a policy would move the economy from its 1961 position at G toward H in Figure 13-4.

The second response was to try to figure out a way to do even better. The problem posed by the Phillips curve was that inflation would creep up before the 4% unemployment target was achieved. To prevent this, President Kennedy introduced *wage and price guideposts*. By directly restraining wages and prices as the economy expanded, he hoped to move to a point such as B (Fig. 13-4), where the economy would reach *both* goals of full employment and reasonably stable prices.

The details of the wage-price guideposts are deferred until the next chapter. For the moment, it is enough to note that they did not work as well as hoped. As the economy expanded and the unemployment rate declined, inflation began to accelerate. Inflation had averaged about 1% per year in the early 1960s. It was more than 3% in 1967 and more than 4% in 1968.

THE RECORD SINCE 1970: HIGHER INFLATION AND HIGHER UNEMPLOYMENT

Since 1970, the behavior of the economy has been disconcerting. The previous decade had begun with high hopes that we could get the best of both worlds, achieving full employment together with price stability. But since 1970, we have suffered the worst of both worlds. High rates of unemployment and inflation have occurred simultaneously, particularly between 1974 and 1981. What went wrong? Two principal explanations have been offered.

COST-PUSH VERSUS DEMAND-PULL INFLATION

The age of Keynesian economics is over; the macroeconomic revolution in fiscal and monetary management we owe to Keynes has run afoul of the microeconomic revolution in trade union and corporate power.

JOHN KENNETH GALBRAITH

The first explanation of stagflation is based on the distinction between **demand-pull** and **cost-push** inflation. This distinction can be illustrated most easily with the simple aggregate demand and aggregate supply curves in Figure 13-5. The left panel shows what happens when aggregate demand increases—that is, when the aggregate demand curve shifts to the right. Output increases and unemployment declines, but the rising demand also pulls up prices. The economy moves upward to the right, from G to H. This is the typical inflation—rising prices are accompanied by rising output. (It can also be illustrated with a Phillips curve diagram. Rising demand causes a movement upward to the left along a Phillips curve. The increase

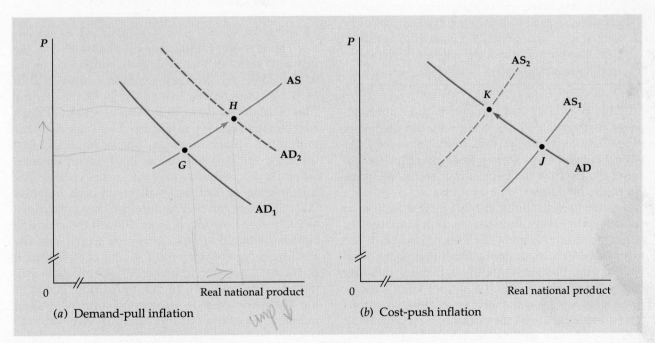

FIGURE 13-5   Demand-pull inflation versus cost-push inflation

When the demand curve shifts upward, higher prices are accompanied by an increase in output (left panel). When the supply curve shifts upward, higher prices are accompanied by a decrease in output (right panel).

in demand causes a decrease in the unemployment rate but a rise in inflation.)

Demand-pull inflation occurs when demand is rising rapidly. Buyers bid eagerly for goods and services, "pulling up" their prices.

Now suppose that strong labor unions and monopolistic companies have the power to influence wages and prices. Even during a period of economic slack, when the demand for labor is low and the unemployment rate is high, a strong union may be able to use the threat of a strike to negotiate higher wages. A firm with few competitors may raise its prices even though demand is sluggish. If this firm is producing basic materials, parts, or other intermediate goods, its higher prices will push up the costs of other companies using its products. Businesses with higher costs of labor and materials may pass them along to the consumer in the form of higher prices. In other words, there is *cost-push* inflation.

Cost-push or *supply-side* inflation occurs when wages or other costs rise and these costs are passed along in the form of higher prices. Prices are "pushed up" by rising costs. Cost-push inflation is also sometimes known as *market power* inflation.

This possibility is illustrated in the right-hand panel of Figure 13-5. As costs rise, the aggregate supply curve shifts upward, from AS_1 to AS_2. As the economy moves from J to K, rising prices are accompanied by a *decline* in output and a rise in the unemployment rate.

As far back as the 1950s, cost-push was used to explain why both inflation and unemployment might increase together. The idea of cost-push led to a heated debate. In particular, it invited a search for culprits. Business executives blamed inflation on the "irresponsible" bargaining of labor unions. The higher wages negotiated by aggressive unions forced businesses—so they claimed—to pass along their higher labor costs in the form of higher prices. On the other hand, labor blamed powerful corporations for pushing up prices in their desire for "fantastic profits."

Oil. While labor and management blamed each other for cost-push inflation during the 1950s, one cost-push culprit stood out in the 1970s: the Organization of Petroleum Exporting Countries (OPEC). In a brief period during 1973 and 1974, OPEC doubled and then redoubled the prices importers had to pay for oil. In 1979-1980, oil prices more than doubled again.

Because of the importance of oil as a source of power for industry, as a fuel for our transportation system, and as a source of heat for our homes and factories, the skyrocketing price of oil had a powerful effect on the United States, and, indeed, on all oil-importing countries. Businesses faced higher costs for power, heating, and transportation, and tried to pass these higher costs along to consumers in the form of higher prices. In response to this **supply shock,** inflation soared into the "double-digit" range—that is, above 10%—in 1974, 1979, and 1980.

A *supply shock* is a sudden, unexpected change in the price or availability of inputs that can push up costs and shift the aggregate supply curve upward.

The cost-push idea can be illustrated by the upward shift of the aggregate supply curve in Figure 13-5*b*, or, alternatively, by the upward shift of the Phillips curve from PC_1 to PC_2 in Figure 13-6. Earlier, we saw that even a stable Phillips curve—such as PC_1 in Figure 13-6—presents the authorities with a dilemma. They can choose low inflation, but this will mean high unemployment (at point G). Alternatively, they can choose low unemployment, but this will mean high inflation (at H). Or they can pick an intermediate point, such as J. Observe how much more difficult the situation becomes when cost-push forces are strong, and the Phillips curve shifts upward. If aggregate demand is steady, both unemployment and inflation will increase, as illustrated by the move from J to K. If the authorities decide to prevent any increase in inflation, regardless of the cost, they will have to restrain aggregate demand. The result will be a move from J to L. Although inflation will be no higher at L than it was at J, there will be a large increase in unemployment. On the other hand, if the

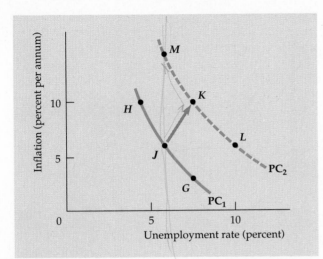

FIGURE 13-6   Cost-push inflation: The policy problem

Cost-push shifts the Phillips curve upward, from PC_1 to PC_2. If demand is restrained in order to fight inflation, the unemployment rate will increase from J to L. If demand is expanded in order to keep the unemployment rate from rising, the rate of inflation will increase from J to M.

authorities aim at preventing any increase in unemployment, they will stimulate aggregate demand, and the rate of inflation will go even higher as the economy moves to M.

The sharp upward shift of the Phillips curve led to a major policy disagreement following the oil price increases of 1973–1974. On the one hand, the Ford administration and the Federal Reserve were worried by the prospect of runaway inflation and leaned toward tight aggregate demand policies. The rate of increase in the money stock was reduced, and the president recommended a tax *increase* in late 1974. Thus the Fed and the president apparently were aiming at a point between K and L in Figure 13-6. However, congressional concern over this strategy grew as the recession of 1974–1975 deepened, and Congress moved to expand aggregate demand by *cutting* taxes. During 1974 and 1975, the net result of the oil price shock and the policy response was a combination of high unemployment and high inflation rates (as illustrated by point K).

Between 1975 and 1978, oil price increases were much more moderate than in 1973 and 1974. This

helped to reduce inflation during the sustained economic recovery that began in mid-1975. But then, when the revolution in Iran interrupted Iranian oil supplies in 1979, OPEC took the opportunity to raise prices, shifting the Phillips curve up once more. Again, a difficult question arose as to appropriate aggregate demand policies. The Fed became alarmed about the possibility of a runaway inflation and took strong steps to tighten monetary policy. The result was a major recession.

Not all price surprises are unpleasant, however. In 1986, the international price of oil unexpectedly fell below $10 per barrel—far below the 1985 price of $26. Partly as a result, the Phillips curve moved downward, and there was a sharp decline in the inflation rate even as unemployment continued its downward trend. The following year, however, saw a reversal: Oil prices bounced back up to the high teens, contributing to the rise of inflation in 1987.

In summary, the first explanation of stagflation depends on disturbances from the cost side. The Phillips curve can be shifted up by aggressive wage and pricing activities by unions and businesses, or by shocks from abroad, such as the increase in the price of imported oil. When such a shift occurs, the economy is likely to suffer an increase in both inflation and unemployment, with the mix depending on aggregate demand policies.

PRICE EXPECTATIONS AND THE WAGE-PRICE SPIRAL: THE ACCELERATIONIST THEORY

The second explanation of stagflation goes further, suggesting that the Phillips curve is highly unstable. It *shifts whenever people's expectations of inflation change*. In particular, it shifts upward as inflation gathers momentum. If the makers of monetary and fiscal policies attempt to choose a low-unemployment point on the Phillips curve, they will be disappointed. Inflation will not remain at a low, steady rate. Instead, it will accelerate to higher and higher rates. Hence, this is known as the **accelerationist** theory.

The easiest way to explain this theory is to

assume initially that prices have been stable for a long period of time. On the basis of past experience, they are expected to remain stable into the indefinite future. The economy rests at a stable equilibrium at G on the initial Phillips curve (Fig. 13-7) where the inflation rate is zero.

Now suppose that the government decides that the unemployment rate at G is unacceptable. Expansive fiscal and monetary policies are introduced in order to increase aggregate demand and reduce the unemployment rate to a target of U_T.

What happens? To meet the higher demand, producers need more workers. Those looking for jobs get them easily and quickly. Production increases and unemployment falls. In the face of higher demand, producers gradually begin to raise prices. In the early stages of inflation, however, little change takes place in money wages. Most collective bargaining contracts are for three years, and union wages change only slowly as a result. Nonunion wages are also sticky. People may work on individual contracts that run for one year or more. Even where there is no written contract, it is customary to review wages only periodically—say, once a year. With prices rising and wages responding slowly, profits increase rapidly. The initial reaction to the increase in demand is therefore an increase in output and employment, only a moderate increase in prices and wages, and a rise in profits. The economy moves along the Phillips curve to point H (Fig. 13-7).

Point H is not stable, however. The initial Phillips curve (PC₁) reflects *wage contracts that were negotiated when employers, workers, and unions believed that prices would remain stable.* But prices are no longer stable, and the contracts do not last forever. As new contract negotiations begin, workers observe that their real wages—the amount of goods and services their wages will buy—have been eroded by inflation. They demand a cost-of-living catchup. As long as aggregate demand rises rapidly enough to keep the economy operating at full blast at the low target unemployment rate U_T, the unions are in a good position to get their demands. With booming markets, employers capitulate to strike threats. Nonunion employees are likewise granted raises to keep them from quitting to look for more highly paid work. Because demand is high and rising, businesses can easily pass along the higher wages in the form of higher

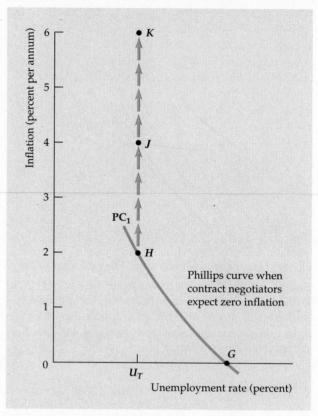

FIGURE 13-7   The acceleration of inflation: The wage-price spiral

If demand is continuously increased by enough to maintain the low target rate of unemployment U_T, the result is an ever-increasing rate of inflation. The economy moves successively to points H, J, K, and higher. The original Phillips curve PC₁ applies only to the short-run period *when the initial wage contracts remain in force.*

prices, and they do so. The rate of inflation accelerates; the economy moves to point J, above the original Phillips curve. With a higher rate of inflation, however, workers find that once again they have been cheated by inflation; once again their real wages are less than expected. At the next round of wage negotiations, they demand a larger cost-of-living catchup. The **wage-price spiral** gathers momentum. As long as demand is expanded enough to keep unemployment at the low target rate U_T, inflation will *continue to accelerate*, from H to J to K, and so on.

The Phillips curve therefore gives the wrong impression. It creates the illusion that there is a simple tradeoff between inflation and unemployment, that a low rate of unemployment can be "bought" with a moderate, steady rate of inflation. In fact, the cost of trying to achieve a low rate of unemployment is much more serious: *an ever-accelerating inflation.* Wages and prices spiral upward, with higher prices leading to higher and higher wage demands, and higher wages being passed along in the form of higher and higher prices.

LIMITING INFLATION

An ever-accelerating inflation is intolerable. If prices rise faster and faster, sooner or later the whole monetary system will break down and the economy will revert to an inefficient barter system. (The rate required for a complete breakdown is very high indeed—thousands of percent per annum. Nevertheless, severe disruptions may be caused even by rates of inflation of 10% or 15%.) At some time, therefore, the monetary and fiscal policymakers will decide to draw the line; they will refuse to increase aggregate demand without limit.

To keep this illustration simple, assume that (1) the monetary and fiscal line is drawn sooner rather than later, and (2) aggregate demand policies can be adjusted quickly and precisely. As soon as the economy gets to point H, the government recognizes the danger of an ever-accelerating inflation. It therefore switches aggregate demand policies. Instead of increasing aggregate demand by whatever amount is necessary to maintain a low target rate of unemployment, the authorities limit aggregate demand to whatever degree is necessary to prevent inflation from rising above the 2% reached at H. In other words, the authorities *change the policy target.* Their objective is no longer to keep the unemployment rate low at U_T, but instead to keep inflation from rising above the 2% target level I_T (Fig. 13-8).

What happens? Workers continue to push for higher wages because the 2% rate of inflation is still eroding their purchasing power. Employers are now in a bind. They cannot easily pass along higher wages because of the restraint on demand. Furthermore, the restraint on demand means that output begins to fall and unemployment rises. The economy moves to the right. The question is: how far?

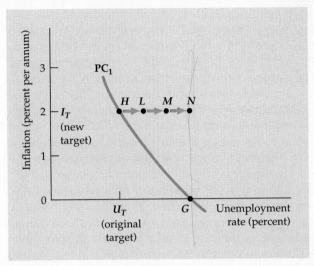

FIGURE 13-8   Limiting inflation

If the policymakers switch targets, limiting demand to prevent inflation greater than I_T, then the economy will begin to move to the right.

THE VERTICAL LONG-RUN PHILLIPS CURVE

If demand is restrained to keep inflation permanently at a target rate of 2%, where will the ultimate equilibrium be in Figure 13-8? At L? At M? Further to the right? There are reasons to believe that the economy will stop at N, directly above the original equilibrium G.

To see why, let us go back to the initial point, G. This represented a stable equilibrium. It was the result of an extended experience with a zero rate of inflation. Both businesses and labor had a chance to adjust completely to the stable price level. If they now get a chance to adjust completely to a 2% rate of inflation—with workers receiving 2% more in money wages to compensate—then the new equilibrium should be at N, where both labor and business are in the same *real* position as at G. At G, prices were stable. Now, at N, prices are rising by 2%. However, workers are just as well off as at G because they are receiving enough additional money income to compensate for the inflation. Consequently, they should be neither more nor less eager to work. Businesses are also in the same real situation at N as at G. They pay 2% more for labor and for material inputs each year than they would have paid at *G*, but they are compensated by the average increase of 2% in their prices. Therefore they should hire the same number of workers at *N* as they did at *G*. Thus *N* lies directly above *G*, and the unemployment rate is the same at *N* as at *G*.

With a steady 2% rate of inflation, the economy eventually moves to an equilibrium at *N*, where the unemployment rate is the same as at *G* and workers and businesses are in the same real position as at *G*. Alternatively, if the rate of inflation rises to 4% before monetary and fiscal policymakers draw the line to prevent more rapid inflation, the economy eventually moves to *R* (Fig. 13-9), or with a steady 6% rate of inflation, to *T*. All these are points of stable equilibrium. In each case, people have adjusted completely to the prevailing rate of inflation. In contrast, point *H* was unstable because workers had not yet had a chance to renegotiate their wages to reflect the new inflation.

In other words, the points of long-run equilibrium trace out a vertical line; the **long-run Phillips curve** (PC$_L$) is *perfectly vertical. In the long-run, there is no tradeoff* between inflation and unemployment. By accepting more inflation, we cannot *permanently* achieve a lower rate of unemployment. Expansive demand policies cause a lower rate of unemployment only during a temporary period of disequilibrium—at *H*, for example. During the temporary disequilibrium, workers and others are committed to contracts they would not have accepted if they had correctly anticipated the rate of inflation. As people have time to adjust, unemployment gravitates toward the equilibrium or **natural rate.**

The *long-run Phillips curve* is the curve (or line) traced out by the possible points of long-run equilibrium—that is, the points where people have adjusted completely to the prevailing rate of inflation. At such points, actual inflation is the same as expected inflation.

The *natural rate of unemployment* is the equilibrium rate that exists when people have adjusted completely to the prevailing rate of inflation. Alternatively, it may be defined as the equilibrium rate that exists when the public gets the rate of inflation it expects.

Through each of the long-run equilibrium points—such as *N*, *R*, or *T* in Figure 13-9—there is a

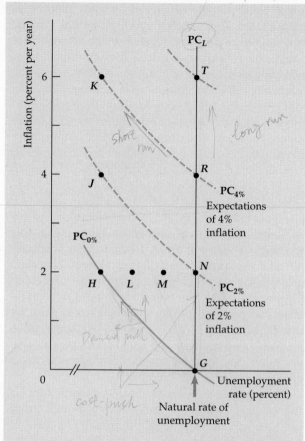

FIGURE 13-9   The vertical long-run Phillips curve

The economy gravitates toward the vertical long-run Phillips curve (PC$_L$) as the negotiators of wages and other contracts adjust to the prevailing rate of inflation. There is no long-run tradeoff between unemployment and inflation.

However, the short-run Phillips curve is *not* vertical. For example, once contracts have adjusted completely to a 4% rate of inflation at *R*, then an unexpected disturbance in aggregate demand will cause the economy to move along the short-run Phillips curve (PC$_{4\%}$) running through *R*. Thus a spurt in demand will cause an increase in output, a fall in unemployment, and an increase in inflation as the economy moves from *R* to *K*.

short-run Phillips curve, reflecting contracts based on the prevailing rate of inflation. For example, the short-run Phillips curve (PC$_{4\%}$) running through *R* is based on the expectation by contract negotiators that there will be a continuing rate of inflation of 4% per year. Suppose that after a number of years at R, the authorities adjust monetary and fiscal policies to make aggregate demand grow more rapidly. Faced with a high demand, businesses increase output, hire more workers, and begin to raise prices by more than 4% per annum. The economy moves along the short-run Phillips curve $PC_{4\%}$ to a point such as K, with a low rate of unemployment.

However, K is unstable for the same reason that H was unstable. Point K results from wage contracts that were agreed to when inflation was expected to be 4%. But actual inflation is 6%. Workers will feel cheated by the unexpectedly high inflation. During the next round of negotiations, they will press for higher wages to compensate for the high inflation. When wage contracts are adjusted upward, there are two possible outcomes. (1) If the authorities continue to follow expansive aggregate demand policies, there will be an accelerating wage-price spiral. (2) Alternatively, if policymakers take steps to prevent any further increase in inflation, the economy will move to the right, back toward the long-run Phillips curve and the natural rate of unemployment at T.

The *accelerationist* theory includes the following two propositions:

1. The long-run Phillips curve is vertical. There is an equilibrium or *natural* rate of unemployment that is independent of the rate of inflation.

2. If demand is stimulated in an effort to keep the unemployment rate below the natural rate, the result will be a continuous acceleration of inflation.

Because of point (1), the accelerationist theory is also known as the *natural rate hypothesis.*

Note that there is a similarity between the accelerationist theory and the theory of cost-push inflation. In each case, the Phillips curve shifts upward, and in each case, higher wage contracts can play an important role in the shift. But here the similarity between the two theories ends. Whereas cost-push theorists see higher wages as a major *cause* of inflation, accelerationists believe that *both*

wage and price increases are the result of a *single* underlying cause: excess demand. The government should not go looking for culprits in the form of powerful unions or powerful businesses or OPEC. Rather, the culprit is right in Washington: the government itself (including the Federal Reserve), which has generated the inflationary demand in the first place with excessively expansionist policies.

The vertical long-run Phillips curve brings us back to the view of classical quantity theorists. *In the long run*, changes in aggregate demand affect prices (P) and not the quantity of output (Q) or employment. Thus, the vertical long-run Phillips curve turns out to be the same as the vertical aggregate supply curve of classical economics (originally shown in Fig. 8-2), but in another guise.

Because we are brought back to the classical view, it is not surprising that the case for the vertical long-run Phillips curve—together with other aspects of the accelerationist theory—came from the pen of one of the leading monetarists, Milton Friedman of the University of Chicago. (Another early proponent was Edmund Phelps of Columbia University.)[3] Friedman wrote, "There is *always* a *temporary tradeoff* between inflation and unemployment; there is *no permanent tradeoff*." The short-run Phillips curve slopes downward to the right; in contrast, the long-run Phillips curve is vertical. A steady long-run increase in aggregate demand will lead to the same rate of unemployment—namely, the natural rate—whether demand is being increased by 4% per year or 14%. The only difference will be in the rate of inflation, not in output and employment.

During the 1970s, the idea of a vertical long-run Phillips curve became widely accepted by those in the Keynesian and classical traditions alike. Now, it would be difficult to find any economist who believes that the original, curved Phillips curve represents a stable, long-run relationship. By 1975,

---

[3]Milton Friedman, "The Role of Monetary Policy," *American Economic Review*, March 1968, pp. 1–17; and Edmund S. Phelps, "Phillips Curves, Expectations of Inflation and Optimal Unemployment over Time," *Economica*, August 1967, pp. 254–281.

Arthur Okun was willing to concede on behalf of the original Phillips curve school: "We are all accelerationists now."[4]

THE PROBLEM OF UNWINDING INFLATIONARY EXPECTATIONS

If policymakers believe they can count on a stable short-run Phillips curve, they may fall into a trap. They may think they can achieve low rates of unemployment to the left of the long-run Phillips curve by expansive monetary and fiscal policies. In fact, they will be able to maintain such a low rate of unemployment only if they allow inflation to spiral higher and higher.

Furthermore, the problem is even worse than that. Once inflation becomes engrained in negotiators' expectations, it can be eliminated with demand-management policies only at the cost of a high rate of unemployment, to the *right* of the long-run Phillips curve.

This is illustrated in Figure 13-10. Suppose that the economy has reached point T on the long-run Phillips curve, with inflation consistently running at 6% year after year. This point is stable; inflation will neither rise nor fall, and unemployment will remain at the natural rate. Now, suppose that policymakers decide that an inflation rate of 6% is too high. They are determined to reduce it by restrictive monetary and fiscal policies.

As aggregate demand is restrained, businesses find their sales falling. Production is cut back and workers are laid off. The unemployment rate rises. Because of intensifying competitive pressures as businesses scramble to make sales, businesses no

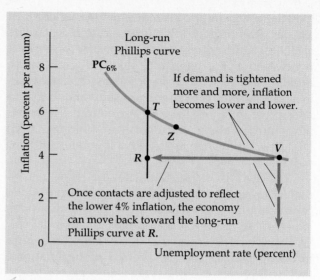

FIGURE 13-10 High unemployment while inflation is being unwound

Once inflation becomes built into contracts, it is painful to unwind. The short-run Phillips curve shown here reflects contracts based on the expectation of 6% inflation. It takes a period of high unemployment at V before wage contracts are adjusted downward.

longer insist on such large price increases. The rate of inflation begins to subside. However, this does not happen quickly. Businesses are still committed to pay the hefty wage increases under the old labor contracts; their costs continue to rise even though demand is slack. As a result, the short-run effect of the restrained demand shows up most strongly in a fall in output and a rise in unemployment, and only to a limited extent in lower inflation. The economy moves to point V.

Because point V is off the long-run Phillips curve, it is unstable. It is on the short-run Phillips curve running through point T, reflecting wage contracts negotiated when people expected that inflation would continue at 6% per year. But actual inflation is now only 4%. Because inflation is lower, workers are willing to settle for more moderate wage increases at the next round of wage negotiations. This willingness is reinforced by their desire to protect their jobs during a period of high unemployment. Furthermore, employers take a strong bargaining stance because of disappointing sales and low profits.

---

[4] Okun, "Inflation: Its Mechanics and Welfare Costs," *Brookings Papers on Economic Activity* 2:1975, p. 356. Okun was paraphrasing an earlier concession of Friedman: "In one sense, we are all Keynesians now." (Friedman had, however, tacked on a qualification: "in another [sense], no one is a Keynesian any longer." From Milton Friedman, *Dollars and Deficits* [Englewood Cliffs, N.J.: Prentice-Hall, 1968], p. 15.)

Okun pointed out that the data fit a Phillips curve "like a glove" during the 1960s. However, he observed that, since 1970, "the Phillips curve has become an unidentified flying object."

When wage settlements become more moderate, the economy moves from point V. If monetary and fiscal policies are kept tight, the rate of inflation will continue to drop. The economy will move down from V to progressively lower points, as shown by the arrows. The argument here is similar to that in Figure 13-7, except that inflation is now falling rather than rising in each successive period; everything is operating in the opposite direction. (A complication is explained in Box 13-1.)

On the other hand, if monetary and fiscal restraint is eased as the economy reaches 4% inflation, sales will begin to revive, the unemployment rate will fall, and the economy will move back toward the long-run Phillips curve at point R. This argument corresponds to the earlier one in Figure 13-8, again operating in the opposite direction.

This theory provides part of the explanation for the high rates of unemployment and inflation in the period from 1974 to 1981. (There also were other factors, such as the cost-push forces in the international oil market.) During the late 1960s, demand inflation was allowed to gather steam, both because of the desire to get unemployment down and because of government spending for the Vietnam War. The inflationary momentum accelerated because of expansive aggregate demand policies in 1971–1973 and 1977–1979. Then, when high and rising rates of inflation became a matter of grave concern, demand was restrained in 1974 and at the beginning of the 1980s. The anti-inflationary policies led to major recessions in 1974–1975 and 1981–1982. In each case, the inflation rate was driven down, but at the cost of a very high rate of unemployment.

Because the unemployment cost can be very high if inflation is hammered out of the economy in this way, governments have searched for other policies to supplement tight aggregate demand, and thus make the transition to a lower rate of inflation less painful. Most of these policies will be deferred until the next chapter, but one is considered here—namely, the policy of gradualism.

GRADUALISM

Very high rates of unemployment can be avoided if inflation is unwound gradually by initially picking a point such as Z rather than V (Fig. 13-10). It is true, of course, that the process will take much

---

BOX 13–1 The Natural Rate Theory and the Great Depression

The accelerationist or natural rate theory is accepted by most economists as a framework for explaining changes in inflation and unemployment during the past four decades. But an important warning is necessary: Not all available evidence supports the natural rate theory. In particular, the behavior of the economy during the Great Depression is inconsistent with it.

To see why, consider Figure 13-10 in more detail. If demand remains weak once the economy reaches point V, then inflation will be lower and lower during each succeeding period. Facing slack demand, firms will be in a poor position to raise prices, and workers will agree to smaller increases in nominal wages. The rate of inflation will fall from 4% to 2% to zero. But that should not be the end of it. If demand remains weak, prices should begin to fall; firms are under pressure to cut prices to increase their lagging sales. The results should be an accelerating *deflation*—with prices falling at 2%, then 4%, and so on, for as long as demand remains depressed and unemployment remains greater than the natural rate. So says the theory.

Things didn't happen that way in the 1930s, however. It is true that prices did fall during the early years of the depression, between 1930 and 1933, but the deflation didn't accelerate as predicted by the theory. Rather, prices rose between 1934 and 1937, even though unemployment rates remained between 10% and 20%—far greater than any reasonable estimate of the natural rate.

Thus the natural rate theory that is useful in explaining recent periods of inflation was apparently not valid during the Great Depression. Let us hope that this point will be of historical interest only; let us hope that there will be no future depression to test the validity of the natural rate theory during such a period.

longer if the inflation rate is decreased by only 1/4% or so each period. But those advocating gradualism believe that the total long-run costs will be smaller. Very high unemployment rates will be avoided, and such rates would be especially demoralizing for those who cannot find jobs even though they are very eager to work.

Gradualism was the anti-inflationary policy of the early Nixon administration. In practice, the strategy ran into two difficulties. First, it was not possible to follow a precise policy aimed at suppressing aggregate demand only slightly. In fact, the restraint of 1969 turned out to be greater than desired and led to the recession of 1970. Second, the gradualist policy became politically untenable when people saw that little progress was being made against inflation. President Nixon lost patience with gradualism in 1971 and abruptly introduced a wage-price freeze. Details of the freeze will be provided in the next chapter.

KEY POINTS

1. Data for the 1960s trace out a *Phillips curve.* Observations since 1969 are above and to the right of this curve.

2. Since 1970, a high rate of unemployment and a high rate of inflation have sometimes occurred at the same time. This means that the economy is no longer on the Phillips curve of the 1960s; the (short-run) Phillips curve has shifted upward.

3. There are two major explanations for the upward shift of the short-run Phillips curve:

(a) Higher oil prices have created cost-push pressures.

(b) People have responded to a higher rate of inflation by negotiating higher wages, causing the short-run Phillips curve to shift upward.

4. The short-run Phillips curve is unstable. There is a different curve for every expected rate of inflation.

5. In the short run, there is a *tradeoff* between inflation and unemployment. Expansive aggregate demand policies lead to less unemployment but more inflation. Restrictive aggregate demand policies lead to less inflation but more unemployment.

6. Natural rate theorists argue that people adjust completely to a steady, expected rate of inflation. As they adjust, unemployment moves to its equilibrium or *natural* rate.

7. As a consequence, the long-run Phillips curve is a vertical straight line. There is *no long-run tradeoff* between inflation and unemployment. Even if policymakers are willing to accept inflation, they cannot permanently keep the unemployment rate below its natural rate.

KEY CONCEPTS

Phillips curve
stagflation
policy dilemma
tradeoff between inflation and
    unemployment

demand-pull inflation
cost-push inflation
supply shock
accelerationist theory
wage-price spiral

long-run Phillips curve
    tural, or equilibrium, rate of
    unemployment
gradualism

PROBLEMS

13-1. Why might expansive demand policies aimed at a low rate of unemployment cause a wage-price spiral, with an ever-accelerating rate of inflation?

13-2. For each of the following statements, state whether you agree or disagree, and explain why. If the statement is incorrect, fix it.

(a) On each short-run Phillips curve, there is one and only one stable point, namely, the point at which the short-run Phillips curve intersects the long-run Phillips curve.

(b) According to accelerationist or natural-rate theory, the rate of unemployment will be less than the natural rate whenever inflation is less than the expected rate, and it will be greater than the natural rate whenever inflation is greater than the expected rate.

(c) According to accelerationist or natural rate theory, there is no tradeoff between the objectives of high employment and stable prices in the short run. Such a tradeoff occurs only in the long run, after the economy has adjusted to the prevailing rate of inflation.

(d) Short-run fluctuations in aggregate demand can affect prices, output, and employment. But long-run trends in aggregate demand are unimportant; they do not affect prices, output, or employment.

13-3. When prices rise more than wages, what generally happens to profits? What is likely to happen to output and unemployment as a result?

13-4. Now, suppose that prices rise more than wages as a result of a rise in the price of imported oil. How would your answers to question 13-3 be modified?

*__13-5.__ If the Phillips curve—such as that shown in red in Figure 13-7—is stable only in the short run, how was it possible for Phillips to find a curve for Britain that was stable for almost a full century?

CHAPTER 14
HOW DO WE DEAL WITH THE UNEMPLOYMENT-INFLATION DILEMMA?

The connection between [unemployment and inflation] . . . is the principal domestic burden of presidents and prime ministers, and the major area of controversy and ignorance in macroeconomics.

JAMES TOBIN

The coexistence of unemployment and inflation has created a painful dilemma for monetary and fiscal policymakers. No matter what they do, their decisions may seem wrong in the short run. If they expand aggregate demand in order to reduce unemployment, the result can be higher inflation. If they tighten policy to fight inflation, they may depress the economy and make unemployment worse.

Nevertheless, they must do something. Even standing pat—continuing past policies—is a policy. What are policymakers to do? This chapter discusses several suggestions for easing the unemployment-inflation dilemma:

■ Reduce the natural rate of unemployment by policies to improve the labor market.

■ Restrain inflation directly with wage and price controls or other policies.

■ If inflation has already gained momentum, do not try to stop it by relying exclusively on tight demand policies, which can cause an extended period of high unemployment. Look for ways to add flexibility to the economy in order to achieve a

quicker adjustment to stable prices, with a shorter period of high unemployment.

In the final sections of the chapter, we will look in detail at the way in which people's expectations of inflation can change. We will see that, if expectations change rapidly, it may be possible to unwind inflation in a relatively painless way, with relatively little unemployment.

WHAT CAN BE DONE TO REDUCE THE NATURAL RATE OF UNEMPLOYMENT?

No matter how successful policymakers may be in stabilizing aggregate demand to remove cyclical unemployment, there will still be a sizable amount of unemployment owing to frictional and structural causes. Not all of this represents voluntary unemployment while people search for appropriate jobs. Some workers—particularly teenagers—have trouble finding jobs no matter how hard they look. Accordingly, it is appropriate to study ways of reducing the natural rate of unemployment— that is, ways of shifting the long-run Phillips curve to the left.

INCREASES IN THE NATURAL RATE OF UNEMPLOYMENT

First, however, we must consider an unfortunate fact. The long-run Phillips curve shifted in the opposite direction—to the right—during the late 1960s and 1970s; there was an increase in the natural rate of unemployment, below which inflation would accelerate. During the Kennedy administration (1961–1963), an unemployment target of 4% was chosen; the Council of Economic Advisers believed that this rate could be achieved without unleashing inflationary pressures. By the mid-1970s, the Council of Economic Advisers was suggesting that the natural rate had risen at least as high as 5%; trying to drive the unemployment rate below 5% would lead to an acceleration of inflation.[1] By the end of the 1970s, the evidence indicated that the natural rate of unemployment was even higher—above 6%. Specifically, the unemployment rate was consistently above 6% in 1977 and the first half of 1978, yet the rate of inflation was nevertheless accelerating.

By the late 1980s, there was some indication that the natural rate might again be down below 6%. Specifically, the rate of unemployment fell to 5.5% in 1988 without causing an acceleration of inflation. (In 1988, the inflation rate was 4.4%, the same as in 1987.)

Such changes in the natural rate of unemployment do not conflict with the accelerationist theory that the long-run Phillips curve is vertical. According to that theory (presented in Chapter 13), there is no long-run tradeoff between inflation and unemployment; the equilibrium or natural rate of unemployment is not affected by changes in aggregate demand. However, it *can* change if conditions in the labor market change. In this case, the whole long-run Phillips curve can shift to the right or left.

Several explanations have been offered for the increase in the natural rate of unemployment during the late 1960s and 1970s, and for its decline in the 1980s.

1. The changing composition of the labor force. In 1960, teenagers (that is, 16 to 19 year olds) made up only 7.0% of the civilian labor force; by 1977, this figure had increased to 9.4%. Teenagers have higher unemployment rates than adults; they are more likely to move from job to job, trying various options before settling down to their life's work. This is not necessarily bad. A period of experimentation may pay off in terms of long-term satisfaction with the jobs they finally choose. But it does mean that frictional unemployment is relatively high among teenagers. As teenagers became a larger proportion of the labor force in the 1960s and 1970s, the natural rate of unemployment rose.

However, because of changes in the birthrate, the percentage of teenagers in the labor force has been falling since 1977. By 1987, it was down to 6.7%. This decline in the number of teenagers may explain why the natural rate of unemployment appears to have fallen in the 1980s. Indeed, this downward pressure on the natural rate will continue for the next few years, as the percentage of 16 to 19 year olds in the population will continue to decline until 1993.

2. The minimum wage. During the 1960s and 1970s, the height of the minimum wage was increased periodically, and more workers were covered. This increased the natural rate of unemployment because employers were discouraged from hiring low-productivity workers. They were particularly reluctant to hire teenagers with limited training and work experience.[2]

Between 1980 and 1988, the minimum wage declined in real terms—that is, after adjustment for inflation. This decline may have contributed to a lower natural rate of unemployment.

---

[1]*Economic Report of the President, 1962*, pp. 44–47, and *Economic Report of the President, 1975*, pp. 94–97.

---

[2]For example, Edward Gramlich of the University of Michigan found that the 25% increase in the minimum wage in 1974 caused an increase of 4 percentage points in the unemployment rate of teenagers. Gramlich, "Impact of Minimum Wages on Other Wages, Employment, and Family Income," *Brookings Papers on Economic Activity*, 1976, 2, pp. 409–451. See also Charles Brown, Curtis Gilroy, and Andrew Cohen, "The Effect of the Minimum Wage on Employment and Unemployment," *Journal of Economic Literature*, June 1982, pp. 487-528.

3. Unemployment insurance and welfare. Improvements in unemployment insurance and welfare provide a third possible explanation for the increase in the natural rate of unemployment during the 1960s and 1970s. These programs help to maintain the incomes of the unemployed. As a consequence, the unemployed are less desperate to take the first jobs available. Frictional unemployment may rise when those out of work engage in a more leisurely search for jobs.

There is some evidence to support this conclusion. For example, benefits for unemployed workers generally last only 6 months in the United States, compared with a year or more in Britain, France, and Germany. In each of these European countries, unemployment lasts *much* longer than in the United States. This suggests that long-lasting unemployment benefits do indeed make unemployment last longer, thereby pushing up the unemployment rate.

Nevertheless, other evidence suggests that unemployment insurance has little or no tendency to raise unemployment rates. Swedish unemployment benefits have been high and rising, yet the Swedish unemployment rate has remained far below that of the rest of Europe. Britain has cut unemployment benefits, but British unemployment has risen sharply.[3]

Even if there were a clear and strong relationship between unemployment insurance and the rate of unemployment, it is not obvious what, if anything, should be done about it, since there is a conflict of objectives. It is desirable to reduce the hardship of the unemployed by providing unemployment insurance. But their incentive to take unattractive jobs is thereby lessened, which makes it more difficult to achieve the goal of lower unemployment. However, one thing is clear. Government programs should be designed, insofar as possible, to maintain incentives to get a job. In particular, care should be taken to avoid programs that allow people to be better off not working.

---

[3]Gary Burtless, "Jobless Pay and High European Unemployment," in Robert Z. Lawrence and Charles L. Schultze, eds., *Barriers to European Growth* (Washington, D.C.: Brookings Institution, 1987), p. 143.

STEPS TO REDUCE THE NATURAL RATE OF UNEMPLOYMENT

A number of steps have been suggested to reduce the natural rate of unemployment.

1. Abolish the minimum wage? Some economists suggest that the minimum wage be abolished because it can cause unemployment. Sometimes this suggestion is combined with a proposal for more government grants to low-income families.

The government is unlikely to take the strong, symbolic step of abolishing the minimum wage. However, if it simply does nothing, the result will eventually be the same: The minimum wage is set in dollar terms, and its real value is gradually eroded by inflation. In fact, this happened between 1981 and 1988, when the wage remained fixed at $3.35. (In 1989, Congress passed an increase to $4.55 to compensate for inflation, but President Bush vetoed the increase on the ground that it would raise unemployment.)

Proponents of the minimum wage believe that it is only fair to raise the wage at least enough to compensate for inflation. They argue that the minimum wage has little effect on unemployment. They believe that, whatever the small unemployment effect may be, it is more than outweighed by the need to provide a living wage to the unskilled.

In rejoinder, opponents of a minimum wage point out that many of those working at the minimum wage do not have families to support; many are teenagers in prosperous families. The Congressional Budget Office estimates that about 70% of minimum wage earners come from families with incomes at least 50% above the poverty level.

2. A two-tiered minimum wage? The minimum wage is most likely to push up the unemployment rate of teenagers; many have little experience and limited skills. This has led some economists to suggest a two-tiered minimum wage, with a lower minimum for new workers during a training period. President Bush pushed for such a lower training wage when the minimum wage legislation was being reconsidered in 1989. This proposal does not, however, have universal support; it is opposed by those who fear that employers would simply replace older workers with new, low-waged workers.

3. Less discrimination. The unemployment rate of minorities has been about twice as high as the national average. A reduction in discrimination will not only make the economy more fair, but also reduce the unemployment rate.

4. Training programs. A lack of skills is one reason why some workers have difficulty finding jobs. In order to help workers develop skills and thus reduce structural unemployment, the Job Training Partnership Act of 1982 (JTPA) provides grants to subsidize training. This act had broad political support, and was sponsored by Senators Dan Quayle and Edward Kennedy. One main advantage of the JTPA, compared to the previous training programs that it replaced, is that the JTPA provides for much closer cooperation with businesses. The objective is to ensure that workers are trained for jobs actually available in the local labor market.

5. Government as the employer of last resort? A very ambitious program is sometimes suggested to reduce the unemployment rate. The government might act as the **employer of last resort,** standing ready to provide jobs for all those who want work but are unable to find it in the private sector.

There was not much discussion of this option during the 1980s, when many government programs were being cut back. But it was explicitly proposed in 1976. The original draft of the Humphrey-Hawkins bill, officially known as the *Full Employment and Balanced Growth Bill,* would have committed the government to offer enough jobs to get unemployment down to 3%. However, the last-resort provision was dropped before Humphrey-Hawkins became law.

Proponents of public employment programs point out that the unemployed could be given something useful to do. They might carry out conservation and public works projects similar to those of Roosevelt's recovery program in the 1930s.

Opponents object that such programs are expensive. Just how expensive was indicated by the Public Service Employment Program of the Carter administration, which provided 725,000 jobs at a cost of $8.4 billion. That works out to more than $11,500 per job—or $19,500 in 1989 dollars.

(The average worker got considerably less than $11,500—in fact, only $7,200. The rest went into administration and supporting services.)

If people are unemployed, it might seem obviously worthwhile for the government to hire them for, say, $4 per hour even if they can produce only $3 worth of output. Society at least gets the $3 in output, which is better than the zero output that society would get if they remained unemployed. However, critics argue that they won't necessarily remain unemployed. Without last-resort jobs, people might look harder for work in the private sector. Thus, over time, public employment could come to include people who would otherwise have found jobs in the private sector, where workers typically produce at least as much as they earn. Consequently, public employment could be a drag on the economy.

There seems to be no simple, painless, and uncontroversial way to lower the high natural rate of unemployment.

DIRECT RESTRAINTS ON WAGES AND PRICES: INCOMES POLICIES

Governments sometimes attempt to restrain inflation with direct controls or guideposts and thus improve the tradeoff between unemployment and inflation. Direct restraints on money wages and prices are sometimes known as **incomes policies.** Wage restraints affect the money incomes of workers. Price restraints affect other incomes, such as profits and rent.

Price and wage controls have often been introduced during wartime to suppress inflationary pressures. During the past three decades, the government has used incomes policies on a number of occasions: the guideposts of the Kennedy and Johnson administrations, the wage-price freeze introduced by President Nixon in 1971, and President Carter's guideposts.

The circumstances and objectives of these policies were somewhat different. The aim of the Kennedy-Johnson guideposts was to prevent inflation from gaining steam in the first place. The purpose of the Nixon freeze was to roll back existing inflation. The objective of the Carter guideposts was to prevent an already high inflation from becoming even higher, and perhaps also to bring it down. President Reagan was intent on reducing the role of government, and avoided such incomes policies.

THE KENNEDY-JOHNSON GUIDEPOSTS

To restrain wages and prices as expansive fiscal policies were applied, the Kennedy administration announced two guideposts:

1. On average, prices should not rise.

2. In general, money wages should not rise by more than the increase in labor productivity in the economy as a whole, estimated at 3.2% per year in the early 1960s.

These two guideposts are consistent. If wages increase by no more than productivity, no inflation need result. Labor can be paid more because labor produces more. Employers can afford to pay the higher wages and still keep prices constant on average.

Of course, there would still be some changes in relative prices. Where productivity was increasing very rapidly—for example, in the computer industry—prices could and did fall, even while the producers were paying higher wages. On the other hand, prices of some other products would increase, particularly where productivity was sluggish.

The idea of the guideposts was that restraint by labor and management would contribute to the general good; the economy could expand without inflation. The guideposts were to be enforced by public pressure on offenders and by exhortations or *jawboning*. There were no legal teeth to back them up.

When the guideposts were developed in the early 1960s, the rate of inflation was very low—less than 1%. As long as inflation remained very low, the wage-price guideposts constituted a consistent package. Labor could settle for an increase of 3.2% in money wages and still enjoy rising real incomes. However, by 1966–1967, a rapid expansion of aggregate demand was pulling consumer prices up about 3% per year. Workers could scarcely be expected to stick to a 3.2% wage increase. If they did so, their real wages would remain approxi-

mately constant. They would not get a share of the rising national product.

One way to deal with this problem would have been to protect labor's real income by permitting the money wage to increase by the estimated 3.2% productivity increase *plus* the rate of inflation. But the administration rejected this idea; the larger wage increase would have perpetuated inflation, not cured it. After 1965, both labor and business paid less and less attention to the guideposts. They became irrelevant.

THE WAGE-PRICE FREEZE OF 1971

In his early months in office, President Nixon was determined to combat inflation by dealing with the fundamental cause: excess aggregate demand. But, when aggregate demand was restrained, the economy slipped into recession in early 1970. Because inflation was already built into contracts and into people's expectations, the administration faced an extended period of high unemployment while inflation was being reduced.

By the middle of 1971, the president was becoming impatient. Unemployment, at 6%, was well above the average for the previous decade, and progress against inflation was painfully slow. Nixon abruptly shifted gears, introducing his *New Economic Policy*. To get inflation down quickly, a 90-day *freeze* on wages, prices, and rents was imposed, followed by less rigid controls. To stimulate output and employment, demand policies were shifted in an expansive direction.

Like other experiments with incomes policies, these controls were controversial. In one way, they seemed to work well. The inflation rate did drop sharply in late 1971 and 1972, and the unemployment rate declined slightly. However, inflation soon spiraled up again after the controls were relaxed. By 1973, the rate of inflation was 6.2%, substantially above the 4.4% rate when the controls were imposed. By 1975, inflation was 9.1% and unemployment 8.5%—both far above their 1971 levels.

INCOMES POLICIES UNDER CARTER: PAY AND PRICE STANDARDS

In his first year in office, President Carter confined himself to low-keyed statements that he hoped business and labor would show restraint. "Wish-boning," the critics called it. It was not very effective; the rate of inflation accelerated in 1977. Then, in 1978, the president announced pay and price standards, somewhat similar to those of the Kennedy-Johnson administrations. However, prices were already rising at almost 7% per year. Therefore it was obviously unreasonable to use the increase in productivity as the wage guidepost. The Carter standard for wage increases was set at 7%, with those earning less than $4.00 per hour being exempted. Price increases were also to be limited.

A novel aspect of Carter's program was a proposal for **real wage insurance.** Workers who agreed to the 7% money wage increase would get tax rebates in the event prices rose by more than 7%. Thus they would be protected against a fall in real wages in the event of rapid inflation. However, Congress refused to go along with this proposal. Critics pointed out that, if prices in fact rose by more than 7%, the automatic tax rebates would stimulate demand and increase inflation even more. Notice that the automatic tax cuts would be the opposite of the automatic fiscal stabilization explained in Chapter 10, whereby tax collections automatically increase in the event of booming demand and inflation.

During the 1970s, other proposals included the **tax-based incomes policy** (TIP). According to this concept, the government would use tax incentives to encourage businesses as well as labor to comply with guideposts. Government might offer a "carrot" in the form of tax rebates to firms and workers who complied with the guideposts. Alternatively, it might use a "stick"—a tax surcharge on violators. Critics doubted that TIP would be effective enough to justify the complications it would introduce into the tax system. What would the government do if firms kept their same wage scales but nevertheless paid workers more by simply promoting them into higher paying job classifications?

INCOMES POLICIES: CONTROVERSIAL ISSUES

The desirability of guideposts or more formal controls on wages and prices has been the subject of continuing and heated debate. Three main points are at issue.

1.   *Workability.* Skeptics point to the breakdown of the Kennedy-Johnson guideposts, to the inflation that followed Nixon's price freeze, to the failure of Carter's guideposts to prevent double-digit inflation, and to disappointing experiences with incomes policies in foreign countries.[4] In the United States and in foreign countries, this disappointment caused a move away from incomes policies during the 1980s.

Proponents of guideposts point to the successes of the 1960s. During the period when the wage-price guideposts were in force, the United States had an unusually long period of steady expansion. The rate of inflation remained below 2% until 1966, when excess demand was generated by spending for the Vietnam War. However, opponents of guideposts point out that the expansion of the 1960s was rivalled by that of the 1980s, when there were no price guideposts. Furthermore, the rate of inflation remained stable during the long expansion of the 1980s.

In more detail, critics argue that incomes policies may be counterproductive. Governments that use incomes policies may suffer from the illusion that they can indeed control prices in this way, and that they are therefore free to increase aggregate demand rapidly. If they do so, the incomes policies will collapse under the intense pressures of excess demand, and prices and wages will shoot up. This is one interpretation of the events of 1971–1974 and 1977–1980. Furthermore, incomes policies may be taken as warning of even more stringent controls to come, causing businesses to "jump the gun." If prices are about to be frozen, won't businesses raise prices now, while there is still time? There is some evidence that some businesses did in fact jump the gun in late 1976, when President-elect Carter announced that he would ask Congress for authority to impose price and wage controls.

---

[4]Robert J. Flanagan, David W. Soskice, and Lloyd Ulman, *Unionism, Economic Stabilization, and Incomes Policies: European Experience* (Washington, D.C.: Brookings Institution, 1983).

The United Kingdom's early experience is critically evaluated by Hugh Clegg (who served as a member of the old British Prices and Incomes Board), *How to Run an Incomes Policy, and Why We Made Such a Mess of the Last One* (London: Heinemann, 1970).

In addition, price controls can cause shortages, particularly if they are enforced over long periods of time. Goods in high demand may be channeled into *black markets,* where prices are above the legal limits. Because sellers are breaking the law, they may charge higher prices to compensate for their risk of being fined or imprisoned. Thus price controls can make inflation worse.

2. *Allocative efficiency.* Opponents of guideposts and controls point out that they interfere with the function of the price system in allocating production. As explained in Chapter 4, prices provide information and incentives to producers. When goods are scarce, prices rise, encouraging producers to make more. If prices are controlled, they no longer can perform this important role.

A particular problem arises because controls or guideposts may be enforced erratically. Responding to political pressures, the government may enforce price restraints most vigorously for essential goods. As a result of the low prices, businesses will switch to the production of more profitable items. Thus *price controls may end up by creating shortages of the very goods the society considers most essential.* For example, rent controls are the most common form of price control, since housing is so important. But in cities with rent controls, it is generally extremely difficult to find an apartment for rent.

Proponents of incomes policies recognize this danger but believe it can be dealt with. Advocates of guideposts or controls generally propose that a government agency be given the authority to grant exemptions, permitting higher wages and prices in industries where there are shortages.

3. *Economic freedom.* The proposal for a powerful government agency to control prices and grant exemptions is viewed with alarm by opponents. If officials are allowed to decide whether a firm will be able to raise its prices, they may gain the power to decide whether or not the firm will survive. Furthermore, in pressing for compliance, the government may pick on politically unpopular businesses—as happened when President Kennedy went on television to denounce steel executives for raising prices.

Proponents of controls point out that these dangers must be kept in perspective. In the absence of incomes policies, the government will have to restrain aggregate demand and generate high rates of unemployment if it wants to suppress inflation. The unemployed will be used as cannon fodder in the war against inflation. Thus the freedom of business executives and labor leaders to do as they please must be weighed against the need for workers to have jobs.

INCOMES POLICIES: A FINAL WORD

A discussion of incomes policies would be incomplete without noting that governments also follow policies that *raise* prices. For example, agricultural price supports keep farm prices up, while restraints on imports reduce competition and raise the U.S. prices of products such as textiles and steel. In the face of political lobbies, it is easy for the government to take the line of least resistance and extend such price-raising policies. But to do so is to sabotage its fight against inflation. Thus, in evaluating an administration's anti-inflationary policies, several related questions should be kept in mind: What policies has it been following to benefit specific industries or specific groups of workers? To what extent have these policies raised prices and wages? By adding to inflationary pressures, do such policies signal the need for monetary and fiscal restraint, and thus make it more difficult to achieve high employment in the economy as a whole?

OTHER PROPOSALS TO EASE THE TRANSITION TO LOWER INFLATION

Inflation is like toothpaste. Once it's out, you can hardly get it back in again.

KARL-OTTO POHL,
PRESIDENT OF THE WEST GERMAN CENTRAL BANK

If tight aggregate demand policies are used to wring inflation out of the economy, the result can be a long period of high unemployment. Incomes policies are sometimes used in an attempt to shortcut this painful process (for example, in 1971). Two other suggestions have been made to ease the transition to lower inflation.

INDEXATION OF WAGES

In the face of inflation, workers can protect themselves in several ways. One way, discussed in

Chapter 13, is for workers to negotiate an adjustment for inflation in their wage contracts. For example, during a period when inflation is running at 6%, they might negotiate a wage increase of 7.5%—a 6% adjustment for the inflation, plus a 1.5% real increase.

For workers, this approach has a major defect. It protects them only from *expected* inflation, not from *unexpected* inflation. If, for example, the inflation rate unexpectedly rises to 8%, they will find that their 7.5% nominal wage increase means a reduction in the real wage.

One way to deal with this problem is through the **indexation of wages,** which adjusts nominal wages during the life of the contract to compensate for inflation. For example, a contract might include a 1.5% basic increase in wages, with an **escalator clause** providing automatic adjustment for inflation. Thus workers would be protected from inflation, even though they could not tell ahead of time what it might be.

During the 1970s, when the rate of inflation was accelerating rapidly and unpredictably, indexed contracts became quite common in the United States—although they generally were **capped** and accordingly provided only a limited adjustment for inflation. In 1970, only 25% of workers covered by major collective bargaining contracts were protected by escalator clauses. By 1978, that figure had risen to 60%. As inflation declined during the 1980s, unions became less anxious to include these clauses. By 1988, only 40% of workers were covered.

An *indexed* wage contract contains an *escalator clause* that provides workers with additional money wages to compensate for inflation. The additional wage is often referred to as a *cost-of-living allowance* (COLA).

Often, there is a *cap* on the cost of living adjustment, which limits the increase to no more than a specified percentage.

The primary reason for wage indexation is to protect workers from inflation. Some economists have suggested a second reason: Indexation can increase the flexibility of nominal wages and thus help to break an inflationary spiral. If wage contracts are not indexed, years of abnormally high unemployment may pass before inflation can be sweated out of an economy, as noted in Chapter 13. With wage indexation, the transitional period may be shorter. Instead of negotiating a wage increase of 7.5% during a period when inflation is 6%, workers may settle for a real wage increase of 1.5%; that is, an increase of 1.5% plus the increase in the price index. If initial success is achieved in reducing inflation—from, say, 6% to 4%—then indexing will *automatically* reduce the increase in nominal wages from 7.5% to 5.5%. Upward pressures on prices will be reduced further, and the inflationary spiral will be broken in a relatively rapid and painless way.

Indexation is dangerous, however. It is a two-edged sword; rather than helping, it can make the spiral worse. If inflation begins to increase, indexation makes wages respond more quickly, generating even more inflation.

The danger of escalating inflation can become particularly acute if wages are fully indexed and if other incomes are too—for example, social security pensions. The problem is that the public may be promised more income than the economy can possibly produce. In a nonindexed economy, this problem is solved by inflation. Inflation cheats people out of some of their income, and the public ends up with no more than the economy can actually produce. However, if everything is fully indexed, price increases cause automatic increases in nominal income. If more has been promised than can possibly be delivered, there is no limit to how high inflation can spiral.

The risk of promising more than can be delivered will increase if real production or real income of society falls short of expectations. Two examples might be cited:

1. *The rate of increase of labor productivity slowed down* in the 1970s. The increase in output was less than expected, for reasons that will be studied in Chapter 16. The combination of indexation and weak productivity added to the wage-price spiral.

2. An *external shock* can extract real income from the economy. The prime examples were the rapid increases in the international price of oil in 1973–1974 and 1979–1980.

Somebody has to pay the higher cost of imported oil. If wages and other incomes are stable in dollar terms, then everybody will bear some of the burden of higher prices at the gas pump. But if people are protected by indexing, then wages and other nominal incomes will increase automatically. The burden will be passed along to someone else at the end of the line whose income is not indexed—such as a retired person with a pension fixed in dollar terms. Thus, in the face of an external shock, indexing leads to two problems: a speeding up of the inflationary effect, and an even heavier burden on those "at the end of the line" who are not protected from inflation.

In this regard, Britain had a particularly unfortunate experience. In 1973, Prime Minister Edward Heath encouraged the use of escalator clauses in labor contracts in the belief that they would make it easier for unions to settle for moderate wage increases and thus help to reduce inflation. The timing could not have been worse. The new indexation clauses added to the inflationary effects of the first oil shock in late 1973 and 1974.

Because of such problems, some early advocates of indexing have become less enthusiastic in recent years. Although indexing undoubtedly contributed to the rapid fall in the rate of inflation in the United States in 1981–1982, it has in many cases made inflation worse, not better.

THE SHARE ECONOMY

Indexing can make the wage-price spiral worse by making real incomes more rigid (even while it makes nominal incomes more flexible). A more promising policy is to move in the opposite direction, making real incomes *more flexible.*

One way to do this is through **profit sharing,** with workers being paid a base wage plus a share of the corporation's profits as a bonus. During a recession, firms would lay off fewer workers because the cost per worker (wage plus bonus) would automatically fall as profits fall. Furthermore, with lower costs per worker, firms would be encouraged to cut prices during recessions in order to stimulate sales. This would help to break the inflationary spiral and might also reduce cyclical fluctuations in output. For example, if the public recognized that car prices were unusually low during recessions, they would be encouraged to buy at that time.

Profit-sharing has been strongly recommended by Martin Weitzman of MIT, who bolsters his case by pointing to the low inflation and low unemploy-

ment in Japan, where profit-sharing makes up a sizable fraction of total labor income. Historically, U.S. unions have been cool to the idea, because they see it as a way to keep the base wage down.

However, profit-sharing has begun to take hold in the United States in recent years. The United Auto Workers' Union has negotiated profit-sharing agreements with GM, Ford, and Chrysler, and the idea has spread to other important sectors, including parts of the steel, aerospace, banking, and telephone industries. One reason is the growing realization that, to survive in a highly competitive world economy, U.S. labor and management must cooperate more closely. Profit-sharing provides workers with a clear and obvious stake in the success of the firm. In order to make the idea more acceptable, it has been renamed. Among labor negotiators, it is generally known as *gain-sharing* or *pay for performance* rather than profit-sharing, and Weitzman entitles his program *The Share Economy.*[5] Profit-sharing is sometimes combined with a no-layoff policy, making it even more similar to the Japanese system.

Some of the shares have been big enough to really count. At a Nucor steel minimill in North Carolina, base pay is only half that at the big Pittsburgh mills, but Nucor workers have averaged as much as $30,000 in bonuses in some years. Ford's workers received an average bonus of $2,100 in 1987, $3,700 in 1988, and $2,800 in 1989. Not all is rosy, however. Some years ago, GM's workers were angry to learn that executives had been given fat bonuses, even though profits were too low to trigger profit-sharing for them.

With *profit-sharing* or *gain-sharing,* workers receive both a base wage and a share of the company's profits.

EXPECTATIONS WHEN PEOPLE ANTICIPATE POLICIES

An influential group of economists believe that expectations are the key to any successful anti-

---

[5]Martin Weitzman, *The Share Economy: Conquering Stagflation* (Cambridge, Mass.: Harvard University Press, 1984).

inflationary policy. Because of the way expectations adjust, it may be possible to unwind inflation in a relatively painless way, without long periods of abnormally high unemployment.

LARGE SHIFTS IN THE SHORT-RUN PHILLIPS CURVE

To see how important expectations can be, let us reconsider the accelerationist theory outlined in the last chapter. If the authorities adopt an expansive aggregate demand policy in an effort to hold unemployment below the natural rate, the result will be an ever-accelerating inflation. To recapitulate briefly: From an initial point of equilibrium G in Figure 14-1, an increase in aggregate demand causes unemployment to decrease and prices to rise. The economy moves to H. But H is not a stable equilibrium. H is on the short-run Phillips curve $PC_{0\%}$ which is based on the expectation of zero inflation. However, actual inflation is running at 2% per annum. Contracts are adjusted upward to compensate for the 2% inflation, causing the short-run Phillips curve to shift up to $PC_{2\%}$. If the government wants to keep unemployment at the low target rate of U_T, it will increase aggregate demand again, moving the economy from H to J in the next period.

Suppose that we have gotten to J in this manner, with actual inflation at 4%. What rate of inflation will people expect to occur in the next period? What rate of inflation will unions and businesses expect when they negotiate wage contracts?

The answer, according to the original accelerationist theory, is that the expected rate for the future will be the same as the *actual* rate today—in our example, the 4% rate of inflation that people are experiencing at point J. This is an example of **adaptive expectations:** People's expectations adapt to the inflation they actually experience. If people adjust to the existing rate of inflation of 4%, the short-run Phillips curve will shift up to $PC_{4\%}$. If the authorities want to keep unemployment at the low rate U_T, they can increase aggregate demand enough to move the economy from J to K, just like the earlier move from H to J.

If expectations of inflation are *adaptive,* they depend on the inflation actually observed.

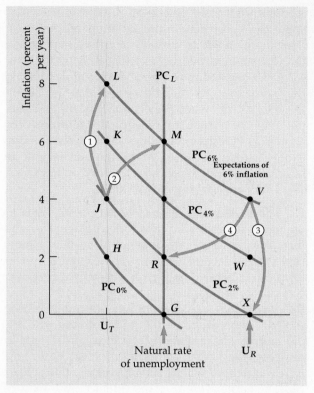

FIGURE 14-1 The acceleration of inflation when policies are anticipated.

In this example, people are fooled by rising inflation—when the economy moves from G to H and when it moves from H to J. In each case, they expect the current rate of inflation to continue, when in fact it is rising. However, when they get to J, they may expect that future inflation will be higher than the current rate of 4%. As a result, the short-run Phillips curve may shift up even more than in the simple accelerationist theory presented in Chapter 13 (Fig. 13-9). Similarly, if declining inflation is anticipated at V, then the short-run Phillips curve shifts down more rapidly, easing the inflation-unemployment problem.

This is not necessarily the correct answer, however. When the economy is at J, people do not necessarily expect that the actual inflation rate of 4% will continue. The reason is that they have already been fooled twice. They expected zero inflation but got 2% inflation at H instead. Then they expected 2% inflation and were wrong again. Inflation rose to 4% as the economy moved to J. Once people figure out the authorities' strong commitment to a low rate of unemployment, they may anticipate further inflationary policies in the future; they may come to expect that future inflation will be *worse* than inflation today. Hence, at *J*, they may expect that inflation in the future will be *higher* than the 4% that exists today. Suppose, for example, that at *J* they come to expect that future inflation will be 6%. In other words, when the economy is at *J* and people have a chance to renegotiate contracts, the short-run Phillips curve does *not* simply shift up from $PC_{2\%}$ to $PC_{4\%}$, based on the current rate of inflation. Instead, it jumps all the way up to $PC_{6\%}$.

There are now two possibilities:

1. The authorities remain determined to keep unemployment at the small percentage U_T, and they expand aggregate demand at an increasingly rapid rate in order to do so. The economy moves from *J* to *L* (arrow 1 in Fig. 14-1), leapfrogging over *K*. The rate of inflation has jumped from 4% at *J* all the way to 8% at *L*. People have once again been fooled: They expected 6% inflation but got 8%. No matter what inflation they have anticipated in the past, they have gotten more. Next time, how much inflation will they anticipate? 15%? 20%? More? The next jump in the inflation rate may be huge.

2. The second possibility at point *J* is that the authorities recognize the danger of runaway inflation, and accordingly do not expand aggregate demand so rapidly. If they expand demand only enough to create the 6% inflation the public expects, but not enough to keep unemployment down to U_T, the economy will move from *J* to *M* (arrow 2). At *M*, the inflation rate is at least stable. Equilibrium exists: The public expects 6% inflation and gets it.

In summary:

1. If the public comes to expect that future inflation will exceed current inflation, then the wage-price spiral may explode.

2. If the public *correctly* anticipates future inflation, then unemployment will return to its natural or equilibrium rate (arrow 2 in Fig. 14-1).

The first conclusion was important in the late 1970s. People did begin to fear that inflation was getting out of hand, and this fear speeded up the wage-price spiral.

UNWINDING INFLATION

Now consider what happens if the authorities take a further step and try to unwind inflation by following restrictive demand policies, starting from the equilibrium at M in Figure 14-1.

Chapter 13 has already described what will happen if people have adaptive expectations and therefore expect the current rate of inflation to continue. To quickly review: At equilibrium point *M*, expected inflation is equal to the actual rate of 6%; the economy is not only on the long-run Phillips curve but also on the short-run Phillips curve $PC_{6\%}$. When the authorities tighten aggregate demand in the fight against inflation, the economy moves down $PC_{6\%}$ from *M* to *V*. Inflation drops from 6% to 4%. If people expected current inflation to continue (as assumed in Chapter 13), the next contracts would be written on the expectation of 4% inflation. Thus the short-run PC curve would shift down to $PC_{4\%}$. If the authorities continued to pursue tight enough policies to keep the unemployment rate at U_R, substantially greater than the natural rate, the economy would move to *W* in the next period, and then, by a similar process, to *X*. Thus inflation would be reduced, but very slowly. The unemployment rate would be very high and inflation would come down only 2% each time period. This painful problem is what this chapter is all about.

The process need not be this slow, however, if people figure out what is going on and recognize that the authorities are firmly committed to reducing inflation, even at the cost of heavy unemployment. Then people come to expect that future inflation will not be the same as today's inflation but will instead be *less*. When they sign contracts based on this assumption, the PC curve shifts down rapidly. For example, if they figure out that the authorities are committed to an anti-inflationary policy when the economy is at *V*, they will be willing to sign contracts based, not on the assumption that inflation will stay at its current rate of 4%, but will instead be lower, say 2%. Thus, when contracts are renegotiated at *V*, the short-run Phillips curve will shift all the way down to $PC_{2\%}$.

The authorities then have the option of reducing inflation rapidly, leapfrogging from *V* over *W* and all the way to *X* in Figure 14-1, as illustrated by arrow 3. (Alternatively, they can ease their tight policies, causing a movement along arrow 4 back to the natural rate of unemployment at *R*.) In short, people's ability to figure out what is going on will make it possible to bring inflation down more rapidly. *Long, costly periods with high unemployment may not be necessary to unwind inflation.*

CREDIBILITY 可信性

If a policy is to be believed, it should be believable.
WILLIAM FELLNER

Note that the *credibility* of an anti-inflationary policy can be the key to its success. Paradoxically, the way to stop inflation *without* long periods of high unemployment is to convince the public that the Federal Reserve *will* tolerate long periods of high unemployment if necessary. People will be ready to sign contracts based on lower inflation rates only if they believe that inflation will, in fact, come down.

Recent U.S. history gives some support to this view. The inflation rate came down quite rapidly between 1980 and 1982, as the public came to recognize that the Federal Reserve really was determined to fight inflation. Nevertheless, the reduction in inflation was far from costless; during the recession of 1981-1982, the unemployment rate rose above 10%—the highest rate since the Great Depression. This suggests that, even when the Fed takes a strong anti-inflationary stand, the unwinding of inflation can cause high unemployment. A strong stand can speed the process of adjustment but not eliminate it.

To sum up the main ideas thus far:

1. If people figure out that policymakers are trying to achieve lower unemployment with an inflationary policy, the wage-price spiral may become explosive. The authorities will find that they cannot achieve a lower rate of unemployment for any extended period.

2. If people figure out that policymakers are determined to push down the rate of inflation by following tight aggregate demand policies, the wage-price spiral may come down quickly, with a relatively low cost in unemployment. *Credibility* is the key to a successful anti-inflationary policy.

In addition, this analysis is based on the key ideas of the original accelerationist theory presented in Chapter 13:

1. When people get the inflation they expected when they wrote their contracts, unemployment will be at the natural rate.

2. When people get more inflation than they expected when they wrote their contracts, unemployment will be less than the natural rate (as illustrated by point *H* or *J* in Fig. 14-1).

3. When people get less inflation than they expected when they wrote their contracts, unemployment will be greater than the natural rate (point *V*).

RATIONAL EXPECTATIONS

The idea that the public may anticipate policies has been formalized and extended by **rational expectations** theorists, who believe that people make the best forecasts with the information available to them.

Rational expectations are the best forecasts that can be made with available information, including information on (1) what the authorities are doing and (2) how the economy works. People with rational expectations may make mistakes, but they do not make *systematic* mistakes. The errors in their forecasts are random, chance occurrences.

To see why the best forecast may nevertheless be mistaken, consider what happens if a coin is tossed 10 times. Clearly, the best forecast is: 5 heads and 5 tails. But when the experiment is actually carried out, 7 tails may come up. The two extra tails have occurred by chance.

INEFFECTIVE POLICIES?

In the hands of Thomas Sargent and Neil Wallace, rational expectations led to the controversial conclusion that aggregate demand policies are *worthless* as a way of reducing unemployment. By adjusting the quantity of money, the Federal Reserve can have a powerful effect on prices. But it cannot systematically affect output and employment.[6] To see why Sargent and Wallace came to this conclusion, consider two cases.

Case 1. In the first—admittedly unrealistic—case, the public knows exactly what the Federal Reserve is doing. The Fed announces its target for the money stock each period and hits the target precisely.

Suppose that the economy in Figure 14-2 begins at point G, an equilibrium on the long-run Phillips curve PC_L. Inflation has been zero for some time. Suppose, now, that the Fed announces that it will increase the rate of growth of the money stock by 5%. People therefore expect higher aggregate demand and expect prices to rise by, say, 5% in the future.

According to rational expectations theory, people won't wait until the higher inflation actually arrives before they adjust their contracts upward. While the economy is still at G, people adjust as soon as they see the policies that will cause future inflation. Therefore the short-run Phillips curve shifts upward to $PC_{5\%}$. If people now get the 5% inflation they *expect*, the economy will stay on PC_L, moving directly from point G to R. In this case, the inflationary policy will cause no change in output or employment *even in the short run*.

Even though 5% is the *best* estimate of inflation, it is not necessarily *correct*. People do not know exactly how the economy works; they do not know how much inflation will be caused by the faster growth in the money stock. They may get more inflation than they expect—say, 6%. In this case, the economy will end up at K rather than R. On the other hand, they may get less inflation (say, 4%), putting the economy at W. The economy may depart from the point R but only in a random way; it is just as likely to move to the right as to the left of R.

With rational expectations, notice how easily the rate of inflation may be reduced—*if* the Fed's policies are credible. Suppose the Fed announces a

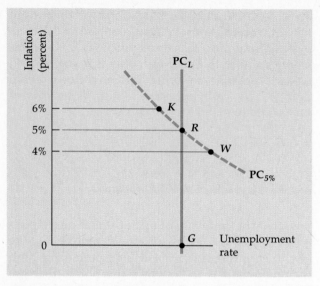

FIGURE 14-2 Rational expectations.

If expectations are rational, people make the best estimate of inflation. Their errors are random, and therefore departures from the natural rate of unemployment are random.

For example, if the Federal Reserve pursues an inflationary policy when the economy is at G, the public will make the best estimate of the inflationary effect of that policy. If the estimate is correct, then the economy will move directly to R, with no increase or decrease in unemployment. Because mistakes are random, the economy is as likely to move to W as to K.

reduction in money growth and carries through with an actual reduction. Anticipating a lower inflation, the public will revise their contracts. The economy will move directly to a lower point on the long-run Phillips curve (again, plus or minus a random error). This move is similar to the move from G to R but in the opposite direction. Inflation falls quickly, with only a random disturbance in the unemployment rate. Rational expectations theorists are hawks in the war against inflation. They believe that inflation can be unwound with little or no cost in terms of high unemployment.

Case 2. In practice, the public does not know exactly what the Fed will do. This complication is taken into account in case 2, in which people have two things to figure out—what the Fed will do and how the economy will respond. But once again, rational expectations mean that people will make

[6]Thomas Sargent and Neil Wallace, "Rational Expectations, the Optimal Monetary Instrument, and the Optimal Money Supply Rule," *Journal of Political Economy*, April 1975, pp. 241–254.

the best forecasts. Their errors will still be random. However, they are now forecasting two things rather than just one. Therefore their errors will generally be larger than in case 1, and random departures from the natural rate of unemployment will accordingly be larger.

Consider a hypothetical example. Suppose that, in each presidential election year, the party in power decides to stimulate aggregate demand in order to increase employment and put people in a good mood when they go to the polls. What will happen? People will figure this out (although they will not do so perfectly; they will make random errors). They will say to themselves, "Now that an election year is coming, the authorities will follow an inflationary policy." Workers will demand higher wage contracts in anticipation of this. Wages and prices will increase. However, because the increase in aggregate demand and prices is expected, there will be no systematic (non-random) change in output or unemployment.

The Fed may nevertheless be able to push unemployment temporarily below the natural rate by trickery—that is, by misleading the public. For example, the Fed might say it was going to reduce the quantity of money but actually increase it. Then inflation would be greater than expected and the unemployment rate less than the natural rate. However, this would be a bad policy. Having been fooled, people would have a hard job figuring out the Fed's policy in the future. They would make larger errors in forecasting inflation, causing larger fluctuations in output and employment.

Rational expectations theorists conclude that, instead of using trickery, the Fed should do the opposite. It should make aggregate demand and prices as stable and *predictable* as possible, in order to reduce the random fluctuations in employment. The best way to do this is to follow a monetary rule, increasing the money stock by a slow, constant rate of (say) 3% per year. Thus they advocate the same policy rule as the earlier monetarists.

CRITICISMS

The policy ineffectiveness theory of Sargent and Wallace has attracted much attention but remains a minority viewpoint. Critics raise several objections.

1. The theory assumes that people make detailed calculations of what the Fed is doing and how this will affect the economy. But, as Stanley Fischer of MIT observes, "It is absurd to assume individuals can make the necessary calculations since most economists still cannot do so."[7]

2. Rational expectations alone are not enough to establish the proposition that policies are ineffective. There is also another assumption embedded in Figure 14-2—namely, that people can quickly renegotiate wage and other contracts. But many labor contracts last two or three years. During a two- or three-year period when wages are sticky, the economy is stuck on a short-run Phillips curve. Changes in aggregate demand policy can affect output and employment, even if expectations are rational.

3. The facts don't fit the theory. The theory predicts that unemployment will fluctuate randomly; it will not remain consistently above (or below) the natural rate for very long. But in fact, unemployment was very high throughout the 1930s. More recently, unemployment was 7.5% or more for four consecutive years (1981-1984).

4. The policy conclusion doesn't necessarily follow. Rational expectations theorists say that, to get the most stable, predictable path of aggregate demand and prices, the authorities should adopt a monetary rule. But this is not necessarily so. If the Fed actively manages monetary policy, it may be able to make demand and prices even more stable and predictable. Specifically, this could occur if the Fed is able to offset disturbances in the economy. Therefore, rational expectations theory has left macroeconomists facing the same old question: In practice, *can* the authorities stabilize aggregate demand through active management? This key question will be studied in Chapter 18.

Table 14-1 provides a summary of the similarities and differences between the the rational expectations school and the earlier monetarists of the 1960s.

---

[7]Stanley Fischer, "Recent Developments in Monetary Policy," *American Economic Review,* May 1975, p. 164.

tradeoff
权衡

TABLE 14-1 Early Monetarism and Rational Expectations Theory: A Comparison

Issue	Early Monetarism	Rational Expectations Theory
1. Key to aggregate demand	Money	Money
2. Best policy	Monetary rule (steady increase in money stock)	Monetary rule (steady increase in money stock)
3. Which generates a more stable, predictable demand: monetary rule or discretion?	Rule	Rule
4. How public forms expectations	Adaptively	Rationally
5. Public's ability to figure out Federal Reserve	Unspecified (not a central issue)	Great if policy is consistent; not great if Fed resorts to trickery
6. Price flexibility	Moderately high but not high enough to prevent sizable recessions if aggregate demand is unstable	Very high
7. Long-run Phillips curve	Vertical; no long-run tradeoff	Vertical; no long-run tradeoff
8. Short run	There is a tradeoff; inflationary policies cause low unemployment for a time.	There is no tradeoff. Systematic policies will be anticipated. Erratic policies (trickery) will increase the random deviations from the natural rate of unemployment.

稳定的 (handwritten note near row 2)

LIVING IN A GLOBAL ECONOMY

WHY IS THE UNEMPLOYMENT RATE SO HIGH IN EUROPE?

Twenty-five years ago, economists used to ask: Why is the unemployment rate so much lower in Europe than in the United States? Now the ques-

tion is the opposite: Why is the unemployment rate so much higher in Europe? (See Fig. 14-3.)

Three possible explanations are debated by European economists:

1. *Big government?* Many blame big government, pointing out that it can inhibit economic adjustment in many ways. For example, generous unemployment insurance reduces the incentives for the unemployed to look for work. Workers who

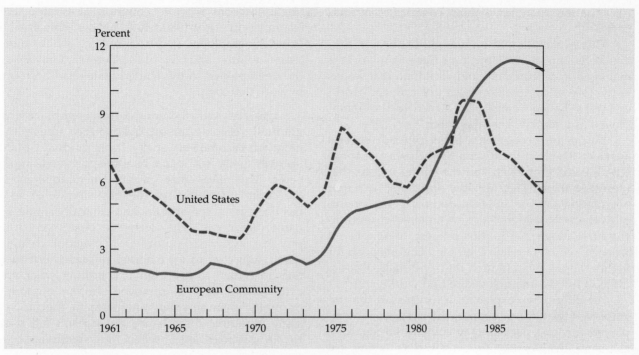

FIGURE 14-3 Unemployment in Western Europe and the United States.

In the 1960s, the European unemployment rate was less than the U. S. rate. However, since 1983, it has been higher. (*Source:* Organization for Economic Cooperation and Development, *Main Economic Indicators.* Data for the European Community include Belgium, France, Germany, Italy, Luxemburg, the Netherlands, and the United Kingdom, but exclude recently admitted members such as Greece.)

already have jobs can push aggressively for higher wages with little fear of the consequences. Laws restrict the right of employers to fire or lay off workers, and employers are therefore reluctant to hire people in the first place. A prominent critic of big government is Herbert Giersch of Kiel University, who believes that, as a result, the continent suffers from *Eurosclerosis*—a collective hardening of its economic arteries.

One difficulty with this explanation is that there are some obvious exceptions—most notably, Sweden. The Swedish government is the champion spender, reaching a peak of almost 60% of gross domestic product in the early 1980s. (Not all of this represented a direct government claim on the nation's output; transfer payments amounted to 25%.) Yet, in the mid-1980s, when the average unemployment rate in Western Europe was about 11%, it was only 3% in Sweden.[8]

2. *Excessive real wages?* The second explanation for the high unemployment rate is the high level of real wages in Western Europe. Employers won't hire more workers because they would have to pay them more than they could produce.

Support for this view is provided by the remarkable ability of the European labor force to protect its real wage in the face of inflation or other disturbances. European workers have been much more successful in capturing quick compensation

_____

[8]A detailed analysis is provided in Robert Z. Lawrence and Charles L. Schultze, eds., *Barriers to European Growth* (Washington, D.C.: Brookings Institution, 1987).

for inflation than have their American counterparts.

This explanation also raises difficulties, in particular the question, "How have European workers managed to capture and hold such high real wages in the face of competition from unemployed workers? Why haven't employers turned to the unemployed as a source of cheaper labor?"

European economists have offered several answers. The first focuses on the behavior of those who are still employed and the strong unions that represent them. They are the "insiders" in labor negotiations and in political decisions. The unemployed are "outsiders" and are in effect disenfranchised. Unions act in the interest of employed workers who will retain their jobs. Unions push for higher wages, even though they will make it more difficult for the unemployed to find work.

An alternative explanation focuses on the unemployed themselves. People who have been unemployed for long periods may come to be regarded as unemployable; they are perceived as having lost the skills and motivation needed to be productive workers. Whether or not this perception is correct, it means that the long-term unemployed may gradually become unemployable.

This explanation may be important. Long-term unemployment is quite common in Europe. For example, in 1979-1980, 40% of the French and British unemployed had been out of a job for more than 6 months, and 55% of the German. Only 9% of the unemployed in the United States had been out of work that long.

3. *Hysteresis?* If the long-term unemployed *do* gradually become unemployable, then unemployment can become very sticky. It can gradually build up over many years and be unresponsive to rapid cures. This idea—that current unemployment is the cumulative effect of the past decade or so—has been given the obscure and clinically sounding name, *hysteresis*. The term is borrowed from physics; hysteresis occurs if a material changes when subjected to an external influence but then fails to return to its original condition when the external influence is removed. In the economic example, unemployment increases in the face of some economic disturbance but doesn't fall back to its original level when the disturbance is removed.

Economists have not reached a consensus on which of these three points provides the best explanation of the high unemployment rate. They may all be important.

KEY POINTS

1. A number of suggestions have been made to deal with the inflation-unemployment dilemma:

  (a) Develop labor market policies aimed at reducing the natural rate of unemployment.

  (b) Use wage and price guideposts or controls to restrain inflation directly.

  (c) Do not depend solely on aggregate demand restraint as a way to reduce inflation, since it can cause high unemployment. Look for ways to make the transition to lower inflation less painful. Wage indexation is one proposal.

2. Between 1960 and the late 1970s, the natural rate of unemployment increased. Several controversial explanations have been offered for this increase:

  (a) Increases in the percentage of teenagers in the population. Teenagers have a higher unemployment rate than older workers.

  (b) Increases in the height and coverage of the minimum wage, which priced some workers with low skills out of the market.

  (c) Improvements in unemployment benefits. They may have increased frictional employment, since they reduced the pressures on the unemployed to take jobs quickly.

3. During the 1980s, there may have been a decrease in the natural rate of unemployment. One factor working for a decrease has been the decline in the percentage of teenagers in the labor force.

4. Proposals to reduce the natural rate of unemployment include:

(a) Abolition of the minimum wage.

(b) A two-tiered minimum wage, with a lower wage for teenagers.

(c) Steps to combat discrimination against minorities.

(d) Training programs for the unemployed.

(e) A program in which the government acts as the employer of last resort.

5. Incomes policies were used during the 1960s and 1970s by Presidents Kennedy, Johnson, Nixon, and Carter in the attempt to suppress inflation directly.

6. Incomes policies are controversial; they raise several important questions:

(a) Do they work?

(b) Do they adversely affect efficiency?

(c) Are they consistent with economic freedom?

7. A number of policies have been suggested to ease the transition to a lower rate of inflation, without causing a long period of high unemployment:

(a) Incomes policies.

(b) Indexed wages.

(c) Profit-sharing.

8. If the public anticipates what the policymakers are going to do, the inflation rate will become more volatile. An attempt to keep the unemployment rate below the natural rate will quickly lead to very rapid inflation. A tight policy will reduce inflation with relatively little unemployment. *Credibility* is the key to a successful anti-inflationary policy.

9. According to the rational expectations theory, there will be only random deviations from the natural rate of unemployment. Systematic demand management policies will be useless as a way of keeping the unemployment rate consistently low.

10. However, *if* the authorities are able to stabilize aggregate demand, they should do so, thereby reducing *fluctuations* from the natural rate of unemployment.

11. In the 1960s, the unemployment rate was lower in Western Europe than in the United States. However, it rose rapidly in the 1970s and 1980s.

KEY CONCEPTS

employer of last resort	tax-based incomes policies (TIP)	profit-sharing
incomes policies	indexation of wages	the share economy
guideposts	escalator clause	adaptive expectations
jawboning	cost-of-living allowance	rational expectations
wage-price freeze	escalator cap	

PROBLEMS

14-1. Teenagers have a much higher rate of unemployment than older workers. How might this be the result of government policies? In the absence of such government policies, would you expect the teenage unemployment rate to be equal to, above, or less than the rate for older workers? Why?

14-2. For each of the following statements, state whether you agree or disagree, and explain why. If you disagree with the statement, revise it.

(a) An increase in the minimum wage makes the unemployment rate higher. Therefore it should not be increased.

(b) Unemployment insurance also makes the unemployment rate higher. Therefore it should be abolished.

(c) The Kennedy-Johnson wage guidepost provided for an increase of wages of approximately 3%. The objective of this wage increase was to provide labor with a gradually increasing share of national product, in order to make up for past exploitation of workers.

14-3. Guideposts and wage-price controls are often opposed both by labor unions and by business executives. Why might labor leaders oppose them, when the objective of these policies is to make possible a combination of low inflation and low unemployment? Why might business executives oppose them, when one of the main objectives is to restrain nominal wage increases without having to put the economy through a period of recession and falling profits?

14-4. In late 1976, when President-elect Carter announced his intention to ask Congress for stand-by authority to impose wage and price controls, he gave people an incentive to "jump the gun." Why? Would people have an incentive to jump the gun before the Kennedy-Johnson guideposts were imposed? Before the Nixon freeze?

14-5. Indexed wages can create inflationary problems in the face of a "supply shock," such as an increase in the price of oil.

(a) Explain why.

(b) Will it create the same problem in a country that exports oil? Why or why not?

(c) Suppose that, at a time when unemployment and inflation are already high, there is a *favorable* supply shock, such as a decline in the price of oil or a bumper crop. Will indexation make the inflation-unemployment problem worse or better in this case? Explain why.

* **14-6.** President Carter's proposal for real wage insurance might have destabilized fiscal policy, since it would have provided for automatic tax cuts when inflation was unexpectedly high. Does the same criticism apply to tax-based incomes policies, whereby the tax rates of corporations depend on whether they adhere to guideposts? Explain your answer.

* **14-7.** Would you favor the government's acting as the employer of last resort? Why or why not? If you are in favor, what jobs would you give to those hired under a last-resort program? How much would you pay them? Would you place any time limit on how long they could work for the government under this program?

* **14-8.** At the end of the previous chapter, we saw that the accelerationist hypothesis was not consistent with what actually happened during the Great Depression of the 1930s. Is the rational expectations theory supported by the events of the Great Depression? Why or why not?

CHAPTER 15
HOW DOES INFLATION AFFECT THE ECONOMY?

Inflation is the time when those who have saved for a rainy day get soaked.

Inflation ranks with unemployment as one of the two major macroeconomic diseases. Every trip to the car dealer's or the department store is a nagging reminder of how much the value of the dollar has shrunk.

Only a few decades ago, inflation was considered a problem of secondary importance—and with good reason. In 1965, the price level was only 18% higher than it had been in 1953, reflecting an average rate of inflation of only 1.4% per year. This was in keeping with the long historical experience: During peacetime, U.S. prices had showed no strong upward trend. In 1914, prices on average were no higher than in 1875. On the eve of the Second World War in the late 1930s, the average level of prices was *below* the level of 1920.

It was only during wartime that inflation had been a major problem. The Civil War, World War I, World War II, and the Vietnam conflict all caused large increases in the price level, as shown in Figure 15-1. Inflation was particularly rapid during the Revolutionary War. The quip "not worth a continental" reflected the precipitous decline in the value of money issued by the new "continental" government of the United States.

In the 1970s, a fundamental change took place. The rapid inflation between 1973 and 1981 was

new; it occurred during peacetime and could not be attributed to military spending. As the United States extricated itself from the Vietnam conflict in the early 1970s, defense spending declined, but the rate of inflation nevertheless increased. Other countries with similar economies—such as Britain and Canada—also experienced high rates of inflation in spite of extended peace and low military expenditures.

It is true that since 1982, inflation has been lower—only about 4%. But our willingness to look on 4% inflation as a success shows just how much our attitudes have changed. A few decades ago, inflation of 4% would have been considered very high indeed. In 1971, President Nixon became so concerned about an inflation rate of 4.4% that he imposed wage-price controls.

In this chapter, we will study the problems created by inflation and the ways in which people can respond to inflation in order to protect themselves. Specifically, we will

■ See how *unexpected* inflation can cause capricious shifts in income and wealth among various segments of the population.

■ See how losers can protect themselves when inflation is *expected*. Thus we will confirm the con-

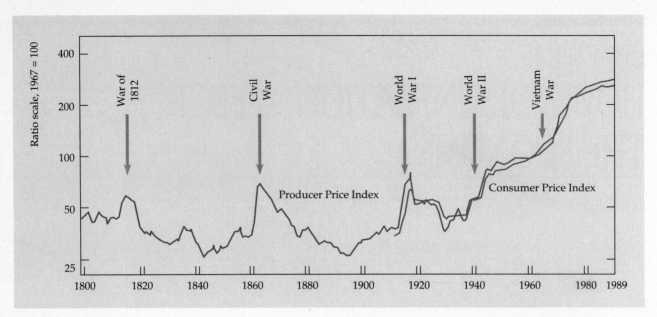

FIGURE 15-1   Prices.

Rapid inflation has usually been associated with wars or their immediate aftermath. The rapid inflation of the 1970s was a notable exception.

This figure shows both the familiar Consumer Price Index (CPI) and the Producer Price Index (PPI), which is an index of the prices of goods produced in the economy. The CPI includes the prices of services, but the PPI does not.

clusion of Chapter 13, that *expected* or *anticipated* inflation has smaller effects than does *unexpected* or *unanticipated* inflation.

■   See why inflation can nevertheless have substantial, continuing effects even when it is anticipated. Taxes are one reason.

■   See that *when inflation is rapid,* it tends to be *highly variable* from year to year. Consequently, it is hard to anticipate what the inflation rate will be. As a result, a rapid inflation can have serious consequences.

■   Study the effects of high inflation on the government's budget, and see why it becomes so *difficult to figure out the best macroeconomic policies* during periods of rapid and changing inflation.

In this chapter, a recurring theme will be the effects of inflation on the cost of buying a home. The importance of housing scarcely needs to be emphasized. In 1989, the average urban household spent almost 30% of its income on housing (over 35% if utilities are included). The largest asset that the typical family acquires is its home, and paying off the mortgage rivals the pension fund as the most important way to save. The housing market is particularly significant for college students; many will be buying their first homes in the next decade. Because of inflation, it will be more difficult to do so, for reasons that will be explained in this chapter.

UNEXPECTED INFLATION: WHO LOSES AND WHO GAINS?

Inflation gives people a feeling that they have no basis for planning, no sense of fairness and justice.

ARTHUR OKUN

The costs of inflation are much less clear than the costs of unemployment. That may seem surprising, as people are almost unanimous in expressing dislike of inflation. But, in any transaction, there is a buyer and a seller. When a price rises, the buyer loses but the seller gains. Thus the analysis of inflation is quite different from the study of unemployment. Unemployment represents an obvious loss; fewer goods and services are produced. However, inflation creates both losers *and* gainers.

LOSERS

During inflation, money loses its value. Thus the losers are those whose income or receipts are stable in money terms. These include

■ People who are working for a wage or salary that is fixed in dollar terms.

■ Any business that has undertaken to deliver goods or services in the future at fixed prices.

■ Retirees who receive pensions fixed in dollar terms.

■ Those who have bought bonds or have loaned money in other ways. They are eventually paid back in dollars that are worth less.

Consider the individual who purchased a $10,000 government bond in 1965 which came due in 1990. In addition to interest of 5% percent per annum, the bond purchaser expected to get $10,000 back when the bond reached maturity. In a formal sense, that expectation was fulfilled: The government did pay the bondholder $10,000 in 1990. But that $10,000 represented a pale shadow of its original value. In 1990, $10,000 bought no more goods and services than $2,600 bought in 1965. In 25 years, money had lost 74% of its value. For bondholders, unexpected inflation is bad news.

Some people might say that this doesn't matter much because only wealthy people own bonds. But this is not so. Many elderly people of moderate means hold bonds or savings accounts, whose purchasing power also declines as a result of inflation. During the rapid inflation of 1979–1980, the elderly became so angry over the losses inflicted on bondholders that one of their organizations (the Grey Panthers) pressured the U.S. Treasury into changing its ads for U.S. savings bonds. No longer are these bonds touted as "the one sure way to make your dreams come true." Now, the claim is much more modest. If you have trouble saving, the Treasury will help you. It will arrange for deductions from your paycheck to buy bonds, thus providing a "way to save dough that runs right through your fingers."

The elderly are hard-hit by unexpected inflation in yet another way: They have saved through private pension funds, which in turn hold bonds. With inflation, pensions financed by these bonds provide less real income for retirees. For the private pension system, the unexpected acceleration of inflation during the 1970s was a calamity. (However, social security and other government pensions have been adjusted upward to compensate for inflation.)

WINNERS

Although almost everyone understands that some people lose from unexpected inflation, it is not as well understood that other people win. Businesses that employ workers at stable wages will win if the prices of what they sell rise more rapidly than their costs.

Just as bondholders and other lenders lose from unanticipated inflation, so bond issuers and other borrowers win. When $10,000 is repaid after a period of rapid inflation, we have seen how the lender is worse off. He or she is repaid in dollars whose value has declined. For exactly the same reason, the borrower is better off. He or she repays the debt with dollars that have decreased in value.

Among the big winners are people who borrowed money to buy homes in the early 1960s, when inflation was expected to remain at low levels. The rapid, *unexpected* inflation of the last three decades wiped out much of their debt; they had an easy time paying off their mortgages. (However, as we will soon see, the *expected* inflation of recent years makes it more difficult for their children to buy homes now.)

Because *unexpected inflation* can lead to a capricious reshuffling of wealth—away from lenders and toward debtors—it makes the economic system *less fair*.

ADJUSTING TO EXPECTED INFLATION: THE REAL RATE OF INTEREST

When inflation is expected, those who are hurt can take steps to protect themselves. We have already seen in Chapter 13 how the labor market may adjust: Wage contracts may include a compensation for inflation. Financial markets may also adjust, with changes in interest rates providing a compensation for inflation.

Because inflation has such a strong effect on borrowers and lenders, it affects the interest rate that lenders charge and borrowers pay. We have already seen how inflation can harm lenders; they are repaid in money whose value has declined. Consequently, inflation makes them reluctant to make loans. The quantity of funds that lenders are willing to supply to the financial markets decreases, as illustrated by the move from S_1 to S_2 in Figure 15-2. At the same time, inflation benefits borrowers. Therefore the demand for loanable funds by businesses, home buyers, and others increases from D_1 to D_2. Equilibrium moves from E_1 to E_2. There is an increase in the price of loans (the interest rate).

The question is, how much does the interest rate rise? One common argument—traced back a half century to the work of Irving Fisher of Yale—

is that the interest rate will rise by the amount of inflation, thus leaving borrowers and lenders in the same real position as before. That is, borrowers and lenders will face the same **real rate of interest** as before, with this real rate calculated in a manner similar to that used for the real wage in Chapter 6. Specifically:

The *real rate of interest* $\approx$
    the nominal rate of interest –
    the expected rate of inflation[1]   (15-1)

Figure 15-2 illustrates the reason for believing that the nominal rate of interest will include a full compensation for inflation, bringing the real interest rate back to its original level. The noninflationary equilibrium is at E_1, with a nominal rate of interest of 3%. With zero inflation, the real rate of interest is likewise 3%.

With a steady, expected inflation of 5% per year, how much does the supply of loanable funds (S_1) shift? Point A on supply curve S_1 shows us that, before inflation, lenders had to receive 2% interest to induce them to provide C units of loanable funds. This suggests that, once there is an inflation of 5%, those lenders will be willing to lend the same C units only if they receive an interest rate of 7%, at point B. This provides them with a 5% compensation for inflation—shown by arrow f—and the same 2% real rate of interest as before. No matter what point we consider on S_1, the corresponding point on S_2 is 5% higher. Thus the entire supply curve shifts up by the amount of the inflation arrow f.

A similar argument applies to borrowers. With inflation, their enthusiasm for borrowing increases, since they will repay with money whose value has declined. Their demand for loans shifts up by 5%. No matter how much they borrow, they will be willing to pay 5% more for it, because this is the benefit they get from inflation.

With both curves shifting up by the same 5%, new equilibrium E_2 is 5% above original equilibrium E_1. In this simple case of a stable, predictable inflation, the nominal rate of interest should there-

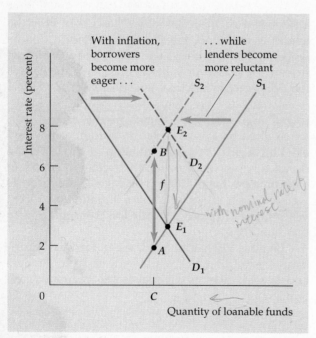

FIGURE 15-2   Inflation and the demand and supply of loanable funds.

As a result of inflation, people are eager to borrow; the demand for funds increases to D_2. Lenders are reluctant, causing the supply of loanable funds to decrease to S_2. As a result, the rate of interest rises.

---

[1]This is only an approximation. As in the case of the real wage (Eq. 6-10, p. 93), a precise calculation requires division.

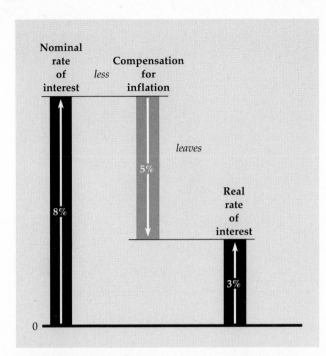

FIGURE 15-3   Nominal and real rates of interest, with 5% inflation.

On a $100 loan, $5 is required to compensate the lender for the yearly loss of value of the $100 loaned. With a nominal payment of $8, this leaves the lender ahead by $3. Thus the real rate of interest is 3%.

fore rise to 8% to compensate for the 5% inflation, leaving the real interest rate unaffected at 3%. Of the 8% total, 3% can be regarded as a net payment to lenders, while the other 5% compensates them for the decline in the value of the money they have loaned (Fig. 15-3).

THE REAL INTEREST RATE IN THE UNITED STATES

The previous section suggests that, as inflation was increasing during the late 1960s and 1970s, nominal rates of interest should have been rising. Figure 15-4 confirms that this did in fact happen. Moreover, as inflation fell during the 1980s, nominal interest rates fell, as predicted by the theory.

Unfortunately, it is difficult to go further and determine whether the nominal rate of interest includes a full compensation for inflation. One major problem is that people look to the *future* when they borrow or lend; the theory says that nominal interest rates should include compensation for *expected* inflation. The difficulty is that we do not live in the simple world we have assumed thus far, where the rate of inflation is perfectly stable and predictable. In the real world, we don't know the expected rate of inflation with any degree of precision. Therefore we have no straightforward way to calculate the real rates of interest that bond buyers and other lenders expect to receive.

The situation is not hopeless, however. There are two ways to obtain an estimate of expected inflation:

■   First is the traditional method. This is based on the reasonable idea that expected future inflation depends on what has been happening recently. Thus actual inflation over a recent period—the previous two years, say—can be taken as a rough-and-ready estimate of expected inflation. This can then be deducted from the nominal rate to provide an estimate of the real rate of interest, as shown for 1965–1978 on the left side of Figure 15-4.

■   The second way is superior. To find out what people expect, the best method is presumably to ask them. Since late 1978, financial experts have been surveyed to discover what inflation they expect. Their estimates of future inflation are deducted from the nominal rate of interest to find the real rate of interest, as shown in the right part of Figure 15-4 for the years since 1978.

Three broad conclusions may be drawn from this figure:

1. Before 1971, the estimated real rate of interest was quite stable in the range between 1% and 2%. The evidence therefore suggests that, until 1971, nominal rates of interest did contain a full compensation for expected inflation.

2. In the mid-1970s, nominal interest rates responded to higher inflation, but they did not compensate fully. As the inflation rate soared, real rates of interest were depressed, falling below zero between 1974 and 1976. In the words of Lawrence Summers of Harvard University, the data for the 1970s "suggest some tendency for interest rates to adjust to inflation, but far less than predicted by

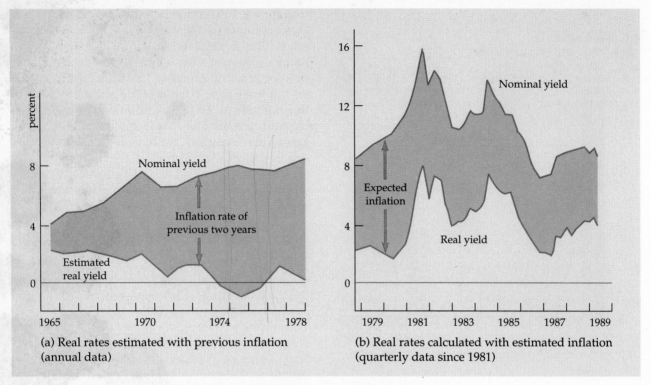

(a) Real rates estimated with previous inflation
(annual data)

(b) Real rates calculated with estimated inflation
(quarterly data since 1981)

FIGURE 15-4   Yields on long-term U.S. Treasury bonds.

Yields have risen sharply in the past two decades. Until the early 1980s, the increases could be fully explained by more rapid inflation. The real return on long-term U.S. government bonds did not exceed 3% until the end of 1980. (*Sources:* Real yields in both panels are calculated from Equation 15-1. In the left panel, the estimated rate of inflation is assumed to be equal to the actual rate for the preceding two years. In the right panel, inflationary expectations are taken from the survey data of Richard B. Hoey, David Rolley, and Helen Hotchkiss, *Decision-Makers Poll*, New York: Drexel Burnham Lambert, Inc.)

the theory."[2] To the degree that nominal interest rates failed to adjust fully, inflation helped borrowers and harmed lenders.

3. Finally, the very large swings in nominal interest rates in the 1980s cannot be explained by changes in expected inflation. In particular, the very rapid increase in the nominal rate of interest in 1980–1981 occurred at a time when expected inflation was *declining* about 1%. Something other

than expected inflation was causing the interest rate to change. What could that something else be?

Major changes in monetary and fiscal policies provide the most obvious answer. In 1980–1981, the Fed was determined to stop inflation; its tight monetary policy pushed nominal and real interest rates upward. On the fiscal side, Congress was working on a major cut in tax rates by 1981. This was expected to cause larger budget deficits and more borrowing by the government, and this put further upward pressure on interest rates.

Then, in 1982, both monetary and fiscal policies changed direction. The Fed shifted toward a much more expansive monetary policy in order to fight the recession. At the same time, Congress partially reversed the tax cuts of 1981 in order to reduce

[2]Lawrence Summers, "The Nonadjustment of Nominal Interest Rates," in James Tobin, ed., *Macroeconomics, Prices and Quantities* (Washington, D.C.: Brookings Institution, 1983), p. 232.

deficits and government borrowing. Both monetary expansion and the tax increases worked to lower real interest rates.

Of these three points, the second is particularly important. Nominal interest rates do not always compensate fully for inflation. Thus inflation can depress real interest rates, thereby helping borrowers and harming lenders. The resulting transfer of wealth from lenders to borrowers is one of the real effects of inflation.

This is not the only real effect of inflation, however. Even if inflation has *no* effect on real interest rates, it can *still* have real effects—as we will see in the following sections.

INFLATION AND THE TAXATION OF INTEREST

Inflation increases the tax burden on bondholders and gives a tax break to many borrowers. To illus-

trate, consider a noninflationary situation in which the interest rate is 3% in both nominal and real terms. A bondholder in the 33% tax bracket pays one-third (that is, 1%) of the interest in taxes, leaving an after-tax return of 2% in both nominal and real terms.

Now suppose there is a continuing inflation of 9%, which gets built into the interest rate. The results are shown in Figure 15-5. The nominal interest rate rises to 12%, leaving a constant pretax real rate of interest of 3%. The bondholder in the 33% tax bracket pays one-third of the 12% interest in taxes, leaving 8% after taxes. Note what has happened to the **real after-tax return.** When we subtract the 9% inflation, we find that the real after-tax return has not only disappeared; it has become *negative.* The reason is that the tax is collected not only on the 3% real rate of interest that represents the bondholders' real income, but also on the 9% that is simply offsetting inflation and is not real income at all.

A negative after-tax real return is not just a the-

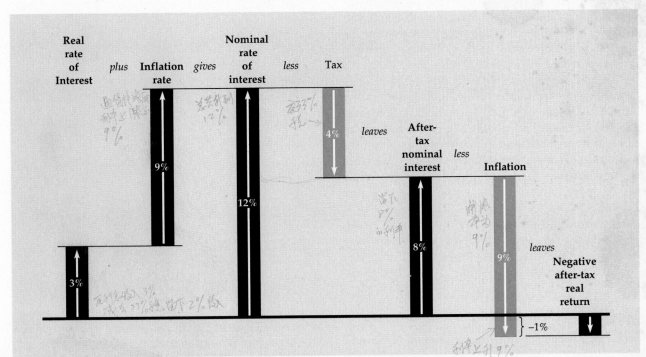

FIGURE 15-5   Effect of 33% tax, with 3% real rate of interest.

When inflation is 9% per year, the individual or corporation in the 33% tax bracket is not left with enough to compensate for inflation. The real after-tax interest rate is negative.

oretical possibility. After-tax real returns on short-term U.S. Treasury securities were less than zero during most of the period from 1968 to 1981.[3]

Although the tax system adds to the woes of bondholders and other lenders, it lessens the interest burden on borrowers. The reason is that interest payments reduce the taxable incomes of many borrowers. For example, interest payments represent a business expense; they reduce profits and therefore the taxes that corporations pay. Similarly, households may deduct interest payments on most mortgages from their income, thereby reducing the tax they pay. Just as lenders must add the full 12% of nominal interest to their taxable income, so too the borrowers can subtract the full 12% of nominal interest from their income, thus lowering their tax. (The calculations of Fig. 15-5 also apply to a borrower in the 33% tax bracket. The tax advantage more than compensates for the real interest paid; the real after-tax interest payment is negative.)

Thus the combination of taxes and inflation penalizes bondholders and discourages saving, while it encourages businesses and others to borrow.

The penalty to bondholders and the advantage to borrowers depend on their tax bracket. For example, the higher the tax bracket, the greater the advantage in borrowing to buy a house during a period of inflation. Upper income people have a particularly strong incentive to buy homes. They view housing "primarily as an investment rather than as necessary shelter."[4] Thus the inflation-taxation combination can distort the housing market. Builders may construct too many oversized houses to provide tax advantages to the wealthy, and not enough housing for lower income people. When this happens, inflation has a real impact on the economy.

Inflation introduces many quirks and inequities into the tax system, which was developed on the assumption that the average level of prices would remain reasonably stable. In the 1980s, *two*

major developments have made the tax system more rational: the tax act of 1986, which explicitly closed loopholes and made the tax system more equitable; and the reduction of inflation, which had the fortunate side effect of reducing the inequities in the tax system.

INFLATION CAUSES UNCERTAINTY

The chief evil of an unstable dollar is uncertainty.

IRVING FISHER

When the average rate of inflation is high, it generally is erratic and unpredictable. A country with a very rapid inflation may, for example, find that inflation bounces from 100% one year to 50% the next and to 90% the next. On the other hand, a country with a low average rate of inflation will find that the inflation rate is quite stable from year to year. Observe in Figure 15-6 that the year-to-year

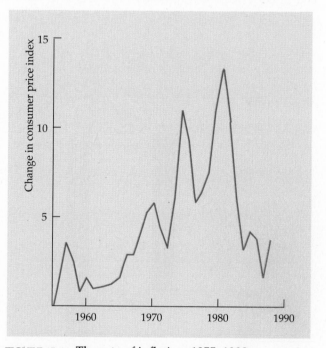

FIGURE 15-6   The rate of inflation, 1955–1988.

When inflation was low, in the late 1950s and early 1960s, there was little change in its rate from year to year. Between 1968 and 1981, the average rate of inflation was higher on average, and it also varied considerably from year to year. Since 1982, both the height and variability of inflation have been less than during the previous decade.

---

[3]Joe Peek, "Inflation and the Excess Taxation of Personal Interest Income," *New England Economic Review* (Federal Reserve Bank of Boston), March 1988, pp. 46-52.

[4]Anthony Downs, *Rental Housing in the 1980s* (Washington, D.C.: Brookings Institution, 1983), p. 33.

change in the U.S. rate of inflation was small between 1955 and 1965, when the average rate was low. Between 1968 and 1982, U.S. inflation was more rapid *and* more erratic. After 1982, it once more became lower and less erratic.

When inflation is erratic and unpredictable, it causes the shifts in income and wealth noted at the beginning of this chapter. An unexpected increase in inflation creates a windfall for borrowers and inflicts a penalty on lenders. An unexpected decrease in inflation creates a windfall for lenders and inflicts a penalty on borrowers.

ERRATIC INFLATION MAKES THE BOND MARKET SHRINK

Bonds are generally bought by people interested in a stable income; those who are willing to take risks are more likely to go into the stock market. Although increases in nominal interest rates help compensate bond buyers for *predictable* inflation, an unpredictable inflation makes the real return on bonds very uncertain. If the rate of inflation shoots up above the nominal interest rate, the bondholder will be "soaked"; the interest won't even cover the dollar's loss of value through inflation. On the other hand, if the inflation rate unexpectedly comes down, the bondholder will receive a windfall.

Because of the risks, potential buyers of bonds may be frightened away if inflation becomes erratic. Similarly, potential borrowers become reluctant to issue bonds; they also are uncertain whether erratic inflation will make them winners or losers. Thus erratic inflation can make the long-term bond market shrink. In 1980, for example, there was great uncertainty whether inflation would accelerate, and, if so, by how much. For this reason (and also because of the recession), the number of new bonds issued in the United States fell sharply. Businesses had difficulty issuing bonds to finance long-term projects. Thus erratic inflation imposed a real cost on the economy.

ADJUSTABLE-RATE MORTGAGES

There is, however, a way to reduce risks. A clause may be inserted in home mortgages, corporate bonds, or other debt contracts to periodically adjust the nominal interest. The interest payable can be tied to a current rate of interest, such as that on U.S. Treasury bills or newly issued bonds. In this way, nominal interest payments can be adjusted in the face of changing conditions.

With the large changes in inflation and interest rates during the past two decades, savings and loan associations have put increasing emphasis on **adjustable-rate mortgages,** also known as **variable-rate mortgages.** By the late 1980s, approximately 80% of newly granted mortgages had adjustable rates. Because such mortgages reduce the risks faced by savings and loan associations and other lenders, they are generally offered on favorable terms and are therefore often preferable for borrowers, too. Thus a reduction in risk can provide benefits to *both* borrowers and lenders.

An *adjustable-rate mortgage* (ARM) has an interest rate that is adjusted periodically in response to changes in the market rate of interest.

Adjustable-rate mortgages are similar to the indexed wage contracts discussed in Chapter 14. In each case, the objective is to protect people from capricious shifts in income when the rate of inflation unexpectedly changes during the life of a contract.

INFLATION CAUSES A FRONT-LOADING OF DEBT

Now let us return to the simple case in which inflation is steady and predictable, and the nominal interest rate adjusts to keep the real rate constant. Even in this case, we have seen that inflation can have arbitrary effects: Taxes are increased for bondholders and reduced for borrowers.

Such steady, predictable inflation can also have a second important effect. Here, however, it is the *borrower* who faces a major problem. To see how the borrower can be hurt, suppose a family buys a home. They take out a mortgage of $100,000, to be repaid over a 30-year period.

First, consider their situation in a noninflationary world, with nominal and real interest rates at 4%. Their payments are approximately $475 per month for 30 years. This monthly payment covers both interest and the repayment of the $100,000 loan. Because there is no inflation, the burden of the debt is spread evenly over the 30-year period. The $475 that they pay in the last month has the same purchasing power as the $475 paid in the first month.

Now, consider what happens with an expected inflation of 10%. If the real interest rate remains at 4%, the nominal rate will be 14%. With a traditional mortgage—requiring the same dollar payment each month over a 30-year period—the payments will be approximately $1,500 per month. This $1,500 represents a *huge* burden at first, since prices have not yet risen very much. However, by the final year, the $1,500 will be trivial. It will represent less purchasing power than $100 in the first year. To restate this point: If *nominal* payments are constant every month, then *real* payments decline through time as prices rise and the value of money falls.

Thus inflation and high nominal rates of interest result in the burden of mortgages being shifted forward to the early years. The mortgages are **front-loaded.**

A debt is *front-loaded* if the payments, measured in real terms, are greater at the beginning than at the end of the repayment period.

Many people who could buy a home in a noninflationary situation find they cannot do so if inflation is rapid. The burdens of the early years may be impossibly heavy; people may simply be unable to afford the early payments, even though they would be compensated by very light real payments in future years. This is an important real effect of inflation—*even if the real interest rate remains unchanged.*

In the early 1980s, young families faced great difficulties in financing their first homes:

■ Real interest rates were high (as seen in Fig. 15-4).

■ Nominal interest rates were even higher, causing a front-loading of mortgages.

■ Most houses were expensive. One reason was the eagerness of high-income people to buy homes for the tax advantages; their demand created upward pressures on home prices.

These three factors combined to discourage home purchases. In 1978, 53% of the households in the 35-44 age bracket lived in their own homes. A decade later, only 45% did.

Inflation presents an interesting paradox. People who bought houses in the early 1960s—while inflation was still low—gained from the *unexpected* inflation in the following years. They paid their low-interest mortgages off with dollars whose value had declined. More recently, however, expected inflation and the resulting high nominal rates of interest have created difficulties for home buyers. Home buyers now face front-loaded mortgages, with very high real payments in the early years. The older generation benefited from unexpected inflation. The younger generation suffers from expected inflation.

GRADUATED-PAYMENT MORTGAGES

Why not remove front-loading by starting with low dollar payments, increasing them gradually as prices rise? In our example, in which prices rise steadily at 10% per annum, home buyers would have an initial payment of approximately $480 at the end of the first month. The monthly payment would then rise gradually, in line with inflation, to reach $8,400 by the time the final payment was made at the end of the thirtieth year. In this way, the real burden would be the same every month—*provided that inflation continued at a steady 10% per year.* (The figures are correct. With 10% inflation, $8,400 at the end of 30 years has the same purchasing power as $480 at the beginning. See Box 15-1.)

However, a family with such a **graduated-payment mortgage** would be in trouble if inflation slowed down. To see why, consider the extreme case in which inflation fell to zero. The monthly payment would continue to increase by 10% per year in dollar terms. But now the *real* payment would also increase by 10% per year. Similar, but less dramatic, increases in real payments would occur if inflation only slowed down.

Although some lending institutions have experimented with mildly graduated mortgages, these experiments have been rare, and the graduation falls *far* short of the amount that would be

BOX 15–1   The Rule of 70: How Long Does It Take for Prices to Double?

Consider the effects of a steady inflation at 10%. During an initial base year, the index of prices is 100; in the second year, it becomes 110. During the third year, the index rises again by 10%. That is, it rises to 110% of the previous year's height, or to 121 (= 110 x 110%). Because the index grows at a compound rate, it increases by a larger number each year. As a result, the index reaches 200 in less than 10 years. But how long does it take? The answer is: about 7 years.

This answer is found by using the **rule of 70**:

$$\text{Approximate number of years required to double} = \frac{70}{\text{percentage rate of growth per year}}$$

In our example, where the rate of growth was 10% per year:

$$\text{Approximate number of years required to double} = \frac{70}{10} = 7$$

Because it is a general formula, the rule of 70 has broad applicability. It can be used to estimate not only how long prices take to double, but also how long an interest-bearing bank account takes to double, or how long a GNP growing at a constant real rate takes to double. For example, if GNP grows at 3.5% per year, it will double in about $70/3.5 = 20$ years.

The rule of 70—reflecting the underlying phenomenon of compounding—would lead to spectacular results in the event of persistent inflation of 6.4% per year, the average rate since 1970. Between 1990 and 2001, prices would double, and then redouble by year 2012. By 2023, they would be eight times their 1990 level; by 2034, sixteen times. If you wanted to earn $43,000 in 1990 dollars by the time of your retirement in 2040, you would have to be earning a million dollars a year by 2040. But that would be just a hint of things to come. If all prices were to rise at the same average rate, by 2070 your grandchildren would be paying $80 for a cup of coffee. It would cost them $2.5 million to send one of their kids to a private college for one year!

---

needed to level out the real burden. As a consequence, home buyers continue to face front-loaded mortgages, and many therefore have to settle for smaller homes than they could afford in the longer run.

A *graduated-payment mortgage* is one whose money payments rise as time passes. A *fully graduated* mortgage is one whose money payments will rise enough to keep real payments constant if the present rate of inflation continues. (There are no fully graduated mortgages.)

To sum up: Full graduation of mortgages does *not* occur. Therefore inflation continues to result in the front-loading of mortgages. Even after inflation has continued for some time and has been built into people's expectations, it continues to have an effect on real aspects of the economy. Most notably, it increases the real burden faced by home owners in the early years. In this important way, our financial institutions have not adjusted fully to an inflationary environment.

GRADUATED-PAYMENT MORTGAGES AND ADJUSTABLE-RATE MORTGAGES: A COMPARISON

Note that the graduated-payment mortgage and the adjustable-rate mortgage are designed to deal with different problems. The adjustable-rate mortgage (ARM) is designed to deal with the problem of *variable* inflation and interest rates. It does not solve the problem of front-loading. (If inflation is high and stable, nominal interest rates will be high and stable. The interest-rate adjustments on an ARM will be small, and the nominal interest rate will remain high and stable. The mortgage will be front-loaded.) In contrast, graduated-payment mortgages *are* designed to reduce the problem of front-loading. As we have seen, they are appropriate when interest rates are high and stable, but inappropriate when inflation and interest rates are erratic.

Adjustable-rate mortgages have become common, whereas graduated-rate mortgages are exceedingly rare. Thus the mortgage market has dealt with the problem of *variable* inflation and interest rates much more effectively than with the problem of *high* rates and front-loading. *Front-loading remains a major problem for home buyers.*

MACROECONOMIC POLICY IN AN INFLATIONARY ENVIRONMENT

Inflation not only creates uncertainties for borrowers and lenders. It also means that policymakers have difficulty in figuring out what is going on and what policies are most appropriate. In particular, inflation changes the value of outstanding government debt and therefore complicates the measurement and evaluation of fiscal policy.

To see why, we will have to begin with the fundamental relationship between deficits and debt. Recall that, when the government runs a deficit of $1 billion, it is spending $1 billion more than its revenues. It must borrow the $1 billion. Therefore its debt increases by $1 billion. Thus the *deficit* equals the *increase in debt*.

With this background, let us reconsider some of the major facts about the federal government's finances in a recent year. At the beginning of fiscal 1988, the government's total outstanding debt was $2,446 billion. During that year, government expenditures were $1,064 billion, receipts were $909 billion, and the deficit was accordingly $155 billion. The deficit necessitated additional government borrowing, which raised the national debt to $2,601 billion by the end of the fiscal year. That is, the debt rose by the amount of the deficit. Of the government's expenditures, $152 billion were interest payments on the national debt. The inflation rate was approximately 4.5%.

CALCULATING THE REAL DEFICIT

Here's one possible interpretation of these facts. With 4.5% inflation, the beginning debt of $2,446 billion could grow by a similar 4.5%—or by $110 billion—without its real size changing at all. Thus the first $110 billion of the deficit is not really a deficit. It does not add to the government's obligations in real terms; it simply offsets the effects of inflation. Thus the true deficit was not the $155 billion commonly reported. Rather, it was $110 billion less, or only $45 billion. That is, the **real deficit** was

only the amount by which the real debt of the government rose. According to this line of argument, the standard figures greatly overstate the real deficit and therefore greatly overstate the stimulus coming from the fiscal side.

The **real deficit** of the government is measured by the increase in the real debt of the government. If the debt falls in real terms, then the government has a *real surplus.*

Proponents of this view include Robert Eisner of Northwestern University and Paul J. Pieper of the University of Illinois, who argue that "in government accounts as in private accounts, inflation plays vast tricks." They recalculate the government deficit as the increase in the real value of the debt and find that this greatly alters the picture of fiscal policy, particularly during the high-inflation years of 1978–1981. Rather than sizable deficits—as shown in the standard figures—Eisner and Pieper estimate that the real budget was in *surplus* between 1978 and 1980 (Fig. 15-7). They argue that many economists have been mistaken in concluding, on the basis of the standard figures, that the federal budget became perversely expansionary after 1966, when inflation was increasing. On the contrary, "the federal budget may properly be viewed as more frequently in surplus than in deficit . . . . The view that fiscal policy has generally been too easy and overstimulatory is contradicted." Furthermore, "the 1981–'82 recession cannot be properly interpreted as the triumph of all-powerful monetary constraints over relatively ineffective fiscal ease." Why not? Because, say Eisner and Pieper, the real, inflation-adjusted budget was not very stimulative at that time. In 1980, the real budget was in surplus, and in 1981, the real deficit was very small.[5]

AN ALTERNATIVE VIEW

An alternative view is that it is a great mistake to measure fiscal policy in real terms, even though it

---

[5]Robert Eisner and Paul J. Pieper, "A New View of the Federal Debt and Budget Deficits," *American Economic Review,* March 1984, pp. 11-29. The quotations are from pp. 11 and 23.

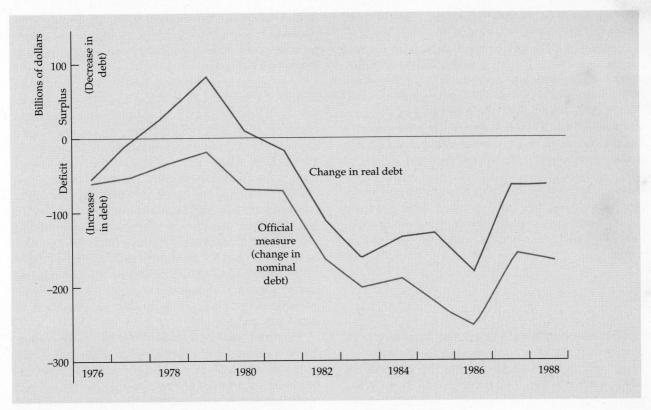

FIGURE 15-7   Adjusting the federal budget for inflation.

Federal deficits add to outstanding government debt. Calculated in the standard way, as an increase in the nominal debt outstanding, the federal budget has been substantially in deficit in recent years. However, when the deficit is recalculated as the increase in the real value of the debt outstanding, then some of the deficits of recent years are transformed into *surpluses.* Because of inflation, the real value of government debt declined in 1978, 1979, and 1980. (*Source:* For 1976–1980, Robert Eisner and Paul J. Pieper, "A New View of the Federal Debt and Budget Deficits," *American Economic Review,* March 1984, p. 16. Updated by authors, 1981–1988.)

is of course perfectly correct that inflation lowers the real value of outstanding government debt.[6]

According to this alternative view, it is reasonable and desirable for individuals and corporations to recalculate their debt and other liabilities and assets in real terms, to get a better idea of how they are doing. Individuals and corporations may *adjust* and *respond* to inflation in this way. However, the government is fundamentally different. The government should not simply respond to inflation. Through its monetary and fiscal policies it is primarily *responsible* for inflation. If it keeps its accounts in real terms, it is likely to make inflation worse and *destabilize the economy.*

To see why, consider what happens if the economy enters a period of inflation. As a result, the real value of the debt falls. As calculated by Eisner and Pieper, the real budget automatically swings into surplus. Measured in this way, fiscal policy is judged to be moving in a restrictive direction. To offset this unexpected restraint, the government

---

[6]The authors of this book take the alternative view. Paul Wonnacott, "The Nominal Deficit Really Matters," *Challenge,* September 1986, pp. 48-51.

may cut taxes or increase spending. But this will add to the inflation.

Similarly, if the government focuses on the real deficit or surplus, it may destabilize the economy during a deflationary period such as the early 1930s. Between 1929 and 1933, prices fell approximately 25%. As a result, the real value of the government debt rose. In real terms, the government's budget was moving even more deeply into deficit. If the government focused on this real deficit, it might erroneously assume that it was already providing a large stimulus, and it might fail to make the needed shift toward expansion. It might even cut expenditures to limit the increase in the real debt. But such cuts would make the depression worse.

MONETARY POLICY IN AN INFLATIONARY ENVIRONMENT

Similar issues arise with respect to monetary policy. The real quantity of money in the economy is important; it helps to determine the quantity of goods and services that people will buy. What would happen if the Fed were to concentrate on the real quantity of money? To make things simple, suppose that the Fed follows a policy of slowly increasing the real money stock, in line with the slow increase of the productive capacity of the economy.

Again, the focus on *real* magnitudes could have destabilizing results. Consider again an economy entering a period of inflation. The nominal quantity of money has undoubtedly been rising. However, when we adjust it for inflation, we may find that the real amount of money has not been rising much. It may even have been falling.[7] If the central

bank is focusing on the real quantity, it may conclude that monetary policy is too tight, and create more money. This is precisely the wrong way to respond to inflation.

Similarly, concentrating on the real quantity of money can be the wrong thing to do during a period of deflation. Again, consider what happened between 1929 and 1933. Prices fell approximately 25%, while the nominal quantity of money fell about 27%. Thus, in real terms, the quantity of money declined only slightly. A central bank focusing on the real quantity might conclude that there was only a small problem with monetary policy. In fact, the large decline in the nominal quantity of money was having catastrophic effects. The central bank should not focus on the real quantity of money. Furthermore, outside observers should not use changes in the real quantity of money as the primary way of judging the tightness or looseness of monetary policy.

In brief, real accounting—which makes sense for individuals and corporations—does not make nearly as much sense for the government and central bank, since they are responsible for the overall operation of the economy. Real accounting can lead to destabilizing actions.

It is going too far to argue that real magnitudes are not important. They are. But the use of real magnitudes as guides for macroeconomic policy is problematic, to say the least. Even in the best of times, policymakers face difficulties in determining the best macroeconomic policies. When inflation is rapid, it greatly adds to their difficulties.

In conclusion, we now have found a total of *four policy traps*—apparently plausible policy guides that can cause destabilizing actions:

■ The annually balanced budget rule (Chapter 10).

■ The use of a real, inflation-adjusted budget as a guide for fiscal policy (this chapter).

■ An attempt by the Federal Reserve to stabilize interest rates (the end of Chapter 12).

■ An attempt by the Federal Reserve to stabilize the real quantity of money (this chapter).

---

*[7]Indeed, if the inflation is rapid, the real quantity of money is *likely* to decline. Suppose, for example, that the nominal quantity of money doubles during a year and prices rise rapidly. Because money is quickly losing its value, people have an incentive to spend it quickly. Thus a 100% increase in the money stock may cause aggregate demand and prices to rise by more than 100%. With prices rising by a greater percentage than the nominal quantity of money, the real quantity of money declines.

KEY POINTS

1. Unexpected inflation causes a capricious redistribution of wealth, away from lenders (bondholders) and toward borrowers.

2. During periods of high expected inflation, people are eager to borrow and reluctant to lend. This causes nominal rates of interest to rise.

3. The *real* rate of interest is (approximately) the nominal rate less the expected rate of inflation.

4. Real rates of interest have not been very stable. They were low during the 1970s—indeed, they were negative for several years. They were high during most of the 1980s.

5. The combination of high inflation, high nominal interest rates, and taxation means that lenders in high tax brackets end up with low or even negative after-tax returns. Borrowers in high tax brackets end up gaining in real terms. Thus, during periods of rapid inflation, well-to-do people are discouraged from lending and encouraged instead to borrow—for example, by purchasing large houses with big mortgages.

6. High inflation is usually erratic inflation.

7. One way to limit the redistribution of wealth from erratic, unexpected changes in inflation is through adjustable-rate mortgages.

8. When inflation pushes up nominal rates of interest, the effect is that borrowers have to repay loans more quickly. For example, the normal mortgage, with the same dollar payment each month, becomes "front-loaded." People have difficulty buying homes, since higher real payments are required in the early years.

9. One way to deal with this problem would be with graduated-payment mortgages, whose money payments rise over the life of the mortgage, thus lessening the front-loading. However, graduated-payment mortgages are very rare. As a result, the front-loading of mortgages remains a major problem for home buyers.

10. If the government's deficit or surplus is measured as the increase or decrease in the *real* value of government debt, then the government has been running surpluses, not deficits, during many of the past 20 years.

11. It is, however, questionable whether fiscal policy should be measured in this way, as the change in the real debt. In particular, governments that focus on this real measure may engage in destabilizing fiscal actions. Similarly, a central bank may destabilize the economy if it focuses on what is happening to the real quantity of money.

12. Thus far, four policy *traps* have been identified:

■ The annually balanced budget rule (Chapter 10).

■ The use of a real, inflation-adjusted budget as a guide for fiscal policy (this chapter).

■ An attempt by the Federal Reserve to stabilize interest rates (the end of Chapter 12).

■ An attempt by the Federal Reserve to stabilize the real quantity of money (this chapter).

If the authorities follow any one of these apparently plausible guidelines, they can make the economy more unstable.

KEY CONCEPTS

nominal rate of interest	adjustable-rate mortgage	graduated-payment mortgage
real rate of interest	front-loaded mortgage payments	real deficit of the government
real after-tax return		

PROBLEMS

15-1. Which of the following would gain from unexpected inflation, and which would lose? In each case, explain why.

    (a) The person who has put $10,000 in a savings account and intends to use it as a downpayment on a house.

    (b) The person who has used $10,000 as a downpayment on a house, just before the unexpected inflation occurred.

    (c) An airline that has borrowed large amounts to buy 50 new airplanes.

15-2. How would your answers to Problem 15-1 change if the inflation were expected?

15-3. How does inflation make it difficult for people to acquire their first homes, even if they have assurance that their future incomes will rise with the general price level? Why are the problems less severe for those who already own a home and are selling it to move into a larger one?

15-4. Suppose that, after a period of stable prices, inflation rises gradually to a rate of 10% per annum. At 10%, it hits a peak and then gradually disappears.

    (a) How will this affect home owners who acquired their homes before the inflation began?

    (b) How will those who acquire homes when inflation peaks at 10% be affected as inflation decreases?

15-5. What problem can be reduced with graduated-payment mortgages? What problem with variable-rate mortgages?

15-6. In the early 1970s, the maximum marginal tax rate on unearned income (including interest) was 98% in Britain. (Top marginal rates have since been reduced.) During that period, the rate of inflation in Britain rose to more than 20% per annum.

    (a) With 20% inflation and 98% tax rates, what would the nominal interest rate have to be to leave the high-income bondholder with a zero real after-tax return? With a 3% real after-tax return?

    (b) Without looking up the facts, can you make an educated guess as to whether nominal interest rates in Britain rose by enough to leave high-income individuals with a positive after-tax real return? If you looked at the list of holders of bonds of a British corporation, would you expect to find many high-income individuals?

15-7. How did Eisner and Pieper measure the real deficit of the government? Consider an alternative. Suppose the real deficit is calculated as the nominal deficit, deflated by a price index (similar to the way real GNP can be calculated from nominal GNP back in Eq. 6-7, p. 93). Would the two approaches lead to the same estimate of the real deficit? Explain your answer.
(*Hint:* consider the case in which the nominal deficit is zero during a period of inflation.)

15-8. What difficulties arise if the government's deficit or surplus is used as a guide in the making of fiscal policies? Does the same problem arise if the real stock of money is used as a guide by the central bank? Explain your answer.

CHAPTER 16
GROWTH AND PRODUCTIVITY
Why Have They Varied So?

Not to go back, is somewhat to advance,
And men must walk, at least, before they dance.
ALEXANDER POPE

When economists study aggregate supply, they are interested in two quite different issues. One issue, discussed in Chapter 13, is the way in which the economy can fluctuate around its full-employment equilibrium in response to short-run changes in demand. The other issue is what happens to the full-employment, potential output of the economy through time. How and why does an economy grow? That is the question to be addressed in this chapter.

In recent decades, this second question has attracted attention because of two major problems. One has been the slow growth and sluggish productivity of the United States and other high-income nations in the years since 1973. The other has been the pattern of growth in low-income nations. Whereas some nations have grown at a remarkable rate, others seem caught in an apparently inescapable trap of poverty, low productivity, and low growth.

This chapter will focus on the question: Why do growth and productivity vary so much? Specifically:

■ Why have growth and productivity varied so much *through time*? Why have growth and productivity in the U.S. economy been so much weaker in the years since 1973 than in the preceding decades?

■ Why do growth and productivity vary so much *among countries?* Why do some countries grow slowly, while others grow rapidly? Most notably, why have the "four tigers" of East Asia—South Korea, Taiwan, Hong Kong, and Singapore—enjoyed such spectacular growth?

PRODUCTIVITY AND ECONOMIC GROWTH IN THE UNITED STATES

The key to growth is an increase in productivity. When the typical worker produces more in an hour—that is, when the **average productivity of labor** increases—then total output grows. This follows from the basic relationship:

$$\text{Total output } (Q) = \text{labor hours } (L) \times \text{average productivity of labor} \left(\frac{Q}{L}\right) \quad (16\text{-}1)$$

The solid lines in Figure 16-1 show the average annual rates of change of the three items in this equation, namely, the quantity of output, labor hours, and the average productivity of labor. (The average productivity of labor is often known as

277

"labor productivity" or, even more simply, as "productivity.")

In this figure, observe that labor productivity in the United States increased between 1948 and 1966 by more than 3% per year, far above the historical average. In contrast, the performance between 1973 and 1979 was poor, with labor productivity increasing by less than 1% per year. During the 1980s, productivity rebounded, although it remained far below the 1948–1966 peak.

INCREASES IN LABOR HOURS AND PRODUCTIVITY

Observe in Figure 16-1 how the increase in labor productivity generally has moved in the opposite direction to the increase in labor hours. When the input of labor hours has risen slowly, productivity has generally increased rapidly. In particular, the most rapid increase in productivity (1948–1966) coincided with the slowest rate of increase in labor hours. The long upward trend in productivity growth from 1800 into the 1960s corresponded to a long downward trend in the rate of growth of labor hours.

There is a good reason for this inverse relationship. The fewer workers entering the labor force, the more capital each one has to work with. With more capital, each worker can produce more.

Therefore one of the explanations for the slowdown in productivity growth after 1966 is straightforward. The labor force grew rapidly. As a result, there was only a slow increase in the amount of capital at the disposal of the average worker, and productivity likewise increased slowly.

The two reasons for the rapid growth in the labor force were:

■ The "baby boom" after World War II. Following a long depression and war, many people felt free to have children. By the late 1960s, these children were reaching working age.

■ The increasing participation of women in the labor force. In 1970, only 43% of women over 16 years of age were in the labor force. By 1980, the figure had risen to 52%, and by 1988, to 57%.

Most of the new entrants into the labor force found jobs. The number of civilians with jobs rose from 79 million in 1970 to 99 million in 1980 and

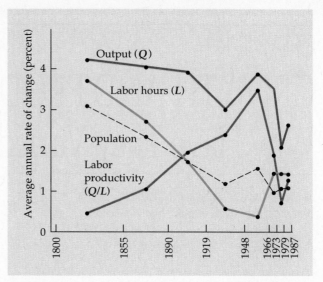

FIGURE 16-1   Average annual rates of change of output, labor hours, and productivity in the United States, 1800–1987.

Between 1800 and the mid-1960s, there was a long upward trend in the rate of growth of labor productivity (Q/L). This coincided with a downward trend in the rate of growth of total labor hours worked (L). Between 1966 and 1979, the long-term trends were reversed: The input of labor hours grew rapidly, and productivity grew more slowly. Since 1980, productivity has recovered somewhat. (This figure includes only output in the private domestic sector; the government sector is excluded. The dates on the horizontal axis indicate the beginning and end of each period, with the points representing the average for the period. Thus the point at the top left of Figure 16-1 shows that the average annual rate of increase in output was 4.2% over the period from 1800 to 1855.) *Sources:* John W. Kendrick, "Survey of Factors Contributing to the Decline in U.S. Productivity Growth," in Federal Reserve Bank of Boston, *The Decline in Productivity Growth* (1980), p. 3; Martin N. Baily and Alok K. Chakrabarti, *Innovation and the Productivity Crisis* (Washington, D.C.: Brookings Institution, 1988), p. 3; and *Economic Report of the President, 1989*, Appendix B.

115 million in 1988—an increase of 45% in less than two decades.

Thus the slow increase in productivity in the 1970s was partly attributable to the normal working of the economy. More people wanted jobs. On the whole, the economy was successful in providing these jobs. The result was less capital for each worker than there otherwise would have been and consequently a less rapid increase in productivity. To the extent that this was the explanation for the slower improvement in productivity, there is no cause for alarm. On the contrary, the economy worked well because it provided jobs for new entrants into the labor force. However, a rapid growth in employment was *only partly* responsible for the disappointing productivity performance. Other, less reassuring, forces were at work, as we will see later in the following sections.

THE INCREASE IN U.S. PRODUCTIVITY, 1948–1973

Why does productivity increase? Some of the most notable work on this topic has been done by Edward F. Denison of the Brookings Institution, a policy-oriented research organization in Washington, D.C. Denison's findings for the period 1948–1973 are summarized in the first column of Table 16-1. (Denison studied output *per worker*, whereas Figure 16-1 shows output per *hour*. However, output per worker changes in roughly the same way as output per hour.)

Between 1948 and 1973, there was an average annual increase of 2.5% in output per worker. Of this increase, Denison attributed 0.3% to changes in

the labor force. The average worker put in fewer hours per week, which, by itself, would have depressed output per worker by 0.2%. However, Denison found that an improvement in the quality of the labor force, as measured by education, raised productivity by 0.5% per year and thus more than made up for the decline in the length of the workweek. Over the past four decades, the percentages of the labor force who have graduated from high school and college have risen steadily.

Denison found that the increase in physical capital contributed 0.4% to the increase in output per worker, or slightly less than the amount attributable to education. An improved allocation of resources—primarily from reduced discrimination against minorities and lower barriers to international trade—added 0.3%. Economies of scale added another 0.4%. Even though our economy is already large, we have not yet exhausted all the advantages of size.

Finally, advances in knowledge—as well as a residual not explained elsewhere—accounted for 1.1%, or almost half of the total increase. A significant source of growth is an *improvement in technology*—that is, inventions, better designs of machinery, and better methods of production.

TABLE 16-1 Changes in Output per Person Employed
(Nonresidential Business Sector)

	(1) 1948–1973	(2) 1973–1981	(3) Difference (2) – (1)
Average annual change in output per person employed	2.5%	–0.2%	–2.7%
Percent attributable to			
Labor	0.3	0.2	–0.1
Divided into changes in			
Hours at work	–0.2	–0.4	–0.2
Education	0.5	0.6	0.1
Physical capital	0.4	0.2	–0.2
Improved allocation of resources	0.3	0.0	–0.3
Economies of scale	0.4	0.3	–0.1
Legal and human environment	0.0	–0.2	–0.2
Advances in knowledge and not elsewhere classified	1.1	–0.7	–1.8

Source: Edward F. Denison, "The Interruption of Productivity Growth in the United States," *Economic Journal*, March 1983, p. 56.

The most important conclusion of Denison's study was that growth resulted from a *combination* of causes. No single determinant held the key to growth, nor could any simple strategy—such as increasing the investment in plant and equipment—hold out hope for a major acceleration of growth. Observed Denison: "The tale of the kingdom lost for want of a horseshoe nail appears in poetry, not in history."

THE PUZZLE OF THE 1970s: WHAT WENT WRONG?

The last two columns of Table 16-1 show the results of Denison's effort to explain why output per worker became stagnant between 1973 and 1981. The most striking feature of these columns is that Denison's "explanations" *don't explain most of this change.* Between the earlier period and 1973–1981, the change totaled –2.7% per year (shown in col. 3)—that is, the swing from +2.5% to –0.2% in the annual growth of output per worker. Denison's detailed estimates account for only a third of this swing; the remaining 1.8% is in the unexplained residual (the final item in Table 16-1). Ruefully, Denison concludes: "What has happened is, to be blunt, a mystery."[1] Other researchers have likewise been unable to explain most of the change.

Changes identified by Denison. Before we investigate the large, mysterious residual, let us consider the changes that Denison does identify. During the 1973–1981 period, more people worked part time, causing a pronounced *decline in the average number of hours at work.* This accounted for a 0.4% decline in output per worker, compared with the more moderate 0.2% decline during the earlier period.

A *slowdown in investment* provided Denison's second explanation. Although physical capital per worker increased between 1973 and 1981, it did so at a slower rate than in the previous period.

Of the remaining estimates, most interesting is the *legal and human environment,* to which Denison

attributes a 0.2% decline in output per worker. This category includes government regulations that have required the diversion of a growing share of the nation's labor and capital to reducing pollution and increasing safety during the 1973–1981 period. (Because resources were used this way, the nation's total output grew less rapidly. But there were important environmental and safety benefits. Such benefits do not appear as part of measured output—and hence do not appear in this table. Thus our economic performance was better than this table suggests.) Also included in the legal and human environment category are the depressing effects of more crime, which has forced businesses to divert resources to crime prevention.

The mysterious residual. Because of the very large (1.8%) unexplained residual, Denison looks in some detail at frequently mentioned possibilities that are not identified in Table 16-1. These include a decrease in *research and development* (R&D) expenditures and an increase in *energy prices.*

Denison is skeptical that lower R&D explains much of the disappointing performance. As a percentage of GNP, R&D expenditures did decline, from a peak of 3.0% in 1964 to 2.3% in 1977. But most of this decline in R&D was concentrated in the government category, mostly for weapons and space research, and can scarcely account for the slower growth in productivity in the private sector.

The increase in energy prices. The rise in energy prices is perhaps the most interesting of the possibilities left out of Table 16-1. Energy prices are an obvious scapegoat. The first oil price shock occurred in 1973–1974 and could thus explain the slowdown in productivity that began at that time. Moreover, higher oil prices might explain why the growth rate declined after 1973 in *many* countries, including Britain, France, Germany, and Japan.

Nevertheless, Denison is again skeptical that higher oil prices account for much of the decline. He points out that oil consumption did not fall much, particularly in the 1973–1976 period when output per worker was very weak. If oil consumption had fallen sharply, this would have indicated the adoption of different and probably less productive methods of doing business. Since oil use did not fall much, however, it is difficult to explain the deterioration in this way.

[1]Edward F. Denison, *Accounting for Slower Economic Growth: The United States in the 1970s* (Washington, D.C.: Brookings Institution, 1979), p. 4.

promoted
text

There are several reasons why oil prices could have had a more damaging effect on productivity than Denison estimated. Considerable new investment was required in response to the higher oil prices in the 1970s—for example, in the automobile industry, which undertook a complete retooling to produce smaller cars. Such investments did not show up in large current reductions in oil consumption by industry, the measure which Denison used to estimate the disruptive effects of increases in the price of oil. Yet these investments did use resources that could have gone into other capital projects, thereby increasing productivity. Furthermore, business executives have spent much time and effort trying to figure out the best response to changing energy prices. Dale Jorgenson of Harvard concludes that the oil price increases and the related increases in the price of electricity "contributed to a marked slowdown in productivity growth."[2]

In brief, we have a fair idea of some of the causes of the poor productivity performance of the 1973-1981 period. But we simply do not know with any degree of precision the reasons for the poor productivity performance of the U.S. economy in the late 1970s.[3]

Nevertheless, the research of recent decades identifies three key reasons why productivity improves:

■ Investment in machinery and other forms of real capital.

■ Investment in human beings, in the form of education and training.

■ Technological improvement.

---

[2]Dale Jorgenson, "The Role of Energy in Productivity Growth," in John W. Kendrick, ed., *International Comparisons of Productivity and Causes of the Slowdown* (Cambridge, Mass.: Balinger, 1984), p. 309.

[3]Paul Romer, "Crazy Explanations of the Productivity Slowdown," in Stanley Fischer, ed., *NBER Macroeconomics Annual, 1987* (Cambridge, Mass.: MIT Press for the National Bureau of Economic Research, 1987). Romer (pp. 182, 198) emphasizes the point made early in this chapter: Part of the slowdown in productivity can be attributed to the unusually rapid growth of the labor force.

INTERNATIONAL COMPARISONS

Countries are often classified into three groups:

1. *High-income industrialized countries* with market economies: Western European nations, the United States, Canada, Japan, Australia, and New Zealand.

2. *Centrally planned economies:* the Soviet Union and Eastern Europe. Because of the central role of the government in these economies, they are considered separately in Chapter 40.

3. *Less-developed countries* (LDCs): mainly in Africa, Asia, and Latin America. They are also often known as the *developing nations* or *Third World nations.* (The high-income countries are the First World, and the centrally planned countries are the Second World. China, Vietnam, and Cuba are sometimes classified in the Second World, sometimes in the Third.)

Oil-exporting countries are sometimes classified as a separate group because their experience has been so different from that of other countries. For a few countries with low populations, oil has been a quick and easy path to riches. During the first half of the 1980s, when oil prices were high, the highest income country in the world was not the United States, Sweden, or Japan, but the United Arab Emirates. The fortunes of the oil-exporting countries can, however, change very rapidly as the price of oil fluctuates.

There are major differences within groups, particularly among the less-developed countries. For example, Ethiopia, the poorest country in the world with a per capita income of $120 in 1986, was far poorer than Singapore, where per capita income was $7,410.[4] In fact, Singapore and Hong Kong, which are classified as members of the Third World for geographic and historical reasons, have higher per capita incomes than Ireland or Spain.

---

[4]Such comparisons are not very precise. There are major difficulties in comparing output per person in various countries. See Irving B. Kravis et al., *A System of International Comparisons of Gross Products and Purchasing Power* (Baltimore: Johns Hopkins University Press, 1975). The numbers cited here are from the World Bank, *World Development Report* (Washington, D.C.: 1988), pp. 223–224.

The most important generalization about the Third World is this: One should be careful about generalizations.

Figure 16-2 illustrates how much growth in per capita income differs among countries. Since 1965, per capita GNP has increased at an annual average of more than 4% in Japan and more than 6% in Singapore and South Korea. Unfortunately, some of the poor countries have made little or no progress in improving their incomes—for example, Ethiopia and Bangladesh. Since 1965, GNP per capita has not increased at all in Ethiopia and only by 0.4% per year in Bangladesh.

THE LEAST DEVELOPED COUNTRIES: THE VICIOUS CIRCLE OF POVERTY

Why is it so difficult for people in the poorest countries to improve their lot? Are they poor simply because they are poor? Figure 16-3 illustrates some of the reasons why countries can be caught in a **vicious circle of poverty.**

1. *Low saving and investment.* When incomes are very low, people are preoccupied with survival; when they are hungry, they may be unwilling and unable to save and invest. As a result, they have

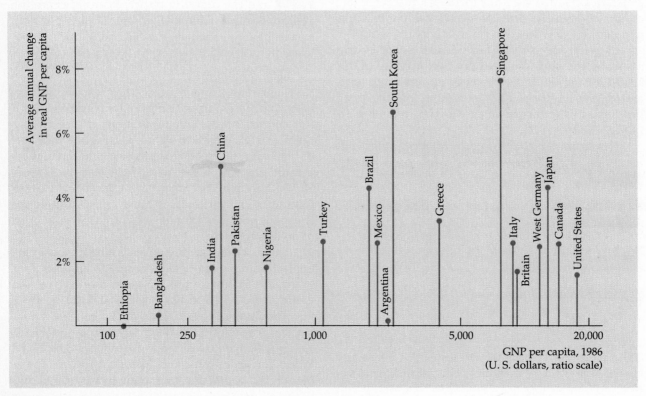

FIGURE 16-2   Increases in per capita output: International comparisons, 1965–1986.

Growth in real GNP per capita has varied considerably among countries. A number of countries have enjoyed very rapid increases—for example, Singapore and South Korea. A wide range of countries at quite different levels of development have been at or near the world average of 2.5%—for example, Pakistan, Turkey, Mexico, Italy, West Germany, and Canada. Particularly disappointing has been the nonexistent or very small improvement in the two countries with very low per capita incomes, Ethiopia and Bangladesh. (*Source:* World Bank, *World Development Report 1988*, pp. 222-223.)

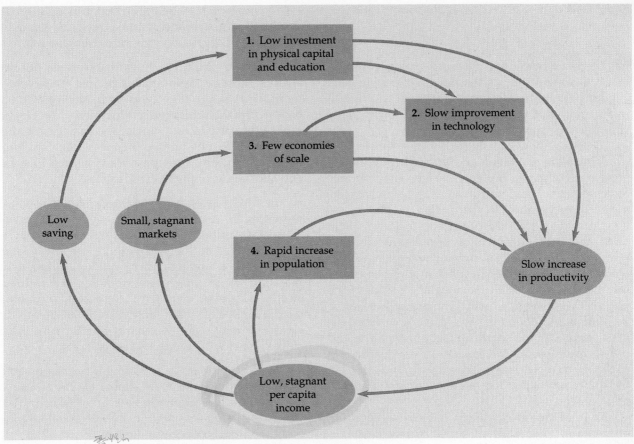

FIGURE 16-3   The vicious circle of poverty.

Low-income countries may have great difficulty in breaking out of the circle of poverty.
Low incomes result in low saving and investment, slow changes in technology, and small
markets, and these all act as a drag on growth.

difficulty accumulating the capital that is so important for growth. The outside loop in Figure 16-3
illustrates this point. Low incomes mean low saving; low saving means low investment; and low
investment means a slow rate of increase in productivity and in per capita incomes. Low saving is
a *result* of poverty. It is also a *cause* of continuing
poverty.

2. *Slow technological progress.* Low investment not
only limits the amount of capital, but also retards
technological progress (Fig. 16-3, box #2). The reason is that technology is often embodied in physical equipment. To adopt new ways of doing things,
it is often necessary to acquire new machinery or

equipment. Therefore low investment can mean
slow technological advance.

3. *Small, stagnant markets.* In many sectors of the
economy, particularly manufacturing, firms have to
produce in high volume to gain economies of scale
and produce efficiently. If a country has low and
stagnant incomes, businesses will not be able to sell
in large quantities. Productivity will suffer as a
result (Fig. 16-3, box #3).

4. *Rapid increase in population.* Many low-income
countries have a rapid growth in population. As a
result, the already low quantities of capital and
other resources must be spread even more thinly.

Once again, this can act as a drag on output per person (box #4, Fig. 16-3).

Paradoxically, a high rate of infant mortality has been one reason for the rapid growth of population in some LDCs. In these regions people need children for economic support in their old age. If infant mortality is high, couples may have many children to be sure some will survive.

There is, however, hope for the future. Improvements in sanitation and public health almost always accompany the early stages of economic development. These improvements not only make a direct contribution to the quality of life. In the long run, they can also contribute to lower birthrates and a stabilization of population. Fertility rates have already fallen from an average of 6.5 per woman in 1965 to 3.9 in 1985 in the very low-income countries (with incomes of less than $500 per year). However, it will be many years before the rate of population growth shows a corresponding decrease. In the short run, better sanitation and public health programs lead to lower death rates and a more rapid rate of growth of population. In the short run, they add urgency to the development process.

One important caution is necessary regarding population. The oft-heard term, *overpopulation*, is fuzzy and imprecise. A high and growing population can put pressure on resources and slow the development process. But we cannot identify any particular population as "too high." Hong Kong and Singapore are two of the most densely populated areas on earth. Yet their per capita incomes have grown very rapidly. (The population question is considered in more detail in the appendix to this chapter.)

In addition to the barriers to development shown in Figure 16-3, several others might be noted:

5. *Social and cultural barriers.* For economic development to take place, individuals and social groups must want it badly enough to change their old ways of doing things; they must be willing to bear the costs. The process of development can cause profound changes in social and political relationships. A political elite may be indifferent or even hostile to economic development; a growing merchant and manufacturing class may challenge their power. In some developing countries, *entrepreneurship* may be the critical missing ingredient. New industries do not take root and grow by themselves; they need vigorous entrepreneurs.

Negative attitudes toward business do not always raise an insuperable barrier to development. During the eighteenth and nineteenth centuries, British industry and commerce developed rapidly in spite of the view of the upper class that gentlemen do not pursue business careers. Other groups in society were quite ready to step forward and take a lead in the new industries.

6. *Lack of social capital.* To develop, countries need more capital. A particularly strategic role is played by **social capital** or **infrastructure,** such as roads, electric power, and telephones. If these are lacking, even the most talented and ambitious entrepreneur may fail. Most machinery requires an assured, steady source of electricity. A smoothly running telephone system can contribute to business efficiency in many ways—in particular, by permitting close contact with suppliers and markets.

In all countries, roadbuilding is the responsibility of the government. In almost all countries, so are railroads and electric power. In most countries, the government has responsibility for telephones and other forms of communication.

The central role of the government provides one huge advantage: The government may be able to raise the large amounts of financing necessary for a new power plant or for a telephone system. Private entrepreneurs might be unable to do so because most LDCs have poorly developed markets for bonds and other financial capital. But heavy government involvement can have disadvantages, too. Government ownership can lead to cronyism and poor management. If government enterprises receive large subsidies, they may lack a strong incentive to cut costs and increase efficiency.

7. *War.* Finally, peace and a reasonably stable society are prerequisites for vigorous economic growth. The success stories—South Korea, Hong Kong, Singapore, and Taiwan—have enjoyed 30 or more years of uninterrupted peace. The most depressing story comes from Ethiopia. Its already low income fell during the long civil war of the 1980s. (Fig. 16-2 shows an average increase of zero, but this includes both the prewar years of growth and the wartime years of decline.) Fragmentary information suggests that per capita income also declined in Iran and Iraq during the war of the 1980s.

BREAKING THE VICIOUS CIRCLE

One path out of the vicious circle of poverty lies in saving, hard work, and vigorous entrepreneurship. Although progress may be very slow and difficult at first, it becomes easier as the economy grows. As incomes rise, it is easier to save: Saving may be taken out of the increase in income, with no actual fall in consumption.

DEVELOPMENT AND THE INTERNATIONAL ECONOMY

Contacts with the international economy provide another path out of the vicious circle. The rest of the world can help in a number of ways, by providing:

1. *Financial capital,* which can be used to pay for imported machinery, equipment, and other inputs. When foreign funds are available, investment is no longer limited to the level of domestic saving.

Foreign capital comes in various forms and from various sources. It can come in the form of *grants, loans,* or *direct investment.* It can come from foreign governments, from international organizations such as the World Bank, or from foreign corporations and other private sources.

Needless to say, grants provide one clear advantage over loans: They don't have to be repaid. For borrowing to be advantageous in the long run, the funds must be invested in projects that will generate future payoffs sufficient to pay interest and retire the loan. If loans are used simply to finance consumption, they will make matters worse: The nation will face a future burden of interest and repayment, without any corresponding increase in its productive capacity. At the end of this chapter, we will consider the problems that foreign debt can create.

Direct investment occurs when a business in one country establishes operations in another—for example, when a U.S. or Japanese auto firm establishes a manufacturing operation in Mexico. The U.S. or Japanese company owns the Mexican subsidiary, either in whole or in partnership with Mexicans. Such direct investment carries major advantages for the host country, since it comes as a package, together with management. Direct investment is quite controversial, however, since host countries often fear that the foreign company will extract excessive profits and possibly delay the development of domestic entrepreneurship and management.

2. *Technology.* Other nations can likewise be a source of technology. It is unnecessary for every country to reinvent the wheel—or the computer, or advanced methods of production.

In this respect, the developing nations have an advantage. Because much of their technology is outmoded, they have a great opportunity to borrow foreign technology. Borrowed technology is one of the secrets of success in Taiwan, Korea, and a number of other rapidly growing economies. However, as countries catch up, the technological gap closes. Because there is less foreign technology still to be borrowed, growth may slow down.

3. *Markets.* By exporting into the world market, firms may be able to achieve *economies of scale* in spite of limited domestic markets. Thus, for example, the fledgling Korean automobile industry is exporting much of its output in order to bring its per-unit costs down.

The United States has contributed in each of the above ways to the growth of the developing nations. It has provided grants, loans, direct investment, technology, and markets. Each of these is helpful to the developing countries, but they certainly do not all fall under the category of "aid." Many loans, most trade, and practically all direct investment are motivated by commercial considerations, with both sides expecting to gain.

LIVING IN A GLOBAL ECONOMY

THE "FOUR TIGERS" OF EAST ASIA

Development can be a slow and painful process. What can be learned from economies that have broken out of the vicious circle and grown very rapidly? Specifically, what can be learned from the group of four new industrializing economies of East Asia—Hong Kong, Singapore, South Korea, and Taiwan—whose output per capita has grown by more than 6% per year over the past two decades?

The first message is that an economy does not have to be richly endowed with natural resources to grow rapidly. None of the four has plentiful mineral resources, and two—Hong Kong and Singapore—have only minimal amounts of land.

Their secret lies in the two paths out of the vicious circle noted in the previous section: (1) saving, hard work, and vigorous entrepreneurship; and (2) contacts with the world economy.

In each of the four economies, high saving rates provide the resources for high investment. For the four as a group, gross saving averages almost 30% of **gross domestic product** (Fig. 16-4).[5] In one year, 1985, saving in Singapore reached an astonishing 42% of GDP! Furthermore, the work ethic is deeply engrained and constantly reinforced. Koreans awake to hear radio announcers urging them to "work hard to make our nation better." They work an average of 2,700 hours a year—25% more than Japanese and 40% more than Americans. Furthermore, each of the four economies has a vigorous group of entrepreneurs. In some respects, however, they are dissimilar. Large conglomerates (*chaebol*)—such as Daewoo and Hyundai—dominate the Korean economy, and have been actively encouraged by the government. In contrast, Taiwanese firms are mostly small or medium-sized.

Gross domestic product (GDP) is the same as GNP, except that earnings on international investments are treated differently. (For example, U.S. GDP does not include profits of U.S. firms abroad.)

THEIR INTERNATIONAL ECONOMIC RELATIONS

Each of the four is strongly *export oriented*. Korea exports 40% of GDP, and the others, even more. (In comparison, Japan exports 13% of its GDP and the

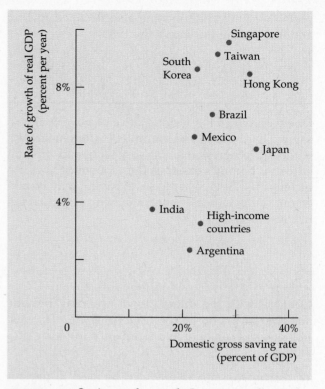

FIGURE 16-4   Saving and growth: International comparisons, 1963–1985.

High saving is generally associated with rapid growth. The association is not a tight one, however. Growth depends not only on how much is saved, but also on how efficiently the saving is invested. (The dot for the high-income countries represents the average for the members of the Organization for Economic Cooperation and Development—an association that includes the United States, Canada, Japan, and the countries of Western Europe.) *Source:* Bela Balassa and John Williamson, *Adjusting to Success: Balance of Payments Policy in the East Asian NICs* (Washington, D. C.: Institute for International Economics, 1987), p. 3. (A NIC is a newly industrializing country.)

United States 7%.) Indeed, the exports of Singapore and Hong Kong are *greater* than GDP; Singapore and Hong Kong export more goods than they produce. How can that be? These two ports operate as major transshipment centers, reexporting many goods they have previously imported. Hong Kong plays a particularly important role as a transshipment port for many of China's exports and imports.

---

[5]This is gross saving and includes saving by corporations and government as well as by individuals. It represents an overstatement in the sense that it includes the saving needed to cover depreciation.

All four tigers are voracious users of *foreign technology* and *foreign equipment*. In the late 1980s, the most modern fleet of aircraft in the world was owned by Singapore Airlines. Korea produces video cassette recorders (VCRs); the United States doesn't, even though the VCR was invented here. The Daewoo group of Korea is in the process of hiring 1,000 Ph.D.s by 1990, many of them trained in U.S. universities. The fledgling Korean auto industry has close contacts with Japan and the United States, as sources of both technology and markets.

Although foreign markets and foreign technology have made substantial contributions to the rapid growth of these four economies, access to foreign *financial capital* has on average not been very important. In fact, these four export much more than they import; their exports are more than sufficient to pay for their imports, and they have no need to be net borrowers on the world financial markets. During the 1980s, the **trade surpluses** of Taiwan and Korea became large enough to cause frictions with their trading partners, particularly the United States; the United States would like to export more to those countries in order to help pay for its imports. In 1986, the excess of Taiwan's exports over imports amounted to almost 20% of its GDP, one of the highest ratios ever recorded.

A country has a *trade surplus* when its exports exceed its imports. If its exports are less than its imports, it has a *trade deficit*.

This is not to say that foreign financial capital can be completely ignored as a contributor to growth. At an early stage, both Korea and Taiwan were major recipients of aid from the U.S. government. During the 1960s and 1970s, Korea was a sizable borrower; by 1985, its foreign debt amounted to almost $50 billion. Since that time, Korea has repaid some of this debt with the proceeds from its trade surpluses.

Why have the four been so successful in exporting? One important reason is that they have kept their products highly competitive through their **exchange rate** policies. That is, they have kept the price of their currencies low and have thus kept the prices of their goods low on world markets.

(When Americans can buy Korean currency cheaply, they can buy Korean goods cheaply.)

An *exchange rate* is the price of one currency in terms of another.

The experience of the four East Asian economies is the opposite of a number of other developing countries that have kept their currencies overvalued (priced too high in terms of other currencies). Overvaluation has made their goods expensive to foreign buyers and has resulted in a chronic tendency for exports to fall short of imports. Because their exports aren't large enough to pay for their imports, they may directly restrict imports through licensing arrangements, thereby adding to the woes of their producers. For example, Indian manufacturers sometimes face difficulty in obtaining licenses to import needed spare parts for their machines. It is obviously inefficient when the government delays the import of spare parts and expensive machines are left out of service as a result.

THE ROLE OF THE GOVERNMENT

In addition to keeping their exports competitively priced through their exchange rate policies, what role have the governments played in the four rapidly developing economies of East Asia?

In each, the government has provided excellent social capital and extensive services to the public in the form of free education, subsidized health services, and large programs of subsidized housing. In other areas of the economy, however, the "four tigers" take quite different attitudes toward government regulation and intervention. Singapore follows a policy of free trade. Korea and Taiwan still maintain significant barriers to imports, although they have been reducing these barriers in recent years. With regard to domestic industries, Hong Kong has followed a policy close to laissez faire. The Korean government has been much more interventionist, fostering large-scale industry, promoting government-business cooperation along Japanese lines, and setting export targets for individual firms. Even in Korea, however, the government has taken some steps away from regulation. Regulations on capital markets—including interest rate ceilings—have been relaxed, thereby stimulating domestic saving and investment.

In conclusion, what lessons can be learned from the experience of these four? We should be careful; what works in one time or place will not necessarily work in another. In particular, the emphasis on exports will work only if other countries are willing to take the exports; it will not work if foreign nations are highly protectionist. Nevertheless, the experience of the four economies suggests the following lessons:

1. Domestic *saving* can be a major engine of growth.

2. Access to *foreign technology* and *foreign markets* can similarly contribute to growth.

3. An *export-oriented* strategy can be very effective. Exports provide a quick way to capture economies of scale. Each of the four governments has sent a clear message to businesses: It is your responsibility to get out and compete on world markets. In contrast, less success has been achieved by countries that have followed an import-substitution strategy—that is, a strategy of restricting imports in order to stimulate domestic production of goods previously bought abroad. Import-substitution policies generally result in a high-cost, inefficient industry—for example, the Indian industry that sometimes can't run its machines because it can't get spare parts.

4. An *undervalued currency* can promote exports. However, there is a danger if export-promotion policies are pursued too vigorously. In the face of large trade imbalances, trading partners may raise their barriers to imports in order to protect their own domestic industries.

5. Rapid growth is *consistent with a variety of approaches by government.* Government may intervene extensively; on the other hand, it may lean in the direction of laissez faire. However, in each of the four cases, government provides high-quality social capital and extensive programs in education, health, and housing. The governments that do intervene heavily—most notably, in Korea—do so in order to spur business to greater achievements; few of their regulations are anti-business. Indeed, each of the four governments takes a strongly pro-business stance.

Finally, the picture is not completely rosy. Not everybody shares fully in the rising incomes. Strains are especially apparent in South Korea. That nation has a somewhat more equal distribution of income than most countries, but the rapid changes of recent decades have provided special advantages to those with jobs in the export industries. It is true people in the export industries have worked very hard, but they have also earned incomes far above those of their compatriots. Particularly in the late 1980s, their incomes rose very rapidly. Employers were willing to pay higher wages because their exports were selling so well in foreign countries; they were eager to avoid strikes that would interrupt their lucrative business. Rapid wage increases seem likely to continue. If Korean cars sell in world markets, why should Korean auto workers not hope for wage rates approaching those in the auto industries of Japan, North America, or Europe? As the incomes of auto workers rise, however, other Koreans feel left behind.

THE INTERNATIONAL DEBT CRISIS

The story of the developing nations has been a mixture of success and problems. One of the greatest problems is the crushing debt burden that a number of them face.

Between 1973 and 1982, many developing nations borrowed heavily from foreign countries. As a result, their external debt expanded at a very rapid and unsustainable rate, increasing almost fivefold. In 1982, a crisis shook the international financial system when Mexico became unable to make payments of interest and principal to foreign lenders. After tense negotiations, Mexican debt was **rescheduled**—that is, repayment was postponed. In the following months and years, a number of other developing countries went through similar rescheduling exercises, which reduced the immediate pressures to repay. However, many Third World countries are still saddled with staggering foreign debts—totaling over $1 trillion in 1988. Table 16-2 lists countries with major debt problems. (Countries were included in this table if their debt exceeded GNP, or if they spent more than 40% of

TABLE 16-2 External Debt of Selected Nations, 1970 and 1986

| | Long-term Debt | | | | Debt Service in 1986 as a Percentage of[†] | |
| | Billions of Dollars | | As Percentage of GNP | | | |
Country	1970	1986	1970	1986	GNP	Exports
Malawi	0.1	0.9	43.2	78.6	9.4	40.1
Burma	0.1	3.7	4.9	45.3	3.0	55.4
Madagascar	0.1	2.6	10.4	105.6	4.5	27.7
Somalia	0.1	1.4	24.4	54.4	2.0	62.1
Mauritania	0.0	1.6	13.9	210.0	9.9	17.4
Jamaica	1.0	3.1	73.1	147.5	21.4	32.7
Chile	2.6	17.9	32.1	120.1	13.1	37.1
Brazil	5.1	97.2	12.2	37.6	4.1	41.8
Mexico	6.0	91.1	17.0	76.1	10.2	51.5
Argentina	5.2	43.0	23.2	51.7	6.8	64.1

Source: World Bank, *World Development Report 1988*, pp. 256-257. Nations are listed in order of their GNP per capita in 1986.

[†]Debt service is the sum of the actual payments of interest plus the actual repayment of principal. A number of countries missed scheduled payments of interest and principal; their debt service was therefore low compared to the size of the debt.

their export earnings to make payments on the debt in 1986.) Their long-run ability to pay interest on these debts remains in doubt, to say nothing of the repayment of principal.

Borrowing from foreign nations can play an important and constructive role in the development process. By borrowing, countries—like business firms—can obtain the funds needed to buy machinery and equipment. When such capital is put to good use, it not only results in greater production and higher living standards at home. It can also be used to produce goods for export, thus providing the funds to repay the debt.

Unfortunately, the developing nations expanded their debt not only to finance investment and growth, but also for consumption and other spending that did not contribute to the growth of productive capacity. When the price of oil skyrocketed in 1973–1974, most countries were unable to cut back their oil consumption quickly. In order to pay for expensive oil imports, many went deeply into

debt. They were borrowing to finance current consumption—a situation that could not continue indefinitely.

Paradoxically, the oil-importing countries were not the only ones to borrow more when the price of oil increased rapidly. Some of the oil *exporters*—such as Mexico—also incurred large new debts. The Mexicans expected that the price of oil would continue to go higher, compared to the average price of other products. If the future promised large and growing oil revenues, why not benefit now by borrowing? Furthermore, Mexicans were actively encouraged to borrow by U.S. banks, which took the same unrealistic view of Mexican prospects and therefore believed that such loans were safe. If problems arose, the banks expected that the U.S. government, the IMF, or other official bodies would step in to prevent a default.

The recession in the United States and elsewhere in the early 1980s caused a sharp reduction in the demand by the high-income countries for the exports of the developing nations. As a result, the developing nations had difficulty earning the foreign currencies needed to make payments on their debt. Monetary conditions in the United States also had adverse effects on the developing world. When U.S. interest rates rose, so did the interest that the developing countries had to pay on much of their debt.

The rescheduling of the debt of Mexico and other countries eased the immediate crisis of 1982. However, the huge debts of the developing countries continued to grow during the last half of the 1980s, when the overall world economy was relatively stable and prosperous. By 1986, Mexico was using over 50% of its receipts from exports to make payments on its foreign-held debt (Table 16-2, last column). The huge debt burden raises disturbing questions. During the next recession, when imports of the high-income countries decline, will the developing countries find it impossible to make payments on their debt? Will this lead to an international financial crisis, disrupting the economies of the rich and poor countries alike?

The debt problem has been papered over. But it continues to grow, posing a threat to the prosperity of the international economy.

KEY POINTS

1. The growth of output depends on the combined effect of increases in (a) the number of hours worked, and (b) labor productivity.

2. Productivity grew most rapidly in the 1948–1966 period. This corresponded to the slowest rate of growth of labor hours. Productivity growth was slow during the late 1970s, when labor hours were increasing rapidly.

3. Denison found a number of important causes for the rapid growth between 1948 and 1973, especially investment in education and in physical capital. However, no single cause was the "key" to rapid growth.

4. Denison was unable to explain about two-thirds of the deterioration in the productivity performance of the U.S. economy in the 1973–1981 period. Other economists are also puzzled by the deterioration.

5. Productivity has improved during the 1980s, but it is still improving much less slowly than it did during the golden age of growth in the two decades after World War II.

6. There are three principal explanations for rising productivity: (a) investment in machines and other real capital, (b) improvements in the education and training of the labor force, and (c) technological improvements.

7. A number of the lowest income countries have grown very slowly; some seem caught in a vicious circle. Saving is low because incomes are low, and incomes remain low because saving and investment are low.

8. There are two main paths out of the vicious circle of poverty: the domestic path of hard work, saving, and investment; and ties with the world economy.

9. The world economy can be a source of funds, permitting countries to invest more than they save. Foreign technology may be copied. Foreign markets can permit a new industry to gain economies of scale even if the domestic market is small.

10. Hard work, high rates of domestic saving, access to foreign technology, and an emphasis on exports have contributed to the rapid development of the "four tigers" of East Asia—Hong Kong, Singapore, South Korea, and Taiwan.

11. A number of the developing countries face a heavy burden of foreign debt.

KEY CONCEPTS

average productivity of labor
technological improvement
investment in education and
   training

investment in real capital
the vicious circle of poverty
social capital or infrastructure
gross domestic product

export oriented
exchange rate
rescheduling of debt

PROBLEMS

16-1. Why might a rapid increase in population cause a drag on productivity? Are there any circumstances in which a rapid increase in population might encourage a rapid increase in productivity?

16-2. Observe in Figure 16-1 that the rate of growth of labor hours in the 1919–1948 period was almost as slow as in 1948–1966. But the rate of growth of productivity was substantially less rapid. That is, productivity did not grow as rapidly between 1919 and 1948 as we might expect simply by looking at the low rate of growth of labor hours. What events during this period acted as a drag on productivity? Explain how they kept productivity from increasing more rapidly.

16-3. Most people think that rapid growth is desirable. Can you think of any reason why rapid growth might be undesirable? Is the best policy the one that leads to the most rapid growth? (*Hint:* Review Fig. 2-5.)

16-4. What is the "vicious circle of poverty?" How can nations get out of it?

16-5. What are the advantages of an "export-oriented" growth strategy? What can be done to encourage exports?

*16-6. Keeping the value of the home currency low in terms of foreign currencies will promote exports. Are there any disadvantages?

WILL POPULATION EXPLODE?
The Malthusian Problem

There is a wide variation among the less-developed countries. In some, per capita output has risen rapidly in the past two decades; in others, it has remained relatively stagnant. The very poorest are haunted by the grim prospect described by the young English clergyman Thomas Malthus in his *Essay on the Principle of Population* (1798). Malthus emphasized the scarcity of natural resources—particularly land—which limits the production of food. Specifically, he argued that the output of food increases at best at an arithmetic rate (1, 2, 3, 4, 5, 6, and so on). However, the "passion between the sexes" means that population tends to increase at a geometric rate (1, 2, 4, 8, 16, 32, etc.):

> It may safely be pronounced that population, when unchecked, goes on doubling itself every twenty-five years, or increases in a geometrical ratio. The rate according to which the productions of the earth may be supposed to increase, will not be so easy to determine. Of this, however, we may be perfectly certain, that the ratio of their increase in a limited territory must be of a totally different nature from the ratio of the increase in population. A thousand millions are just as easily doubled every twenty-five years by the power of population as a thousand. But the food to support the increase from the greater number will by no means be obtained with the same facility. . . .
>
> It may be fairly pronounced, therefore, that considering the present average state of the earth, the means of subsistence, under circumstances the most favorable to human industry, could not possibly be made to increase faster than in an arithmetic ratio. . . . The ultimate check to population appears then to be a want of food, arising necessarily from the different ratios according to which population and food increase.[6]

Because of the tendency of population to outstrip food production, the per capita income of the working class will be driven down to the subsistence level. During the nineteenth century, this proposition came to be known as the **iron law of wages.**

After the wage reaches the subsistence level, population growth cannot continue at the same rate; there isn't enough food. Famine, pestilence, or war will keep the population in check. Malthus' theory pointed to a cruel conclusion. Public relief for the poor would do nothing in the long run to improve their condition. It would simply result in an upsurge in population; there would be more people to starve in the future.

As a general forecast, Malthus' theory proved inaccurate. The standard of living in most countries has risen markedly in the past 200 years. Birth control has been a much greater constraint on population growth than Malthus anticipated. Food production has increased beyond Malthus' expectation, because of the technological revolution that has extended to agriculture as well as manufacturing. Nevertheless, Malthus' theory—that there can be a race between population growth and the ability to produce—is worth remembering in a world that is becoming more crowded.

---

[6]Thomas Malthus, *An Essay on the Principle of Population* (London: 1798).

PART V

GREAT MACRO-ECONOMIC ISSUES:
Aggregate Demand

Part 3 dealt with complications on the aggregate supply side. Aggregate demand may also be complicated:

- There are two main aggregate demand tools—monetary policy and fiscal policy. Which is more important? (Chapter 17)

- How actively should the government try to manage aggregate demand? Should it try to fine tune the economy, in an attempt to prevent recessions and inflation? Would it be better to adhere to a long-run policy rule instead? (Chapter 18)

- Should exchange rates—that is, the prices of foreign currencies—be held stable, or should they be allowed to fluctuate? The ability of the government and central bank to manage aggregate demand depends on this decision. (Chapter 19)

CHAPTER 17
MONETARY POLICY AND FISCAL POLICY
Which Is the Key to Aggregate Demand?

Nothing in excess
ANCIENT GREEK ADAGE
(DIOGENES)

Part 3 described the two major tools with which aggregate demand can be controlled: fiscal policy and monetary policy. When there are two tools, the question naturally arises: "Which one should we rely on?"

Views on that question have changed considerably in recent decades. The Keynesian Revolution of the 1930s not only emphasized the responsibility of government to manage aggregate demand. It also identified fiscal policy as the primary tool to do so. Monetary policy was considered much less important. Keynes and his followers argued that, in the deepest pit of a depression, expansive monetary policies might be completely useless as a means of stimulating aggregate demand. An increase in the money stock might have no effect on spending. In more normal times, Keynes was less skeptical regarding the effects of monetary policy. In fact, he emphasized the importance of money in his earlier works, especially *Monetary Reform* (1924) and *A Treatise on Money* (1930). Nevertheless, the *General Theory* left a strong legacy in favor of fiscal policy as the primary tool to control aggregate demand.

In the two decades between 1945 and 1965,

when Keynesian theory still dominated macroeconomic analysis in the United States, fiscal policy was at the center of attention, with monetary policy being considered much less important. Some Keynesians went as far as Warren Smith of the University of Michigan, who dismissed the control of aggregate demand through monetary policy as "a mirage and delusion."[1]

During the 1960s, there was a resurgence of interest in monetary policy and in the pre-Keynesian, classical theory that had identified money as *the* determinant of aggregate demand. The most prominent role in this classical revival was played by Milton Friedman, then a professor at the University of Chicago (now retired). Friedman summarized his position: "Money is extremely important for nominal magnitudes, for nominal income, for the level of income in dollars." Furthermore, Friedman was skeptical about the

---

[1] In *Staff Report on Employment, Growth, and Price Levels* (Washington, D.C.: Joint Economic Committee, U.S. Congress, 1959), p. 401. Smith served as a member of President Johnson's Council of Economic Advisers.

effectiveness of fiscal policy as a tool for controlling aggregate demand. He of course recognized that the government budget has an important influence on the allocation of resources: The budget determines how much of national product is taken by the government and how much is left for the private sector. But Friedman doubted that fiscal policy has an important effect on aggregate demand: "In my opinion, the state of the budget by itself has no significant effect on the course of nominal income, on inflation, on deflation, or on cyclical fluctuations."[2]

Those who trace their intellectual heritage back to the classical school are generally known as **monetarists** because of their emphasis on money. While monetarists such as Friedman have had a profound effect, they have not attained the dominant position enjoyed by Keynesian economists in the decades following the Second World War. Most macroeconomists are eclectic, agreeing with some parts of Keynesian analysis and with some parts of monetarism. In response to the question posed back in the first paragraph, most present-day macroeconomists would answer: "Both monetary and fiscal policies are important. We should not rely exclusively on either."

To understand current thinking on monetary and fiscal policies, it is important to study both Keynesian and monetarist theory. Each theory provides a sensible framework for the orderly investigation of macroeconomic developments. Each can heighten our understanding of how the economy works. Chapter 10 explained the Keynesian view of how fiscal policy can affect aggregate demand. To complete our discussion of fiscal and monetary policies, this chapter will explain:

■ The Keynesian view of how monetary policy can affect aggregate demand, and the circumstances in which the effect may not be very strong.

■ The monetarist view on how monetary policy affects aggregate demand, and why monetarists expect a change in the quantity of money to have a powerful effect on aggregate demand.

■ The reasons why monetarists have doubts about fiscal policy; specifically, why they doubt that fiscal policy has the strong and predictable effect on aggregate demand suggested by the Keynesian theory outlined in Chapter 10.

■ The advantages of using a *combination* of monetary and fiscal policies as part of an overall strategy of stabilizing aggregate demand.

■ Why monetary policy has in fact been the predominant demand-management tool since the late 1970s, in spite of the widely recognized advantages of using a balanced combination of monetary and fiscal policies.

THE EFFECTS OF MONETARY POLICY: THE KEYNESIAN VIEW

Keynes identified a three-step process by which an expansive monetary policy could increase aggregate demand (Fig. 17-1):

1. An open market purchase generally causes a *lower interest rate.*

2. A lower interest rate encourages businesses to *invest more.* It is cheaper for them to borrow money to buy new machines or build new factories.

3. Higher investment demand will have a *multiplied effect* on aggregate demand and national product.

The third step is the familiar multiplier process explained in Chapter 9. Here, we will look at steps 1 and 2.

STEP 1. MONETARY POLICY AND THE INTEREST RATE: THE STOCK OF MONEY AND THE DEMAND FOR IT

The first step in the process—how an open market purchase can lower interest rates—was discussed briefly in Chapter 12. Because this step is important in the Keynesian evaluation of monetary policy, we consider it in more detail here.

In Keynes' theory, the interest rate reaches equilibrium when the quantity of money demanded is equal to the quantity in existence—that is, *when people are willing to hold the amount of money that exists in the economy.*

[2]Milton Friedman and Walter Heller, *Monetary vs. Fiscal Policy: A Dialogue* (New York: W. W. Norton, 1969), pp. 46, 51.

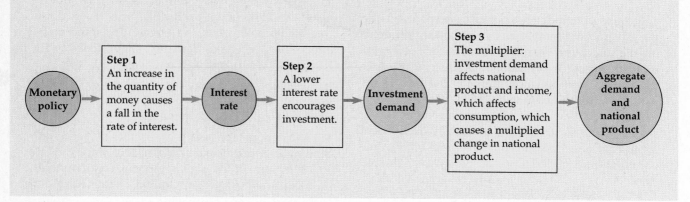

FIGURE 17-1   How monetary policy affects aggregate demand and national product: The Keynesian approach.

People hold money in order to buy goods and services. As a result, the demand for money *depends on national income.* The reason is straightforward. The higher is income, the more purchases people will plan to make, and the more money they will consequently want to hold.

The demand for money also *depends on the interest rate.* Whenever money is held rather than used to buy a bond or other interest-bearing security, the holder of money gives up the interest that could have been earned on the security. Suppose that interest rates are high. The treasurers of corporations will try to keep as little money on hand as is conveniently possible, putting the rest into interest-bearing securities. At an interest rate of 10% per annum, for example, $10 million earns almost $20,000 in interest per week—a tidy sum. On the other hand, if interest rates are low, people have less incentive to buy interest-bearing securities and they are willing to hold more money.

The willingness of people to hold more money at a lower rate of interest is illustrated by the downward-sloping demand curve in Figure 17-2. Suppose that $200 billion of money has been created by the banking system. S_1 illustrates this money supply. The equilibrium interest rate is 8%, at the intersection of the demand and supply curves.

Consider next what happens if the Federal Reserve purchases securities on the open market, causing an expansion of the money stock to $300 billion, as shown by S_2. At the old 8% interest rate, there is a surplus of money shown by the arrow;

people have more than they are willing to hold at this interest rate. People with excess money are eager to lend it. They bid the interest rate down to its new equilibrium, 6%. At E_2, the public is just willing to hold the $300 billion of money.

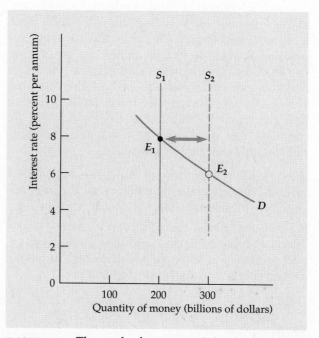

FIGURE 17-2   The stock of money and the demand for it.

The equilibrium interest rate occurs when the quantity of money demanded is equal to the stock in existence.

$M_s\uparrow \rightarrow I_r\downarrow$

An increase in the stock of money can thus lead to a fall in the interest rate. Now consider the second step: How a fall in the interest rate can lead to an increase in investment.

STEP 2. THE INTEREST RATE AND INVESTMENT DEMAND 影响

A number of factors influence the eagerness of business executives to buy new machinery or to invest in other capital. One influence is the productivity of the capital. For example, a new generation of larger, fuel-efficient aircraft can encourage airlines to reequip their fleets. A second influence is the level of sales that executives expect in the future. If their markets are booming, they will want more machinery in order to be able to produce more goods. A third influence is the cost of financing the new investment—that is, the interest rate.

Monetary policy affects investment primarily through the interest rate. To concentrate on this variable, assume for the moment that all the other determinants of investment—such as the productivity of capital—remain unchanged.

The effect of the interest rate on the quantity of investment demanded is illustrated in Figure 17-3. As the interest rate falls from, say, 8% to 6%, it is cheaper to finance investment projects, and business executives are therefore encouraged to undertake new ones. The desired quantity of investment (I^*) increases from $100 billion to $125 billion.

We may now summarize the Keynesian view as to how monetary policy works:

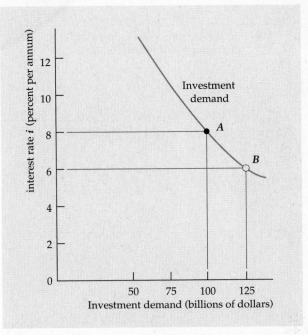

FIGURE 17-3   The investment demand curve.

The investment demand curve slopes downward to the right. At a lower interest rate, it is cheaper for businesses to finance their investment projects. More projects are therefore undertaken.

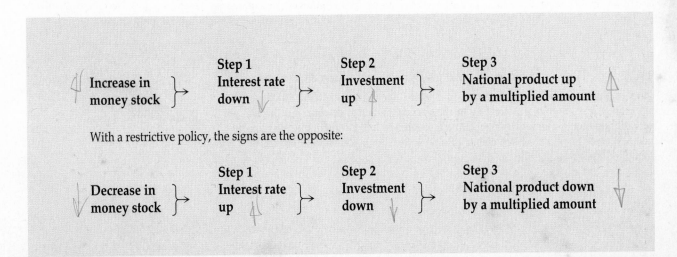

With a restrictive policy, the signs are the opposite:

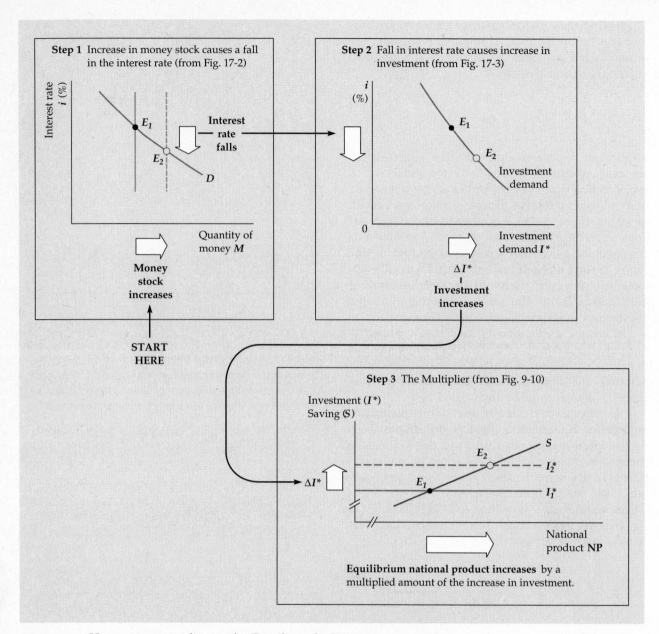

FIGURE 17-4   How monetary policy works: Details on the Keynesian approach.

This figure fills out the details in Figure 17-1. At step 1, the fall in the interest rate depends on the amount of additional money and on the slope of the money demand function. At step 2, the amount of extra investment that is generated by a reduction in the interest rate depends on the slope of the investment demand curve. At step 3, the investment has a multiplied effect on aggregate demand.

PROBLEMS WITH MONETARY POLICY

By this three-step process, shown in detail in Figure 17-4, a change in the quantity of money can affect aggregate demand. Why, then, were early Keynesians skeptical regarding the possible effectiveness of monetary policy as a tool for managing demand? The answer is: We cannot be certain that the effects at either of the first two steps will be very strong.

Step 1. Keynes himself was particularly concerned that an expansive monetary policy might be ineffective at the very first step, and therefore could not be counted on as a way of getting out of the deep depression that existed when the *General Theory* was written. During a deep depression, interest rates may be very low—for example, in the 2% to 3% range that prevailed during much of the depression of the 1930s. In such circumstances, the ability of the Fed to push the rates down even further is not very great. Clearly, interest rates cannot be pushed all the way down to zero. (At a zero interest rate, nobody would be willing to hold bonds. They would be giving up the use of their money and getting nothing in return. It would be better to hold money in the bank instead.) Thus, when interest rates are already very low, it may become impossible for the Federal Reserve to move them much lower. Expansive monetary policy cannot have much effect on interest rates; it fails at step 1.

In more normal times, open market operations can significantly affect the interest rate, and the second step becomes the principal concern in the operation of monetary policy.

Step 2. As Figure 17-3 is drawn, investment is quite responsive to a change in the rate of interest. For example, a fall in the interest rate from 8% to 6% will cause a 25% increase in investment demand, from $100 billion to $125 billion. An alternative possibility is illustrated in Figure 17-5. Here, the investment demand curve falls much more steeply than it did in Figure 17-3. Now, even with a sharp drop in the interest rate from 8% to 6%, investment does not increase very much—only by $5 billion. This, then, is the second reason why monetary policy may be ineffective.

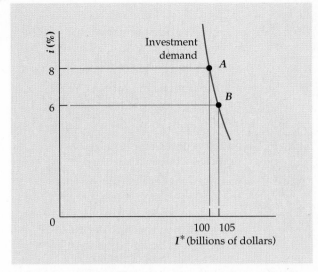

FIGURE 17-5   An ineffective monetary policy at step 2.

If the investment demand curve is steep, investment does not increase much when the interest rate falls. Therefore, the effect of monetary policy on aggregate demand is not very powerful.

This view—that investment would not respond very strongly to changes in the interest rate—was widely held during the 1940s and 1950s, and contributed to the prevailing skepticism regarding the effectiveness of monetary policy as a demand-management tool.

MONETARY POLICY: THE MONETARIST VIEW

During the 1960s, there was a major revival of the old classical school, which made money the centerpiece of aggregate demand theory.

In contrast to Keynes, who started his analysis of aggregate demand by looking at its components (consumption, investment, government purchases of goods and services, and net exports), classical economists began from quite a different starting point. Their analysis was based on the equation of exchange:

$$MV = PQ \qquad (17\text{-}1)$$

where

M = quantity of money in the hands of the public

P = average level of prices

Q = quantity of output—that is, real national product or real national income

Thus PQ = national product, measured in nominal (dollar) terms

and V = income velocity of money—that is, the average number of times that the money stock (M) is spent to buy final output during a year. Specifically, V is defined as being equal to PQ/M.

Suppose that the money stock is $100 billion. Assume that, in the course of a year, the average dollar bill and the average checking deposit are spent six times to purchase final goods and services. In other words, V is 6. Then, total spending for final output is $100 billion times 6, or $600 billion. In turn, this total spending (MV) equals the total quantity of goods and services (Q) times the average price (P) at which they were sold.

But how can the same dollar be used over and over to purchase final goods? Very simply. When you purchase groceries at the store, the $50 you pay does not disappear. Rather, it goes into the cash register. From there, it is used to pay the farmer for fresh vegetables, the canning factory for canned goods, or the clerk's wages. The farmer or the clerk or the employee of the canning factory will in turn use the money to purchase goods. Once more, the money is used for final purchases. The same dollar bill can circulate round and round.

THE QUANTITY THEORY OF MONEY

The equation of exchange, by itself, does not get us very far, because it is a **tautology** or *truism*. That is, it *must* be true because of the way the terms are defined. Note that velocity is defined as $V = PQ/M$. Thus, by definition, $MV = PQ$. (Just multiply both sides of the first equation by M.)

However, in the hands of classical economists, the equation of exchange became more than a tautology; it became the basis of an important theory.

This theory—the **quantity theory of money**—was based on the proposition that *velocity (V) is stable*.

The **quantity theory of money** is the proposition that velocity (V) is stable. A change in the quantity of money (M) will cause nominal national product (PQ) to change by approximately the same percentage.

If, for example, the money stock (M) increases by 20%, then as a consequence, nominal national product (PQ) will also rise by about 20%.

Building on the old quantity theory of money, modern monetarists put forward a number of major propositions:

1. A change in the quantity of money (M) is the key to changes in aggregate demand. When people have more M, they spend more on the nation's output. Specifically, an increase in M will cause an approximately proportional increase in nominal national product (PQ).

2. *In the long run*, real output (Q) moves to the full-employment, capacity level. The long-run Phillips curve is vertical. Therefore the long-run effect of a change in M is on P, not on Q. Most notably, a rapid increase in the quantity of money causes a rapid inflation.

3. Nevertheless, *in the short run* (over periods of months or quarters), a change in M can have a substantial effect on both P and Q. For example, a decline in the quantity of money can cause a decline in output (Q) and the onset of a recession. During a recession, a growth of M can cause a short-run increase in Q, moving the economy back toward full employment. In the short run, the Phillips curve is not vertical.

4. Monetary disturbances are a major cause of unstable aggregate demand and of business cycles. If M is kept stable, a market economy will be quite stable.

5. Thus the major macroeconomic responsibility of the authorities is to provide a stable money supply. Specifically, the money supply should be steadily increased at a rate that is adequate to buy the full-employment output of the economy at stable prices. As the capacity of the economy grows gradually, monetarists argue that the authorities

should adhere to a *policy rule*, increasing the money stock at a slow, steady rate of 3 or 4% per year. The gradually rising money stock will cause a slow, steady increase in aggregate demand, and, as a result, it will be possible to sell the rising output at stable prices.

In brief, monetarists believe that money has a powerful effect on aggregate demand. Nevertheless, they believe that the Federal Reserve should *not* attempt to combat business cycles by adjusting monetary policy. The economy is too complex, and our understanding too limited, for such an active policy to help. Instead, the Fed should follow a **monetary rule.** These monetarist views will be explained in the rest of this chapter and in Chapter 18.

WHY SHOULD VELOCITY BE STABLE? THE DEMAND FOR MONEY

The quantity theory may be traced back over 200 years, at least as far back as the writings of philosopher David Hume in the eighteenth century. The early quantity theorists attributed the inflation of the time to the inflow of gold and silver from the New World. The exact mechanism by which money affected aggregate demand and prices was not spelled out in detail by these early theorists. They believed that it was self-evident that, when people have more money, they spend more. When they spend more—with more money chasing a given quantity of goods—prices rise.

More recently, particularly in response to criticisms by Keynesians, monetarists have been more explicit about their theory. Velocity is stable, they argue, because *the demand for money is stable.* The demand for money arises because of the usefulness of money in purchasing goods and services. Money is held only temporarily, from the time people receive income until they spend it to purchase goods and services. The higher are people's incomes, the more money they will need to make purchases. Therefore the quantity of money demanded depends on the size of national income. And it is national income in current dollars (that is, PQ rather than simply Q) that is important in determining the demand for money: If prices rise, people will need more money to pay for the more expensive goods and services. Thus monetarists

focus on nominal national income as the principal determinant of the demand for money.

Figure 17-6 illustrates this relationship. The higher the current-dollar or nominal national product (measured up the vertical axis), the greater the quantity of money demanded (measured along the horizontal axis). Suppose that the actual amount of money in the economy is initially at S_1, and the current-dollar national product is at A. Then the supply S_1 and demand for money will be in equilibrium, at point E_1.

Now, suppose that the money stock increases to S_2. At the existing national product (A), the quantity of money that people have (AB) is greater than the amount they want to hold (AE_1); there is a temporary surplus of money of E_1B. With more money than they want, people spend it to buy more goods and services. In other words, aggregate demand goes up. If the economy is initially in a

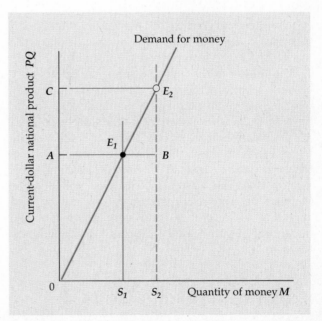

FIGURE 17-6   The demand for money: The monetarist view.

Monetarists believe that the demand for money is stable and depends primarily on current-dollar national product. If the stock of money which people hold exceeds the demand for money, then people will increase their spending.

depression, with large amounts of excess capacity, output (Q) will respond strongly to the increase in money. But if the economy is already at or near full employment, Q can't increase substantially. Higher aggregate demand will therefore cause a rise in prices (P). In either case, current-dollar national product (PQ) will increase. As this happens, people become willing to hold more money. The process continues until current-dollar national product rises to C, where the quantity of money and the demand for it are again in equilibrium at E_2. In this way, a change in the quantity of money causes an approximately proportional change in national product PQ. But this in turn means that V is stable. (If a 10% increase in PQ occurs whenever there is a 10% increase in M, then the ratio PQ/M is constant. That is, V is constant.)

Thus the theoretical underpinning of the quantity theory of money—the proposition that V is stable—is this: There is a stable demand for money, similar to the straight line shown in Figure 17-6.

In conclusion, note that when there is an increase in the quantity of money, Keynesians and monetarists present quite different ideas as to what can happen. According to Keynesian theory, an increase in the quantity of money will start the complicated, three-step process outlined in Figure 17-4. At either of the first two steps, the effects may be very weak. In this case, the increase in money will not stimulate aggregate demand very much; most of the additional money will simply be held in idle balances. Not so, say monetarists. If people have more money, they have a very straightforward option. Instead of simply holding their money, they can spend it. This they will do. For monetarists, the connection between money and spending is very tight and very short, not the uncertain, complicated process described by Keynes.

MONETARIST DOUBTS ABOUT FISCAL POLICY: CROWDING OUT

Prior to the appearance of Keynes' *General Theory*, many economists were skeptical about the effects of fiscal policy on aggregate demand, output, and

employment.[3] For example, the British Treasury opposed additional government spending during the Great Depression on the ground that it would do no good, since it would merely displace or **crowd out** an equivalent amount of private investment demand. (One of Keynes' principal objectives in writing the *General Theory* was to combat this view of the British Treasury.) Modern monetarists—the inheritors of the classical tradition—are likewise skeptical about the effects of fiscal policy on aggregate demand.

Expansive fiscal policies may crowd out investment demand in the following way. When the government increases its expenditures or cuts taxes, its deficit rises. To finance its deficit spending, the government sells new bonds or shorter term securities. That is, it borrows from the financial markets. The additional borrowing pushes up interest rates. Higher interest rates, in turn, cause a decrease in desired investment, as businesses move along the investment demand curve (Fig. 17-7). The decline in investment acts as a drag on aggregate demand, counteracting the direct stimulative effects of government spending or tax cuts.

Crowding out occurs when an expansive fiscal policy causes higher interest rates, and these higher interest rates in turn depress investment demand.

There is little doubt that some crowding out takes place. The question is, how much? Keynesian economists—and particularly early Keynesians—have often argued that investment is not very responsive to interest rates. This view was illustrated back in Figure 17-5, where investment decreases only a little in a move from B to A. As a result, not much crowding out of investment takes place.

---

[3]However, some classical economists recognized that budget deficits could stimulate aggregate demand. For example, Jacob Viner of the University of Chicago argued that "The outstanding though unintentional achievement of the Hoover Administration in counteracting the depression has in fact been its deficits of the last two years." Viner, *Balanced Deflation, Inflation, or More Depression* (Minneapolis: University of Minnesota Press, Day and Hour Series, 1933), p. 18.

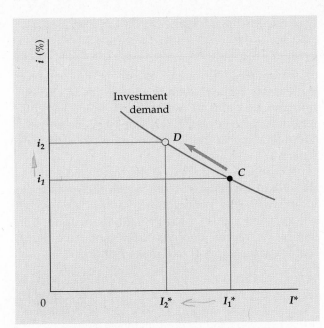

FIGURE 17-7   Crowding out: The monetarist view.

Government deficits may push up the interest rate—from i_1 to i_2, for example. This causes a movement along the investment demand curve from C to D, with investment decreasing from I_1^* to I_2^*.

Consequently, fiscal policy is a powerful tool for controlling aggregate demand. (Note that, if the investment demand curve is steep, as shown in Fig. 17-5, monetary policy will be weak, but fiscal policy will be strong.) Monetarists, on the other hand, generally believe that the investment demand curve is quite flat, as shown in Figure 17-7, and that deficit spending by the government crowds out a large amount of private investment. Thus fiscal policy has little if any effect on aggregate demand.

In casting doubt on the effectiveness of deficit spending, monetarists make one important qualification. If the central bank buys any of the additional bonds that the government has to sell to finance its deficit, the central bank will be conducting open market purchases and thus increasing the money stock. The new money will have a powerful expansive effect on aggregate demand. But monetarists attribute the higher demand to a change in the money stock, not to the government deficit itself. They see **pure fiscal policy** as having little effect on aggregate demand.

Pure fiscal policy involves a change in government spending or tax rates, unaccompanied by any change in the rate of growth of the money stock.

LIVING IN A GLOBAL ECONOMY

BUDGET DEFICITS AND TRADE DEFICITS

In this chapter, we have thus far been summarizing the long-lasting debate that began with Keynes' attack on classical economics in the 1930s. The possible "crowding out" of investment was part of that debate.

In recent years, and particularly with the ballooning of government deficits during the early 1980s, there has been another reason to doubt that deficit spending by the government will have a strong stimulative effect. Specifically, a *budget deficit* can cause a *trade deficit*—that is, an excess of imports over exports. Instead of stimulating U.S. production, the additional spending may be directed toward foreign products.

To see why, we must follow through the detailed effects of the government deficits caused by an expansive fiscal policy. Again, we will be considering a *pure* fiscal policy, unaccompanied by any change in monetary policy.

Once more, we start by assuming that the government increases its deficit spending. To finance its deficits, the government borrows from the financial markets, thereby increasing the demand for funds and pushing up interest rates. The higher U.S. interest rates encourage foreigners to buy U.S. bonds. (Thus foreigners are financing some of the U.S. budget deficit.) In order to buy these bonds, foreigners need dollars. As they buy dollars, they bid up the price of the dollar in terms of their currency. For example, the price of the dollar is bid up from ¥200 to ¥220. (¥ is the symbol for the Japanese yen.)

Now consider how this affects Japanese who wish to buy American goods, such as a computer selling for $1 million. Initially, when a dollar was worth ¥200, this $1 million computer would cost the Japanese buyer ¥200 million. After the price of the dollar was bid up, the same computer would cost the Japanese ¥220 million. Because U.S. computers have thus become more expensive to foreign buyers, they buy fewer. There is a decline in U.S. exports of computers and other goods.

A high value of the dollar causes a similar loss of sales by U.S. companies that compete with imports. When the dollar is worth more—that is, when foreign currencies are worth less in terms of dollars—Americans can buy Japanese and other foreign goods more cheaply. They therefore switch away from U.S. goods and buy more imports instead.

In brief, the deficit spending causes a decline in sales by U.S. firms that export and those that compete with imported goods. The loss of sales partially offsets and weakens the stimulative effect of the government's deficit spending.

This argument may be summarized as follows:

An increase in deficit spending by the government → Interest rate up → Purchase of U.S. bonds by foreigners → Rise in price of dollar in terms of foreign currencies → Fall in exports and rise in imports, that is, an increase in the U.S. trade deficit.

The effect of budget deficits on trade deficits was particularly strong between 1981 and 1985. Rising budget deficits were accompanied by a soaring U.S. dollar and by soaring U.S. trade deficits. Thus government deficits affected the *composition* of output, depressing sales and output of industries facing international competition (that is, both export industries and import-competing industries such as cars). The early expansion of 1983–1985 was *lopsided*, with manufacturing remaining depressed while most other parts of the economy recovered. As the budget came under somewhat better control during the last half of the decade, the price of the U.S. dollar declined in terms of the yen and other currencies, and manufacturing expanded vigorously.

THE UNCERTAIN LESSON OF RECENT HISTORY

To summarize the major debate in this chapter: Monetarists argue that money is the key to changes in aggregate demand, while fiscal policy has little net effect. In contrast, Keynesians believe that fiscal policy has a powerful impact on aggregate demand.

It would seem easy to settle this dispute—simply look at the facts and see which theory is more in line with the observations of the real world. Unfortunately, this is easier said than done. The history of recent decades does not give clear, unambiguous support to either position.

THE RISE AND FALL OF MONETARISM

Monetarism was given a boost in the late 1960s, when events tended to confirm the quantity theory and cast doubts on the Keynesian view. In mid-1968, Congress imposed an income tax surcharge and placed a limitation on federal government spending in order to cool down the inflation generated by the Vietnam conflict. Economists using the Keynesian approach expected a powerful restrictive effect on aggregate demand. In fact, they expressed fears that Congress had engaged in "fiscal overkill" and that a recession would be caused by the shift toward fiscal restraint. In order to soften the expected recession, the Federal Reserve eased monetary policy, allowing a rapid rate of growth of the money stock. Thus monetary policy was expansive, while fiscal policy was restrictive. What happened? Aggregate demand followed the path set by monetary policy and continued to expand vigorously throughout late 1968. In fact, the boom continued until after monetary policy was shifted sharply toward restraint in early 1969. Monetarists seemed vindicated, and Keynesians were shaken in their beliefs. In the words of Princeton's Alan Blinder and MIT's Robert Solow, the events of the late 1960s threatened to send Keynesian economic advisers "scurrying back to their universities with their doctrinal tales [sic] between their legs."[4] (For more on the ineffectiveness of fiscal policy, see the appendix.)

In 1974, monetarism was given a further boost. The tight monetary policies of that year were followed by the worst recession in decades, confirming the view that money has a powerful effect on aggregate demand.

The decade from 1965 to 1974 thus provided considerable support to monetarists. But their triumph was short-lived. A strong upswing in GNP began in 1975 in spite of a slow growth in the money stock. According to the quantity theory, this strong upswing should not have occurred with so little increase in the quantity of money—"the case of the missing money," in the words of Princeton's Stephen Goldfeld.[5] Because GNP grew much more rapidly than the money stock, velocity rose sharply, as can be seen in Figure 17-8. In the late 1970s, the velocity of M1 rose more rapidly than it had in previous years, and the velocity of M2 also rose rapidly. Thus doubts were cast on the monetarists' view that velocity is stable.

When the expansion of the late 1970s ended in an inflationary binge, the Federal Reserve became alarmed. In 1979, the Fed announced that it would reduce its target for the growth of the money stock and would try harder to meet that new, lower target.

In deciding to pay more attention to a monetary target, the Fed took a major step toward the monetarist position. However, the argument put forward by monetarists provided only one reason for this change. Perhaps equally significant was the political problem faced by the Fed. If the exploding inflation were to be stopped, the Fed would have to tighten policy. The result would be higher interest rates, which were bound to generate criticism. By explicitly targeting the money stock, the Fed

[4]Alan Blinder and Robert Solow, "Analytical Foundations of Fiscal Policy," in Blinder, Solow, and others, *The Economics of Public Finance* (Washington, D.C.: Brookings Institution, 1974), p. 10.

[5]Stephen Goldfeld, "The Case of the Missing Money," *Brookings Papers on Economic Activity* 3:1976, pp. 683–730.

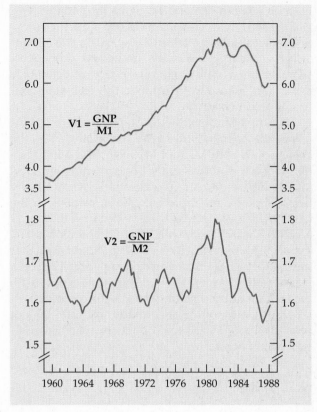

FIGURE 17-8   The velocity of money.

The income velocity of money is the ratio of gross national product to the quantity of money. If M1 (currency plus checking deposits) is taken as the definition of money, there was an upward trend in velocity (V1) between 1960 and 1981, especially in the late 1970s. If M2 is taken as the definition of money, then velocity (V2) showed no major trend between 1960 and 1977, when it began to rise rapidly. Since 1981, both V1 and V2 have declined.

was declaring war on inflation and hoping to deflect criticisms over higher interest rates.

This policy experiment represented the high-water mark of monetarist influence; thereafter it receded. The monetarist case requires that velocity be stable; if it is not, a stable growth in the quantity of money will not lead to a stable growth in aggregate demand. In the late 1970s, velocity had already shown signs of instability. But worse was soon to come. During the recession of 1982, the velocity of both M1 and M2 fell substantially (Fig. 17-8). Faced with a deep recession and the unexpected weakness of velocity, the Fed in 1982 abandoned its target of slow monetary growth. It switched to a more vigorous policy of monetary expansion in order to combat the recession and promote recovery.

Figure 17-8 illustrates how much the behavior of velocity changed after 1976. In the late 1970s, the velocities of both M1 and M2 rose; after 1980, they fell. Indeed, in terms of the fundamental equation $MV = PQ$, increases in velocity V were largely responsible for the rapid increase in prices P in the late 1970s, and decreases in velocity were largely responsible for the slowing down of inflation in the early 1980s. By 1987, the Fed began to despair that the velocity of M1 was stable enough for M1 to be a useful policy target. For the first time since 1975, the Fed announced no target for M1 growth.

The history of the past quarter century has not been kind to doctrinaire economists, whether monetarist or Keynesian.

THE RECENT RELIANCE ON MONETARY POLICY

During the past decade, changes in velocity have complicated the task of the Federal Reserve. Unstable velocity means that, when the Fed changes its monetary policy, it is less able to predict the effect on aggregate demand. In spite of this, the United States has come to rely more heavily on monetary policy than it did in previous decades. Since 1981, monetary policy has been at center stage because of problems with fiscal policy. The tax cuts and increases in military spending, which provided the cornerstone of President Reagan's economic policy, resulted in such large deficits in the federal budget that the government no longer feels free to use an active fiscal policy to stabilize the economy.

Although many political leaders believed that it was important to reduce the deficits, there was little agreement on how to do so. Each spending program had its supporters, and the campaigns of Ronald Reagan and George Bush against tax in-

creases made it almost impossible for any politician to recommend them. Fiscal policy became stuck in a political gridlock: Conflicting pressures made it very difficult to cut spending or explicitly raise taxes (although some disguised taxes—or "revenue enhancements"—were considered). Because of the fiscal gridlock, monetary policy was the only macroeconomic "game left in town." Monetary policy became the principal demand-management tool by default.

THE CASE FOR USING MONETARY AND FISCAL POLICIES TOGETHER

This concentration on monetary policy has been unfortunate. A substantial case can be made that the best macroeconomic policy includes both fiscal and monetary policies, used cooperatively.

The controversy described in this chapter provides the first reason. Although economists have generally moved away from the extremes and toward the center, they still disagree over the relative strengths of monetary and fiscal policies. Historical evidence does not provide a sharp, clean resolution to this disagreement. Continuing uncertainties over the relative effectiveness of monetary and fiscal policies strengthen the case for using both. It is unwise to put all our eggs in one basket, particularly when we're not sure which basket it should be.

Furthermore, there is a second important reason for favoring a combined monetary-fiscal strategy. During a boom in aggregate demand, restrictive steps are desirable. Such steps are painful. Cuts in government spending hurt various groups in the economy. Nobody wants an increase in their taxes. A tighter monetary policy and higher interest rates can put a squeeze on housing construction and other types of investment. If a combination of policies is used, the effects of each may be kept moderate and the costs of restrictive policies may be spread more widely over the population. Thus it may be possible to avoid placing a very heavy burden on any single segment of the economy.

KEY POINTS

1. Most present-day economists take a central position, believing that both fiscal and monetary policies have substantial effects on aggregate demand. However, some economists have taken polar positions. Early Keynesians not only focused on fiscal policy; some also believed that monetary policy might have little effect on aggregate demand. On the other side is the monetarist view that money is the predominant force determining aggregate demand, and that fiscal policy has little effect.

2. Keynes proposed that the effects of monetary policy be analyzed by looking at three steps:

    (a) The effect of monetary policy on the rate of interest.

    (b) The effect of the interest rate on investment.

    (c) The effect of a change in investment on aggregate demand (the multiplier).

3. Keynes himself believed that expansive monetary policies could not be counted on to get the economy out of the depression of the 1930s because of a problem at the very first step. Interest rates were already very low and could not be pushed down much further by an expansive monetary policy.

4. Some early followers of Keynes had more general doubts about the effectiveness of monetary policies—not just in a depression, but also in more normal times. Specifically, they argued that a problem would arise at the second step because investment is not very responsive to changes in the rate of interest. That is, the investment demand schedule is steep, as illustrated in Figure 17-5.

5. Classical macroeconomics was based on the equation of exchange ($MV = PQ$) and on the proposition that velocity V is stable (the quantity theory). If velocity is stable, a change in money M will cause current-dollar national product (PQ) to change by approximately the same percentage.

6. Monetarists—the modern inheritors of the classical tradition—believe that, in the long run, the principal effect of a change in the rate of growth of M will be a change in the price level P. In the short run, however, changes in the growth of M can also affect real national product Q.

7. Indeed, monetarists believe that monetary disturbances are one of the principal causes of fluctuations in real output.

8. The view that velocity is stable is based on the belief that there is a stable demand for money. If, after a period of equilibrium, people get more money, their holdings of money will exceed their demand for it (Fig. 17-6). They will use the surplus to buy goods and services, thus increasing current-dollar national product (PQ).

9. Monetarists doubt that fiscal policy has a substantial effect on aggregate demand, unless the fiscal policy is accompanied by changes in M. That is, they have doubts about the effectiveness of *pure* fiscal policy. These doubts are based on the belief that an increase in deficit spending will push up interest rates and therefore *crowd out* private investment.

10. The crowding out effect is powerful, and fiscal policy is therefore weak, if investment is very responsive to changes in interest rates (the investment demand function is relatively flat). Strong monetarists believe the investment demand function is quite flat, and therefore fiscal policy is weak. Some years ago, strong Keynesians believed the investment demand function was quite steep, and therefore monetary policy was weak.

11. In addition to the crowding out of investment, there is a second way in which the expansive effects of an increase in deficit spending may be partially offset. Higher interest rates may encourage foreigners to buy U.S. bonds, raising the price of the U.S. dollar in terms of foreign currencies. As a result, U.S. producers will be less competitive; exports will fall and imports will rise. The increase in deficit spending will stimulate the sales of foreign producers, not U.S. producers. This complication was important during the first half of the 1980s.

12. Recent history does not give a clear, unambiguous confirmation of either the strong Keynesian or the strong monetarist view. At times—1968, for example—the evidence supported the quantity theory, and at other times—much of the 1980s—the evidence tended to contradict it.

13. Because of this uncertainty—and for other reasons—it is undesirable to place exclusive reliance on either monetary or fiscal policy. Instead,

it is wiser to use a combined monetary-fiscal strategy.

14. Nevertheless, there has been a very heavy reliance on monetary policy since 1979. One reason was the desire of the Fed to control the rapidly accelerating inflation of the late 1970s. Another was the great difficulty in changing fiscal policy during the 1980s.

KEY CONCEPTS

demand for money
responsiveness of investment to a change in the interest rate
equation of exchange

income velocity of money (V)
quantity theory of money
monetary rule
crowding out

pure fiscal policy
trade deficit

PROBLEMS

17-1. In the Keynesian framework, there are three separate steps in the process by which monetary policy affects aggregate demand.

(a) What are these three steps?

(b) Keynes argued that expansive monetary policy would be ineffective in getting the economy out of the depression of the 1930s because of a problem at one of these three steps. Which step? What was the nature of the problem?

(c) Some of the followers of Keynes argued that monetary policy is generally a weak and ineffective tool for controlling aggregate demand. They foresaw a problem at another one of the steps. Which step? What was the nature of the problem?

17-2. The Keynesian theory of the demand for money (shown in Fig. 17-2) was developed at a time when no interest was paid on checking deposits. There was an obvious cost in holding money: namely, the interest that could otherwise have been earned by buying a security.

Now banks and other institutions are permitted to pay interest on checking deposits, as we saw in Chapter 11. When banks pay interest on such

deposits, how would you expect the demand for money to be affected as a result?

17-3. How do strong Keynesians and strong monetarists disagree on the way in which the investment demand curve should be drawn? How does the way a strong Keynesian draws the investment demand curve cast doubt on the effectiveness of monetary policy? How does the way a strong monetarist draws the investment demand curve cast doubt on the effectiveness of fiscal policy in controlling aggregate demand?

17-4. "I accept the equation of exchange as valid. But I do not accept the quantity theory of money." Is it consistent for an economist to hold such a position? Why or why not?

17-5. Suppose that the quantity of money demanded is initially equal to the quantity in existence. Then suppose that the quantity of money is doubled because of action by the central bank. According to a Keynesian economist, what will happen? According to a monetarist, what will happen?

17-6. Explain how a budget deficit might cause a trade deficit. (A trade deficit is an excess of imports over exports.)

DOUBTS ABOUT FISCAL POLICY
How Do Consumers Respond?

The 1960s began with high hopes that fiscal policy could be used to manage aggregate demand. By the end of the decade, doubts were widespread. The temporary tax surcharge of 1968 had failed to slow down consumption expenditures as much as predicted.

The reason was that the predictions were based on a simple consumption function, similar to that presented in Chapter 9. That consumption function was a good place to begin a study of macroeconomics; consumption does depend primarily on disposable income. But reality is somewhat more complicated.

To see why, consider why people save (that is, consume less than their disposable incomes). Presumably, they do so in order to be able to consume more at a later date. Saving is a way of rearranging consumption through time. If their current income is abnormally low—less than they can reasonably expect in the future—they have an incentive to dissave. Thus students often borrow in order to consume more than their current income. They expect to repay in the future when their incomes will be higher. On the other hand, when incomes are abnormally high—during the peak earning years of middle age, in particular—people have an incentive to save for their future, when they expect lower incomes.

Thus consumption depends not simply on *current* income. Rather, it depends on the income that people consider to be normal—or, in the jargon of economists, on their **permanent income.**

Now, let us return to the income tax surcharge of 1968. This was a *temporary* extra tax, intended to cool the overheating economy. Suppose that you have to pay $400 extra to the government as a result of such a surcharge. What is your reaction likely to be? While your present disposable income is down by $400, the government has already said that this reduction is temporary. Your permanent income—what you consider normal—will be changed little, if at all. Why should you cut back your consumption in the face of this temporary disturbance? You are likely to respond by reducing your consumption only a little, and simply save less. In this way, you will spread the effects of the tax over a number of years. Thus a *temporary* tax change has only a weak effect on consumption. It is only when a tax change is expected to be *permanent* that consumers will respond strongly.

The 1968 tax surcharge was temporary, and therefore it came mostly out of people's saving, not consumption. Similarly, the tax cuts of 1975 were temporary. Near the bottom of the recession, Congress rebated part of 1974 taxes and temporarily reduced taxes for 1975. Again, the results were disappointing. There wasn't much stimulus. People simply saved most of the tax rebates. By 1977, when President Carter again proposed a temporary tax rebate to stimulate the economy, Congress rejected the idea because of skepticism that it would do much good.

The history of 1968 and 1975 throws into question the whole idea of changing tax rates in an attempt to stabilize aggregate demand. Such changes by their very nature are for the short run and are likely to be reversed when conditions change. Because the public recognizes that they are temporary, they won't have much effect on consumption or on aggregate demand.

BARRO-RICARDO

Some economists go much further and question whether a longer run, fundamental change in the tax code will have much effect on consumption. The most prominent proponent of this view is

Robert Barro of Harvard University, who traces his argument back to David Ricardo (1772–1823).

Barro observes that a tax cut, unaccompanied by any change in government spending, has implications for the future. The resulting deficit means that the government will have to borrow. Therefore it will have to raise taxes in the future to pay interest on the additional debt. People recognize this. They realize that they will have to pay higher taxes in the future. How can they protect themselves? The answer is, by saving more. Suppose the government cuts taxes by $100 and issues $100 in debt. The only way the public can protect themselves completely is by saving the whole $100 current tax cut; this will provide a future flow of interest just large enough to cover their additional future taxes. This, says Barro, is what they will do. A $100 tax cut will lead to a $100 increase in saving. There will be *no* effect on consumption or aggregate demand.[6]

The Barro conclusion is based on a number of very strong assumptions. One is that people see *very* far into the future—past their lifetimes to the lifetimes of their children and grandchildren. If their grandchildren are going to be burdened with $100 more in debt, people will save $100 more now to enable them to bear that burden. If we depart from Barro's theory and assume that people do not look beyond their own lifetimes, a $100 tax cut *will* have an effect on consumption. For example, a sixty year old whose tax is cut will spend part of the tax cut. There is no need to save the full amount,

since much of the burden of the debt can be left to future generations.

Many economists are skeptical of Barro's conclusion; they are skeptical that people are foresighted enough to increase their saving by $100 for every $100 cut in taxes. If the skeptics are correct, a fundamental tax cut—not aimed at temporary demand-management objectives—*will* affect consumption expenditures; people will not simply save the whole tax cut. The experience of the 1980s supports this conclusion and undercuts Barro's argument. The major cuts in tax rates in 1981–1984 were clearly intended to be long run. When people found their taxes falling, they spent more; they did not save the whole amount. In fact, personal saving was only 4.2% of disposable personal income between 1985 and 1987—much *less* than in the early 1980s (6.6%) or in the 1970s (8.0%). Furthermore, evidence from other countries provides "striking" support for the view that "government deficits stimulate private consumption."[7]

In summary, we have a paradoxical conclusion: A short-run cut in taxes, intended to manage aggregate demand, has little effect on demand. (It leaves permanent income—and therefore consumption and aggregate demand—practically unchanged.) Most of the tax cut is saved.

On the other hand, when a long-run, permanent cut is made in tax rates (as in 1981), then permanent income, consumption, and aggregate demand do increase. Thus, paradoxically, the tax cuts that have the greatest effect on aggregate demand are the permanent cuts that are not intended to affect demand!

------

[6]This is sometimes known as the *Ricardian equivalence theorem*. The path of consumption will be equivalent, whether the government finances its spending by taxes or by issuing debt.

Although Ricardo originated this idea, he was somewhat skeptical of its applicability. He noted that taxes and debt *might* be equivalent in this way, but it is not clear that he believed they *would* be.

------

[7]B. Douglas Bernheim, "Ricardian Equivalence: An Evaluation of Theory and Evidence," in Stanley Fischer, ed., *NBER Macroeconomics Annual, 1987* (Cambridge, Mass.: MIT Press, 1987), p. 299.

CHAPTER 18

FINE TUNING OR STABLE POLICY SETTINGS?

If something works, don't fix it.
MODERN AMERICAN PROVERB

In the study of macroeconomics, successful policies are the ultimate goal. It is not clear whether the policies of the past 30 years should be judged a success or a failure. In part, the answer depends on the question: Successful compared to what?

Certainly, compared to the depressed decade of the 1930s, the economy has performed very well during the three decades. The unemployment rate has never gotten anywhere near the 24.9% of 1933. However, we have not been doing better and better as time passes. The recessions of 1974 and 1982 were much more severe than any during the 1940s, 1950s, or 1960s. During the recession of 1982, the unemployment rate rose to 10.8%, the highest since the Great Depression. With regard to inflation, the U.S. experience of recent decades has also been worse than that of the preceding period. Bursts of inflation occurred during the late 1960s and the 1970s, with inflation hitting a peak of 13.3% by 1979. Although inflation has been brought under much better control since 1981, it has still averaged about 4%—substantially above the average annual rate of 1.6% between 1955 and 1965.

The mediocre performance of the economy in the three decades has revitalized an old debate that goes back to the Great Depression of the 1930s. On the one side are those in the Keynesian tradition, who argue that aggregate demand policies should be *actively managed* in order to achieve high employment and stable prices. As the economy heads toward recession, expansive policies should be adopted. As the economy heads toward an inflationary boom, restraint should be exercised.

On the other side are monetarists, who argue that activist, discretionary policies are more likely to do harm than good, no matter how well intentioned policymakers might be. Consequently, they argue that **discretionary** policies should be avoided. Instead, permanent policy settings should be chosen and maintained regardless of the short-term fluctuations in economic activity. That is, a **policy rule** should be followed. It is of course important that the rule be chosen carefully and, in particular, that it be consistent with economic stability. For example, it would be a mistake to adhere to the rules of the old gold standard, which made the banking system vulnerable to runs.

However, monetarists suggest that there is a policy rule that *is* consistent with a high degree of economic stability. Specifically, they suggest that the Federal Reserve should aim at a slow, steady increase in the money supply, at something like 3%

313

or 4% per year. This increase would provide the money needed to purchase the expanding national output at stable prices.

> *Discretionary* fiscal and monetary policies are policies that the government and the central bank adjust periodically in order to deal with changing conditions in the economy.

As in Chapter 17, the sharp contrast between Keynesians and monetarists may be illustrated by comparing the statements of Warren Smith (a Keynesian) and Milton Friedman (a monetarist). The flavor of the activist, hands-on-the-helm view was given by Smith:

> The only good rule is that the budget should never be balanced—except for an instant when a surplus to curb inflation is being altered to a deficit to fight deflation.[1]

Friedman explicitly criticized the activist policy of attempting to *fine tune* the economy:

> Is fiscal policy being oversold? Is monetary policy being oversold? . . . My answer is yes to both of those questions. . . . Monetary policy is being oversold. . . . Fiscal policy is being oversold. . . . Fine tuning has been oversold.[2]

Skepticism over activist policies was likewise expressed by Murray Weidenbaum of Washington University (St. Louis), who served as chairman of the Council of Economic Advisers under President Reagan. Quipped Weidenbaum: "Don't just do something. Stand there."

We introduce this debate over the active management of demand by looking more closely at the Keynesian approach, in which aggregate demand policies are adjusted in pursuit of the goals of full employment and stable prices. Later sections of this chapter will explain criticisms of that policy

and describe some problems with the alternative of following a monetary rule.

AIMING FOR A STABLE, HIGH-EMPLOYMENT ECONOMY: THE ACTIVE KEYNESIAN APPROACH

As we have seen, Keynes believed that a market economy would suffer from two major diseases. (1) It was likely to move toward an equilibrium where there would be inadequate aggregate demand and high unemployment. (2) Even if the economy did get to a position of full employment, it would be unlikely to stay there, primarily because of the instability of investment demand. In short, demand would tend to be both *inadequate* and *unstable*. Therefore the policy problem, as seen by Keynesian economists, was (1) to stimulate aggregate demand to the full-employment level, and then (2) to adjust or fine tune it whenever needed to combat business fluctuations.

The Keynesian strategy is illustrated in Figure 18-1. Suppose that the economy in year 1 begins at a position of high unemployment. The actual production of the economy, at *A*, is well below the

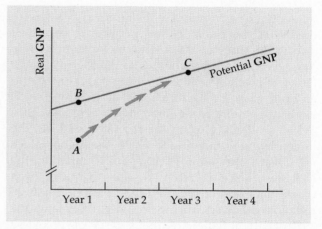

FIGURE 18-1   The Keynesian strategy: An active policy.

The activist Keynesian strategy is to move to the potential GNP path. Fiscal and monetary policies should then be adjusted as needed to keep the economy as close as possible to potential GNP.

[1]Warren Smith, statement to a meeting of Treasury consultants, as quoted by Paul A. Samuelson, *Economics*, 11th ed. (New York: McGraw-Hill, 1976), p. 222.

[2]Milton Friedman and Walter Heller, *Monetary vs. Fiscal Policy* (New York: W. W. Norton, 1969), p. 47.

potential at full employment (*B*). Of course, the potential output of the economy does not remain constant. As time passes, the labor force grows, the capital stock increases, and technology improves. Thus the path of full-employment or potential GNP trends upward. The objective of policy in year 1 should be to aim the economy toward the full-employment path. However, full employment cannot be achieved immediately; there are lags in the implementation and effect of policy. Thus policy in year 1 should be aimed at stimulating the economy so that it approaches full employment at some time in the reasonably near future, as shown by the arrows in Figure 18-1.

AN EXAMPLE

By going back to the early 1960s, we can find a clear and explicit illustration of this Keynesian strategy. The black parts of Figure 18-2 were presented by the Council of Economic Advisers (CEA) in its *Annual Report* in early 1962. The thin dashed lines show three possible outcomes. *A*, the most favorable, would eliminate the GNP gap within two years. On the other hand, a growth path toward *C* would not represent any improvement; the GNP gap would remain just as wide in 1963 as it was in 1961. The policy problem was to try to make the economy follow path *A*, or close to it.

The outcome in the following years is shown in the red parts of Figure 18-2. The red curve showing actual GNP traces out a very impressive performance. Although the GNP gap was not eliminated within two years, it was eliminated within four. By the end of 1965, the economy was right on target. What remained then was to fine tune the economy, keeping it as close as possible to the potential growth path.

There were, of course, problems. One was the well-recognized problem of lags: How do you adjust policies when the actions taken today do not affect the economy until some future time, when they may no longer be appropriate? Keynesians believed that they had an adequate—though far from perfect—answer. By forecasting, policymakers can get a fairly good idea of where the economy is headed. Thus they should be able to lead their

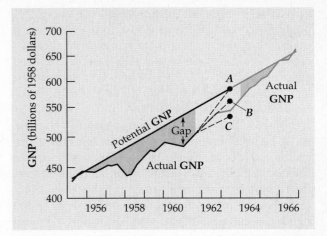

FIGURE 18-2   The active strategy in practice, 1962–1966.

The black parts of the diagram are taken from the Council of Economic Advisers, *Annual Report, 1962*, p. 52. They show the gap between the actual and potential GNP, and illustrate how various future paths (*A*, *B*, and *C*) would affect the gap. The red parts of the diagram show what actually happened. Although the economy did not move quickly back to its potential path, the gap had been eliminated by late 1965.

moving target, just as a quarterback can lead a receiver whose pattern he can predict.

Details of forecasting are deferred until a later section in this chapter. Here, we turn to the way in which lags are used as an argument against an active demand-management policy.

THE CASE AGAINST ACTIVISM: LAGS

The case against activism is based on the belief that active policies are more likely to destabilize than to stabilize the economy. Often, they are badly timed; they are designed to fight the battles of last year and are inappropriate to deal with the problems of the future.

There are *three lags* between the time that aggregate demand should be changed and the time when the change actually occurs. To illustrate, suppose that the economy begins to slide into a recession. This fact may not be recognized for some time. It takes time to gather statistics on what is happening. Initial signs of weakness may be dismissed as temporary disturbances; not every little jiggle in economic activity grows into a recession or boom. Thus the first lag is the *recognition lag*, which occurs between the time the weakness in the economy begins and the time when it is recognized. Furthermore, even after the decline is recognized, policymakers take some time to act; this is the *action lag*. For example, congressional hearings must be held before taxes are cut. Spending programs must be designed before they can be implemented. Finally, after action is taken, there is some delay before the major *impact* on the economy is felt. For example, when government spending finally is increased, the various rounds of consumer spending in the multiplier process take time. For monetary policy, there is a lag between the open market purchase that pushes down interest rates and the actual investment that is stimulated as a consequence. These, then, are the lags that occur before aggregate demand actually changes: the **recognition lag**, the **action lag**, and the **impact lag.**

Consider how these lags can lead to incorrect policies and add to the instability of the economy. Suppose, for example, that the ideal path of aggregate demand is shown by the solid line in Figure 18-3. Actual demand follows the dashed curve, however. Starting at point *A*, aggregate demand starts to slip below the desired level; the economy begins to move into a recession. This problem is not recognized for some time, however—not until point *B*. Even then, taxes are not cut immediately; action does not take place until point *C*. By this time, it may be too late. There is a further lag before the action affects demand (between points *D* and *E*), and by then the economy has already recovered. Fuel is added to the inflationary fire. Then, as the severity of inflation is recognized, policies are shifted in a restrictive direction. But once again there are lags; the policies can come too late, making the next recession worse. Rather than trying to adjust to changing conditions, it might be better to follow a stable set of policies. So say the monetarists.

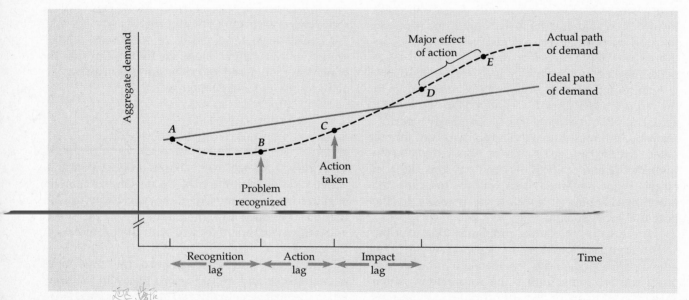

FIGURE 18-3 **Lags and economic instability.**

Policy changes may make things worse because of the recognition, action, and impact lags. Expansive steps aimed at fighting the recession at point *C* may add to a later inflationary boom at *E*. Similarly, policies aimed at restraining inflation may make the next recession worse.

THE HELMSMAN'S DILEMMA

Because the economy is slow to respond, the policymaker faces a problem similar to that of a helmsman who finds his ship drifting off course. If he turns the wheel just slightly, the ship will not respond quickly. In his anxiety, he may then turn the wheel more sharply. Clearly, the more sharply the wheel is turned, the more quickly the ship will return to its desired course. But if the wheel is swung hard, a new problem will arise. Once the ship is back on course, it will be turning with considerable momentum; it will swing to the opposite side. In his panic, the helmsman may be tempted to swing the wheel back. We can imagine the voyage of the anxious mariner—zigzagging across the ocean.

Of course, ships do not zigzag all over the ocean. With practice, the helmsman learns not to lean too hard on the wheel. He learns to move the wheel back to the center *before* the ship gets back to its intended course; the ship's momentum will complete the turn. Policymakers face the same type of problem. They must try to switch toward restraint *before* an economic expansion turns into an inflationary boom. William McChesney Martin, who served as chairman of the Federal Reserve for most of the 1950s and 1960s, sadly observed that the Fed has an unpopular task—to take away the punch bowl just when the party really gets going.

Not only do policymakers have the helmsman's problem; they also face a few more that provide extra excitement. One of the additional complications is that the helm and the rudder of the economic ship are connected by elastic bands and baling twine. Unlike the mechanism connecting the ship's wheel to the rudder, the mechanism connecting monetary and fiscal policies to aggregate demand does not work in a precise, highly predictable manner. Furthermore, the economic policymaker may have to chart a course across turbulent and stormy seas. Over the past quarter century, there have been large shocks to the U.S. economy: first, the war in Vietnam; then the oil embargo and the quadrupling of oil prices in 1973 and 1974; then the second big jump in oil prices in 1979–1980. If the ship is being guided across placid seas, the policymaker has the luxury of turning the wheel meekly so as not to overcorrect. But in stormy seas, this is not good enough. Gentle policies will be overwhelmed by other forces. This, then, is the helmsman's dilemma: How hard should the wheel be swung, and how soon should it be moved back toward center?

THE CASE AGAINST ACTIVISM: THE OVERESTIMATION OF POTENTIAL

The danger of overreaction is increased by a fourth type of lag. The three lags in the previous section represented delays *before* aggregate demand changes. The fourth lag occurs *after* aggregate demand changes. It involves the differing speeds with which real GNP and inflation respond to changes in demand. Specifically, when aggregate demand rises, the short-run effect on real output is generally powerful. Unless producers are already straining hard against their capacity limitations, they respond to an increase in demand by producing more. (The economy moves along a relatively flat short-run Phillips curve.) However, as time passes, the higher demand is reflected more and more in terms of more rapid inflation and less and less in terms of real output. (As time passes, the Phillips curve becomes steeper.) Thus, *when aggregate demand is stimulated, the favorable output effects come quickly; the unfavorable inflationary effects are delayed.* The lag creates a temptation to stick with expansive fiscal and monetary policies too long, in order to gain their short-term benefits in terms of higher output.

Figure 18-4 illustrates this lag. Note that the response of inflation in the lower panel comes after the change in output shown in the top panel. Figure 18-4 also illustrates some of the criticisms directed at the activist Keynesian approach. The first step in the Keynesian approach is to estimate potential GNP. Policymakers tend to be optimistic, overestimating potential GNP and the amount by which unemployment can be reduced by expansive demand policies. Such an overly optimistic estimate is shown by the blue potential GNP line in Figure 18-4. The red line shows the true potential path that can be followed without causing an overheating of the economy and an acceleration of inflation.

Now let us see what the critics fear if activists are in charge. Beginning at *A,* the economy is re-

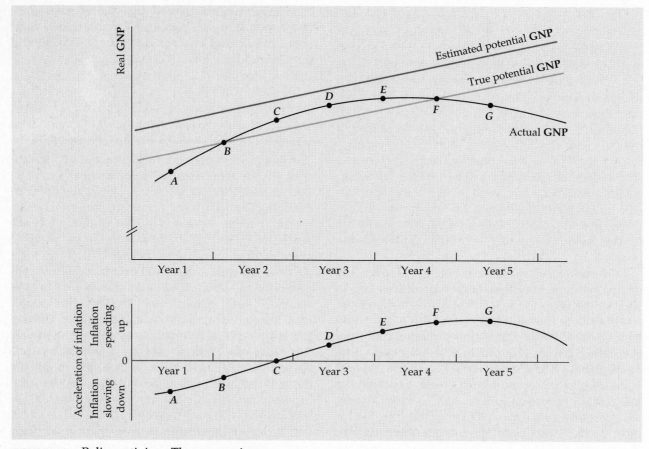

FIGURE 18-4   Policy activism: The case against.

Because of the delayed response of prices and overly ambitious goals, aggregate demand will be overstimulated, say the critics of active demand management. When inflation finally does become an obvious problem, policymakers often overreact, causing a recession.

covering from a recession. Monetary and fiscal policies are set for the expansion of aggregate demand. Real output is rising briskly, the unemployment rate is falling, and inflation—with its delayed response—is still slowing down because of the previous period of slack. Everything is going well. The expansive policy settings are retained. But, without anyone noticing, the economy moves past *B*, crossing the true potential path. The error in estimating the potential path means that policymakers incorrectly believe that aggregate demand is still too low. (GNP is still below the optimistic blue estimate of potential.) As a result, expansive policies are continued. In reality, however, aggregate demand is too high, since the economy is

above the true potential path shown in red. Therefore a less expansive policy is appropriate.

As the economy crosses the true potential path, the seeds of a more rapid inflation are being sown, although the inflationary result does not appear for some time. As the curve in the lower diagram illustrates, inflation does not begin to accelerate until time *C*.

If the error in estimating the blue potential GNP path has been large, the economy may never actually reach it. The expanding demand shows up increasingly in terms of inflation and less in terms of real output. The expansive fiscal and monetary policies cause an increase in aggregate demand, but they do not control the extent to which the higher demand will cause higher output and the extent to which it will cause higher prices.

Between C and D, a sharp policy debate is likely. Those focusing on the optimistic blue path argue that to reach it, aggregate demand should be increased even more. But, as inflation is by now accelerating (to the right of point C in the lower part of the diagram), others urge caution. As time passes and inflation gets worse, it eventually becomes evident that restraint is necessary. With inflation now rising rapidly, the policy adjustment may be abrupt.

As a result, the economy may start to move into a recession after point E. But, as always, inflation responds with a lag. *Inflation is still accelerating, even though tight policies have been introduced. Everything goes wrong during the period between E and G*—just as everything went right during the expansion between A and C. The economy is slipping into recession, while inflation is still getting worse. Skeptics charge that demand restraint simply won't stop inflation. They argue that inflation has become "built in," and nothing much can be done about it with monetary and fiscal policies. Aggregate demand policies are turned in an expansive direction in order to increase output and reduce unemployment. After a lag, a new upswing begins. But, in most cases, inflation accelerates more as a result of the extended period of rising demand than it falls as a result of the shorter period of declining demand. Thus there is a tendency for each successive upswing to begin with a higher rate of inflation than the previous one. This, then, is the case against activism.

Just as the case in favor of active policies can be supported with real-world evidence (as shown in Fig. 18-2), so critics can point to real-world failures. First, they note that, during the 1961–1981 period when aggregate demand was managed most actively, each succeeding recovery did in fact begin with a higher inflation than the previous recovery. Inflation was less than 1% in the early recovery year of 1961; about 3% in the early recovery of 1971; about 7% in the early recovery of 1975; and over 10% as the economy started coming out of recession in late 1980. The recovery starting at the end of 1982 was a notable exception; the inflation rate was only 4%. The previous expansion of 1980–1981 had been unusually short and the recession of 1981–1982 unusually severe.

Second, the 1970s and early 1980s provide a real-world illustration of the principal point of Figure 18-4—that is, how an overestimation of potential GNP can lead to policy errors. Specifically, consider Figure 18-5, which includes official estimates of potential GNP. The original estimate—made in 1968 and shown in blue—indicated that actual GNP in 1972 was still below potential. Accordingly, expansive monetary and fiscal policies were maintained through 1972 to stimulate the economy. Even at the peak of the expansion in 1973, GNP was still below the current estimate of potential shown in blue.

In fact, however, GNP was not still below its potential. Later, more realistic estimates of potential GNP made in 1977—shown as the green path in Figure 18-5—indicate that actual GNP had reached its potential by the middle of 1972. If the authorities had known this at the time, they presumably would have followed less expansive policies in 1972–1973. Instead, they acted on the mistaken belief that there was still slack in the economy, and continued to increase aggregate demand. This caused an inflationary burst, which led to a much tighter monetary policy in late 1973. In turn, the tighter policy contributed to the depth of the 1974–1975 recession.

Potential GNP was again overestimated in 1977–1978. Although the estimates of potential had already been revised downward in early 1977 (from the blue path to the green path in Fig. 18-5), even this revised series was too high. In 1979 and 1982, the estimates of potential were again adjusted downward, as shown by the brown and red paths.

Once again, the overestimate of potential led to an overly expansive aggregate demand policy in 1977–1978, which caused a rapid acceleration of inflation. Then monetary policy was switched in a much tighter direction, precipitating the recession of 1980. In short, the overestimation of potential GNP again contributed to policies that destabilized the economy.

The question arises as to how the potential GNP could have been overestimated so much. Some monetarists argue that Keynesians generally overestimate both potential GNP and their ability to stimulate high levels of production and employment without causing inflation. But surely there is something wrong with this broad generalization.

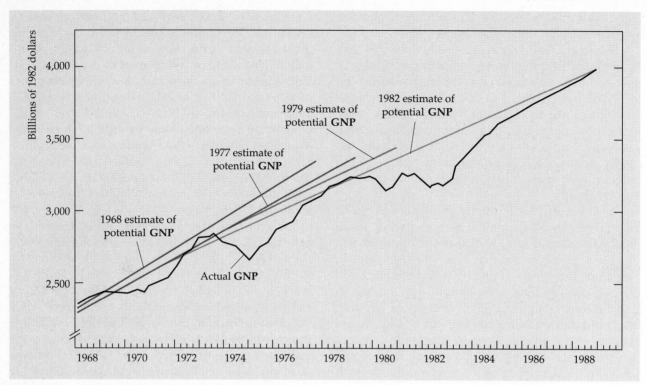

FIGURE 18-5   Actual and potential GNP, 1968–1988.

According to estimates of potential GNP available at the time, shown in blue, actual GNP still fell short of potential in 1973, suggesting that aggregate demand was still too low. Later (1977) revisions of potential GNP, shown in green, indicate that the economy had reached potential by the end of 1972 and that aggregate demand was too high by early 1973. Likewise, policymakers erroneously thought that GNP was below its potential in 1978, and pursued overly expansive policies. (*Sources:* Except for the 1982 estimate, the estimates of potential are from the *Economic Report of the President, 1979*, p. 75. The 1982 estimate is from the Congressional Budget Office, *The Outlook for Economic Recovery*, February 1983, p. 56, and is extended into the late 1980s by the authors.)

After all, there was no similar overestimate of potential GNP in the 1960s. In the 1970s, fundamental changes were occurring in the economy which misled the Council of Economic Advisers (CEA). The growth of potential was slowing down for reasons that are only imperfectly understood (Chapter 16).

The CEA summarized its experience in its *Annual Report, 1980* (p. 76): "Projecting potential GNP growth into the future is subject to large errors." But if potential GNP cannot be forecasted accurately, it is not very useful as a target at which to aim aggregate demand policy. Therefore the strategy of active aggregate demand management is thrown into question. (For other problems with policy targets, see Box 18-1.)

THE CASE FOR A MONETARY RULE

There are widespread doubts about how well discretionary demand-management policies have worked. However, discretionary policies cannot be judged in a vacuum. It is also necessary to compare them to the alternative suggested by monetarists—that the quantity of money be increased at a steady, moderate rate. There are several points in the monetarist case:

1. The desirable path of aggregate demand is one of steady, moderate growth, which will make possible the purchase of the growing output of the economy at approximately stable prices.

2. The best way to ensure a steady, moderate increase in aggregate demand is with a steady, moderate increase in the money stock. Velocity is, of course, not perfectly constant, and therefore even a perfectly stable growth of money would not lead to a perfectly stable growth in demand. But, say the advocates of a monetary rule, the amount of instability would be less than the instability caused by discretionary policies. Furthermore, a rule specifying a slow growth of the money stock would avoid the strong inflationary tendencies that have resulted from discretionary policies during the past quarter century. That is, monetarists have two objectives: to reduce the *instability* of aggregate demand and to avoid an inflationary *trend* in demand.

3. Some proponents of a policy rule base their case on political as well as economic considerations. They believe that a policy rule will result in less interference by government in the free enterprise system. Several decades ago, Henry C. Simons of the University of Chicago made rules a cornerstone of his *Economic Policy for a Free Society:*

> In a free enterprise system we obviously need highly definite and stable rules of the game, especially as to money. The monetary rules must be compatible with the reasonably smooth working of the system. Once established, however, they should work mechanically, with the chips falling where they may. To put our present problem as a paradox—we need to design and establish with the greatest intelligence a monetary system good enough so that, hereafter, we may hold to it unrationally—on faith—as a religion, if you please.[3]

THE CASE AGAINST A MONETARY RULE

On behalf of discretionary policy making, we will examine three major criticisms of a fixed monetary rule: (1) In practice, there cannot be a rigid rule that is followed regardless of the consequences. (2) The proponents of a monetary rule generally aim for a slow rate of increase in aggregate demand, in order to ensure price stability. The critics argue that, in practice, the result may be an unnecessarily high rate of unemployment. That is, the *trend* of demand may be too low if the monetarist proposal is followed. (3) Even though there is much to be said for a stable rate of growth of aggregate demand, a monetary policy rule will not provide it. Velocity is not stable. In other words, there are substantial nonmonetary sources of disturbance in the economy. Policies should be changed from time to time to combat these disturbances and smooth out aggregate demand. (One major nonmonetary cause of instability is presented in the appendix.)

Let us consider each of these three points in detail.

1. CAN THERE BE A RIGID RULE?

Monetarists have traditionally argued for a policy rule that should be followed regardless of current conditions. In Simons' view, it should be followed regardless of how the chips fall. However, this rigid position can scarcely be taken literally. After all, evidence regarding economic institutions and economic behavior should be taken into account in establishing any rule; not to do so would be foolish. Yet these institutions and patterns of behavior change. When they do, any rule based on them should be reconsidered—not held steadfastly, like a religion. There used to be a monetary "religion" based on the gold standard. However, it contributed to the disaster of the 1930s. As Simons himself observed, "The utter inadequacy of the old gold standard, either as a definite system of rules or as the basis of a monetary religion, seems beyond intelligent dispute."[4] But that is exactly the point—the evidence indicated that the gold standard was a bad rule. Rules should not be maintained regard-

---

[3]Henry C. Simons, *Economic Policy for a Free Society* (Chicago: University of Chicago Press, 1948), p. 169.

[4]Ibid., p. 169.

BOX 18–1   *The Problem of Goals: Is There a Political Business Cycle?*

In previous chapters, we have seen how the economy can be destabilized when policymakers pursue what seem to be plausible goals. To sum up thus far:

■   Chapter 10 explained how policymakers can fall into a trap and destabilize the economy if they attempt to balance the budget every year.

■   Chapter 13 explained how policymakers can similarly fall into a trap if they attempt to stabilize interest rates.

■   This chapter has explained the problems that can arise if policymakers aim at an unattainable estimate of potential GNP.

However, these are not the only cases in which the pursuit of certain goals can lead to economic instability. Most notably, government expenditures during wartime are generally so high that they cause rapid inflation. Inflation in such circumstances does not necessarily mean that the government is making a mistake, however. The inflation of the 1940s was not too high a price to pay for the defeat of Hitler.

A "POLITICAL" BUSINESS CYCLE?

Another objective of policymakers—namely, the desire to get reelected—may also contribute to economic instability. Officeholders want the voters in a mellow mood when they enter the polling booths; the economy is an important determinant of voting behavior. Unemployment was a major factor in Herbert Hoover's defeat, and inflation was instrumental in Jimmy Carter's. Moreover, the evidence suggests that the recent *trend* of the economy is more important than its *position*. Consider, for example, Roosevelt's landslide victory in 1936. The economy was still in miserable shape, with the unemployment rate averaging 16.9%. Nevertheless, unemployment was down from the 24.9% of 1933. Things were improving; Roosevelt offered hope.

Because recent developments in the economy can be important to voters, a rather cynical strategy may be used by a president who wants to maximize the chances of reelection. The political game is not simply to create sustained prosperity. Even though times will be good, they will not be noticeably improving, and there is a danger that extended prosperity will eventually push the rate of inflation upward. In its crudest form, the game is to have an election in an early recovery—one to two years after a trough—when everything will be going well. The unemployment rate will be falling, while inflationary forces will not yet have had time to gather momentum. But, of course, an early recovery requires a preceding recession. Thus, in the words of Yale's Raymond Fair, a vote-maximizing strategy "requires that the economy be first brought into a recession. From the recession trough, the policy is then to stimulate the economy strongly until election day." [†]

The evidence is inconclusive as to whether such a strategy is actually followed. Sometimes the economy is in an early recovery during an election year; sometimes it is not. Three historical cases are particularly interesting.

---

less of the evidence, regardless of how the chips fall.

As MIT's Paul Samuelson has observed, a set of rules is "set up by discretion, is abandoned by discretion, and is interfered with by discretion."[5] Monetary rules do not exist in a vacuum. They involve questions of alternatives, of evidence, of analysis—not of theology.

2. WOULD AGGREGATE DEMAND BE INSUFFICIENT?

Monetarists generally propose a rule designed to prevent aggregate demand from increasing more rapidly than the productive capacity of the economy. If successful, the rule would result in long-run price stability.

Critics of a monetary rule fear that monetarists would keep the trend of aggregate demand too low, creating extended periods of high unemployment. Monetarists believe that this danger is not very severe because the economy has a strong tendency to return to equilibrium on the vertical long-run Phillips curve. Furthermore, monetarists be-

[5]"Principles and Rules in Modern Fiscal Policy," *Collected Papers of Paul A. Samuelson* (Cambridge, Mass.: MIT Press, 1966), vol. 2, p. 1278.

The first was the four-year term of President Nixon, from 1969 to 1972. In the first year of his administration, monetary policy was adjusted in a restrictive direction, while fiscal restraint continued. As a result, a recession began late in 1969, with recovery starting about a year later. In 1971–1972, policies were expansive. By the election year, the recovery was proceeding nicely. There were widespread rumors that the White House was pressuring the Fed to keep monetary conditions easy. However, even though the events fit the vote-maximizing strategy, we cannot be sure that policies were in fact motivated by a desire to maximize votes. There were other plausible explanations. As we have seen earlier in this chapter, GNP was still substantially below existing estimates of potential in 1971–1972. It is possible that this shortfall below the estimated potential, and not the desire to maximize votes, was the reason for the expansive policies of those years.

The second case was the presidency of Jimmy Carter, from 1977 to 1980, when policy was almost exactly the opposite of the vote-maximizing strategy. Early in his administration, stimulative steps were taken. Then, as the expansion increasingly put upward pressures on prices, policy was moved in a restrictive direction in 1979, leading to a recession in the election year 1980. Carter's experience may be taken as a political lesson in what not to do. In the last year of his administration, the economy was suffering from double-digit inflation and rising unemployment. He became the first elected president since Hoover to be defeated in a bid for reelection.

The third case was the first Reagan administration, when events were consistent with a vote-maximizing strategy. There was an early recession in 1981–1982, followed by a strong expansion in the two years preceding the 1984 election. As we read the evidence, however, the recession was not the result of a vote-maximizing strategy. It seems to have come as a genuine surprise to the president.

Finally, it is too early to judge the Bush administration. In his first few months in office, however, President Bush seemed to be following Jimmy Carter's approach rather than the more successful Nixon-Reagan pattern. Like Carter, the early emphasis of Bush was on a relatively expansive policy. He became involved in a mild disagreement with the Federal Reserve, suggesting that the Fed's policies were too restrictive. His support of expansive policies may have been dictated by his difficult budgetary problem. He was struggling with the intractable problem of bringing down government deficits. Tight monetary policies, with their higher interest rates in the short run, would increase government interest expenditures and thus make the short-run deficits larger.

To the question of whether a political business cycle exists, the most we can say is, "perhaps." Sometimes presidents follow a policy designed to put the economy in an early recovery during election year; sometimes they do not.

[†]Raymond Fair, "Growth Rates Predict November Winners," *New York Times*, January 25, 1976. See also Thomas Havrilesky, "Electoral Cycles in Economic Policy," *Challenge*, July-August 1988, pp. 14–21.

lieve that an active policy is worse: Policymakers will take the path of least resistance, creating too much demand and persistent inflation.

3. WOULD A MONETARY RULE MAKE THE GROWTH OF AGGREGATE DEMAND MORE STABLE?

The case for a monetary rule is based in part on the view that velocity is reasonably stable. As noted in Chapter 17, velocity in the 1980s has departed substantially from its historical trend, thus weakening the case for a firm monetary rule.

However, the debate over a "rule versus discretion" cannot be settled simply by looking at one of the options. The issue is not whether a monetary rule would work well in some absolute sense. The question is, which works *better*: a discretionary policy *or* a monetary rule? To rephrase the question: do discretionary policies on average stabilize or destabilize the economy, when compared to a rule? Both sides in the debate find some support in the actual behavior of the money stock, shown in Figure 18-6.

Those who favor rules point particularly to the fall in the growth rate of the money stock that has preceded or accompanied every recent recession. In fact, since 1907—the first year for which monthly

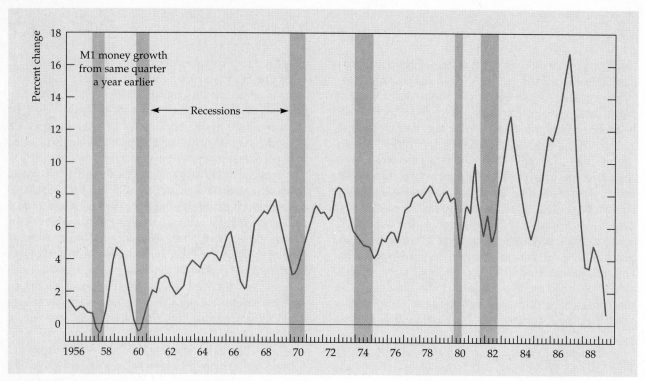

FIGURE 18-6   Money and the business cycle.

Monetarists point out that the rate of growth of the money stock slows down before and during recessions. Presumably, recessions would be less severe if the rate of growth of the money stock were more stable.

money stock data are available—there has never been a recession when the rate of growth of the money stock (M1) was rising. Presumably, recessions would have been less severe if the rate of growth of money had been more stable. Milton Friedman, the most prominent monetarist, is blunt in his condemnation of the Federal Reserve: "No major institution in the United States has so poor a record of performance over so long a period yet so high a public reputation."[6]

Those who favor discretionary policies point to the years since 1982. The money stock has grown rapidly. In fact, M1 grew more rapidly between 1982 and 1986 than between 1967 and 1978, when high and rising money growth was roundly criti-

cized as the cause of accelerating inflation. Yet in the 1980s, the unprecedented increase in the quantity of M1 was accompanied by a decline in velocity; it did not cause an inflationary explosion. Since 1982, the rate of inflation has been quite stable, at about 4% per year. If the Federal Reserve had adhered rigidly to a monetary rule and held the increase in money to a low, stable rate, there would have been a drag on aggregate demand. This would have slowed the expansion out of the deep recession of 1982. Thus, say the proponents of discretionary policy, the Federal Reserve should be applauded for its 1982 decision to permit a more rapid growth of the money stock. This decision contributed to the long expansion of the 1980s.

Some of those in the monetarist tradition agree. In the face of the instability of velocity in the 1980s, some now agree that discretionary changes in poli-

___

[6]Milton Friedman, "The Case for Overhauling the Federal Reserve," *Challenge,* July-August 1985, p. 5.

cy are desirable. Specifically, the Fed should be prepared to increase the rate of growth of money M when velocity V is declining, or decrease the rate of growth of M when V is increasing, in order to stabilize overall spending ($M \times V$).

In the late 1960s and 1970s, as evidence of the power of monetary policy grew, Keynesian economists retreated from the view that fiscal policy is much more important than monetary policy. In the 1980s, as evidence of unstable velocity accumulated, some monetarists retreated from the idea of a firm rule (while still emphasizing the importance of money as a determinant of aggregate demand). Thus there has been a tendency over the years for economists to move toward the center, and away from the more extreme Keynesian and monetarist viewpoints.

THE OUTCOME OF THE DEBATE

Advocates of a rigid monetary rule remain in the distinct minority; because of the instability of velocity in the past decade, their influence has waned. Nevertheless, the debate over "rules versus discretion" has had important, lasting consequences:

■ There has been increased awareness that demand management itself may be a cause of economic instability. Overly ambitious demand management may cause accelerating inflation. Furthermore, substantial lags may result in actions that are too late and add to the magnitude of cyclical swings.

■ There is more widespread recognition of the long-term consequences of policies. In particular, the long lag between a change in aggregate demand and a change in inflation means that anti-inflation policies should be made with the long run in mind.

Since 1975—and particularly between 1979 and 1982—the Federal Reserve has used monetary targets in its decision-making process. However, targets for monetary growth are quite different from a monetary rule in two important ways:

1. The Federal Reserve from time to time "rebases" its targets—that is, it picks a new starting point for measuring monetary growth. When a new starting point is picked, the Fed escapes the discipline of a monetary rule.

2. The Fed has from time to time targeted a number of different measures of the money stock (both M1 and M2, plus some others). Switching from one target to another is another way the Fed can avoid being bound by a rigid monetary rule.

WHICH TARGET?

In using a monetary rule or monetary target, the objective is to achieve a steady rate of growth in aggregate demand and in nominal GNP. But if a steady growth in nominal GNP is the objective, why not target it directly? Specifically, why not tighten policy whenever nominal GNP grows at a rate of more than, say, 5%; why not switch to a more expansive policy whenever nominal GNP grows more slowly?

The answer lies in lags. A change in monetary or fiscal policy today will have its major effect some months in the future. If the Federal Reserve targets nominal GNP, it risks overreactions and may end up following the zigzag path of the anxious helmsman. In other words, the case for a monetary target depends on a basic idea: a monetary target will result in a more stable growth of nominal GNP than would a direct targeting of nominal GNP.

For the idea of a monetary target to be valid, there must be a stable relationship between the targeted item—such as M1—and nominal GNP. More precisely, the lags mean that *there must be a stable relationship between the targeted item today and nominal GNP at some time* (perhaps 6 to 12 months) *in the future.* This suggests an answer to the question: What should be targeted? The target should be the item with the most stable relationship to nominal GNP.

Because of the instability of the velocity of M1 in the 1980s, M1 has lost favor; the Fed no longer uses M1 as a target. It is not clear that a targeting of M1 is superior to a direct targeting of nominal GNP itself. M2 is the most obvious alternative target, but the velocity of M2 has been quite unstable, too. As a result, an old search has been renewed: Can some other magnitude be found with a more stable relationship to GNP—such as a broader definition of money (M3), or an even broader concept such as liquid assets or total debt?

In 1983, Frank Morris, president of the Federal Reserve Bank of Boston, suggested that the answer was yes. Instead of M1 and M2, he recommended that the Federal Open Market Committee target liquid assets (L) and total debt (D). He was particularly impressed by the historical stability of the relationship between debt (D) and GNP. But he had scarcely made this suggestion when the close relationship broke down. Debt began to increase much faster than GNP, in part because of a rash of corporate takeovers financed with newly issued bonds. This raises a fundamental problem in *any* monetary rule or monetary targeting: There is no assurance that a close relationship of the past will continue into the future.[7]

Table 18-1 summarizes the main points of difference between economists in the Keynesian and classical traditions, as explained in Chapters 8, 17, and 18.

FORECASTING 预测

Because of lags, policies adopted today will not have their full effect until some months in the future. As a result, the Fed and fiscal policymakers have *no alternative but to forecast*. The question is not *whether* to forecast but *how*. Anyone who thinks that forecasting can be avoided is, in fact, forecasting in a naive way. By implying that policy be designed for the needs of the moment, such a person is making the simple forecast that the problems of the future will be the same as those of today. Even the proponents of a monetary rule are forecasting in a sense. Their case is based on the forecast that velocity will be stable in the future.

FORECASTING WITH A MODEL

In developing a forecast for the coming months, economists in and out of government use computer-based statistical—or *econometric*—models of the economy. Typically, forecasters estimate future consumption, investment, government expenditures, and net exports. The relationship between consumption and disposable income is estimated from past experience. The path of investment is forecast

on the basis of current and expected future interest rates and other important influences. The president's budget and spending authorizations by Congress are used to estimate the probable course of government spending. Exports are estimated on the basis of expected economic activity abroad; the more prosperous foreign economies are, the more likely they are to buy our exports.

A simple example will give a general idea of how a forecast is made. We begin by repeating the fundamental GNP equation:

$$GNP = C + I + G + X - M \qquad (18\text{-}1)$$

Suppose that two-thirds of GNP goes to consumers in the form of disposable income. (The rest goes to taxes, etc.) Suppose, also, that statistical evidence indicates that consumers in the past have spent 90% of their disposable income. That means that consumption is 60% of GNP (that is, 90% × 2/3). Formally:

$$C = 0.6 \, GNP \qquad (18\text{-}2)$$

Suppose that businesses are expected to invest $600 billion in the coming period:

$$I = \$600 \qquad (18\text{-}3)$$

The budgets of the federal, state, and local governments commit them to $800 billion in purchases of goods and services:

$$G = \$800 \qquad (18\text{-}4)$$

Exports are expected to be $400 billion:

$$X = \$400 \qquad (18\text{-}5)$$

Finally, past information indicates that imports are about 10% of GNP:

$$M = 0.1 \, GNP \qquad (18\text{-}6)$$

Substituting the last five equations into Equation (18-1), we can solve:

$$GNP = 0.6GNP + \$600 + \$800 + \$400 - 0.1GNP$$

$$GNP = 0.5GNP + \$1,800$$

That is:

$$GNP = \$3,600 \qquad (18\text{-}7)$$

We thus forecast GNP to be $3,600 billion.

In practice, of course, economists use substantially more complicated equations. For example, consumption expenditures depend not only on

---

[7]Frank E. Morris, "Monetarism Without Money," *New England Economic Review,* March 1983, and "Rules Plus Discretion in Monetary Policy," *NEER,* September 1985.

TABLE 18-1 Monetarist and Keynesian Views: A Contrast

Issue	Monetarist/Classical View	Keynesian View
Nature of market economy (Ch. 8)	Quite stable, *if* quantity of money *M* is stable	Market economy contains major flaws: 1. Quite unstable 2. May reach equilibrium with large-scale unemployment
Nature of equilibrium (Ch. 8, 9)	Only at full employment	Perhaps at full employment, perhaps with large-scale unemployment
Aggregate supply (Ch. 8, 13)	Vertical in long run, sloped in short run (long- and short-run Phillips curves)	Simple version: Reversed *L* (prices downwardly rigid) (More complex version: Fig. 8-5b)
If aggregate demand is less than aggregate supply (Ch. 8, 13)	Prices sticky in short run; will adjust in long run	Prices are rigid in downward direction; depression will persist until demand recovers
Key to changes in aggregate demand (Ch. 8, 17)	Changes in quantity of money *M*	Fluctuations in investment demand *I**
Cause of Great Depression (Ch. 8)	Collapse in aggregate demand, caused by collapse of money stock *M*	Collapse in aggregate demand, caused by collapse of investment demand *I**
Key macroeconomic equation	$MV = PQ$ (Ch. 17)	Aggregate Expenditures $= C + I^* + G + X - M$ (Ch. 8, 9, 10)
Best tool to control aggregate demand	Monetary policy (Ch. 17)	Fiscal policy, especially changes in government spending *G* (Ch. 10, 17)
Best policy (Ch. 10, 17, 18)	Monetary rule	Discretionary fiscal policy, to make aggregate demand: 1. high enough 2. more stable
If people have surplus holdings of money, they will: (Ch. 17)	Spend it	Buy bonds or hoard money
Responsiveness of investment to changes in interest rate (Ch. 17)	Very strong (therefore, crowding out is strong, and fiscal policy is weak)	Very weak (and therefore monetary policy and crowding out are both weak)

consumers' disposable income, but also on their wealth (such as bonds). When forecasting, economists pay particular attention to the time element—for example, *how quickly* does consumption respond to changing levels of disposable income? Taking these two complications into account, we get a more sophisticated consumption function:

$$C_t = 0.5DI_t + 0.2DI_{t-1} + 0.05W_t \qquad (18\text{-}8)$$

where:

> DI stands for disposable income,
>
> W stands for wealth, and
>
> > the subscripts stand for time periods; specifically, $t - 1$ is the quarter before t.

In plain English, Equation (18-8) says that consumption expenditures in any quarter (C_t) depend on disposable income in that quarter (DI_t) and in the previous quarter (DI_{t-1}), and also on wealth in that quarter (W_t).

Although Equation (18-8) is still relatively simple, it is beginning to resemble the consumption function used in actual econometric models. The appendix to this chapter will introduce some of the basic ideas used to explain investment in such models.

Well-known econometric models of the economy include the MPS model (of the Massachusetts Institute of Technology, the University of Pennsylvania, and the Social Science Research Council), the model of Data Resources, Inc. (DRI), and Lawrence Klein's model at the University of Pennsylvania's Wharton School, to name a few.

These models provide a useful starting point for forecasts, and are particularly helpful in cross-checking the various components of GNP (consumption, investment, government spending, and net exports) to make sure that the estimates are consistent. However, models have a major limitation. Essentially, they project the future on the basis of relationships that have held in the past but that may change. The future of the economy depends on many forces, some of which are not easy to incorporate into formal econometric models. Thus forecasters generally adjust the initial results of their econometric models to allow for additional factors that they consider important. The final result is a "judgmental" forecast—using the results of models but with modifications.

In adjusting the raw output of econometric models, forecasters use the results of various surveys of future intentions—for example, Commerce Department questionnaires regarding investment intentions; Conference Board surveys of capital appropriations by businesses; and surveys of consumer attitudes, including those done by the Survey Research Center at the University of Michigan.

TURNING POINTS

One of the hardest problems in forecasting is to tell when a turning point will take place—when an expansion will reach a peak and a decline will begin, or when a recession will hit the trough and a recovery begin. One of the weakest features of econometric models is that they do not forecast turning points very accurately. But turning points are *very* important. If an upswing will end and a recession begin in the next several months, now is the time to consider more expansive policies.

What is needed, then, is something that will signal a coming turn. The search for **leading indicators** has been centered in the National Bureau of Economic Research. A number of leading indicators have been identified; they include such items as common stock prices, new orders for durable goods, and the average number of hours worked per week. An index of **leading indicators** is published monthly by the Department of Commerce in *Business Conditions Digest*.

A *leading indicator* is an economic variable that reaches a turning point (peak or trough) before the economy as a whole changes direction. (New orders for durable goods are an example.)

As Figure 18-7 shows, leading indicators have been helpful: They have predicted every recession since 1948. However, even when they correctly signal a future recession, they don't tell *when* it will occur; they don't provide the same period of advance warning each time. Note that the leading indicators provided a 23-month warning of the 1957 recession but only a 3-month warning of the very severe recession of 1981–1982. Worse still, they sometimes send false signals, indicating a recession even though the economy in fact continues to

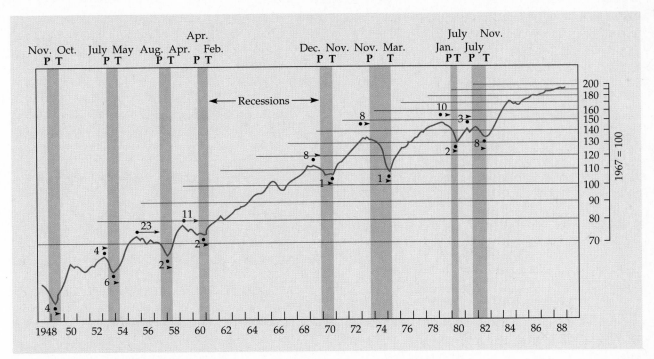

FIGURE 18-7   Index of leading indicators.

The curve shows the behavior of the leading indicators. The *P* and *T* notation along the top dates the peaks and troughs of the economy; the recessions in between are shaded. A signal from the leading indicators usually means a coming turn—but not always. For example, the indicators turned down in early 1984, but no recession occurred. The numbers specify the amount of time by which the indicators preceded the turning points. Sometimes there is a long warning: 23 months elapsed between the time when the indicators turned down in 1955 and when the economy began to decline in 1957. In 1981, however, the indicators gave only 3 months warning of a very severe recession. (*Source:* U. S. Department of Commerce, *Business Conditions Digest.*)

expand. For example, there was no recession following the downturn in the indicators in 1966 and 1984 (although the expansion did slow down in each case). The false signals have led to a common quip: Leading indicators have signaled seven of the last five recessions.

THE PROOF OF THE PUDDING

Figure 18-8 gives the results of five well-known forecasts, one government and four private. The green lines show how much GNP was expected to change over a period of one year, according to the *median* forecast (the middle of the five forecasts). The black lines show the actual changes over the

year. The difference between the two is thus the amount by which forecasters missed the mark.

An inspection of Figure 18-8 indicates that there is a tendency for actual changes in GNP and predicted changes to move together. Thus it is much better to use the median forecast than to rely on a simple procedure, such as extrapolating from recent trends or assuming that the increase over the next year will be the same as the average increase for the past few years. This conclusion is reassuring. Businesses and governments pay substantial amounts for forecasts. They are not wasting their money.

Less reassuring, however, is the record of forecasters during the three recessions of 1973–1975,

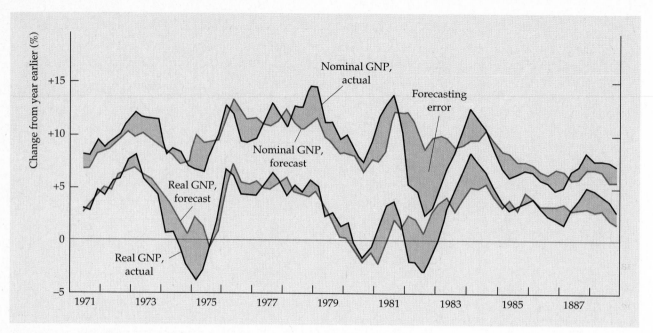

FIGURE 18-8   The forecasting record.

Most of the time, forecasts are reasonably accurate. The biggest errors occur during recessions. Note in particular how forecasters underestimated the fall in real GNP during the recessions of 1973–1975 and 1981–1982.

(The dates on the horizontal axis show the *end* of the year-long forecasting period. For example, the forecast for real GNP for the first quarter of 1982 is shown as +2.2%. This means that, in the first quarter of 1981, forecasters predicted a 2.2% increase for the coming year. The actual change for the year was -2.0%.) *Source:* Stephen K. McNees, "Which Forecast Should You Use?" *New England Economic Review,* July 1985, p. 37. Update provided by Mr. McNees.

1980, and 1981–1982. In only one of these cases (1980) did they anticipate the strength of the downturn in real GNP. During the recession of 1973–1975, the record of forecasters was mixed. Although they anticipated the weakening of the economy in late 1973, they greatly underestimated how much real GNP would fall. They also underestimated how long the recession would last, forecasting a rebound by early 1975. The worst record came in 1981–1982, when forecasters failed to anticipate the worst recession of recent decades.

Forecasting was particularly difficult during 1981–1982 because fiscal policy was moving sharply in an expansive direction, while monetary restraint was being exercised. When monetary policy is pushed in one direction, and fiscal policy in another, the path of the economy becomes particularly uncertain. Howard Baker, who was the Republican leader in the Senate, was right on the money when he referred to the large tax cuts enacted in 1981 as a "riverboat gamble."

It is worrisome that forecasters are not able to do a better job of anticipating recessions, because this is their most important task. If discretionary policies are to be successful, it is particularly important that policy be moved in an expansive direction as the economy is approaching a recession.

KEY POINTS

1. The mediocre record of monetary and fiscal policies in recent decades has enlivened an old debate: Should aggregate demand policies be actively adjusted in the quest for high employment and stable prices? Or should a monetary rule be followed?

2. The activist Keynesian approach involves several steps. First, the full-employment or potential path of GNP is estimated. Second, if actual GNP is significantly below potential GNP, aggregate demand should be expanded until the potential path is approached. Thereafter, fiscal and monetary policies should be adjusted as needed to combat fluctuations.

3. This strategy was followed with success during the first half of the 1960s. However, aggregate demand became too high and inflation accelerated in the last half of the decade.

4. The existence of time lags makes it difficult to design countercyclical policies. Actions taken today may not be appropriate to the economy of tomorrow, when they will have their major effect.

5. There are *three lags* between the time when aggregate demand should be changed and the time when the change actually occurs. The *recognition lag* is the interval before changes in economic conditions are recognized. The *action lag* is the interval between the time when a problem is recognized and the time when fiscal and monetary policies are adjusted. The *impact lag* is the interval between the time when policies are changed and the time when aggregate demand responds. Because of lags, policies implemented today will have their effects in the future, when they may be too late.

6. There is also another important lag. When aggregate demand changes, the effects on inflation lag behind the effects on output. That is, when aggregate demand increases, output generally responds quickly, with inflation increasing only after a lag. When aggregate demand falls, output generally falls quickly, with the economy sliding into a recession. Inflation begins to decelerate only after a lag.

7. Many monetarists believe that discretionary policies are likely to do more harm than good. They recommend a **policy rule**—that the money stock be increased by a fixed percentage, year after year, regardless of current economic conditions. They believe that discretionary adjustments in aggregate demand policies are likely to do more harm than good because:

(a) There are lags before aggregate demand can be adjusted, and between changes in demand and the effect on prices.

(b) People tend to be overly optimistic in estimating the potential path of real GNP (Fig. 18-5).

(c) Because of the lags and overoptimism, expansive policies are generally continued too long. Then, when inflation becomes a clear and present danger, policymakers generally overreact, causing a fall in aggregate demand and a recession. However, inflation does not respond quickly to the lower aggregate demand. The restrictive policies are therefore deemed a failure, and another round of expansive policies is begun. Consequently, discretionary policies are likely to cause instability and an inflationary bias in the economy. Recovery generally begins with a higher rate of inflation than in the previous recovery.

(d) A policy rule will result in less interference by the government, and therefore in more economic freedom.

8. The economy can be destabilized when policymakers pursue what seem to be plausible goals. A number of examples have been provided:

(a) Chapter 10 explained how policymakers can fall into a trap and destabilize the economy if they attempt to balance the budget every year.

(b) Chapter 12 explained how policymakers can similarly fall into a trap if they attempt to stabilize interest rates.

(c) This chapter has explained the problems that arise if policymakers aim at an unattainable estimate of potential GNP.

9. A number of arguments can be made against a monetary rule and in favor of discretionary policies:

(a) In practice, no government will follow a policy rule regardless of the short-run consequences (how the chips fall) and competing objectives (such as wartime finance).

(b) Rulemakers tend to propose a rule that will keep the trend of aggregate demand too low. An unnecessarily high rate of unemployment will be the result. [Compare this with Key Point 7(c), the monetarist view that activist policies will give the economy an inflationary bias.]

(c) A monetary rule does not ensure a stable increase in aggregate demand.

10. In spite of these counterarguments, important changes in attitudes have occurred as a consequence of the monetarist criticisms of fine tuning:

(a) The problem of lags is more clearly recognized.

(b) The importance of keeping long-term objectives in mind is more widely recognized.

11. Because policies have their major effect on aggregate demand some months in the future, a forecast of future conditions must be made—explicitly or implicitly—whenever policy is changed. To forecast, economists use econometric models, supplemented with survey data and "judgmental" adjustments. The experience of recent years suggests that it is very difficult to forecast recessions.

KEY CONCEPTS

policy activism	recognition lag	econometric model
discretionary policy	action lag	turning point
policy rule	impact lag	leading indicator
fine tuning	lag between changes in output	
GNP gap	and changes in inflation	

PROBLEMS

18-1. Explain the various steps in the activist Keynesian strategy.

18-2. If discretionary policies are followed, what are the consequences of overestimating the growth of potential GNP? Use the U.S. experience since 1970 in your answer.

18-3. What case can be made against a monetary policy rule?

18-4. Why do Samuelson and others argue that a policy rule is impossible?

18-5. In the section describing the possible overestimation of potential GNP, we observed that output and prices do not respond at the same rate to changes in aggregate demand. In such circumstances, why do the statistics sometimes give policymakers conflicting signals about the appropriate way to adjust aggregate demand? How do the conflicting signals add to the "recognition lag?"

18-6. Why must future economic conditions be forecast when monetary or fiscal policies are changed? If policymakers do not believe they are forecasting, why may we conclude that they are in fact using implicit forecasts? If someone argues for no change in monetary and fiscal policies, is he or she making any forecast about the future? Why is it particularly important to forecast turning points? Can you think of any reason why it is difficult to forecast turning points accurately?

THE ACCELERATOR
A Nonmonetary Explanation of Business Fluctuations

If business cycles were primarily the result of monetary disturbances, a smooth growth in the money stock would make the economy more stable. However, the stronger the nonmonetary disturbances, the less the economy can be smoothed by a monetary policy rule, and the stronger is the case for discretionary policies to offset the disturbances.

Separating monetary from nonmonetary disturbances is not a simple matter. "Nonmonetary" theories of business cycles generally focus on the investment sector of aggregate demand, since this is the most unstable. The theory of investment presented in this appendix will be nonmonetary in the sense that money is not an integral part of the theory. However, we cannot demonstrate that it is completely nonmonetary. In fact, we will see later that monetary issues are lurking in the background.

INVESTMENT DEMAND: THE SIMPLE ACCELERATOR

Suppose we put ourselves in the business executive's shoes. Why should we want to invest? Why, for example, should we want to acquire more machines?

The simplest answer is that businesses want more machines because they want to produce more goods. *The desired stock of capital depends on the amount of production.* This fundamental proposition lies behind the **acceleration principle,** illustrated in Table 18-2 and Figure 18-9. In the first two years of this example, a bicycle manufacturer sells 200,000 bicycles per year. Suppose that one machine is needed for every 10,000 bicycles produced.

Assume also that the manufacturer initially has the 20 machines needed to produce the 200,000 bicycles. As long as the demand for bicycles remains stable (as shown in Table 18-2, Phase I, years 1 and 2), there is no need for additional machines; there is no net investment.

That does not mean, however, that machine production is zero. Suppose that a machine lasts for 10 years, with 2 of the original 20 machines wearing out each year. As long as the demand for bicycles remains constant at 200,000 per year, gross investment will continue to be 2 machines per year. (That is, 2 machines will be purchased to replace the 2 that wear out each year.)

Now, suppose that the demand for bicycles starts to grow in Phase II. In the third year, sales increase by 10%, from 200,000 to 220,000. As a consequence, the manufacturer needs 22 machines; 2 additional machines must be acquired. Gross investment therefore rises to 4 machines—2 replacements plus 2 net additions. An increase in sales of only 10% has had an *accelerated* or magnified effect on investment. Gross investment has risen from 2 to 4 machines, or by no less than 100%. (This magnified effect on investment provides an important clue as to why investment fluctuates so much more than GNP.) Then in the fourth year, with the growth of sales remaining constant at 20,000 units, gross investment remains constant at 4 machines per year.

Next, see what happens in Phase III. In the fifth year, demand begins to level out. As growth slows to 10,000 bicycles, only one additional machine is needed. Both net and gross investment *decline* as a result of *slowing* of the growth of bicycle sales. We emphasize: *An actual decline in sales is not necessary*

TABLE 18-2 The Acceleration Principle

Time	(1) Yearly Sales of Bicycles (in thousands)	(2) Desired Number of Machines (column 1 ÷ 10,000)	(3) Net Investment (change in column 2)	(4) Gross Investment (column 3 + replacement of 2 machines)
Phase 1: Steady sales				
First year	200	20	0	2
Second year	200	20	0	2
Phase II: Rising sales				
Third year	220	22	2	4
Fourth year	240	24	2	4
Phase III: A leveling off				
Fifth year	250	25	1	3
Sixth year	250	25	0	2
Phase IV: Declining sales				
Seventh year	230	23	−2	0
Eighth year	210	21	−2	0
Phase V: A leveling off				
Ninth year	200	20	−1	1
Tenth year	200	20	0	2

to cause a decline in investment. (Sales did not decline in the fifth year; they merely grew more slowly than in the fourth year.) Then, when the demand for bicycles levels out in the sixth year, there is no longer a need for any additional machines; net investment drops to zero, and gross investment falls back to two. Then, if bicycle sales begin to decline in Phase IV (year 7), the number of machines which the manufacturer needs will decline; the machines that are wearing out will not be replaced. Net investment becomes negative, and gross investment can fall to zero.

This example of the acceleration principle (or *accelerator*) illustrates a number of important points:

1. Investment in machines fluctuates by a much greater percentage than output of the goods for which capital is used (bicycles).

2. Net investment depends on the *change* in the production of the goods for which capital is used.

3. Once output begins to rise, it must continue to grow by the same amount if investment is to remain constant. A reduction in the growth of output will cause a *decline* in investment (year 5). But a very rapid growth of sales may be unsustainable. Therefore a rapid upswing in economic activity contains the seeds of its own destruction. As the growth of consumption slows down, investment will fall.

4. It is possible for gross investment to collapse, even though there is only a mild decline in sales (year 7).

5. For investment to recover, it is not necessary for sales to rise. A smaller decline in sales is sufficient (year 9). Thus a decline in economic activity contains the seeds of recovery.

This illustration is simplified, but the validity of its major points may be shown in a few examples. If business slackens off and fewer goods are shipped, the amount of trucking declines. Consequently, the demand for new trucks will decline sharply. Or consider what happens when the birthrate declines. Construction of schools is cut back. (New schools are needed primarily to

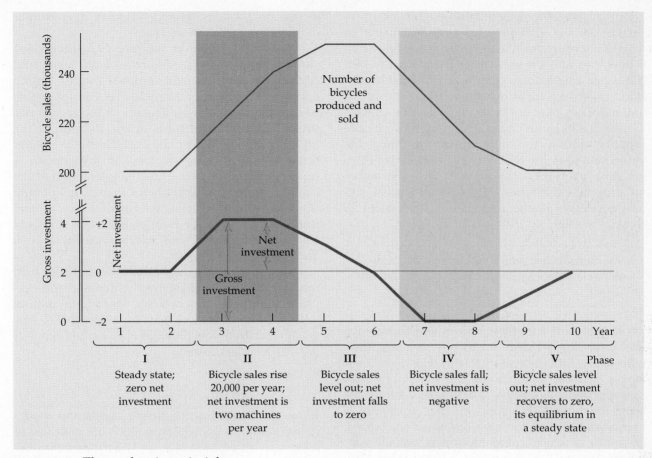

FIGURE 18-9   The acceleration principle.

accommodate an increase in the student population.) Note how the accelerator applies not only to machines, but also to other forms of investment such as school buildings and factories.

The accelerator can also apply to inventory investment, and this can add to the instability of the economy. Merchants may attempt to keep their inventories in proportion to sales. Thus, if sales increase by, say, 10%, orders to the factory may be increased by perhaps 20% in order to bring inventories into line with the higher sales. Nevertheless, inventory investment does not always act as a destabilizing force. There is no need for retailers to keep any rigid relationship between their sales and inventories. On the contrary, the effects of temporary spurts in sales may be cushioned by the existence of inventories: Retailers may meet the increased sales by running down their inventories.

MODIFICATION OF THE SIMPLE ACCELERATOR: LAGS IN INVESTMENT

Even in the case of a manufacturing operation, it is an oversimplification to assume that a rigid relationship exists between sales and the number of machines. In practice, the firm does not need exactly one machine for every 10,000 bicycles produced. Instead of acquiring new machines, a firm can run its factories overtime when demand increases. In this way, it can change its **capital/output ratio.** Furthermore, at the end of 10 years, an old machine does not suddenly disintegrate; it wears out gradually. During a boom, older machines can be kept in use beyond their normal retirement age.

What should businesses take into account in

deciding whether to buy new machinery or to "make do" by patching up old machinery or scheduling overtime? One important consideration is how long an increase in sales is expected to last. If it is just a temporary spurt and will quickly subside, expensive new machines should not be ordered. They may not be received quickly enough to meet the bulge in demand, and may add to idle capacity during the next downturn. Thus the immediate response to increases in sales may be to schedule overtime, and to wait and see before ordering new machines. As a result, there are significant delays in the response of investment to changes in sales.

The *capital/output ratio* is the value of capital (machines, factories, etc.) divided by the value of annual output.

In the short run, these delays add to stability. Businesses do not rush out to buy new machines with every little increase in sales. However, over longer periods, lags can add to the force of an upswing or a downswing. If high sales continue for some time, businesses conclude that prosperity is permanent. Orders for new machines are placed. Once this happens, competitors may become concerned. If they don't jump on the bandwagon, they may lose their place in a growing market. A boom psychology can develop. Although investment demand is initially slow to respond, it can gain momentum.

INTERACTIONS BETWEEN THE ACCELERATOR AND THE MULTIPLIER

Interactions between consumption and investment add to the momentum of the economy. As more machines are ordered, incomes rise in the machinery-producing industries. As incomes rise, people consume more. As they buy more consumer goods, business optimism is confirmed—the rising sales are "for real." As a consequence, orders for plant and equipment increase even more. Once again, the higher incomes resulting from higher investment stimulate consumption; the multiplier process makes the expansion stronger. Thus increases

in investment demand and increases in consumer demand reinforce one another.

Eventually, however, a strong expansion must slow down. Economic resources—land, labor, and capital—are limited, and national output cannot expand indefinitely at a rapid pace. Output begins to increase more slowly. Because of the accelerator principle, investment turns down. Because of the multiplier, national product declines by several times as much as the decrease in investment. A recession is under way. Thus the interaction of the accelerator and multiplier helps to explain not only (1) the *strength* of cycles, but also (2) *why turning points occur*—why, for example, a boom does not continue indefinitely, but instead reaches a peak and turns into a recession.

However, an expansion does not *inevitably* turn into a recession. If the increase in demand and output can be kept moderate and steady, the natural rebound into recession may be avoided. For this reason, *moderate growth can be more healthy and lasting than a business boom.*

THE DOWNSWING AND LOWER TURNING POINT

When the lessons of the simple accelerator model (listed earlier as points 1 through 5) are modified to take account of time lags and the interaction between the multiplier and accelerator, the following sequence occurs as a result of a reduction in the growth of sales:

1. In the short run of a few weeks or months, there is little if any decline in investment in plant and equipment. This is because investment in plant and equipment is cushioned from the effects of changing sales in a number of ways: (a) Inventories are temporarily allowed to increase, with the result that factory orders hold up better than final sales. (b) Overtime is reduced. (c) The opportunity is taken to retire machines that have been kept in service past their normal lifetimes.

2. If sales continue to be weak, business executives begin to fear the worst. Rather than accumulate higher and higher inventories, firms cut back sharply on their orders. As production falls, factories slash new orders for machines. (These are the effects of the accelerator.) Momentum is added to the downswing as laid-off workers reduce their consumption (the multiplier).

3. Consumption demand does not continue to decline indefinitely, however. While some purchases may easily be postponed, consumers try to maintain their expenditures for food and other necessities. Furthermore, as automobiles and other consumer durables wear out, consumers become increasingly anxious to replace them. As the decline in consumer spending moderates, investment in machinery and buildings begins to recover. (However, the recovery may be delayed by the desire of retailers, wholesalers, and manufacturers to work off excessive inventories.)

Each of these three stages is important, and each contains its own valuable lesson. These lessons are, respectively:

1. Investment is not volatile in the face of small and temporary reductions in the rate of growth of sales.

2. If sales remain weak for some time, investment falls. The downswing gathers momentum because of feedbacks between falling investment and falling consumer demand—that is, because of the interaction of the multiplier and the accelerator.

3. However, the downward movement does not continue forever. Even in the worst depressions, economic activity does not collapse toward zero. The accelerator process generates natural forces of recovery even before consumption bottoms out.

In deciding whether to invest, business executives compare the advantages of new machinery with the alternative of "making do" by scheduling overtime and keeping old machines in production. In this decision, a relevant consideration is the cost of new machines. There are two important costs: (1) the price of the machine itself; and (2) the price of the financing—that is, the interest rate. Here is an important place where money comes into the picture. For example, open market purchases can be used to push down interest rates, and thus lower the cost of acquiring new machines, buildings, and inventories. Thus the Federal Reserve can encourage the recovery from a recession. Similarly, open market sales (or less-than-normal purchases) and higher interest rates discourage investment, and thus can help prevent a healthy expansion from turning into an unhealthy boom.

KEY POINTS

12. Investment fluctuates more widely than other segments of GNP. The accelerator principle illustrates why. Investment depends on the change in output, and investment demand can change by a large percentage in the face of relatively small percentage changes in sales. The accelerator also helps to explain why turning points occur in the business cycle. Investment can fall even in a growing economy, if the *growth* of sales slows down. An actual decline in sales is not necessary. During a recession, investment can recover when sales decline at a slower rate. An actual upturn in sales is not necessary.

13. While the acceleration principle illustrates important forces that help to determine invest-

ment demand, it represents a simplification. In practice, there may be delays in the response of investment to changes in sales. These delays contribute to the stability of the economy in the face of small disturbances. However, they mean that, once an expansion or contraction gets going, it can gather momentum.

14. The interaction between the accelerator and the multiplier also adds to the momentum of an upswing or downswing. When investment demand falls, incomes and consumption demand also fall, causing a further decline in output (the multiplier). This decline in output in turn depresses investment (the accelerator).

PROBLEMS

18-7. Complete the table below illustrating the acceleration principle. Assume that one machine is needed to produce every 1,000 automobiles. Assume that a machine lasts 10 years. Assume also that one-tenth of the initial number of machines is scheduled for retirement in each of the next 10 years.

18-8. Suppose, alternatively, that there is a lag in investment. The number of machines desired in any year is calculated by taking the average number of autos produced in that year and the previous year. In other respects, follow the assumptions of Problem 18-7. Then recalculate the table in Problem 18-7. Does this change in assumption make investment demand more or less stable?

18-9. Suppose you are in business and demand for your product has recently increased. You now have to choose among (1) turning away some of your new customers, (2) scheduling overtime, (3) adding a new shift, or (4) expanding your factory and the number of your machines. Explain what you would take into account in choosing among these four options.

Year	(1) Yearly Sales of Autos	(2) Desired Number of Machines	(3) Net Investment	(4) Gross Investment
1	100,000	10	0	1
2	100,000	10	0	1
3	90,000	9	-1	0
4	80,000	8	-1	0
5	80,000	8	0	1
6	80,000	8	0	1
7	90,000	9	1	2
8	100,000	10	1	2
9	100,000	10	0	1

CHAPTER 19
FIXED OR FLEXIBLE EXCHANGE RATES?

As for foreign exchange, it is almost as romantic as young love, and quite as resistant to formulae.

H. L. MENCKEN

Economic efficiency requires specialization. It is efficient to grow wheat and corn in the Midwest, and to grow cotton in the South. The scope for specialization goes far beyond the boundaries of any single country. Even such a large nation as the United States can gain by international specialization. The United States exports products such as wheat, aircraft, and computers. In return, we import cameras, oil, and coffee.

Economic efficiency will be considered in detail in Part 8 of this book. We defer details of the way in which international specialization can contribute to a high standard of living to Chapter 33. In this chapter, we will study the monetary and macroeconomic aspects of international transactions. Specifically:

■ What complications are introduced into monetary and fiscal policies by international transactions?

■ What can be done to minimize international disturbances to the U.S. economy?

■ Why did the United States import so much more than it exported during the 1980s?

EXCHANGE RATES

In many ways, international trade is like domestic trade. It adds to economic efficiency because of comparative advantage and economies of scale. But two major complications make international transactions different from domestic trade:

1. International trade is complicated by *barriers* that do not exist in trade between states, provinces, or cities within the same country. For example, national governments discourage imports through *tariffs* (taxes on imports). Tariffs and other trade barriers will be studied in Chapter 34. Here, we concentrate on the second point.

2. With domestic trade, there is just one currency. For example, when a New Yorker purchases Florida oranges, the consumer pays in dollars, and that is the currency the seller wants. But international trade involves *two currencies*. Consider a British firm importing U.S. cotton. It has British pounds (£) to pay for the cotton. But the U.S. exporter wants to receive payment in dollars. Therefore the British importer will go to the **for-**

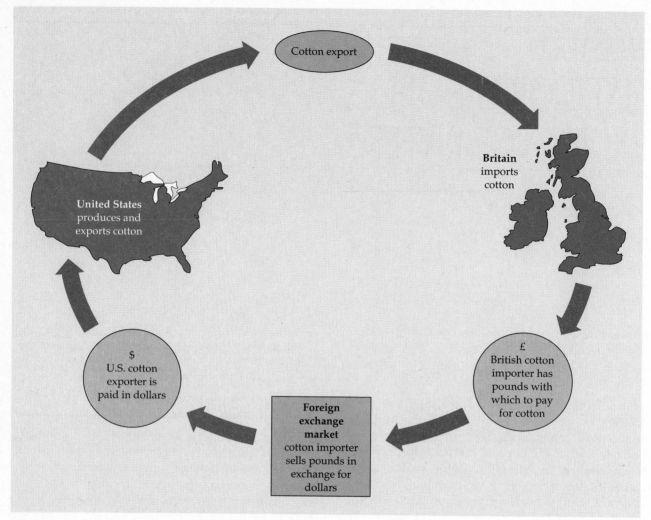

FIGURE 19-1   International trade and the foreign exchange market.

International trade normally involves more than one national currency. The British importer wants to pay in pounds, while the U.S. exporter wants to receive payment in dollars. Consequently, the British import results in a transaction on the foreign exchange market, with pounds being sold for dollars.

eign exchange market in order to sell pounds and buy the dollars needed to pay for the cotton, as illustrated in Figure 19-1. Foreign exchange markets are located in major financial centers, such as London and New York.

> *Foreign exchange* is the currency of another country. For example, British pounds or Japanese yen are foreign exchange to an American. U.S. dollars are foreign exchange to a Briton or German.

A *foreign exchange market* is a market in which one national currency (such as the U.S. dollar) is bought in exchange for another national currency (such as the British pound).

An *exchange rate* is the price of one national currency in terms of another national currency. For example, the price £1 = $1.60 is an exchange rate, and so is $1 = ¥130. (£ is the symbol for the British pound and ¥ the symbol for the Japanese yen.)

THE FOREIGN EXCHANGE MARKET

Like the market for wheat or oranges, the market for foreign exchange can be studied by looking at demand and supply. The demand for British pounds by those now holding dollars arises from three types of transactions:

1. *American imports of British goods.* In order to pay for British goods, an American importer buys the pounds which the British producer wants. This creates a demand for pounds.

2. *American imports of British services.* For example, an American tourist may stay in a British hotel and eat in a British restaurant. In order to pay the hotel or restaurant, the American first buys pounds with dollars. Thus the tourist creates a demand for pounds.

What is the difference between an import of a good and an import of a service? The good—such as a British car or British textiles—physically enters the United States, but a service does not. Obviously, the hotel room and the restaurant stay in London. In either case, however, Americans are buying from the British and thus creating a demand for pounds.

3. *American acquisitions of British assets.* For example, if an American corporation wants to invest in Britain by building a new factory, it will buy pounds to pay the British construction firm.

The quantity of pounds demanded, like the quantity of wheat demanded, depends on the price. Suppose that, instead of being worth, say, $2, the British pound had a lower price of $1. What would this mean? British goods and services would be less expensive to Americans. If the price of the pound were $2, a British hotel room costing £50 would cost an American $100. But if the price of the pound were $1, that same room would cost only $50 in U.S. money. As a result, American tourists would be more likely to go to Britain, and Americans would be more likely to buy British textiles or cars. Thus, when £1 costs $1, the quantity of pounds demanded is greater than when a pound costs $2, as illustrated by the demand curve (*D*) in Figure 19-2.

Observe in this example that the price which an American pays for a British hotel room depends on two things: (1) The British price of the room (£50

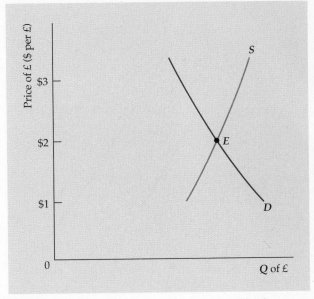

FIGURE 19-2 The demand and supply for British pounds.

The equilibrium exchange rate is determined by the intersection of demand and supply. The demand for pounds in terms of dollars depends on U.S. purchases of British goods, services, and assets. The supply of pounds depends on British purchases of U.S. goods, services, and assets.

in the example); and (2) the exchange rate between the pound and dollar.

Now consider the other side of the market, the supply of pounds to be exchanged for dollars. When British residents want to buy something from the United States, they pay for it in dollars. To acquire these dollars, they offer pounds; they create a supply of pounds in the exchange market. Thus the supply of pounds depends on:

1. British imports of U.S. goods.

2. British imports of U.S. services.

3. British acquisitions of U.S. assets; that is, British investment in the United States.

DISEQUILIBRIUM IN THE EXCHANGE MARKET

At the existing exchange rate, the quantity of pounds demanded may be exactly equal to the

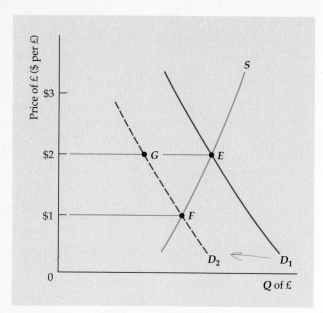

FIGURE 19-3   A shift in the demand for pounds.

If the demand for pounds shifts to the left from D_1 to D_2, there will be an excess supply of pounds (GE) at the old exchange rate. The British can eliminate this excess supply by one or a combination of the following steps: (1) The purchase of pounds in exchange for dollars by British authorities. (2) A change in the exchange rate to its new equilibrium, F. (3) Restrictions on imports and other international transactions. This will reduce the supply of pounds so that the supply curve shifts to the left to pass through point G. (4) Restrictive aggregate demand policies in Britain, which will also reduce the supply of pounds while increasing the demand.

quantity supplied. It is possible, for example, that at an existing exchange rate of £1 = $2, the demand and supply curves intersect, as shown at the initial equilibrium E in Figure 19-3.

However, we live in a changing world. Even if the market is initially in equilibrium, one or both curves may shift as time passes. Suppose that the demand for pounds decreases from D_1 to D_2. It might do so for a number of reasons; anything that decreases the U.S. demand for British products will cause a leftward shift of the demand for pounds. An example was the switch by Americans away from purchasing British cars to buying Japanese cars instead.

As a result of the shift in the demand curve, the initial $2 per pound is no longer an equilibrium price. In the face of this change, the British govern-

ment has the option of taking any one—or a combination—of the following steps:

1. *Intervene in the foreign exchange market.* The British government can keep the price of the pound at $2 by selling some of the U.S. dollars it owns to buy the excess supply of pounds, *GE*. In order to be able to influence exchange rates in this manner, governments and central banks hold **reserves** of foreign currencies.

2. *Impose direct restrictions on international transactions.* In order to maintain the price of £1 = $2, the British government may reduce the supply of pounds so that it shifts leftward and passes through point *G*. This can be accomplished by direct restrictions on international transactions. For example, the British government can increase tariffs and thus reduce British purchases of U.S. goods. Alternatively, it can limit the amount of U.S assets that British residents may acquire. In either case, the British will buy fewer dollars and therefore will supply fewer pounds.

3. *Adopt tighter aggregate demand policies.* The British government may *reduce the supply of pounds* more indirectly by adopting restrictive monetary and fiscal policies. Such policies will reduce British imports—and consequently the supply of pounds on the foreign exchange market—for two reasons. First, tighter policies will slow down British economic activity and reduce incomes. As a result, consumption will fall, including the consumption of imports. Second, the tighter policies will reduce British inflation. As British goods become more competitive in price, British consumers will switch away from imports and buy less expensive domestic goods instead.

In addition, as British goods become more competitive, British exports will increase and this will *increase the demand for pounds*, helping to shift it from D_2 back toward D_1. Finally, a tighter monetary policy in Britain will raise interest rates and therefore encourage Americans to buy British bonds. To do so, they will buy pounds, causing a further rightward shift in the demand curve for pounds.

4. *Allow the exchange rate to adjust.* The British government may allow the exchange rate to fall to the new equilibrium, *F*.

Since the end of the Second World War in 1945,

the central debate in international finance has been over the relative merits of these four options. But before studying recent developments, we will look at the historical gold standard, where reliance was placed on the third option. The idea underlying the gold standard was that exchange rates would be kept stable and international equilibrium would be maintained by changes in aggregate demand.

THE GOLD STANDARD

Prior to the First World War, and again briefly in the period between the two world wars, a number of countries adhered to the international gold standard. Gold coins circulated as part of the money supply, and paper currency was convertible into gold. The dollar was worth a fixed quantity of gold—approximately one-twentieth of an ounce. Similarly, the British pound was worth a fixed quantity of gold—about one quarter of an ounce.

As a result, exchange rates were stable. One British pound was worth about 5 times as much gold as the U.S. dollar—4.86 times as much, to be precise. Consequently, nobody would pay much more than $4.86 for a pound, or take much less. The exchange rate stayed close to £1 = $4.86.

THE ADJUSTMENT MECHANISM OF THE GOLD STANDARD

The international gold standard provided an automatic **mechanism of adjustment.** It worked to prevent a continuing flow of gold from one country to another. Here's how.

Suppose that Britain begins to import much more than it exports. Britain pays for the extra imports with gold; gold flows from Britain to the United States and other countries. The U.S. money stock automatically rises, since gold itself is money. Furthermore, gold flowing into U.S. banks adds to their reserves, since gold also is a bank reserve when countries adhere to the gold standard. With the additional reserves, banks can expand their loans, thereby causing a further increase in the money stock. With a rising money stock, aggregate demand increases in the United States. Prices are bid up.

On the other side, Britain's expenditures abroad exceed its receipts; it has a balance-of-payments **deficit.** It loses gold and its money stock automatically falls. Aggregate demand declines and so do prices. As British goods become cheaper compared with U.S. goods, British exports rise and imports fall. The British stop losing gold.

An *international adjustment mechanism* is a set of forces that operate to eliminate balance-of-payments deficits or surpluses. That is, an adjustment mechanism works to ensure that one country will not continuously lose—or gain—large amounts of gold or other reserves.

A country has a *deficit* in its balance of payments when its foreign expenditures exceed its foreign receipts.

A country has a balance-of-payments *surplus* when its foreign receipts exceed its foreign expenditures.

PROBLEMS WITH THE GOLD STANDARD

The international gold standard provided exchange-rate stability during much of the nineteenth century, when international trade and investment grew rapidly. But the gold standard had two major defects:

1. The process of adjustment could be very painful. For example, gold sometimes flowed out of a country that was already in a recession. The gold standard caused an automatic reduction in the money supply, further depressing aggregate demand and increasing unemployment. In other words, there sometimes was a **conflict** between (1) the *expansive* aggregate demand policies needed for domestic prosperity and (2) the *decrease* in the money stock required by the gold standard to drive down prices and strengthen the country's ability to compete on world markets.

From time to time, gold flows also made the domestic situation worse in the country receiving gold. This happened when there already were strong inflationary pressures. The automatic increase in the quantity of money made the inflation worse.

2. As we saw in Chapter 12, the gold standard could lead to very *unstable* monetary conditions. Under the fractional-reserve system of banking, a large quantity of money was built on a relatively small base of gold. The monetary system was therefore vulnerable to a crisis of confidence and a run on the gold stock. Such a crisis of confidence came during the Great Depression of the 1930s, and the gold standard collapsed. One country after another announced that it would no longer convert its currency into gold.

THE ADJUSTABLE PEG: THE IMF SYSTEM, 1945–1971

In 1944, toward the end of the Second World War, senior financial officials from the allied countries met at Bretton Woods, New Hampshire, and designed a new *adjustable peg* system of exchange rates. It also established two new institutions: the **International Monetary Fund** (IMF), to help make the new exchange-rate system work, and the **World Bank,** to provide financial assistance for postwar reconstruction and for economic development.

The adjustable peg system was designed to provide some of the exchange-rate stability of the old gold standard, while avoiding its major defects. Specifically, under the Bretton Woods system, exchange rates were to be kept stable within a narrow band (±1%) around an officially declared **par value.** For example, between 1949 and 1967, the pound was pegged at an official price or par value of £1 = $2.80.

Under the IMF system prior to 1971, the *par value* of a currency was the official price of the currency, specified in terms of the U.S. dollar or gold.

The founders of the IMF recognized that some provision would have to be made for international adjustment in the event of persistent deficits or surpluses in a nation's balance of payments. Recall from the discussion earlier in the chapter that a country has only four major ways to deal with a disturbance in the foreign exchange market. It may:

1. Keep the exchange rate stable by buying or selling its own currency in exchange for foreign currency.

2. Change tariffs or other restrictions on imports or other international transactions.

3. Change domestic aggregate demand policies in order to shift the demand and supply curves for foreign exchange.

4. Move to a new exchange rate.

The IMF system represented a compromise, with each of these steps playing a part. Increases in tariffs or other restrictions on imports (option 2) were considered undesirable, since they reduce international trade and make the world economy less efficient. However, they were permitted in emergencies, including the severely disrupted period after World War II. The main reliance was to be placed on the other three options.

Exchange market disturbances might be temporary, reflecting such things as strikes, bad weather that affects crops, or other transitory phenomena. In such circumstances, changes in exchange rates were considered undesirable. A swing in the price of the currency would be reversed in the future when the transitory events passed, and such changes in exchange rates would perform no useful function. Rather than allow exchange rates to move, countries should respond to temporary disturbances by buying or selling foreign currencies (option 1). Because temporary swings might be quite large, the IMF was empowered to lend foreign currencies to deficit countries in order to help them stabilize their currencies on the exchange markets. Thus "Fund" is an important part of the title of the IMF. The member countries of the IMF provided it with the funds to lend to deficit countries.

No country has unlimited quantities of foreign exchange, however, and there are limits to the amount the IMF is willing to lend. Therefore a country can intervene in the exchange market to support the price of its currency only as a temporary measure to deal with short-run disturbances. *Sales of foreign exchange cannot be a permanent solution to a continuing deficit.*

Some disturbances in the exchange market are not transitory; some shifts in the demand or supply curves for foreign exchange will not reverse themselves in the future. In such cases, more fundamental steps than exchange market intervention must be taken, such as changes in domestic aggregate demand (option 3). For example, if a country is following excessively expansive aggregate demand policies, the resulting inflation may price its goods out of world markets and cause balance-of-payments deficits. In such cases, there is no conflict between domestic and international objectives. A more restrictive aggregate demand policy is appropriate in order to restrain inflation at home as well as to improve the international payments position. The IMF can require a country seeking a loan to introduce such restraint in its monetary and fiscal policies.

However, an adjustment in domestic demand is not always a desirable way of dealing with a balance-of-payments problem. As we have seen in the discussion of the gold standard, a country with a balance-of-payments deficit might already be suffering from domestic recession. Restrictive aggregate demand policies to solve the balance-of-payments problem would make the recession worse.

In such circumstances, where the first three options had been ruled out or proved inadequate, the country was in a **fundamental disequilibrium,** and the Bretton Woods system approved the only remaining option: Change the exchange rate. For example, the British **devalued** the pound from £1 = $4.03 to a new par of £1 = $2.80 in 1949, and again lowered the par value to $2.40 in 1967. On the other side, the Germans **revalued** their currency (the Deutsche Mark, or DM) upward in 1961 and 1969.

A country *devalues* when it lowers the par value (the official price) of its currency.

A country *revalues* when it raises the par value of its currency.

In brief, exchange rates were *pegged but adjustable.*

THE IMF SYSTEM: THE PROBLEMS OF ADJUSTMENT AND CONFIDENCE

For several decades, the IMF system worked reasonably well—well enough to provide the financial framework for the recovery from the Second World War and for a very rapid expansion of international trade. But it contained major flaws that caused a breakdown in the early 1970s.

In practice, there were defects in the policy of changing the par value of a currency to deal with a fundamental disequilibrium. When a country begins to run a deficit or surplus, it is uncertain whether the deficit or surplus is only temporary—in which case it can be dealt with by selling or buying foreign currency rather than by changing the exchange rate—or whether it represents a fundamental disequilibrium—in which case a change in the par value is appropriate. The IMF agreement itself provided no help in this regard. At no place did it define a fundamental disequilibrium.

Since a fundamental disequilibrium involves a surplus or deficit that will persist, one simple test is to wait and see whether in fact it does persist. But waiting can be a nerve-wracking experience. In particular, deficits cause the loss of foreign exchange reserves. As reserves dwindle, **speculators** add to the problem. As soon as speculators become convinced that the deficits will continue—and that the British, say, may eventually be forced to devalue—they have an incentive to sell pounds. For example, if a speculator sells pounds when the price is $2.80 and the British do devalue the pound to $2.40, the speculator can buy the pounds back for $2.40, making a profit of 40¢ on each pound. Speculators may stampede into the market because the pound is such a fat target. Speculators win if the pound goes down. If the crisis passes without a devaluation, they don't win. But they don't lose much, either. (They lose only small amounts, such as the transactions costs.) In such circumstances, the speculator looks on the foreign exchange market as a great place to bet: Heads I win a lot; tails I lose only a little.

A *speculator* is anyone who buys or sells a foreign currency or any other asset in the hope of profiting from a change in its price.

Once people *lose confidence* that deficits can be controlled, speculators may thus add a flood of pounds for sale on the foreign exchange market. To keep the price of the pound from dropping, the British government has to buy these excess pounds, using its reserves of U.S. dollars to do so. Consequently, the entry of speculators into the market speeds up the loss of British foreign exchange reserves and puts further pressure on the government to devalue. Thus a case of **self-fulfilling expectations** may develop. The expectation by speculators that the pound will be devalued leads them to take an action (selling pounds) that increases the likelihood that the British government will, in fact, have to devalue.

In our example, speculators reap a windfall gain of 40¢ per pound when the British devalue. But this 40¢ represents a transfer from the British government, which loses exactly the same amount by fighting the speculators. (When speculators sold pounds before the devaluation, the British government bought these pounds at $2.80. After the devaluation, the government sells the pounds back to the speculators at $2.40, for a loss of 40¢.) Ultimately, the British taxpayer bears this loss.

Why, then, do the authorities fight speculation as it builds up? Why don't they devalue quickly? The answer is that they are still unsure whether a devaluation is really necessary. They hope to end speculation by restoring confidence that the pound will not be devalued.

To restore confidence, the leaders of the government firmly proclaim their determination to defend the pound. Even if they are almost sure that they will have to devalue the pound tomorrow, they must declare today that they will *not* do so. What choice do they have? If they admit that a devaluation is possible—or even if they refuse to comment—speculators will pour pounds into the market and reap even greater profits at the expense of the government when the devaluation does occur.

Once leaders have staked their reputations on the defense of the currency, it is very difficult for them to back down and change its par value. Therefore, in practice, devaluations were infrequent and long delayed under the IMF system. Once they came, they generally were large, so that the government would not have to go through the painful experience again in the near future. Thus the system of adjustable pegs did not work out as hoped. For long periods the system was one of *rigid* pegs as officials committed themselves firmly to the existing exchange rates. Exchange-rate changes were not playing a major role in the adjustment process, and imbalances in international payments built up. Then, when pressures became intolerable and changes had to be made, *jumping* pegs were

the result, with drastic changes being made in exchange rates.

When countries clung desperately to their existing par values, they were pushed back toward the old gold standard, using changes in aggregate demand as the way to adjust. The British, for example, engaged in a series of **stop-go** domestic policies, restricting aggregate demand when they were losing foreign exchange reserves and turning policies to "go" when their international position improved. Thus a strong destabilizing force was introduced into domestic economic policy.

THE BREAKDOWN OF THE ADJUSTABLE PEG SYSTEM, 1971–1973

Problems with the adjustable peg system came to a head in 1971. The U.S. government was concerned that imports were increasing rapidly because the value of the dollar was too high. Some American goods had been priced out of world markets. In August 1971, the United States introduced a major new policy aimed at encouraging more adjustment in exchange rates and designed, in particular, to lower the value of the dollar on exchange markets—that is, to raise the values of other currencies. A number of countries were uncertain how much to raise the values of their currencies, so they simply abandoned their fixed pegs and allowed their currencies to **float.**

A *floating* or *flexible* exchange rate is one that is allowed to change in response to changing demand or supply conditions.

If governments and central banks withdraw completely from the exchange markets, the exchange rate is *freely flexible*—that is, the float is *clean*. A float is *managed* or *dirty* if a nation's government or central bank intervenes in exchange markets by buying or selling foreign currencies in order to affect its exchange rate.

In December 1971, an attempt was made to patch up the pegged exchange-rate system at a conference at the Smithsonian Institution in Washington. The new pegged rates chosen by most of the countries involved higher prices of their currencies. Thus the United States achieved its goal of dollar devaluation. [When the price of a foreign currency goes up in terms of dollars, the price of the dollar goes down. To see why, first note that an exchange rate can be quoted in two different ways. For example, if 1£ = $2.00, then $1 = £0.50. (Just divide each side of the first equation by 2 and switch the two sides.) If the price of the pound rises from 1£ = $2.00 to 1£ = $2.50, that means that the price of the dollar falls from $1 = £0.50 to $1 = £0.40.]

The Smithsonian patchwork did not last. In 1972, the British let the pound float. Stresses on the exchange-rate system increased. There were such large amounts of internationally mobile funds that some exchange rates could not be held stable in the face of speculation. In an unsuccessful attempt over a four-day period to keep the mark from rising, West German authorities sold enough marks to speculators to buy 2 million Volkswagens. In early 1973, the major trading nations abandoned the pegs of the Smithsonian Agreement and allowed their currencies to float.

FLEXIBLE EXCHANGE RATES

A flexible exchange rate system has several advantages:

1. The principal alternative—a pegged exchange-rate system—broke down in the early 1970s, in part because of an inadequate adjustment mechanism and in part because of huge currency transactions by speculators. Today, it would be even more difficult to maintain pegged rates because the pools of internationally mobile funds are now even larger. One of the main arguments for flexible exchange rates is the *lack of a good alternative.*

2. When exchange rates are allowed to fluctuate, countries do not have to defend the existing exchange rate by adopting restrictive domestic policies. In other words, flexible exchange rates give domestic authorities *more freedom* to follow the aggregate demand policies that are best for the domestic economy. The desire for such freedom explains why both monetarists and Keynesian economists are included among the supporters of flexible exchange rates. Monetarists want exchange-rate flexibility so that the central bank can follow a monetary rule, without having to worry

about exchange rates. Keynesian proponents of flexible exchange rates want the authorities to be free to manage aggregate demand to achieve the domestic goals of high employment and stable prices, rather than to defend a pegged exchange rate.

3. A country following stable domestic policies is *insulated from foreign inflation.* We will see why in just a moment, when we come to the idea of a *virtuous circle.*

However, flexible exchange rates have been criticized on a number of grounds:

1. Changes in exchange rates may *disrupt international trade and investment.* It is a matter of dispute whether this disruption is greater with flexible exchange rates than under the crisis-prone IMF system, with its infrequent but abrupt changes in parity.

2. When exchange rates are allowed to float, an important *discipline* over monetary and fiscal policies is lost. Under the IMF system of adjustable pegs, the fear of balance-of-payments deficits provided a restraint on inflationary domestic policies.

This is the other side of the freedom argument put forward by proponents of flexible exchange rates. What one person considers "freedom" another may consider a "lack of discipline." Proponents of flexible exchange rates emphasize the advantages of freedom to pursue domestic objectives. Specifically, monetary and fiscal policies can be used to stabilize the domestic economy rather than the exchange rate. Opponents of exchange-rate flexibility argue that such freedom is undesirable, because weak and indisciplined governments will be more likely to follow inflationary policies.

3. Exchange-rate movements can contribute to domestic problems. For example, if a country has a weak international payments position, its currency will **depreciate.** True, the depreciation contributes to international adjustment. As the price of the home currency falls, imports become more expensive, and people buy fewer foreign goods as a result. But this increase in the price of imports also causes a problem. It *adds to domestic inflation.* A country can become caught in a **vicious circle,** with domestic inflation causing a depreciation, the depreciation in turn adding to the domestic inflationary spiral, and the higher inflation leading to even more depreciation. The vicious circle is not inevitable: a country may escape by following tighter monetary policies. But the vicious circle can speed up the inflationary process.

A floating currency *depreciates* when its price falls in terms of other currencies. (Note that a pegged currency is *devalued*; a floating currency *depreciates*.)

A floating currency *appreciates* when its price rises in terms of other currencies.

There is, however, another side to this argument, too. With flexible exchange rates, a country following stable domestic policies is insulated from inflationary disturbances originating abroad. Suppose, for example, that West Germany follows restrained policies, keeping its domestic prices stable. Then its goods become more attractive as prices rise in foreign countries. As foreigners eagerly buy German goods, they bid up the price of the mark. That is, they bid down the prices of their own currencies. As a result, imports into Germany remain inexpensive in spite of the foreign inflation. Germany benefits from a **virtuous circle.** Stable domestic prices lead to an appreciation of the mark, keeping the prices of imports down and making it even easier to prevent inflation in Germany.

4. The final criticism of a system of flexible rates is that it has led to *large fluctuations* in exchange rates since 1973. Critics argue that the up-and-down movements have served no useful purpose. Exchange rates have in practice responded to short-run, transitory disturbances. Many of the changes have not been necessary to correct fundamental disequilibria. Large fluctuations in exchange rates can be very disruptive to domestic industries, as we will see by looking at the experience of the United States.

REAL AND NOMINAL EXCHANGE RATES

Before studying the U.S. experience, however, we need to explain the difference between a **nominal exchange rate** and a **real exchange rate.**

A *nominal* exchange rate is simply the price of one currency in terms of another—such as the price of the dollar in terms of the Mexican peso. For example, if the price of the dollar rises from 100 to 200 pesos over a period of time, then the nominal

exchange rate of the dollar has doubled in terms of the peso.

This large increase in the price of the dollar does not, however, necessarily mean that U.S. goods will be driven from the Mexican market. The reason is that exchange-rate changes—particularly large ones—may reflect what is happening to domestic prices. In the above example, it is possible that U.S. domestic prices have been stable while domestic prices have doubled in Mexico. If so, the change in the exchange rate will barely compensate for changes in domestic prices. Because of the change in the exchange rate, a U.S. good costing, say, $100 will now cost a Mexican buyer twice as many pesos. But the Mexican inflation means that a Mexican good will also cost twice as many pesos as before. The competitive position of the U.S. good remains unchanged.

When the change in the nominal exchange rate simply compensates for inflation in this way, the **real exchange rate** remains unchanged.

The *real exchange rate* is the nominal exchange rate adjusted for differences in inflation between countries.

According to the **purchasing-power parity** theory, nominal exchange rates will in fact compensate for differences in domestic rates of inflation, leaving real exchange rates stable. This theory is reasonably close to what actually happens during periods of very rapid inflation, when inflation becomes the dominant force driving exchange-rate changes. However, the theory has not held up for the U.S. dollar during the past two decades. The wide swings in the exchange rate of the dollar have *not* simply reflected differences in inflation. Instead, the real exchange rate has also fluctuated strongly, causing major changes in the competitive position of U.S. goods on world markets.

THE FLUCTUATING DOLLAR

Figure 19-4 shows the price of the dollar in terms of an average of 10 other major currencies (the British pound, French franc, Japanese yen, and so on). Since 1971, three major movements have occurred in the price of the dollar: a decline of 30% between 1971 and 1980; a rise of 80% between 1980 and early 1985; and then a sharp decline between 1985 and

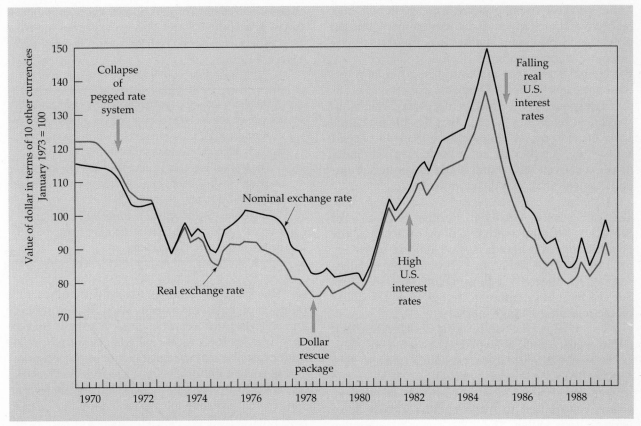

FIGURE 19-4 The rollercoaster ride of the dollar, 1971–1989.

During the 1970s, the average price of the dollar moved lower in terms of other currencies. Between 1981 and 1984, the dollar moved sharply higher. One reason was the high U.S. interest rates, which encouraged foreigners to buy U.S. bonds. Between 1985 and 1987, the dollar declined rapidly. (To calculate this average, the currency of each of the 10 foreign nations is weighted according to the amount of trade the country has with the United States.) (*Source:* Board of Governors of Federal Reserve System.)

1987 that took the dollar almost back to its low of 1980. The real exchange rate has followed a broadly similar pattern.

The declining dollar, 1971–1980. The first stage of the decline, between 1971 and 1973, occurred as the Bretton Woods system was breaking down. Exchange rates were no longer pegged at unrealistic levels, and the decline in the value of the dollar improved the competitiveness of U.S. goods on world markets. This early decline was generally desirable. Since 1976, however, the large changes in exchange rates have been much more controversial.

Between 1976 and 1978, aggregate demand rose rapidly in the United States, partly because of expansive monetary and fiscal policies. Output rose, while the rate of inflation accelerated from less than 5% in 1976 to 9% in 1978 and more than 13% in 1979. Soaring inflation was one factor dragging the dollar down. In turn, the rapid decline in the dollar added to U.S. inflationary pressures.

In the fall of 1978, the administration and the Federal Reserve became concerned that the United States was slipping into a vicious circle. If nothing were done, would inflation escalate to 15% or 20% or even more? Alarmed by this prospect, President Carter announced a "dollar rescue package."

Monetary and fiscal policies were switched in a restrictive direction, and the government bought dollars in the exchange market to support its price.

Note that, in spite of flexible exchange rates, the United States was not completely free of international complications. Domestic policy was shifted in response to the collapsing dollar. What can we conclude? It may be true that flexible exchange rates provide more independence than do pegged rates. However, they do not provide complete independence. Even the United States is strongly influenced by international developments.

The soaring dollar, 1980–1984. Further steps toward monetary restraint were taken in 1979, when the Fed announced a new policy of limiting monetary growth to fight inflation. The rate of inflation responded strongly, falling below 4% by 1982. Success in fighting inflation strengthened the dollar on the foreign exchange markets.

The rise in the dollar was, however, much stronger than could be explained by what was happening to inflation; the real exchange rate also rose rapidly. The U.S. tax cuts enacted in 1981 were one reason. They led to more government borrowing, which contributed to the high real interest rates (shown back in Fig. 15-4). As a result, foreigners flocked to buy U.S. bonds, thereby increasing the demand for dollars and driving its price upward. This upward movement was reinforced by a lackluster economic performance in Western Europe and problems in the developing countries. The United States became a *safe haven* for anxious foreign investors. Why take chances in other countries, particularly when U.S. bonds paid such high rates of interest?

By early 1985, the dollar reached a peak. Foreigners had to pay much more for American goods because the dollar had become so expensive. At the same time, foreign goods became cheaper to American buyers. The consequence was a profound change in the U.S. economic position in the world. American imports soared while exports stagnated. The U.S. **trade deficit**—which had hovered around $30 billion between 1977 and 1981—increased to more than $100 billion by 1984, as shown in Figure 19-5. (Details on balance-of-payments accounts are provided in the appendix.) The United States was selling bonds and other assets to foreign countries and using the proceeds to buy huge quantities of foreign goods, such as Japanese autos. The United States was quickly moving from its position as a large **creditor** nation toward being a large **debtor.**

A *trade surplus* is the amount by which a country's exports of goods exceeds its imports of goods.

A *trade deficit* is the amount by which a country's imports of goods exceeds its exports of goods.

The United States was a *creditor* when U.S.-owned assets in foreign nations exceeded foreign nations' assets in the United States.

The United States became a *debtor* when foreign nations' assets in the United States came to exceed U.S.-owned assets in foreign nations.

The surge of imports led to difficulties in a number of basic industries, such as automobiles and steel. Some observers feared that the U.S. economy was in the process of *deindustrialization.* We might lose the manufacturing core of our economy and become a nation devoted to services. Pressures mounted to do something. The United States persuaded the Japanese to impose "voluntary" export restraints (VERs) on their shipments of cars to the United States. ("Voluntary" is put in quotation marks because the VERs were not exactly voluntary. If the Japanese failed to act, the United States threatened to impose even tighter restrictions.) VERs on the export of steel to the United States were tightened. In spite of its desire for relatively free trade, the Reagan administration was being drawn into protectionism by the high value of the dollar, which was making U.S. producers very vulnerable to foreign competition.

Down again, 1985–1987. In early 1985, the upward trend of the dollar was reversed. By the end of 1987, the dollar had almost fallen back to its lows of 1978–1980.

The rapid decline in real U.S. interest rates was an important reason. Between late 1984 and late 1986, real interest rates on U.S. government bonds declined from 6% to 2%. Foreigners became much less eager to accumulate such bonds, thereby weakening the demand for dollars.

There also was a major change in the attitude of the U.S. government. During the first Reagan

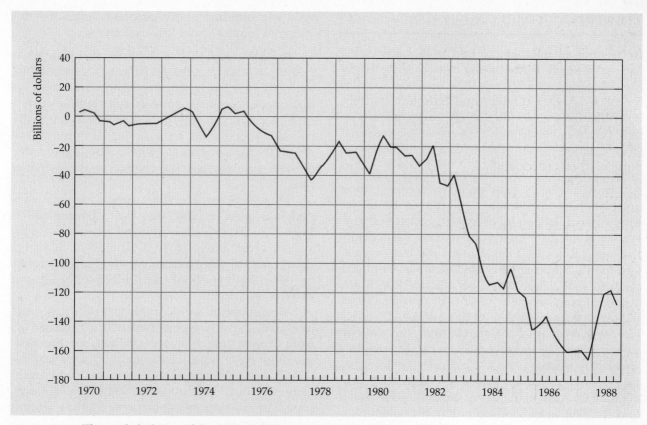

FIGURE 19-5   The trade balance of the United States.

The U.S. trade balance moved in a strongly negative direction between 1981 and 1987.
Between 1981 and 1984, the soaring U.S. dollar (shown in Fig. 19-4) meant that U.S. products were less competitive on world markets. The trade deficit began to shrink in 1988.
This shrinkage represented a lagged response to the fall in the exchange value of the dollar that began in 1985.

administration (1981–1984), the U.S. Treasury took a firm position in favor of *freely* flexible exchange rates. It withdrew from exchange markets and made no effort to resist the upward march of the dollar. In 1985, however, the administration reversed its policy and began to sell dollars. It was fearful that the high dollar would lead Congress to pass a strongly protectionist trade bill. To maintain relatively free trade, it was essential to get the dollar down and thus relieve the competitive pressure that imports were exerting on U.S. producers.

In fact, the fall in the dollar has taken much of the pressure off U.S. industries. It was one reason for the strong recovery of the automobile industry.

For the first time in many decades, the United States even began to sell a few cars in Japan. Nevertheless, the trade balance was painfully slow to adjust. The trade deficit did not begin to decline until 1988—three years after the dollar began to fall. Businesses apparently take a long time to respond to more favorable conditions in world markets. Some observers were concerned that the high dollar of the mid-1980s had done lasting damage to parts of U.S. industry, particularly where firms were driven from business by severe import competition. Now that the dollar has fallen, it may be years before new firms can begin production.

TOWARD A COMPROMISE SYSTEM?

In deciding to intervene in exchange markets, the U.S. government backed away from its support of a *freely* flexible exchange rate. The question that has arisen is whether fundamental reforms are desirable. Should we consider some intermediate system, part way between the old adjustable pegs and freely floating exchange rates? Two possibilities are particularly worth noting.

1. *Target zones?* A number of economists—most notably, John Williamson of the Institute for International Economics—have suggested that governments calculate their Fundamental Equilibrium Exchange Rates (FEERs), that is, the rates consistent with balance of payments equilibrium. Because such rates cannot be estimated with any degree of precision, it would not be desirable to try to force exchange rates to the estimated FEERs. However, Williamson suggests that the governments undertake to keep their exchange rates in a *target zone*, within 10% of the FEERs. In doing so, they would prevent extreme exchange-rate misalignments such as the overvaluation of the dollar in early 1985. In Williamson's view, the equilibrium exchange rate cannot be identified precisely. We can, however, tell when an exchange rate is far out of line.[1]

Target zones have in fact been considered at meetings of finance ministers, but no firm commitments have been made. If this reform were adopted, countries would be expected to keep within the target zones by exchange market intervention, backed up as necessary with changes in domestic monetary and fiscal policies.

2. *Crawling pegs?* An even more radical reform would be a return to pegged exchange rates, with one big difference from the old IMF system. Rather than keeping the pegs rigid, with periodic jumps, the pegs themselves would be changed gradually. For example, the currency of a deficit country would be devalued by 1/4% per month, or 3% per year, as long as the deficit lasted. Such gradual movements in exchange rates would help to prevent the buildup of deficits and surpluses that occurred under the old IMF system.

It might seem that such predictable changes in parities would present fat targets to speculators, who would rush to sell declining currencies. But that is not necessarily so. A country whose currency is declining steadily at 3% per year could discourage speculation by keeping its interest rate about 3% higher than elsewhere. The higher interest rate would offset the change in the exchange rate.

There was considerable support for the idea of crawling pegs within the U.S. government in 1969–1970. The idea was shelved when the pegged system broke down in 1971. There has, however, been a revival of interest in crawling pegs in recent years, as doubts about the flexible exchange rate system intensified.

A number of Latin American countries—such as Brazil—have experimented with crawling pegs from time to time. However, as their inflation rates are often quite high, a change of 3% per year has simply not been enough to maintain equilibrium. Consequently, exchange-rate adjustments have been larger; they are sometimes called "trotting pegs" rather than crawling pegs.

THE EUROPEAN MONETARY SYSTEM

A system of pegs—but less rigid than the old IMF system—has been adopted within the European Community, an association of most of the Western European nations. In order to reduce fluctuations in the exchange rates between the European currencies, and thus provide a more stable basis for trade, they established the *European Monetary System* (EMS) in 1979. The European leaders were, however, mindful of the rigidities that had brought down the IMF's pegged exchange-rate system and had also led to the breakdown of an earlier attempt to stabilize exchange rates within Western Europe in the early 1970s. They therefore allowed for significant flexibility in the EMS. Member nations are encouraged to change their par rates more quickly than they did under the old IMF system. They can also let their currencies move in wide bands, of as much as 6% on either side of par.

The objective of the European countries is to progressively reduce the degree of flexibility

---

[1]John Williamson, *The Exchange Rate System*, 2d ed. (Washington, D.C.: Institute for International Economics, 1985).

among their currencies, perhaps ultimately developing a monetary union, with a single, unified currency. This objective was highlighted in the Delors Report (1989), which outlined the steps that the members of the European Community would have to take if they were, in fact, to achieve monetary union. Most importantly, they would have to give up their independent national monetary policies. There would be only one, unified policy for the whole European Community, just as there is only one monetary policy within the United States. Within Europe, France would have no more freedom to follow its own monetary policy than California or Michigan has within the United States.

KEY POINTS

1. A foreign exchange market is a market for one national currency in terms of another. The demand for a foreign currency depends on:

    (a) Imports of goods.

    (b) Imports of services.

    (c) Acquisitions of foreign assets.

2. Similarly, a nation's supply of a foreign currency depends on exports of goods and services, and acquisitions of its assets by foreigners.

3. The price which an American pays for a British good depends on: (a) the British price of the good, measured in pounds, and (b) the exchange rate between the pound and the dollar.

4. If the quantity of pounds supplied is more than the quantity demanded at the existing exchange rate, the British government can deal with the surplus of pounds by one or a combination of the following steps:

    (a) Intervening in the exchange market; that is, selling U.S. dollars to buy up the surplus pounds.

    (b) Devaluing the pound or permitting it to depreciate in response to market forces.

    (c) Reducing the supply of pounds through restrictions on imports or other international transactions.

    (d) Restraining aggregate demand in Britain.

5. Under the gold standard, the adjustment mechanism worked through changes in aggregate demand. For example, gold would flow out of a deficit country, automatically reducing the quantity of money. Aggregate demand and prices would fall. The country would become more competitive on world markets. Its exports would rise and its imports fall.

6. The gold standard had two major defects:

    (a) The decline in the money stock needed for international adjustment might make it more difficult to maintain full employment.

    (b) The gold standard could result in instability. A crisis of confidence might occur, causing a run on the gold reserves of the banking system.

7. At the end of the Second World War, the IMF system was established, with *pegged but adjustable* exchange rates. There were major problems:

    (a) Exchange rates were often rigid, leaving the system without an adequate *adjustment* mechanism. Deficit countries tended to have continuing deficits, and surplus countries continuing surpluses.

    (b) There could be a crisis of *confidence* when a devaluation was expected. Speculators had an incentive to sell the currency before its official price was reduced.

8. The adjustable peg system broke down in the 1971-1973 period, leading to the present system of flexible exchange rates.

9. The U.S. dollar has fluctuated substantially in the past two decades. The rise in the dollar between 1981 and 1985 caused an increase in the U.S. trade deficit.

10. An intermediate system would be possible, between an IMF-style pegged rate and freely flexible rates:

    (a) Target zones.

    (b) Crawling pegs.

11. The European Monetary System limits fluctuations in exchange rates among the European currencies.

KEY CONCEPTS

exchange rate
foreign exchange
foreign exchange market
imports of goods
imports of services
acquisition of foreign assets
    (investment in foreign
    countries)
foreign exchange reserves
official intervention in the
    exchange market
adjustment mechanism
balance-of-payments deficit

balance-of-payments surplus
gold standard
adjustable peg
par value
fundamental disequilibrium
devalue
revalue
speculator
adjustment problem
confidence problem
"stop-go" policy
flexible or floating exchange rate

clean float
dirty float
depreciation
appreciation
vicious circle
virtuous circle
real exchange rate
purchasing power parity
trade surplus
trade deficit
crawling peg
European Monetary System

PROBLEMS

19-1. Suppose that after a period of equilibrium, the demand for the British pound falls on the exchange markets. What choices does the British government have in dealing with this change?

19-2. Under the old gold standard, what prevents a country from continuously losing gold?

19-3. Why might a country follow a "stop-go" policy under a pegged exchange-rate system?

19-4. The text explains why the finance minister of a deficit country would be unwise to admit that a devaluation was being considered under the old IMF adjustable peg system. Would the finance minister of a surplus country be similarly unwise to admit that a reevaluation was under consideration? Explain why or why not.

19-5. Explain how speculators who bought marks worth "2 million Volkswagens" gained at the expense of the German government when the mark was finally allowed to rise on the exchange markets.

19-6. Why did the U.S. dollar rise between 1981 and 1985. Who was hurt by this increase? Did anyone in the United States benefit?

APPENDIX
BALANCE-OF-PAYMENTS ACCOUNTS

The U.S. balance-of-payments accounts provide a record of transactions between residents of the United States and other countries. A system of **double-entry bookkeeping** is used. That is, a set of accounts with two sides (+) and (−) is constructed, and any single transaction results in equal entries on both sides. Consequently, the accounts logically *must* balance. We have already run into this concept of double-entry bookkeeping in our study of banks in Chapters 11 and 12. For example, if the Fed purchases a $100,000 bond from a commercial bank (Table 12-2), the Fed's assets increase by $100,000 (the bond), while exactly the same change takes place in its liabilities (in the form of the reserve deposit of the commercial bank).

With *double-entry bookkeeping,* each transaction results in equal entries on both sides. When double-entry bookkeeping is used, the two sides of the accounts must balance.

To illustrate how double-entry bookkeeping works with international transactions, consider a simple example where a U.S. company exports a $100,000 computer to Germany. The export is entered on the positive—or *credit*—side of the U.S. balance of payments. But something else also hap-

pens. The German importer has to pay for the computer. Suppose, to make things easy, that the importer pays with a check, which the U.S. computer company deposits in its Frankfurt bank account. (For convenience, a business engaged in international trade may keep accounts in a number of foreign banks.) Then Table 19-1 shows the effects of this single transaction on the U.S. balance-of-payments accounts. Note that an increase in U.S. assets (bank accounts) in Germany appears on the negative side. This must be so, to make the accounts balance.

The overall U.S. balance of payments is subdivided into two main accounts. In one category—the **capital account**—statisticians enter changes in U.S.-owned assets in foreign countries and changes in foreign-owned assets in the United States. For example, the increase in the computer company's deposit in Frankfurt is a U.S.-owned asset in a German bank, and accordingly it is a capital account item. Other capital account items include increases in ownership of foreign stocks or bonds, or of property such as factories and capital equipment. In other words, *international investment* shows up in the capital accounts.

All other items—that is, those that do not represent changes in the ownership of foreign assets—are put in the **current account,** shown at the top of Table 19-2.

TABLE 19-1 An International Transaction   (effects on the U. S. balance of payments)

Positive Items (credits)		Negative Items (debits)	
U. S. export of computer	$100,000	Increase in U. S.-owned bank account in Germany	$100,000

An international transaction—such as this export to Germany—affects both sides of the U. S. balance of payments equally. As a consequence, the two sides of the balance of payments sum to the same total.

TABLE 19-2   U. S. Balance-of-Payments Accounts, 1988   (billions of dollars)

Positive Items (credits)			Negative Items (debits)		
I. Current account					
1. Exports of goods and services		508	5. Imports of goods and services		630
(a) Merchandise exports	320		(a) Merchandise imports	446	
(b) Receipts from U. S.			(b) Payments on foreign		
investments abroad	108		investments in United States	105	
(c) Other	80		(c) Other	79	
			6. Unilateral transfers, net		13
II. Capital accounts					
A. Changes in nonreserve assets					
2. Increase in foreign nonreserve			7. Increase in U. S. nonreserve		
assets in United States		172	assets abroad		88
(a) Direct investment in the			(a) Direct investment	20	
United States	42		(b) Other	68	
(b) Other	130				
B. Changes in reserves					
3. Increase in foreign official assets		39	8. Changes in U. S. reserve assets		4
in United States					
(a) U. S. government securities	43				
(b) Other	−4				
C. Statistical discrepancy					
4. Statistical discrepancy		16			
Total		735	Total		735

THE CURRENT ACCOUNT

Item (1a), merchandise exports, includes the products such as wheat, computers, and aircraft exported by the United States in 1988. Americans receive income—principally dividends and interest—from past investments abroad (item 1b).

Note that *returns from investments appear in the current account*, even though the investments themselves are included in the capital accounts. The reason is this. If General Motors buys a German company, U.S.-owned assets abroad rise. Therefore this investment belongs in the capital account. But when GM receives dividends from this German company, there is no change in ownership. GM receives the dividends, but still owns the German

company. Thus dividends go in the current account (1b). Similarly, interest from a foreign bond is put in the current account. (However, when a foreign bond is paid off, that represents a change in asset holdings and therefore appears in the capital account.) Interest and dividend receipts are considered an export of services. That is, they represent payments by foreigners to Americans for the *use of the services of American capital*.

U.S. exports of goods and services appear on the positive side of the U.S. balance of payments. Our imports of goods and services appear on the negative side.

Unilateral transfers are the final item in the current account. Included in this item are payments immigrants send back to their families in the "old country," grants by the U.S. government and private charities to foreigners, and payments made to those drawing pensions from the United States while living abroad.

THE CAPITAL ACCOUNTS

The capital accounts are divided into three main subcategories: changes in nonreserve assets; changes in reserve assets; and the statistical discrepancy.

A. CHANGES IN NONRESERVE ASSETS

Direct investment in the United States occurs when there is an increase in ownership by foreigners who control a business in the United States. For example, when Honda establishes production facilities in the United States, that appears as direct investment (2a). Similarly, on the other side, when Ford builds a plant in Mexico, that also appears as direct investment (7a). Other investment (2b and 7b) does not involve control: Individuals or corporations are acquiring foreign bonds, or stocks of companies they do not control, or short-term foreign assets such as bank accounts.

Note that, when foreigners increase their assets in the United States, the increase is entered as a *positive* item in the U.S. balance of payments. An increase in U.S.-owned assets abroad is entered as a negative item. (We already saw in Table 19-1 why an increase in U.S. bank deposits in Germany is a negative entry.)

The fact that a *negative* entry is made for an increase in U.S.-owned assets abroad is worth emphasizing. It is advantageous for the United States to own large assets abroad. (Specifically, item 1(b) shows that in 1988 we earned $108 billion on our earlier investments in foreign countries.) Therefore *we should resist the temptation to consider a negative item as necessarily "bad" or a positive item as necessarily "good."*

B. CHANGES IN RESERVE ASSETS

Increases in foreign official assets in the United States (item 3) represent dollars held by foreign governments and central banks, mostly in the form of U.S. Treasury bills.

On the other (debit) side of the accounts, increases in U.S. reserves of foreign currencies are entered; these reserves are owned by the U.S. Treasury or the Federal Reserve. Note that an acquisition of reserves by the United States appears as a *negative* or debit item in this nation's balance of payments. (Remember the earlier warning: Positive doesn't necessarily mean "good" or negative, "bad.") By considering a very simple transaction, we can see why this must be so. Suppose that the United States exports $1 million of goods and acquires $1 million of foreign reserves in exchange. The export appears on the positive side of our balance of payments. To make the accounts come out right, our acquisition of reserves must appear on the negative side.

C. THE STATISTICAL DISCREPANCY

Theoretically, this item should not appear. If government statisticians had a perfect knowledge of international transactions, the sum of the positive items considered thus far would be exactly equal to the sum of the negative items. But they aren't equal. The statistical discrepancy is whatever number is necessary to make them equal. From the size of this discrepancy—$16 billion in 1988—it is obvious that international transactions are not measured perfectly.

THE BALANCE OF PAYMENTS

If the two sides of the balance of payments must be equal, what do we mean when we talk of the balance of payments being in "deficit" or "surplus"? When such terms are used, *we must be excluding certain items from the calculations.* The standard way of calculating the balance of payments is to exclude changes in reserves (category IIB), taking the net amount of all other items. The balance of payments measures the surpluses or shortages that would occur in foreign exchange markets at existing exchange rates in the absence of official intervention.

Two other balances are also commonly calculated. The **current-account balance,** as the name implies, includes only the items in the current account (category I). In 1988, the U.S. had a current-account deficit of $135 billion. In other words, we spent more abroad than we earned. As a result, foreigners accumulated more assets in the United States than we accumulated abroad. The United States was going into debt.

A country has a *balance-of-payments surplus* if it is acquiring net international reserves. (That is, if its international reserves are increasing more rapidly than foreign countries' reserve claims on it.)

A *balance-of-payments deficit* occurs when a country is losing reserves on a net basis.

A country has a *current-account surplus* if its exports of goods and services are greater than the combined sum of its imports of goods and services plus its net unilateral transfers to foreign countries.

Finally, we may subtract merchandise imports ($446 billion) from merchandise exports ($320 billion) to find the trade balance or merchandise account balance—a deficit of $126 billion in 1988.

GLOSSARY

(Not all these terms appear in this book. Some appear in the companion volume, Microeconomics, and some are included because they occur frequently in readings or lectures. Page numbers provide the primary references for the terms. For additional references, see the index.)

ability to pay principle. The view that taxes should be levied according to the means of the various taxpayers, as measured by their incomes and/or wealth. Compare with *benefit principle*. (p. 73)

absolute advantage. A country (or region or individual) has an absolute advantage in the production of a good or service if it can produce that good or service with fewer resources than other countries (or regions or individuals). See also *comparative advantage*. (p. 41)

accelerationist. One who believes that an attempt to keep the unemployment rate low by expansive demand policies will cause more and more rapid inflation, and that a steady inflation will cause the unemployment rate to return to its natural or equilibrium rate. (p. 237)

accelerator. The theory that investment depends on the change in sales. (p. 333)

accommodative monetary policy. (1) A monetary policy that allows the money stock to change in response to changes in the demand for loans. (2) A monetary policy that increases aggregate demand when wages and other costs increase, in order to prevent an increase in unemployment in the face of cost-push forces.

accounts payable. Debts to suppliers of goods or services.

accounts receivable. Amounts due from customers.

action lag. The time interval between the recognition that adjustments in aggregate demand policies are desirable and the time when policies are actually changed. (p. 316)

actual investment. Investment as it appears in the GNP accounts; investment including undesired inventory accumulation. (p. 140)

adaptive expectations. Expectations that depend on past and/or present observations. (p. 251) Contrast with *rational expectations*.

adjustable peg system. A system in which countries peg (fix) exchange rates but retain the right to change them in the event of fundamental disequilibrium. (In the adjustable peg system of 1945-1973, countries generally fixed the prices of their currencies in terms of the U.S. dollar.) (p. 344)

adjustable-rate mortgage. A mortgage whose interest rate is adjusted periodically in response to changes in a market rate of interest. (p. 269)

ad valorem tax. A tax collected as a percentage of the price or value of a good.

aggregate demand. Total quantity of goods and services that would be bought at various average price levels. (p. 120)

aggregate expenditures. Total quantity of goods and services that would be bought at various levels of national income or national product. Total quantity of goods and services demanded as a function of national income or product. (p. 139)

aggregate supply. (1) Total quantity of goods and services that would be offered for sale at various average price levels. (pp. 121, 125) (2) Potential GNP.

allocative efficiency. Production of the best combination of goods with the lowest cost combination of inputs. (p. 11)

annually balanced budget principle. The view that government expenditures should be limited each year to no more than government receipts during that year. (p. 179)

antitrust laws. Laws designed to control monopoly power and practices. Examples: Sherman Act, 1890: Clayton Act, 1914.

appreciation of a currency. In a flexible exchange-rate system, a rise in the price of a currency in terms of another currency or currencies. (p. 348)

arbitrage. A set of transactions aimed at making a profit from inconsistent prices.

arbitration. Settlement of differences between a union and management by an impartial third party (the arbitrator) whose decisions are binding.

arc elasticity of demand. The elasticity of demand between two points on a demand curve, calculated by the midpoint formula.

asset. Something that is owned.

automatic stabilizer. A feature built into the economy that reduces the amplitude of fluctuations, *without any policy change being made* (in contrast to a *discretionary policy action*). For example, tax collections tend to fall during a recession and rise during a boom, slowing the change in disposable incomes and aggregate demand. Thus they are an automatic fiscal stabilizer. (p. 171) Interest rates tend to fall during a recession and rise during a boom because of changes in the demand for funds. These changes in interest rates tend to stabilize investment demand. Thus they are an automatic monetary stabilizer.

average cost pricing. Setting the price where the average-cost curve (including normal profit) intersects the demand curve.

average fixed cost. Fixed cost divided by the number of units of output.

average product. Total product divided by the number of units of the variable input used.

average propensity to consume. Consumption divided by disposable income.

average propensity to save. Saving divided by disposable income.

average revenue. Total revenue divided by the number of units sold. Where there is a single price, this price equals average revenue.

average total cost. Total cost divided by the number of units of output.

average variable cost. Variable cost divided by the number of units produced.

balanced budget. (1) A budget with revenues equal to expenditures. (2) More loosely (but more commonly), a budget with revenues equal to or greater than expenditures. (p. 70)

balanced budget multiplier. The change in equilibrium national product divided by the change in government spending when this spending is financed by an equivalent change in taxes.

balance of payments. (1) The accounts showing transactions between residents of one country and the rest of the world. (2) The summary figure calculated from balance-of-payments credits less balance-of-payments debits, with official reserve transactions excluded from the calculation. (pp. 356, 357)

balance-of-payments accounts. A statement of a country's transactions with other countries. (p. 356)

balance-of-payments surplus (deficit). A positive (negative) balance of payments. (p. 358)

balance of trade (or balance on merchandise account). The value of exports of goods minus the value of imports of goods. (p. 358)

balance sheet. The statement of a firm's financial position at a particular time, showing its assets, liabilities, and net worth.

band. The range within which an exchange rate could move without the government's being committed to intervene in exchange markets to prevent further movement. Under the adjustable peg system, governments were obliged to keep exchange rates from moving outside a band (of 1% either side of parity). (p. 344)

bank rate. The rate of interest charged by the central bank on loans to commercial banks or other institutions. The discount rate. (p. 211)

bank reserve. Bank holding of currency and reserve deposits in the Federal Reserve. (p. 194)

bank run. A situation in which many owners of bank deposits attempt to make withdrawals because of their fear that the bank will be unable to meet its obligations. (p. 192)

bankruptcy. (1) A situation in which a firm (or individual) has legally been declared unable to pay its debts. (2) More loosely, a situation in which a firm (or individual) is unable to pay its debts.

barrier to entry. An impediment that makes it difficult or impossible for a new firm to enter an industry. Examples: patents, economies of scale, accepted brand names.

barter. The exchange of one good or service for another without the use of money. (p. 36)

base year. The reference year, given the value of 100 when constructing a price index or other time series. (p. 92)

beggar-thy-neighbor policy (or beggar-my-neighbor policy). A policy aimed at shifting an unemployment problem to another country. Example: an increase in tariffs.

benefit-cost analysis. The calculation and comparison of the benefits and costs of a program or project.

benefit in kind. Payment, not of cash, but of some good (like food) or service (like medical care).

benefit principle. The view that taxes should be levied in proportion to the benefits that the various taxpayers receive from government expenditures. Compare with *ability to pay principle*. (p. 72)

bilateral monopoly. A market structure involving a single seller (monopolist) and a single buyer (monopsonist).

bill. See *Treasury bill*.

blacklist. A list of workers who are not to be given jobs because of union activity or other behavior considered objectionable by employers.

black market. A market in which sales take place at a price above the legal maximum. (p. 60)

block grant. Grant that may be used in a broad area (such as education) and need not be spent on specific programs (such as reading programs for the handicapped).

bond. A written commitment to pay a scheduled series of interest payments plus the face value (principal) at a specified maturity date. (p. 124)

book value. The book value of a stock is its net worth per share. (It is calculated by dividing the net worth of the firm by the number of its shares outstanding.)

bourgeoisie. (1) In Marxist doctrine, capitalists as a social class. (2) The middle class. (3) More narrowly, shopkeepers.

boycott. A concerted refusal to buy (buyer's boycott) or sell (seller's boycott). A campaign to discourage people from doing business with a particular firm.

break-even point. (1) The lowest point on the average total cost curve. If price is at this height, revenues are just equal to costs, and therefore economic profit is zero. (2) The level of disposable income at which consumption just equals disposable income, and therefore saving is zero.

broker. One who acts on behalf of a buyer or seller.

budget deficit. The amount by which budgetary outlays exceed revenues. (p. 70)

budget line (or income line or price line). The line on a diagram that shows the various combinations of commodities that can be bought with a given income at a given set prices.

budget surplus. The amount by which budgetary revenues exceed outlays. (p. 70)

built-in stabilizer. See *automatic stabilizer*.

burden of tax. The amount of the tax ultimately paid by different individuals or groups. (For example, how much does a cigarette tax raise the price paid by buyers, and how much does it lower the net price received by sellers?) The incidence of the tax.

business cycle. The more or less regular upward and downward movement of economic activity over a period of years. A cycle has four phases: recession, trough, expansion, and peak. (p. 102)

capital. (1) Real capital: buildings, equipment, and other materials used in the production process that have themselves been produced in the past. (p. 26) (2) Financial capital: either funds available for acquiring real capital *or* financial assets such as bonds or common stock. (p. 26) (3) Human capital: the education, training, and experience that make human beings more productive. (p. 27)

capital account. In international economics, changes between countries in the ownership of assets. (p. 355)

capital consumption allowance. Depreciation, with adjustments for the effects of inflation on the measurement of capital. Loosely, depreciation. (p. 88n)

capital gain. The increase in the value of an asset over time.

capitalism. A system in which individuals and privately owned firms are permitted to own large amounts of capital, and decisions are made primarily in private markets, with relatively little government interference. (p. 47)

capitalized value. The present value of the income stream that an asset is expected to produce. (p. 213)

capital market. A market in which financial instruments such as stocks and bonds are bought and sold.

capital-output ratio. The value of capital divided by the value of the annual output produced with this capital. (p. 335)

capital stock. The total quantity of capital.

cartel. A formal agreement among firms to set price and share the market.

categorical grant. A federal grant to a state or local government for a specific program. Such a grant generally requires the recipient government to pay part of the cost of the program.

cease-and-desist order. An order from a court or government agency to an individual or company to stop a specified action.

central bank. A banker's bank, whose major responsibility is the control of the money supply. A central bank also generally performs other functions, such as check clearing and the inspection of commercial banks.

central planning. Centralized direction of the resources of the economy, with the objective of fulfilling national goals. In a centrally planned economy, the government owns most of the capital. (p. 47)

certificate of deposit (CD). A marketable time deposit.

ceteris paribus. "Other things unchanged." In demand-and-supply analysis, it is common to make the *ceteris paribus* assumption, that is, to assume that none of the determinants of the quality demanded or supplied is allowed to change, with the sole exception of price. (p. 52) We may also speak of how income affects the quantity demanded, *ceteris paribus*—that is, if nothing but income changes.

check clearing. The transfer of checks from the bank in which they were deposited to the bank on which they were written, with the net amounts due to or from each bank being calculated. (p. 197)

checking deposit. A deposit against which an order to pay (that is, a check) may be written.

checking deposit multiplier. The increase in checking deposits divided by the increase in bank reserves. (p. 201)

checkoff. The deduction of union dues from workers' pay by an employer, who then remits the dues to the union.

circular flow of payments. The flow of payments from businesses to households in exchange for labor and other productive services and the return flow of payments from households to businesses in exchange for goods and services. (p. 39)

classical economics. (1) In Keynesian economics, the accepted body of macroeconomic doctrine prior to the publication of Keynes' *General Theory*. According to classical economics, a market economy tends toward an equilibrium with full employment; a market economy tends to be stable if monetary conditions are stable; and changes in the quantity of money are the major cause of changes in aggregate demand. (pp. 128–130, 327) (2) The accepted view, prior to about 1870, that value depends on the cost of production. [In the late nineteenth century, this was replaced with the "neoclassical" view that value depends on both costs of production (supply) and utility (demand).]

class struggle. In Marxist economics, the struggle for control between the proletariat and the bourgeoisie.

clean float. A situation in which exchange rates

are determined by market forces, without intervention by central banks or governments. (p. 346)

clearing of checks. See *check clearing*.

closed economy. An economy with no international transactions.

closed shop. A business that hires only workers who are already union members. Compare with *union shop* and *right-to-work law*.

cobweb cycle. A switching back and forth between a situation of high production and low price and one of low production and high price. A cobweb cycle can occur if there are long lags in production and if producers erroneously assume that price this year is a good indicator of price next year.

coincidence of wants. This exists when *A* is willing to offer what *B* wants, while *B* is willing to offer what *A* wants. (p. 37)

collective bargaining. Negotiations between a union and management over wages, fringe benefits, hiring policies, or working conditions.

collective goods. Goods that, by their very nature, provide benefits to a large group of people.

collusion. An agreement among sellers regarding prices and/or market shares. The agreement may be explicit or tacit.

commercial bank. A privately owned, profit-seeking institution that accepts demand and savings deposits, makes loans, and acquires other earning assets (particularly bonds and shorter term debt instruments). (p. 193)

commons. Land that is open for use by all or by a large group. Example: commonly owned pastureland.

common stock. Each share of common stock represents part ownership in a corporation.

communism. (1) In Marxist theory, the ultimate stage of historical development in which (a) all are expected to work and no one lives by owning capital, (b) exploitation has been eliminated and there is a classless society, and (c) the state has withered away. (2) A common alternative usage: the economic and political systems of the People's Republic of China, the Soviet Union, and other countries in which a Communist party is in power.

company union. A union dominated by the employer.

comparable. Of equal value, requiring equivalent effort, responsibility, training, and skills. The *comparable worth issue* is the question of whether employers should be required to pay women as much as men working in different but comparable jobs. Comparable worth—also sometimes known as *pay equity*—takes the anti-discrimination idea beyond the requirement that people be paid the same amount for doing the same job.

comparative advantage. A nation (or city or individual) has a comparative advantage in a good or service if it can produce the good or service at a lower opportunity cost than its trading partner.

compensating wage differential. Wage difference that may result if labor views a job as less attractive than an alternative. (Employers have to pay a higher wage to fill the unattractive job.)

competition. See *perfect competition*.

competitive devaluations. A round of exchange-rate devaluations in which each of a number of countries tries to gain a competitive advantage by devaluing its currency. (Not all can be successful; each must fail to the extent that other countries also devalue.)

complementary goals. Goals such that the achievement of one helps in the achievement of the other. (Contrast with *conflicting goals*.) (p. 13)

complementary goods, or complements in consumption. Goods such that the rise in the price of one causes a leftward shift in the demand curve for the other. (Contrast with *substitute*.) (p. 53)

complements in production. Goods such that the rise in the price of one causes a rightward shift in the supply curve of the other. Joint products. (p. 55)

concentration ratio. Usually, the fraction of an industry's total output produced by the four largest firms. (Sometimes a different number of firms—such as eight—is chosen in calculating concentration ratios, and sometimes a different measure of size—such as sales or assets—is chosen.)

conflicting goals. Goals such that working toward one makes it more difficult to achieve the other. (p. 16)

conglomerate merger. See *merger*.

consent decree. An agreement whereby a defendant, without admitting guilt, undertakes to desist from certain actions and abide by other conditions laid down in the decree.

conspicuous consumption. Consumption whose purpose is to impress others. A term originated by Thorstein Veblen (1857–1929).

constant dollars. A series is measured in constant dollars if it is measured at the prices existing in a specified base year. Such a series has been adjusted to remove the effects of inflation or deflation. (p. 92) Contrast with *current dollars.*

constant returns (to scale). Occurs when an increase of $x\%$ in all inputs causes output to increase by the same $x\%$.

consumer price index (CPI). A weighted average of the prices of goods and services commonly purchased by families in urban areas, as calculated by the U.S. Bureau of Labor Statistics. (p. 93)

consumer surplus. The net benefit that consumers get from being able to purchase a good at the prevailing price; the difference between the maximum amounts that consumers would be willing to pay and what they actually do pay. It is estimated as the triangular area under the demand curve and above the market price.

consumption. (1) The purchase of consumer goods and services. (p. 85) (2) The act of using goods and services to satisfy wants. (3) The using up of goods (as in capital consumption allowances).

consumption function. (1) The relationship between consumer expenditures and disposable income. (p. 136) (2) More broadly, the relationship between consumer expenditures and the factors that determine these expenditures.

contestable market. A market with only one or a few producers, whose market power is nevertheless severely limited by the ease with which additional producers may enter.

convergence hypothesis. The proposition that the differences between communistic and capitalistic societies is decreasing.

convertible bond. A bond that can be exchanged for common stock under specified terms and prior to a specified date, at the option of the bondholder.

cornering a market. Buying and accumulating enough of a commodity to become the single (or at least dominant) owner, and thus acquire the power to resell at a higher price.

corporation. An association of stockholders with a government charter that grants certain legal powers, privileges, and liabilities separate from those of the individual stockholder-owners. The major advantages of the corporate form of business organization are limited liability for the owners, continuity, and relative ease of raising capital for expansion.

correlation. The tendency of two variables (like income and consumption) to move together.

cost-benefit analysis. The calculation and comparison of the benefits and costs of a program or project. Also called *benefit-cost analysis.*

cost-push inflation. Inflation caused principally by increasing costs—in the form of higher prices for labor, materials, and other inputs—rather than by rising demand. (p. 232) Contrast with *demand-pull inflation.*

countercyclical policy. (1) Policy that reduces fluctuations in economic activity. (2) Policy whose objective is to reduce fluctuations in economic activity.

countervailing power. Power in one group which has grown as a reaction to power in another group. For example, a big labor union may develop to balance the bargaining power of a big corporation. The term was originated by Harvard's John Kenneth Galbraith.

Nash equilibrium. Equilibrium that exists when each firm has made its best choice, on the assumption that the other firms stick to their existing strategies.

craft union. A labor union whose members have a particular craft (skill or occupation). Examples: an electricians' union or a plumbers' union. Contrast with *industrial union.*

crawling peg system. An international financial system in which par values would be changed frequently, by small amounts, in order to avoid large changes at a later date.

credit crunch. Severe credit rationing, where demand for loans substantially exceeds the available supply.

credit instrument. A written promise to pay at some future date.

credit rationing. Allocation of available funds among borrowers when the demand for loans exceeds the supply at the prevailing interest rate.

creeping inflation. A slow but persistent upward movement of the average level of prices (not more than 2% or 3% per annum).

cross-section data. Observations taken at the same time. Example: the consumption of different income classes in the United States in 1986.

crowding out. A reduction in private investment demand caused when an expansive fiscal policy results in higher interest rates. (p. 304)

currency. (1) Coins and paper money (dollar bills). (p. 188) (2) In international economics, a national money, such as the dollar or the yen. (p. 340).

current account surplus. The amount by which a country's export of goods and services is greater than the combined sum of its imports of goods and services plus its net unilateral transfers to foreign countries. (p. 358)

current dollars. A series (like GNP) is measured in current dollars if each observation is measured at the prices that prevailed at the time. Such a series reflects both real changes in GNP *and* inflation (or deflation). Contrast with *constant dollars.* (p. 92)

current liabilities. Debts that are due for payment within a year.

customs union. An agreement among nations to eliminate trade barriers (tariffs, quotas, etc.) among themselves and to adopt common tariffs on imports from nonmember countries. Example: the European Community.

cutthroat competition. Selling at a price below cost, with the objective of driving competitors out of the market (at which time prices may be raised and monopoly profits reaped).

cyclically balanced budget. A budget whose receipts over a whole business cycle are at least equal to its expenditures over the same cycle. Unlike an annually balanced budget, a cyclically balanced budget permits the use of countercyclical fiscal policies. Surpluses during prosperity may be used to cover deficits during recessions. (p. 179).

cyclical unemployment. Unemployment caused by a general downturn in the economy. (p. 112)

deadweight loss. A loss of allocative efficiency, owing to the wrong pattern of production or the wrong combination of inputs.

debasement of currency. (1) Reduction of the quantity of precious metal in coins. (p. 40) (2) More broadly, a substantial decrease in the purchasing power of money.

debt. The amount owed. (p. 70)

debt instrument. A written commitment to repay borrowed funds.

declining industry. An industry whose firms make less than normal profits. (Firms will therefore leave the industry.)

decreasing returns (to scale). Occurs if an $x\%$ increase in all inputs results in an increase of output of less than $x\%$.

deficiency payment. The government's payment of the difference between the market price and its target price.

deficit. A *budget deficit* is the amount by which government expenditures exceed government revenues. (p. 70) A *trade deficit* is the amount by which imports exceed exports. (p. 287)

deflation. (1) A decline in the average level of prices; the opposite of inflation. (p. 9) (2) The removal of the effects of inflation from a series of observations by dividing each observation with a price index. The derivation of a constant-dollar series from a current-dollar series. (p. 93)

deflationary bias. Exists in a system if, on average, monetary and fiscal authorities are constrained from allowing aggregate demand to increase as rapidly as productive capacity. (The classical gold standard was criticized on the ground that it created a deflationary bias.)

deflationary gap. See *recessionary gap.*

deindustrialization. A reduction in the size of the manufacturing sector, usually as a result of competition from imports.

demand. A schedule or curve showing how much of a good or service would be demanded at various possible prices, *ceteris paribus.* (p. 50)

demand deposit. A bank deposit withdrawable on demand and transferable by check. (p. 194)

demand management policy. A change in monetary and/or fiscal policy aimed at affecting aggregate demand.

demand-pull inflation. Inflation caused by excess aggregate demand. (p. 231) Contrast with *cost-push inflation.*

demand schedule. A table showing the quantities of a good or service that buyers would be willing and able to purchase at various market prices, *ceteris paribus.* (p. 50)

demand shift. A movement of the demand curve to the right or left as a result of a change in income or any other determinant of the quantity demand (with the sole exception of the price of the good). (p. 52)

demand shifter. Anything except its own price that affects the quantity of a good demanded. (p. 53)

depletion allowance. A deduction, equal to a percentage of sales, that certain extractive industries are permitted in calculating taxable profits.

depreciation. (1) The loss in the value of physical capital owing to wear and obsolescence. (2) The estimate of such loss in business or economic accounts. (3) The amount that tax laws allow businesses to count as a cost of using plant or equipment. (p. 87)

depreciation of a currency. A decline in the value of a floating currency measured in terms of another currency or currencies. (p. 348)

depression. An extended period of very high unemployment and much excess capacity. (There is no generally accepted, precise numerical definition of a depression. This text suggests that a depression requires unemployment rates of 10% or more for two years or more.) (pp. 7, 103)

derived demand. The demand for an input that depends on the demand for the product or products it is used to make. For example, the demand for flour is derived from the demand for bread.

desired investment. (Also known as *investment demand* or *planned investment.*) This is the amount of new plant, equipment, and housing acquired during the year, plus additions to inventories that businesses wanted to acquire. Actual investment less undesired inventory accumulation. (p. 140)

devaluation. In international economics, a reduction of the par value of a currency. (p. 345)

dictatorship of the proletariat. In Marxist economics, the state after a revolution has eliminated the capitalist class and power has fallen into the hands of the proletariat.

differentiated products. Similar products that retain some distinctive difference(s); close but not perfect substitutes. Examples: Ford and Chevrolet automobiles, different brands of toothpaste.

diminishing returns, law of eventually. See *law of eventually diminishing returns.*

dirty float. See *floating (or flexible) exchange rate.*

discounting. The process by which the present value of one or more future payments is calculated, using an interest rate. (See *present value.*) (p. 213) (2) In central banking, lending by the central bank to a commercial bank or other financial institution. (p. 211)

discount rate. (1) In central banking, the rate of interest charged by the central bank on loans to commercial banks or other institutions. (p. 211) (2) The interest rate used to calculate present value. (p. 213)

discouraged worker. Someone who wants a job but is no longer looking because work is believed to be unavailable. A discouraged worker is not included in either the labor force or the number of unemployed. (p. 108)

discretionary policy. Policy that is periodically changed in the light of changing conditions. The term is usually applied to monetary or fiscal policies that are adjusted with the objectives of high employment and stable prices. Contrast with *monetary rule.*

diseconomies of scale. Occur when an increase of $x\%$ in all inputs results in an increase in output of less than $x\%$.

disposable (personal) income. Income that households have left after the payment of taxes. It is divided among consumption expenditures, the payment of interest on consumer debt, and saving. (p. 91)

dissaving. Negative saving.

dividend. The part of a corporation's profits paid out to its shareholders.

division of labor. The breaking up of a productive process into different tasks, each done by a different worker (for example, on an automobile assembly line).

dollar standard. An international system in which many international transactions take place in dollars and many countries hold sizable factions of their reserves in dollars. Also, other currencies may be pegged to the dollar.

double-entry bookkeeping. An accounting system in which each transaction results in equal entries on both sides. When double-entry bookkeeping is used, the two sides of the accounts must balance. (p. 355)

double taxation. The taxation of corporate dividends twice—once as part of the profits of the corporation, and once as the income of the dividend recipient.

dual labor market. A double labor market, where workers in one market are excluded from taking jobs in the other market.

dumping. The sale of a good at a lower price in a foreign market than in the home market—a form of price discrimination.

duopoly. A market in which there are only two sellers.

duty. A tax on an imported good as it enters the country. (p. 5)

dynamic efficiency. Efficient change in an economy, particularly the most efficient use of resources, the best rate of technological change, and the most efficient rate of growth.

dynamic wage differential. A wage difference that arises because of changing demand or supply conditions in the labor market. It tends to disappear over time as labor moves out of relatively low-wage jobs and into those that pay a relatively high wage.

econometrics. The application of statistical methods to economic problems. (p. 329)

economic efficiency. See *allocative efficiency; dynamic efficiency;* and *technological (or technical) efficiency.*

economic integration. The elimination of tariffs and other barriers between nations. The partial or complete unification of the economies of different countries.

economic problem. The need to make choices because our resources are scarce while our wants are virtually unlimited. (p. 25)

economic profit. Above-normal profit. Profit in excess of the amount needed to keep capital in the industry.

economic rent. The return to a factor of production in excess of its opportunity cost.

economics. (1) The study of the allocation of scarce resources to satisfy alternative, competing human wants. (p. 25) (2) The study of how people acquire material necessities and comforts, the problems they encounter in doing so, and how these problems can be reduced.

economies (diseconomies) of scale. Occur when an increase of $x\%$ in all inputs results in an increase in output of more (less) than $x\%$. (p. 43)

economies of scope. Occur when the addition of a new product reduces the cost of existing products.

economize. To achieve a specific benefit at the lowest cost in terms of the resources used. (p. 25) To make the most of limited resources. To be careful in spending.

economy. (1) A set of interrelated production and consumption activities. (2) The act of reducing the cost of achieving a goal.

efficiency. The goal of getting the most out of our productive efforts. See also *allocative efficiency; dynamic efficiency;* and *technological efficiency.* (p. 10)

effluent charge. A tax or other levy on a polluting activity based on the quantity of pollution discharged.

elastic demand. Demand with an elasticity whose absolute value exceeds 1. A fall in price causes an increase in total expenditure on the product in question, because the percentage change in quantity demanded is greater than the percentage change in price.

elasticity of demand. The price elasticity of demand is

$$\frac{\text{Percentage change in quantity demanded}}{\text{Percentage change in price}}$$

Similarly, the income elasticity of demand is

$$\frac{\text{Percentage change in quantity demanded}}{\text{Percentage change in income}}$$

The unmodified term "elasticity" usually applies to price elasticity. (pp. *84–99*)

elasticity of supply. The (price) elasticity of supply is

$$\frac{\text{Percentage change in quantity supplied}}{\text{Percentage change in price}}$$

elastic supply. Supply with an elasticity of more than 1. A supply curve which, if extended in a straight line, would meet the vertical axis.

emission fee. See *effluent charge.*

employer of last resort. The government acts as the employer of last resort if it provides jobs for all those who are willing and able to work but cannot find jobs in the private sector. (p. 245)

employment rate. The percentage of the labor force employed.

endogenous variable. A variable explained within a theory.

Engel's laws. Regularities between income and consumer expenditures observed by nineteenth-century statistician Ernst Engel. Most important is the decrease in the percentage of income spent on food as income rises.

entrepreneur. One who organizes and manages production. One who innovates and bears risks. (p. 27)

envelope curve. A curve that encloses, by just touching, a series of other curves. For example, the long-run average-cost curve is the envelope of all the short-run average-cost curves (each of which shows costs, given a particular stock of fixed capital).

equation of exchange. MV = PQ. (p. 301)

equilibrium. A situation in which there is no tendency to change. (p. 51)

equity. (1) Ownership, or amount owned. (2) Fairness.

escalator clause. A provision in a contract or law whereby a price, wage, or other monetary quantity is increased at the same rate as a specified price index (usually the consumer price index). (p. 249)

estate tax. A tax on property owned at the time of death.

Eurodollars. Deposits in European banks that are denominated in U.S. dollars.

ex ante. Planned or desired (as contrasted to actual or *ex post*). Example: *ex ante* investment.

excess burden of a tax. The decrease in efficiency that results when people change their behavior to reduce their tax payments. Distinguish from *primary burden of a tax*. (p. 177)

excess demand. The amount by which the quantity demanded exceeds the quantity supplied at the existing price. A shortage. (p. 52)

excess reserves. Reserves held by a bank in excess of the legally required amount. (p. *197*)

excess supply. The amount by which the quantity supplied exceeds the quantity demanded at the existing price. A surplus. (p. 52)

exchange rate. The price of one national currency in terms of another. (p. 340)

exchange-rate appreciation (depreciation). See *appreciation (depreciation) of a currency.*

excise tax. A tax on the sale of a particular good. An *ad valorem tax* is collected as a percentage of the price of the good. A *specific tax* is a fixed number of cents or dollars on each unit of the good.

exclusion principle. The basis for distinguishing between public and nonpublic goods. If those who do not pay for a good can be excluded from enjoying it, then it is not a public good.

exogenous variable. A variable not explained within a theory; its value is taken as given. Example: investment in the simple Keynesian theory.

expansion. The phase of the business cycle when output and employment are increasing. (p. 102)

export (E). Good or service sold to foreign nationals.

export of capital. Acquisition of foreign assets.

ex post. Actual (as contrasted to desired or *ex ante*). Example: *ex post* investment.

external benefit. Benefit enjoyed by someone other than the buyers or sellers of a product; a spillover benefit.

external cost. Cost borne by someone other than the buyers or sellers of a product; a spillover cost. Example: pollution. (p. 76)

externality. An adverse or beneficial side effect of production or consumption. Also known as a *spillover* or *third-party effect*. (p. 76)

externally held public debt. Government securities held by foreigners. (p. 177)

Fabian socialism. Form of socialism founded in Great Britain in the late nineteenth century, advocating gradual and evolutionary movement toward socialism within a democratic political system.

face value. The stated amount of a loan or bond. The amount that must be paid, in addition to interest, when the bond comes due. The principal. (p. 213)

factor mobility. Ease with which factors can be moved from one use to another.

factor of production. Resource used to produce a good or service. Land, labor, and capital are the three basic categories of factors. (p. 26)

fair return. Return to which a regulated public utility should be entitled.

fallacy of composition. The unwarranted conclusion that a proposition which is true of a single sector or market is necessarily true for the economy as a whole. (p. 161)

featherbedding. (1) Commonly: Make-work rules designed to increase the number of workers or the number of hours on a particular job. (2) As defined in the Taft-Hartley Act: Payment for work not actually performed.

federal funds rate. The interest rate on very short-term (usually overnight) loans between banks.

Federal Reserve Bank interest rate. The rate of interest charged by the Federal Reserve on loans to commercial banks or other institutions. The discount rate. (p. 211)

fiat money. Paper money that is neither backed by nor convertible into precious metals but is nevertheless legal tender. Money that is money solely because the government says it is. (p. 217)

final product. A good or service purchased by the ultimate user, and not intended for resale or further processing. (p. 119)

financial capital. Financial assets such as bank accounts, bonds, and common stock. Funds available for acquiring real capital. Distinguish from *real capital,* such as buildings or equipment. (p. 26)

financial instrument. A legal document representing claims or ownership. Examples: bonds; Treasury bills.

financial intermediary. An institution that issues financial obligations (such as checking deposits) in order to acquire funds from the public. The institution then pools these funds and provides them in larger amounts to businesses, governments, or individuals. Examples: commercial banks; savings and loan associations; insurance companies.

financial investment. The acquisition of financial capital, such as bonds or common stock. Distinguish from *real investment*—the accumulation of real capital, such as buildings or equipment. (p. 26)

financial market. A market in which financial instruments (stocks, bonds, etc.) are bought and sold.

fine tuning. An attempt to smooth out mild fluctuations in the economy by frequent adjustments in monetary and/or fiscal policies. (p. 314)

firm. A business organization that produces goods and/or services. A firm may own one or more plants. (p. 49)

fiscal dividend. A budget surplus, measured at the full-employment national product, that is generated by the growth of the productive capacity of the economy. (This term was most commonly used during the 1960s.)

fiscal drag. The tendency for rising tax collections to impede the healthy growth of aggregate demand that is needed for the achievement and maintenance of full employment. (This term was most commonly used during the 1960s.)

fiscal policy. The adjustment of tax rates or government spending in order to affect aggregate demand. (pp. 129, 164) *Pure fiscal policy* is a change in government spending or tax rates, unaccompanied by any change in the rate of growth of the money stock. (p. 305)

fiscal year. A twelve-month period selected as the

year for accounting purposes.

Fisher equation. The equation of exchange: MV = PQ. (p. 301)

fixed asset. A durable good, expected to last at least a year.

fixed cost. A cost that does not vary with output.

fixed exchange rate. An exchange rate that is held within a narrow band by the monetary authorities or by the operation of the gold standard.

fixed factor. A factor whose quantity cannot be changed in the short run.

flat tax. A tax with only one rate applying to all income. A proportional tax.

floating (or flexible) exchange rate. An exchange rate that is not pegged by monetary authorities but is allowed to change in response to changing demand or supply conditions. If governments and central banks withdraw completely from the exchange markets, the float is *clean.* (That is, the exchange rate is *freely flexible.*) A float is *dirty* when governments or central banks intervene in exchange markets by buying or selling foreign currencies in order to influence exchange rates. (p. 346)

focal point pricing. Occurs when independent firms quote the same price even though they do not explicitly collude. They are led by convention, rules of thumb, or similar thinking to the same price. Example: $39.95 for a pair of shoes.

forced saving. A situation in which households lose control of part of their income, which is directed into saving even though they would have preferred to consume it. This can occur if the monetary authorities provide financial resources for investment, creating inflation that reduces the purchasing power of households' incomes (and therefore reduces their consumption). Alternatively, forced saving occurs if taxes are used for investment projects (such as dams).

foreign exchange. The currency of another country. (p. 340)

foreign exchange market. A market in which one national currency is bought in exchange for another national currency. (p. 340)

foreign exchange reserves. Foreign currencies held by the government or central bank. (p. 342)

forward price. A price established in a contract to be executed at a specified time in the future (such as three months from now). See also *futures market.*

fractional-reserve banking. A banking system in which banks keep reserves (generally in the form of currency or deposits in the central bank) equal to only a fraction of their deposit liabilities. (p. 191)

freedom of entry. The absence of barriers that make it difficult or impossible for a new firm to enter an industry.

free enterprise economy. An economy in which individuals are permitted to own large amounts of capital, and decisions are made primarily in private markets, with relatively little government interference. (p. 47)

free good. A good or service whose price is zero, because at that price the quantity supplied is at least as great as the quantity demanded.

free market economy. An economy in which the major questions "What?" "How?" and "For whom?" are answered by the actions of individuals and firms in the marketplace rather than by the government. (p. 47)

free rider. Someone who cannot be excluded from enjoying the benefits of a project, but who pays nothing or pays a disproportionately small share to cover its costs.

free trade. A situation in which no tariffs or other barriers exist on trade between countries.

free-trade area (or free-trade association). A group of countries that agree to eliminate trade barriers (tariffs, quotas, etc.) among themselves, while each retains the right to set its own tariffs on imports from nonmember countries. Compare with *customs union.* (p. 44)

frictional unemployment. Temporary unemployment associated with adjustments in a changing, dynamic economy. It arises for a number of reasons. For example, some new entrants into the labor force take time to find jobs, some with jobs quit to look for better ones, and others are temporarily unemployed by such disturbances as bad weather. (p. 113)

front-loaded debt. A debt on which the payments, measured in constant dollars, are greater at the beginning than at the end of the repayment period. (p. 270)

full employment. (1) A situation in which the unemployment rate is brought down as low as possible, without causing an increase in the rate of inflation. (2) A situation in which there is no unemployment attributable to insufficient aggregate demand, that is, in which all unemployment is due to frictional or structural causes. See also *natural rate of unemployment*. (p. 114)

full-employment budget (or high-employment budget). The size that the government's surplus (or deficit) would be with existing spending programs and tax rates, if the economy were at full employment. Full-employment government receipts (that is, the receipts that would be obtained with present tax rates if the economy were at full employment) minus full-employment government expenditures (that is, actual expenditures less expenditures directly associated with unemployment in excess of the full-employment level). (p. 172)

full-employment GNP. The GNP that would exist if full employment were consistently maintained. Potential GNP. (p. 115)

full-line forcing. See *tying contract*.

fundamental disequilibrium (in international economics). A term used but not defined in the articles of agreement of the International Monetary Fund. The general idea is that a fundamental disequilibrium exists when an international payments imbalance cannot be eliminated without increasing trade restrictions or imposing unduly restrictive aggregate demand policies. (p. 345)

futures market. A market in which contracts are undertaken today at prices specified today for fulfillment at some specified future time. For example, a futures sale of wheat involves the commitment to deliver wheat, say three months from today at a price set now.

gain from trade. Increase in real income that results from specialization and trade.

game theory. Theory dealing with conflict, in which alternative strategies are formally analyzed. Sometimes used in the analysis of oligopoly.

general equilibrium. Situation in which all markets are in equilibrium simultaneously.

general equilibrium analysis. Analysis taking into account interactions among markets.

general glut. Occurs when excess supply is a general phenomenon. The quantity of goods and services that producers are willing to supply greatly exceeds the quantity buyers are willing and able to purchase.

general inflation. An increase in all prices (including wages) by the same percentage, leaving relative prices unchanged. (p. 121)

general price level. Price level as measured by a broad average, such as the consumer price index or the GNP deflator.

Giffen good. A good whose demand curve slopes upward to the right.

Gini coefficient. A measure of inequality derived from the Lorenz curve. It is the "bow" area between the curve and the diagonal line divided by the entire area beneath the diagonal line. It can range from zero (if there is no inequality and the Lorenz curve corresponds to the diagonal line) to one (if there is complete inequality and the Lorenz curve runs along the horizontal axis).

GNP (price) deflator. Current-dollar GNP divided by constant dollar GNP, times 100. Measure of the change in prices of the goods and services included in GNP. (p. 93)

GNP gap. Amount by which actual GNP falls short of potential GNP. (p. 116)

gold certificate. Certificate issued by the U.S. Treasury to the Federal Reserve, backed 100% by Treasury holdings of gold.

gold exchange standard. International system in which most countries keep their currencies pegged to, and convertible into, another currency that in turn is pegged to and convertible into gold.

gold point. Under the old gold standard, an exchange rate at which an arbitrageur can barely cover the costs of shipping, handling, and insuring gold.

gold standard. System in which the monetary unit is defined in terms of gold, the monetary authorities buy and sell gold freely at that price, gold acts as the ultimate bank reserve, and gold may be freely exported or imported. If central banks follow the "rule of the gold standard game," they allow changes in gold to be reflected in changes in the money stock. (pp. 217, 343)

gold sterilization. Occurs when the central bank takes steps to cancel out the automatic effects of the gold flow on the country's money supply (that is, when the "rule of the gold standard game" is broken).

good. Tangible commodity, such as wheat, a shirt, or an automobile. (p. 26)

graduated-payment mortgage. A mortgage on which the money payments rise as time passes, in order to reduce front loading. If the money payments rise rapidly enough to keep real payments constant, then the mortgage is *fully* graduated. (p. 271)

greenmail. The premium over the market price that a firm pays to purchase its stock from a holder who is threatening to take over the company or engage in a proxy fight.

Gresham's law. Crudely, "Bad money drives out good." More precisely: If there are two types of money whose values in exchange are equal while their values in another use (like consumption) are different, the more valuable item will be retained for its other use while the less valuable item will continue to circulate as money. (p. 40)

gross domestic product (GDP). U.S. GDP = U.S. GNP *less* U.S. income from American investments in foreign countries *plus* income earned by foreigners on investments in the United States. (p. 286)

gross national product (GNP). Personal consumption expenditures plus government purchases of goods and services plus gross private domestic investment plus net exports of goods and services. The total product of the nation, excluding double counting. (p. 88)

gross private domestic investment (I_g). Expenditures for new plant, equipment, and new residential buildings, plus the change in inventories. (p. 87)

growth. An increase in the productive capacity of an economy; an outward shift of the production possibilities curve. (p. 30)

Herfindahl-Hirschman index. A measure of concentration. Specifically, the sum of the squared percentage market shares of each of the firms.

high-employment GNP. The GNP that would exist if a high rate of employment were consistently maintained. Potential GNP. (p. 116)

holding company. A company that holds a controlling interest in the stock of one or more other companies.

horizontal merger. See *merger.*

human capital. Education and training that make human beings more productive. (p. 27)

hyperinflation. Very rapid inflation, at a rate of 1,000% per year or more. (p. 10)

hysteresis. The property of not returning to the original state when a disturbance is removed. (p. 258)

identification problem. The difficulty of determining the effect of variable a alone on variable b when b can also be affected by variables c, d, and so on.

impact lag. The time interval between policy changes and the time when the major effects of the policy changes occur. (p. 316)

imperfect competition. A market in which any buyer or seller is able to have a noticeable effect on price. (p. 48)

implicit (or imputed) cost. The opportunity cost of using an input that is already owned by the producer.

implicit GNP deflator. See *GNP (price) deflator* (p. 93)

implicit tax. A tax built into a welfare program. The benefits a family or individual loses when another $1 of income is earned. For example, if benefits are reduced by 46¢, the implicit tax is 46%.

import (M). Good or service acquired from foreign nationals.

import of capital. Sale of assets to foreign nationals.

import quota. A restriction on the quantity of a good that may be imported.

incidence of a tax. The amount of the tax ultimately paid by different individuals or groups. (For example, how much does a cigarette tax raise the price paid by buyers, and how much does it lower the net price received by sellers?)

income-consumption line. The line or curve traced out by the points of tangency between an indifference map and a series of parallel budget (income) lines. It shows how a consumer responds to a changing income when relative prices remain constant.

income effect. Change in the quantity of a good demanded as a result of a change in real income with no change in relative prices.

income elasticity of demand. See *elasticity of demand*.

income line. See *budget line*.

incomes policy. A government policy (such as wage-price guideposts or wage and price controls) aimed at restraining the rate of increase in money wages and other money incomes. The purpose is to reduce the rate of inflation. (p. 245)

income statement. An accounting statement that summarizes a firm's revenues, costs, and income taxes over a given period of time (usually a year). A profit-and-loss statement.

increasing returns to scale. Occurs when an increase of $x\%$ in all inputs results in an increase in output of more than $x\%$. Economies of scale.

incremental cost. The term that business executives frequently use instead of "marginal cost."

incremental revenue. The term that business executives frequently use instead of "marginal revenue."

index. A series of numbers, showing how an average (of prices, or wages, or some other economic measure) changes through time. Each of these numbers is called an index number. By convention, the index number for the base year is set at 100. (p. 93)

indexation. The inclusion of an *escalator clause* in a contract or law. An increase in the wage rate, tax brackets, or other dollar measure by the same proportion as the increase in the average level of prices. (p. 249)

indifference curve. A curve joining all points among which the consumer is indifferent.

indifference map. A series of indifference curves, each representing a different level of satisfaction or utility.

indirect tax. A tax that is thought to be passed on to others, and not borne by the one who originally pays it. Examples: sales taxes; excise taxes; import duties.

induced investment. Additional investment demand that results from an increase in national product.

industrial union. A union open to all workers in an industry, regardless of their skill. Example: the United Auto Workers. Contrast with *craft union*.

industry. The producers of a single good or service (or closely similar goods or services). (p. 49)

inelastic demand. Demand with an elasticity whose absolute value is less than 1. A fall in price causes a fall in total expenditure on the product in question, because the percentage change in quantity demanded is less than the percentage change in price.

inelastic supply. Supply with an elasticity of less than 1. A supply curve which, if extended in a straight line, would meet the horizontal axis.

infant-industry argument for protection. The proposition that new domestic industries with economies of scale or large requirements of human capital need protection from foreign producers until they can become established.

inferior good. A good for which the quantity demand decreases as income rises, *ceteris paribus*. (p. 53).

inflation. A rise in the average level of prices. (p. 9)

inflationary gap. The vertical distance by which the aggregate demand line is above the 45° line at the full-employment quantity of national product. The opposite of a *recessionary gap*.

infrastructure. Basic facilities such as roads, power plants, and telephone systems. (p. 284)

inheritance tax. Tax imposed on property received from a person who has died.

injection. Expenditure for a GNP component other than consumption. Example: investment or government expenditures for goods and services. (p. 143)

injunction. Court order to refrain from certain practices or requiring certain action.

innovation. A change in products or in the techniques of production.

inputs. Materials and services used in the process of production.

interest. Payment for the use of money.

interest rate. Interest as a percentage per annum of the amount borrowed.

interlocking directorate. Situation in which one or more directors of a company sit on the boards of directors of one or more other companies that are competitors, suppliers, or customers of the first company.

intermediate good or intermediate product. A product intended for resale or further processing. (p. 84)

internal cost. Cost incurred by those who actually produce (or consume) a good. Contrast with *external cost.*

internalization. A process that results in a firm or individual being penalized (or rewarded) for an external cost (or benefit) of its actions.

international adjustment mechanism. Any set of forces that tends to reduce surpluses or deficits in the balance of payments. (p. 343)

international liquidity. The total amount of international reserves (foreign exchange, special drawing rights, etc.) held by the various nations.

inventories. Stocks of raw materials, intermediate products, and finished goods held by producers or marketing organizations. (p. 86)

investment. (1) Accumulation of capital. Unless otherwise specified, economists use the term "investment" to mean *real* investment (the accumulation of real capital such as machinery or buildings) rather than financial investment (such as the acquisition of bonds). (p. 28) See also *gross private domestic investment* and *net private domestic investment.*

investment bank. A firm that markets common stocks, bonds, and other securities.

investment demand. (Also known as *desired investment* or *planned investment*). This is the amount of new plant, equipment, and housing acquired during the year, plus additions to inven-

tories that businesses wanted to acquire. Actual investment less undesired inventory accumulation. (p. 140)

investment good. A capital good; plant, equipment, or inventory.

investment, private domestic. See *gross private domestic investment* and *net private domestic investment.*

investment tax credit. A provision at one time in the tax code providing a reduction in taxes to those who acquire capital goods.

invisible. An intangible; a service (as contrasted with a good).

invisible hand. Adam Smith's phrase expressing the idea that the pursuit of self-interest by individuals will lead to a desirable outcome for society as a whole. (p. 5)

iron law of wages. The view, commonly held in the nineteenth century, that the human propensity to reproduce causes a tendency for the supply of labor to outrun the productive capacity of the economy and the demand for labor. As a consequence, an iron law of nature was at work to drive wages down to the subsistence level. (Any excess population at that wage would die from starvation, pestilence, or war.) (p. 292)

jawbone. To persuade; to attempt to persuade, perhaps using threats.

joint products. Goods such that the rise in the price of one causes a rightward shift in the supply curve of the other. Complements in production. Products produced together. Examples: meat and hides. (p. 55)

joint profit maximization. Formal or informal cooperation by oligopolists to pick the price that yields the most profit for the group.

jurisdictional dispute. Dispute between unions over whose workers will be permitted to perform a certain task.

key currency. A national currency commonly used by foreigners in international transactions and by foreign monetary authorities when intervening in exchange markets. Examples: the U.S. dollar, and, historically, the British pound.

Keynesian economics. The major macroeconomic propositions put forward by John Maynard Keynes in *The General Theory of Employment, Interest, and*

Money (1936), namely: A market economy may reach an equilibrium with large-scale unemployment; steps to stimulate aggregate demand can cure a depression; and fiscal policies are the best way to control aggregate demand. (p. 327) Contrast with *classical economics*.

kinked demand curve. A demand curve that an oligopoly firm faces if its competitors follow any price cut it makes but do not follow any of its price increase. The kink in such a demand curve occurs at the existing price.

L. M3 + U.S. savings bonds + short-term Treasury securities + short-term marketable securities issued by corporations; liquid assets.

labor. The physical and mental contributions of people to production. (p. 26)

labor force. The number of people employed plus those actively seeking work. (p. 108)

labor-intensive product. A good whose production uses a relatively large quantity of labor and a relatively small quantity of other resources.

labor participation rate. See *participation rate*.

labor productivity. See *productivity of labor*.

labor theory of value. Strictly, the proposition that the sole source of value is labor (including labor "congealed" in capital). Loosely, the proposition that labor is the principal source of value.

labor union. See *union*.

Laffer curve. A curve showing how tax revenues change as the tax rate changes. (p. 185)

laissez faire. Strictly translated, "let do." More loosely, "leave it alone." An expression used by the French physiocrats and later by Adam Smith, meaning the absence of government intervention in markets. (p. 5)

land. A term used broadly by economists to include not only arable land, but also the other gifts of nature (such as minerals) that come with the land. (p. 26)

law of diminishing marginal utility. As a consumer gets more and more of a good, the marginal utility of that good will (eventually) decrease.

law of eventually diminishing returns. If technology is unchanged, then the use of more and more units of a variable input, together with one or more fixed inputs, must eventually lead to a declining marginal product of the variable input.

leading indicator. A time series that reaches a turning point (peak or trough) before the economy as a whole. (p. 328)

leakage. (1) A withdrawal of potential spending from the circular flow of income and expenditures; saving, taxes, and imports. (p. 143) (2) A withdrawal from the banking system that reduces the potential expansion of the money stock.

leakages-injections approach. The determination of equilibrium national product by finding the size of the product at which leakages are equal to injections. (p. 145)

legal tender. An item that creditors must, by law, accept in payment of a debt. (p. 216)

leverage. The ratio of debt to net worth.

leveraged buyout. The purchase of a corporation, financed in such a way as to increase leverage— that is, by borrowing.

liability. (1) What is owed. (2) The amount that can be lost by the owners of a business if that business goes bankrupt.

life-cycle hypothesis. The proposition that consumption depends on expected lifetime income (as contrasted with the early Keynesian view that consumption depends on current income).

limited liability. The amount an owner-shareholder of a corporation can lose in the event of bankruptcy. This is limited to the amount paid to purchase shares of the corporation.

limited partnership. An organization that avoids the corporate disadvantage of double taxation, while providing the corporate advantage of limited liability to some of its owners.

line of credit. Commitment by a bank or other lender to stand ready to lend up to a specified amount to a customer on request.

liquid asset. An asset that can be sold on short notice, at a predictable price, with little cost or bother. (p. 190)

liquidity. Ease with which an asset can be sold on short notice, at a predictable price, with little cost.

liquidity preference. The demand for money—that is, the willingness to hold money as a function of the interest rate.

liquidity preference theory of the interest rate. The theory put forward by J. M. Keynes that the interest rate is determined by the willingness to hold money (liquidity preference) and the supply of money (that is, the stock of money in existence). (p. 298) Contrast with *loanable funds theory of interest.*

liquidity trap. In Keynesian theory, the situation in which individuals and businesses are willing to hold all their additional financial assets in the form of money—rather than bonds or other debt instruments—at the existing interest rate. In such circumstances, the creation of additional money by the central bank cannot depress the interest rate further, and monetary policy cannot be effectively used to stimulate aggregate demand. (All additional money created is caught in the liquidity trap and is held as idle balances.) In geometric terms, the liquidity trap exists where the liquidity preference curve (the demand for money) is horizontal.

loanable funds theory of interest. The theory that the interest rate is determined by the demand for and the supply of funds in the market for bonds and other forms of debt. Contrast with *liquidity preference theory of interest.*

lockout. Temporary closing of a factory or other place of business in order to deprive workers of their jobs. A bargaining tool sometimes used in labor disputes; the employer's equivalent of a strike.

logarithmic (or log or ratio) scale. A scale in which equal proportional changes are shown as equal distances. For example, the distance from 100 to 200 is equal to the distance from 200 to 400. (Each involves a doubling.) (p. 20)

long run. (1) A period long enough for prices and wages to adjust to their equilibrium levels. (p. 123) (2) A period long enough for equilibrium to be reached. (3) A period of time long enough for the quantity of all inputs, including capital, to be adjusted to the desired level. (4) Any extended period.

long-run Phillips curve. The curve (or line) traced out by the possible points of long-run equilibrium, that is, the points where people have adjusted completely to the prevailing rate of inflation.

long-run production function. A table showing various combinations of inputs and the maximum output that can be produced with each combination. For a simple firm with only two inputs (labor and capital), the production function can be shown by a two-dimensional table.

Lorenz curve. A curve showing cumulative percentages of income or wealth. For example, a point on a Lorenz curve might show the percentage of income received by the poorest half of the families. (The cumulative percentage of income is shown on the vertical axis. The family with the lowest income is counted first, and then other families are successively added in the order of their incomes. The cumulative percentage of families is on the horizontal axis). Such a curve can be used to measure inequality; if all families have the same income, the Lorenz curve traces out a diagonal line. See also *Gini coefficient.*

lump-sum tax. A tax of a constant amount. The revenues from such a tax do not change when income changes. (p. 166)

M1. The narrowly defined money stock; currency (paper money plus coins) plus checking deposits plus travelers' checks held by the public (that is, excluding holdings of currency, etc., by the federal government, the Federal Reserve, and commercial banks). (p. 188)

M2. A more broadly defined money stock; M1 plus noncheckable savings deposits plus small time deposits plus money market mutual fund accounts. (p. 190)

M3. An even more broadly defined money stock; M2 plus large time deposits.

macroeconomics. The study of the overall aggregates of the economy, such as total employment, the unemployment rate, national product, and the rate of inflation. (p. 81)

Malthusian problem. The tendency for population to outstrip productive capacity, particularly the capacity to produce food. This is the supposed consequence of a tendency for population to grow geometrically (l, 2, 4, 8, etc.) while the means of subsistence grows arithmetically (l, 2, 3, 4, etc.). The pressure of population will tend to depress the wage rate to the subsistence level and keep it there, with the excess population being eliminated by war, pestilence, or starvation. A problem described by Thomas Malthus in his *Essay on the Principle of Population* (l798). (p. 292)

managed float. A dirty float. *See floating (or flexible) exchange rate.*

marginal. The term commonly used by economists to mean "additional." For example, *marginal cost* is the additional cost when one more unit is produced; *marginal revenue* is the addition to revenue when one more unit is sold; and *marginal utility* is the utility or satisfaction received from consuming one more unit of a good or service.

marginal cost pricing. Setting price at the level where marginal cost intersects the demand curve.

marginal efficiency of investment. The schedule or curve relating desired investment to the rate of interest. The investment demand curve.

marginal physical product. The additional output when one more unit of an input is used (with all other inputs being held constant). For example, the *marginal physical product of labor* (often abbreviated to the *marginal product of labor*) is the additional output when one more unit of labor is used.

marginal product. (1) Strictly, the marginal physical product. (2) Sometimes, the value of the marginal physical product.

marginal propensity to consume (MPC). The change in consumption expenditures divided by the change in disposable income. (p. 138)

marginal propensity to import. The change in imports of goods and services divided by the change in GNP.

marginal propensity to save (MPS). The change in saving divided by the change in disposable income. 1 – MPC. (p. 138)

marginal rate of substitution. The slope of the indifference curve. The ratio of the marginal utilities of two goods.

marginal revenue product. The additional revenue when the firm uses one additional unit of an input (with all other inputs being held constant).

marginal tax rate. The fraction of additional income paid in taxes. (p. 69)

marginal utility. The satisfaction an individual receives from consuming one additional unit of good or service.

margin call. The requirement by a lender who holds stocks (or bonds) as security that more money be put up or the stocks (or bonds) will be sold. A margin call may be issued when the price of the stocks (or bonds) declines, making the stocks (or bonds) less adequate as security for the loan.

margin requirement. The minimum percentage that purchasers of stocks or bonds must put up in their own money. For example, if the margin requirement on stock is 60%, the buyer must put up at least 60% of the price in his or her own money and can borrow no more than 40% from a bank or stockbroker. (p. 214)

market. An institution in which purchases and sales are made. (p. 46)

market economy. See *free market economy.*

market failure. The failure of market forces to bring about the best allocation of resources. For example, when production of a good generates pollution, too many resources tend to go into the production of that good and not enough into the production of alternative goods and services.

market mechanism. The system whereby prices and the interaction of demand and supply help to answer the major economic questions "What will be produced?" "How?" and "For whom?" (p. 59)

market power. The ability of a single firm or individual to influence the market price of a good or service. (p. 48)

market-power inflation. See *cost-push inflation.* (p. 232)

market share. Percentage of an industry's sales accounted for by a single firm.

market structure. Characteristics that affect the behavior of firms in a market, such as the number of firms, the possibility of collusion, the degree of product differentiation, and the ease of entry.

Marxist economy. An economy in which most of the capital is owned by the government. (Individuals may, of course, own small capital goods, such as hoes or hammers, but the major forms of capital—factories and heavy machinery—are owned by the state.) Political power is in the hands of a party pledging allegiance to the doctrines of Karl Marx.

measure of economic welfare (MEW). A comprehensive measure of economic well-being. Per capita real national product is adjusted to take into account leisure, pollution, and other such influences on welfare. (p. 94)

median. The item in the middle (that is, half of all items are above the median and half are below).

medium of exchange. Money; any item that is generally acceptable in exchange for goods or services; any item that is commonly used in buying goods or services. (p. 39)

member bank. A bank that belongs to the Federal Reserve System.

mercantilism. The theory that national prosperity can be promoted by a positive balance of trade and the accumulation of precious metals.

merchandise account surplus. The excess of merchandise exports over merchandise imports.

merger. The bringing together of two or more firms under common control through purchase, exchange of common stock, or other means. *A horizontal merger* brings together competing firms. *A vertical merger* brings together firms that are each others' suppliers or customers. *A conglomerate merger* brings together firms that are not related in any of these ways.

merit good. A good or service that the government considers particularly desirable and that it therefore encourages by subsidy or regulation—such as the regulation that children must go to school to get the merit good of education. (p. 76)

microeconomics. The study of individual units within the economy—such as households, firms, and industries—and their interrelationships. The study of the allocation of resources and the distribution of income.

midpoint formula. The elasticity formula that uses the average of price and average of quantity, rather than either end point.

military-industrial complex. The combined political power exerted by military officers and defense industries; those with a vested interest in military spending. (In his farewell address, President Eisenhower warned against the military-industrial complex.)

minimum efficient scale. The output at which the average total cost curve reaches its minimum and becomes level.

minimum wage. The lowest wage that an employer may legally pay for an hour's work.

mint parity. The exchange rate calculated from the official prices of gold in two countries under the gold standard.

mixed economy. An economy in which the private market and the government share the decisions as to what will be produced, how, and for whom.

model. The essential features of an economy or economic problem, explained in terms of diagrams, equations, or words—or some combination of these.

monetarism. A body of thought that has its roots in classical economics and that rejects much of the teaching of Keynes' *General Theory*. According to monetarists, the most important determinant of aggregate demand is the quantity of money; the economy is basically stable if monetary growth is stable; and the authorities should follow a monetary rule, aiming for a steady growth of the money stock. Many monetarists also believe that the effects of fiscal policy on aggregate demand are weak (unless accompanied by changes in the quantity of money), that the government plays too active a role in the economy, and that the long-run Phillips curve is vertical. (p. 327)

monetary base. Currency held by the general public and by commercial banks plus the deposits of commercial banks in the Federal Reserve.

monetary policy. Central bank policies aimed at changing the rate of growth of the money stock or of interest rates. Examples: open market operations or changes in required reserve ratios. (p. 206)

monetary rule. The rule, proposed by monetarists, that the central bank should aim for a steady rate of growth of the money stock. (p. 321)

money. Any item commonly used in buying goods or services. Frequently, M1.

money illusion. Strictly defined, people have money illusion if their behavior changes in the event of a proportional change in prices, money incomes, and assets and liabilities measured in money terms. More loosely, people have money illusion if their behavior changes when there is a proportional change in prices and money incomes.

money income. Income measured in dollars (or, in another country, income measured in the currency of that country).

money market. The market for short-term debt instruments.

money multiplier. The number of dollars by which the money stock can increase as a result of a $1 increase in the reserves of commercial banks. (p. 201)

money stock (or supply). Narrowly, M1. More broadly and less commonly, M2 or M3. (pp. 188–190)

monopolistic competition. A market structure with many firms selling a differentiated product, with low barriers to entry. Individual firms have some small influence over price.

monopoly. (1) A market in which there is only a single seller. (p. 48) (2) The single seller in such a market. A *natural monopoly* occurs when the average total cost of a single firm falls over such an extended range that one firm can produce the total quantity sold at a lower average cost than could two or more firms. (p. *194*)

monopoly rent. Above-normal profit of a monopoly.

monopsony. A market in which there is only one buyer.

moral hazard. Any tendency for those who are protected (for example, by guarantees or insurance) to behave less carefully because they are protected. (p. 219)

moral suasion. Appeals or pressure by the Federal Reserve Board intended to influence the behavior of commercial banks. (p. 215)

most-favored-nation clause. A clause in a trade agreement that commits a country to impose no greater barriers (tariffs, etc.) on imports from a second country than it imposes on imports from any other country.

multinational corporation. A corporation that carries on business (either directly or through subsidiaries) in more than one country.

multiplier. The change in equilibrium real national product divided by the change in desired investment (or in government expenditures or exports). In the simplest economy (with a marginal tax rate of zero and no imports), the multiplier is $1 \div$ (the marginal propensity to save). (pp. 145, 148, 169n, 170n) See also *checking deposit multiplier.*

municipals. Bonds or shorter term securities issued by municipal governments.

national bank. A commercial bank chartered by the national government.

national debt. (1) The outstanding debt of the federal government. (2) The outstanding federal government debt excluding that held by federal government trust funds. (3) The outstanding federal government debt excluding that held by federal government trust funds and the 12 Federal Reserve Banks.

national income. The sum of all income of a nation, derived from providing the factors of production. It includes wages and salaries, rents, interest, and profits. (p. 83)

national product. The money value of the goods and services produced by a nation during a specific time period, such as a year. (p. 82) See *gross national product* and *net national product.*

natural monopoly. See *monopoly.*

natural oligopoly. See *oligopoly.*

natural rate of interest. The equilibrium rate of interest; the rate of interest consistent with a stable price level.

natural rate of unemployment. The equilibrium rate of unemployment that exists when people have adjusted completely to the existing rate of inflation. The rate of unemployment to which the economy tends when those making labor and other contracts correctly anticipate the rate of inflation. The rate of unemployment consistent with a stable rate of inflation. (p. 237)

near money. A highly liquid asset that can be quickly and easily converted into money. Examples: a savings deposit or a Treasury bill. (p. 190)

negative income tax. A reverse income tax whereby the government makes payments to individuals and families with low incomes. (The lower the income, the greater the payment from the government.)

negotiable order of withdrawal (NOW). A check-like order to pay funds from an interest-bearing savings deposit. (p. 194)

neocolonialism. The domination of the economy of a nation by the business firms or government of another nation or nations.

net exports. Exports minus imports.

net national product (NNP). Personal consumption expenditures plus government purchases of goods and services plus net private domestic investment plus net exports of goods and services. GNP minus capital consumption allowances. (p. 88).

net private domestic investment (I_n). Gross (private domestic) investment minus capital consumption allowances.

net worth. Total assets less total liabilities. The value of ownership. (pp. 191, *132*)

neutrality of money. Occurs when a change in the quantity of money affects only the price level without affecting relative prices or the distribution of income or wealth.

neutrality of taxes. (1) A situation in which taxes do not affect relative prices, and therefore disturb market forces as little as possible. (p. 72) (2) The absence of an excess burden of taxes.

New Left. Radical economists; Marxists of the 1960s and 1970s.

nominal. Measured in money terms. Current dollar as contrasted to constant dollar or real. (p. 92)

noncompeting groups. Groups of workers that do not compete with each other for jobs because their training or skills are different.

nonprice competition. Competition by means other than price. Example: advertising or product differentiation.

nontariff barrier (NTB). Government-imposed impediment to trade other than tariffs. Example: an import quota.

normal good. A good for which the quantity demanded rises as income rises, *ceteris paribus*. Contrast with an *inferior good*. (p. 53)

normal profit. The opportunity cost of capital and/or entrepreneurship. (Normal profit is considered a cost by economists but not by business accountants.)

normative statement. A statement about what should be. (p. 33) Contrast with a *positive statement*.

NOW account. A savings account against which a negotiable order of withdrawal (a check) may be written.

official settlements surplus. The balance-of-payments surplus of a country acquiring net international reserves (that is, a country whose international reserves are increasing more rapidly than foreign countries' reserve claims on it).

Okun's law. The observation that a change of 2% to 3% in real GNP (compared with its long-run trend) has been associated with a 1% change in the opposite direction in the unemployment rate. (Named after Arthur M. Okun.) (p. 110)

old age, survivors, and disability insurance. Social security.

oligopoly. A market that is dominated by a few sellers; they may sell either a standardized or differentiated product. (p. 48) A *natural oligopoly* occurs when the average total costs of individual firms fall over a large enough range that a few firms can produce the total quantity sold at the lowest average cost. (Compare with *natural monopoly*.)

oligopsony. A market in which there are only a few buyers.

open economy. An economy that has transactions with foreign nations.

open market operation. The purchase (or sale) of government (or other) securities by the central bank on the open market (that is, not directly from the issuer of the security). A purchase of securities causes an increase in bank deposits; a sale causes a decrease. (p. 208)

open shop. A business that may hire workers who are not (and need not become) union members. Contrast with *closed shop* and *union shop*.

opportunity cost. (1) The alternative that must be foregone when something is produced. (p. 29) (2) The amount that an input could earn in its best alternative use.

optimal purchase rule. A rule for maximizing the utility from a given income, by choosing the consumption pattern in such a way as to equalize the ratio of marginal utility to price for all goods and services purchased.

output gap. The amount by which output falls short of the potential or full-employment level. The GNP gap. (p. 165)

panic. A rush for safety, historically marked by a switch out of bank deposits into currency and out of paper currency into gold. A run on banks. (p. 192) A *stock market panic* occurs when there is a rush to sell and stock prices collapse.

paradox of thrift. The paradoxical situation, pointed out by Keynes, whereby an increase in the desire to save can result in a decrease in the equilibrium quantity of saving. (p. 161).

paradox of value. The apparent contradiction, pointed out by Adam Smith, when an essential (such as water) has a low price while a nonessential (such as a diamond) has a high price.

Pareto improvement. Making one person better off without making anyone else worse off. (Named after Vilfredo Pareto, 1848–1923.)

Pareto optimum. A situation in which it is impossible to make any Pareto improvement. That is, it is impossible to make any individual better off without making someone else worse off.

parity price. The price of a farm product (such as wheat) that would allow a farmer to exchange it for the same quantity of nonfarm goods as in the 1910–1914 base period. (A concept of fair price used in American agricultural policy since the Agricultural Adjustment Act of 1933.)

partial equilibrium analysis. Analysis of a particular market or set of markets, ignoring feedback from other markets.

participation rate. Number of people in the civilian labor force as a percentage of the civilian population of working age. (p. 109)

partnership. An unincorporated business owned by two or more people.

par value of a currency. Up to 1971, under the IMF adjustable peg system, the par value was the official price of a currency specified in terms of the U.S. dollar or gold. (p. 344)

patent. Exclusive right, granted by the government to an inventor, to use an invention for a specified time period. (Such a right can be licensed or sold by the patent holder.)

payoff matrix. A grid showing the various possible outcomes when two or more individuals are engaged in a cooperative or competitive activity.

payroll tax. A tax levied on wages and salaries, or on wages and salaries up to a specified limit. Example: social security tax.

peak. The month of greatest economic activity prior to the onset of a recession; one of the four phases of the business cycle. (p. 102)

peak-load pricing. Setting the price for a good or service higher during periods of heavy demand than at other times. The purpose is to encourage buyers to choose nonpeak periods and/or to raise more revenue. Examples: electricity; weekend ski tow.

pegged. Fixed by the authorities, at least temporarily. Examples: pegged interest rates (1941–1951); pegged exchange rates (1945–1973).

penalty rate. A discount rate kept consistently above a short-term market rate of interest (such as the rate on Treasury bills).

perfect competition. A market with many buyers and many sellers, with no single buyer or seller having any (noticeable) influence over price. That is, every buyer and every seller is a *price taker.*

permanent income. Normal income; income that is thought to be normal. (p. 311)

permanent-income hypothesis. The proposition that the principal determinant of consumption is permanent income (rather than current income). (p. 311)

perpetuity (or "perp"). A bond with no maturity date that pays interest forever. (p. 213).

personal consumption expenditures. See *consumption.*

personal income. Income received by households in return for productive services, and from transfers. (p. 91)

personal saving. (1) Loosely but commonly, disposable personal income less consumption expenditures. (p. 136) (2) More strictly, disposable personal income less consumption expenditures less payment of interest on consumer debt. (pp. 89, 91)

petrodollars. Liquid U.S. dollar assets held by oil-exporting nations, representing revenues received from the export of oil.

Phillips curve. The curve tracing out the relationship between the unemployment rate (on the horizontal axis) and the inflation rate or the rate of change of money wages (on the vertical axis).

(p. 228) The *long-run Phillips curve* is the curve (or line) tracing out the relationship between the unemployment rate and the inflation rate when the inflation rate is stable and correctly anticipated. (p. 236)

planned investment. Desired investment; investment demand; *ex ante* investment. (p. 140)

plant. A physical establishment where production takes place. (p. 49)

policy dilemma. Occurs when a policy that helps to solve one problem makes another worse.

political business cycle. A business cycle caused by actions of politicians designed to increase their chances of reelection. (p. 322)

positive statement. A statement about what is (or was) or about how something works. (p. 33) Contrast with a *normative statement.*

potential output (or potential GNP). The GNP that would exist if a high rate of employment were consistently maintained. (p. 116)

poverty. A condition that exists when people have inadequate income to buy the necessities of life. (p. 11)

poverty level (or poverty standard). An estimate of the income needed to avoid poverty. In 1988 it was $12,075 for a family of four. (p. 11)

precautionary demand for money. The amount of money that households and businesses want to hold to protect themselves against unforeseen events.

preferred stock. A stock that is given preference over common stock when dividends are paid. That is, specified dividends must be paid on preferred stock before any dividend is paid on common stock.

premature inflation. Inflation that occurs before the economy reaches full employment.

present value. The value now of a future receipt or receipts, calculated using the interest rate, i. The present value (PV) of $X to be received n years hence is $\$X \div (1 + i)^n$. (p. 213)

price ceiling. The legally established maximum price.

price discrimination. The sale of the same good or service at different prices to different customers or in different markets, provided the price differences are not justified by cost differences such as differences in transportation costs.

price-earnings ratio. The ratio of the price of a stock to the annual (after-tax) earnings per share of the stock.

price elasticity of demand (supply). See *elasticity of demand (supply).*

price floor. (1) The price at which the government undertakes to buy all surpluses, thus preventing any further decline in price. (2) The legally established minimum price.

price index. A weighted average of prices, as a percentage of prices existing in a base year. (p. 93)

price leadership. A method by which oligopolistic firms establish similar prices without overt collusion. One firm (the price leader) announces a new price, expecting that the other firm or firms will follow.

price line. See *budget line.*

price maker. A monopolist (or monopsonist) who is able to set price because there are no competitors.

price mechanism. See *market mechanism.*

price parity. See *parity price.*

price searcher. A seller (or buyer) who is able to influence price, and who has competitors whose responses can affect the profit-maximizing price. An oligopolist (or oligopsonist).

price support. A commitment by the government to buy surpluses at a given price (the support price) in order to prevent the price from falling below that figure.

price system. See *market mechanism.*

price taker. A seller or buyer who is unable to affect the price and whose market decision is limited to the quantity to be sold or bought at the existing market price. A seller or buyer in a perfectly competitive market.

price-wage flexibility. The ease with which prices and wages rise or fall (especially fall) in the event of changing demand and supply. Contrast with *price-wage stickiness.*

price-wage stickiness. The resistance of prices and wages to a movement, particularly in a downward direction. (p. 122)

primary burden of a tax. The amount of tax collected. Compare with *excess burden of a tax*.

prime rate of interest. (1) a bank's publicly announced interest rate on short-term loans. (2) Historically, the interest rate charged by banks on loans to their most creditworthy customers. (p. 214)

prisoners' dilemma. The dilemma as to whether or not you should confess, when a confederate may implicate you. The dilemma arises when a person who confesses receives a smaller penalty than a person who is implicated by a confederate.

private domestic investment. The production of private (nongovernmental) capital during a time period, including (1) plant and equipment, (2) residential buildings, and (3) additions to inventories. (p. 86)

privatization. The sale of government-owned businesses and assets to private firms or individuals. (p. 77)

procyclical policy. A policy that increases the amplitude of business fluctuations. ("Procyclical" refers to results, not intentions.)

producer surplus. Net benefit that producers get from being able to sell a good at the existing price. Returns to capital, entrepreneurship, workers, and others in the productive process in excess of their opportunity costs. Economic rent. Measured by the area left of the supply curve and below the existing price.

product differentiation. See *differentiated products*.

production function. The relationship showing the maximum output that can be produced with various combinations of inputs.

production possibilities curve. A curve showing the alternative combinations of outputs that can be produced if all productive resources are used. The boundary of attainable combinations of outputs. (p. 27)

productivity. Output per unit of input.

productivity of labor. The *average* productivity of labor is total output divided by the units of labor input. (pp. 109, 277) The *marginal* productivity of labor is the additional output when one more unit

of labor is added, while all other factors are held constant.

profit. In economics, return to capital and/or entrepreneurship over and above normal profit. In business accounting, revenues minus costs. Also sometimes used to mean profit after the payment of corporate income taxes.

profit-and-loss statement. An accounting statement that summarizes a firm's revenues, costs, and income taxes over a given period of time (usually a year). An income statement.

progressive tax. A tax that takes a larger percentage of income as income rises. (p. 69)

proletariat. Karl Marx's term for the working class, especially the industrial working class.

proportional tax. A tax that takes the same percentage of income regardless of the level of income. (p. 69)

proprietors' income. The income of unincorporated firms. (p. 90)

prospectus. A statement of the financial condition and prospects of a corporation, presented when new securities are about to be issued.

protectionism. The advocacy or use of high or higher tariffs or other trade barriers to protect domestic producers from foreign competition.

protective tariff. A tariff intended to protect domestic producers from foreign competition (as contrasted with a *revenue tariff*, intended as a source of revenue for the government).

proxy. A temporary written transfer of voting rights at a shareholders' meeting.

proxy fight. A struggle between competing groups in a corporation to obtain a majority vote (and therefore control of the corporation) by collecting proxies of shareholders.

public debt. See *national debt*.

public good. See *pure public good*.

public utility. A firm that is the sole supplier of an essential good or service in an area and is owned or regulated by the government.

pump priming. Short-term increases in government expenditures aimed at generating an upward momentum of the economy toward full employment.

purchasing power of money. The value of money in buying goods and services. The change in the purchasing power of money is measured by the change in the fraction l ÷ the price index. (p. 121) *General purchasing power* is something that can be used to buy any of the goods and services offered for sale; money. (p. 37)

purchasing-power parity theory. The theory that changes in exchange rates reflect and compensate for differences in the rate of inflation in different countries, leaving real exchange rates stable. (p. 348)

pure fiscal policy. A change in government spending or tax rates, unaccompanied by any change in the rate of growth of the money stock. (p. 305)

pure public good. A good (or service) with inexhaustible benefits that people cannot be excluded from enjoying, regardless of who pays for the good.

qualitative controls. In monetary policy, controls that affect the supply of funds to specific markets, such as the stock market; selective controls. (p. 214) Contrast with *quantitative controls.*

quantitative controls. In monetary policy, controls that affect the total supply of funds and the total quantity of money in an economy. (p. 214)

quantity theory (of money). The proposition that velocity is reasonably stable and that a change in the quantity of money will therefore cause nominal national product to change by approximately the same percentage. (p. 302)

quota. A numerical limit. Example: a limit on the amount of a good that may be imported.

random sample. A sample chosen from a larger group in such a way that every member of the group has an equal chance of being chosen.

rate base. Allowable capital of a public utility, to which the regulatory agency applies the allowable rate of return.

rate of exchange. The price of one national currency in terms of another. (p. 340)

rate of interest. Interest as a percentage per annum of the amount borrowed.

rate of return. (1) Annual profit as a percentage of

net worth. (2) Additional annual revenue from the sale of goods or services produced by plant or equipment, less depreciation and operating costs such as labor and materials, expressed as a percentage of the value of the plant or equipment.

rational expectations. The best forecasts that can be made with available information, including information on (1) what the authorities are doing, and (2) how the economy works. If expectations are rational, people may make mistakes, but they do not make *systematic* mistakes. Their errors are random. (p. 253)

rationing. (1) A method for allocating a good (or service) when the quantity demand exceeds the quantity supplied at the existing price. (2) More loosely, any method for allocating a scarce resource or good. In this sense, we may speak of the market *rationing by price.*

ratio (or logarithmic) scale. A scale in which equal proportional changes are shown as equal distances. For example, the distance from 100 to 200 is equal to the distance from 200 to 400. (Each involves a doubling.) (p. 20)

Reaganomics. The economic program of President Reagan, including (1) tax cuts, (2) restraint in domestic spending, (3) increases in defense spending, and (4) less regulation. (p. 70)

real. Measured in quantity terms; adjusted to remove the effects of inflation. (p. 93)

real capital. Buildings, equipment, and other materials used in production, which have themselves been produced in the past. Buildings, equipment, and inventories.

real exchange rate. The nominal exchange rate adjusted for differences in inflation. (p. 348)

real wage. The quantity of goods and services that a money wage will buy; the money wage adjusted for inflation. (p. 93)

recession. A decline in output, income, employment, and trade, usually lasting six months to a year and marked by widespread contractions in many sectors of the economy. (pp. 9, 102)

recessionary gap. The vertical distance by which the aggregate expenditures line is below the 45° line at the full-employment quantity of national product. (p. 165)

recognition lag. The time interval between the beginning of a problem and the time when the problem is recognized. (p. 316)

regression analysis. A statistical calculation of the relationship between two or more variables.

regressive tax. A tax that takes a smaller percentage of income as income rises. (p. 69)

rent. (1) In economics, any payment to a factor of production in excess of its opportunity cost. (2) A payment by the user of land to the owner. (3) Payments by users to the owners of land, buildings, or equipment.

replacement-cost depreciation. Depreciation based on the current replacement cost of buildings and equipment rather than their original acquisition cost.

required reserve ratio. The fraction of deposit liabilities that a bank must keep in reserves. (p. 194)

required reserves. The reserves that a bank legally must keep. For members of the Federal Reserve System, these reserves are held in the form of currency or deposits with a Federal Reserve Bank. (p. 194)

rescheduling of debt. The renegotiation of the terms of the debt, to give the debtor more time to repay, sometimes including a reduction in the interest rate. (p. 288)

reservation price of a resource. The cost of harvesting the resource today plus the amount necessary to compensate for the reduction in the quantity of the resource available in the future.

reserves. See *required reserves* and *foreign exchange reserves*.

resource. Basic inputs used in the production of goods and services, namely, labor, land, and capital. (p. 26)

restrictive agreement. Agreement among companies to restrain competition through practices such as price fixing or market sharing.

retail price maintenance. Practice whereby a manufacturer sets the minimum retail price of a product, thereby eliminating price competition among retailers of that product.

return to capital. See *rate of return*.

revaluation of a currency. An increase in the par value of the currency. (p. 345)

revenue sharing. Grant by the federal government to a state or local government. *General revenue sharing* involves grants whose use is (practically) unrestricted.

revenue tariff. A tariff intended to provide revenues for the government (as contrasted with a *protective tariff*, intended to protect domestic producers from foreign competition).

Ricardian equivalence theorem. The theorem that the path of consumption will be the same, whether the government finances its spending by taxes or by issuing debt. (p. 312)

right-to-work law. State law making it illegal to require union membership as a condition of employment. State prohibition of closed shops and union shops.

risk premium. The difference between the yields on two grades of bonds (or other securities) because of differences in their risk. The additional interest or yield needed to compensate the holder of bonds (or other securities) for risk.

roundabout production. The production of capital goods and the use of these capital goods in the production of consumer goods. The production of goods in more than one stage.

rule of the gold standard game. The understanding that each country would permit its money stock to change in the same direction as the change in its gold stock. That is, if a country's gold stock were to rise, it should allow its money supply to increase, and vice versa.

rule of 70. A rule that tells approximately how many years it will take for something to double in size if it is growing at a compound rate. For example, a deposit earning 2% interest approximately doubles in $70 \div 2 = 35$ years. In general, a deposit earning $x\%$ interest will double in about $70 \div x$ years. (p. 271)

run. A rush to switch into safer assets. Example: a *run on banks*. (p. 192)

satisficing theory. The theory that firms do not try to maximize profits but rather aim for reasonable target levels of profits, sales, and other measures of performance.

saving. (1) Loosely but commonly, disposable personal income less consumption expenditures. (p. 136) (2) More strictly, disposable personal income less consumption expenditures less payment of interest on consumer debt. (pp. 89, 91) (3) National saving—that is, personal saving plus business saving plus government saving.

saving function. (1) The relationship between personal saving and disposable income. (p. 138) (2) More broadly, the relationship between personal saving and the factors (like disposable income) that determine saving.

Say's law. The discredited view that supply in the aggregate creates its own demand (regardless of the general price level). (p. 158)

scarcity. (1) The inability to satisfy all wants because they exceed what we can produce with our available resources. (p. 27) (2) A shortage—that is, the amount by which quantity supplied is less than quantity demanded at the existing price. (p. 52)

SDRs. See *special drawing rights*.

seasonal adjustment. The removal of regular seasonal movements from a time series. (p. 103)

secondary boycott. Boycott against a firm to discourage it from doing business with a second firm, in order to exert pressure on the second firm (which may be in a strong position to withstand other forms of pressure).

secondary reserves. Bank holdings of liquid assets (Treasury bills, etc.) that can readily be converted into primary reserves (currency or reserve deposits).

second best, theory of the. The theory of how to get the best results in remaining markets when one or more markets have defects about which nothing can be done.

secular stagnation. A situation of inadequate aggregate demand extending over many years. Consequently, large-scale unemployment persists, and it may even become increasingly severe. (This was considered a major problem half a century ago.)

secular trend. The trend in economic activity over an extended period of years.

selective controls. In monetary policy, controls that affect the supply of funds to specific markets, such as the stock market; qualitative controls. (p. 214)

sell short. See *short sale*.

seniority rules. Rules giving preference to those who have been longest on the job. Individuals with seniority are typically the last to be discharged or laid off, and the first to be rehired.

shortage. (1) The amount by which quantity supplied is less than quantity demanded at the existing price; the opposite of a *surplus*. (2) Any deficiency. (p. 52)

short run. (1) The period before the price level has adjusted to its equilibrium. (2) The period in which the quantity of plant and equipment cannot change. (3) The time period before equilibrium can be reestablished. (4) Any brief time period.

short-run production function. The table showing the relationship between the amount of variable factors used and the amount of output that can be produced, in a situation where the quantity of capital is constant. For the simple case of a firm with just two inputs—capital and one variable factor—the short-run production function is one row in the long-run production function.

short sale. A contract to sell something at a later date for a price specified now.

shutdown point. The lowest point on the average variable cost curve. If the price is lower than this point, the firm will shut down.

single-tax proposal. The proposal of Henry George (1839–1897) that all taxes be eliminated except one on land. (George argued that all returns to land represent an unearned surplus.)

slope. The vertical rise in a function divided by the horizontal run. (p. 23)

snake. An agreement among some Western European countries to keep their currencies within a narrow band of fluctuation (the snake). Prior to 1973, they allowed their currencies to move jointly in a wide band with respect to the dollar. (This was called the *snake in the tunnel*.) Since 1973, the snake has not been tied to the dollar.

socialism. An economic system in which the means of production (capital equipment, buildings, and land) are owned by the state.

soil bank program. A government program under which the government pays farmers to take land out of production (in order to reduce crop surpluses).

sole proprietorship. A business owned by an individual person. Contrast with *partnership* and *corporation*.

special drawing rights (SDRs). Bookkeeping accounts created by the International Monetary Fund to increase the quantity of international reserves held by national governments. SDRs can be used to cover balance-of-payments deficits.

specific tax. A fixed number of cents or dollars of tax on each unit of the good. Contrast with *ad valorem tax.*

speculation. The purchase (or sale) of an asset in the hope of making a profit from a rise (fall) in its price. (p. 345)

speculative demand for money. The schedule or curve showing how the rate of interest affects the amount of assets that firms and households are willing to hold in the form of money, rather than in bonds or other interest-bearing securities.

speculator. Anyone who buys or sells an asset in the hope of profiting from a change in its price. (p. 345)

spillover. See *externality.*

stagflation. The coexistence of a high rate of unemployment (stagnation) and inflation. (p. 228)

standard of value. The item (money) in which the prices of goods and services are measured. (p. 188)

state bank. A commercial bank chartered by a state government.

sterilization of gold. See *gold sterilization.*

store of value. An asset that may be used to store wealth through time; an asset that may be used to finance future purchases. (p. 188)

structural budget (or high-employment budget). The size that the government's surplus (or deficit) would be with existing spending programs and tax rates, if the economy were at full employment. Full-employment government receipts (that is, the receipts that would be obtained with present tax rates if the economy were at full employment) minus full-employment government expenditures (that is, actual expenditures less expenditures directly associated with unemployment in excess of the full-employment level). (p. 172)

structural unemployment. Unemployment resulting from a mismatch between the skills or location of the labor force and the skills or location required by employers. Unemployment resulting from a changing location or composition of jobs. (p. 113)

subchapter S corporation. A corporation treated in the tax code as if it were a partnership. Advantage: It avoids double taxation.

subsidy. A negative tax.

subsistence wage. Minimum living wage. A wage below which population will decline because of starvation or disease. (p. 292)

substitute, or substitute in consumption. A good or service that satisfies similar needs. Two commodities are substitutes if a rise in the price of one causes a rightward shift in the demand curve for the other. (p. 53)

substitute in production. A good or service whose production uses the same inputs. Two commodities are substitutes if a rise in the price of one causes a leftward shift in the supply curve of the other. (p. 55)

substitution effect. The change in the quantity of a good demanded because of a change in its price when the real income effect of the change in price has been eliminated. That is, a change in the quantity demanded as a result of a movement along a single indifference curve. See also *income effect.*

sunspot theory. The theory put forward in the late nineteenth century that cycles in sunspot activity cause cycles in agricultural production and hence cycles in business activity.

supply. The schedule or curve showing the quantities of a good or service that sellers would be willing and able to sell at various prices, *ceteris paribus.* (p. 51)

supply of money. See *money stock.*

supply schedule. A table showing the quantities of a good or service that sellers would be willing and able to sell at various prices, *ceteris paribus.* (p. 51)

supply shift. A movement of the supply curve of a good (or service) to the right or left as a result of a change in the price of inputs or any other determinant of the quantity supplied (except the price of the good or service itself). (p. 54)

supply shifter. Anything that affects the quantity of a good or service supplied except its own price. (p. 55)

supply shock. A sudden and unexpected change in the price or availability of inputs that can push costs and the aggregate supply curve upward. (p. 232)

supply side. The view that it is supply factors—such as the quantity of capital and the willingness to work—that are the principal constraints to growth. According to this view, a lack of aggregate demand is not the main constraint. (p. 175)

surplus. (1) The amount by which quantity supplied exceeds quantity demanded at the existing price. (p. 52) (2) A *budget surplus:* an excess of government revenues over expenditures. (p. 70) (3) Any excess or amount left over. Contrast with *shortage.*

surplus value. In Marxist economics, the amount by which the value of a worker's output exceeds the wage; a measure of capitalist exploitation.

sustainable yield. The amount of a renewable resource (like fish) that can be harvested while still leaving the population constant.

sympathy strike. A strike by a union that does not have a dispute with its own employer but rather is trying to strengthen the bargaining position of another striking union.

syndicate. An association of investment bankers to market a large block of securities.

tacit collusion. The adoption of a common policy by sellers without explicit agreement.

takeoff. The achievement of the situation of sustained growth, in which capital can be accumulated without depressing the standard of living below its existing level.

target price. Agricultural price guaranteed to farmers by the government. (If the market price falls short of the target price, the government pays farmers the difference.)

tariff. (1) A tax on an imported good; a duty. (2) A schedule or list of duties.

tax-based incomes policy (TIP). An incomes policy backed up with tax penalties on violators or tax incentives for those who cooperate. (p. 247)

tax credit. A subtraction from the tax payable.

tax deduction. A subtraction from taxable income. Suppose an individual pays $1,000 in interest on a home mortgage. This $1,000 can be deducted from taxable income. For someone in the 28% tax bracket, this results in a $280 reduction in taxes.

tax incidence. See *incidence of a tax.*

tax neutrality. (1) A situation in which taxes do not affect relative prices. (2) A situation in which the excess burden of taxes is zero. (p. 72)

tax shifting. Occurs when the initial taxpayer transfers all or part of a tax to others. (For example, a firm that is taxed may charge a higher price.)

technological (or technical) efficiency. Providing the maximum output with the available resources and technology, while working at a reasonable pace. The avoidance of wasted motion and sloppy management. (p. 10)

terms of trade. The average price of goods sold divided by the average price of goods bought.

theory of games. See *game theory.*

theory of public choice. Theory of how government spending decisions are made and how they should be made.

third world. Countries that are neither in the "first" world (the high-income countries of Western Europe and North America, plus a few others such as Japan) nor in the "second" world (the countries of Eastern Europe). Low-income countries. (p. 281)

time preference. The desire to have goods now rather than in the future. The amount by which goods now are preferred over goods in the future.

time series. A set of observations taken in successive time periods. Examples: GNP in 1988, in 1989, in 1990, etc. (p. 18)

TIP. See *tax-based incomes policy.*

total cost. The sum of fixed costs and variable costs.

total revenue. Total receipts from the sale of a product. Where there is a single price, that price times the quantity sold.

transactions demand for money. The amount of money that firms and individuals want to cover the time between the receipt of income and the making of expenditures.

transfer payment. A payment, usually made by the government to private individuals, that does not result from current productive activity and is not compensation for services rendered. (p. 67)

transfer price. The price necessary to attract a factor of production.

Treasury bill. A short-term (less than a year, often three months) debt of the U.S. Treasury. It carries no explicit interest payment; a purchaser gains by buying a bill for less than its face value. (p. 212)

trough. The month of lowest economic activity prior to the beginning of a recovery; one of the four phases of the business cycle. (p. 102)

turnover tax. A tax on goods or services (whether they are intermediate or final products) whenever they are sold.

turning point. The trough or peak of a business cycle.

tying contract. Contract that requires the purchaser to buy another item or items in a seller's line of products in order to get the one that is really wanted.

underemployed. (1) Workers who can find only part-time work when they want full-time work. (2) Workers who are being paid full time but are not kept busy because of low demand for output. (p. 109)

underground economy. Economic activity unobserved by tax collectors and government statisticians. (p. 96)

underwrite. To guarantee that a new issue of stock will all be sold. (An investment banker who underwrites stock but is unable to sell it all must buy the remainder.)

undesired inventory accumulation. Actual inventory accumulation less desired inventory accumulation. (p. 142)

undistributed corporate profits. After-tax corporate profits less dividends paid.

unemployment. The condition of people who are willing to work but cannot find jobs. More generally, the condition of any underutilized resource. (p. 108)

unemployment rate. The percentage of the labor force unemployed. (p. 109)

union. An association of workers, formed to negotiate over wages, fringe benefits, and working conditions.

union shop. A business where all nonunion workers must join the union soon after they are employed. Compare with *closed shop* and *right-to-work law.*

unit elasticity. Elasticity of 1. If a demand curve has unit elasticity, total revenue remains unchanged as price changes. (The demand curve is a rectangular hyperbola.) If a supply curve has unit elasticity, it is a straight line that would, if extended, go through the origin.

unlimited liability. Responsibility for debts without limit.

utility. The ability to satisfy wants.

value added. Value of the product sold less the cost of intermediate products bought from outside suppliers. (p. 85)

variable cost. Any cost that increases as output increases.

variable rate mortgage. A mortgage whose interest rate is adjusted periodically in response to changes in a market rate of interest. (p. 269)

velocity of money. The average number of times per year that the average dollar in the money stock is spent. There are two principal ways of calculating velocity. (1) *Income velocity* is the number of times the average dollar is spent on final products (that is, GNP ÷ M). (2) *Transaction velocity* is the number of times the average dollar is spent on *any* transaction (including those for intermediate goods and financial assets). That is, total spending ÷ M. (pp. 302, 307)

vertical merger. See *merger.*

vicious circle of inflation and depreciation. The tendency for inflation to cause a depreciation of the currency, which can lead to more inflation and more depreciation. (p. 347)

vicious circle of poverty. The interrelationships that make it difficult to escape from poverty. For example, a poor country has difficulty saving and investing. (p. 282)

virtuous circle. The tendency for a lower-than-average rate of inflation to cause an appreciation of the currency, which can help to keep inflation low. (p. 348)

wage-price spiral. A tendency for inflation to lead to higher nominal wages, which can lead to even more inflation. (p. 234)

workable competition. A compromise that limits monopoly power while allowing firms to become big enough to reap the economies of scale. A practical alternative to the often unattainable goal of perfect competition.

yellow-dog contract. Contract in which an employee agrees not to become a member of a union.

yield. The annual rate of discount that would make the present value of a stream of future payments equal to the price or present value of an asset. (p. 213) The *rate of return*.

zero-base budgeting. A budgeting technique that requires items to be justified anew "from the ground up," without regard to how much has been spent on them in the past.

INDEX

Aaron, Henry J., 181n.
Accelerationist theory, 233-237
Accelerator, 333-336
    interaction with multiplier, 336-337
Action lag, 316
Activist, (*see* Fine tuning)
Adaptive expectations, 251
Adjustable peg exchange rate system, 344
    breakdown of, 346-347
Adjustable-rate mortgage, 269
Aggregate demand, 119-133
    Classical, 120-121
    Keynesian, 124, 127
Aggregate expenditure *vs.* aggregate
    demand, 139
Aggregate supply, 119-130, 226-228
    Classical, 121
    Keynesian, 125-127
    relation to Phillips curve, 226-228
Allocative efficiency (*see* Efficiency,
    allocative)
Annually-balanced budget, 179
Appreciation of currency, 348
Automatic stabilizers, 170-171
    vs. discretionary action, 171
    government expenditures as, 171
    taxes as, 170-171

Baily, Martin N., 278n.
Baker, Howard, 330
Balanced budget, 70, 171-181
    annually, 179
    over the business cycle, 179
    as a trap, 171-172
Balance of payments, 355-358
    U.S. figures for 1988, 356
Balance of trade, 287, 350, 358
Band of an exchange rate, 344, 352
Banking, 190-202
    fractional-reserve, 192
    historical development of, 190-193
    (*See also* Banks)
Bank rate, 211
Banks, 192-197
    assets and liabilities of, 193-194
    balance sheet, 194
    cheque clearing, 197-198
    excess reserves, 196-197
    and money creation, 195-202
    multiple expansion of deposits, 198-
        202
    regulation of, 195
    required reserves, 193-194, 196-197

    runs on, 192
    (*See also* Commercial banks)
Barro, Robert, 311-312
Barter, 36
Belsley, David A., 228n.
Bernheim, B. Douglas, 312
Black death, 58
Black market (*see* Price controls, and black
    markets)
Blinder, Alan, 306
Bosworth, Barry, 181n.
Boulding, Kenneth E., 94n.
Brenner, Harvey, 115
Britain (*see* United Kingdom)
Brown, Charles, 243n.
Burns, Arthur F., 207
Burtless, Gary, 181n., 244n.
Bush, George, 71, 323
Business cycle:
    four phases of, 101-103
    history of, 100-101, 103-112, 315, 320,
        324
    political, 322

Canada:
    free trade agreement with, 43-44
Capital:
    and growth, 279-280, 282-284
    human, 27
    in international payments, 357
    physical, 26
    real *vs.* financial, 26
    social, 284
Capital account, 355
Capitalism, 47
Capitalized value, 213
Capital/output ratio, 336
Caplan, Mortimer, 73
Carter, Jimmy, 75, 179, 323
    incomes policies, 246-247
Central bank (*see* Federal Reserve)
Central planning *vs.* free enterprise, 47
Ceteris paribus assumption, 52
Chakrabarti, Alok K., 278n.
Circular flow, 37-39, 57, 83, 143, 144
Civil Aeronautics Board (CAB), 75
Civilian Conservation Corps (CCC), 66
Classical theory, 120-124
    aggregate demand, 120-121
    aggregate supply, 121
    equilibrium at full employment, 121-
        122
    and the Great Depression, 122-123

    (*See also* Keynesian theory, *vs.* Classical
        theory)
Clean float, 346
Clegg, Hugh, 247n.
Cohen, Andrew, 243n.
Colbert, Jean Baptiste, 72
Commercial banks, 193-194
    (*See also* Banks)
Complements (complimentary goods)
    in consumption, 53
    in production (joint products), 55
Compound growth, 213, 271
Conflicting goals:
    full employment *vs.* price stability, 230-
        231, 242-255
    price controls *vs.* efficiency, 248
Consumer price index, 93
Consumption, 85, 89, 135-142
    function, 135-136
        long run *vs.* short run, 311
    influences on, 135-137, 154-155
        expectations (permanent income), 155
        income, 135-137
        time, 154
        wealth (money balances), 155
    in Keynesian theory, 135-142
    recession and, 105-107
    and saving, 136-137
Cost of living allowance (COLA), 249
Cost-push inflation, 231-233
Crawling peg exchange rate system, 352
Credibility, 253
Crowding out, 304-305
Currency, 188, 202
    depreciation of, 347-348
    devaluation of, 345
    in international exchange, 339-340
Current account, 356-358
Cycles:
    business:
        four phases of, 101-102
        history of, 100-101, 103-112, 315, 320,
            324
        political, 322

Debasement of currency, 40
Debt:
    duration of, 269-270
    front-loaded, 269-270
    of the government, 176-177
    international crisis, 288-290
    rescheduling, 288

Deficit:
  of the government, 70, 176-177
    and Social Security surplus, 181-182
    in international trade, 287, 350, 358
    interrelation between these two
      deficits, 305-306, 350-351
    real, 272
Deflation, 9
Deindustrialization, 350
Delors Report (1989), 353
Demand, 49-50
  for money, 297-298, 303
  shifters of, 52-54
  and supply, 51
Demand–pull inflation, 231-233
Denison, Edward F., 279-281
Depreciation, 87-90
  of capital, 87
  of a currency, 347-348
Depression, 7
Deregulation:
  of financial institutions, 194-195, 218
Devaluation, 345
Diagrams in economics:
  bar charts, 16
    when misleading, 17-18
  slope, meaning of, 23
  time series, 18
Dilemma, 230, 242-258
Diogenes, 296
Dirty float, 346
Discount rate, 211
Discretionary policies
  criticisms of, 315-320
  vs. stable policy settings, 313-330
Disposable income, 89, 91
Dissaving, 138
  (See also Saving)
Double-entry bookkeeping, 355
Downs, Anthony, 268n.
Duesenberry, James, 155

Econometric models, 326-327
Economic growth (see Growth)
Economies of scale, 42-43, 279, 283
Education:
  as a cause of growth, 279
Efficiency, 11
  allocative, 11
    and incomes policies, 248
  technical (technological), 10, 11
Eisner, Robert, 85n., 272-273
Employer of last resort, 245
Employment Act of 1946, 8
Entrepreneur, 27
Equal Employment Opportunities
  Commission (EEOC), 74
Equation of exchange, MV = PQ, 301-302
Escalator clause, 249
European Community (EC):
  unemployment in, 256-258
European Monetary System, 352-353
Exchange rate, 287, 339-353
  appreciation of, 348
  band, 344, 352
  crawling peg, 352

depreciation of, 347-348
devaluation of, 345
flexible (floating), 347-351
fluctuations of, 348-351
fundamental equilibrium, 352
under gold standard, 343
pegged, 344-347
real and nominal, 348
revaluation of, 345
Expectations:
  adaptive, 251
  of inflation, 250-255
  when policies are anticipated, 250-255
  rational, 253-255
  self-fulfilling, 346
Exports, 87, 89, 169-170

Fair, Raymond, 323
Fallacy of composition, 161
Federal Aviation Administration (FAA), 74
Federal Deposit Insurance Corporation
  (FDIC), 74, 217-219
Federal Drug Administration (FDA), 74
Federal Open Market Committee
  (FOMC), 208
Federal Reserve, 193, 206-222
  balance sheet, 215
  board of governors, 207-208
  discount rate, 211
  as the federal government's bank, 193
  Federal Open Market Committee
    (FOMC), 208
  and margin requirement, 214
  moral suasion, 215
  open market operations, 208-211
  organization, 206-208
  regional banks, 207
  reserve requirements, 211-212
  roles of, 193
Federal Reserve Act, 193
Federal Reserve Board, 207-208
Federal Savings and Loan Insurance
  Corporation (FSLIC), 217-219
  recent losses, 218-219
Federal Trade Commission, 74
Feige, Edgar L., 96
Fellner, William, 253
Fiat money, 217
Final products, 84
Fine tuning:
  criticisms of, 315-320
  vs. stable policy settings, 313-330
Fiscal policy, 164-186
  Classical vs. Keynesian view of, 129
  compared to monetary policy, 296-305
  multiplier and, 164-165
  pure, 305
  tax cuts vs. government expenditures,
    167-168
Fischer, Stanley, 255, 281n.
Fisher, Irving, 268
Flanagan, Robert J., 247n.
Floating (flexible) exchange rate (see
  Exchange rate)
Fluctuations, business, 100-101, 103-112,
  315, 320, 324

(See also Business cycles)
Fluctuations in economic activity, 100-116
Forecasting, 326-330
Foreign exchange, 340
  demand for, 341
  par value, 344
  policies to cure disequilibrium, 341-343
  reserves, 342
  supply of, 341
  (See also Exchange rate)
Four tigers, 285-288
Free enterprise vs. central planning, 47
  (See also Free markets)
Free markets:
  strengths, 59
  weaknesses, 60-62
Friedman, Milton, 122n., 155n., 237, 238n.,
  296-297, 314, 324
Friedman, Rose, 6, 129n.
Front-loaded mortgages, 269-270
Full-employment budget, 172-174
  full employment deficit vs. cyclical
    deficit, 173
Full employment, 114-115
Full line forcing (see Tying contracts)
Fundamental disequilibrium (of exchange
  rate), 245

Gain-sharing, 250
Gilroy, Curtis, 243n.
GNP, potential, 320
GNP gap, 116, 320
GNP price deflator, 93
Galbraith, John Kenneth, 6, 61
Goals:
  complementality of, 13
  conflict among, 13
Goldfeld, Stephen M., 307
Gold standard, 217-220, 343-344
  collapse of, 217-218
  and domestic policy conflict, 343
  international adjustment under, 343
  and monetary instability, 217-220
Government expenditure:
  as an automatic stabilizer, 171
  as a countercyclical policy, 165-166
  federal vs. state and local, 67
  on national defense, 67, 68
  purchases vs. transfer payments, 66-67
Government regulation (see Regulation)
Government's role, 65-78
  Classical vs. Keynesian view of, 129-130
  in providing merit goods, 76
  (See also Government expenditure;
    Privatization; Regulation; Taxes)
Gradualism, 239-240
Graduated-payment mortgage, 270-271
Gramlich, Edward, 243n.
Gramm-Rudman Act, 180-181
Great Britain (see United Kingdom)
Greenspan, Alan, 207
Gresham's law, 40
Gross domestic product (GDP), 286
Gross national product (GNP), 87, 89, 106
  full employment GNP (or potential
    GNP), 115-116

real *vs.* nominal, 91-92
Growth, 30-31
 disappointing record (1973-1979), 278-281
 and environment, 13
 and human capital, 279
 and improvements in technology, 279, 283
 international comparisons, 281-282
 in labor force, 279
 population and, 283-284
 and research and development, 280
 sources of, 279-288
Gutman, Peter M., 96

Havrilesky, Thomas, 323
Heath, Edward, 250
Helfrich, Harold, 94*n.*
Heller, Walter W., 164, 297*n.*, 314*n.*
Hemingway, Ernest, 226
Henry, O., 206
Hong Kong, 58, 285-288
Housing:
 and inflation, 268-272
 as investment, 86
Houthakker, H.S., 370
Huff, Darrell, 17
Hume, David, 36
Humphrey–Hawkins bill, 245
Hyperinflation, 10, 187
Hysteresis, 258

Impact lag, 316
Imports, 87, 169-170
Income:
 national, 82-83, 89, 90
 permanent, 311
 personal, 89, 91
Incomes policy, 230, 245-248
Income statement, 414
Indexation:
 cap on, 249
 of wages, 248-250
Indivisibility, 37
Inferior goods, 53
Inflation, 9
 adjustment for, 163-267
 anticipated *vs.* unanticipated, 262-265
 and bonds, 263-267, 269-270
 vs. change in relative prices, 10
 cost-push *vs.* demand-pull, 231-233
 and front-loading of debt, 269-270
 historical record of, 262
 and home ownership, 268-272
 and interest rates, 263-268
 and rational expectations, 253-255
 and the taxation of interest income, 267-268
 and tradeoff with unemployment, 230-231, 242-258
 and uncertainty, 268-269
 unwinding of, 238-240, 252-255
 winners and losers from, 263
Information:
 role of prices in providing, 48

Infrastructure, 284
Injections and leakages, 169-170
Innovation (*see* Technological change)
Interest rate:
 and bond prices, 213
 and the demand for money, 298
 effect of monetary policy on, 212-214, 297-298
 and inflation, 263-267
 as an influence on investment, 299-301, 305
 as a policy target, 220-222
 prime rate, 214
 real *vs.* nominal, 263-267
 taxation of, 267-268
Interest rate target, 220-222
Intermediate products, 84
International adjustment mechanism, 343
International Bank for Reconstruction and Development, 282, 344
International Monetary Fund, 344-347
International trade:
 collapse in Great Depression, 104
Inventories, 86, 140-142
 undesired accumulation of, 140, 142
 undesired decrease in, 141-142
Investment, 86, 89
 as appearing in international payments, 357
 desired *vs.* actual, 140-142
 during recession, 106, 107
 and growth, 279-280, 282-284
 in housing, 86
 in inventories, 86
 in Keynesian theory, 139
 lags in, 335
 net *vs.* gross, 88
 in plant and equipment, 86
 social, 284
Invisible hand, 5
Iron law of wages, 292

Jackson, Andrew, 206
Japan, 3, 58
Jawboning, 215
Jobs, Steve, 27
Job Training Partnership Act (JTPA), 245
Johnson, Lyndon, B., wage-price guideposts, 246
Joint products (complements), 55
Jorgenson, Dale, 281*n.*

Kendrick, John W., 278*n.*, 281*n.*
Kennedy, Edward, 245
Kennedy, John F., 167
 wage-price guideposts, 246
Keynes, John Maynard, 6, 119, 134, 184
 (*See also* Keynesian theory)
Keynesian theory, 124-161
 aggregate demand, 127, 132-133
 aggregate supply, 125-127
 vs. Classical theory, 127-130, 156-158
 areas of agreement, 128-129
 areas of disagreement, 129-130
 equilibrium with large-scale unemployment, 124, 142

role of government spending, 124, 127, 164-165
 role of monetary policy, 297-301
 unstable investment in, 127
Kindleberger, Charles, 104
Korea, 285-288
Kravis, Irving B., 281
Labor productivity, 277-279
 its disappointing increase (1973-1979), 278-281
Laffer curve, 185-186
Lags:
 in accelerator theory, 335
 action lag, 316
 impact lag, 316
 in monetary and fiscal policies, 317
 in prices, relative to real output, 318-319
 recognition lag, 316
Laissez faire, 5
 (*See also* Free markets)
Lawrence, Robert Z., 244*n.*, 257*n.*
Leading indicator, 328-329
Leakages-injections approach, 145
Legal tender, 216
Less-developed countries (LDCs)
 problems in development, 282-285, 288-290
 successes in development, 285-288
Levy, Frank, 181*n.*
Liquidity preference theory, 298
Litan, Robert, 219

M1, M2, definitions of money, 188-190
McNees, Stephen K., 330
Malthus, Thomas, 292
Margin requirement, 214-215
Marginal propensity to consume (MPC), 138
 and the marginal propensity to save, 139
 and the multiplier, 147-148
Marginal propensity to save (MPS), 138
 and the marginal propensity to consume, 139
 and the multiplier, 148-149
Marshall, Alfred, 1
Martin, William McChesney, 207
Marxism, 6
Measure of economic welfare (MEW), 93-96
Mechanism of adjustment, 343
Merchandise account surplus or deficit, 358
Merit goods, 76-77
Mexico, 289
Minimum wage, 243-244
 and teenage unemployment, 243-244
Mobility of labor, 110, 112
Model, econometric, 326-327
Monetarism, 129, 256, 301-308
 compared to Keynesianism, 327
Monetary policy, 206-240, 297-303
 Classical *vs.* Keynesian view of, 129
 (*See also* Federal Reserve)
Monetary pyramid, 203
Monetary rule, 303
 criticisms of, 321-325

vs. fine-tuning, 313-330
Money, 38-40, 187-202
    creation of, 195-202
    definitions of, 188-190
    demand for, 297-298, 303
    functions of, 188
    velocity of, 302
Money market deposits and mutual
    funds, 190
Moore, Geoffrey H., 101, 102*n*.
Moore, John, 78*n*.
Moral suasion, 215
Morris Frank, 326
Mortgages:
    graduated payment, 270-271
    variable rate, 269
Multiplier, 145-150, 164, 168-170
    MPC and, 147-148
    MPS and, 148-149
    when prices change, 149-150
    effect of taxes on, 168-169

National Bureau of Economic Research
    (NBER), 101, 102, 328
National debt, 176-178
    when a future burden, when not, 176-
        177
National income, 82-83, 89, 90
National Monetary Commission, 193
National product, 82-87
National Recovery Act, 126
Natural rate of unemployment, 236
Near money, 190
Negotiable order of withdrawal (NOW),
    194-195
Net national product, 87, 89, 90
Nixon, Richard M., 323
    wage-price freeze, 246, 261
Nordhaus, William, 94, 95
Normative statement, 33

Oil, 232-233, 280
Okun, Arthur, 95, 238, 262
Open market committee, 208
Open market operations, 208-211
Opportunity cost, 28-29, 30
Output-expenditures approach, 144-145
Output gap, 165-166

Par value of a currency, 344
Paradox of thrift, 160-161
Peckman, Joseph, 73*n*.
Peek, Joe, 268
Permanent income hypothesis, 311
Perpetuity, 213
Personal income, 89, 91
Peter, Lawrence J., 75*n*.
Phelps, Edmund S., 237
Phillips curve, 228-231
    short-run *vs.* long-run, 235-238
Pieper, Paul J., 272-273
Pigou effect, 158
Pohl, Karl-Otto, 248
Policy dilemma, 230
Policy rule, 303
    criticisms of, 321-325
    vs. fine-tuning, 313-330

Political business cycle, 322
Pope, Alexander, 277
Population:
    and growth, 283-284
    Malthusian theory, 292
Positive statement, 33
Potential GNP, tendency to overestimate,
    317-320
Poverty, 11-12
    vicious circle of, 282-285
Present value, 213
Prestowitz, Clyde, 58
Price controls, 59-60
    and black markets, 60
Price index, 92-93
Price-wage controls, 246
Price-wage guideposts, 230, 246
Price-wage freeze, 246, 251
Price-wage spiral, 233-235
    unwinding of, 238-240, 252-255
Prime rate of interest, 214
Privatization, 77-78
    in Britain, 77-78
    objectives, 77-78
Procyclical policy, 220-222
Production possibilities curve (PPC), 27-32
Productivity of labor, 109, 277-279
    its disappointing increase (1973-1979),
        278-281
Profit sharing, 250
Public good, 76
Public Service Employment Program, 245
Purchasing power of money, 121
Purchasing power of parity theory, 348
Pure fiscal policy, 305

Qualitative monetary controls, 214-215
Quantitative monetary controls, 214
Quantity theory of money, 301-304
Quayle, Dan, 245

Radford, R.A., 38
Rate of exchange, 340
Rational expectations, 253-255
Reagan, Ronald, 65, 70, 75, 179, 180, 186,
    323
Real balance (Pigou) effect, 158
Real deficit, 272
Real wage insurance proposal, 247
Recessionary gap, 165-166
Recessions, 8-9, 101-102, 105-107, 115-116
Recognition lag, 316
Regulation, 66, 74-75
Research and development (R&D), 280,
    529
Revaluation of currency, 345
Ricardo, David, 42-43
    equivalence theorem, 312
Robbins, Lionel, 25
Romer, Paul, 281*n*.
Roosevelt, Franklin D., 65, 171
Rules *vs.* active management, 129
Rule of seventy, 271

Sagan, Carl, 25
Samuelson, Paul A., 314*n*., 322
Sargent, Thomas, 254

Saving:
    consumption and, 136-137
    and the paradox of thrift, 160-161
    related to income (the saving function),
        137
Savings and loan associations (S&Ls), 194,
    218-219
Say's law, 158-159
Scarcity and choice, 25-34
Schlesinger, Arthur M., Jr., 209
Schultze, Charles L., 244*n*., 257*n*.
Schwartz, Anna, 122*n*.
Seasonal adjustment, 103
Seuling, Barbara, 75*n*.
Share economy, 250
Sherman Act, 74
Shortage, 51-52
Simons, Henry C., 321
Singapore, 285-288
Smith, Adam, 5, 6, 43
Smith, Warren, 296, 314
Smithsonian Agreement, 346-347
Social capital, 284
Social security, 68-69, 180-182
    and the federal deficit, 181-182
Solow, Robert M., 228*n*., 306
Soskice, David W., 247*n*.
Specialization and exchange, 36-43
Stagflation, 229
Stein, Herbert, 13, 186
Stop-go policies, 346
Subsistence wage, 292
Substitutes:
    in consumption, 53
    in production, 55
Summers, Lawrence, 266*n*.
Supply, 50-51
    and demand, 51
    shifters, 54-56
Supply side, 167, 185-186
    and tax cuts, 173-182, 177
Supply shock, 232, 249-250
Surplus, 51-52
    in balance of payments, 357-358
    in balance of trade, 287, 350, 358

Taiwan, 285-288
Tariffs, 5
Tax-based incomes policy (TIP), 247
Tax Reform Act of 1986, 69, 73-74
    loopholes plugged, 73
    reduction in income tax rates, 73-74
Taxes:
    as an automatic stabilizer, 170-171
    and the consumption function, 166-168
    excess burden *vs.* primary burden of,
        177
    and the multiplier, 168-169
    neutrality and nonneutrality of, 72
    principles of, 72-73
        ability to pay, 73
        benefit, 72-73
    progressive, 69
    proportional, 69
    proportional *vs.* lump sum, 166-168
    regressive, 69, 70
    types of:

corporation income, 69
  excise, 70
  personal income, 69
  social insurance, 69, 70
Technical efficiency (*see* Efficiency,
  technical (technological))
Technological change, 30-31, 279, 283
Teenage unemployment,
  and minimum wage, 243-244
Theory, economic, 31
  normative *vs.* positive, 33
Tobin, James, 94, 95, 242, 266*n.*
Third world, 281
  (*See also* Less-developed countries
    (LDCs))
Trade balance, 287, 350, 358
Tradeoff, between inflation and
  unemployment, 230-231, 242-255
Transfer payment, 67
Treasury bill, 212

Underemployment, 108
Underground economy, 96-97

Unemployment, 7, 8, 106, 108-115
  duration and sources of, 112
  incidence of, 110-111
  and inflation tradeoff, 230, 242-258
  natural rate of, 236, 242-245
  types of, 108-114
    cyclical, 108-112
    frictional, 112-113
    structural, 113-114
United Kingdom:
  demand management policies, 346
  incomes policies, 250
U.S./Canada free trade agreement, 43-44

Value added, 84
Variable rate mortgage, 269
Velocity of money, 302, 307
Vernon, Raymond, 78
Vicious circle:
  of inflation and exchange depreciation,
    347-348
  of poverty, 283
Viner, Jacob, 304*n.*

Virtuous circle, 348
Volcker, Paul, 207
"Voluntary" export restraints (VERs), 350

Wage indexation, 248-250
Wage–price controls, 246
Wage–price guideposts, 230, 246
Wage–price freeze, 246, 251
Wage–price spiral, 233-235
  unwinding of, 238-240, 252-255
Wages and salaries:
  in national accounts, 89
Wages, iron law of, 292
Wallace, Neil, 254
Weidenbaum, Murray, 314
Weitzman, Martin, 250
Williamson, John, 352
Wonnacott, Paul, 273n.
World Bank, 3, 282, 344

Yield, on a bond, 212-213